Generic Goals and Generic Practices

GG 1 Achieve Specific Goals
    GP 1.1   Perform Specific Practices

GG 2 Institutionalize a Managed Process
    GP 2.1   Establish an Organizational Policy
    GP 2.2   Plan the Process
    GP 2.3   Provide Resources
    GP 2.4   Assign Responsibility
    GP 2.5   Train People
    GP 2.6   Control Work Products
    GP 2.7   Identify and Involve Relevant Stakeholders
    GP 2.8   Monitor and Control the Process
    GP 2.9   Objectively Evaluate Adherence
    GP 2.10   Review Status with Higher Level Management

GG 3 Institutionalize a Defined Process
    GP 3.1   Establish a Defined Process
    GP 3.2   Collect Process Related Experiences

CMMI® for Acquisition

Second Edition

The **SEI Series in Software Engineering** represents is a collaborative undertaking of the Carnegie Mellon Software Engineering Institute (SEI) and Addison-Wesley to develop and publish books on software engineering and related topics. The common goal of the SEI and Addison-Wesley is to provide the most current information on these topics in a form that is easily usable by practitioners and students.

Books in the series describe frameworks, tools, methods, and technologies designed to help organizations, teams, and individuals improve their technical or management capabilities. Some books describe processes and practices for developing higher-quality software, acquiring programs for complex systems, or delivering services more effectively. Other books focus on software and system architecture and product-line development. Still others, from the SEI's CERT Program, describe technologies and practices needed to manage software and network security risk. These and all books in the series address critical problems in software engineering for which practical solutions are available.

CMMI® for Acquisition
Guidelines for Improving the Acquisition of Products and Services

Second Edition

Brian P. Gallagher
Mike Phillips
Karen J. Richter
Sandy Shrum

✦✦Addison-Wesley

Upper Saddle River, NJ • Boston • Indianapolis • San Francisco
New York • Toronto • Montreal • London • Munich • Paris • Madrid
Capetown • Sydney • Tokyo • Singapore • Mexico City

Software Engineering Institute | **Carnegie Mellon**

The SEI Series in Software Engineering

CONTENTS

FOREWORD

In today's increasingly global economy, it is imperative that organizations discover, sustain, and improve methods that consistently provide the highest quality products and services at the lowest possible cost. In the aerospace industry, this necessity is more critical than ever. Our nation faces a multitude of challenges, from preventing terrorist attacks to fighting wars on multiple fronts against enemies both foreign and domestic. Industry is adapting by incorporating new technology, becoming more agile, and building the flexibility to combat both physical and cyber threats against our customers and ourselves. It is essential that defense contractors employ methods for the entire lifecycle of ever more complex systems to optimize cost, schedule, technical, and workmanship standards and focus on enhancing the warfighter's ability to succeed the first time, every time.

Northrop Grumman Corporation and our Aerospace Sector are extremely proud to provide the nation with aerospace and defense capabilities. We strive to continually improve our ability to meet and exceed our customers' expectations and deliver best-in-class products and services. Specifically, in our role as the Prime Integration Contractor for the Minuteman III Intercontinental Ballistic Missile (ICBM) weapon system, the majority of our products are acquired from subcontractors, suppliers, and sub-tier suppliers. We partner with our customer and our entire supply chain to enhance the reliability, availability, and sustainability of the weapon system, while ensuring requirements are accurately defined, allocated, maintained, and realized. Through this team dynamic, we have updated, enhanced, integrated, and maintained our nation's ability to provide a highly robust and available deterrent against nuclear attack on the United States or its allies.

CMMI for Acquisition (CMMI-ACQ) enables a predictable, consistent, and reliable process for defining the requirements, defining an acquisition strategy, and capturing the best sources. The abilities to identify the right sources, execute properly defined subcontracts, and validate critical requirements are key contributors to ensure customers' critical needs are satisfied. Our acquisition processes are the cornerstone by which we have managed a wide array of requirements and complex technical solutions to deliver high quality, robust products. Our success is largely due to our implementation of fundamental CMMI concepts within our processes. By achieving CMMI-ACQ maturity level 5, our customers have confidence in our processes as well as our products.

I encourage you to read this book with one goal in mind—continual improvement of your organization's acquisition performance. This book can guide you to improve every tier of your supply chain and thereby improve the products and services you ultimately deliver to your customers.

—*Anthony W. Spehar*
VP Missile Systems (MXS)
Strike & Surveillance Systems Division
Northrop Grumman Aerospace Systems
Clearfield, Utah

PREFACE

CMMI (Capability Maturity Model Integration) models are collections of best practices that help organizations to improve their processes. These models are developed by product teams with members from industry, government, and the Software Engineering Institute (SEI).

This model, called CMMI for Acquisition (CMMI-ACQ), provides a comprehensive integrated set of guidelines for acquiring products and services.

Purpose

The CMMI-ACQ model provides guidance for applying CMMI best practices in an acquiring organization. Best practices in the model focus on activities for initiating and managing the acquisition of products and services to meet the needs of customers and end users. Although suppliers can provide artifacts useful to the processes addressed in CMMI-ACQ, the focus of the model is on the processes of the acquirer.

The CMMI-ACQ V1.3 model is a collection of acquisition best practices from government and industry that is generated from the CMMI V1.3 Architecture and Framework.[1] CMMI-ACQ is based on the CMMI Model Foundation or CMF (i.e., model components

---

1. The CMMI Framework is the basic structure that organizes CMMI components and combines them into CMMI constellations and models.

common to all CMMI models and constellations[2]), the CMMI Acquisition Module, and the Software Acquisition Capability Maturity Model (SA-CMM) [SEI 2002].CMMI-ACQ also incorporates work by acquisition organizations to adapt CMMI for use in an acquisition organization.

CMMI-ACQ provides a comprehensive set of best practices for acquiring products and services. CMMI for Development (CMMI-DEV) can be treated as a reference for supplier-executed activities in an acquisition initiative [SEI 2010a]. In those cases where the acquirer also has a role as a product or service developer (e.g., taking responsibility for the first few layers of product development and integration), CMMI-DEV (in particular the Requirements Development, Technical Solution, and Product Integration process areas) should also be used to improve the acquirer's product or service development processes.

Model Acknowledgments

Many talented people were involved in the development of the V1.3 CMMI Product Suite. Three primary groups were the CMMI Steering Group, Product Team, and Configuration Control Board (CCB).

The Steering Group guided and approved the plans of the Product Team, provided consultation on significant CMMI project issues, and ensured involvement from a variety of interested communities.

The Steering Group oversaw the development of the Acquisition constellation, recognizing the importance of providing best practices to acquirers.

The Product Team wrote, reviewed, revised, discussed, and agreed on the structure and technical content of the CMMI Product Suite, including the framework, models, training, and appraisal materials. Development activities were based on multiple inputs. These inputs included an A-Specification and guidance specific to each release provided by the Steering Group, source models, change requests received from the user community, and input received from pilots and other stakeholders.

The CCB is the official mechanism for controlling changes to CMMI models, appraisal related documents, and *Introduction to CMMI* training. As such, this group ensures integrity over the life of the product suite by reviewing all proposed changes to the baseline

---

2. A constellation is a collection of CMMI components that are used to construct models, training materials, and appraisal related documents for an area of interest (e.g., development, acquisition, services).

and approving only those changes that satisfy identified issues and meet criteria for the upcoming release.

Members of the groups involved in developing CMMI-ACQ V1.3 are listed in Appendix C.

Audience

The audience for CMMI-ACQ includes anyone interested in process improvement in an acquisition environment. Whether you are familiar with the concept of Capability Maturity Models or are seeking information to begin improving your acquisition processes, CMMI-ACQ will be useful to you. This model is also intended for organizations that want to use a reference model for an appraisal of their acquisition related processes.[3]

Organization of This Document

This document is organized into three main parts:

- Part One: About CMMI for Acquisition
- Part Two: Generic Goals and Generic Practices, and the Process Areas
- Part Three: The Appendices and Glossary

Part One: About CMMI for Acquisition, consists of six chapters:

- Chapter 1, Introduction, offers a broad view of CMMI and the Acquisition constellation, concepts of process improvement, and the history of models used for process improvement and different process improvement approaches.
- Chapter 2, Process Area Components, describes all of the components of the CMMI-ACQ process areas.[4]
- Chapter 3, Tying It All Together, assembles the model components and explains the concepts of maturity levels and capability levels.
- Chapter 4, Relationships Among Process Areas, provides insight into the meaning and interactions among the CMMI-ACQ process areas.

---

3. An appraisal is an examination of one or more processes by a trained team of professionals using a reference model (e.g., CMMI-ACQ) as the basis for determining strengths and weaknesses.
4. A process area is a cluster of related practices in an area that, when implemented collectively, satisfies a set of goals considered important for making improvement in that area. This concept is covered in detail in Chapter 2.

- Chapter 5, Using CMMI Models, describes paths to adoption and the use of CMMI-ACQ for process improvement and benchmarking of practices in an acquisition organization.
- Chapter 6, Essays on CMMI-ACQ in Government and Industry, contains essays from invited contributors about topics related to CMMI-ACQ.

Part Two: Generic Goals and Generic Practices, and the Process Areas, contains all of this CMMI model's required and expected components. It also contains related informative components, including subpractices, notes, examples, and example work products.

Part Two contains 23 sections. The first section contains the generic goals and practices. The remaining 22 sections each represent one of the CMMI-ACQ process areas.

To make these process areas easy to find, they are organized alphabetically by process area acronym. Each section contains descriptions of goals, best practices, and examples.

Part Three: The Appendices, consists of four sections:

- Appendix A: References, contains references you can use to locate documented sources of information such as reports, process improvement models, industry standards, and books that are related to CMMI-ACQ.
- Appendix B: Acronyms, defines the acronyms used in the model.
- Appendix C: CMMI Version 1.3 Project Participants, contains lists of team members who participated in the development of CMMI-ACQ V1.3.
- Appendix D: Glossary, defines many of the terms used in CMMI-ACQ.

Finally, the Book Contributors section, provides information about the book's authors and those who contributed essays for Chapter 6.

How to Use This Document

Whether you are new to process improvement, new to CMMI, or already familiar with CMMI, Part One can help you understand why CMMI-ACQ is the model to use for improving your acquisition processes.

Readers New to Process Improvement

If you are new to process improvement or new to the Capability Maturity Model (CMM) concept, we suggest that you read Chapter 1 first. Chapter 1 contains an overview of process improvement that explains what CMMI is all about.

Next, skim Part Two, including generic goals and practices and specific goals and practices, to get a feel for the scope of the best practices contained in the model. Pay close attention to the purpose and introductory notes at the beginning of each process area.

In Part Three, look through the references in Appendix A and select additional sources you think would be beneficial to read before moving forward with using CMMI-ACQ. Read through the acronyms and glossary to become familiar with the language of CMMI. Then, go back and read the details of Part Two.

Readers Experienced with Process Improvement

If you are new to CMMI but have experience with other process improvement models, such as the Software Acquisition CMM, you will immediately recognize many similarities in their structure and content [SEI 2002].

We recommend that you read Part One to understand how CMMI is different from other process improvement models. If you have experience with other models, you may want to select which sections to read first. Read Part Two with an eye for best practices you recognize from the models that you have already used. By identifying familiar material, you will gain an understanding of what is new, what has been carried over, and what is familiar from the models you already know.

Next, review the glossary to understand how some terminology can differ from that used in the process improvement models you know. Many concepts are repeated, but they may be called something different.

Readers Familiar with CMMI

If you have reviewed or used a CMMI model before, you will quickly recognize the CMMI concepts discussed and the best practices presented. As always, the improvements that the CMMI Product Team made to CMMI for the V1.3 release were driven by user input. Change requests were carefully considered, analyzed, and implemented.

Some significant improvements you can expect in CMMI-ACQ V1.3 include the following:

- High maturity process areas are significantly improved to reflect industry best practices, including a new specific goal and several new specific practices in the process area that was renamed from

Organizational Innovation and Deployment (OID) to Organizational Performance Management (OPM).

- Improvements were made to the model architecture that simplify the use of multiple models.

- The informative material was improved, including adding guidance about using preferred suppliers in SSAD and AM.

- Glossary definitions and model terminology were improved to enhance the clarity, accuracy, and usability of the model.

- The level 4 and 5 generic goals and practices were eliminated as well as capability levels 4 and 5 to appropriately focus high maturity on the achievement of business objectives, which is accomplished by applying capability levels 1–3 to the high maturity process areas (Causal Analysis and Resolution, Quantitative Project Management, Organizational Performance Management, and Organizational Process Performance).

For a more complete and detailed list of improvements, see www.sei.cmu.edu/cmmi/tools/cmmiv1-3/.

Additional Information and Reader Feedback

Many sources of information about CMMI are listed in Appendix A and are also published on the CMMI website—www.sei.cmu.edu/cmmi/.

Your suggestions for improving CMMI are welcome. For information on how to provide feedback, see the CMMI website at www.sei.cmu.edu/cmmi/tools/cr/. If you have questions about CMMI, send email to cmmi-comments@sei.cmu.edu.

BOOK ACKNOWLEDGMENTS

This book wouldn't be possible without the efforts of a multitude of dedicated people working together on CMMI-based process improvement. The complete CMMI-ACQ model is contained in this book, which was created by the CMMI Product Team. This team included members from different organizations and backgrounds. Ultimately, without the work of those involved in the CMMI project since it began in 1998, this book would not exist.

We would also like to acknowledge those who directly contributed to this book. The contributing authors who wrote essays for Chapter 6 added significantly to the book's value. All of these authors were willing to share their insights and experiences and met aggressive deadlines to do so: Richard Freeman, Richard Frost, Tom Keuten, Ashok Gurumurthy, Claude Bolton, Dan Lutrell, Steve Kelley, Mary Ann Lapham, Madhav Panwar, and Craig Meyers. We are delighted that they agreed to contribute their experiences to our book.

We are grateful to Anthony W. Spehar for his kind words in the foreword.

Special thanks go to Addison-Wesley Publishing Partner, Peter Gordon, for his assistance, experience, and advice. We'd also like to thank Kim Boedigheimer, Curt Johnson, Stephane Nakib, Julie Nahil, Megan Guiney, and Jill Hobbs for their help with the book's publication and promotion.

From Brian Gallagher

I would like to thank Valerie, Caitlin, Rachel, and Gabriel for their patience and understanding, and my parents Ed and Earlene and in-laws Alice and Lynn for their wisdom. Special thanks to my daughter Ashley for her bravery and her service in Iraq as the U.S. Army's #1 Medic. Finally, as always, I would like to dedicate my contribution to this book to my son Brian. Not a day goes by without you in our thoughts, prayers, and hearts.

From Mike Phillips

For this second edition, I would again like to thank my wife Connie for her understanding and acknowledging the time needed to help create this update. It has been a delight to work again with two great teams—one that helped us all refine the three "constellations" for the CMMI Product Suite, and my three coauthors of the additional perspectives we have sought to provide. I'd like to dedicate my contribution to the Chief Architect of our approach to CMMI, the late Dr. Roger Bate. His friendship and guidance over the years keep him close in my memories.

From Karen Richter

I would like to thank my sponsors from the Office of the Under Secretary of Defense for Acquisition, Technology and Logistics (OUSD [AT&L]), Mr. Mark Schaeffer and Ms. Kristen Baldwin, for their unwavering and continued support for my CMMI work over the past 12 years. At the Institute for Defense Analyses (IDA), I would like to thank the Vice President for Programs, Mr. Philip Major, and my Division Director, Mr. Michael Dominguez, for their support to coauthor this book.

From Sandy Shrum

Working simultaneously on three CMMI books has tested my limits in many ways. Those who have helped me along the journey provided both professional and personal support.

Many thanks to Rhonda Brown and Mike Konrad for their partnership during CMMI model development. They are peerless as team members and friends. Our joint management of the CMMI Core Model Team was not only effective, but also enjoyable.

Affectionate thanks to my boyfriend Jimmy Orsag for his loving support and for helping me keep my focus and sense of humor through all the hours of work preparing three manuscripts. Heartfelt thanks to my parents, John and Eileen Maruca, for always being there for me no matter what and for instilling my strong work ethic.

Finally, thanks to the coauthors of all three CMMI books: Brandon Buteau, Mary Beth Chrissis, Eileen Forrester, Brian Gallagher, Mike Konrad, Mike Phillips, and Karen Richter. They are all terrific to work with. Without their understanding, excellent coordination, and hard work, I would never have been able to participate.

PART ONE

About CMMI for Acquisition

CHAPTER 1

INTRODUCTION

Now more than ever, organizations are increasingly becoming acquirers[1] of needed capabilities by obtaining products and services from suppliers and developing less and less of these capabilities in-house. This widely adopted business strategy is designed to improve an organization's operational efficiencies by leveraging suppliers' capabilities to deliver quality solutions rapidly, at lower cost, and with the most appropriate technology.

> **AUTHORS' NOTE**
> A May 2010 report from the Government Accountability Office (GAO) found that only 21 percent of programs in the U.S. Department of Defense's 2008 major defense acquisition portfolio appeared to be stable and on track with original cost and schedule goals [GAO: Defense Acquisition, 2010].

Acquisition of needed capabilities is challenging because acquirers have overall accountability for satisfying the end user while allowing the supplier to perform the tasks necessary to develop and provide the solution.

Mismanagement, the inability to articulate customer needs, poor requirements definition, inadequate supplier selection and contracting processes, insufficient technology selection procedures, and uncontrolled requirements changes are factors that contribute to project failure. Responsibility is shared by both the supplier and the acquirer. The majority of project failures could be avoided if the acquirer learned how to properly prepare for, engage with, and manage suppliers.

---

1. In CMMI-ACQ, the terms *project* and *acquirer* refer to the acquisition project; the term *organization* refers to the acquisition organization.

> **AUTHORS' NOTE**
> General Motors Information Technology is a leader in working with its suppliers. See Chapter 6 for an essay about GM's use of CMMI-ACQ to learn more about how sophisticated the relationships and communication with suppliers can be.

In addition to these challenges, an overall key to a successful acquirer–supplier relationship is communication.

Unfortunately, many organizations have not invested in the capabilities necessary to effectively manage projects in an acquisition environment. Too often acquirers disengage from the project once the supplier is hired. Too late they discover that the project is not on schedule, deadlines will not be met, the technology selected is not viable, and the project has failed.

The acquirer has a focused set of major objectives. These objectives include the requirement to maintain a relationship with end users to fully comprehend their needs. The acquirer owns the project, executes overall project management, and is accountable for delivering the product or service to the end users. Thus, these acquirer responsibilities can extend beyond ensuring the product or service is delivered by chosen suppliers to include activities such as integrating the overall product or service, ensuring it makes the transition into operation, and obtaining insight into its appropriateness and adequacy to continue to meet customer needs.

CMMI for Acquisition (CMMI-ACQ) enables organizations to avoid or eliminate barriers in the acquisition process through practices and terminology that transcend the interests of individual departments or groups.

> **AUTHORS' NOTE**
> If the acquirer and its suppliers are both using CMMI, they have a common language they can use to enhance their relationship.

CMMI-ACQ contains 22 process areas. Of those process areas, 16 are core process areas that cover Process Management, Project Management, and Support process areas.[2]

---

2. A core process area is a process area that is common to all CMMI models. A shared process area is shared by at least two CMMI models, but not all of them.

AUTHORS' NOTE

The CMF concept is what enables CMMI to be integrated for both supplier and acquirer use. The shared content across models for different domains enables organizations in different domains (e.g., acquirers and suppliers) to work together more effectively. It also enables large organizations to use multiple CMMI models without making a huge investment in learning new terminology, concepts, and procedures.

Six process areas focus on practices specific to acquisition, addressing agreement management, acquisition requirements development, acquisition technical management, acquisition validation, acquisition verification, and solicitation and supplier agreement development.

All CMMI-ACQ model practices focus on the activities of the acquirer. Those activities include supplier sourcing; developing and awarding supplier agreements; and managing the acquisition of capabilities, including the acquisition of both products and services. Supplier activities are not addressed in this document. Suppliers and acquirers who also develop products and services should consider using the CMMI-DEV model.

About Process Improvement

In its research to help organizations to develop and maintain quality products and services, the Software Engineering Institute (SEI) has found several dimensions that an organization can focus on to improve its business. Figure 1.1 illustrates the three critical dimensions that organizations typically focus on: people, procedures and methods, and tools and equipment.

What holds everything together? It is the *processes* used in your organization. Processes allow you to align the way you do business. They allow you to address scalability and provide a way to incorporate knowledge of how to do things better. Processes allow you to leverage your resources and to examine business trends.

AUTHORS' NOTE

Another advantage of using CMMI models for improvement is that they are extremely flexible. CMMI doesn't dictate which processes to use, which tools to buy, or who should perform particular processes. Instead, CMMI provides a framework of flexible best practices that can be applied to meet the organization's business objectives no matter what they are.

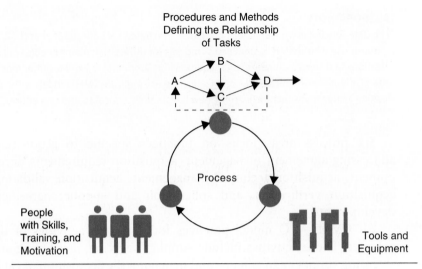

FIGURE 1.1
The Three Critical Dimensions

This is not to say that people and technology are not important. We are living in a world where technology is changing at an incredible speed. Similarly, people typically work for many companies throughout their careers. We live in a dynamic world. A focus on process provides the infrastructure and stability necessary to deal with an ever-changing world and to maximize the productivity of people and the use of technology to be competitive.

Manufacturing has long recognized the importance of process effectiveness and efficiency. Today, many organizations in manufacturing and service industries recognize the importance of quality processes. Process helps an organization's workforce to meet business objectives by helping them to work smarter, not harder, and with improved consistency. Effective processes also provide a vehicle for introducing and using new technology in a way that best meets the business objectives of the organization.

About Capability Maturity Models

A Capability Maturity Model (CMM), including CMMI, is a simplified representation of the world. CMMs contain the essential elements of effective processes. These elements are based on the concepts developed by Crosby, Deming, Juran, and Humphrey.

In the 1930s, Walter Shewhart began work in process improvement with his principles of statistical quality control [Shewhart 1931].

These principles were refined by W. Edwards Deming [Deming 1986], Phillip Crosby [Crosby 1979], and Joseph Juran [Juran 1988]. Watts Humphrey, Ron Radice, and others extended these principles further and began applying them to software in their work at IBM (International Business Machines) and the SEI [Humphrey 1989]. Humphrey's book, *Managing the Software Process*, provides a description of the basic principles and concepts on which many of the Capability Maturity Models (CMMs) are based.

The SEI has taken the process management premise, "the quality of a system or product is highly influenced by the quality of the process used to develop and maintain it," and defined CMMs that embody this premise. The belief in this premise is seen worldwide in quality movements, as evidenced by the International Organization for Standardization/International Electrotechnical Commission (ISO/IEC) body of standards.

CMMs focus on improving processes in an organization. They contain the essential elements of effective processes for one or more disciplines and describe an evolutionary improvement path from ad hoc, immature processes to disciplined, mature processes with improved quality and effectiveness.

Like other CMMs, CMMI models provide guidance to use when developing processes. CMMI models are not processes or process descriptions. The actual processes used in an organization depend on many factors, including application domains and organization structure and size. In particular, the process areas of a CMMI model typically do not map one to one with the processes used in your organization.

The SEI created the first CMM designed for software organizations and published it in a book, *The Capability Maturity Model: Guidelines for Improving the Software Process* [SEI 1995].

Today, CMMI is an application of the principles introduced almost a century ago to this never-ending cycle of process improvement. The value of this process improvement approach has been confirmed over time. Organizations have experienced increased productivity and quality, improved cycle time, and more accurate and predictable schedules and budgets [Gibson 2006].

Evolution of CMMI

The CMM Integration project was formed to sort out the problem of using multiple CMMs. The combination of selected models into a single improvement framework was intended for use by organizations in their pursuit of enterprise-wide process improvement.

Developing a set of integrated models involved more than simply combining existing model materials. Using processes that promote consensus, the CMMI Product Team built a framework that accommodates multiple constellations.

The first model to be developed was the CMMI for Development model (then simply called "CMMI"). Figure 1.2 illustrates the models that led to CMMI Version 1.3.

Initially, CMMI was one model that combined three source models: the *Capability Maturity Model for Software* (SW-CMM) v2.0 draft C, the *Systems Engineering Capability Model* (SECM) [EIA 2002], and the *Integrated Product Development Capability Maturity Model* (IPD-CMM) v0.98.

These three source models were selected because of their successful adoption or promising approach to improving processes in an organization.

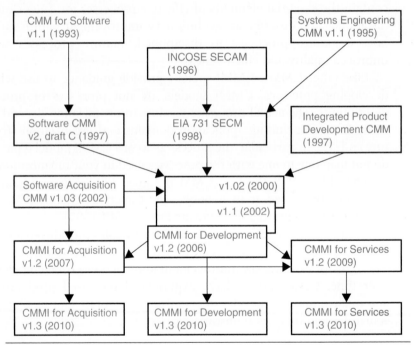

FIGURE 1.2
The History of CMMs[3]

___

3. EIA 731 SECM is the Electronic Industries Alliance standard 731, or the Systems Engineering Capability Model. INCOSE SECAM is the International Council on Systems Engineering Systems Engineering Capability Assessment Model [EIA 2002a].

> **AUTHORS' NOTE**
> Every CMMI model must be used within the framework of the organization's business objectives. An organization's processes should not be restructured to match a CMMI model's structure.

The first CMMI model (V1.02) was designed for use by development organizations in their pursuit of enterprise-wide process improvement. It was released in 2000. Two years later version 1.1 was released and four years after that, version 1.2 was released.

By the time that version 1.2 was released, two other CMMI models were being planned. Because of this planned expansion, the name of the first CMMI model had to change to become CMMI for Development and the concept of constellations was created.

The CMMI for Acquisition model was released in 2007 [SEI 2007a]. Since it built on the CMMI for Development Version 1.2 model, it also was named Version 1.2. Two years later the CMMI for Services model was released. It built on the other two models and also was named Version 1.2.

> **AUTHORS' NOTE**
> The Acquisition Module was updated after CMMI-ACQ was released. Now called the CMMI for Acquisition Primer, Version 1.2, it continues to be an introduction to CMMI-based improvement for acquisition organizations. The primer is an SEI report (CMU/SEI-2008-TR-010) that you can find at www.sei.cmu.edu/library/reportspapers.cfm.

In 2008 plans were drawn to begin developing Version 1.3, which would ensure consistency among all three models and improve high maturity material. Version 1.3 of CMMI for Acquisition [Gallagher 2011], CMMI for Development [Chrissis 2011, SEI 2010a], and CMMI for Services [Forrester 2011, SEI 2010b] were released in November 2010.

CMMI Framework

The CMMI Framework provides the structure needed to produce CMMI models, training, and appraisal components. To allow the use of multiple models within the CMMI Framework, model components are classified as either common to all CMMI models or applicable to a specific model. The common material is called the "CMMI Model Foundation" or "CMF."

The components of the CMF are part of every model generated from the CMMI Framework. Those components are combined with material applicable to an area of interest (e.g., acquisition, development, services) to produce a model.

A "constellation" is defined as a collection of CMMI components that are used to construct models, training materials, and appraisal related documents for an area of interest (e.g., acquisition, development, services). The Acquisition constellation's model is called "CMMI for Acquisition" or "CMMI-ACQ."

CMMI for Acquisition

The CMMI Steering Group initially approved a small introductory collection of acquisition best practices called the *Acquisition Module* (*CMMI-AM*), which was based on the CMMI Framework. While it described best practices, it was not intended to become an appraisable model nor a model suitable for process improvement purposes. A similar, but more up-to-date document, *CMMI for Acquisition Primer*, is now available [Richter 2008].

General Motors partnered with the SEI to create the initial Acquisition model draft that was the basis for this model. The model now represents the work of many organizations and individuals from industry, government, and the SEI.

When using this model, use professional judgment and common sense to interpret it for your organization. That is, although the process areas described in this model depict behaviors considered best practices for most acquirers, all process areas and practices should be interpreted using an in-depth knowledge of CMMI-ACQ, your organizational constraints, and your business environment [SEI 2007b].

This document is a reference model that covers the acquisition of needed capabilities. Capabilities are acquired in many industries, including aerospace, banking, computer hardware, software, defense, automobile manufacturing, and telecommunications. All of these industries can use CMMI-ACQ.

CHAPTER 2

PROCESS AREA COMPONENTS

This chapter describes the components found in each process area and in the generic goals and generic practices. Understanding these components is critical to using the information in Part Two effectively. If you are unfamiliar with Part Two, you may want to skim the Generic Goals and Generic Practices section and a couple of process area sections to get a general feel for the content and layout before reading this chapter.

Core Process Areas and CMMI Models

All CMMI models are produced from the CMMI Framework. This framework contains all of the goals and practices that are used to produce CMMI models that belong to CMMI constellations.

All CMMI models contain 16 core process areas. These process areas cover basic concepts that are fundamental to process improvement in any area of interest (i.e., acquisition, development, services). Some of the material in the core process areas is the same in all constellations. Other material may be adjusted to address a specific area of interest. Consequently, the material in the core process areas may not be exactly the same.

Required, Expected, and Informative Components

Model components are grouped into three categories—required, expected, and informative—that reflect how to interpret them.

Required Components

Required components are CMMI components that are essential to achieving process improvement in a given process area. This achievement must be visibly implemented in an organization's processes. The required components in CMMI are the specific and generic goals. Goal satisfaction is used in appraisals as the basis for deciding whether a process area has been satisfied.

Expected Components

Expected components are CMMI components that describe the activities that are important in achieving a required CMMI component. Expected components guide those who implement improvements or perform appraisals. The expected components in CMMI are the specific and generic practices.

Before goals can be considered to be satisfied, either their practices as described, or acceptable alternatives to them, must be present in the planned and implemented processes of the organization.

> **AUTHORS' NOTE**
> The required and expected components are also referred to as normative material (versus informative material).

Informative Components

Informative components are CMMI components that help model users understand CMMI required and expected components. These components can be example boxes, detailed explanations, or other helpful information. Subpractices, notes, references, goal titles, practice titles, sources, example work products, and generic practice elaborations are informative model components.

The informative material plays an important role in understanding the model. It is often impossible to adequately describe the behavior required or expected of an organization using only a single goal or practice statement. The model's informative material provides information necessary to achieve the correct understanding of goals and practices and thus cannot be ignored.

For CMMI-ACQ, example supplier deliverables are added informative components that are not found in other CMMI models. These components are included in this model because of the interaction between supplier and acquirer processes.

Components Associated with Part Two

The model components associated with Part Two are summarized in Figure 2.1 to illustrate their relationships.

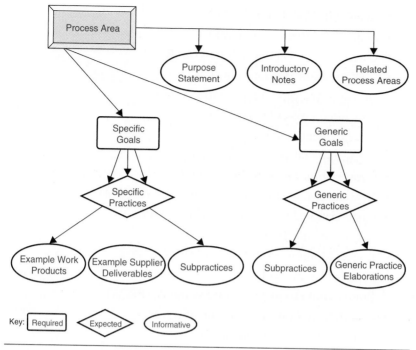

FIGURE 2.1
CMMI Model Components

AUTHORS' NOTE
All model components are important. The informative material helps you to understand the expected and required material. It is best to take these model components as a whole. If you understand the entire model, you can then understand what all the pieces are and how they fit together to form a framework that can benefit your organization.

The following sections provide detailed descriptions of CMMI model components.

Process Areas

A process area is a cluster of related practices in an area that, when implemented collectively, satisfies a set of goals considered important for making improvement in that area. (See the definition of "process area" in the glossary.)

The 22 process areas are presented in alphabetical order by acronym:

- Agreement Management (AM)
- Acquisition Requirements Development (ARD)
- Acquisition Technical Management (ATM)

- Acquisition Validation (AVAL)
- Acquisition Verification (AVER)
- Causal Analysis and Resolution (CAR)
- Configuration Management (CM)
- Decision Analysis and Resolution (DAR)
- Integrated Project Management (IPM)
- Measurement and Analysis (MA)
- Organizational Process Definition (OPD)
- Organizational Process Focus (OPF)
- Organizational Performance Management (OPM)
- Organizational Process Performance (OPP)
- Organizational Training (OT)
- Project Monitoring and Control (PMC)
- Project Planning (PP)
- Process and Product Quality Assurance (PPQA)
- Quantitative Project Management (QPM)
- Requirements Management (REQM)
- Risk Management (RSKM)
- Solicitation and Supplier Agreement Development (SSAD)

AUTHORS' NOTE
Every time we release a model, someone inevitably tells us that the process areas are not in alphabetical order. Because most users after a short time refer to the process areas by their acronyms, it made sense to list them alphabetically by acronym instead of by full name.

Purpose Statements

A purpose statement describes the purpose of the process area and is an informative component.

For example, the purpose statement of the Organizational Process Definition process area is "The purpose of Organizational Process Definition (OPD) is to establish and maintain a usable set of organizational process assets, work environment standards, and rules and guidelines for teams."

AUTHORS' NOTE
All purpose statements follow the same sentence structure and always contain the process area acronym. An easy way to find a process area in an electronic file is to search for part or all of the purpose statement.

Introductory Notes

The introductory notes section of the process area describes the major concepts covered in the process area and is an informative component.

An example from the introductory notes of the Project Monitoring and Control process area is "When actual status deviates significantly from expected values, corrective actions are taken as appropriate."

Related Process Areas

The Related Process Areas section lists references to related process areas and reflects the high-level relationships among the process areas. The Related Process Areas section is an informative component.

An example of a reference found in the Related Process Areas section of the Project Planning process area is "Refer to the Risk Management process area for more information about identifying and analyzing risks and mitigating risks."

Specific Goals

A specific goal describes the unique characteristics that must be present to satisfy the process area. A specific goal is a required model component and is used in appraisals to help determine whether a process area is satisfied. (See the definition of "specific goal" in the glossary.)

For example, a specific goal from the Configuration Management process area is "Integrity of baselines is established and maintained."

Only the statement of the specific goal is a required model component. The title of a specific goal (preceded by the goal number) and notes associated with the goal are considered informative model components.

Generic Goals

Generic goals are called "generic" because the same goal statement applies to multiple process areas. A generic goal describes the characteristics that must be present to institutionalize processes that implement a process area. A generic goal is a required model component and is used in appraisals to determine whether a process area is satisfied. (See the Generic Goals and Generic Practices section in Part Two for a more detailed description of generic goals. See the definition of "generic goal" in the glossary.)

An example of a generic goal is "The process is institutionalized as a defined process."

Only the statement of the generic goal is a required model component. The title of a generic goal (preceded by the goal number) and notes associated with the goal are considered informative model components.

Specific Goal and Practice Summaries

The specific goal and practice summary provides a high-level summary of the specific goals and specific practices. The specific goal and practice summary is an informative component.

> **AUTHORS' NOTE**
> The specific goal and practice summary shows you at a glance a high-level summary of what is contained in a process area.

Specific Practices

A specific practice is the description of an activity that is considered important in achieving the associated specific goal. The specific practices describe the activities that are expected to result in achievement of the specific goals of a process area. A specific practice is an expected model component. (See the definition of "specific practice" in the glossary.)

For example, a specific practice from the Project Monitoring and Control process area is "Monitor commitments against those identified in the project plan."

Only the statement of the specific practice is an expected model component. The title of a specific practice (preceded by the practice number) and notes associated with the specific practice are considered informative model components.

Example Work Products

The example work products section lists sample outputs from a specific practice. An example work product is an informative model component. (See the definition of "example work product" in the glossary.)

For instance, an example work product for the specific practice "Monitor Project Planning Parameters" in the Project Monitoring and Control process area is "Records of significant deviations."

Example Supplier Deliverables

To aid the acquirer, example supplier deliverables are also provided. An example supplier deliverable represents an artifact that is input into or supports the acquirer's implementation of the practice. An example supplier deliverable is an informative model component.

For instance, an example supplier deliverable for the specific practice "Perform activities with the supplier as specified in the supplier agreement" in the Agreement Management process area is "Supplier project progress and performance reports."

AUTHORS' NOTE
CMMI-ACQ includes a model component called "example supplier deliverables." This component presents lists of often valuable inputs to the acquirers' processes that yield, in turn, the example work products of the acquirers' activities. Example supplier deliverables were included in the model to enable synergy across the acquirer–supplier team, particularly when both organizations are using the same CMMI best practices. Supplier deliverables do not become evidence for appraisals as example work products often do, but providing these deliverables may aid project team members during early planning and acquisition requirements development so that a more complete solicitation can be prepared.

Subpractices

A subpractice is a detailed description that provides guidance for interpreting and implementing a specific or generic practice. Subpractices can be worded as if prescriptive, but they are actually an informative component meant only to provide ideas that may be useful for process improvement. (See the definition of "subpractice" in the glossary.)

For example, a subpractice for the specific practice "Take Corrective Action" in the Project Monitoring and Control process area is "Determine and document the appropriate actions needed to address identified issues."

Generic Practices

Generic practices are called "generic" because the same practice applies to multiple process areas. The generic practices associated with a generic goal describe the activities that are considered important in achieving the generic goal and contribute to the institutionalization of the processes associated with a process area. A generic practice is an expected model component. (See the definition of "generic practice" in the glossary.)

For example, a generic practice for the generic goal "The process is institutionalized as a managed process" is "Provide adequate resources for performing the process, developing the work products, and providing the services of the process."

Only the statement of the generic practice is an expected model component. The title of a generic practice (preceded by the practice number) and notes associated with the practice are considered informative model components.

Generic Practice Elaborations

Generic practice elaborations appear after generic practices to provide guidance on how the generic practices can be applied uniquely to process areas. A generic practice elaboration is an informative model component. (See the definition of "generic practice elaboration" in the glossary.)

For example, a generic practice elaboration after the generic practice "Establish and maintain an organizational policy for planning and performing the process" is "This policy establishes organizational expectations for planning and performing the process, including not only the elements of the process addressed directly by the acquirer but also the interactions between the acquirer with suppliers."

Additions

Additions are clearly marked model components that contain information of interest to particular users. An addition can be informative material, a specific practice, a specific goal, or an entire process area that extends the scope of a model or emphasizes a particular aspect of its use. There are no additions in the CMMI-ACQ model.

Supporting Informative Components

In many places in the model, further information is needed to describe a concept. This informative material is provided in the form of the following components:

- Notes
- Examples
- References

Notes

A note is text that can accompany nearly any other model component. It may provide detail, background, or rationale. A note is an informative model component.

For example, a note that accompanies the specific practice "Implement Action Proposals" in the Causal Analysis and Resolution process area is "Only changes that prove to be of value should be considered for broad implementation."

Examples

An example is a component comprising text and often a list of items, usually in a box, that can accompany nearly any other component and provides one or more examples to clarify a concept or described activity. An example is an informative model component.

The following is an example that accompanies the subpractice "Document noncompliance issues when they cannot be resolved in the project" under the specific practice "Communicate and Resolve Noncompliance Issues" in the Process and Product Quality Assurance process area.

Examples of ways to resolve noncompliance in the project include the following:

- Fixing the noncompliance
- Changing the process descriptions, standards, or procedures that were violated
- Obtaining a waiver to cover the noncompliance

References

A reference is a pointer to additional or more detailed information in related process areas and can accompany nearly any other model component. A reference is an informative model component. (See the definition of "reference" in the glossary.)

For example, a reference that accompanies the specific practice "Compose the Defined Process" in the Quantitative Project Management process area is "Refer to the Organizational Process Definition process area for more information about establishing organizational process assets."

AUTHORS' NOTE
The difference between a reference that appears in the Related Process Areas section of a process area and one that appears elsewhere in the process area is that the references in the Related Process Areas section represent more fundamental or important relationships and apply to the whole process area.

Numbering Scheme

Specific and generic goals are numbered sequentially. Each specific goal begins with the prefix "SG" (e.g., SG 1). Each generic goal begins with the prefix "GG" (e.g., GG 2).

Specific and generic practices are also numbered sequentially. Each specific practice begins with the prefix "SP," followed by a number in the form "x.y" (e.g., SP 1.1). The x is the same number as the goal to which the specific practice maps. The y is the sequence number of the specific practice under the specific goal.

An example of specific practice numbering is in the Project Planning process area. The first specific practice is numbered SP 1.1 and the second is SP 1.2.

Each generic practice begins with the prefix "GP," followed by a number in the form "x.y" (e.g., GP 1.1). The x corresponds to the number of the generic goal. The y is the sequence number of the generic practice under the generic goal. For example, the first generic practice associated with GG 2 is numbered GP 2.1 and the second is GP 2.2.

Typographical Conventions

The typographical conventions used in this model were designed to enable you to easily identify and select model components by presenting them in formats that allow you to find them quickly on the page.

Figures 2.2, 2.3, and 2.4 are sample pages from process areas in Part Two; they show the different process area components, labeled so that you can identify them. Notice that components differ typographically so that you can easily identify each one.

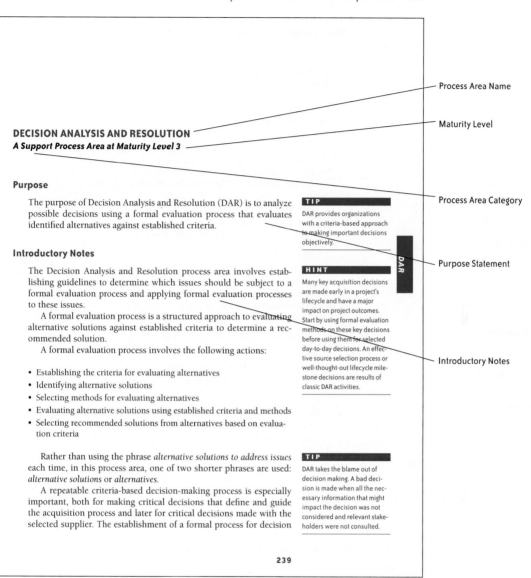

Process Area Name

Maturity Level

Process Area Category

Purpose Statement

Introductory Notes

DECISION ANALYSIS AND RESOLUTION
A Support Process Area at Maturity Level 3

Purpose

The purpose of Decision Analysis and Resolution (DAR) is to analyze possible decisions using a formal evaluation process that evaluates identified alternatives against established criteria.

> **TIP**
>
> DAR provides organizations with a criteria-based approach to making important decisions objectively.

Introductory Notes

The Decision Analysis and Resolution process area involves establishing guidelines to determine which issues should be subject to a formal evaluation process and applying formal evaluation processes to these issues.

A formal evaluation process is a structured approach to evaluating alternative solutions against established criteria to determine a recommended solution.

A formal evaluation process involves the following actions:

- Establishing the criteria for evaluating alternatives
- Identifying alternative solutions
- Selecting methods for evaluating alternatives
- Evaluating alternative solutions using established criteria and methods
- Selecting recommended solutions from alternatives based on evaluation criteria

Rather than using the phrase *alternative solutions to address issues* each time, in this process area, one of two shorter phrases are used: *alternative solutions* or *alternatives*.

A repeatable criteria-based decision-making process is especially important, both for making critical decisions that define and guide the acquisition process and later for critical decisions made with the selected supplier. The establishment of a formal process for decision

> **HINT**
>
> Many key acquisition decisions are made early in a project's lifecycle and have a major impact on project outcomes. Start by using formal evaluation methods on these key decisions before using them for selected day-to-day decisions. An effective source selection process or well-thought-out lifecycle milestone decisions are results of classic DAR activities.

> **TIP**
>
> DAR takes the blame out of decision making. A bad decision is made when all the necessary information that might impact the decision was not considered and relevant stakeholders were not consulted.

DAR

239

FIGURE 2.2
Sample Page from Decision Analysis and Resolution

Specific Goal

Specific Practice

Reference

Example Work Product

Example Supplier Deliverable

Subpractice

Specific Practices by Goal

SG 1 *SATISFY SUPPLIER AGREEMENTS*

The terms of the supplier agreement are met by both the acquirer and the supplier.

SP 1.1 *EXECUTE THE SUPPLIER AGREEMENT*

Perform activities with the supplier as specified in the supplier agreement.

This specific practice covers internal and external communication as well as the use of information by the acquirer and supplier regarding the relationship, performance, results, and impact to the business. The acquirer manages the relationship with the supplier to maintain effective communication on key issues (e.g., changes in the acquirer's business), new supplier products and technologies, and changes in the organizational structure.

Refer to the Project Monitoring and Control process area for more information about monitoring projects and taking corrective action.

Example Work Products

1. Integrated list of issues
2. Supplier project progress and performance reports
3. Supplier review materials and reports
4. Action items tracked to closure
5. Records of product and document deliveries

Example Supplier Deliverables

1. Supplier project progress and performance reports
2. Corrective action results for supplier issues
3. Correspondence with the acquirer

Subpractices

1. Monitor supplier project progress and performance (e.g., schedule, effort, and cost) as defined in the supplier agreement.
2. Conduct management reviews with the supplier as specified in the supplier agreement.
   Reviews cover both formal and informal reviews and include the following steps:
   • Preparing for the review
   • Ensuring that relevant stakeholders participate
   • Conducting the review
   • Identifying, documenting, and tracking all action items to closure
   • Preparing and distributing to the relevant stakeholders a summary report of the review

FIGURE 2.3
Sample Page from Agreement Management

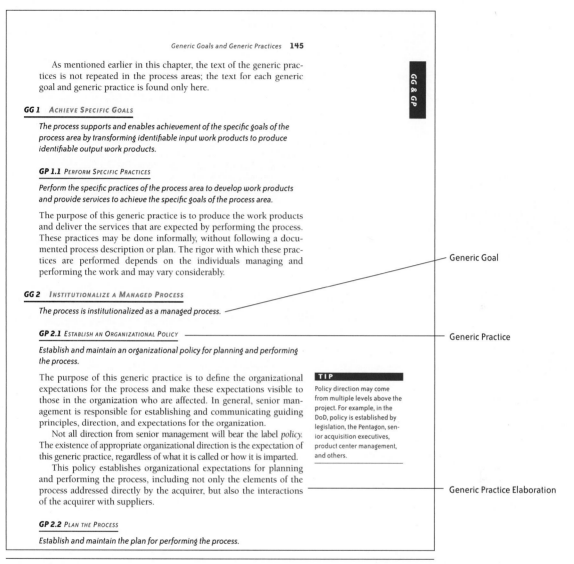

As mentioned earlier in this chapter, the text of the generic practices is not repeated in the process areas; the text for each generic goal and generic practice is found only here.

GG 1   ACHIEVE SPECIFIC GOALS

The process supports and enables achievement of the specific goals of the process area by transforming identifiable input work products to produce identifiable output work products.

GP 1.1   PERFORM SPECIFIC PRACTICES

Perform the specific practices of the process area to develop work products and provide services to achieve the specific goals of the process area.

The purpose of this generic practice is to produce the work products and deliver the services that are expected by performing the process. These practices may be done informally, without following a documented process description or plan. The rigor with which these practices are performed depends on the individuals managing and performing the work and may vary considerably.

GG 2   INSTITUTIONALIZE A MANAGED PROCESS

The process is institutionalized as a managed process. — Generic Goal

GP 2.1   ESTABLISH AN ORGANIZATIONAL POLICY — Generic Practice

Establish and maintain an organizational policy for planning and performing the process.

The purpose of this generic practice is to define the organizational expectations for the process and make these expectations visible to those in the organization who are affected. In general, senior management is responsible for establishing and communicating guiding principles, direction, and expectations for the organization.

> **TIP**
>
> Policy direction may come from multiple levels above the project. For example, in the DoD, policy is established by legislation, the Pentagon, senior acquisition executives, product center management, and others.

Not all direction from senior management will bear the label *policy*. The existence of appropriate organizational direction is the expectation of this generic practice, regardless of what it is called or how it is imparted.

This policy establishes organizational expectations for planning and performing the process, including not only the elements of the process addressed directly by the acquirer, but also the interactions of the acquirer with suppliers. — Generic Practice Elaboration

GP 2.2   PLAN THE PROCESS

Establish and maintain the plan for performing the process.

FIGURE 2.4
Sample Page from the Generic Goals and Generic Practices

CHAPTER 3

TYING IT ALL TOGETHER

Now that you have been introduced to the components of CMMI models, you need to understand how they fit together to meet your process improvement needs. This chapter introduces the concept of *levels* and shows how the process areas are organized and used.

CMMI-ACQ does not specify that a project or organization must follow a particular acquisition process flow or that a certain number of deliverables per day or specific project performance targets be achieved. The model does specify that a project or organization should have processes that address acquisition related practices. To determine whether these processes are in place, a project or organization maps its processes to the process areas in this model.

The mapping of processes to process areas enables the organization to track its progress against the CMMI-ACQ model as it updates or creates processes. Do not expect that every CMMI-ACQ process area will map one to one with your organization's or project's processes.

AUTHORS' NOTE
Think of CMMI-ACQ practices as characteristics that should be present in your processes to help reduce risk, not as checklist items to be blindly followed.

Understanding Levels

Levels are used in CMMI-ACQ to describe an evolutionary path recommended for an organization that wants to improve the processes it uses to acquire capabilities, including products and services. Levels can also be the outcome of the rating activity in appraisals.[1] Appraisals

---

1. For more information about appraisals, refer to *Appraisal Requirements for CMMI* and the *Standard CMMI Appraisal Method for Process Improvement Method Definition Document* [SEI 2006c, SEI 2006b].

can apply to entire organizations or to smaller groups such as a group of projects or a division.

> **AUTHORS' NOTE**
> Levels are useful for benchmarking your capabilities against a publicly reviewed set of practices and establishing improvement priorities. However, be sure to consider the entire team's capabilities (e.g., acquirer, supplier, and end user) when trying to maximize the outcomes and reduce risk on a particular project.

> **AUTHORS' NOTE**
> For guidance on how to use CMMI to help reduce project risk across the entire team, see the SEI report, "Understanding and Leveraging a Supplier's CMMI Efforts: A Guidebook for Acquirers" (CMU/SEI-2007-TR-004).

CMMI supports two improvement paths using levels. One path enables organizations to incrementally improve processes corresponding to an individual process area (or group of process areas) selected by the organization. The other path enables organizations to improve a set of related processes by incrementally addressing successive sets of process areas.

These two improvement paths are associated with the two types of levels: capability levels and maturity levels. These levels correspond to two approaches to process improvement called "representations." The two representations are called "continuous" and "staged." Using the continuous representation enables you to achieve "capability levels." Using the staged representation enables you to achieve "maturity levels."

To reach a particular level, an organization must satisfy all of the goals of the process area or set of process areas that are targeted for improvement, regardless of whether it is a capability or a maturity level.

Both representations provide ways to improve your processes to achieve business objectives, and both provide the same essential content and use the same model components.

Structures of the Continuous and Staged Representations

Figure 3.1 illustrates the structures of the continuous and staged representations. The differences between the structures are subtle but significant. The staged representation uses maturity levels to

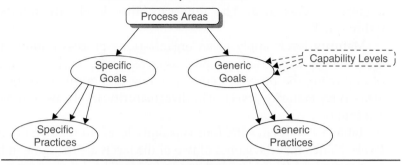

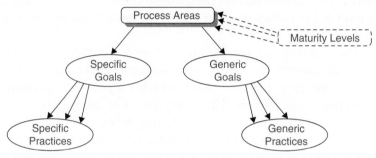

FIGURE 3.1
Structure of the Continuous and Staged Representations

characterize the overall state of the organization's processes relative to the model as a whole, whereas the continuous representation uses capability levels to characterize the state of the organization's processes relative to an individual process area.

What may strike you as you compare these two representations is their similarity. Both have many of the same components (e.g., process areas, specific goals, specific practices), and these components have the same hierarchy and configuration.

What is not readily apparent from the high-level view in Figure 3.1 is that the continuous representation focuses on process area capability as measured by capability levels and the staged representation focuses on overall maturity as measured by maturity levels. This dimension (the capability/maturity dimension) of CMMI is used for benchmarking and appraisal activities, as well as guiding an organization's improvement efforts.

Capability levels apply to an organization's process improvement achievement in individual process areas. These levels are a means for incrementally improving the processes corresponding to a given process area. The four capability levels are numbered 0 through 3.

Maturity levels apply to an organization's process improvement achievement across multiple process areas. These levels are a means of improving the processes corresponding to a given set of process areas (i.e., maturity level). The five maturity levels are numbered 1 through 5.

Table 3.1 compares the four capability levels to the five maturity levels. Notice that the names of two of the levels are the same in both representations (i.e., Managed and Defined). The differences are that there is no maturity level 0; there are no capability levels 4 and 5; and at level 1, the names used for capability level 1 and maturity level 1 are different.

The continuous representation is concerned with selecting both a particular process area to improve and the desired capability level for that process area. In this context, whether a process is performed or incomplete is important. Therefore, the name "Incomplete" is given to the continuous representation starting point.

The staged representation is concerned with selecting multiple process areas to improve within a maturity level; whether individual processes are performed or incomplete is not the primary focus. Therefore, the name "Initial" is given to the staged representation starting point.

Both capability levels and maturity levels provide a way to improve the processes of an organization and measure how well organizations can and do improve their processes. However, the associated approach to process improvement is different.

TABLE 3.1 Comparison of Capability and Maturity Levels

Level	Continuous Representation Capability Levels	Staged Representation Maturity Levels
Level 0	Incomplete	
Level 1	Performed	Initial
Level 2	Managed	Managed
Level 3	Defined	Defined
Level 4		Quantitatively Managed
Level 5		Optimizing

Understanding Capability Levels

To support those who use the continuous representation, all CMMI models reflect capability levels in their design and content.

The four capability levels, each a layer in the foundation for ongoing process improvement, are designated by the numbers 0 through 3:

0. Incomplete
1. Performed
2. Managed
3. Defined

A capability level for a process area is achieved when all of the generic goals are satisfied up to that level. The fact that capability levels 2 and 3 use the same terms as generic goals 2 and 3 is intentional because each of these generic goals and practices reflects the meaning of the capability levels of the goals and practices. (See the Generic Goals and Generic Practices section in Part Two for more information about generic goals and practices.) A short description of each capability level follows.

Capability Level 0: Incomplete

An *incomplete* process is a process that either is not performed or is partially performed. One or more of the specific goals of the process area are not satisfied and no generic goals exist for this level since there is no reason to institutionalize a partially performed process.

Capability Level 1: Performed

A capability level 1 process is characterized as a *performed process*. A performed process is a process that accomplishes the needed work to produce work products; the specific goals of the process area are satisfied.

Although capability level 1 results in important improvements, those improvements can be lost over time if they are not institutionalized. The application of institutionalization (the CMMI generic practices at capability levels 2 and 3) helps to ensure that improvements are maintained.

Capability Level 2: Managed

A capability level 2 process is characterized as a *managed process*. A managed process is a performed process that is planned and executed in accordance with policy; employs skilled people having adequate resources to produce controlled outputs; involves relevant stakeholders; is monitored, controlled, and reviewed; and is evaluated for adherence to its process description.

The process discipline reflected by capability level 2 helps to ensure that existing practices are retained during times of stress.

Capability Level 3: Defined

A capability level 3 process is characterized as a *defined process*. A defined process is a managed process that is tailored from the organization's set of standard processes according to the organization's tailoring guidelines; has a maintained process description; and contributes process related experiences to the organizational process assets.

A critical distinction between capability levels 2 and 3 is the scope of standards, process descriptions, and procedures. At capability level 2, the standards, process descriptions, and procedures can be quite different in each specific instance of the process (e.g., on a particular project). At capability level 3, the standards, process descriptions, and procedures for a project are tailored from the organization's set of standard processes to suit a particular project or organizational unit and therefore are more consistent, except for the differences allowed by the tailoring guidelines.

Another critical distinction is that at capability level 3 processes are typically described more rigorously than at capability level 2. A defined process clearly states the purpose, inputs, entry criteria, activities, roles, measures, verification steps, outputs, and exit criteria. At capability level 3, processes are managed more proactively using an understanding of the interrelationships of the process activities and detailed measures of the process and its work products.

Advancing Through Capability Levels

The capability levels of a process area are achieved through the application of generic practices or suitable alternatives to the processes associated with that process area.

Reaching capability level 1 for a process area is equivalent to saying that the processes associated with that process area are *performed processes*.

Reaching capability level 2 for a process area is equivalent to saying that there is a policy that indicates you will perform the process. There is a plan for performing it, resources are provided, responsibilities are assigned, training to perform it is provided, selected work products related to performing the process are controlled, and so on.

In other words, a capability level 2 process can be planned and monitored just like any project or support activity.

Reaching capability level 3 for a process area is equivalent to saying that an organizational standard process exists associated with that process area, which can be tailored to the needs of the project. The processes in the organization are now more consistently defined and applied because they are based on organizational standard processes.

After an organization has reached capability level 3 in the process areas it has selected for improvement, it can continue its improvement journey by addressing high maturity process areas (Organizational Process Performance, Quantitative Project Management, Causal Analysis and Resolution, and Organizational Performance Management).

The high maturity process areas focus on improving the performance of those processes already implemented. The high maturity process areas describe the use of statistical and other quantitative techniques to improve organizational and project processes to better achieve business objectives.

When continuing its improvement journey in this way, an organization can derive the most benefit by first selecting the OPP and QPM process areas, and bringing those process areas to capability levels 1, 2, and 3. In doing so, projects and organizations align the selection and analyses of processes more closely with their business objectives.

After the organization attains capability level 3 in the OPP and QPM process areas, the organization can continue its improvement path by selecting the CAR and OPM process areas. In doing so, the organization analyzes the business performance using statistical and other quantitative techniques to determine performance shortfalls, and identifies and deploys process and technology improvements that contribute to meeting quality and process performance objectives. Projects and the organization use causal analysis to identify and resolve issues affecting performance and promote the dissemination of best practices.

Understanding Maturity Levels

To support those who use the staged representation, all CMMI models reflect maturity levels in their design and content. A maturity level consists of related specific and generic practices for a predefined set of process areas that improve the organization's overall performance.

The maturity level of an organization provides a way to characterize its performance. Experience has shown that organizations do their best when they focus their process improvement efforts on a manageable number of process areas at a time and that those areas require increasing sophistication as the organization improves.

A maturity level is a defined evolutionary plateau for organizational process improvement. Each maturity level matures an important subset of the organization's processes, preparing it to move to the next maturity level. The maturity levels are measured by the achievement of the specific and generic goals associated with each predefined set of process areas.

The five maturity levels, each a layer in the foundation for ongoing process improvement, are designated by the numbers 1 through 5:

1. Initial
2. Managed
3. Defined
4. Quantitatively Managed
5. Optimizing

Remember that maturity levels 2 and 3 use the same terms as capability levels 2 and 3. This consistency of terminology was intentional because the concepts of maturity levels and capability levels are complementary. Maturity levels are used to characterize organizational improvement relative to a set of process areas, and capability levels characterize organizational improvement relative to an individual process area.

Maturity Level 1: Initial

At maturity level 1, processes are usually ad hoc and chaotic. The organization usually does not provide a stable environment to support processes. Success in these organizations depends on the competence and heroics of the people in the organization and not on the use of proven processes. In spite of this chaos, maturity level 1 organizations acquire products and services that work, but they frequently exceed the budget and schedule documented in their plans.

Maturity level 1 organizations are characterized by a tendency to overcommit, abandon their processes in a time of crisis, and be unable to repeat their successes.

Maturity Level 2: Managed

At maturity level 2, projects establish the foundation for an organization to become an effective acquirer of needed capabilities by institutionalizing selected Project Management and Acquisition Engineering processes. Projects define a supplier strategy, create project plans, and monitor and control the project to ensure the product or service is delivered as planned. The acquirer establishes agreements with suppliers supporting the projects and manages these agreements to ensure each supplier delivers on commitments. The acquirer develops and manages customer and contractual requirements. Configuration management and process and product quality assurance are institutionalized, and the acquirer develops the capability to measure and analyze process performance.

Also at maturity level 2, projects, processes, work products, and services are managed. The acquirer ensures that processes are planned in accordance with policy. To execute the process, the acquirer provides adequate resources, assigns responsibility for performing the process, trains people on the process, and ensures the designated work products of the process are under appropriate levels of configuration management. The acquirer identifies and involves relevant stakeholders and periodically monitors and controls the process. Process adherence is periodically evaluated and process performance is shared with senior management. The process discipline reflected by maturity level 2 helps to ensure that existing practices are retained during times of stress.

Maturity Level 3: Defined

At maturity level 3, acquirers use defined processes for managing projects and suppliers. They embed tenets of project management and acquisition best practices, such as integrated project management and acquisition technical management, into the standard process set. The acquirer verifies that selected work products meet their requirements and validates products and services to ensure they meet the needs of the customer and end user. These processes are well characterized and understood and are described in standards, procedures, tools, and methods.

The organization's set of standard processes, which is the basis for maturity level 3, is established and improved over time. These standard processes are used to establish consistency across the organization. Projects establish their defined processes by tailoring the organization's set of standard processes according to tailoring guidelines. (See the definition of "organization's set of standard processes" in the glossary.)

A critical distinction between maturity levels 2 and 3 is the scope of standards, process descriptions, and procedures. At maturity level 2, the standards, process descriptions, and procedures can be quite different in each specific instance of the process (e.g., on a particular project). At maturity level 3, the standards, process descriptions, and procedures for a project are tailored from the organization's set of standard processes to suit a particular project or organizational unit and therefore are more consistent except for the differences allowed by the tailoring guidelines.

Another critical distinction is that at maturity level 3, processes are typically described more rigorously than at maturity level 2. A defined process clearly states the purpose, inputs, entry criteria, activities, roles, measures, verification steps, outputs, and exit criteria. At maturity level 3, processes are managed more proactively using an understanding of the interrelationships of process activities and detailed measures of the process, its work products, and its services.

At maturity level 3, the organization further improves its processes that are related to the maturity level 2 process areas. Generic practices associated with generic goal 3 that were not addressed at maturity level 2 are applied to achieve maturity level 3.

Maturity Level 4: Quantitatively Managed

At maturity level 4, acquirers establish quantitative objectives for quality and process performance and use them as criteria in managing processes. Quantitative objectives are based on the needs of the customer, end users, organization, and process implementers. Quality and process performance is understood in statistical terms and is managed throughout the life of processes.

For selected subprocesses, specific measures of process performance are collected and statistically analyzed. When selecting subprocesses for analyses, it is critical to understand the relationships between different subprocesses and their impact on achieving the objectives for quality and process performance. Such an approach helps to ensure that subprocess monitoring using statistical and other quantitative techniques is applied to where it has the most overall value to the business. Process performance baselines and models can be used to help set quality and process performance objectives that help achieve business objectives.

A critical distinction between maturity levels 3 and 4 is the predictability of process performance. At maturity level 4, the performance of processes is controlled using statistical and other quantitative techniques and predictions are based, in part, on a statistical analysis of fine-grained process data.

Maturity Level 5: Optimizing

At maturity level 5, an organization continually improves its processes based on a quantitative understanding of its business objectives and performance needs. The organization uses a quantitative approach to understand the variation inherent in the process and the causes of process outcomes.

Maturity level 5 focuses on continually improving process performance through incremental and innovative process and technological improvements. The organization's quality and process performance objectives are established, continually revised to reflect changing business objectives and organizational performance, and used as criteria in managing process improvement. The effects of deployed process improvements are measured using statistical and other quantitative techniques and compared to quality and process performance objectives. The project's defined processes, the organization's set of standard processes, and supporting technology are targets of measurable improvement activities.

A critical distinction between maturity levels 4 and 5 is the focus on managing and improving organizational performance. At maturity level 4, the organization and projects focus on understanding and controlling performance at the subprocess level and using the results to manage projects. At maturity level 5, the organization is concerned with overall organizational performance using data collected from multiple projects. Analysis of the data identifies shortfalls or gaps in performance. These gaps are used to drive organizational process improvement that generates measurable improvement in performance.

Advancing Through Maturity Levels

Organizations can achieve progressive improvements in their maturity by achieving control first at the project level and continuing to the most advanced level—organization-wide continuous process improvement—using both qualitative and quantitative data to make decisions.

Since improved organizational maturity is associated with improvement in the range of expected results that can be achieved by an organization, maturity is one way of predicting general outcomes of the organization's next project. For instance, at maturity level 2, the organization has been elevated from ad hoc to disciplined by establishing sound project management. As the organization achieves generic and specific goals for the set of process areas in a maturity level, it increases its organizational maturity and reaps the benefits of process improvement. Because each maturity level forms a necessary foundation for the next level, trying to skip maturity levels is usually counterproductive.

At the same time, recognize that process improvement efforts should focus on the needs of the organization in the context of its business environment and that process areas at higher maturity levels can address the current and future needs of an organization or project.

For example, organizations seeking to move from maturity level 1 to maturity level 2 are frequently encouraged to establish a process group, which is addressed by the Organizational Process Focus process area at maturity level 3. Although a process group is not a necessary characteristic of a maturity level 2 organization, it can be a useful part of the organization's approach to achieving maturity level 2.

This situation is sometimes characterized as establishing a maturity level 1 process group to bootstrap the maturity level 1 organization to maturity level 2. Maturity level 1 process improvement activities may depend primarily on the insight and competence of the process group until an infrastructure to support more disciplined and widespread improvement is in place.

Organizations can institute process improvements anytime they choose, even before they are prepared to advance to the maturity level at which the specific practice is recommended. In such situations, however, organizations should understand that the success of these improvements is at risk because the foundation for their successful institutionalization has not been completed. Processes without the proper foundation can fail at the point they are needed most—under stress.

A defined process that is characteristic of a maturity level 3 organization can be placed at great risk if maturity level 2 management practices are deficient. For example, management may commit to a poorly planned schedule or fail to control changes to baselined requirements. Similarly, many organizations prematurely collect the detailed data characteristic of maturity level 4 only to find the data uninterpretable because of inconsistencies in processes and measurement definitions.

Process Areas

Process areas are viewed differently in the two representations. Figure 3.2 compares views of how process areas are used in the continuous representation and the staged representation.

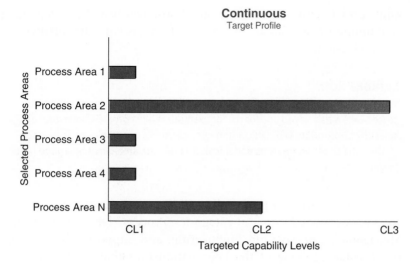

Continuous
Target Profile

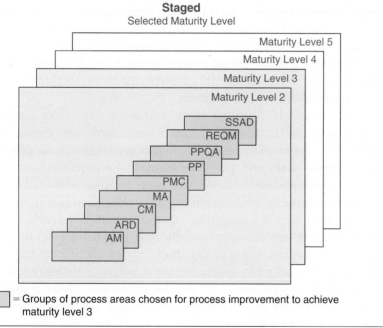

Staged
Selected Maturity Level

= Groups of process areas chosen for process improvement to achieve maturity level 3

FIGURE 3.2

Process Areas in the Continuous and Staged Representations

The continuous representation enables the organization to choose the focus of its process improvement efforts by choosing those process areas, or sets of interrelated process areas, that best benefit the organization and its business objectives. Although there are some limits on what an organization can choose because of the dependencies among process areas, the organization has considerable freedom in its selection.

> **AUTHORS' NOTE**
> When selecting which process areas to use to improve your organization's processes, take a risk-based approach. For example, if most projects have difficulty selecting appropriate acquisition strategies or cannot effectively perform trade studies, the Decision Analysis and Resolution process area might be a good place to start.

To support those who use the continuous representation, process areas are organized into four categories: Process Management, Project Management, Acquisition Engineering, and Support. These categories emphasize some of the key relationships that exist among the process areas.

Sometimes an informal grouping of process areas is mentioned: high maturity process areas. The four high maturity process areas are Organizational Process Performance, Quantitative Project Management, Organizational Performance Management, and Causal Analysis and Resolution. These process areas focus on improving the performance of implemented processes that most closely relate to the organization's business objectives.

Once you select process areas, you must also select how much you would like to mature processes associated with those process areas (i.e., select the appropriate capability level). Capability levels and generic goals and practices support the improvement of processes associated with individual process areas. For example, an organization may wish to reach capability level 2 in one process area and capability level 3 in another. As the organization reaches a capability level, it sets its sights on the next capability level for one of these same process areas or decides to widen its view and address a larger number of process areas. Once it reaches capability level 3 in most of the process areas, the organization can shift its attention to the high maturity process areas and can track the capability of each through capability level 3.

> **AUTHORS' NOTE**
> Consider improving processes that cross acquirer–supplier boundaries, such as the requirements process, and perform joint acquirer–supplier improvement activities.

The selection of a combination of process areas and capability levels is typically described in a "target profile." A target profile defines all of the process areas to be addressed and the targeted capability level for each. This profile governs which goals and practices the organization will address in its process improvement efforts.

Most organizations, at minimum, target capability level 1 for the process areas they select, which requires that all of these process areas' specific goals be achieved. However, organizations that target capability levels higher than 1 concentrate on the institutionalization of selected processes in the organization by implementing generic goals and practices.

The staged representation provides a path of improvement from maturity level 1 to maturity level 5 that involves achieving the goals of the process areas at each maturity level. To support those who use the staged representation, process areas are grouped by maturity level, indicating which process areas to implement to achieve each maturity level.

For example, at maturity level 2, there is a set of process areas that an organization would use to guide its process improvement until it could achieve all the goals of all these process areas. Once maturity level 2 is achieved, the organization focuses its efforts on maturity level 3 process areas, and so on. The generic goals that apply to each process area are also predetermined. Generic goal 2 applies to maturity level 2 and generic goal 3 applies to maturity levels 3 through 5.

Table 3.2 provides a list of CMMI-ACQ process areas and their associated categories and maturity levels.

Equivalent Staging

Equivalent staging is a way to compare results from using the continuous representation to results from using the staged representation. In essence, if you measure improvement relative to selected process areas using capability levels in the continuous representation, how do you translate that work into maturity levels? Is this translation possible?

Up to this point, we have not discussed process appraisals in much detail. The SCAMPI method[2] is used to appraise organizations using CMMI, and one result of an appraisal is a rating [SEI 2011a, Ahern 2005]. If the continuous representation is used for an appraisal, the rating is a "capability level profile." If the staged representation is used for an appraisal, the rating is a "maturity level rating" (e.g., maturity level 3).

---

2. The Standard CMMI Appraisal Method for Process Improvement (SCAMPI) method is described in Chapter 5.

TABLE 3.2 Process Areas, Categories, and Maturity Levels

Process Area	Category	Maturity Level
Agreement Management (AM)	Project Management	2
Acquisition Requirements Development (ARD)	Acquisition Engineering	2
Acquisition Technical Management (ATM)	Acquisition Engineering	3
Acquisition Validation (AVAL)	Acquisition Engineering	3
Acquisition Verification (AVER)	Acquisition Engineering	3
Causal Analysis and Resolution (CAR)	Support	5
Configuration Management (CM)	Support	2
Decision Analysis and Resolution (DAR)	Support	3
Integrated Project Management (IPM)	Project Management	3
Measurement and Analysis (MA)	Support	2
Organizational Process Definition (OPD)	Process Management	3
Organizational Process Focus (OPF)	Process Management	3
Organizational Performance Management (OPM)	Process Management	5
Organizational Process Performance (OPP)	Process Management	4
Organizational Training (OT)	Process Management	3
Project Monitoring and Control (PMC)	Project Management	2
Project Planning (PP)	Project Management	2
Process and Product Quality Assurance (PPQA)	Support	2
Quantitative Project Management (QPM)	Project Management	4
Requirements Management (REQM)	Project Management	2
Risk Management (RSKM)	Project Management	3
Solicitation and Supplier Agreement Development (SSAD)	Project Management	2

A capability level profile is a list of process areas and the corresponding capability level achieved for each. This profile enables an organization to track its capability level by process area. The profile is called an "achievement profile" when it represents the organization's actual progress for each process area. Alternatively, the profile is called a "target profile" when it represents the organization's planned process improvement objectives.

Figure 3.3 illustrates a combined target and achievement profile. The gray portion of each bar represents what has been achieved. The unshaded portion represents what remains to be accomplished to meet the target profile.

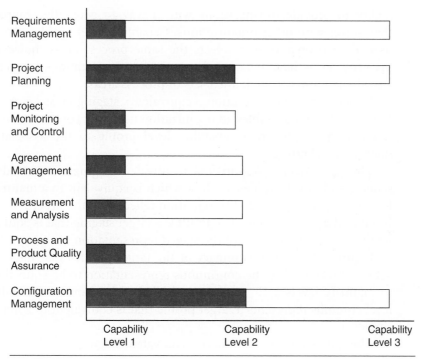

FIGURE 3.3

Example Combined Target and Achievement Profile

An achievement profile, when compared with a target profile, enables an organization to plan and track its progress for each selected process area. Maintaining capability level profiles is advisable when using the continuous representation.

Target staging is a sequence of target profiles that describes the path of process improvement to be followed by the organization. When building target profiles, the organization should pay attention to the dependencies between generic practices and process areas. If a generic practice depends on a process area, either to carry out the generic practice or to provide a prerequisite work product, the generic practice can be much less effective when the process area is not implemented.[3]

Although the reasons to use the continuous representation are many, ratings consisting of capability level profiles are limited in their

3. See Table 7.2 in the Generic Goals and Generic Practices section of Part Two for more information about the dependencies between generic practices and process areas.

ability to provide organizations with a way to generally compare themselves with other organizations. Capability level profiles can be used if each organization selects the same process areas; however, maturity levels have been used to compare organizations for years and already provide predefined sets of process areas.

Because of this situation, equivalent staging was created. Equivalent staging enables an organization using the continuous representation to convert a capability level profile to the associated maturity level rating.

The most effective way to depict equivalent staging is to provide a sequence of target profiles, each of which is equivalent to a maturity level rating of the staged representation reflected in the process areas listed in the target profile. The result is a target staging that is equivalent to the maturity levels of the staged representation.

Figure 3.4 shows a summary of the target profiles that must be achieved when using the continuous representation to be equivalent to maturity levels 2 through 5. Each shaded area in the capability level columns represents a target profile that is equivalent to a maturity level.

The following rules summarize equivalent staging:

- To achieve maturity level 2, all process areas assigned to maturity level 2 must achieve capability level 2 or 3.
- To achieve maturity level 3, all process areas assigned to maturity levels 2 and 3 must achieve capability level 3.
- To achieve maturity level 4, all process areas assigned to maturity levels 2, 3, and 4 must achieve capability level 3.
- To achieve maturity level 5, all process areas must achieve capability level 3.

Achieving High Maturity

When using the staged representation, you attain high maturity when you achieve maturity level 4 or 5. Achieving maturity level 4 involves implementing all process areas for maturity levels 2, 3, and 4. Likewise, achieving maturity level 5 involves implementing all process areas for maturity levels 2, 3, 4, and 5.

When using the continuous representation, you attain high maturity using the equivalent staging concept. High maturity that is equivalent to staged maturity level 4 using equivalent staging is attained when you achieve capability level 3 for all process areas

Name	Abbr	ML	CL1	CL2	CL3
Agreement Management	AM	2			
Acquisition Requirements Development	ARD	2			
Configuration Management	CM	2			
Measurement and Analysis	MA	2		Target	
Project Monitoring and Control	PMC	2		Profile 2	
Project Planning	PP	2			
Process and Product Quality Assurance	PPQA	2			
Requirements Management	REQM	2			
Solicitation and Supplier Agreement Development	SSAD	2			
Acquisition Technical Management	ATM	3			
Acquisition Validation	AVAL	3		Target	
Acquisition Verification	AVER	3		Profile 3	
Decision Analysis and Resolution	DAR	3			
Integrated Project Management	IPM	3			
Organizational Process Definition	OPD	3			
Organizational Process Focus	OPF	3			
Organizational Training	OT	3			
Risk Management	RSKM	3			
Organizational Process Performance	OPP	4		Target	
Quantitative Project Management	QPM	4		Profile 4	
Causal Analysis and Resolution	CAR	5		Target	
Organizational Innovation and Deployment	OID	5		Profile 5	

FIGURE 3.4
Target Profiles and Equivalent Staging

except for Organizational Performance Management (OPM) and Causal Analysis and Resolution (CAR). High maturity that is equivalent to staged maturity level 5 using equivalent staging is attained when you achieve capability level 3 for all process areas.

CHAPTER 4

RELATIONSHIPS AMONG PROCESS AREAS

In this chapter we describe the key relationships among process areas to help you see the acquirer's view of process improvement and how process areas depend on the implementation of other process areas.

The relationships among multiple process areas, including the information and artifacts that flow from one process area to another—illustrated by the figure and descriptions in this chapter—help you to see a larger view of process implementation and improvement.

Successful process improvement initiatives must be driven by the business objectives of the organization. For example, a common business objective is to reduce the time it takes to get a product to market. The process improvement objective derived from that might be to improve the project management processes to ensure on-time delivery. Those improvements rely on best practices in the Project Planning and Project Monitoring and Control process areas.

Although we group process areas in this chapter to simplify the discussion of their relationships, process areas often interact and have an effect on one another regardless of their group, category, or level. For example, the Decision Analysis and Resolution process area (a Support process area at maturity level 3) contains specific practices that address the formal evaluation process used in the Solicitation and Supplier Agreement Development process area (a Project Management process area at maturity level 2) to select suppliers to deliver a product or service.

Being aware of the key relationships that exist among CMMI process areas will help you apply CMMI in a useful and productive way. Relationships among process areas are described in more detail in the references of each process area and specifically in the Related Process Areas section of each process area in Part Two. Refer to Chapter 2 for more information about references.

Figure 4.1 illustrates key relationships among CMMI-ACQ process areas.

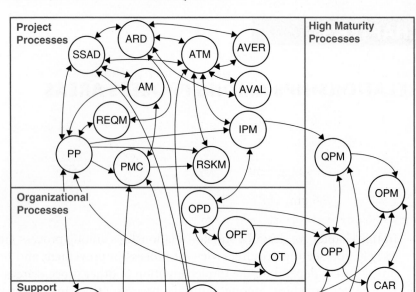

FIGURE 4.1
Key Relationships Among Process Areas

AUTHORS' NOTE

The model uses the process area categories of Project Management, Process Management, and Support, and Acquisition. This nomenclature is useful for building and sharing models; however, in this chapter the process areas are organized into groups that are more functional and descriptive to support process implementation. These groups—Project, Organizational, Support, and High Maturity—are depicted in Figure 4.1.

AUTHORS' NOTE

The grouping of process areas is not intended to dictate where organizationally the practices within a process area must be performed in the context of your organizational construct. For example, some acquisition organizations may develop acquisition strategies (a Project Planning practice) as part of an organizational function apart from individual projects to ensure that strategies remain consistent among similar projects.

Project Processes

The project process areas contain practices that address acquirer activities related to establishing, executing, and ensuring the transition of an acquisition project.

The project process areas of CMMI-ACQ contain the following process areas from the Project Management and Acquisition Engineering categories:

Project Management

- Project Planning (PP)
- Requirements Management (REQM)
- Solicitation and Supplier Agreement Development (SSAD)
- Agreement Management (AM)
- Project Monitoring and Control (PMC)
- Integrated Project Management (IPM)
- Risk Management (RSKM)

Acquisition Engineering

- Acquisition Requirements Development (ARD)
- Acquisition Technical Management (ATM)
- Acquisition Verification (AVER)
- Acquisition Validation (AVAL)

The Project Planning process area includes practices for determining the acquisition strategy, developing the project plan, involving stakeholders appropriately, obtaining commitment to the plan, and maintaining the plan.

Planning begins with the acquisition strategy, which provides the framework for the acquisition project and its plans. The project plan covers the project management and acquisition activities performed by the project. Other plans (e.g., plans for transition to operations and support, configuration management, verification, and measurement and analysis) from relevant stakeholders that affect the project are reviewed, and commitments with those stakeholders for their contributions to the project are established.

Once the acquisition strategy is established using Project Planning practices, the strategy is used to focus on specifying customer and contractual requirements that express customer value in Acquisition Requirements Development practices. Customer needs are established and translated into customer requirements. The set of customer requirements is prioritized and a set of contractual requirements, including design constraints, is developed.

Development of contractual requirements and operational scenarios also depends on the acquisition strategy developed using Project Planning practices. This set of contractual requirements is used in Solicitation and Supplier Agreement Development practices to select suppliers and establish a supplier agreement to acquire the product or service. The product or service is designed and implemented by the supplier consistent with the acquirer's contractual requirements and design constraints.

Requirements are maintained using Requirements Management practices. These practices describe activities for obtaining and controlling requirement changes and ensuring that other relevant plans and data are kept current. They also describe the traceability of requirements from customer to contractual requirements and supplier agreements. Requirements Management practices interact with Acquisition Requirements Development practices. All changes to contractual requirements must be reflected in the supplier agreements established and maintained using Solicitation and Supplier Agreement Development practices.

The Solicitation and Supplier Agreement Development process area defines practices for preparing a solicitation package, selecting a capable supplier, and establishing and maintaining the supplier agreement. The acquisition strategy developed using Project Planning practices and contractual requirements developed using Acquisition Requirements Development practices are a prerequisite to prepare for Solicitation and Supplier Agreement Development practices. An agreement is developed to acquire the product or service by identifying potential suppliers, developing the solicitation package, and distributing it to the potential suppliers. The acquirer evaluates the proposed solutions and negotiates with the supplier to finalize the agreement so that both the acquirer and supplier have a mutual understanding of the agreement. This agreement is established and maintained using Solicitation and Supplier Agreement Development, but the execution of the agreement is performed using Agreement Management practices.

The acquirer uses Agreement Management practices to manage the supplier agreement by performing the acquirer activities defined in the supplier agreement, monitoring selected supplier processes, accepting the product or service, and managing supplier invoices.

After a supplier is selected and a supplier agreement is established, the acquirer continues to apply Requirements Management practices to manage customer and contractual requirements, while the selected supplier is managing the refined product and product component requirements. Using Requirements Management practices ensures that changes to requirements are reflected in project plans, activities, and work products. This cycle of changes can affect or be affected by other processes; thus, the requirements management process is a dynamic and often recursive sequence of events.

The Project Monitoring and Control process area contains practices for monitoring and controlling acquirer activities and overseeing the supplier's project progress and performance according to project plans. The process area includes coverage of monitoring and controlling the transition to operations and support that was planned using Project Planning practices.

Project Monitoring and Control practices also cover taking corrective action. The project plan specifies the frequency of progress reviews and the measures used to monitor progress. Progress is determined primarily by comparing project status to the plan. When the actual status deviates significantly from expected values, corrective actions are taken as appropriate. These actions can include replanning, which requires using Project Planning practices.

As the acquirer's processes improve in capability, Integrated Project Management practices are used to manage the project using a defined process tailored from the organization's set of standard processes (Organizational Process Development). The project uses and contributes to organizational process assets, the project's work environment is established and maintained from the organization's work environment standards, and teams are established using the organization's rules and guidelines. The project's relevant stakeholders coordinate their efforts in a timely manner through the identification, negotiation, and tracking of critical dependencies and the resolution of coordination issues.

In the acquirer–supplier relationship, the need for an early and aggressive detection of risk is compounded by the complexity of projects acquiring products or services. The purpose of Risk Management is to identify and assess project risks during the project planning process and to manage these risks throughout the project.

The acquirer has a dual role: first, to assess and manage overall project risks for the duration of the project, and second, to assess and manage risks associated with the performance of the supplier. As the acquisition progresses to the selection of a supplier, the risks specific to the supplier's technical and management approach become more important to the success of the acquisition.

Although risk identification and monitoring are covered in the Project Planning and Project Monitoring and Control process areas, using the Risk Management process area enables the acquirer to take a continuing, forward-looking approach to managing risks with activities that include identification of risk parameters, risk assessments, and risk mitigation.

Acquisition Technical Management practices are used to combine the project's defined process and risk management activities to perform technical and interface management. This management includes activities such as managing the technical evaluation of selected supplier products and services, conducting technical reviews with the supplier, and managing selected interfaces throughout the project's lifecycle. Acquisition Technical Management practices, Agreement Management practices, and the Project Monitoring and Control practices are all used in concert, as they all contain reviews that are conducted throughout the project.

Using Acquisition Verification practices ensures that the acquirer's selected work products meet specified requirements. Using Acquisition Verification practices also enables the acquirer to select work products and verification methods to verify acquirer work products against specified requirements.

Acquisition Verification practices also are used to address peer reviews. Peer reviews are a proven method for removing defects early and provide valuable insight into the work products and product components being developed and maintained by the acquirer.

The acquirer uses Acquisition Validation processes to ensure that the products or services received from the supplier will fulfill the relevant stakeholders' needs. Products and services are incrementally validated against the customer's needs.

Validation can be performed in the operational environment or in a simulated operational environment. Coordination with the customer on the validation requirements is an important element of this process area.

The scope of the Acquisition Validation process area includes the validation of products, product components, selected intermediate work products, and processes. These validated elements can often require reverification and revalidation. Issues discovered during validation are usually resolved using Acquisition Requirements Development practices or by working with the supplier through the supplier agreement and technical reviews.

As mentioned above, Integrated Project Management processes establish a defined process and integrated plan for managing all the activities of the project. These activities include all project processes described above, from Project Planning through Acquisition Validation. The organization's set of standard processes and other process assets provide critical guidance to projects for establishing a defined process and plan. How the organization creates and deploys such process assets for use by the whole organization, along with other forms of critical project support, is the subject of the next section.

Organizational Processes

Organizational process areas contain the cross-project activities related to defining, planning, deploying, implementing, monitoring, controlling, appraising, measuring, and improving processes.

The organizational process areas contain practices that provide the acquiring organization with a capability to develop and deploy processes and supporting assets and to document and share best practices and learning across the organization.

The three organizational process areas in CMMI-ACQ are as follows:

- Organizational Process Focus (OPF)
- Organizational Process Definition (OPD)
- Organizational Training (OT)

Organizational Process Focus practices help the acquiring organization to plan, implement, and deploy organizational process improvements based on an understanding of the current strengths and weaknesses of the organization's processes and process assets. Candidate improvements to the organization's processes are obtained through activities in the processes of related projects. These activities include generating process improvement proposals, measuring processes, collecting lessons learned in implementing the processes, and evaluating products and services.

Using Organizational Process Focus practices, the acquirer encourages participation of suppliers in process improvement activities. Suppliers can be involved in developing process action plans if processes that define interfaces between the acquirer and supplier are targeted for improvement.

Organizational Process Definition practices form the basis for establishing and maintaining the organization's set of standard processes, work environment standards, rules and guidelines for the operation of teams, and other assets based on the process needs and objectives of the organization.

These other assets include descriptions of lifecycle models, process tailoring guidelines, and process related documentation and data. Projects tailor the organization's set of standard processes to create their defined processes using Integrated Project Management practices. Experiences and work products from performing these defined processes, including measurement data, process descriptions, process artifacts, and lessons learned, are incorporated, as appropriate, into the organization's set of standard processes and other assets.

The acquirer's set of standard processes can also describe standard interactions with suppliers. Supplier interactions are typically characterized by the deliverables expected from suppliers, acceptance criteria applicable to those deliverables, standards (e.g., architecture and technology standards), and standard milestone and progress reviews. The acquirer defines in the supplier agreement how changes to organizational process assets that affect the supplier (e.g., standard supplier deliverables, acceptance criteria) are deployed.

The purpose of implementing Organizational Training practices is to develop the skills and knowledge of people so they can perform their roles effectively and efficiently. For example, an acquiring organization may want to develop its project managers' capabilities in managing supplier agreements.

Using Organizational Training practices helps the acquirer identify the strategic training needs of the organization as well as the tactical training needs that are common across projects and support groups. In particular, training is created or obtained to develop the skills required to perform the organization's set of standard processes. The main components of training include a managed training development program, documented plans, staff with appropriate knowledge, and mechanisms for measuring the effectiveness of the training program.

Support Processes

The Support process areas address acquisition project processes and can address processes that apply more generally to the organization. For example, Process and Product Quality Assurance practices can be used to provide an objective evaluation of the processes and work products described in all the process areas.

Although all Support process areas rely on other process areas for input, some Support process areas provide support functions that also help implement several generic practices.

The four Support process areas in CMMI-ACQ are as follows:

- Measurement and Analysis (MA)
- Process and Product Quality Assurance (PPQA)
- Configuration Management (CM)
- Decision Analysis and Resolution (DAR)

The Measurement and Analysis process area is related to other process areas because its practices guide projects and organizations in aligning measurement needs and objectives with a measurement approach that is used to support management information needs. The results can be used in making informed decisions and taking appropriate corrective actions.

An acquirer uses Measurement and Analysis practices to support the information needs of the organization and project. Some of this information may be needed from the acquirer, some from the supplier, and some from all parts of a project. Supplier Solicitation and Agreement Development describes how these measures are specified in the solicitation process and supplier agreement. The measurement results from the acquirer and supplier support project, supplier, and technical reviews through project monitoring and control, agreement management, and acquisition technical management.

The Process and Product Quality Assurance process area is related to all process areas because it describes specific practices for objectively evaluating performed processes and work products against applicable process descriptions, standards, and procedures, and by ensuring that issues arising from these evaluations are addressed. Process and Product Quality Assurance practices support the acquisition of high quality products and services by providing the acquirer with appropriate visibility into, and feedback on, the processes and associated work products throughout the life of the project.

The Configuration Management process area is related to all process areas because its practices describe establishing and maintaining the integrity of work products using configuration identification, configuration control, configuration status accounting, and configuration audits. The work products placed under configuration control include the products that are delivered to the customer, designated internal work products, acquired products, tools, and other items that are used in creating and describing these work products.

Examples of work products that can be placed under configuration control include plans, process descriptions, and requirements. Suppliers can play a part in any of these activities on behalf of the acquirer, so the supplier agreement should specify the configuration management roles and responsibilities of the acquirer and supplier. Configuration management of acquired products (both final and interim products) created by the suppliers requires monitoring to ensure that project requirements are met.

The Decision Analysis and Resolution process area is related to all process areas because its practices describe determining which issues should be subjected to a formal evaluation process and applying a formal evaluation process to them. A repeatable Decision Analysis and Resolution process is important for an acquirer when making the critical decisions that define and guide the acquisition process and later when critical decisions are made with the selected supplier.

High Maturity Processes

High maturity process areas describe practices that further align organizational, project, and support processes with the business objectives of the organization. These process areas describe practices at both the organizational and project level for establishing objectives for quality and process performance, monitoring variation in the organization's and projects' processes, evaluating the impacts of proposed changes to those processes, and systematically deploying processes across the organization. To effectively implement these practices, mature measurement and analysis processes are needed.

The acquirer achieves an effective implementation of high maturity practices by ensuring that all members of the organization collect and analyze measurements and propose and evaluate changes to processes. In other words, high maturity practices should be integrated as much as possible with the practices in other process areas.

The four high maturity process areas in CMMI-ACQ are as follows:

- Organizational Process Performance (OPP)
- Quantitative Project Management (QPM)
- Causal Analysis and Resolution (CAR)
- Organizational Performance Management (OPM)

At the organizational level, the acquirer uses the Organizational Process Performance practices to derive quantitative objectives for quality and process performance from the organization's business objectives and the customer. Processes and subprocesses critical to achieving the quality and process performance objectives are identified along with measurements to characterize performance. Using collected measurement data, process performance models and process performance baselines are created, updated, and used to analyze process performance.

Quantitative Project Management practices describe applying statistical and other quantitative techniques to manage process performance and product quality. The project's quality and process performance objectives are based on the objectives established by the organization. The project's defined process is composed based, in part, on an analysis of historical process performance data. Process performance baselines and models enable the project to predict whether or not it can achieve its quality and process performance objectives. Based on the prediction, the project can adjust its defined process, subprocesses, plans, or may negotiate changes to its objectives. The project monitors process performance throughout the project and takes corrective action as needed.

In Organizational Performance Management, process performance baselines and models are analyzed to understand the organization's ability to meet its business objectives and to derive quality and process performance objectives. Based on this understanding, the organization proactively selects and deploys incremental and innovative improvements that measurably improve the organization's performance. The identification of promising incremental and innovative improvements should involve the participation of an empowered workforce aligned with the business values and objectives of the organization. The selection of improvements to deploy is based on a quantitative understanding of the likely benefits and predicted costs of deploying candidate improvements. The organization can also adjust business objectives and quality and process performance objectives as appropriate.

Acquirers use Causal Analysis and Resolution practices to identify causes of selected outcomes and take action to prevent negative outcomes from occurring in the future or to leverage positive outcomes. While the project's defined processes are the initial targets for root cause analysis and action plans, effective process changes can result in process improvement proposals submitted to the organization's set of standard processes.

Together, the high maturity processes enable the organization to achieve its quantitative objectives for quality and process performance.

CHAPTER 5

USING CMMI MODELS

The complexity of products today demands an integrated view of how organizations do business. CMMI can reduce the cost of process improvement across enterprises that depend on multiple functions or groups to achieve their objectives.

To achieve this integrated view, the CMMI Framework includes common terminology, common model components, common appraisal methods, and common training materials. This chapter describes how organizations can use the CMMI Product Suite not only to improve their quality, reduce their costs, and optimize their schedules, but also to gauge how well their process improvement program is working.

Adopting CMMI

Research has shown that the most powerful initial step to process improvement is to build organizational support through strong senior management sponsorship. To gain the sponsorship of senior management, it is often beneficial to expose them to the performance results experienced by others who have used CMMI to improve their processes [Gibson 2006].

For more information about CMMI performance results, see the SEI website at www.sei.cmu.edu/cmmi/research/results/.

The senior manager, once committed as the process improvement sponsor, must be actively involved in the CMMI-based process improvement effort. Activities performed by the senior management sponsor include but are not limited to the following:

- Influence the organization to adopt CMMI
- Choose the best people to manage the process improvement effort
- Monitor the process improvement effort personally

- Be a visible advocate and spokesperson for the process improvement effort
- Ensure that adequate resources are available to enable the process improvement effort to be successful

Given sufficient senior management sponsorship, the next step is establishing a strong, technically competent process group that represents relevant stakeholders to guide process improvement efforts [Ahern 2008].

For an organization with a mission to develop software-intensive systems, the process group might include those who represent different disciplines across the organization and other selected members based on the business needs driving improvement. For example, a systems administrator may focus on information technology support, whereas a marketing representative may focus on integrating customers' needs. Both members could make powerful contributions to the process group.

Once your organization decides to adopt CMMI, planning can begin with an improvement approach such as the IDEAL (Initiating, Diagnosing, Establishing, Acting, and Learning) model [McFeeley 1996]. For more information about the IDEAL model, see the SEI website at www.sei.cmu.edu/library/abstracts/reports/96hb001.cfm.

> **AUTHORS' NOTE**
> The SEI's Mastering Process Improvement course combines the use of CMMI models and the IDEAL model to establish a process improvement program that can result in real, positive changes.

Your Process Improvement Program

Use the CMMI Product Suite to help establish your organization's process improvement program. Using the product suite for this purpose can be a relatively informal process that involves understanding and applying CMMI best practices to your organization. Or, it can be a formal process that involves extensive training, creation of a process improvement infrastructure, appraisals, and more.

Selections That Influence Your Program

You must make three selections to apply CMMI to your organization for process improvement:

1. Select a part of the organization.

2. Select a model.
3. Select a representation.

Selecting the projects to be involved in your process improvement program is critical. If you select a group that is too large, it may be too much for the initial improvement effort. The selection should also consider organizational, product, and work homogeneity (i.e., whether the group's members all are experts in the same discipline, whether they all work on the same product or business line, and so on).

Selecting an appropriate model is also essential to a successful process improvement program. The CMMI-DEV model focuses on activities for developing quality products and services. The CMMI-ACQ model focuses on activities for initiating and managing the acquisition of products and services. The CMMI-SVC model focuses on activities for providing quality services to the customer and end users. When selecting a model, appropriate consideration should be given to the primary focus of the organization and projects, as well as to the processes necessary to satisfy business objectives. The lifecycle processes (e.g., conception, design, manufacture, deployment, operations, maintenance, disposal) on which an organization concentrates should also be considered when selecting an appropriate model.

Select the representation (capability or maturity levels) that fits your concept of process improvement. Regardless of which you choose, you can select nearly any process area or group of process areas to guide improvement, although dependencies among process areas should be considered when making such a selection.

As process improvement plans and activities progress, other important selections must be made, including whether to use an appraisal, which appraisal method should be used, which projects should be appraised, how training for staff should be secured, and which staff members should be trained.

CMMI Models

CMMI models describe best practices that organizations have found to be productive and useful to achieving their business objectives. Regardless of your organization, you must use professional judgment when interpreting CMMI best practices for your situation, needs, and business objectives.

This use of judgment is reinforced when you see words such as "adequate," "appropriate," or "as needed" in a goal or practice. These words are used for activities that may not be equally relevant in all situations. Interpret these goals and practices in ways that work for your organization.

Although process areas depict the characteristics of an organization committed to process improvement, you must interpret the process areas using an in-depth knowledge of CMMI, your organization, the business environment, and the specific circumstances involved.

As you begin using a CMMI model to improve your organization's processes, map your real-world processes to CMMI process areas. This mapping enables you to initially judge and later track your organization's level of conformance to the CMMI model you are using and to identify opportunities for improvement.

To interpret practices, it is important to consider the overall context in which these practices are used and to determine how well the practices satisfy the goals of a process area in that context. CMMI models do not prescribe nor imply processes that are right for any organization or project. Instead, CMMI describes minimal criteria necessary to plan and implement processes selected by the organization for improvement based on business objectives.

CMMI practices purposely use nonspecific phrases such as "relevant stakeholders," "as appropriate," and "as necessary" to accommodate the needs of different organizations and projects. The specific needs of a project can also differ at various points in its life.

Using CMMI Appraisals

Many organizations find value in measuring their progress by conducting an appraisal and earning a maturity level rating or a capability level achievement profile. These types of appraisals are typically conducted for one or more of the following reasons:

- To determine how well the organization's processes compare to CMMI best practices and identify areas where improvement can be made
- To inform external customers and suppliers about how well the organization's processes compare to CMMI best practices
- To meet the contractual requirements of one or more customers

AUTHORS' NOTE

You can find guidance for an acquirer on interpreting the results of a supplier's appraisal in the SEI report, "Understanding and Leveraging a Supplier's CMMI Efforts: A Guidebook for Acquirers" (CMU/SEI-2007-TR-004), at www.sei.cmu.edu/library/reportspapers.cfm.

Appraisals of organizations using a CMMI model must conform to the requirements defined in the *Appraisal Requirements for CMMI* (ARC) [SEI 2011b] document. Appraisals focus on identifying improvement opportunities and comparing the organization's processes to CMMI best practices.

Appraisal teams use a CMMI model and ARC-conformant appraisal method to guide their evaluation of the organization and their reporting of conclusions. The appraisal results are used (e.g., by a process group) to plan improvements for the organization.

Appraisal Requirements for CMMI

The *Appraisal Requirements for CMMI* (ARC) document describes the requirements for several types of appraisals. A full benchmarking appraisal is defined as a *Class A* appraisal method. Less formal methods are defined as *Class B* or *Class C* methods. The ARC document was designed to help improve consistency across appraisal methods and to help appraisal method developers, sponsors, and users understand the tradeoffs associated with various methods.

Depending on the purpose of the appraisal and the nature of the circumstances, one class may be preferred over the others. Sometimes self-assessments, initial appraisals, quick-look or mini-appraisals, or external appraisals are appropriate; at other times a formal benchmarking appraisal is appropriate.

A particular appraisal method is declared an ARC Class A, B, or C appraisal method based on the sets of ARC requirements that the method developer addressed when designing the method.

More information about the ARC is available on the SEI website at www.sei.cmu.edu/cmmi/tools/appraisals/.

SCAMPI Appraisal Methods

The SCAMPI A appraisal method is the generally accepted method used for conducting ARC Class A appraisals using CMMI models. The *SCAMPI A Method Definition Document* (MDD) defines rules for ensuring the consistency of SCAMPI A appraisal ratings [SEI 2011a]. For benchmarking against other organizations, appraisals must ensure consistent ratings. The achievement of a specific maturity level or the satisfaction of a process area must mean the same thing for different appraised organizations.

The SCAMPI family of appraisals includes Class A, B, and C appraisal methods. The SCAMPI A appraisal method is the officially recognized and most rigorous method. It is the only method that can result in benchmark quality ratings. SCAMPI B and C appraisal methods provide organizations with improvement information that is less formal than the results of a SCAMPI A appraisal, but nonetheless helps the organization to identify improvement opportunities.

More information about SCAMPI methods is available on the SEI website at www.sei.cmu.edu/cmmi/tools/appraisals/.

Appraisal Considerations

Choices that affect a CMMI-based appraisal include the following:

- CMMI model
- Appraisal scope, including the organizational unit to be appraised, the CMMI process areas to be investigated, and the maturity level or capability levels to be appraised
- Appraisal method
- Appraisal team leader and team members
- Appraisal participants selected from the appraisal entities to be interviewed
- Appraisal outputs (e.g., ratings, instantiation specific findings)
- Appraisal constraints (e.g., time spent on site)

The SCAMPI MDD allows the selection of predefined options for use in an appraisal. These appraisal options are designed to help organizations align CMMI with their business needs and objectives.

CMMI appraisal plans and results should always include a description of the appraisal options, model scope, and organizational scope selected. This documentation confirms whether an appraisal meets the requirements for benchmarking.

For organizations that wish to appraise multiple functions or groups, the integrated approach of CMMI enables some economy of scale in model and appraisal training. One appraisal method can provide separate or combined results for multiple functions.

AUTHORS' NOTE
Some organizations manage projects that develop products, perform services, and acquire products and services within the same organization, managed by a common leadership team, and guided by a common set of policies. The SCAMPI appraisal method allows economies (e.g., joint document reviews and interviews, shared team leaders and team members) while preserving unique appraisal outputs when working with multiple CMMI models.

The following appraisal principles for CMMI are the same as those principles used in appraisals for other process improvement models:

- Senior management sponsorship[1]
- A focus on the organization's business objectives
- Confidentiality for interviewees
- Use of a documented appraisal method
- Use of a process reference model (e.g., a CMMI model)
- A collaborative team approach
- A focus on actions for process improvement

CMMI Related Training

Whether your organization is new to process improvement or is already familiar with process improvement models, training is a key element in the ability of organizations to adopt CMMI. An initial set of courses is provided by the SEI and its Partner Network, but your organization may wish to supplement these courses with its own instruction. This approach allows your organization to focus on areas that provide the greatest business value.

The SEI and its Partner Network offer an introductory course that provides a basic overview of CMMI for Acquisition. The SEI also offers advanced training to those who plan to become more deeply involved in CMMI adoption or appraisal—for example, those who will guide improvement as part of a process group, those who will lead SCAMPI appraisals, and those who will teach the introductory course.

Current information about CMMI related training is available on the SEI website at www.sei.cmu.edu/training/.

---

1. Experience has shown that the most critical factor influencing successful process improvement and appraisals is senior management sponsorship.

CHAPTER 6

ESSAYS ON CMMI-ACQ IN GOVERNMENT AND INDUSTRY

This chapter provides insights, guidance, and recommendations useful for organizations looking to improve their acquisition processes by using the CMMI for Acquisition (CMMI-ACQ) model.

The first set of essays describes successes and challenges experienced by organizations that have adopted CMMI-ACQ within the public sector, primarily government defense and civil agencies in the United States and in France. Included is analysis from the organization that achieved the first-ever CMMI-ACQ maturity level 5 rating.

The second set of essays discusses private-sector adoption and the unique challenges faced by industry when outsourcing IT products and services.

The third set of essays highlights some important lifecycle aspects of CMMI-ACQ that help reduce program risk. These risks can arise anywhere in the lifecycle—from planning the acquisition strategy to transitioning products and services into use.

The next set of essays covers special topics that include acquiring interoperable systems, Agile acquisition, and process improvement.

The chapter closes with a view toward how the future of CMMI might evolve and how the CMMI constellations can be used to enable enterprise-wide improvement.

Critical Issues in Government Acquisition

Mike Phillips, Brian Gallagher, and Karen Richter

Since the first edition of this book was published, even more activity has taken place to reform acquisition in the Department of Defense (DoD). Before discussing this activity, we have updated our discussion

65

of the earlier "Defense Acquisition Performance Assessment Report" (the DAPA report) [Kadish 2006] to this new version of the model.

"Big A" Versus "Little a" Acquisition

In his letter delivering the report to Deputy Secretary of Defense Gordon England, the panel chair, Gen Kadish, noted:

> *Although our Acquisition System has produced the most effective weapon systems in the world, leadership periodically loses confidence in its efficiency. Multiple studies and improvements to the Acquisition System have been proposed—all with varying degrees of success. Our approach was broader than most of these studies. We addressed the "big A" Acquisition System because it includes all the management systems that [the] DoD uses, not [just] the narrow processes traditionally thought of as acquisition. The problems [the] DoD faces are deeply [e]mbedded in the "big A" management systems, not just the "little a" processes. We concluded that these processes must be stable for incremental change to be effective—they are not.*

In developing the CMMI-ACQ model—a model we wanted to apply to both commercial and government organizations—we considered tackling the issues raised in the DAPA report. However, successful model adoption requires an organization to embrace the ideas (i.e., best practices) of the model for effective improvement of the processes involved.

As the preceding quote illustrates, in addition to organizations traditionally thought of as the "acquisition system" ("little a") in the DoD, there are also organizations that are associated with the "big A," including the Joint Capabilities Integration and Development System (JCIDS) and the Planning, Programming, Budgeting, and Execution (PPBE) system. These systems are governed by different stakeholders, directives, and instructions. To be effective, the model would need to be adopted at an extremely high level—by the DoD itself. Because of this situation, we resolved with our sponsor in the Office of the Secretary of Defense to focus on the kinds of "little a" organizations that are able to address CMMI best practices once the decision for a materiel solution has been reached.

In reality, we often find that models can have an impact beyond what might be perceived to be the "limits" of process control. The remainder of this essay highlights some of the clear leverage points at which the model supports DAPA recommendations for improvement.

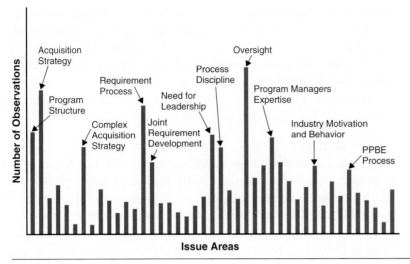

FIGURE 6.1
Observations by Issue Area

Figure 6.1 illustrates some of the issues and their relative importance as observed by the DAPA project team in reviewing previous recommendations and speaking to experts [Kadish 2006]. The issue areas in Figure 6.1 are discussed next. Although we would never claim that the CMMI-ACQ model offers a complete solution to all of the key issues addressed in the DAPA report, building the capabilities covered in the CMMI-ACQ model offers opportunities to address many of the risks in these issue areas.

Acquisition Strategy

Acquisition Strategy is one of the more significant additions to the CMMI Model Foundation (CMF) to support the acquisition area of interest. Multiple process area locations (including Acquisition Requirements Development and Solicitation and Supplier Agreement Development) were considered before placing the acquisition strategy practice into Project Planning. Feedback from various acquisition organizations noted that many different organizational elements are stakeholders in strategy development, but its criticality to the overall plan suggested an effective fit as part of this process area. We also found that some projects might develop the initial strategy before the formal establishment of full acquisition offices, which would then accept the long-term management responsibility for the strategy. Note that the practice does not demand a specific strategy, but does expect the strategy to be a planning artifact. The full practice, "Establish and maintain the acquisition strategy," in Project Planning specific practice 1.1, recognizes that maintenance may require strategy updates if the changing environment reflects that need. The DAPA report (p. 14) calls out some recommended strategies in the DoD environment [Kadish 2006].

Additional discussion is contained in the Acquisition Strategy: Planning for Success essay, found later in this chapter.

Program Structure

Although a model such as CMMI-ACQ should not direct specific organizational structures, the CMMI Product Team looked for ways to encourage improved operations on programs. Most significant might be practices for creating and managing teams with effective rules and guidelines such as those suggested in the Organizational Process Definition process area. The DAPA report (p. 76) noted deficiencies in operation. Organizations following model guidance may be better able to address these shortfalls.

Requirement Process

The CMMI-ACQ Product Team, recognizing the vital role played by effective requirements development in acquisition, assigned Acquisition Requirements Development to maturity level 2.[1] Key to this effectiveness is specific goal 2, "Customer requirements are refined and elaborated into contractual requirements." The importance of this activity cannot be overemphasized, as poor requirements are likely to be the most troubling type of "defect" that the acquisition organization injects into the system. The DAPA report notes that requirement errors are often injected late into the acquisition system. Examples in the report included operational test requirements unspecified by the user. Although the model cannot address such issues directly, it does provide a framework that aids in the traceability of requirements to the source, which in turn facilitates the successful resolution of issues. (The Requirements Management process area also aids in this traceability.)

Oversight

Several features in CMMI-ACQ should help users address the oversight issue. Probably the most significant help is found in the

---

1. The Requirements Development process area is at maturity level 3 in the CMMI for Development (CMMI-DEV) model; the Requirements Development practices are in a maturity level 3 process area in the CMMI for Services (CMMI-SVC) model called Service System Development.

Acquisition Technical Management process area, which recognizes the need for the effective technical oversight of development activities. Acquisition Technical Management is coupled with the companion process area of Agreement Management, which addresses business issues with the supplier via contractual mechanisms. For those individuals familiar with CMMI model construction, the generic practice associated with reviewing the activities, status, and results of all the processes with higher level management and resolving issues offers yet another opportunity to resolve issues.

Need for Leadership, Program Manager Expertise, and Process Discipline

We have grouped leadership, program manager expertise, and process discipline issues together because they reflect the specific purpose of creating CMMI-ACQ—to provide best practices that enable leadership to develop capabilities within acquisition organizations, and to instill process discipline where clarity might previously have been lacking. Here the linkage between DAPA report issues and CMMI-ACQ is not specific, but very general.

Complex Acquisition System and PPBE Process

Alas, for complex acquisition system and PPBE process issues, the model does not have any specific assistance to offer. Nevertheless, the effective development of the high maturity elements of process-performance modeling, particularly if shared by both the acquirer and the system development team, may help address the challenges of "big A" budgetary exercises with more accurate analyses than otherwise would be produced.

Continuing Acquisition Reform in the Department of Defense

In 2009, the Weapon System Acquisition Reform Act of 2009 (WSARA) was passed by Congress. This act was of interest to the CMMI-ACQ community because of its emphasis on systems engineering within DoD acquisition. The CMMI-ACQ Product Team recognized the importance of systems engineering in acquisition by giving the model a solid foundation in the Acquisition Engineering process areas: Acquisition Requirements Development, Acquisition Technical Management, Acquisition Verification, and Acquisition Validation. Acquisition Engineering is designated as a new category in CMMI-ACQ V1.3 to stress its importance.

The National Defense Acquisition Act (NDAA) for fiscal year 2010 required a new acquisition process for information technology

(IT) systems. This new process must be designed to include the following elements:

- Early and continual involvement of the user
- Multiple, rapidly executed increments or releases of capability
- Early, successive prototyping to support an evolutionary approach
- A modular, open-systems approach

Of course, the CMMI-ACQ model is designed with sufficient flexibility so that it may be applied to all kinds of systems and services, including IT systems. For example, the last three elements identified above are all requirements that would need to be included in the acquisition strategy developed at the very beginning of the Project Planning process area, as discussed earlier in this essay and in the Acquisition Strategy: Planning for Success essay later in this chapter.

The first new requirement for IT system acquisition—early and continual involvement of the user—is addressed pervasively throughout the CMMI-ACQ model. Clearly, in the new IT acquisition process, the "relevant stakeholder" group would always include the user.

Involvement of all relevant stakeholders in the execution of the acquisition processes is discussed throughout all process areas in various activities. Specifically, institutionalizing a process at capability or maturity level 2 requires the generic practice, "Identify and involve the relevant stakeholders of the process as planned."

Involvement of stakeholders is an important consideration in activities including, but not limited to, the following:

- Planning
- Decision making
- Making commitments
- Communicating
- Coordinating
- Reviewing
- Conducting appraisals
- Defining requirements
- Resolving problems and issues

A specific practice in Project Planning, "Plan the involvement of identified stakeholders," sets up the involvement early in the project.

Another specific practice, "Monitor stakeholder involvement against the project plan," in Project Monitoring and Control ensures that the project carries out the plan for the stakeholder involvement. Finally, a specific goal, "Coordination and collaboration between the project and relevant stakeholders are conducted," in Integrated Project Management ensures this behavior is carried throughout the project.

In 2010, Secretary of Defense Robert Gates began an initiative to deliver better value to the warfighter and the taxpayer by improving the way the DoD does business. Under Secretary of Defense (Acquisition, Technology and Logistics) Ashton Carter's implementation of this initiative included measures focused on improving the tradecraft in the acquisition of services. When planning the CMMI-ACQ model, we made a concerted effort to cover the acquisition of both products and services. Best practices that may help the DoD in its efforts in improving the acquisition of services are found throughout the model.

Although the CMMI-ACQ model cannot address all of the problems in the complex DoD acquisition process, it can provide a firm foundation for improvement in acquisition offices in line with the intent of further improvement initiatives.

Systems-of-Systems Acquisition Challenges

Although CMMI-ACQ is aimed primarily at the acquisition of products and services, it also outlines some practices that would be especially important in addressing systems-of-systems issues. Because of the importance of this topic in government acquisition, we decided to add this discussion and the Interoperable Acquisition section later in this chapter to assist readers who are facing the challenges associated with systems of systems.

A source document for this discussion is *Interoperable Acquisition for Systems of Systems: The Challenges* [Smith 2006], which describes the ever-increasing interdependence of systems necessary to provide needed capabilities to the user. As an example cited in the document, in one key satellite communications program, at least five separate and independent acquisition programs needed to be completed successfully before the actual capability could be delivered to the various military services. The increasing emphasis on net-centric operations and service-oriented architectures added to the challenge. Figure 6.2 provides a visual depiction of some of the complexity in this program.

Figure 6.2 shows the many ways that complexity grows quickly as the number of critical programmatic interfaces increases. Each dependency creates a risk for at least one of the organizations. The figure suggests that for two of the programs, a shared reporting directorate can aid in mitigating risks. This kind of challenge can be described as one in which applying recursion is sufficient to meet the demands. The system is composed of subsystems, and a single overarching management structure controls the subordinate elements. For some large program offices, for example, the system might be an aircraft with its supporting maintenance systems and required training systems. All elements may be separate programs, but coordination occurs within a single management structure. Figure 6.2, however, shows the additional challenges evident when no single management structure has been established. Critical parts of the capability are delivered by separate management structures, often with widely different motivators and priorities.

Although the CMMI-ACQ model was not constructed to specifically solve these challenges, especially the existence of separate management structures, the complexity was familiar to CMMI-ACQ authors. Those individuals who have used the CMM or CMMI

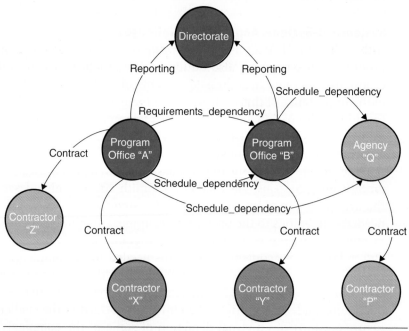

FIGURE 6.2
Systems-of-Systems Acquisition Challenges

model in the past will recognize the Risk Management process area in this model. In addition to noting the existence of significant risks in managing the delivery of a system through any outside agent, such as a supplier, the model emphasizes the value of recognizing both internal and external sources of risk. The following note is part of Risk Management specific practice 1.1:

> *Identifying risk sources provides a basis for systematically examining changing situations over time to uncover circumstances that impact the ability of the project to meet its objectives. Risk sources are both internal and external to the project. As the project progresses, additional sources of risk may be identified. Establishing categories for risks provides a mechanism for collecting and organizing risks as well as ensuring appropriate scrutiny and management attention to risks that can have serious consequences on meeting project objectives.*

Varying approaches to addressing risks across multiple programs and organizations have been taken. One of these, Team Risk Management, has been documented by the SEI [Higuera 2005]. CMMI-ACQ anticipated the need for flexible organizational structures to address these kinds of issues and chose to expect that organizations would establish and maintain teams crossing organizational boundaries. The following is part of Organizational Process Definition specific practice 1.7:

> *In an acquisition organization, teams are useful not just in the acquirer's organization but between the acquirer and supplier and among the acquirer, supplier, and other relevant stakeholders, as appropriate. Teams may be especially important in a systems of systems environment.*

Perhaps the most flexible and powerful model feature used to address the complexities of systems of systems is the effective employment of the specific practices in the second specific goal of Acquisition Technical Management: Perform Interface Management. The practices under this specific goal require successfully managing needed interfaces among the system being focused on and other systems not under the project's direct control. The foundation for these practices is established in Acquisition Requirements Development:

> *Develop requirements for the interfaces between the acquired product and other products in the intended environment. (ARD SP 2.1.2)*

The installation of the specific goal in Acquisition Technical Management as part of overseeing effective system development from the acquirer's perspective is a powerful means of addressing systems-of-systems problems. The following note is part of Acquisition Technical Management specific goal 2:

> *Many integration and transition problems arise from unknown or uncontrolled aspects of both internal and external interfaces. Effective management of interface requirements, specifications, and designs helps to ensure implemented interfaces are complete and compatible.*

The supplier is responsible for managing the interfaces of the product or service it is developing. At the same time, the acquirer identifies those interfaces, particularly external interfaces, that it will manage.

Although these model features provide a basis for addressing some of the challenges of delivering the capabilities desired in a systems-of-systems environment, the methods best suited for various acquisition environments await further development in future documents. CMMI-ACQ is positioned to facilitate that development and mitigate the risks inherent in these acquisitions.

The IPIC Experience

Daniel J. Luttrell and Steven Kelley

A Brief History

The Minuteman III system now deployed is the pinnacle of more than 50 years of rocket science applied to Intercontinental Ballistic Missiles (ICBM). In 1954, the U.S. Air Force awarded the Systems Engineering and Technical Direction (SETD) contract to the Ramo-Wooldridge Corporation (now Northrop Grumman) for Ballistic Missile support. That contract award was the seed that eventually grew to become the ICBM Prime Integration Contract (IPIC).[2]

As ICBMs were developed, from the early Atlas, Thor, and Titan missiles into the Minuteman and Peacekeeper systems and then continuing with the Minuteman III missiles today, Northrop Grumman has built and maintained detailed mathematical models to predict missile flight path, accuracy, and probability of success. In the beginning, these models consisted of technical papers and reports on the current system's abilities and predictions for future systems being proposed. After the systems were fielded, the predictive models were

---

2. Principal products throughout IPIC and prior program development are the mathematical models and the statistical analysis that goes with them. Everything else derives from those efforts. In IPIC, statistical analysis is not simply the routine practice of checking a box; it is the heart of what the program is about.

sustained and continually upgraded with each new data set. Modeling and statistical analysis served as the basis of the original contract and remains the heart of today's IPIC program.

Due to Minuteman's success, this system will maintain operational readiness for the foreseeable future. Its ability to continue its mission well beyond its original service life is evidence of its robust design and sustainment activities. Over the years, many of the components and subsystems have been replaced or upgraded, while many other elements of the system remain with limited or no refurbishment.

Transition from Advisor to Integrator and Sustainer

The Northrop Grumman Missile Systems organization, based primarily in Clearfield, Utah, has used statistical analysis to build, sustain, and improve the ICBM weapon system and the organization's engineering and business processes since ICBMs were first developed. In 1997, the Air Force moved away from managing all of the separate pieces of the ICBM system to using a single prime integrator. Northrop Grumman was awarded the contract, and the IPIC Team (consisting of Northrop Grumman plus more than a dozen subcontractors, including Boeing, Lockheed-Martin, ATK, and Aerojet) assumed responsibility for the integration and sustainment of the end-to-end ICBM system. As the prime integrator, Northrop Grumman manages the contract and the IPIC Team shares responsibility for fulfillment of the ICBM mission with the Air Force. This contract is unique because it is based on system performance with a focus on weapon system health. This contract structure for prime integration has worked effectively over a long period of performance.

The Minuteman III missile is a three-stage, solid-propellant rocket motor with a liquid-propellant fourth stage; it is housed in an underground silo. The service life for the IPIC Minuteman system is being extended through 2030, which presents a technical challenge: The system was originally fielded in the 1970s with an expected service life of 10 years.

The IPIC Team has been the sole integrator of the complete ICBM weapon system, including all subsystems, since program inception. IPIC efforts include sustainment engineering, systems engineering, research and development, modifications, and repair programs.

Through joint technical integration, the IPIC Team advises the Air Force, which makes all decisions on proposed technical approaches. This separation of responsibility allows industry, including the prime integrator and subcontractors, the freedom to deliver a best-value product that meets the customer's weapon system performance requirements and ensures mission success. The IPIC contract has established a weapon system management approach that empowers both the government and the contractor team, holding them jointly accountable to deliver warfighting capability to the end user.

The Air Force provides incentives for the IPIC Team to maintain system performance as measured by key readiness parameters. The focus is on weapon system capability, with government direction addressing *what* to do, but not specifying *how* to do the job. Northrop Grumman has been given the flexibility to manage weapon system risk and streamline processes to achieve the desired outcome.

The IPIC contract was part of the Air Force "Lightning Bolt" acquisition initiative and delivers significant cost savings to the Air Force. While other prime integration contracts have not performed as well as expected on development efforts, Northrop Grumman's prime integration approach on IPIC has been very successfully applied to Minuteman sustainment and life extension. This contract vehicle establishes a framework that allows for all analysis, advisory, and solution development efforts to be tied to one contract, thereby providing a unified industry position for the decisions the Air Force must make for system sustainment. To a large degree, the same industry base benefits from the ongoing sustainment and upgrade work identified by analysis under the contract. This framework allows the contractors to retain engineering talent and data developed with the original system and keep them up-to-date on system improvements as they happen. It also allows industry to bring in new personnel and train them, alongside seasoned veterans, in the systems and processes used to maintain and enhance the system.

The advantage to the Air Force of this arrangement is that it can rely on a stable team that performs well together and has done so for more than a decade. Today, the IPIC Team continues to evolve, improve teaming relationships, and deliver performance in support of the Air Force customer.

IPIC consists of two major types of efforts, as illustrated in Figure 6.3: (1) sustainment to analyze the aging Minuteman system and (2) development of modification programs to modernize the system as required to extend its service life through the year 2030. Modification programs are integrated into the IPIC contract individually as they are approved and negotiated.

Sustainment consists of sustaining engineering and weapon system assessment. The sustaining engineering function responds to issues with the operational system as they arise. The weapon system assessment function analyzes system subelement data proactively

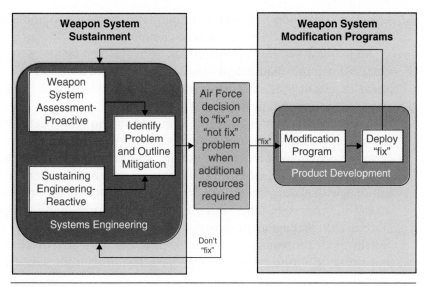

FIGURE 6.3
Two Major Types of Efforts Handled by IPIC

gathered from testing. Data from all sources are fed into performance models that enable the team to identify weapon system risks far enough in advance of system impact that team members can fully characterize the extent of the risk, determine appropriate short-term mitigation actions, create a plan, and ultimately mitigate the risk entirely. System risk assessment is driven by statistical models for missile performance to support the key readiness parameters: availability, reliability, accuracy, and hardness. Analyzing these performance models in conjunction with aging models enables the IPIC Team to determine whether all subsystems and the system as a whole will function correctly through the target dates (2030 and beyond).

How IPIC Works

Effective sustainment of the Minuteman force requires the government and Northrop Grumman to continually balance dual priorities: keeping the missiles on alert, while fielding vital new hardware and software upgrades that extend the service life of the system. All elements of the system are involved— millions of custom software lines, thousands of computers, all types of communications, and thousands of mission hardware items. All must be maintained and enhanced both safely and cost-effectively. Engineering productivity has been increased by consolidating contractor statements of work, eliminating redundant tasking, and employing commercial best practices. When combined with innovative procurement approaches for major subsystem upgrades, Northrop Grumman's approach significantly reduces the overall cost of system sustainment.

Applying a systems approach has been the key factor in ICBM success for more than a half century, since the first strategic land-based deterrent was introduced in the 1950s. The ICBM Systems Approach is pictured in Figure 6.4.

Applying systems engineering requires a complete spectrum of engineering and science disciplines to understand and manage complex interdependencies. Systems engineering also interacts with the goal of achieving overall weapon system optimization. A full review of all considerations is completed prior to every relevant action on the system. This review employs a comprehensive weapon system risk management process. As experience has shown, the Northrop Grumman systems approach is the best way to identify and mitigate unintended consequences resulting from subsystem changes.

To further enhance the systems approach, Northrop Grumman has developed mature and disciplined processes that have improved with time to provide consistent and reliable results. Documented in an easily accessible organizational command media and program data site, these processes are essential for maintaining the quality demanded of such a mission-critical system. These processes have been tested by time and improved through measurement against industry best practices such as ISO standards, AS9100, CMMI, and Lean Six Sigma.

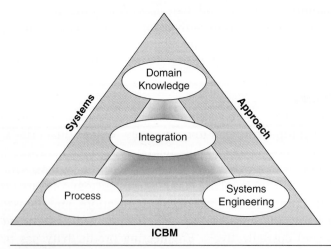

FIGURE 6.4
A Systems Approach

Domain knowledge consists of extensive and sustained expertise about the system—from the beginning of concept development through deployment and decommissioning. Northrop Grumman maintains a full history of data for all aspects of the system (i.e., ICBM performance data, system configurations, and upgrades) along with long-term human expertise in the concept, design, development, deployment, modification, infrastructure, operations, and support functions used to maintain system viability.

Engineers employed at the beginning of the ICBM program are still on the job today. Northrop Grumman systematically hires new graduates and assigns them to work alongside these experienced engineers, from whom they absorb domain knowledge; this practice ensures that the new-generation engineers will be ready to carry on when older generations retire. This domain knowledge enables thorough analysis when issues arise.

The final ingredient of ICBM's success is total weapon system integration—the control and coordination of separate complex elements and activities (e.g., interfaces, resources, milestones) to achieve required system performance. Integration is the activity that enables IPIC to avoid gaps, overlaps, and system suboptimization. Complete integration of all related subsystem activities is vital to avoid disconnects or unintended consequences when implementing changes and upgrades.

When so many changes are taking place across the system concurrently, the system engineering, integration, and process functions become critical as means to avoid adverse impacts. Management of individual efforts is also critical to performance and reporting on cost and schedule, as each effort is tracked and rolled up to the system level for top-level customer review. The complex system and contract include parallel activities both in the execution of modifications and in deployment. Integration and optimization of deployment activity minimizes resource expenditure while ensuring that operational readiness is maintained at acceptable levels.

Industry Process Standards and Models

The IPIC mission is to maintain the total ICBM weapon system and modernize the Minuteman III to extend its useful life to 2030. The expected product of this mission is an ICBM weapon system that maintains its readiness to launch 24/7/365 while at the same time undergoing testing, evaluation, and upgrades. Success, in this case, is measured by comparing predicted results with observed results and getting no surprises from year to year. Process discipline,

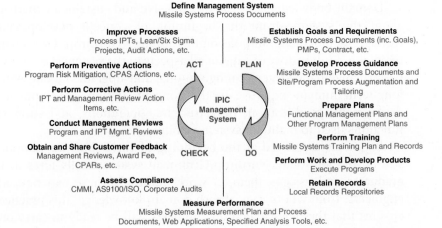

FIGURE 6.5
Northrop Grumman Operating Philosophy

predictability, and improvement are vital across the enterprise to enable mission success.

Over its lifetime, the IPIC program has examined process standards and models from DoD, IEEE, ISO/AS9100, CMMI-DEV, CMMI-SVC, and CMMI-ACQ to help frame its internal process development and improvement activities. As with all programs, some standards have proved more useful than others. Nearly all share the same fundamental "Plan, Do, Check, Act" construct. Northrop Grumman arranged the AS9100 framework (a contractual compliance requirement) around the simple "Plan, Do, Check, Act" core to codify a broad process framework for management. Illustrated in Figure 6.5, this operating philosophy is the essence of what Northrop Grumman and its subcontract team must do to succeed.

This operating philosophy includes the following elements:

Define Management System: Documented on a website accessible by all Program Team members (including teammates, subcontractors, and the Air Force) are assets that include program requirements establishing local policy for performing work, implementation plans, additional clarification on how processes are to be implemented, and other plans to establish a framework for operations. The site also contains handbooks, guides, templates, and tools to support the processes.

Establish Goals and Requirements: In the Management System diagram, IPIC's primary goal is to meet or exceed all customer expectations and achieve excellent award fees. All other goals flow from the primary goal and from government contract direction.

Develop Process Guidance: Accessed via the website, the process guidance documentation includes mandatory items plus handbooks, guides, forms, tools, and templates. Each mandatory document has a process leader, a subject matter expert, and a process reviewer who has the authority to approve or reject changes after review by the appropriate change control board.

Prepare Plans: IPIC plans are a subset of process guidance, also accessed via the web page, that is mandatory for compliance. Each program element and key function has an approved plan for execution (e.g., Measurement, Program Management, Data Management).

Perform Training: Mandatory and optional classes and online computer-based training are available, along with informal mentoring and attendance at seminars and conferences.

Perform Work and Develop Products: The primary product of assessment engineering is ongoing weapon system modeling and risk analysis. As subsystems are sustained and upgraded, new issues may arise that also require mitigation. Some mitigations may consist of small corrective efforts or simple updates to technical orders. Others may require significant product development such as the design and manufacture of one or more system components.

Retain Records: Records are retained in a variety of databases and web tools with appropriate levels of configuration control.

Measure Performance: IPIC maintains a plan describing what to measure, how to measure it, how to analyze the data, and where the data and analysis are to be reported and stored. A strong measurement and statistical analysis program is in place to measure and predict future costs and schedule performance as well as weapon system health and readiness.

Assess Compliance: Northrop Grumman has an active internal assessment program. If a recurring lack of compliance is identified, the team first evaluates the underlying process documentation to determine if the process should be updated or improved before assuming that poor discipline is the source of the problem. Northrop Grumman measures IPIC against the ISO/AS9100 standard and the CMMI-ACQ model with both internal and external audits, and has completed most audits without negative findings. Northrop Grumman Missile Systems/IPIC was the first organization externally appraised at maturity level 5 for CMMI-ACQ and published by the SEI on the Published Appraisal Results (PAR) website in 2009.

Obtain and Share Customer Feedback: Customer feedback comes in the form of both praise and constructive criticism on a daily basis. Two formal feedback mechanisms are Contract Performance

Assessment Reports (CPAR) and Award Fee Letters. These reports require formal response and action items to address negative remarks. Award fee results are also analyzed for recurring themes and shared with the IPIC employees.

Conduct Management Reviews: Northrop Grumman conducts internal and external reviews at various program levels. Staff meetings, contractor Integrated Product Team (IPT) meetings, joint IPT meetings, and program-level management reviews are conducted on a recurring basis.

Perform Corrective and Preventive Actions: Corrective actions are required for cost, schedule, or technical variances, and are also created at all levels of the program and the organization to address internal or external audit findings, negative customer feedback, and other issues that arise. Preventive actions may also be required depending on the issue or in instances where the issue appears in more than one place.

Improve Processes: An ongoing improvement activity serves to enhance program performance and customer/employee satisfaction with the process architecture. IPIC maintains a database that can be used by any employee, teammate, or customer to submit a problem discovered or a suggestion for improvement. The process integration team reviews and prioritizes suggestions for action. Northrop Grumman uses the Lean and Six Sigma tool sets along with Theory of Constraints thinking processes to guide data collection and process improvement planning and execution.

IPIC and CMMI Models

Starting with the "Plan, Do, Check, Act" core with an encircling AS9100 framework, which provides the broad basis for the IPIC management system (as outlined in the preceding section), CMMI models—with their narrower focus—add a much-needed depth of guidance for management activities.

IPIC was successfully appraised both internally and externally against CMMI-DEV for applicable process areas (excluding Technical Solution and Product Integration). Because Northrop Grumman does not develop products on IPIC, but rather acquires them from subcontractors that develop those products from system-directed requirements, other CMMI models were investigated as they were released. After examining and ruling out the CMMI-SVC model, Missile Systems evaluated the CMMI-ACQ model. The Acquisition model is a more suitable evaluation structure for the pure acquisition work performed by Northrop Grumman on this contract.

Mathematical models and statistical analysis were developed as a technical solution to support the customer (i.e., the Air Force) for decades with a proven track record of success. The voice of the process on the technical side supplied good historical data to support and update technical baselines. Modeling future expectations from these baselines was a logical extension that provided solid information for technical decisions.

When Northrop Grumman began to investigate CMMI models for use on IPIC, it became evident that these same data analysis, baseline development, and mathematical modeling techniques could be applied successfully in the nontechnical arena to manage the program, the business, and the underlying processes. Significant process improvements were derived from high maturity elements of CMMI models using baselines discovered in existing program data as a source for new model development.

As an example, applying moving range analysis to program management data produced a predictive model that could accurately forecast when program work accomplishment trends were eroding compared to plan, even though the standard program metrics might show no cause for concern. Analysis of payment cycle time data, stratified by contract type, yielded stable baselines to provide the basis for another new model to analyze payment trends—a key business process output.

For acquisition, Northrop Grumman "discovered" another baseline in readily available data for mitigation plan development. Combining these data with an existing technical model yielded another new model around the key function of what to acquire and when. Baselines for first-pass acceptance and internal assessment processes led to further acquisition related models that produced actionable information enabling the organization to improve acquired product acceptance to an essentially error-free state and to gain an improved understanding of enterprise-wide process performance.

Generic practices provided another opportunity to expand process maturity. Rather than institutionalizing only CMMI processes, Northrop Grumman chose to apply generic practices to all of its process areas (e.g., Human Resources, Business Development). Beyond expanding the application of CMMI within Northrop Grumman, generic practices such as Process and Product Quality Assurance (PPQA) facilitated even more improvements by helping the organization to develop a more objective and useful QA process.

Prior to adopting CMMI, audits were focused merely on outputs, with only the government Data Item Description (DID) serving as the standard. Process audits did not "feel" objective to those being audited. With CMMI, Northrop Grumman separated product from process audits and developed standards for each. Key steps were identified for each process, and the audits became much less confrontational and easier to complete. Process audit findings are never directed toward the performer, but are focused instead on the key steps. The organization cross-trains audit volunteers who want to understand other parts of the business, thereby helping engineers learn about business processes, and business process employees learn about engineering. Audits are no longer viewed as contentious events to be avoided, but rather as a chance to discuss work and ideas with a fellow employee who wants to learn and ensure the success of the program.

The focus of Acquisition Requirements Development (ARD) and Acquisition Requirements Management (ARM) in the CMMI-ACQ model versus Requirements Development (RD) and Requirements Management (REQM) in the CMMI-DEV model is a good example of how the change in focus provided a much better fit for IPIC at Northrop Grumman. ARD and ARM specific practices dive deep into the way in which requirements flow down the supply chain and suppliers are held accountable for meeting them, while RD and REQM focus on deriving lower level requirements from user needs.

Managing supplier development and delivery to requirements is a substantial process area that Northrop Grumman executes on the contract, for which no credit could be taken using the CMMI-DEV model. Solicitation and Supplier Agreement Development (SSAD) was also a good fit. Northrop Grumman (on IPIC) does not directly develop any product components, but does frequently initiate new supplier agreements. Having a process area focused on the critical aspects of the solicitation and agreement development process from an acquirer's viewpoint is a new and useful tool for both government and industry acquirers. From a contract value perspective, acquisition accounts for 81 percent of the total contract value, and "getting it done right" in the beginning pays dividends later in the acquisition.

Coming up to speed on CMMI-ACQ has been a rewarding experience. Northrop Grumman began a pilot of the model on IPIC in the summer of 2008. In the same time frame, the Air Force independently requested a SCAMPI B appraisal. Only the ACQ processes were evaluated, and even with little time to prepare and no experience with this new model, the outcome was generally positive. In May 2009, with an improved understanding of the model,

Northrop Grumman conducted an internal SCAMPI C appraisal covering all process areas. Again, the results were positive, leading to success in the first ever recorded SCAMPI A maturity level 5 against the CMMI-ACQ model in December 2009. The Lead Appraiser was also one of the model developers.

Given this resounding success, is there anything about the CMMI-ACQ model that could be improved? It has been our experience that contract organizations such as Northrop Grumman (on IPIC) and military organizations that perform acquisition have very small staffs who are assigned to any single acquisition. Staff numbers typically range from one or two to four or five people, supported by larger organizations that supply staff augmentation for short periods such as Solicitation and Supplier Agreement Development or Validation. The day-to-day work is carried out by a small team whose size is not equivalent to that of the project teams in an average development organization. Therefore, some of the process areas normally handled within a typical development project would more naturally be performed outside the acquisition project team.

Some of these process areas are obvious (CM and PPQA), but others are ambiguous (AVAL and QPM). Goals for quantitative management are driven by the larger organization, and not by the small acquisition teams. For example, Northrop Grumman's acquisition project data for IPIC are aggregated across multiple acquisitions and not analyzed by each project. This approach is intentional because of insufficient data inside each acquisition project and because many process improvements are intended for the larger organization and not just for the specific project. Perhaps, then, QPM in the CMMI-ACQ model could be described as Quantitative Process Management (rather than Project Management), and the decision of where the practices are performed might be left to the organization.

Conclusion

Northrop Grumman's unique approach to Minuteman III sustainment and modernization has provided the following objective, tangible results:

- Consistently high award fee scores—averaging 95.5 percent
- High Contractor Performance Assessment Reports (CPARs)—average score of purple or better
- Favorable cost performance—a 3 percent favorable cost variance on more than $6 billion worth of executed program

- Technical performance resulting in weapon system readiness far above threshold specifications
- Consistently reliable flight test demonstrations since program inception

This contract structure, with its integration of prime integrator and customer decision makers, enhanced by management systems and implemented models for organizational management in addition to technical and programmatic variables, is an excellent approach for any mature, fielded weapon system.

CMMI: The Heart of the Air Force's Systems Engineering Assessment Model and Enabler to Integrated Systems Engineering—Beyond the Traditional Realm

George Richard Freeman, Technical Director, U.S. Air Force Center for Systems Engineering[3]

When the U.S. Air Force (AF) consolidated various systems engineering (SE) assessment models into a single model for use across the entire AF, the effort was made significantly easier by the fact that every model used to build the expanded AF model was based on Capability Maturity Model Integration (CMMI) content and concepts. This consolidation also set into motion an approach toward addressing information used across the enterprise in ways that were previously unimagined.

In the mid-1990s, pressure was mounting for the Department of Defense (DoD) to dramatically change the way it acquired, fielded, and sustained weapons systems. Faced with increasingly critical Government Accounting Office (GAO) reports, and with a barrage of media headlines reporting on program multi-billion-dollar cost overruns, late deliveries, and systems that failed to perform at desired levels, the DoD began implementing what was called *acquisition reform.*

Many believed that the root of the problem originated with the government's hands-on approach, which called for it to be intimately involved in requirements generation, design, and production processes. The DoD exerted control primarily through government-published

---

3. The views expressed herein are those of the author and do not reflect the official policy or position of the U.S. Air Force, Department of Defense, or U.S. government.

specifications, standards, methods, and rules, which were then codified into contractual documents. These documents directed—in often excruciating detail—how contractors were required to design and build systems.

This approach resulted in the government unnecessarily bridling contractors. In response, the contractors vehemently insisted that if they were free of these inhibitors, they could deliver better products at lower costs. This dual onslaught from the media and contractors resulted in sweeping changes that included the rescinding of a large number of the military specifications and standards, slashing of program documentation requirements, and a major reduction in the size of government acquisition program offices.

The language of contracts was changed to specify the desired "capability," with contractors being given the freedom to determine "how" to best deliver this capability. This action effectively transferred systems engineering to the sole purview of the contractors. The contractors were being relied upon to deliver the desired products and services, while the responsibility for the delivery of viable solutions remained squarely with the government.

What resulted was a vacuum in which neither the government nor the contractors accomplished the necessary systems engineering. Over the following decade, the government's organic SE capabilities virtually disappeared. This absence of SE capability became increasingly apparent in multiple-system (systems-of-systems) programs in which more than one contractor was involved.

Overall acquisition performance did not improve; indeed, in many instances, it became even worse. While many acquisition reform initiatives were beneficial, it became increasingly clear that the loss of integrated SE was a principal driver behind continued cost overruns, schedule slips, and performance failures.

In response to these problems, on February 14, 2003, the AF announced the establishment of the Air Force Center for Systems Engineering (AF CSE). The CSE was chartered to "re-vitalize SE across the AF." Simultaneously, major AF Acquisition Centers initiated efforts to swing the SE pendulum back the other way.

To regain some level of SE capability, many centers used a process-based approach to address the challenge. Independently, three of these centers turned to the CMMI construct and began tailoring it to create a model to be used within their various program offices, thereby molding CMMI to meet the specific needs of these separate acquisition organizations.

Recognizing the potential of this approach and with an eye toward standardizing SE processes across the entire AF enterprise, in 2006 the AF CSE was tasked to do the following:

- Develop and field a single Air Force Systems Engineering Assessment Model (AF SEAM)
- Involve all major AF centers (acquisition, test, and sustainment)
- Leverage current SE CMMI-based assessment models in various stages of development or use at AF centers

Following initial research and data gathering, in the summer of 2007 the AF CSE established a working group whose members came from the eight major centers across the AF (four Acquisition Centers, one Test Center, and three Sustainment Centers). Assembled members included those who had either built their individual center models or would be responsible for the AF SEAM going forward.

The team's first objective was to develop a consistent understanding of SE through mutual agreement of process categories and associated definitions. Once this understanding was established, the team members used these process areas and, building on the best practices of existing models, together developed a single AF SEAM. Desired characteristics included the following:

- Be viewed as adding value by Program Managers and therefore "pulled" for use to aid in the following:
  - Ensuring standardized core SE processes are in place and being followed
  - Reducing technical risk
  - Improving program performance
- Scalable for use by all programs and projects across the entire AF
  - Self-assessment based
  - Independent verification capable
- A vehicle to share SE lessons learned and best practices
- Easily maintained

To ensure a consistent understanding of SE across the AF and provide the foundation on which to build AF SEAM, the working group clearly defined ten SE process areas (presented in alphabetical order here):

CM	Configuration Management
DA	Decision Analysis
D	Design
M	Manufacturing

PP	Project Planning
R	Requirements
RM	Risk Management
S	Sustainment
TMC	Technical Management and Control
V	Verification and Validation

The model's structure is based on the CMMI construct of process areas (PAs), specific goals (SGs), specific practices (SPs), and generic practices (GPs). The AF SEAM development team subsequently amplified the 10 PAs listed above with 33 SGs, 119 SPs, and 7 GPs.

Each practice includes a title, description, typical work products, references to source requirements and/or guidance, and additional considerations to provide context. While some PAs are largely an extract from CMMI, others are combinations of SPs from multiple CMMI PAs and other sources. Additionally, two PAs not explicitly covered in the CMMI model were added—namely, Manufacturing and Sustainment.

It is equally important to understand where AF SEAM fits within the assessment continuum (depicted in Figure 6.6). The "low" end of this continuum is best defined as an environment where policies are published and "handed off" to the field, with the expectation that they will be followed and in turn yield the desired outcomes. In contrast, the "high" end of the assessment continuum is best defined as an environment replete with a high degree of independent engagements, including highly comprehensive CMMI assessments. AF SEAM was designed to target the "space" between the two ("CMMI Light") and provides one more potential tool for use, when and where appropriate.

Defining the Methodology

Low ⬅ ***Assessment Continuum*** ➡ *High*

- Hands Off
- Promulgate Policy
  - Directives
  - Instructions
  - Checklists
  - Guidance
- Expect Compliance

- **AF SEAM**
  - Collaborative and Inclusive
  - Leanest Possible Best Practices "Must Dos"
  - Clearly Stated Expectations
  - Program Team and Assessor Team
  - Training
- **Self-Assessment of Program with Optional Validation**

- Hands On
- Comprehensive Continuous Process Improvement
  - Highly Detailed Process Books
  - Training
- Independent Assessment
  - Deep Dives

Assessment Methods That Balance Time and Effectiveness

FIGURE 6.6
The Assessment Continuum

To aid in the establishment of a systems engineering process baseline and, in turn, achieve the various aims stated above, programs and projects are undergoing one or more assessments followed by continuous process improvement. An assessment focuses on process existence and use; thus it serves as a leading indicator of potential future performance.

The assessment is not a determination of product quality or a report card on the people or the organization (i.e., lagging indicators). To allow for full AF-wide scalability, the assessment method is intentionally designed to support either a one- or two-step process.

In the first step, each program or project performs a self-assessment using the model to verify process existence, identify local references, and identify work products for each SP and GP—in other words, the program or project "grades" itself. If leadership determines that verification is beneficial, an independent assessment is performed.

This verification is conducted by an external team that confirms the self-assessment results, adds other applicable information, and rates each SP and GP as either "satisfied" or "not satisfied." The external assessment is conducted in a *coaching style,* which facilitates and promotes continuous process improvement.

Results are provided to the program or project as an output of the independent assessment. The information is presented in a manner that promotes the sharing of best practices and facilitates reallocation of resources to underperforming processes. The AF SEAM development working group has also developed training for leaders, self-assessors, and independent assessors, who undergo this training on a "just-in-time" basis.

Since it was originally fielded, the use of AF SEAM continues to grow across the AF. With a long history of using multiple CMMI-based models across the AF, significant cultural inroads have been made to secure the acceptance of this process-based approach. The creation and use of a single AF-wide Systems Engineering Assessment Model is playing a significant role in the revitalization of sound SE practices and the provision of mission-capable systems and systems-of-systems on time and within budget.

Additionally, this process-based methodology has opened up an entirely new frontier—specifically, the advancement of a disciplined systems engineering approach to other areas across the enterprise, otherwise known as *integrated systems engineering: looking beyond the traditional realms.*

Figure 6.7 illustrates the traditional "product" focus of systems engineering, which AF SEAM applies to. The process begins with the

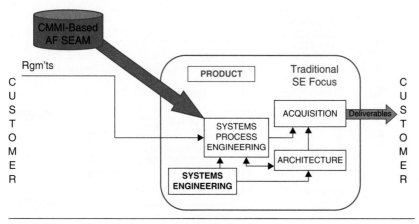

FIGURE 6.7
Traditional "Product" Focus of Systems Engineering

identification of requirements by the customer. Using the various SE processes applied to *Systems Process Engineering,* these requirements are broken down and allocated to various subelements that are then processed through the *Acquisition* process. Both areas are supported by *Architecture*. The end result is a *Deliverable* to the customer. This view, which is commonly referred to as the "product view," illuminates the application of AF SEAM in the context of other associated activities.

An enterprise must continually make resource allocation decisions in its never-ending drive to deliver the highest "value" to the customer at the lowest possible total ownership cost (TOC), within acceptable levels of risk.[4] To achieve this goal, the data and information that are produced within the product view must be fed back to leadership.

This provision of information to leadership is achieved through the addition of the "enterprise view" depicted in Figure 6.8. Note the addition of the *Business Process Engineering* activity adjacent to the *Systems Process Engineering* activity. Also note that although systems process engineering deals with customer requirements, more often than not these requirements are communicated through enterprise business processes.

Gaining an increased understanding of how process-based assessments are executed in the context of other influencing activities is vitally important. Understanding the context of assessments also points one toward potential avenues for expansion of process-based analysis and improvement—hence the designation of continuous

---

4. Adedeji B. Badiru and Marlin U. Thomas, *Handbook of Military Industrial Engineering,* Boca Raton, FL, CRC Press, Taylor & Francis Group, 2009; George R. Freeman, *Achieving Strategic Aims: Moving Toward a Process-Based Government Enterprise,* Chapter 27, p. 27-2.

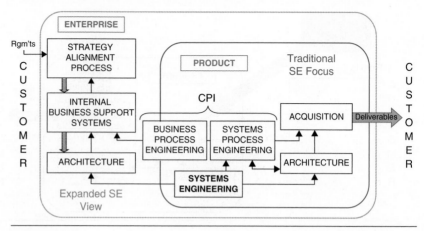

FIGURE 6.8
Continuous Process Improvement

process improvement (CPI) and its applicability to both *Business* and *Systems Process Engineering*.

Data and information that are created within an enterprise are used to support resource allocation and other business decisions. However, this information is incomplete without inclusion of the customer's voice. In Figure 6.9, the customer's voice is depicted through the addition of the "service view." Note the feedback loops, including where they traditionally enter into the various processes. Also note the inherent challenges in transmitting this feedback to the activities that would truly impart change upon the processes supporting each of the views.

Appropriately visualizing and addressing process activities as the heartbeat of the enterprise is another aid to the AF in its goal to deliver needed capabilities on time and within budgetary constraints. Beginning in 2007 with the CMMI-based AF SEAM development effort that focused on the SE processes primarily supporting the product view, this approach set into motion an entirely new way of examining this complex enterprise.

The path ahead for AF SEAM continues to look promising. Individual users are finding value in using AF SEAM, and even in an environment of austere resources it has taken hold as the SE process analysis tool of choice at the practitioner level. This "grassroots" support is directly attributable to the firm foundation upon which the model was constructed combined with the collaborative way in which it was built. Policy makers and leaders are also looking for ways to capitalize further on this process-based leading indicator approach. Figure 6.10 depicts the current state of AF SEAM in many

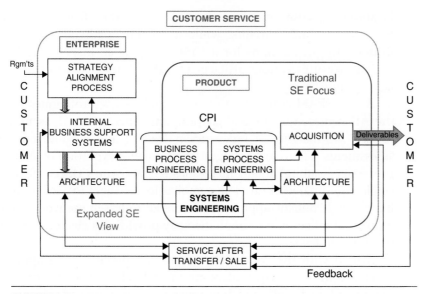

FIGURE 6.9
The Service View

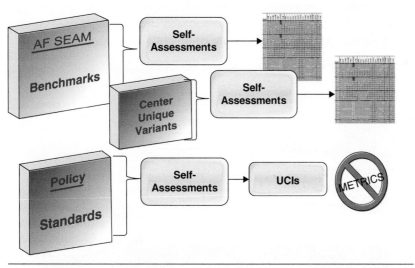

FIGURE 6.10
Current State of AF SEAM in Many Locations

locations as its use continues to mature. AF SEAM is being augmented by various center variants, while a separate path takes an office through its preparations for a Unit Compliance Inspection (UCI). A UCI measures various artifacts and, therefore, is an assessment of lagging indicators.

As AF SEAM continues to mature and its use proliferates across the AF centers and individual program offices, the AF is moving toward the merging of independent leading and lagging indicator assessments. Figure 6.11 suggests how further evolution of standard processes (leading) might merge desired outcomes (lagging) into a single coordinated effort. The combination of these two assessments into a single holistic approach is intended to lessen the workload on individual offices while simultaneously providing a clearer picture of processes to leaders.

Armed with the continually improving process-based approach described in this essay, leaders are more likely to take advantage of these combined tools, which promise to yield improved information with less overall effort. This evolution will, in turn, facilitate improved allocation of resources. Finally, as the challenge of working within highly complex systems-of-systems environments becomes the norm, it is increasingly important that the associated supporting processes have the ability to integrate with one another in ways previously unimagined. The standardization of AF SEAM and the associated processes it describes across the AF enterprise represents a positive step toward achieving these aims.

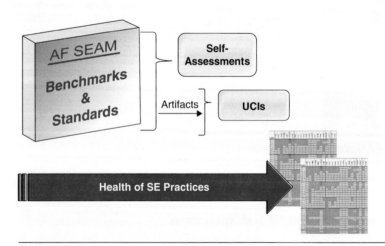

FIGURE 6.11
Evolution of Standard Processes

Lessons Learned by DGA on CMMI-ACQ

*Dominique Luzeaux, Eric Million-Picallion, and
Jean-René Ruault*

General Context and Motivations for CMMI-ACQ

The Direction Générale de l'Armement (DGA) is part of the French Ministry of Defense and is responsible for the design, acquisition, and evaluation of the systems that equip the armed forces, the export of these systems, and the preparation of future weapon systems. Its action encompasses the whole lifecycle of these systems.

The DGA is organized into seven directorates: strategy, operations, technique, international development, planning and budget, quality and modernization, and human resources. The Operations directorate is directly responsible for the design and acquisition of the equipment used by the armed forces and the corresponding budget. Operations is divided into ten divisions: land systems, helicopters, missiles, aircraft systems, naval systems, space and C4ISR systems, deterrence, nuclear and bacteriological protection, the "Coelacanthe" weapon system, and the "Rafale" weapon system. The Land Systems division, which is the focus of this essay, is in charge of all land systems (i.e., combat, transportation, and bridging vehicles; direct and indirect fire systems; ammunitions; infantry and paratrooper equipment; various equipment for troop sustainment; and training and simulation).

The DGA passed ISO 9001 certification four years ago at the enterprise level and is engaged in continuously improving its main processes. The quality process implemented by the DGA relies on a long-term vision aimed at improving the value of acquired systems. Therefore, the decision was made in 2007 to obtain a CMMI level rating, starting with level 2 and then addressing higher levels.

The expected benefits of CMMI-ACQ for the DGA included the following:

- Improved efficiency achieved by measuring tried and tested practices, capitalizing them into documented process references, and increasing professionalism
- Organization improvement by the optimization of estimation, planning, and monitoring and skills development and resource allocation
- Improved operational results through better respect of foreseen budgets and delays and productivity gains
- Recognition by partners, through objective proof of acquisition efficiency

To reach level 2 of the CMMI-ACQ model, an enterprise should implement project and acquisition management processes, such as Requirements Management (REQM), Configuration Management (CM), and Acquisition Requirements Development (ARD). These process areas implement DGA's Stakeholder Requirements Definition Process and the Requirements Analysis Process.

These process areas are very important topics for DGA because they concern its core acquisition activities. Indeed, DGA's architects take as input the needs expressed by the Joint Staff, as well as other stakeholder requirements, such as regulations and laws. They translate these needs and requirements into technical requirements to elaborate technical specifications. These technical specifications form the core of the acquisition agreement between the DGA and its suppliers. They allow the DGA to acquire solutions that satisfy stakeholder needs within the allotted budget and schedule constraints. Furthermore, the DGA's architects must maintain the systems' definition throughout the whole lifecycle.

It is the systems architect's job to account for the flow of evolving needs and to assess their impacts on the definition of the current system architecture. The architect must upgrade the current systems' architectures, maintain operational capabilities, and manage the systems to the budget. These tasks imply that the architect analyzes the impact of all critical dimensions (i.e., operational, financial, schedule, security, and safety) and decides how to implement these requirements and elaborate adequate technical specifications. To achieve these goals, the architect must have an up-to-date architecture definition of the baseline system, a clear set of baseline requirements with their rationale, and appropriate system engineering methods and tools.

In this context, systems engineering processes and activities must be defined and applied. Moreover, these activities must be more and more agile and efficient, allowing the systems architect to master both the architecture definition of the system and evolving requirements to assess the effects of change requests, and to make the best decision.

The CMMI-ACQ model gives the DGA an opportunity to improve its systems engineering practices aimed at achieving this agility and efficiency. Current guidelines and procedures are mapped to CMMI-ACQ specific goals and practices. If necessary, the lack of relevant documents is identified and corrected, and appropriate sets of measurements are defined and applied to activities to enable these activities to reach a higher efficiency level.

CMMI Level 2 Certification Project

The CMMI certification process was launched in 2007. The first assessment focused on management practices and highlighted the differences between the practices implemented by the DGA and the recommendations of the CMMI-ACQ model. Three divisions were chosen among the ten in a first stage. All of these divisions have submitted to a Standard CMMI Appraisal Method for Process Improvement (SCAMPI B) evaluation. The goal in mind was a level 2 certification with evaluation on activities such as process management, project management, and contract and supplier management. This evaluation process ended with a successful SCAMPI A evaluation at the end of 2009 for two divisions; evaluation of the third division was scheduled to be completed at the end of 2010.

For the Land Systems division, several major projects have been evaluated (i.e., infantry combat vehicle, soldier combat system, large-caliber indirect fire system, armored light vehicle, light battle tank, main battle tank, future crossing bridge system), which are in different phases of their lifecycle. Half of the projects have been evaluated on all nine process areas required to achieve level 2 certification. Objective evidence has been submitted to the evaluators and interviews of the integrated project teams have been conducted.

For each project, all the available documents were analyzed before the interviews were conducted. Both divisions were evaluated on very different projects, but the evaluation yielded similar results— which is not especially surprising given that the DGA has been focusing on sharing common methods for quite some time and relies on a matrix organization that fosters such a fruitful exchange. Besides, both divisions have taken advantage of DGA's CMMI project to share and harmonize their practices and to apply common improvements on a short-term basis in a true continuous improvement process.

Lessons Learned

The bottom-up approach underlying CMMI, which consists of identifying and sharing good practices as observed in everyday life, has been widely appreciated by DGA's various teams. These teams are convinced that the CMMI approach supports a quality approach, an internal improvement process, and a standardization of identified best practices. For instance, the reporting spreadsheets developed for some of the projects have been generalized to the various projects.

Several DGA team members have dedicated a large part of their time to the CMMI project. (The word "project" is not misused here: The management processes have been applied in a recursive manner to the CMMI-based improvement effort with planning, resource estimation, project meetings, resource management, and so on.) Working groups have been established to find solutions when gaps between performance and the model are identified.

A special effort is dedicated to the collection of meaningful artifacts in each project. As the DGA's experience demonstrates, the resource investment involved in CMMI-based improvement is not a negligible one. The amount of work on average for both of the DGA's SCAMPI evaluations can be estimated at one person-day per sector per project per evaluation, if the project is already mature in its management. Because the DGA's integrated project teams encompass various skills (e.g., project manager, technical experts, quality experts, finance experts, procurement specialists), the workload differs from one member of the team to the other; for this reason, most preparation work for the evaluations was performed by the quality experts.

Several opportunities for process improvement have been found—for example, in the documentation management, resource allocation, and objective evaluations. Some of them were not a real surprise, and the CMMI project has helped to implement solutions to these issues. A side effect of the whole approach has been the forging of a much closer relationship between the evaluated divisions. Usually they deal with completely different customers and systems, but within the CMMI project they had to share their practices to achieve success within the given schedule.

The main criticism that could be raised about the effectiveness of this evaluation relates to the proof collection process, in that the definition of "proof" seemed rather subjective depending on the experts involved. The proof required from the divisions differed for the experts whom the teams relied on at the beginning of the project and the lead appraiser at the end of the project. This problem was exacerbated because the model (CMMI-ACQ V1.2) and the context of its implementation (a state-owned procurement agency) were new. We sometimes had the feeling that we were required to submit a "proof of a proof." A lot of time was spent on that issue, and the return on investment for that first stage was rather low because most of the time the proofs already existed but were recorded differently.

CMMI-ACQ As the Driver for an Integrated Systems Engineering Process Applied to "Systems of Systems"

For "systems of systems," DGA experts based the systems engineering processes on the ISO/IEC 15288:2008 standard. However, this standard describes high-level processes and does not describe in an explicit manner the means to measure and improve them. In this context, CMMI-ACQ complements ISO/IEC 15288:2008 by defining key systems engineering processes and enabling their measurement and improvement.

Requirements Management (REQM), Acquisition Requirements Development (ARD), and Configuration Management (CM), as defined by the CMMI-ACQ model, are the keystones of DGA systems engineering processes and activities.

The Requirements Management process area details the following specific practices: Understand Requirements, Obtain Commitment to Requirements, Manage Requirements Change, Maintain Bidirectional Traceability of Requirements, and Identify Inconsistencies Between Project Work and Requirements. This process area is of great importance to DGA because it deals with understanding input requirements, obtaining commitments from stakeholders, and managing requirements changes. These activities are based on bidirectional traceability and consistencies between requirements and product work, and they help the architect of the DGA complete his or her work.

Although this process area is necessary, it is not sufficient by itself. There is a huge gap between customer requirements from the Joint Staff that expresses its needs with an operational capability point of view and the contractual requirements. Integrated teams must translate these operational customer requirements into functional requirements. To achieve this feat, they use functional analysis to elaborate functional architecture that supports attended operational capabilities.

After verifying the functional architecture and functional requirements with the Joint Staff using simulations and battle labs, the team translates them into technical requirements, which will be necessary for the acquisition process (e.g., tender, selection of a contractor) to follow.

The acquisition process can be modeled as the following activities:

- Operational requirements are translated into functional requirements.
- Functional requirements are translated into technical requirements.
- Technical requirements are used as the basis of the technical specification.

Every requirement is traceable from any one level to the one above and the one below. Likewise, each requirement, at each level, is traceable between engineering activities and integration activities, and follows a complete validation process.

Thus the Acquisition Requirements Development process area complements the REQM process area by specifying activities in three specific goals: Develop Customer Requirements, Develop Contractual Requirements, and Analyze and Validate Requirements.

During these activities, changes happen both as a result of evolving customer requirements and from compliance with suppliers' requirements (e.g., unavailability of a technology, changing regulation). These changes have many effects. To avoid loss of the consistency of the architecture definition, each change triggers a change request procedure. An impact assessment is made based on the architecture definition of the current baseline. A review translates this information into a change request. If the change request is accepted, it implies an evolution of the architecture definition. These activities are controlled by the Configuration Management process area. The configuration control board is very important for tracking change and controlling consistency.

Once the mapping between the various activities of the systems engineering process is complete, improving the CMMI level at the enterprise level provides a mechanism for improving systems engineering. The mapping takes advantage of the measurement and continuous improvement possibilities provided by the CMMI-ACQ model, while sticking to a standardized engineering process. The various tools and technical standards developed for systems engineering can be related to the best practices promoted by CMMI-ACQ.

CMMI-ACQ and the "Three R's" of DoD Acquisition

Claude Bolton

Much has been written about the state of program management, often called "acquisition" in the U.S. Department of Defense (DoD), and much of this discussion has not been flattering or positive. Acquisition is described as constantly late to schedule. It does not acquire what was needed. Its performance is less than expected. It spends grossly over original cost estimates.

As a result, a number of laws, rules, policies, and regulations have been produced over the years in an attempt to fix—or at least improve—the DoD acquisition process. In addition, a number of studies, commissions, think tank reviews, and other analyses have been chartered to determine the cause of the poor state of the DoD acquisition process. At last count, more than 100 such studies had been conducted, out-briefed, and "shelved," with no apparent actual improvement in sight.

One has to ask, "Why hasn't there been any significant progress? Why does the DoD acquisition process continue to struggle and underperform? Why is it, according to a 2008 GAO report, that of the nearly 100 major DoD programs reviewed, the majority of them experienced cost overruns of 27 percent on average and were 18 to 24 months behind schedule?"

While the GAO report's methodology has been challenged with no rebuttal from the GAO, the fact remains that many programs are not performing adequately despite years of focus on improving the DoD acquisition process. Again, the question is "Why?" Are we not asking the right questions when it comes to DoD acquisition improvement? Are we not addressing the real root problem, but rather focusing on its symptoms? Are we collectively personifying Einstein's definition of insanity—that is, are we continuing to do the same thing, yet expecting a different outcome? When it comes to the DoD acquisition process, Einstein may be on to something: From my vantage point, with rare exception, virtually all of the studies to date have not addressed the real problem.

"And what is the real problem?" you ask. If I were to tell you now, you might not bother to read the rest of this essay. And given that I may have to "prepare the battlefield" so that you will better understand the answer, let me give you my thoughts first and then explain the answer.

Would you be surprised if I were to tell you that all this fuss over the DoD acquisition process could end in a heartbeat and the process improve almost overnight by just following the "three R's"? Or that actually executing acquisition in the DoD is as simple as the "three R's"? It's true. Don't believe me? Let me tell you about the "three R's" and how they, combined with CMMI-ACQ, could change DoD acquisition forever.

Most of us heard about and studied the "three R's" when we attended grammar school: reading, writing, and arithmetic. If you could master those skills, you were well on your way to a great education and much success in the U.S. school system. Everything we learned involved the basics of the "three R's." Just look at what we are doing at this very moment. I am writing an essay that you are reading, so we are collectively using two of the "three R's." The idea is very basic, but without a good understanding of the basics early in our formative years, we would have a tough time communicating today. The same is true with arithmetic. Earlier in this essay, I shared some simple arithmetic regarding the GAO. Again, without learning the basics early in our lives, you and I would be lost by now.

What does all of this have to do with DoD acquisition? My view is that DoD acquisition, when reduced to its basics and practiced accordingly, is as simple as the "three R's." I know, I know. You are probably saying, "Bolton is crazy and must have lost a few brain cells once he retired." Well, I may have lost a few brain cells, but not when it comes to acquisition and doing it right.

Let's take a look at DoD acquisition and let's see how the "three R's" apply. First, I will admit that the "three R's" for acquisition are different from those for grammar school. The "three R's" in DoD acquisition have different meanings but are still quite simple. The following is a brief description of what I mean by the acquisition "three R's":

Requirements: This "R" stands for not only having formal, written operational requirements, but also—and even more importantly— understanding the requirements. In short, does everyone involved in the "big A" understand the requirement? At a minimum, does the warfighter who wrote the operational requirement understand it? Does the resource manager (i.e., the source of funding) understand the same requirement? Does the acquirer (i.e., the Program Manager) understand the same requirement? Does the test community understand the same requirement, particularly the DoD office of the Director, Operational Test and Evaluation (DOT&E)? Does the sustaining/logistics community understand the same requirement? And does the contractor (i.e., the builder) understand the same requirement? Preferably, all of the aforementioned community representatives of the "big A" should meet in the same room at the same time and make sure all have a common understanding of the formal requirement. If this is not done, *do not* proceed with the program.

Resources: While most would believe this "R" is only funding, my definition of "resources" takes it a bit further. Aside from adequate funding, this "R" includes appropriate management tools, practices, processes, policies, regulations, strategies, and other guidelines for all members of the "big A" team who will be involved in meeting the requirement and getting the appropriate capability to the warfighter. This need for adequate resources also includes industry.

Right People: This is perhaps the most important of the "three R's." Without the right people, nothing will be accomplished as planned, even if the requirements and resources are in place. The "right people" are those on both the government and industry sides of the team who are educated, trained, mentored, experienced, creditable, empowered, and trusted to do the job at hand (with the resources given), meet the requirements, and deliver the capability to the warfighter.

In my 30-plus years in DoD acquisition, every program that I have led, studied, or assisted (that has succeeded) followed these "three R's." Those that have violated one or more of the "three R's", at a minimum, have not met expectations and, at worst, have failed and been terminated after much delay and cost. While we could go on and on discussing each of the "three R's" and apply them to various good and bad programs of today, the remainder of this essay will focus on just one of the "three R's," including how it relates to CMMI-ACQ.

Let's turn our attention to the second of the "three R's"—resources. Resources include, among other things, the tools, processes, and practices needed to meet the requirements. To this end, CMMI-ACQ is a natural fit. CMMI-ACQ is a process-oriented tool that lays out an orderly way of describing a program in terms of elements that can be devolved, managed, improved, benchmarked, and assimilated into an integrated whole, which is what the customer wanted, when the customer wanted it, and at the agreed-to price. "Resources," when managed properly, actually integrate all of the "three R's."

For an example that illustrates this point, I will pick on an Army program that was on my watch during my tenure as the Assistant Secretary of the Army for Acquisition, Logistics and Technology (ASAALT). In this case, CMMI-ACQ was not used because it was not then available. Had it been available, the results might have been different. The program was called the Aerial Common Sensor (ACS) program. It was a joint Army–Navy program, for which the Army served as the lead. It was chartered to deliver an aircraft to the Army and Navy that would replace the Army's Guardrail aircraft and the Navy's EP-3 aircraft. Both of these aircraft provided airborne electronic surveillance for the services.

Because of the age of the aircraft, the increasing sophistication of electronic threat and surveillance, and the need to drive lifecycle costs down, the ACS program was conceived and approved. The pre-Milestone B activity, which included technology demonstrations, went well. It appeared as if all of the processes and the "three R's" were in place and performing as expected. However, as Milestone B approached, changes were made to the operational requirements, which drove the size and weight of the aircraft. The effects were so dramatic that, during source selection for Milestone B, one of the competitors was eliminated because its aircraft was too heavy.

Within three months of the start of post-Milestone B activities, the program manager recommended termination of the contract. Why? The winning contractor's aircraft weight had grown to the point that the ACS could not take off! Why did this happen? The interpretation of the operational requirements by the warfighter had changed.

Had the ACS project used the CMMI-ACQ tool from its inception and, in particular, throughout the activities leading to the Milestone B decision, ACS would likely be flying today. Had ACS followed the CMMI-ACQ methodology, it would have discovered the requirements issues early in its inception; it would have established procedures and processes to identify and resolved requirements challenges early in the pre-Milestone A program phase. Those new procedures and processes would have led to better use of the technology demonstrations and provided valuable knowledge about the feasibility of the warfighter requirements. All of these issues could have been resolved early in the program and led to success.

Let's dwell here for a moment. We will consider what would have happened if the ACS had used the CMMI-ACQ tool—which actions would have taken place that would have resulted in a better outcome.

Because the ACS contract was terminated before system development and demonstration could occur, I will focus my remaining remarks on the requirements process. This focus is most appropriate because the change in the interpretation of the operational requirements at the start of the system development and demonstration (SDD) phase was the factor that ultimately caused contract termination shortly after the start of SDD as previously mentioned.

Had ACS been able to adopt and use the CMMI-ACQ model, it would have accomplished the following actions. First, it would have established an Acquisition Requirements Development (ARD) process to collaborate with the warfighter in the development and analysis of the operational requirements, and the translation of those requirements into a contractual arrangement with industry. The model would have insisted on the following goals and practices specially illustrated in the CMMI-ACQ text:

Specific Goal and Practice Summary

SG 1 Develop Customer Requirements
    SP 1.1   Elicit Stakeholder Needs
    SP 1.2   Develop and Prioritize Customer Requirements

SG 2 Develop Contractual Requirements
    SP 2.1   Establish Contractual Requirements
    SP 2.2   Allocate Contractual Requirements
SG 3 Analyze and Validate Requirements
    SP 3.1   Establish Operational Concepts and Scenarios
    SP 3.2   Analyze Requirements
    SP 3.3   Analyze Requirements to Achieve Balance
    SP 3.4   Validate Requirements5

Second, it would have established an Acquisition Technical Management (ATM) process to manage all the technical reviews needed to ensure that the technical aspects of the program were on course. Establishing this process in the pre-Milestone B phase of ACS would have provided early recognition of the impacts of the changing requirements. It would have required the planning and scheduling of technical reviews early in the program history and ensured that all parties involved understood what knowledge was required and at what time—not just during the pre-Milestone B program phase, but throughout the SDD, production, fielding, and sustainment phases.

I believe CMMI-ACQ could have made a considerable difference in the ACS program and allowed it to continue successfully. Just by reading the purpose of each process area and reflecting on what could have been if the ACS had followed and realized each process area's goals, it is clear that, if this program had been developed using CMMI-ACQ, the ACS would undoubtedly be in the Army and Navy inventories today.

Use of CMMI at the U.S. Government Accountability Office

Madhav Panwar

Building, managing, and acquiring information technology systems are not easy tasks. Unless the product you want is commercially available in a box and meets all of your organization's needs, a number of tasks need to be performed to ensure that you build or acquire a system that enables your organization to meet its business objectives.

The Software Engineering Institute (SEI) has provided guidance on building and acquiring systems for more than two decades. As the

---

5. *CMMI-ACQ: Guidelines for Improving the Acquisition of Products and Services*, p. 175.

technology has matured, so has the guidance. Using appropriate portions of the various models that the SEI and its partners in the CMMI Product Development team offer enables your organization to increase its success rate in implementing information technology solutions.

The U.S. Government Accountability Office (GAO) has worked with the SEI to ensure that the best practices captured in the model used earlier by the GAO, the Software Acquisition CMM, were both preserved and improved with the broadening of coverage in CMMI. Since then, the CMMI-ACQ model has proved itself to the GAO, and has become a valuable tool for our work.

At the GAO, we have been using the CMMI-ACQ model to evaluate federal agencies' acquisition efforts. This use of CMMI enables the GAO to evaluate acquisition activities across the government using a common methodology. The GAO does not require that a certain level of CMMI certification be achieved or even recommend which practices to implement when a project is acquiring a good or service. Instead, the program manager makes those decisions based on the level of risk, criticality, funding, and other criteria.

The practices provided in CMMI are a reasonable set that assist the program manager and the organization by increasing the likelihood of success. Given our vast experience in looking at processes across the government, we are confident that the ones in CMMI-ACQ will help organizations with their acquisition efforts, particularly when they are tailored to meet the specific needs of the product or service being considered.

Over the years, the GAO has reported on the acquisition of large IT systems and their cost overruns, failures in meeting customer needs, midstream redefinition of requirements, and even outright project termination. These issues are really part of the history of IT systems in general; what the GAO reports reflects larger industry trends. Over the years, the success rate of acquisition programs has gradually improved.

The GAO has recommended that projects be defined in smaller increments, provide customers with quicker releases, and get feedback to improve the product. Defining requirements for a product that will be released in 5 to 7 years is a complex and difficult task. The recent encouragement to speed the IT acquisition cycle to match the commercial 18-month cycle puts yet more pressure on the acquisition office. When that is the case, a disciplined approach to acquisition like that contained in CMMI-ACQ is required.

CMMI-ACQ deals primarily with processes that result in the acquisition of goods and services. Today, more and more organizations are contracting out for their IT solutions. Federal agencies in the United States, for example, put out numerous solicitations for contractors to offer solutions. This competition ensures that the government gets the best value for its money and also enables the government to keep up-to-date with new technologies and work processes, thereby becoming more efficient. However, to ensure that contractors understand what is required, to monitor the development of the solution, to ensure that various parts are integrated and tested correctly, and to ensure that a working solution is delivered requires that the organization follow practices in this model.

The GAO has been working with various agencies to ensure that systems acquisition is done in a manner that provides the most likely chance of success. For example, the GAO sought to get a data management strategy as a key part of acquisition efforts into legislation. Furthermore, current efforts are underway to make sure that in addition to following a data management strategy, acquisition program managers routinely consult with key stakeholders and actively solicit their input during the entire acquisition lifecycle.

The CMMI models address both of these areas. For its part, the GAO uses the model practices associated with data management and involvement of stakeholders as well as other process areas and practices in the model as appropriate during our reviews of government acquisition efforts. The GAO has used CMMI-ACQ when evaluating agency efforts to acquire software solutions, for example—these reports are available on the GAO website (www.gao.gov/). CMMI-ACQ is the model that GAO uses when evaluating acquisition practices.

While there is no set of practices that will work for every possible situation, experience has shown that managing requirements is critical. Many projects proceed with vaguely defined requirements; do not consult adequately (if at all) with users, customers, and other stakeholders; and put out a solicitation only to find that it is incomplete or not what the user wanted.

Other areas that typically are not addressed adequately include risk management, communications within and outside the team, planning and tracking the work, and senior management oversight. These are all basic management activities. CMMI-ACQ includes practices that can help your organization with these and other areas of the acquisition lifecycle. The GAO recommends that organizations use this model to guide their efforts to successfully acquire solutions and to provide their customers or the organization itself with the tools needed to better accomplish the mission at hand.

An Industry Perspective on CMMI-ACQ

Rich Frost, Ashok Gurumurthy, and Tom Keuten

Overview

Large corporations have been outsourcing all or pieces of their information technology functions for years. Any organization that is not in the IT business is likely buying some form of IT that is necessary for its business to be successful. Most companies buy their core business systems (e.g., enterprise resource planning [ERP] or time management) from commercial providers. Even IBM now buys its laptops from someone else, as the firm is no longer in that business. Organizations must buy at least some IT products and services from someone else because it just doesn't make good business sense to make or do everything themselves. Unfortunately, IT acquisitions don't always go well, as evidenced by the large number of articles discussing IT and outsourcing gone wrong.

Many IT functions have been outsourced by company management because executives are led to believe that they can hire other companies to develop their software, run their help desk and support, manage their infrastructure, and do anything else related to IT, all at a fraction of the cost that these companies pay for their current employees. This "story" makes sense because most companies are in business to do something other than IT, and IT service companies are in business to help other companies with their IT. However, history and statistics on IT outsourcing have shown that many of these deals fall through or are not successful, which leaves some companies with expensive deals that they want to wriggle out of.

On the one hand, many IT organizations that acquire their technology or outsource the whole IT function blame their suppliers when those acquisitions subsequently fail. They complain that the suppliers did not meet their end of the deal and could not deliver what they, the customer, expected. On the other hand, IT suppliers that have tried to help such companies complain that the customers didn't specify what they needed and did not hold up their end of the bargain.

The IT environment is very complex in almost all commercial organizations. Many struggle with issues related to security, cost, scalability, and integration. Countless IT suppliers stand ready to provide all kinds of products and services that are intended to help solve these problems. Those products and support services must somehow seamlessly connect with others that are currently in the IT environment of the acquiring organization. Companies that mostly "insource" their IT functions also run into comparable complex connection issues, but outsourcing some or all of these functions increases that complexity. Consequently, companies that acquire more IT products and services must be exceptional at IT acquisition (which includes holding suppliers and their internal stakeholders accountable) if they expect to achieve positive results.

CMMI-ACQ is the most robust, publicly available solution for organizations that are seeking to improve their acquisition processes. To leverage this model to achieve positive results in acquisition, organizations must internalize CMMI-ACQ best practices so that they fully understand how to apply them. This essay provides some insights based on our observations when working with companies using CMMI-ACQ. It describes how using multiple suppliers increases the complexity of the commercial IT environment, and it provides tips about using preferred vendors, lessons learned on contract management, and insights on implementation. The essay concludes with some recommendations for acquirers about when and how to conduct appraisals using the CMMI-ACQ model and ideas for future versions of CMMI-ACQ.

Multi-supplier Challenges

The definition of outsourcing has matured over time and has become more complex to reflect the changing needs of businesses. When organizations outsource their enterprise IT services, new issues and risks are introduced as various "outsiders" provide IT services. Recently, organizations have started using a "multi-supplier" strategy, which means they use more than one supplier to provide IT services. This strategy adds further complexity to an outsourced environment. Because so many suppliers define a specific niche for themselves and none serves as a one-stop shop for everything a company needs, it is impossible to avoid the multi-supplier environment given today's changing business needs.

Unfortunately, a perfect outsourcing contract may not exist, as so many unwritten expectations must be met in running a large IT environment. During the execution of contracts in a multi-supplier environment, the following issues and challenges typically arise:

- Separate contract terms and conditions and segregated responsibility across suppliers (IT solutions require integrated responsibility)
- Suppliers' unwillingness to work with other suppliers ("not in my contract" responses)

- Suppliers' inability to work together with other suppliers in a multi-supplier environment
- Separate supplier tools and methods for delivery of work artifacts
- Lack of a governance model across multiple suppliers to execute the organizations' policies
- Lack of incentive for suppliers to come up with innovative solutions to drive costs down (the motivation to meet the contractual commitments drives simplicity and commonality of processes, not the idea of being flexible in service delivery)

The solution to the challenges arising from implementing the multi-supplier strategy is to use an organization that provides governance oversight and integrates services from multiple suppliers. Such a solution provides structured oversight and governance across all IT suppliers on behalf of the acquirer based on proven system integration principles.

A system integrator is a person or organization that specializes in bringing together component subsystems into a whole and ensuring that those subsystems function together smoothly. The principles of systems integration should be considered in the context of a multi-supplier outsourcing environment. The resultant "office of multi-supplier governance" provides thought leadership across the IT landscape, from strategy to operations, by using its knowledge and experience of the organization's multi-supplier environment. In addition, the office of multi-supplier governance provides the following key services to address the challenges in an outsourced multi-supplier environment:

- Multi-supplier communication management
- Cross-supplier governance
- Compliance management (e.g., standards and policies)
- Process and technology assurance
- Business-aligned IT strategy and thought leadership
- Enterprise architecture

The office of multi-supplier governance ensures that suppliers receive standard communication, operate consistently within defined policies and standards, and perform required quality checks before delivering something to the customer. This office can also provide thought leadership and research based on external best practices. Most importantly, the office of multi-supplier governance can help overcome challenges that arise when multiple suppliers are working in the same environment.

Preferred Supplier Dos and Don'ts

Many organizations will use multiple suppliers that can provide similar service offerings when they acquire resources either for a project (e.g., software development) or for ongoing operations (e.g., help desk). Some of these organizations maintain a list of prequalified "preferred" vendors that the organization will turn to when it has a need to acquire new products and services. This section discusses why organizations should consider having a list of preferred suppliers and some best practices to consider when engaging them. This topic is addressed here rather than more specifically in the CMMI-ACQ model because some organizations that use CMMI-ACQ may be constrained by regulatory or other organizational requirements that prevent them from being able to engage in this practice.

Development of a list of preferred vendors makes a lot of sense for some companies because it allows the acquiring organization and the suppliers to agree to terms once for a series of acquisitions rather than having to repeat the same process individually each time. This process helps the project team go faster and can provide motivation for the suppliers to invest in longer-term relationships. These elements can help ensure a successful acquisition.

During an acquisition, a lot of time can be spent in solicitation and supplier agreement development (SSAD in CMMI-ACQ). The acquiring organization needs to determine which suppliers are capable of doing the work. If the organization has acquired a similar product or service in the past, and the supplier executed its end of the deal in an acceptable manner, then it is natural that the supplier would be added to a preferred supplier list in that area. Also, if a supplier is able to handle one type of project well, it may be able to handle other types of projects. Once those capabilities are qualified, it would be natural to place that supplier on a preferred vendor list.

When the next project comes along, if the organization has a prequalified list of preferred vendors, that project will go faster. The acquisition will also go faster if the preferred vendors have all agreed in advance to contract terms and conditions. Many contracts are held up by attorneys on either side of the acquisition due to disagreements regarding terms and conditions. If terms and conditions are already agreed on, this risk is avoided. If projects can be timed so that a preferred supplier team "rolls off" one project and starts another one right away, both parties win: Acquirers will benefit from continuity of the team, and suppliers will benefit from knowing where their resources will be allocated.

As these types of win-win scenarios are developed, both suppliers and acquirers get used to working with each other, making it easy to collaborate on innovation and engage in a more productive delivery model. Suppliers may be willing to make critical investments in infrastructure. For example, suppliers may be willing to establish test laboratories with hardware that has the same configuration as the customer to conduct testing in a customer-like environment.

To optimize the value of using preferred suppliers, it is important that agreements with these suppliers include some protections for the acquirer. For example, the acquirer may want to name specific critical employees whom the supplier needs to keep on acquirer projects unless prior written authorization is received from the acquirer not to do so. This term of the agreement will ensure that the acquirer is not paying for new employees to learn the environment and will drive continuity across engagements.

Contract terms (or at least the terms and conditions) should focus on the long-term relationship so that the acquirer can plan for and the supplier can count on more predictability across the time frame of the contract. Finally, the acquirer should specify which tools (e.g., standard test tool) are required to work in the acquirer's environment and that the supplier must use to provide the service. As part of the tools aspect of the contract, there should be specific language about licensing for those tools so that these costs are not included for each project.

Preferred lists of suppliers can be very beneficial to organizations that engage suppliers for similar types of projects. These lists can help the project team go faster and motivate suppliers to work with acquirers to create more effective delivery models. Agreements with suppliers on these preferred lists should contain clauses that protect the acquirer and ensure that the acquirer is receiving the benefits of having preferred suppliers.

Contract Management

Industry surveys on outsourcing show that, in many cases, the outsourcing benefits of IT organizations have not met their initial expectations. The primary drivers for organizations to outsource these operations include a lack of in-house expertise and the ability to transfer the risk to the vendor. At the same time, organizations also view cost savings, flexibility, best practices, and innovation as key supporting drivers of outsourcing IT. As industry research makes clear, many of these organizations do not realize the benefits they expected from outsourcing.

In the real world, outsourcing often does not deliver on its promise. There is rarely a single reason why a contract fails; instead, a combination of reasons is typically to blame. Some of these problems can be attributed to contracting processes. Stipulating basic discipline around contract management processes plays an important role in outsourcing deals. The contract lifecycle spans various phases such as contract planning, solicitation, evaluation of supplier response, negotiation, and contract finalization.

Communication plays a vital role across the contract management lifecycle. Historically, IT organizations have focused on different models and frameworks within the software engineering and project management disciplines. As IT organizations have adopted outsourcing as their key strategy, it has become clear that similar process discipline is needed in the contract management area. Some of the major challenges faced in the outsourcing industry are addressed by CMMI-ACQ process elements, which clearly stipulate many of these activities within the contract management process.

We often hear from outsourcing organizations that expected cost savings are not achieved through outsourcing, because hidden costs are associated with the services that were not considered properly when contracts were written. If proper discipline is followed in creating a solicitation package (which is then used to seek proposals/responses from potential suppliers), these ambiguities in contracts can be avoided.

Solicitation packages need to be reviewed with the appropriate stakeholders to ensure that they provide the correct scope of coverage. Involving the right people in developing and reviewing the solicitation package is critical to avoid discrepancies in contract coverage. For example, not specifically covering the decommissioning of a system in a contract for developing a new solution may lead to potential discrepancies in the contract and may trigger contract change requests and lead to additional costs. Involving the right people in developing and reviewing the solicitation package is covered in the CMMI-ACQ model in the Solicitation and Supplier Agreement Development (SSAD) process area. (*CMMI-ACQ reference:* The SSAD process area specifies preparation, review, and distribution of solicitation packages by involving the right stakeholders. This process area helps the acquirer avoid discrepancies in the contract.)

Outsourcing adds a level of rigidity to normal organizational activities because contracts are binding and suppliers may choose not to accommodate changes without charging the customer additional cost. This problem becomes more significant when a multi-year contract is in place, but the contract does not react to the changes that the acquirer needs to act on based on its changing user requirements. When developing contracts, there is a need to create a win-win situation for both acquirer and supplier. The SSAD process area in the CMMI-ACQ model describes how supplier agreements should elaborate on how scope changes and supplier agreement changes can be determined, communicated, and addressed. The agreement may be either a stand-alone agreement or part of a master agreement. When it is a part of a master agreement, the project agreement may take the form of an addendum, work order, or service request to the master agreement. (*CMMI-ACQ reference:* The SSAD process area specifies how to establish and maintain a supplier agreement.)

Some outsourcing problems are attributed to a lack of contract management governance. Problems in this area may arise because of improper communication, incorrect document versioning, or inadequate reviews done by senior management during the contract lifecycle. By adopting the generic practices of the CMMI-ACQ model, important practices such as communication planning, configuration control, stakeholder and senior management reviews, and process verification can address any issues in the areas early on, allowing the parties to avoid contract disputes. (*CMMI-ACQ reference:* The generic practices are intended to ensure that you address issues that could lead to contract disputes or problems.)

Often, contract approvals take too long to complete. If contracting plans and strategies are not clearly known and communicated by the acquisition organization, the supplier may waste resources by not planning to provide services as soon as the contracts are signed. SSAD emphasizes communicating with potential suppliers concerning the forthcoming solicitation. The acquirer outlines the plans for the solicitation, including the projected schedule for solicitation activities and expected dates for responses from suppliers, which helps suppliers plan to bring their resources on board once contracts are signed. (*CMMI-ACQ reference:* The SSAD process area specifies means to establish and maintain the supplier agreement.)

Implementation Considerations

There are many ways to leverage the CMMI-ACQ model. It is important that the implementation of the practices identified in CMMI-ACQ matches the culture and goals of the organization. While applying CMMI-ACQ in large organizations with a wide variety of acquisitions in the form of commercial off-the-shelf (COTS) software and custom-developed software to infrastructure and hardware, the following points should be considered:

- Develop the process and tailoring approach in a way that ensures that projects do only the right things and neither skip quality steps nor add non-value-added activities into the process.
- Wherever possible, automate process steps so that they automatically collect metrics while the project teams are doing their work.
- Provide oversight where necessary, at the appropriate level of the organization.

When organizations keep processes lean but rigorous and optimized for project teams to deliver, they are more likely to see greater returns on their investment in their adoption of CMMI-ACQ practices.

Even though organizations may pursue a wide variety of acquisitions, each acquisition project can follow a common process that serves as its foundation. Each acquisition project will need to plan the acquisition, elicit and manage customer requirements, engage suppliers through a supplier agreement, verify work products, validate supplier deliverables, and monitor the project against its plan and risk factors. Each of those steps can be either very complex or quite simple, however—its level of complexity will match the characteristics of the acquisition.

For example, if the acquirer simply wants to purchase a new computer server, those requirements are quite different from the requirements for a new handheld device that service technicians can use for requesting parts and tracking outstanding jobs. A requirements specification is needed in both situations, but the latter would include a significant number of user interface and mobility requirements that would not be considered important when purchasing the typical server. When standardizing a process (Organizational Process Definition [OPD] in CMMI-ACQ) for an organization that has such a variety of projects, it is important to implement tailoring to the work products themselves; they need to be tailorable to match what a project needs to be successful.

Processes that have standard quality checkpoints can also have very positive effects on project performance. Throughout any acquisition project, it is important to have someone outside the project review the team's work to ensure its alignment with standard processes and overall quality. During the assessment that takes place at these checkpoints, another opportunity for tailoring opens up.

For major investments that include significant budgets and high complexity levels, these independent reviews will likely need to occur at the highest levels of the organization. However, the head of the organization does not have to review the smaller projects with lower levels of complexity. Sometimes team members for a project must review its progress with large numbers of stakeholders to ensure that they all have visibility. Often, these same stakeholders are invited to reviews of other projects that don't require such robust governance. Thus the reviews an organization conducts can also be tailored to fit the project's unique situation, which helps to ensure that the project doesn't do things that do not add value and the organization's leaders still receive the level of visibility necessary to provide the right level of oversight.

Automating processes that are implemented based on CMMI-ACQ can significantly increase productivity and decrease project costs. For example, we worked with one company that had a robust tollgate process at the end of each project phase in which business customer and IT management would review project status and decide whether to proceed. Because this was a global company with project team members and executives located all over the world, significant effort was required to set up tollgate meetings that fit into all of the shareholders' schedules, and the meetings themselves were very expensive due to the level of attendees.

To solve this problem, the company implemented a virtual tollgate process that allowed project teams to show their progress in an online system and allowed tollgate approvers to vote when it was convenient. Reminders were sent out to those persons who did not submit a vote, and if the project information was not clear, the tollgate approver could request a formal meeting. The default situation was to conduct all voting through the virtual tollgate, but there was always an opportunity to have the meeting if the project required more scrutiny or the approvers just needed in-person discussion. By automating this process, the company was able to reduce the cost of the meeting infrastructure and administration, and it made the process more convenient for both the project teams and approvers.

Organizations that are following the CMMI-ACQ model will at some point strive to gather metrics (if they don't consider them when they first get started). Project teams typically will not mind providing or reviewing metrics if the data are collected as a part of doing normal project work. If the project has to do additional work to gather the metrics and report them, however, team members rarely see the value in doing so and often will do whatever possible to not participate.

For example, many organizations write change requests on forms. As part of the change request analysis, the team often determines the impact to customer requirements as a result of the requested change. If the project then needs to report metrics related to requirements volatility, team members have to go back through the change request forms and determine which ones affected business requirements. If the project instead has a requirements management tool that tracks changes, oftentimes volatility data can be pulled directly from that tool.

Alternatively, if the change request is part of a change management system and data about business requirements changes can be summarized, metrics can be generated rather quickly. Both of these potential solutions do not require the project team members to do extra work to create metrics. Minimizing the non-value-added work and keeping processes lean helps to ensure that projects follow processes because they will find them valuable instead of obstructive.

Another key area to consider when implementing CMMI-ACQ practices is supporting projects with the right level of oversight. Much in the same way that project documents and processes can be tailored, the amount of oversight from senior management through technical leadership can be customized based on the needs of the project. For instance, the CIO of a large organization may be required to attend the project review for the largest IT project in the company, but his or her attendance is likely not necessary for review of the project that is simply upgrading some servers in a data center.

Many organizations invite people to reviews because they have been invited before or because they might know something that could help the project. Other organizations address many projects at a single meeting so that they can be reviewed sequentially. With this policy, half of the people in the meeting care about only half of the projects, yet they are required to attend the whole time. There are lots of opportunities to tailor oversight, just like there are many opportunities to tailor processes and work products. Each of these opportunities should be evaluated when adopting CMMI-ACQ practices.

Organizations that go through major changes like adopting CMMI-ACQ practices often experience many stops and starts. One major reason for delays in making changes is the tendency to implement processes that force projects to do things that do not add value or that create extra work. The more that organizations can improve their tailoring (from processes to work products to approvals), and the more they can automate the collection of metrics so that this task does not create an extra burden for projects, the faster they will be able to implement CMMI-ACQ practices and see the benefits of adoption. Those organizations that do not consider these opportunities may see some of the challenges that many organizations before them have encountered and, one hopes, will have the wherewithal to notice history repeating itself so that they can change course.

CMMI-ACQ Appraisals: Why?

Acquiring organizations have been using CMMI-DEV appraisal results for years to qualify suppliers. To get the best result for the customer, both the acquirer and the supplier must be capable. Acquirers should conduct appraisals of their own organization using CMMI-ACQ to identify opportunities to reduce cost, improve quality, and increase customer satisfaction.

As mentioned earlier in this section, one of the motivating factors for commercial organizations to outsource software development and other IT functions is to reduce cost. Vendors that perform those functions as their primary business should be able to do so less expensively than a company that focuses on providing energy, building trucks, or selling clothing. However, to ensure that costs are as low as they can be, the acquirer must be effective at communicating requirements and engaging suppliers. An appraisal using the SCAMPI method with CMMI-ACQ as the source model will help organizations identify gaps in their ability to elicit requirements, communicate those requirements to suppliers, and subsequently engage them through contracts. If the requirements are vague, conflicting, or not testable, then suppliers bidding on such engagements will raise their prices to account for the work that will inevitably have to be done to clarify and potentially rewrite the acquirer-developed requirements. If the acquirer can eliminate defects in requirements by closing gaps identified in appraisals, the acquirer can expect to see its costs of acquisitions go down, as suppliers can bid more aggressively due to the clarity of acquirer intent.

Acquirers can also increase their quality by conducting appraisals and identifying and closing gaps related to verification and process and product quality assurance from an acquirer's perspective. Suppliers develop a perception of the acquirer's level of quality expectations from the initial engagement, which then builds through the contracting phase and into the delivery phase. If the acquirer does not enforce internal verification steps for the work products that the acquirer develops (e.g., requirements specifications, contract statements of work), then it will become apparent to the supplier that the company has a low expectation—and the supplier will likely deliver products and services geared toward that expectation.

Conversely, if the acquirer produces very clear deliverables that have been reviewed and are well understood, the supplier will develop a perception that the acquirer expects a high level of quality and will strive to match that level of quality so that it can impress the acquirer and win more business. If the supplier also knows that its own quality results may be reviewed by the acquirer at any time (which should be specified in any supplier agreement), the supplier team will have additional motivation to achieve higher quality on its end, resulting in a higher-quality product or service being delivered to the acquiring customer.

Just as suppliers develop perceptions of acquirers, so customers of acquirers can develop perceptions of their acquisition support. For example, many commercial organizations that outsource large portions of their IT function still retain a team of employees to manage the suppliers engaged by the company. These teams often gather requirements from the business and engage suppliers to develop solutions to meet these requirements.

If these internal IT teams do not know how to professionally engage their customers to elicit requirements and appropriately manage expectations through project planning, monitoring, and control, the customers may develop the perception that the acquirer teams are in the way and not able to help them. They may even question whether the internal team roles can also be outsourced to someone who *can* help them. SCAMPI appraisals of these internal IT teams using the CMMI-ACQ model can identify some of these potential pitfalls and help IT leadership understand where to invest in additional capability for better customer engagement. These investments can lead to higher performance by the internal IT team and result in a higher level of customer satisfaction.

Many IT organizations that outsource much of their software development and other functions have been looking for a mechanism that can assess whether they are effective at their remaining function—namely, engaging suppliers to deliver solutions. A CMMI-ACQ appraisal helps acquirers ensure that they have their side of the transaction in order, similar to how results from a CMMI-DEV appraisal can give acquirers confidence that suppliers are prepared to deliver. Acquisitions can fall apart if either side is not prepared, so acquirers need to conduct internal appraisals similar to the way they demand appraisals from their suppliers. Acquirers conducting appraisals of their own organization using CMMI-ACQ can identify many performance opportunities, including those related to cost reduction, quality improvement, and higher customer satisfaction.

What Industry Needs from the Next CMMI-ACQ Model

Like all great concepts, the CMMI-ACQ model needs to continue to evolve to support industry needs as they change. Many of the underlying principles focused on project management, supplier engagement, and acquisition verification and validation have stood the test of time and will likely continue to do so for many years. At the same time, CMMI-ACQ does not address some things that are important to commercial organizations that acquire technical products and services—but a revised version could address those issues in the future.

There will likely be as yet unknown areas that emerge in the future that CMMI-ACQ will need to address as well. This section discusses practices that are needed by industry that CMMI-ACQ could address or that organizations will have to address in other ways to meet their objectives. These practices include "pre-project" analysis and work as well as management of the organizational portfolio of projects. This section also addresses integration with other CMMI models as another opportunity to improve and operationalize the use of CMMI-ACQ.

CMMI-ACQ is focused on improving acquisition projects. The process areas in this model describe practices that projects should follow and practices that organizations should follow to help projects be successful. These practices are all valuable, and they should be implemented by commercial organizations that acquire technical products and services. However, to ensure that the project adds value to the organization, it has to be the right project in the first place.

CMMI-ACQ today does not specifically address project selection by the organization. There are many project investments that an organization can make. Those organizations that select the right projects that are best aligned to organizational goals are more likely to achieve their goals. This selection may be based on criteria such as return on investment, risk, strategic fit, or ability to deliver based on available capacity in terms of resources and capability. Each project investment should be evaluated using standard criteria to ensure that the right projects for the organization are selected in the first place.

Every organization also has scarce resources. CMMI-ACQ captures many good specific and generic practices at the project level. If projects follow these practices, they should have adequate resources to allow them to be effectively and successfully executed. If all of the projects in the organization follow these practices, then the organization should perform at a higher level of maturity. For that to happen effectively, organizations must have a resource management system in place that accomplishes the following:

- Enables senior management to make decisions about which projects should have resources allocated to them
- Provides visibility into the resources that will be finishing their projects and potential projects where they could be used
- Identifies over- or underutilized resources for resource leveling

If resource management happens only at the project level, then the organization will not optimize its resources and may experience higher costs or lower performance. In the future, CMMI-ACQ could include practices for resource management at an organizational level in addition to the project level to help organizations in this area.

The CMMI Product Team has done a fantastic job in ensuring continuity across the CMMI model series. Recognizing that certain core process areas are common to development, acquisition, and services helps customers of those models align their operations using a common language. As the set of models evolves, more guidance on how customers of the models might integrate their efforts to work with one another will be necessary to ensure that when customers and developers decide to work together, a positive result ensues for both organizations.

For example, both CMMI-DEV and CMMI-ACQ include Project Planning (PP) as a process area, and most people would agree that development and acquisition organizations need to be effective in these activities. To effectively implement these process areas when the customer is using the CMMI-ACQ model and the supplier is using the CMMI-DEV model, it is important to clearly understand "who is planning what" to ensure that nothing is missed and that significant duplication of effort does not occur. This understanding requires effective communication between the two organizations, which could be more focused if more guidance is provided in CMMI.

From another perspective, when companies cross their organizational boundaries to work with other companies, they typically enter that partnership with the desire to obtain a positive financial outcome for both companies. CMMI-ACQ has excellent guidance in how to engage suppliers and manage their contractual agreements. The CMMI-DEV model has a Supplier Agreement Management (SAM) process area, but it does not have a Customer Agreement Management process area. If developers don't have the engagement skills necessary to work with their customers, they may not deliver a positive financial return for their own company or develop a positive customer relationship—even if they have great development teams that produce quality products.

CMMI-ACQ is a very powerful tool for commercial organizations that engage suppliers to acquire technical products and services for their own use, for their customers' use, or as components that are integrated into a larger overall solution. To realize the most value from investing in the practices referenced by the model, an organization must take into account many factors, including how to manage multiple suppliers, contracts, preferred vendors, appraisals, and tailoring for both rigor and speed.

As with many great offerings, there are numerous opportunities to continue to improve the CMMI-ACQ model. Because CMMI-ACQ is part of the CMMI model series and integrated with the CMMI Product Suite, it is the most robust publicly available solution for organizations seeking improvement in this area. CMMI-ACQ will be very useful to commercial organizations that buy technical products and services for many years to come.

CMMI-ACQ in Industry: Future Possibilities

Mike Phillips and Brian Gallagher

Since the release of CMMI-ACQ, various types of nongovernment organizations have found the practices contained in this constellation to be a better fit for their quality improvement efforts than the CMMI-DEV predecessor. This essay explores some of the industry examples, and then considers some future possibilities for use of this model.

From a historical perspective, the initial contributions to CMMI were made by industry representatives who noted that often the contracting "arm" of their organizations had contract experts, but lacked a technical skill set for ensuring effective technical content in the contract as well as the skills needs to oversee progress during the supplier's development lifecycle. One organization created a group to assist this effort that was called "procurement engineering." The industry sponsor of CMMI-ACQ, General Motors' CIO, had a similar need for new competencies when the company divested its software development unit and created a "hub and spoke" network of software suppliers. Another essay in this chapter discusses this particular company's current use of the model.

Another essay describes a different path to acquisition. In this case, a defense contractor had been closely involved with a government sponsor in developing critical elements of the DoD's ballistic missile capabilities. Strategic changes have led to a need to extend the life-cycles of the existing systems rather than developing new systems. This requires a commitment to careful modernization of the capabilities, in the face of very limited resources. The government chose to award a contract to one company to oversee all of these acquisition efforts, and the essay describes some of its specific uses of CMMI-ACQ's high maturity capabilities.

Some current industry users of the constellation must deliver whole systems to clients, but engage in little or no development of the elements to be delivered. In some cases, they may have significant integration efforts. In others, they may be better characterized as assemblers of the subsystems, with integration aspects being relatively "low risk." An example might be a company that provides railway cars for urban transit. Many suppliers are at work producing alternative subsystems, but typically only a few companies deliver the final integrated vehicles. CMMI-ACQ provides a valuable "lens" for the oversight of the collection of suppliers that demand the most management attention.

Where might some new applications of the constellation next be seen? One opportunity that appears likely to emerge is when an organization assumes responsibility for the "enterprise," including management of the acquisition of a large suite of services from various supplying organizations. Just as the CMMI-DEV constellation covers the development activities of organizations for both products and services, so CMMI-ACQ is designed to cover the activities necessary for the acquisition of both products and services. To date, most of the "early adopters" seem to be acquiring products. Acquiring services adds a dimension that has been challenging for many organizations on both sides of these agreements. Satisfying service agreements often brings up significant issues, as most of these deals require service level agreements that are difficult to apply successfully. Incidents associated with perceived failures to deliver the needed service levels abound. Now that we have a complementary constellation with CMMI-SVC, we believe there are new areas between acquirers and service providers that are ripe for improvement.

Modern engineering practices, new technologies, and architectural patterns may provide interesting opportunities for industry. Cost savings or efficiencies may be realized in commercial organizations that acquire components and deliver value-added products and services to the general public, those organizations that acquire products and services for internal use, and those organizations that acquire and integrate products for government use. Take, for example, a service-oriented architecture (SOA) architectural pattern that logically decouples services from applications developed using services through an enterprise infrastructure. This decoupling allows acquirers to develop acquisition strategies for each of these three parts (services, applications, infrastructure) that optimize contractual relationships and acquisition methods based on the acquired part of the enterprise. For example, an acquirer may want to encourage quick reaction or use agile approaches when working with application developers, and may want to encourage a plan-driven approach for infrastructure developers. While this approach provides the acquirer with more flexibility, it also requires more sophistication, more integration skills, and systems engineering skills on the part of the acquisition team.

The move toward "cloud computing," in which resources can be shared among multiple users transparently and "on demand," provides some interesting challenges to acquirers as well. In the case where someone is managing an enterprise that requires general-purpose computing power to run applications with the need to dynamically allocate resources from one project to another based on demand, this approach appears to provide value. The acquirer would then need to construct an acquisition strategy for the cloud resources with a clear eye toward critical quality attributes of the enterprise. For example, nonfunctional requirements such as performance, availability, reliability, security, and assurance would all need special attention and may pose challenges when acquiring cloud computing for an enterprise. Additionally, both expected growth and exploratory growth scenarios would aid in determining cloud computing requirements. As with taking advantage of an SOA pattern, cloud computing allows an acquirer to decouple infrastructure procurement from application procurement with the potential of entering into agreements with suppliers that have particular expertise in application development or cloud computing independently.

As with any new engineering practice, technology, or architectural pattern, the hype is usually larger than the initial benefits. A sophisticated acquirer will carefully weigh the benefits using structured decision processes (see the Decision Analysis and Resolution process area) and pilot any new approach using a fact-based piloting approach (see the Organizational Process Focus and Organizational Performance Management process areas).

Acquisition Strategy: Planning for Success

Brian Gallagher
Adapted from "Techniques for Developing an Acquisition Strategy by Profiling
Software Risks," CMU/SEI-2006-TR-002

CMMI-ACQ's Project Planning process area asks a program to
establish and maintain its own acquisition strategy. There are also
references to the acquisition strategy called out in many other
CMMI-ACQ process areas.

What is an acquisition strategy and how does it relate to other
planning documents discussed in CMMI-ACQ?

The Defense Acquisition University (DAU) defines acquisition
planning as follows:

> *Acquisition planning is the process by which the efforts of all*
> *personnel responsible for an acquisition are coordinated and inte-*
> *grated through a comprehensive plan for fulfilling the agency need*
> *in a timely manner and at a reasonable cost. It is performed*
> *throughout the lifecycle and includes developing an overall acquisi-*
> *tion strategy for managing the acquisition and a written acquisition*
> *plan (AP).*

Acquisition planning is the act of defining and maintaining an
overall approach for a program. Acquisition planning guides all
elements of program execution to transform the mission need into a
fielded system that is fully supported and delivers the desired
capability. The goal of acquisition planning is to provide a road map
that is followed to maximize the chances of successfully fielding a
system that meets users' needs within cost and schedule constraints.
Acquisition planning is an iterative process; feedback loops impact
future acquisition planning activities.

An *acquisition strategy*, when formulated carefully, is a means of
addressing program risks through program structure. The DAU
defines acquisition strategy as follows:

> *An acquisition strategy is a business and technical management*
> *approach designed to achieve program objectives within the resource*
> *constraints imposed. It is the framework for planning, directing,*
> *contracting for, and managing a program. It provides a master*
> *schedule for research, development, test, production, fielding, modifi-*
> *cation, postproduction management, and other activities essential*

for program success. The acquisition strategy is the basis for formulating functional plans and strategies (e.g., test and evaluation master plan [TEMP], acquisition plan [AP], competition, systems engineering, etc.).

The Defense Acquisition Guidebook [DoD 2010] describes an acquisition strategy as "a comprehensive, integrated plan that identifies the acquisition approach and describes the business, technical, and support strategies that management will follow to manage program risks and meet program objectives. The Acquisition Strategy should define the relationship between the acquisition phases and work efforts, and key program events such as decision points, reviews, contract awards, test activities, production lot/delivery quantities, and operational deployment objectives."

The guidebook goes on to state that the acquisition strategy "evolves over the phases and should continuously reflect the current status and desired end point of the phase and the overall program."

A program's best acquisition strategy directly addresses its highest-priority risks. High-priority risks can be technical if no one has yet built a component that meets some critical aspect of the system or has never combined mature components in the way that is required. Risks can be programmatic if the system must be designed to accommodate predefined cost or schedule constraints. Risks can be mission related when the characteristics of a system that meets the need cannot be fully articulated and agreed on by stakeholders. Each program faces a unique set of risks, so the corresponding acquisition strategy must be unique to address them.

The risks a program faces evolve through the life of the program. The acquisition strategy and the plans developed based on that strategy must also evolve. Figure 6.12 shows the iterative nature of acquisition strategy development and planning.

The process usually starts with an articulation of user needs requiring a material solution and identification of alternatives to satisfy those needs (e.g., an analysis of alternatives [AoA]). A technology development strategy is then developed to mature the technologies required for the selected alternative. Next, the acquisition strategy is developed to guide the program. As the strategy is executed, refinements are made. In the DoD, the acquisition strategy is required and formally reviewed at major program milestones (e.g., Milestone B [MS B]).

The terms *acquisition planning, acquisition strategy,* and *acquisition plan* are frequently used interchangeably, which causes confusion.

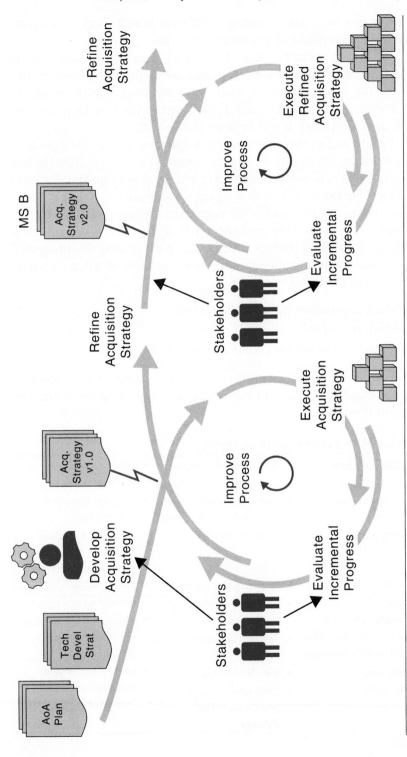

FIGURE 6.12
The Iterative Nature of Acquisition Strategy Development

A program's acquisition strategy is different from its acquisition plan, but both are artifacts of acquisition planning.

All strategies can be plans, but not all plans can be strategies. In the context of acquisition, strategies are high-level decisions that direct the development of more detailed plans, which guide the execution of a program. Careful planning of what is to be done, who will do it, and when it will be done is required.

Developing an all-encompassing acquisition strategy for a program is a daunting activity. As with many complex endeavors, often the best way to begin is to break the complex activity down into simpler, more manageable tasks. When developing an acquisition strategy, a program manager's first task is to define the elements of that strategy. When defining strategy elements, it is useful to ask the question, "Which acquisition choices must I make in structuring this program?"

Inevitably, asking this question leads to more detailed questions such as the following:

- Which acquisition approach should I use?
- Which type of solicitation will work best?
- How will I monitor my contractor's activities?

The result of these choices defines the acquisition strategy, as summarized in Table 6.1. Identifying strategy elements is the first step in this process.

TABLE 6.1 Elements of an Acquisition Strategy

• Acquisition Approach	• Technology Maturation	• Lifecycle Sustainment Planning
• Source and Related Documents	• Industrial Capability and Manufacturing Readiness	• Lifecycle Signature Support Plan
• Capability Needs	• Business Strategy	• Chemical, Biological, Radiological, and Nuclear Survivability
• Top-Level Schedule	• Resource Management	• Human Systems Integration
• Program Interdependency and Interoperability Summary	• Program Security Considerations	• Environment, Safety, and Occupational Health (ESOH)
• International Cooperation	• Test and Evaluation (T&E)	
• Risk and Risk Management	• Data Management	• Military Equipment Valuation and Accountability (MEVA)
	• Corrosion Prevention and Control Plan/ Strategy	

One of the most important strategy considerations is defining the acquisition approach, which in turn dictates the approach the program will use to achieve full capability. Typically, this approach is either evolutionary or a single step, as illustrated in Figure 6.13. (The evolutionary approach is the DoD's preferred approach.)

For readers who are experienced with development approaches, the decision to use a single-step or evolutionary approach seems natural and is driven by program risk. When acquiring a capability that has been developed many times before and for which there are known solutions, a single-step approach may be warranted.

However, most systems are more complex and require an evolutionary approach. The most important aspect to understand is the difference between the acquisition approach and the development approach used by the supplier. You can use a single-step approach as an acquisition strategy if the developer is using an incremental development approach.

At times, a different approach may be selected for different parts of the program. Figure 6.14 depicts the acquirer using a single-step approach while the developer is using an incremental approach.

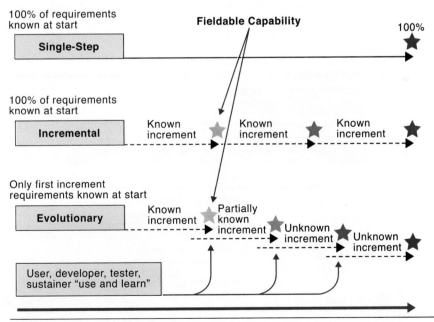

FIGURE 6.13
Defining an Acquisition Approach

Single-Step Acquisition, Contractor Incremental Development

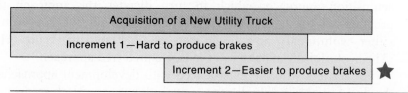

FIGURE 6.14
Single-Step Acquisition with an Incremental Development Approach

Figure 6.15 shows the acquirer using an evolutionary approach and the developer using a mix of single-step, incremental, and evolutionary (spiral) approaches.

The acquisition approach is just one of many decisions an acquirer makes when developing the acquisition strategy. Most choices are made based on a careful examination of risk. Each project is unique, so each acquisition strategy is unique. In the end, the acquisition strategy becomes one of the most important guiding artifacts for all stakeholders.

The decisions made and documented in the acquisition strategy help to mitigate the highest risks to the program and provide a road map that all stakeholders can understand, share, and analyze to help the project succeed.

Evolutionary Acquisition, Contractor Mixed Development—Comms System

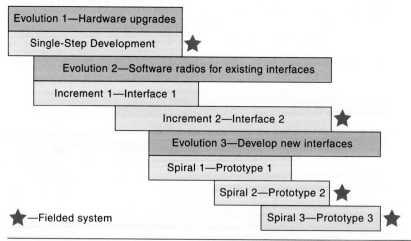

FIGURE 6.15
Evolutionary Acquisition with Mixed Development Approaches

Agreements: They Are Not Just with Suppliers

Mike Phillips

When creating the CMMI-ACQ model, we wrestled with finding ways to properly discuss the myriad agreements that are needed for an acquisition program to be successful. In this essay, I offer some thoughts related to the multiple types of agreements possible in acquisitions based on my experiences in government acquisition over the past 30 years.

Central to a successful acquisition process is the key contractual agreement between the acquirer and the supplier. To describe the agreements for this relationship, we built on the excellent foundation provided by the Supplier Agreement Management (SAM) process area from CMMI-DEV and legacy documents such as the Software Acquisition CMM published in the 1990s [SEI 2002, SEI 2006a]. However, the product team knew that other agreements must be carefully developed and managed over the life of many acquisitions, and that the model had to cover these types of agreements as well. Figure 6.15 is a reminder of the need for multiple agreements given the complexity of many of today's acquisitions.

In many government organizations, the acquisition discipline is established and maintained in specific organizations that are chartered to handle acquisition tasks for a variety of using organizations. Often the acquirers do not simply provide products to customers that the supplier delivers "as is," but instead integrate delivered products with other systems or add services such as training or upgrades, all of which may come from other agencies, departments, or organizations not typically thought of as suppliers. These other acquirer activities increase as product complexity increases.

Because of this known complexity, the product team knew that the definition of supplier agreement had to be broad and cover more than just a contract. So, the product team settled on the following definition: "A documented agreement between the acquirer and supplier (e.g., contract, license, or memorandum of agreement)."

The focus of the Acquisition Requirements Development process area is to ensure that customer needs are translated into customer requirements and that those requirements are used to develop contractual requirements. Although the product team agreed to call these "contractual" requirements, they knew the application of these requirements had to be broader.

Thus, contractual requirements are defined as follows: "The result of the analysis and refinement of customer requirements into a set of requirements suitable to be included in one or more solicitation packages, formal contracts, or supplier agreements between the acquirer and other appropriate organizations."

In another essay, we mention how, in many of our acquisitions, understanding the performance expected in delivering services is important. The service level agreements that are a vital element of the larger contractual agreement have often led to dissatisfaction on the part of both the buyer and the supplier. The disciplined application of the practices contained in ARD can assist in improving the understanding of expectations on both sides of the acquisition team.

Practices in the Solicitation and Supplier Agreement Development and Agreement Management process areas are particularly helpful as the need for other types of documented agreements increases with system complexity. An example of these kinds of agreements is the program-manager-to-program-manager agreement type that the U.S. Navy uses to help integrate combat systems and C4I in surface ships during new construction and modernization.

A recent—and noteworthy—example emerged as we prepared the second edition of this book. As I participated in a workshop with the Navy's Program Executive Office for C4I in San Diego, the commander was somewhat distracted by the challenge he was facing. Haiti had just suffered a massive earthquake, and a Navy task force was to be quickly assembled to provide aid. This situation required rapid, and new, configuration of the various systems that needed to be integrated for a specific task force to meet the specific needs of the deployment.

While the amount of development required for this "systems of systems" was modest, the challenge of ensuring adequate integration of the systems chosen and installed on the ships to be deployed was exceptional. The professional discipline shown by the PEO C4I workforce and their SSC engineering integration teams led to effective and rapid response to the Haiti catastrophe. These are the types of events that remind us of the value of a commitment to quality so that we can meet such challenges successfully.

Another helpful process area to use when integrating a large product is Acquisition Technical Management. Specific goal 2 is particularly useful because it focuses on the critical interfaces that likely have become the responsibility of the acquisition organization. Notes in this goal state: "The supplier is responsible for managing the interfaces of the product or service it is developing. However, the acquirer identifies those interfaces, particularly external interfaces, that it will manage as well."

This statement recognizes that the acquirer's role often extends beyond simply ensuring a good product from a supplier. In the introductory notes of this process area, the acquirer is encouraged to use more of CMMI-DEV's Engineering process areas if "the acquirer assumes the role of overall systems engineer, architect, or integrator for the product."

Clearly many acquisitions are relatively simple and direct, ensuring delivery of a new capability to the customer by establishing contracts with selected suppliers. However, the model provides an excellent starting point for the types of complex arrangements that often are seen in government today.

Acquisition Verification: The Challenges

Mike Phillips

Having been a military test pilot and director of tests for the B-2 Spirit Stealth Bomber acquisition program for the U.S. Air Force (USAF), I am particularly interested in the interactions between the testing aspects contained in the two companion models of CMMI-DEV and CMMI-ACQ. This essay provides some perspectives that will be helpful for those of you who need to work on verification issues across the acquirer–supplier boundary. With this release, we can also reflect on the relationship between CMMI-ACQ and CMMI-SVC, because the acquirer also has to consider some of the unique challenges when the supplier is providing services.

When we created the process areas for the Acquisition category, the product team knew we needed to expand the limited supplier agreement coverage in SAM (in the CMMI-DEV model) to address the business aspects critical to acquisition. We also needed to cover the technical aspects that were "close cousins" to the process areas in the Engineering process area category in CMMI-DEV. We tried to maximize the commonality between the two models so that both collections of process areas would be tightly related in the project lifecycle. For a significant part of the lifecycle, the two models represent two "lenses" observing the same total effort. Certainly testing seemed to be a strongly correlated element in both models.

As you read through the CMMI-ACQ process areas of Acquisition Verification and Acquisition Validation, notice that the wording is either identical or quite similar to the wording in the CMMI-DEV process areas of Verification and Validation. This commonality was intentional—that is, it was meant to maintain bridges between the acquirer and supplier teams, which often must work together effectively.

Throughout my military career, I often worked on teams that crossed the boundaries of government and industry to conserve resources and employ the expertise needed for complex test events such as flight testing. Combined test teams were commonly used. Often these teams conducted flight test missions in which both verification and validation tasks were conducted. The government, in these cases, helped the contractor test the specification and provided critical insight into the usability of the system.

Each model, however, must maintain a distinct purpose from its perspective (whether supplier or acquirer) while maximizing desirable synergies. Consider Validation and Acquisition Validation first. There is little real distinction between these two process areas because the purpose of both is the same: to satisfy the ultimate customer with products and services that provide the needed utility in the end-use environment. The value proposition is not different: Dissatisfied customers are often as upset with the acquisition organization as with the supplier of the product that has not satisfied the users. Thus the difference between Validation and Acquisition Validation is quite small.

With Verification and Acquisition Verification, however, the commonality is strong in one sense—both emphasize assurance that work products are properly verified by a variety of techniques—but each process area focuses on the work products produced and controlled in its own domain. Thus, whereas Verification focuses on the verification of *supplier* work products, Acquisition Verification focuses on the verification of *acquirer* work products.

The CMMI-ACQ product team saw the value of focusing on acquirer work products such as solicitation packages, supplier agreements and plans, requirements documents, and design constraints developed by the acquirer. These work products require thoughtful verification using powerful tools such as peer reviews to remove defects. Given that defective requirements are among the most expensive to find and address because they often are discovered late in development, improvements in verifying requirements have great value.

Verifying the work products developed by the supplier is covered in Verification and is the responsibility of the supplier, who is presumably using CMMI-DEV or CMMI-SVC. The acquirer may *assist* in verification activities because such assistance may be mutually beneficial to both the acquirer and the supplier. Nevertheless, the verification of the product or service developed by the supplier is ultimately performed by the supplier.

The acquirer's interests during supplier verification activities are captured in two other process areas. During much of development, supplier deliverables are used as a way to gauge development progress. Monitoring that progress and reviewing the supplier's technical solutions and verification results are covered by Acquisition Technical Management.

All of the process areas discussed thus far (Verification, Validation, Acquisition Verification, Acquisition Validation, Acquisition Technical Management, and Agreement Management) have elements of the stuff we call "testing." Testing is, in fact, a subset of the wider concept often known as "verification." I'll use my B-2 experience as an example.

Early in B-2 development, the B-2 System Program Office (SPO) prepared a test and evaluation master plan (TEMP). This plan is required in DoD acquisition and demands careful attention to the various methods that the government requires for the contractor's verification environment. The B-2 TEMP outlined the major testing activities necessary to deliver a B-2 to the using command in the USAF. This plan delineated a collection of classic developmental test activities called "developmental test and evaluation." From a model perspective, these activities would be part of the supplier's Verification activities during development. Fortunately, we had the supplier's system test plan, an initial deliverable document to the government, to help us create the developmental test and evaluation portions of the TEMP. Receiving the right supplier deliverables to review and use is part of what the Solicitation and Supplier Agreement Development process area is about.

The TEMP also addressed operational test and evaluation activities, which included operational pilots and maintenance personnel to ensure operational utility. These activities map to both Validation and Acquisition Validation. From a model perspective, many of the operational elements included in the TEMP were the result of mission and basing scenarios codeveloped with the customer. These activities map to practices in Acquisition Requirements Development.

The TEMP also described a large number of ancillary test-related activities such as wind tunnel testing and radar reflectivity testing. These earlier activities are best mapped to the practices of

Acquisition Technical Management. They are the technical activities the acquisition organization uses to analyze the suppliers' candidate solution and review the suppliers' technical progress. As noted in Acquisition Technical Management, when all of the technical aspects have been analyzed and reviewed to the satisfaction of the acquirer, the system is ready for acceptance testing. In the B-2 example, a rigorous physical configuration audit and functional configuration audit were conducted to account for all of the essential elements of the system. The testing and audits ensured that a fully capable aircraft was delivered to the using command. The physical configuration audit activities are part of the "Conduct Technical Reviews" specific practice in Acquisition Technical Management.

Much of the emphasis in CMMI-ACQ reminds acquirers of their responsibilities for the key work products and processes under their control. Many of us have observed the value of conducting peer reviews on critical requirements documents, from the initial delivery that becomes part of a Request for Proposal (RFP) to the oft-needed engineering change proposals. My history with planning the testing efforts for the B-2 leads me to point out a significant use of Acquisition Verification associated with the effective preparation of the TEMP. The test facilities typically were provided by the government, often including a mixture of facilities operated by the DoD and other government agencies such as NASA and what is now the Department of Energy.

Many people have stated that "an untestable requirement is problematic." Therefore, to complete a viable TEMP, the acquisition team must determine the criteria for requirements satisfaction and the verification environment that is needed to enable requirements satisfaction to be judged accurately. Here are a few of the questions that I believe complement Acquisition Verification best practices to help improve the quality of the government work product called the TEMP, or other work products like it in industry:

- What confidence do we have that a specific verification environment—whether it is a government site, an independent site, or the contractor site—can accurately measure the performance we are demanding?
- Are results obtained in a constrained test environment scalable to represent specified performance requirements?
- Can limited experience be extrapolated to represent long-term needs for reliability and maintainability?

- When might it be more cost-effective to accept data gathered at the suppliers' facilities?
- When might it be essential to use an independent (government or buyer) facility to ensure confidence in test results?

These and similar questions demonstrate the need for early attention to Acquisition Verification practices, particularly those under the first Acquisition Verification specific goal, "Prepare for Verification." These practices, of course, then support specific goal 3 activities that verify acquisition work products. These work products, in turn, often provide or augment the verification environment in which the system being acquired demonstrates its performance. These questions also help to differentiate the need to ensure a viable verification environment for the acquiring organization from the more familiar need to support the suppliers' verification of work products.

Now that we have CMMI-SVC to more fully describe the services environment, it makes sense to extend this thinking into that specific domain. In some cases, the extension is easy: The service is developed and delivered much like a tangible work product. More challenging is the situation in which the service to be provided will span a significant period of time, often with multiple service elements being included within the agreement.

Acquisition Verification can assist in the preparation of an effective service level agreement to be part of the contract. Often this work product needs to be a joint effort between the buyer and the supplier of the services. The questions listed previously can guide efforts to ensure satisfaction of the service level agreement. Such collaboration aids both the acquirer and the supplier of the services by ensuring that expectations can be described, measured, and satisfied to the benefit of both parties to the agreement. Based on my own experience, this is an area with major opportunities for research and improvement.

Transition to Operations: Delivering Value

Brian Gallagher

CMMI-ACQ includes two practices—one each in Project Planning and Project Monitoring and Control—related to transitioning products and services into operational use. As shown in Figure 6.16, one of the primary responsibilities of the acquirer, in addition to the

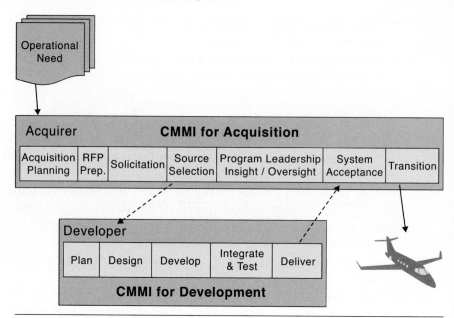

FIGURE 6.16
The Role of the Acquirer

acceptance of products and services from suppliers, is to ensure a successful transition of capability into operational use, including logistical considerations initially as well as throughout the life of the product or service.

Planning and monitoring the transition to operations and support activities involves the processes used to transition new or evolved products and services into operational use, as well as their transition to maintenance or support organizations. Many projects fail during later lifecycle phases because the operational user is ill prepared to accept and integrate the capability into day-to-day operations. Failure also stems from the inability to support the capability delivered due to inadequate initial sparing or the inability to evolve the capability as the operational mission changes.

Maintenance and support responsibilities may not be the responsibility of the original supplier. For example, sometimes an acquisition organization decides to maintain the new capability in-house. In other situations, there may be other reasons, economic or otherwise, why it makes sense to look for more potential providers of support activities. In these cases, the acquisition project must ensure that it has access to everything that is required to sustain the capability. This required access would include all design documentation as well as development environments, test equipment, simulators, and models.

The acquisition project is responsible for ensuring that acquired products not only meet their specified requirements (see the Acquisition Technical Management process area) and can be used in the intended environment (see the Acquisition Validation process area), but also can be transitioned into operational use to achieve the users' desired operational capabilities and can be maintained and sustained over their intended lifecycles.

The acquisition project is responsible for ensuring that reasonable planning for transition into operations is conducted (see Project Planning specific practice 2.7, "Plan for Transition to Operations and Support"), clear transition criteria exist and are agreed to by relevant stakeholders, and planning is completed for product maintenance and support of products after they become operational. These plans should include reasonable accommodation for known and potential evolution of products and their eventual removal from operational use.

This transition planning should be conducted early in the acquisition lifecycle to ensure that the acquisition strategy and other planning documents reflect transition and support decisions. In addition, contractual documentation must reflect these decisions to ensure that operational personnel are equipped and prepared for the transition and that the product or service is supportable after delivery. The project also must monitor its transition activities (see Project Monitoring and Control specific practice 1.8, "Monitor Transition to Operations and Support") to ensure that operational users are prepared for the transition and that the capability is sustainable once it is delivered.

Adequate planning and monitoring of transition activities is critical to success when delivering value to customers. The acquirer plays an important role in these activities by setting the direction, planning for implementation, and ensuring that the acquirer and supplier implement transition activities.

Interoperable Acquisition

Craig Meyers

The term *interoperability* has long been used in an operational context. For example, it relates to the ability of machines to "plug and play." However, there is no reason to limit interoperability to an operational context.

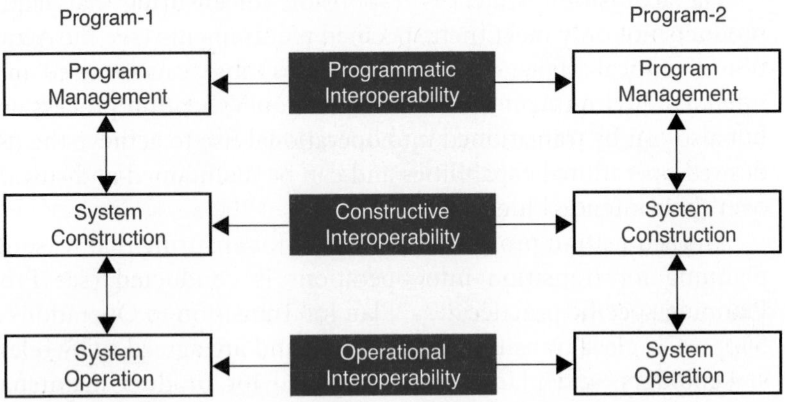

FIGURE 6.17
Systems-of-Systems Interoperability Model

Recent work at the SEI has broadened the concept of interoperability to apply in other contexts. One result of this work is the Systems of Systems Interoperability (SOSI) model [Morris 2004], a diagram of which appears in Figure 6.17. This model is designed for application to a systems-of-systems context that includes more and broader interactions than one typically finds in a program- and system-centric context.

Taking a vertical perspective of Figure 6.17, we introduce activities related to program management, system construction, and system operation. What is important to recognize is the need for interaction among the various acquisition functions. It is this recognition that warrants a broader perspective of the concept of interoperability. Figure 6.17 shows three different aspects of interoperability. Although we recognize that operational interoperability is the traditional use of the term, we also introduce the concepts of programmatic interoperability, constructive interoperability, and interoperable acquisition [Meyers 2008].

Programmatic Interoperability

Programmatic interoperability is interoperability with regard to the functions of program management, regardless of the organization that performs those functions.

It may be natural to interpret programmatic interoperability as occurring only between program offices, but such an interpretation is insufficient. Multiple professionals collaborate with respect to program management. In addition to the program manager, relevant participants may include staff members from a program executive office, a service acquisition executive, independent cost analysts, and so on. Each of these professionals performs a necessary function related to the management of a program. In fact, contractor representation may also be part of this context. The report "Exploring Programmatic Interoperability: Army Future Force Workshop" [Smith 2005] provides an example of the application of the principles of programmatic interoperability.

Constructive Interoperability

The concept of constructive interoperability may be defined in a similar manner as programmatic interoperability. Constructive interoperability is interoperability with regard to the functions of system construction, regardless of which organization actually performs those functions.

Again, it may be natural to think of constructive interoperability as something that occurs between contractors, but that notion would limit its scope. For example, other organizations that may participate in the construction of a system might include a subcontractor, a supplier of commercial off-the-shelf (COTS) products, independent consultants, an independent verification and validation organization, and a testing organization. In addition, a program management representative may participate in the function of system construction. Each of these organizations performs a valuable function in the construction of a system.

An example of programmatic interoperability is the case in which a program is developing a software component that will be used by another program. For this transaction to occur, the program offices must interact with regard to such tasks as schedule synchronization, for example. Other interactions may be required, such as joint risk management. In addition, as noted earlier, other organizations will play a role. For example, the development of an acquisition strategy may require interaction with the organizations responsible for its approval.

This example may be applied to the context of constructive interoperability as well. For one program office to provide a product to another, a corresponding agreement must exist among the relevant contractors. Such an agreement is often expressed in an *associate contractor agreement* (such an agreement would be called a *supplier agreement* in CMMI-ACQ). It is also possible that the separate contractors would seek out suppliers in a collective manner to maximize the chance of achieving an interoperable product.

Integrating Aspects of Interoperability

The preceding example, although focusing on the aspects of interoperability, does not address the integration of those aspects. This topic enlarges the scope of discussion and leads us to define interoperable acquisition.

Interoperable acquisition is the collection of interactions that take place among the functions necessary to acquire, develop, and maintain systems to provide interoperable capabilities.

In essence, interoperable acquisition is the integration of the various aspects of interoperability. For instance, in regard to the previous example, although two program offices may agree on the need for the construction of a system, such construction will require interactions among the program offices and their respective contractors, as well as among the contractors themselves.

There are clearly implications for acquisition in the context of a system of systems[6] and CMMI-ACQ. For example, CMMI-ACQ includes the Solicitation and Supplier Agreement Development and Agreement Management process areas, which relate to agreement management. As the previous discussion illustrates, the nature of agreements—their formation and execution—is important in the context of a system of systems and interoperable acquisition. These agreements may be developed to serve agreement management, or to aid in the construction of systems that must participate in a larger context.

Other areas of relevance deal with requirements management and schedule management, as discussed in the reports "Requirements Management in a System of Systems Context: A Workshop" [Meyers 2006a] and "Schedule Considerations for Interoperable Acquisition" [Meyers 2006c], respectively. Another related topic is that of risk management considerations for interoperable acquisition. This topic is covered in the report "Risk Management Considerations for Interoperable Acquisition" [Meyers 2006b]. Some common threads exist among these topics, including the following:

- Developing and adhering to agreements that manage the necessary interactions
- Defining information, including its syntax, but also (and more importantly) its semantics

---

6. We do not use the expression "acquisition of a system of systems," as it implies acquisition of a monolithic nature that is counter to the concept of a system of systems in which autonomy of the constituents is a prime consideration. As a colleague once said, "Systems of systems are accreted, not designed." This statement may be a bit strong, but it conveys a relevant and meaningful notion.

- Providing mechanisms for sharing information
- Engaging in collaborative behavior necessary to meet the needs of the operational community

Each of these topics must be considered in the application of CMMI-ACQ and CMMI-DEV to a systems-of-systems context, perhaps with necessary extensions, to meet the goals of interoperable acquisition. Therefore, the application of maturity models to acquisition in a systems-of-systems context is quite relevant!

Acquisition Agility

Brian Gallagher

Who can argue that being agile is a bad thing? The implication of not embracing agility is that one appreciates or values bureaucracy and rejects the ability to react quickly to changing environments. Operational parts of organizations, from military fighting units to customer-facing service providers, demand systems that provide operational agility. Developers prefer the increased control that small teams enjoy when implementing agile development methods. Acquisition professionals want to act with speed, agility, and purpose and ensure the systems they acquire meet the evolving needs of their customer while allowing developers the ability to meet technical challenges in new and innovative ways.

Given these desires, the acquisition, development, and operational communities collectively nod their heads in agreement that we need to be more agile. Unfortunately, the interpretation of what agile really means becomes clouded depending on an organization's mission. If the mission is to acquire operationally relevant systems, develop world-class solutions for customers, or execute a set of operational tasks, the thoughts on what agility means will be unique and probably not commonly shared with other enterprise partners.

Figure 6.18 indicates how acquirers, developers, and operational units can all act with agility, and how together, if properly motivated, they can be part of an agile enterprise that ensures each part of the enterprise works in harmony to achieve greater objectives.

The first step in evolving into an agile enterprise is to clearly understand what is needed as an output from the enterprise and then make informed decisions about how much agility, coupled with discipline, is needed to achieve those objectives. For example, if an end

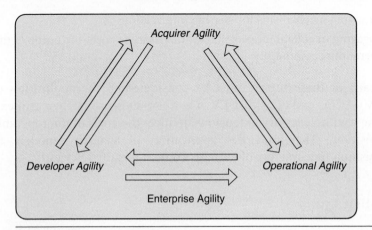

FIGURE 6.18
The Agile Enterprise

user needs a system with the operational characteristic of agility, more time and effort might be required to analyze the problem space, negotiate the solution trade space, and design a system with agility as an operational characteristic.

It doesn't naturally follow that the developer needs to employ formal Agile development methods to deliver an operationally agile system. Consider the following quote by Blaise Pascal: "I have made this [letter] longer than usual, only because I have not had the time to make it shorter."[7] In other words, sometimes it takes longer to deliver a product with certain important characteristics—like a letter with the attributes of being shorter in length and easier to read. Conversely, while the use of Agile development methods may not provide the final solution more quickly than traditional methods, there is a higher probability that the system developed iteratively, with lots of end-user interaction and early-and-often deliveries of working versions, will be more operationally acceptable than a system developed using traditional methods.[8]

The clear conclusion is that the acquirer plays an important role in meeting operational agility needs, in the success of its developers' use of Agile development methods, in the way it uses agile concepts to improve its internal acquisition responsibilities, and in ensuring that all of its partners are able to participate and benefit from operating within an agile enterprise construct.

7. "Lettres Provinciales," No. 16 (1657).
8. Scott Rosenberg, "Dreaming in Code."

Enabling Operational Agility

Most end users of systems and services, whether they are competing in a private commercial environment or a government or military environment, are facing more challenges today than ever before. Competition in the private sector drives organizations to move more quickly to market, to adjust to unforeseen events, and to anticipate market needs. Government end users, whether members of an operational military unit, an agency providing social services, or even an intelligence agency helping to defeat irregular aggressors, are facing similar challenges. They can no longer afford stodgy systems that all too soon become brittle.

When end users discuss "agility," they are usually describing their ability to use the delivered product or service in new and evolving ways without large cost or time impacts. They want the flexibility to quickly reconfigure their systems and services themselves to meet new challenges. What they are describing are quality attributes that are important to meeting their business or mission needs. In the CMMI-ACQ process areas of Acquisition Requirements Development (ARD), Solicitation and Supplier Agreement Development (SSAD), and Acquisition Technical Management (ATM), the acquirer helps elicit the real needs of the end user, translates those needs into contractual requirements that can be fulfilled by developers, and incrementally evaluates progress toward meeting those needs.

Usually, acquirers are very good at capturing functional requirements. However, "agility" needs are not typically described in a functional sense. Instead, their impact drives the acceptability of the system and most certainly will drive the architectural decisions made by both the acquirer and the developer as they analyze requirements and possible solution alternatives. One way to capture the "agility" needs of the end user is through the use of a Quality Attribute Workshop (QAW).[9] QAWs provide a structured method for identifying a system's architecture-critical quality attributes—such as agility, availability, performance, security, interoperability, and modifiability—that are derived from mission or business goals.

These attributes are prioritized and further refined with scenarios that make abstract concepts such as "agility" much more concrete. For example, the end user at a satellite ground station might want an agile system. Through the use of an approach like the QAW, that desire can be explicitly described in the form of some operationally relevant stimuli, expected response, and response measure. When probed, the abstract agile need first articulated by a satellite ground operator might

---

9. www.sei.cmu.edu/architecture/tools/qaw/index.cfm

turn out to be the expectation that when the mission evolves (stimuli), the system will allow insertion of third-party applications or services with no impact to current operations (response) within one month from the identification of the mission change (response measure).

Scenarios like this example can be captured, prioritized, and provided, along with the set of functional requirements, to developers during a competitive source selection activity (involving both ARD and SSAD process areas). The developers can then make key architectural decisions and propose solutions to meet those needs. Another possible approach is to include operational representatives in the program's risk management process to ensure risks to unique end-state agility needs are considered and mitigated proactively.

Enabling Developer Agility

As previously mentioned, the use of Agile development methods, especially for software-intensive systems, provides a higher probability of delivering operationally relevant capabilities. The move toward Agile methods has its roots in the writing of *The Agile Manifesto* (see Figure 6.19). A group of well-respected leaders in the software engineering community, frustrated over the current state of software development, boldly penned the manifesto, which in turn inspired dramatic changes in some approaches to software development, and later system development.

Upon reading the *Manifesto,* it becomes quickly apparent that adoption of Agile methods by developers requires not only changes in the

> *We are uncovering better ways of developing software by doing it and helping others do it. Through this work we have come to value:*
>
> *Individuals and interactions over processes and tools*
> *Working software over comprehensive documentation*
> *Customer collaboration over contract negotiation*
> *Responding to change over following a plan*
>
> *That is, while there is value in the items on the right, we value the items on the left more.*

FIGURE 6.19
The Agile Manifesto[10]

10. www.agilemanifesto.org

way developers behave, but also changes in the way acquirers interact with developers to enable their success. In the past, some acquirers have made the mistake of requiring their developers to use Agile methods, but not changing their interaction with the developer team.

In one program, the direction provided was for the developers to *"Go Agile!"* It became the battle cry and the developers enthusiastically accepted the challenge. It quickly became evident that the cry should have been *"Let's go Agile!"* (to include the acquirers as well as the developers) when the development team expecting "shoulder to shoulder" reviews and strong acquirer presence during daily planning activities were instead faced with the insistence of an arm's-length relationship and high ceremony reviews following a standard "waterfall" lifecycle. Table 6.2 provides some guidance on how the acquirer can evolve its oversight role to increase the probability of success of the development team.

TABLE 6.2 The Acquirer Role in Agile Development

Acquirer Role	Details
Managing scope (REQM, ARD, ATM)	There should be a clear long-term vision or road map (1–3 years) for the product or service. Developers will focus on delivering the highest-priority content after each iteration (90 days or less). The acquirer should keep requirements at a higher level and participate in lower level "story" development for each iteration. The acquirer will have the opportunity at the end of each iteration to review its content and reestablish priorities (based on the latest knowledge) for the next iteration.
Representing the end user (ARD, REQM, ATM, AM, AVAL)	Although it is not always practical to have a real end user participate on a regular basis, the acquirer should identify a customer representative (CR) and then empower/support this CR for the project. The CR is the "single point of contact" a project will use as the "voice of the user." It is preferable for the CR to be colocated with the developer. The CR, as a "voice of the user," needs to meet regularly with the user community to be able to represent their needs and wants.

Continues

TABLE 6.2 The Acquirer Role in Agile Development *(Continued)*

Acquirer Role	Details
Establish "story" priorities (ARD, REQM, ATM, AM)	During each iteration review, the acquirer should reprioritize the story backlog and participate in the planning for the next iteration.
Avoid redirection during an iteration (ARD, REQM, ATM, AM)	Once the "stories" are prioritized for an iteration, the acquirer should not interfere (i.e., reprioritize, add "stories," remove "stories") once the iteration has begun.
Communicate continuously (AM, PMC, MA, IPM)	The acquirer should be in regular (at least weekly, if not daily) communication with the project leader concerning new "stories" for upcoming iterations, the team's current velocity (the amount of work they can perform based on team capability), the upcoming iteration review meeting, and other issues.
Provide key participation (AM, ATM)	At a minimum, the acquirer should be present at all "story writing" workshops, daily meetings, and iteration review meetings.
Witness testing (AVAL)	The acquirer should witness all system-level testing and sign off on test results.
Understand the developer's processes (PP, PMC, AM, IPM)	The acquirer must possess knowledge and understanding of the agile processes used by the developer and their benefits and be comfortable with any unique adaptation.
Develop trust (PMC, IPM)	The acquirer must trust the ability of the development team to carry out agile tenets. Detailed EVMS or inchstone tracking can become counterproductive and slow down the team, making it difficult to adjust to evolving needs.
Decide on iteration length and deployments (PP, PMC, ATM, AM, IPM)	The acquirer must decide the iteration length and deployment schedule. While each iteration should develop some aspects of a working system, not all iterations are deployed to the end user.
Accurately communicate wants and needs (ARD, IPM)	If the acquirer cannot communicate needs and wants to the development staff, agile processes will fail.
Provide rapid turnaround (AM, ATM)	The acquirer must quickly review artifacts and provide timely feedback, approvals, and decisions, thereby enabling the developer to proceed with the next set of tasks.

Embracing Acquisition Agility

The use of agile approaches and methods within the development community is fairly mature. It is no longer the case that only a brave developer tries an agile approach. Instead, use of agile methods is relatively routine, and agile method failures are becoming hard to find. Even so, the acquisition community is still trying to understand what it means to operate an acquisition program or organization in an agile way. The key is to embrace the principles of agility and interpret them for the unique aspects of the acquisition environment, rather than simply adopting the precise practices of agile development.

Table 6.3 lists the principles of agile system development and suggests how these principles might be interpreted for the acquirer.[11]

TABLE 6.3   Relationship Between Agile Development and Agile Acquisition Principles

Agile Development Principles	*Agile Acquisition Principles*
Our highest priority is to satisfy the customer through early and continuous delivery of a valuable system.	Our highest priority is to satisfy the needs of our operational customer through early and continuous delivery of value. (ARD, ATM, AVAL)
A working system is the primary measure of progress.	Meeting the needs of our development partners, operational customers, and acquisition stakeholders is the primary measure of progress. (MA, IPM, QPM)
Welcome changing requirements, even late in development.	We welcome change; we lead change; we inspect and adapt to the needs of our development partners and operational customers. (REQM, ARD, ATM, AM, AVAL)
Deliver a working system frequently, from every couple of weeks to every couple of months, with a preference to the shorter time scale.	We respond to the needs of our development and operational customers frequently, from every couple of weeks to every couple of months, with a preference to the shorter time scale. (ARD, AVAL, AM, ATM, IPM)
Businesspeople and developers must work together daily throughout the project.	We collaborate with our development partners daily and with our operational customers and acquisition stakeholders regularly. (IPM)

Continues

---

11. http://agilemanifesto.org

TABLE 6.3 Relationship Between Agile Development and Agile Acquisition
Principles *(Continued)*

Agile Development Principles	Agile Acquisition Principles
Build projects around motivated individuals. Give them the environment and support they need, and trust them to get the job done.	Build projects to satisfy operationally significant needs staffed with motivated individuals. Give them the environment and support they need, and trust them to get the job done. (ARD, PP, IPM)
The most efficient and effective method of conveying information to and within a development team is face-to-face conversation.	The most efficient and effective method of conveying information is a face-to-face conversation. (PMC, AM, ATM, IPM)
Agile processes promote sustainable development.	An Agile acquisition organization promotes a sustainable pace. (IPM, OPF)
Continuous attention to technical excellence and good design enhances agility.	Continuous attention to process excellence and implementable requirements enhances agility. (ARD, IPM, OPF)
Simplicity—the art of maximizing the amount of work not done—is essential.	Simplicity—the art of maximizing the amount of work not done—is essential. (PMC, IPM)
The best architectures, requirements, and designs emerge from self-organizing teams.	The best work products emerge from self-organizing teams. (PP, IPM, AVER)
At regular intervals, the team reflects on how to become more effective, then tunes and adjusts its behavior accordingly.	At regular intervals, the organization reflects on how to become more effective, then tunes and adjusts its behavior accordingly. (OPF, CAR, OID).

The Agile Enterprise

With a clear understanding of the roles of the acquirer, the developer, and the operational end users and their unique needs for agility, the enterprise can optimize delivery of operationally significant value while meeting critical program timelines. The success of any member of the enterprise depends on the success and cooperation of every other member. The acquisition organization plays a critical role in ensuring delivered systems meet the agility needs of the operational end user as well as enabling its development partners to successfully employ Agile development methods to increase the probability of meeting end-user needs. By interpreting the principles of Agile system development to meet their own needs, the acquisition project can improve its internal focus, operation, and ability to satisfy stakeholder needs.

Employing Agile in DoD Acquisition

Mary Ann Lapham

This essay is adapted from the SEI report "Considerations for Using Agile in DoD Acquisition," which I coauthored with Ray Williams, Bud Hammons, Dan Burton, and Fred Schenker.[12]

Before discussing the use of Agile in DoD, I must provide some context and an assumption we used when we wrote the report. First, within the Agile community of practice, the term "Agile" with a capital "A" is used to represent the entirety of agile concepts and methods used in that community. We have adopted this usage in this essay. Second, we define Agile as follows:

> *An iterative and incremental (evolutionary) approach to software development which is performed in a highly collaborative manner by self-organizing teams within an effective governance framework with "just enough" ceremony that produces high quality software in a cost effective and timely manner which meets the changing needs of its stakeholders.*[13]

We assumed suppliers are either software providers or software-intensive systems providers. Our initial research was designed to determine if the use of Agile is beneficial to the DoD, and if so, to identify the barriers that exist in the acquisition environment and how these barriers might be addressed. Along the way, we found a school of thought that claimed users could and should embrace both the CMMI model and Agile methods [Glazer 2008]. It is not a stretch to conclude that they should embrace the use of CMMI-ACQ as well. However, some accommodations for the concepts used within Agile will most likely be required to have the full use of CMMI-ACQ. With all this in mind, let's explore Agile use within the DoD.

---

12. www.sei.cmu.edu/library/abstracts/reports/10tn002.cfm

13. www.agilemodeling.com/essays/agileSoftwareDevelopment.htm

Agile Use and the DoD

The Agile philosophy has existed for many years and, in fact, is based on concepts that have been around for decades. This philosophy achieved its greatest success in small to mid-sized commercial applications. There has been limited documented use of these concepts in the DoD or larger government arena.

In recent years, Agile has matured, personnel have become more skilled in applying Agile concepts, and some DoD contractors have started to build internal Agile capabilities and use Agile on DoD programs. Some DoD acquisition programs have proposed and used Agile processes, attempting to benefit from contractor capabilities, but without (as yet) any formal DoD guidance, templates, or best practices.

Given this backdrop, can an Agile approach yield a better product developed within cost and schedule parameters? If barriers interfere with the ability of the DoD to adopt Agile, how can they be addressed?

Our interviews and research indicate that Agile can benefit the DoD. Agile *is* another tool that can provide both tactical and strategic benefits. The tactical benefits (i.e., lower cost, met schedules, higher quality) are important; however, the strategic benefits (i.e., responsiveness, the ability to rapidly adjust to the current situation) might be of even greater value. These benefits can be a huge factor in today's world, where the DoD needs to get results faster and be better aligned with changing needs.

In fact, the literature[14] available about Agile use cites impressive results. Even if actual experience provides savings for DoD programs on the low end of the spectrum described in this publication, the savings can be significant. We also found that the DoD 5000 series regulations do not prohibit the use of Agile. In fact, the IEEE[15] is currently working on a standard for Agile development. To date, the standard is unpublished, but the fact that the IEEE has deemed it *worthy* of a standard indicates a step in the direction of obtaining formal guidance for Agile use.

Our research revealed that in the current, traditional "waterfall" method commonly employed within the DoD, there is an established practice that uses some form of controlled experimentation. Current waterfall practices create experimental code or prototypes that are

---

14. Several reported results conclude that by using Agile methods, costs decrease from as little as 5 percent to as much as 61 percent, with schedule decreasing from as little as 24 percent to as much as 58 percent, and cumulative defects decreasing from as little as 11 percent to as much as 83 percent [www.davidfrico.com/agile-book.htm].

15. IEEE P1648 is a draft standard. See www.standards.ieee.org/announcements/pr_1490p1648.html.

later thrown away. Agile methods involve building software iteratively, refining or discarding portions as required to create increments of the product. The goal is to have working code at the end of each iteration that can be deployed. Some programs in the DoD today are employing Agile techniques to do just this.

Embracing Agile Methods

Agile processes are based on good ideas derived from successful industry practices. We believe the DoD should embrace Agile methods for some programs and traditional waterfall methods for others. There is no "one size fits all" Agile process. Just like any set of processes, Agile methods must be tailored to fit the situation and context. For example, Agile teams responsible for developing high-risk, core components of a software architecture might apply not as aggressive release schedules as Agile teams developing less critical pieces of the software system. Some Agile teams might pick a two-week iteration cycle, whereas others might determine that their optimal iteration cycle is three weeks. Agile is not a silver bullet, but rather another technique to be included in the Program Management Office's and contractor's arsenal.

Sometimes a hybrid approach of waterfall and Agile methods is best for a program. For example, due to safety considerations, some mission-critical systems might require certain traditional milestones and documentation deliverables. However, Program Management Offices (PMOs) might work with Agile development teams on a hybrid approach that bridges these requirements with the need for agility and responsiveness. Perhaps the PMO would agree on fewer, less formal reviews and delivery of smaller sets of high-value documentation in exchange for getting a beta version that the user can start evaluating in the field more quickly.

Moving to Agile requires considerable work by the DoD entity (i.e., PMO, DoD, OSD, and perhaps Congress) and is not without hurdles. The most notable of these obstacles are described next.

Acquisition Lifecycle

Each lifecycle phase (e.g., Material Solution Analysis, Technology Development, Engineering and Manufacturing Development, Production and Deployment, and Operations and Support) presents unique challenges and opportunities. Some phases lend themselves to the use of an Agile approach better than others. Consider the Agile processes and practices you want to use early in the acquisition lifecycle; it is critical to make sure that contractually binding documents, such as RFPs and Statements of Work (SOWs), support those processes and practices. For example, if you embrace the Agile philosophy, you must determine how to meet the standard milestone criteria such as PDR and CDR. Typically, the types of documentation expected at these milestone events are not produced using Agile methods. Thus you should create expectations and criteria that reflect the level and type of documentation that are acceptable for those milestones, yet work within Agile constraints.

Team Environment

A central concept in Agile is the small, dynamic, high-performing team. The challenge lies in providing an environment that fosters the creation of self-forming or dynamic teams in a culture that is accustomed to static, centralized organizational structures. To complicate this issue further, the software team might be a small part of an overall system procurement for a tank, ship, or plane. The system environment might call for centralized configuration management, highly defined legacy interfaces, and a predetermined architecture, all of which constrain the software. This environment, then, should be treated as a constraint by the Agile team and can provide boundaries within which the Agile team must operate. These system boundaries could act to encapsulate the Agile team environment.

End-User Access

Access to end users can be complex and difficult when dealing with any single service, but can become even more complex with multi-service programs. Agile developers need to speak with a single voice so that the user can commit to changes for the product being developed. In some Agile approaches, the "one voice" is a product owner or manager who brings decisions to the Agile team that have been made through collaborative interaction with the end users. Within the DoD, the acquisition organization typically acts as the proxy for end users and only duly warranted personnel can commit the program. To mitigate these issues, invite end users to all demonstrations, where they can provide feedback that then becomes binding only with PMO approval. The end users need to work closely with the PMO, as with any acquisition.

Training and Coaching

While Agile concepts may not be new, the subtleties and nuances of each Agile method can be new to the uninformed PMO. To overcome this lack of knowledge, train the PMO staff before starting work with suppliers using Agile methods and employ an experienced coach or knowledgeable advocate for the PMO to help guide the staff throughout the process. Set aside funding for initial and ongoing training and support.

Oversight

Traditional methods have well-defined oversight methods. Agile oversight methods are less defined and require more flexibility to accommodate the fluidity of Agile implementation. Decide on the specific type of oversight needs in advance. One aspect of the Agile management philosophy is that the manager is more of a team advocate than an overseer. The management function of roadblock remover is critical to the success of an Agile team. Update selected day-to-day PMO activities to support this type of change.

Typically, documentation is used by the PMO throughout the development cycle to monitor the progress of the contractor. Documentation produced by Agile teams is just enough to meet this need and provide continuity for the team. It is usually *not* sufficient for capstone reviews or monitoring progress. For this reason, it is important to create different ways to meet the same PMO monitoring objectives while leveraging the advantages of Agile.

Rewards and Incentives

Agile rewards and incentives are different from those associated with traditional methods. In the DoD, the challenge is finding ways to incentivize teams and individuals to support Agile goals such as innovation, rapid software delivery, and customer satisfaction. At the same time, rewards that incentivize the wrong things should be eliminated. For example, rather than rewarding contractors for fixing defects, reward them for early delivery of beta software to a limited set of users in a constrained environment. Using this approach, the beta users get to test the product in the field sooner while providing feedback that helps to improve the quality of the software. Also consider incentives that encourage a collaborative relationship between the PMO and the contractor's staff.

Team Composition

The composition of the PMO staff may need to change to accommodate the use of an Agile approach. Consider adding a knowledgeable Agile advocate or experienced coach to the team. Although end-user representatives are essential for Agile success, these positions are often difficult to fill quickly and consistently. Consider using rotating personnel to fill the end-user positions.

Another challenge is keeping high-performing Agile teams together long enough to achieve peak performance. This issue arises because developers change at the end of a contractual period of performance. Consider putting key Agile technical developers or technical leads under a separate contract vehicle or hiring them to work for the government organization itself.

Culture

The overall organizational culture needs to support the Agile methodology in use. The Agile culture runs counter to the traditional waterfall culture in everything from oversight and team structure to end-user interaction throughout development. This change in approach requires a mindset change for the PMO and other government entities such as OSD. To employ any of the Agile concepts, plan for them, anticipate the changes needed in their environment and business model, and apply the hard work to make the changes a reality. Organizational change management is essential during the transition to Agile.

Conclusion

These hurdles were identified by analyzing the software development environment and determining what needed to change to support adoption of Agile methods. However, these same hurdles exist if one looks at using Agile from an acquisition perspective. If the acquisition and development methods do not work together and complement each other, then the program is doomed before it begins. The tenets of CMMI-ACQ and CMMI-DEV can be and should be applied to meet the goals of a program willing to use Agile. The hurdles that exist need to be addressed and eliminated. As stated before, why not embrace both?

Acquisition Improvement: Identifying and Removing Process Constraints

Brian Gallagher

Most process improvement approaches are based on a similar pedigree that traces back to the same foundation established by process improvement gurus such as Shewhart, Deming, Juran, Ishi-kawa, Taguchi, Humphrey, and others. The improvement approaches embodied in CMMI, Lean Six Sigma, the Theory of Constraints,

Total Quality Management, and other methods all embrace an improvement paradigm that can be boiled down to these simple steps.

1. Define the system you want to improve.
2. Understand the scope of the system.
3. Define the goals and objectives for the system.
4. Determine constraints to achieving objectives.
5. Make a plan to remove the constraints.
6. Learn lessons and do it again.

These simple steps comprise an improvement pattern that is evident in the "Plan, Do, Check, Act" (PDCA) improvement loop; Six Sigma's "Define, Measure, Analyze, Improve, Control" (DMAIC) improvement methodology; the U.S. military's "Observe, Orient, Decide, Act" (OODA) loop; and the SEI's "Initiating, Diagnosing, Establishing, Acting, and Learning" (IDEAL) method shown in Figure 6.20.

All of these improvement paradigms share a common goal: to improve the effectiveness and efficiency of a system. That *system* can be a manufacturing assembly line, the decision process used by military pilots, a development organization, an acquisition project, or any other entity or process that can be defined, observed, and improved.

One mistake individuals and organizations make when embarking on an improvement path is to force a decision to choose one improvement methodology over another, as if each approach must be mutually exclusive. An example is committing an organization to using CMMI or Lean Six Sigma, or the Theory of Constraints, before understanding how to take advantage of the toolkits provided by each approach and selecting the tools that make the most sense for the culture of the organization and the problem at hand. The following case study illustrates how one organization took advantage of using the Theory of Constraints with CMMI.

Case Study: Combining CMMI and the Theory of Constraints

One government agency had just completed a Standard CMMI Appraisal Method for Process Improvement (SCAMPI) appraisal with a CMMI model on its 12 most important customer projects—all managed within a Project Management Organization (PMO) under the direction of a senior executive. The PMO was a virtual organization consisting of a class of projects that the agency decided needed additional focus due to their criticality from a customer perspective. Although the entire acquisition and engineering staff num-

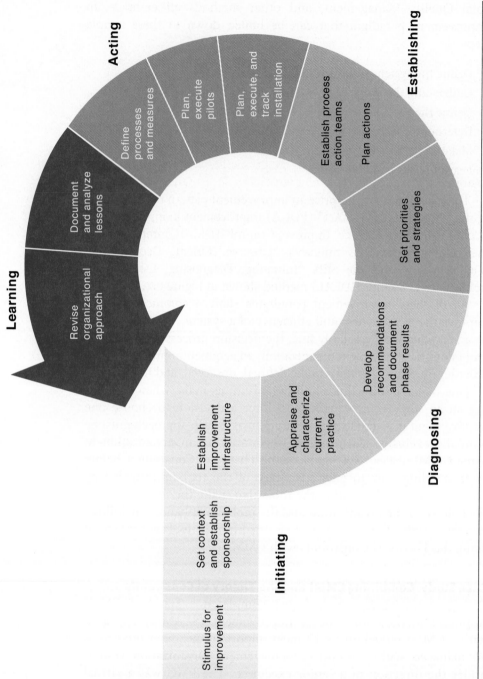

FIGURE 6.20
The SEI's IDEAL Model

bered close to 5,000 employees, the senior executive committed to delivering these 12 projects on time, even at the expense of less important projects. Each project had a well-defined set of process requirements, including those for start-up and planning activities, and was subject to monthly Program Management Reviews (PMRs) to track progress, resolve work issues, and manage risk. With its clear focus on project success, the PMO easily achieved CMMI maturity level 2.

On the heels of the SCAMPI appraisal, the agency was directed to move much of its customer-facing functionality to the Web, enabling customers to take advantage of a wide variety of self-service applications. This web-based system represented a new technology for the agency, as many of its employees and contractors had experience only with mainframe or client/server systems. To learn how to successfully deliver capability using this new technology, the senior executive visited several Internet-based commercial organizations and found that one key factor in their success was the ability to deliver customer value within very short time frames—usually between 30 and 90 days. Armed with this information, the executive decried that all Internet-based projects were to immediately establish a 90-day delivery schedule. Confident with this new direction and eager to see results, he asked that the Internet projects be part of the scope of projects in the next SCAMPI appraisal to validate the approach.

The agency's process improvement consultant realized that trying to do a formal SCAMPI appraisal on an organization struggling to adopt a new, more agile methodology while learning a new web-based technology and under pressure to deliver in 90 days was not the best option given the timing of the recent changes. She explored the idea of conducting a risk assessment or other technical intervention, but found that the word *risk* was overloaded in the agency context. Thus she needed to employ a different approach. She finally suggested using the Theory of Constraints to help identify and mitigate some of the process-related constraints facing the agency.

The Theory of Constraints is a system-level management philosophy that suggests all systems may be compared to chains. Each chain is composed of various links with unique strengths and weaknesses. The weakest link (i.e., the constraint) in the chain is not generally eliminated; rather, it is strengthened by following an organized process, thereby allowing for improvement in the system. By systematically identifying the weakest link and strengthening it, the system as a whole experiences improvement.

The first step in improving the system is to identify all of the system's constraints. A constraint is an obstacle to the successful completion of an endeavor. Think about how constraints would differ depending on the following endeavors:

- Driving from Miami to Las Vegas
- Walking across a busy street
- Digging a ditch
- Building a shed
- Acquiring a new space launch vehicle
- Fighting a battle

Constraints are not context free; you cannot know your constraints until you know your endeavor. For the Internet project endeavor, the senior executive selected a rather wordy "picture of success":

> *The Internet acquisition projects are scheduled and defined based on agency priorities and the availability of resources from all involved components, and the application releases that support those initiatives are planned, developed, and implemented within established time frames using established procedures to produce quality systems.*

The problem the consultant faced was how to systematically identify the constraints. Where should she look, and how would she make sure she covered all the important processes employed by the agency? Because the agency was familiar with CMMI, she decided to use the practices in CMMI as a taxonomy to help identify constraints. Instead of looking for evidence of compliance with the practice statements as one would in a SCAMPI appraisal, she asked interviewees to judge how well the practices were implemented and the impact of implementation on successful achievement of the "picture of success." Consider the difference between the two approaches as demonstrated in an interview session:

SCAMPI Appraisal

Question: "How do you establish estimates?"

Answer: "We follow a documented procedure ... involve stakeholders ... obtain proper sign-off and commitment ..."

CMMI-based Constraint Identification

Question: "Given your 'picture of success,' do you have any concerns about the way you establish estimates?"

Answer: "Our estimates are based on productivity rates that are twice what our contractors have ever been able to accomplish. There's no way we'll meet our current schedule."

After six intense interview sessions involving 40 agency personnel and contractors, 103 individual constraint statements were gathered and affinity-grouped into the following constraint areas:

- Establishing, Communicating, and Measuring Agency Goals
- Legacy Versus Internet
- Lack of Trained and Experienced Resources
- Lack of Coordination and Integration
- Internet-Driven Change
- Product Quality and Integrity
- Team Performance
- Imposed Standards and Mandates
- Requirements Definition and Management
- Unprecedented Delivery Paradigm
- Fixed 90-Day Schedule

Further analysis using cause-and-effect tools helped to identify how each constraint affected the others. This analysis also allowed the consultant to produce the hierarchical interrelationship diagraph depicted in Figure 6.21.

The results of this analysis helped the senior executive decide which constraints needed to be resolved to help improve the quality of the delivered systems. The higher up in the diagram you can affect elements, the more impact you can achieve.

The senior executive decided that the "Imposed Mandates" constraint was outside his span of control. However, many of the other constraints were either directly within his control or at least within his sphere of influence. He decided to charter improvement teams to tackle the following constraints:

- Establishing, Communicating, and Measuring Goals
- Internet Versus Legacy (combined with Coordination and Integration)
- Internet-Driven Changes

The improvement teams used a well-defined improvement approach that helped them explore each constraint in detail, establish an improvement goal, perform root cause analysis, identify barriers

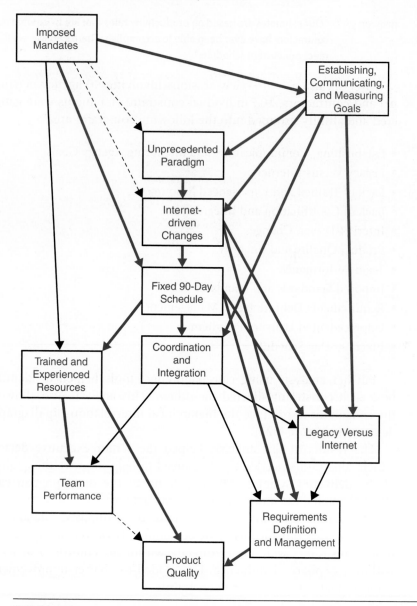

FIGURE 6.21
Hierarchical Interrelationship Diagraph

and enablers to success, and establish strategies and milestones to accomplish the goal.

The process improvement consultant recognized that using CMMI alone was not appropriate for the challenges facing the agency, and imported concepts and tools from another improvement approach—

the Theory of Constraints—to help the agency recognize and remove critical process-related constraints. She sought to establish improvement strategies and helped the agency avert a pending crisis, setting its personnel on an improvement course that served them well. Today, the agency's PMO manages both legacy and Internet-based projects, serves as an exemplar for other agencies, and demonstrated its process prowess by successfully achieving CMMI maturity level 3.

This case study also illustrates how using CMMI for process improvement fits into the DoD-wide Continuous Process Improvement (CPI)/Lean Six Sigma (LSS) Program, which includes the Lean, Six Sigma, and Theory of Constraints tools and methods for process improvement [DoD 2008].

Expanding Capabilities Across the Constellations

Mike Phillips

As we are finishing the details of the current collection of process areas that span three constellations, this essay is my opportunity to encourage "continuous thinking." My esteemed mentor as we began and then evolved the CMMI Product Suite was our Chief Architect, Dr. Roger Bate. Roger left us with an amazing legacy. He imagined that organizations could look at a collection of "process areas" and choose ones they might wish to use to facilitate their process improvement activities.

Maturity levels for organizations were adequate, Roger thought, but not as interesting to him as being able to focus attention on a collection of process areas for business benefit. Small businesses have been the first to realize the advantage of this approach, as they often find the full collection of process areas in any constellation daunting. An SEI report, "CMMI Roadmaps" (www.sei.cmu.edu/library/abstracts/reports/08tn010.cfm), describes some ways to construct thematic approaches to effective use of process areas from the CMMI for Development constellation.

As we created the two new constellations, we took care to refer back to the predecessor collection of process areas in CMMI for Development. For example, in CMMI for Acquisition, we note that some acquisition organizations might need more technical detail in the requirements development effort than we provided in Acquisition Requirements Development (ARD)—in fact, they might need to "reach back" to CMMI-DEV's Requirements Development (RD) process area for more assistance.

In CMMI for Services, we suggest that the Service System Development (SSD) process area is useful when the development efforts are relatively limited, but the full engineering category in CMMI-DEV may be useful if major service systems are being created and delivered.

Now with three full constellations to consider for addressing the complex organizations many of you have as targets for process improvement, many "refer to" possibilities exist. With the release of the V1.3 Product Suite, we will offer the option to describe satisfaction of process areas from any of the process areas in the CMMI portfolio. What are some of the more obvious expansions?

We have already mentioned two expansions—namely, ARD using RD and SSD expanded to capture RD, TS, PI, VER, and VAL. What about situations in which most of the development is done outside the organization, but final responsibility for effective systems integration remains with your organization? Perhaps a few of the acquisition process areas would be useful beyond SAM. A simple start would be to investigate using SSAD and AM as a replacement for SAM to get the additional detailed help. Also, ATM might offer some good technical assistance in monitoring the technical progress of the elements being developed by specific partners.

As we add the contributions of CMMI-SVC to the mix, several process areas offer yet more ways to expand. In V1.2 of CMMI-DEV, for example, we added informative material in Risk Management to begin to address concerns about continuity of operations after some significant risk event occurs. Now, with CMMI-SVC, we have a full process area that provides more robust coverage of continuity concerns. (For those users who need even more coverage, the SEI now has the Resilience Management Model [RMM] to give the greater attention that some financial institutions and similar organizations have expressed as necessary for their process improvement endeavors. For more, see www.cert.org/resilience/rmm.html.)

Another expansion worthy of consideration is inclusion of the contributions in the Service Systems Transition (SST) process area. Organizations that may have been responsible for development of new systems—and maintenance of existing systems until the new system can be brought to full capability—may find the practices contained in SST to be a useful expansion, as this part of the lifecycle is the subject of only limited coverage in CMMI-DEV. In addition, CMMI-ACQ added two practices to PP and PMC to address planning for the transition into use, so the CMMI-ACQ versions of these two core process areas might mesh nicely with the SST expansion.

A topic that challenged the development team for V1.3 was improved coverage of "strategy." Those of us with acquisition experience knew the criticality of an effective acquisition strategy to program success, so the practice was added to the CMMI-ACQ version of PP. In the CMMI-SVC constellation, Strategic Service Management (STSM) has the objective "to get the information needed to make effective strategic decisions about the set of standard services the organization maintains." With minor interpretation, this process area could assist a development organization in determining which types of development projects should be in its product development line. The constellation authors also added a robust practice in the CMMI-SVC version of PP (Work Planning) to "provide the business framework for planning and managing the work."

Two process areas essential for service work were seriously considered for insertion into CMMI-DEV V1.3—Capacity and Availability Management (CAM) and Incident Resolution and Prevention (IRP). In the end, expansion of the CMMI-DEV constellation from 22 to 24 process areas was determined to be less valuable than continuing our efforts to streamline coverage. As a result, these two process areas offer another opportunity for the type of expansion explored in this essay.

Those of you who have experienced appraisals have likely seen the use of target profiles that gather the collection of process areas to be examined. Often these profiles specifically address the necessary collections associated with maturity levels, but this need not be the case. With the release of V1.3, we have ensured that the reporting system (SEI Appraisal System [SAS]) is robust enough to allow depiction of process areas from multiple constellations. As other architecturally similar SEI models, such as the RMM mentioned previously, grow in use, we will be able to develop profiles using the mixtures that give process improvement value to a growing range of complex organizations.

Generic Goals and Generic Practices, and the Process Areas

PART TWO

Generic Goals and

Generic Practices, and

the Process Areas

GENERIC GOALS AND GENERIC PRACTICES

Overview

This section describes in detail all the generic goals and generic practices of CMMI—model components that directly address process institutionalization. As you address each process area, refer to this section for the details of all generic practices.

Generic practice elaborations appear after generic practices to provide guidance on how the generic practice can be applied uniquely to process areas.

TIP

The generic goals and practices apply to every process area; however, they are listed only once in the model document. You will need to refer to this section often for the application of generic goals and generic practice areas to each process area.

Process Institutionalization

Institutionalization is an important concept in process improvement. When mentioned in the generic goal and generic practice descriptions, institutionalization implies that the process is ingrained in the way the work is performed and there is commitment and consistency to performing (i.e., executing) the process.

An institutionalized process is more likely to be retained during times of stress. When the requirements and objectives for the process change, however, the implementation of the process may also need to change to ensure that it remains effective. The generic practices describe activities that address these aspects of institutionalization.

The degree of institutionalization is embodied in the generic goals and expressed in the names of the processes associated with each goal as indicated in Table 7.1.

HINT

Consider institutionalization mismatches when working on process issues that span multiple organizations. An acquirer that has institutionalized a "defined" requirements process, when working with a supplier that has institutionalized a "managed" requirements process, may need to pay attention to negotiating constraints imposed by the acquisition organization across the supplier–acquirer team.

TABLE 7.1 Generic Goals and Process Names

Generic Goal	Progression of Processes
GG 1	Performed process
GG 2	Managed process
GG 3	Defined process

The progression of process institutionalization is characterized in the following descriptions of each process.

Performed Process

A *performed* process is a process that accomplishes the work necessary to satisfy the specific goals of a process area.

Managed Process

A *managed process* is a *performed process* that is planned and executed in accordance with policy; employs skilled people having adequate resources to produce controlled outputs; involves relevant stakeholders; is monitored, controlled, and reviewed; and is evaluated for adherence to its process description.

The process can be instantiated by a project, group, or organizational function. Management of the process is concerned with institutionalization and the achievement of other specific objectives established for the process, such as cost, schedule, and quality objectives. The control provided by a managed process helps to ensure that the established process is retained during times of stress.

The requirements and objectives for the process are established by the organization. The status of the work products and services are visible to management at defined points (e.g., at major milestones, on completion of major tasks). Commitments are established among those who perform the work and the relevant stakeholders and are revised as necessary. Work products are reviewed with relevant stakeholders and are controlled. The work products and services satisfy their specified requirements.

A critical distinction between a *performed process* and a *managed process* is the extent to which the process is managed. A managed process is planned (the plan can be part of a more encompassing plan) and the execution of the process is managed against the plan. Corrective actions are taken when the actual results and execution deviate significantly from the plan. A *managed process* achieves the objectives of the plan and is institutionalized for consistent execution.

Defined Process

A *defined process* is a *managed process* that is tailored from the organization's set of standard processes according to the organization's tailoring guidelines; has a maintained process description; and contributes process related experiences to the organizational process assets.

Organizational process assets are artifacts that relate to describing, implementing, and improving processes. These artifacts are assets because they are developed or acquired to meet the business objectives of the organization and they represent investments by the organization that are expected to provide current and future business value.

The organization's set of standard processes, which are the basis of the defined process, are established and improved over time. Standard processes describe the fundamental process elements that are expected in the defined processes. Standard processes also describe the relationships (e.g., the ordering, the interfaces) among these process elements. The organization-level infrastructure to support current and future use of the organization's set of standard processes is established and improved over time. (See the definition of "standard process" in the glossary.)

A project's defined process provides a basis for planning, performing, and improving the project's tasks and activities. A project can have more than one defined process (e.g., one for developing the product and another for testing the product).

A defined process clearly states the following:

- Purpose
- Inputs
- Entry criteria
- Activities
- Roles
- Measures
- Verification steps
- Outputs
- Exit criteria

A critical distinction between a *managed process* and a *defined process* is the scope of application of the process descriptions, standards, and procedures. For a *managed process*, the process descriptions, standards, and procedures are applicable to a particular project, group, or organizational function. As a result, the managed processes of two projects in one organization can be different.

Another critical distinction is that a *defined process* is described in more detail and is performed more rigorously than a *managed process*. This distinction means that improvement information is easier to understand, analyze, and use. Finally, management of the defined process is based on the additional insight provided by an understanding of the interrelationships of the process activities and detailed measures of the process, its work products, and its services.

Relationships Among Processes

The generic goals evolve so that each goal provides a foundation for the next. Therefore, the following conclusions can be made:

- A *managed process* is a performed process.
- A *defined process* is a managed process.

Thus, applied sequentially and in order, the generic goals describe a process that is increasingly institutionalized from a *performed process* to a *defined process*.

Achieving GG 1 for a process area is equivalent to saying you achieve the specific goals of the process area.

Achieving GG 2 for a process area is equivalent to saying you manage the execution of processes associated with the process area. There is a policy that indicates you will perform the process. There is a plan for performing it. There are resources provided, responsibilities assigned, training on how to perform it, selected work products from performing the process are controlled, and so on. In other words, the process is planned and monitored just like any project or support activity.

Achieving GG 3 for a process area is equivalent to saying that an organizational standard process exists that can be tailored to result in the process you will use. Tailoring might result in making no changes to the standard process. In other words, the process used and the standard process can be identical. Using the standard process "as is" is tailoring because the choice is made that no modification is required.

Each process area describes multiple activities, some of which are repeatedly performed. You may need to tailor the way one of these activities is performed to account for new capabilities or circumstances. For example, you may have a standard for developing or obtaining organizational training that does not consider web-based training. When preparing to develop or obtain a web-based course, you may need to tailor the standard process to account for the particular challenges and benefits of web-based training.

Generic Goals and Generic Practices

This section describes all of the generic goals and generic practices, as well as their associated subpractices, notes, examples, and references. The generic goals are organized in numerical order, GG 1 through

GG 3. The generic practices are also organized in numerical order under the generic goal they support.

GG 1 ACHIEVE SPECIFIC GOALS

The specific goals of the process area are supported by the process by transforming identifiable input work products into identifiable output work products.

GP 1.1 PERFORM SPECIFIC PRACTICES

Perform the specific practices of the process area to develop work products and provide services to achieve the specific goals of the process area.

The purpose of this generic practice is to produce the work products and deliver the services that are expected by performing (i.e., executing) the process. These practices can be done informally without following a documented process description or plan. The rigor with which these practices are performed depends on the individuals managing and performing the work and can vary considerably.

GG 2 INSTITUTIONALIZE A MANAGED PROCESS

The process is institutionalized as a managed process.

GP 2.1 ESTABLISH AN ORGANIZATIONAL POLICY

Establish and maintain an organizational policy for planning and performing the process.

The purpose of this generic practice is to define the organizational expectations for the process and make these expectations visible to those members of the organization who are affected. In general, senior management is responsible for establishing and communicating guiding principles, direction, and expectations for the organization.

Not all direction from senior management will bear the label "policy." The existence of appropriate organizational direction is the expectation of this generic practice, regardless of what it is called or how it is imparted.

> **TIP**
>
> Policy direction may come from multiple levels above the project. For example, in the Department of Defense (DoD), policy is established by legislation, the Pentagon, senior acquisition executives, product center management, and others.

Elaboration for all PAs

This policy establishes organizational expectations for planning and performing the process, including not only the elements of the process addressed directly by the acquirer but also the interactions between the acquirer and suppliers.

GP 2.2 PLAN THE PROCESS

Establish and maintain the plan for performing the process.

The purpose of this generic practice is to determine what is needed to perform the process and to achieve the established objectives, to prepare a plan for performing the process, to prepare a process description, and to get agreement on the plan from relevant stakeholders.

The practical implications of applying a generic practice vary for each process area.

> For example, the planning described by this generic practice as applied to the Project Monitoring and Control process area can be carried out in full by the processes associated with the Project Planning process area. However, this generic practice, when applied to the Project Planning process area, sets an expectation that the project planning process itself be planned.

Therefore, this generic practice can either reinforce expectations set elsewhere in CMMI or set new expectations that should be addressed.

Refer to the Project Planning process area for more information about establishing and maintaining plans that define project activities.

Establishing a plan includes documenting the plan and a process description. Maintaining the plan includes updating it to reflect corrective actions or changes in requirements or objectives.

HINT

This practice does not require a separate plan for each process area. Consider incorporating process area planning requirements into existing project plans (e.g., systems engineering plan, program management plan).

> The plan for performing the process typically includes the following:
> - Process description
> - Standards and requirements for the work products and services of the process
> - Specific objectives for the execution of the process and its results (e.g., quality, time scale, cycle time, use of resources)
> - Dependencies among the activities, work products, and services of the process
> - Resources (e.g., funding, people, tools) needed to perform the process
> - Assignment of responsibility and authority
> - Training needed for performing and supporting the process
> - Work products to be controlled and the level of control to be applied
> - Measurement requirements to provide insight into the execution of the process, its work products, and its services
>
> *Continues*

Continued

- Involvement of relevant stakeholders
- Activities for monitoring and controlling the process
- Objective evaluation activities of the process
- Management review activities for the process and the work products

Subpractices

1. Define and document the plan for performing the process.
   This plan can be a stand-alone document, embedded in a more comprehensive document, or distributed among multiple documents. In the case of the plan being distributed among multiple documents, ensure that a coherent picture of who does what is preserved. Documents can be hardcopy or softcopy.

2. Define and document the process description.
   The process description, which includes relevant standards and procedures, can be included as part of the plan for performing the process or can be included in the plan by reference.

3. Review the plan with relevant stakeholders and get their agreement.
   This review of the plan includes reviewing that the planned process satisfies the applicable policies, plans, requirements, and standards to provide assurance to relevant stakeholders.

4. Revise the plan as necessary.

GP 2.3 PROVIDE RESOURCES

Provide adequate resources for performing the process, developing the work products, and providing the services of the process.

The purpose of this generic practice is to ensure that the resources necessary to perform the process as defined by the plan are available when they are needed. Resources include adequate funding, appropriate physical facilities, skilled people, and appropriate tools.

The interpretation of the term "adequate" depends on many factors and can change over time. Inadequate resources may be addressed by increasing resources or by removing requirements, constraints, and commitments.

GP 2.4 ASSIGN RESPONSIBILITY

Assign responsibility and authority for performing the process, developing the work products, and providing the services of the process.

The purpose of this generic practice is to ensure that there is accountability for performing the process and achieving the specified results

HINT

In addition to a skilled staff, consider other resource needs of the project team and suppliers throughout the lifecycle. Examples include collaboration environments for "systems of systems" acquisition, tools for engineering analysis and decision making, test beds or simulators, access to operational data or environments, benchmark data, and access to targeted "experts" in areas of high risk.

throughout the life of the process. The people assigned must have the appropriate authority to perform the assigned responsibilities.

Responsibility can be assigned using detailed job descriptions or in living documents, such as the plan for performing the process. Dynamic assignment of responsibility is another legitimate way to implement this generic practice, as long as the assignment and acceptance of responsibility are ensured throughout the life of the process.

Subpractices

1. Assign overall responsibility and authority for performing the process.
2. Assign responsibility and authority for performing the specific tasks of the process.
3. Confirm that the people assigned to the responsibilities and authorities understand and accept them.

GP 2.5 *TRAIN PEOPLE*

Train the people performing or supporting the process as needed.

The purpose of this generic practice is to ensure that people have the necessary skills and expertise to perform or support the process.

Appropriate training is provided to those who will be performing the work. Overview training is provided to orient people who interact with those who perform the work.

> Examples of methods for providing training include self-study; self-directed training; self-paced, programmed instruction; formalized on-the-job training; mentoring; and formal and classroom training.

Training supports the successful execution of the process by establishing a common understanding of the process and by imparting the skills and knowledge needed to perform the process.

The organization should conduct a training needs analysis to understand its process training needs at both the organization and project levels. Then, appropriate training vehicles can be identified and provided to minimize process execution related risks.

Refer to the Organizational Training process area for more information about developing skills and knowledge of people so they can perform their roles effectively and efficiently.

HINT

Don't pass the buck to your suppliers. Acquirers must assume responsibility for executing important processes such as managing risk, analyzing measurement indicators, making important trade-study decisions, and managing customer requirements and expectations.

HINT

Consider sharing training opportunities for project-specific needs across the acquirer, supplier, and end-user teams.

Elaboration for all PAs

Determining appropriate skills for people performing roles in the acquisition process can serve as a basis for identifying relevant training for each role.

> Examples of acquisition training include the following:
> - Regulations and business practices related to negotiating and working with suppliers
> - Acquisition planning and preparation
> - COTS products acquisition
> - Supplier evaluation and selection
> - Negotiation and conflict resolution
> - Supplier management
> - Testing and ensuring the transition of acquired products
> - Receiving, storing, using, and maintaining acquired products

GP 2.6 CONTROL WORK PRODUCTS

Place selected work products of the process under appropriate levels of control.

The purpose of this generic practice is to establish and maintain the integrity of the selected work products of the process (or their descriptions) throughout their useful life.

The selected work products are specifically identified in the plan for performing the process, along with a specification of the appropriate level of control.

Different levels of control are appropriate for different work products and for different points in time. For some work products, it may be sufficient to maintain version control so that the version of the work product in use at a given time, past or present, is known and changes are incorporated in a controlled manner. Version control is usually under the sole control of the work product owner (which can be an individual, group, or team).

Sometimes, it can be critical that work products be placed under formal or baseline configuration management. This type of control includes defining and establishing baselines at predetermined points. These baselines are formally reviewed and approved, and serve as the basis for further development of the designated work products.

Refer to the Configuration Management process area for more information about establishing and maintaining the integrity of work products using configuration identification, configuration control, configuration status accounting, and configuration audits.

HINT

Pay special attention to the configuration management of program documentation and products when moving from one phase of the program to another, especially if system development or maintenance responsibility is handed off from supplier to supplier or to an internal maintenance group.

Additional levels of control between version control and formal configuration management are possible. An identified work product can be under various levels of control at different points in time.

Elaboration for all PAs

The acquirer is responsible for establishing and maintaining baselines and ensuring designated acquirer work products and supplier deliverables are placed under appropriate levels of control.

Examples of acquirer work products and supplier deliverables placed under control include the following:

- Project plans
- Solicitation packages
- Measures
- Product documentation

GP 2.7 *IDENTIFY AND INVOLVE RELEVANT STAKEHOLDERS*

Identify and involve the relevant stakeholders of the process as planned.

The purpose of this generic practice is to establish and maintain the expected involvement of relevant stakeholders during the execution of the process.

Involve relevant stakeholders as described in an appropriate plan for stakeholder involvement. Involve stakeholders appropriately in activities such as the following:

- Planning
- Decisions
- Commitments
- Communications
- Coordination
- Reviews
- Appraisals
- Requirements definitions
- Resolution of problems and issues

Refer to the Project Planning process area for more information about planning stakeholder involvement.

The objective of planning stakeholder involvement is to ensure that interactions necessary to the process are accomplished, while not allowing excessive numbers of affected groups and individuals to impede process execution.

HINT

Use surrogates when the relevant stakeholder group is too large. For example, stakeholders for review and acceptance of an environmental impact statement may include the entire population of a given area, so a representative subgroup may need to be selected for practical reasons.

> Examples of stakeholders that might serve as relevant stakeholders for specific tasks, depending on context, include individuals, teams, management, customers, suppliers, end users, operations and support staff, other projects, and government regulators.

Subpractices

1. Identify stakeholders relevant to this process and their appropriate involvement.

    Relevant stakeholders are identified among the suppliers of inputs to, the users of outputs from, and the performers of the activities in the process. Once the relevant stakeholders are identified, the appropriate level of their involvement in process activities is planned.

2. Share these identifications with project planners or other planners as appropriate.

3. Involve relevant stakeholders as planned.

GP 2.8 MONITOR AND CONTROL THE PROCESS

Monitor and control the process against the plan for performing the process and take appropriate corrective action.

The purpose of this generic practice is to perform the direct day-to-day monitoring and controlling of the process. Appropriate visibility into the process is maintained so that appropriate corrective action can be taken when necessary. Monitoring and controlling the process can involve measuring appropriate attributes of the process or work products produced by the process.

Refer to the Measurement and Analysis process area for more information about developing and sustaining a measurement capability used to support management information needs.

Refer to the Project Monitoring and Control process area for more information about providing an understanding of the project's progress so that appropriate corrective actions can be taken when the project's performance deviates significantly from the plan.

Subpractices

1. Evaluate actual progress and performance against the plan for performing the process.

    The evaluations are of the process, its work products, and its services.

2. Review accomplishments and results of the process against the plan for performing the process.

HINT

Use this practice to determine the effectiveness of your processes. A SCAMPI appraisal team may not be able to assess process effectiveness, but it will check whether *you* can judge effectiveness based on your monitoring activities and whether you are making adjustments accordingly.

3. Review activities, status, and results of the process with the immediate level of management responsible for the process and identify issues.

> These reviews are intended to provide the immediate level of management with appropriate visibility into the process based on the day-to-day monitoring and controlling of the process, and are supplemented by periodic and event-driven reviews with higher level management as described in GP 2.10.

4. Identify and evaluate the effects of significant deviations from the plan for performing the process.

5. Identify problems in the plan for performing the process and in the execution of the process.

6. Take corrective action when requirements and objectives are not being satisfied, when issues are identified, or when progress differs significantly from the plan for performing the process.

> Inherent risks should be considered before any corrective action is taken.

Corrective action can include the following:

- Taking remedial action to repair defective work products or services
- Changing the plan for performing the process
- Adjusting resources, including people, tools, and other resources
- Negotiating changes to the established commitments
- Securing change to the requirements and objectives that must be satisfied
- Terminating the effort

---

7. Track corrective action to closure.

Elaboration for all PAs

The project collects and analyzes measurements from the acquirer and from the supplier to effectively monitor and control the project.

OPF Elaboration

Examples of measures and work products used in monitoring and controlling include the following:

- Number of process improvement proposals submitted, accepted, or implemented
- CMMI maturity level or capability level earned
- Schedule for deployment of an organizational process asset
- Percentage of projects using the current organization's set of standard processes (or tailored version of the current set)

Continues

> *Continued*
> - Issue trends associated with implementing the organization's set of standard processes (i.e., number of issues identified, number closed)
> - Progress toward achievement of process needs and objectives

GP 2.9 OBJECTIVELY EVALUATE ADHERENCE

Objectively evaluate adherence of the process and selected work products against the process description, standards, and procedures, and address noncompliance.

The purpose of this generic practice is to provide credible assurance that the process and selected work products are implemented as planned and adhere to the process description, standards, and procedures. (See the definition of "objectively evaluate" in the glossary.)

Refer to the Process and Product Quality Assurance process area for more information about objectively evaluating processes and work products.

People not directly responsible for managing or performing the activities of the process typically evaluate adherence. In many cases, adherence is evaluated by people in the organization, but external to the process or project, or by people external to the organization. As a result, credible assurance of adherence can be provided even during times when the process is under stress (e.g., when the effort is behind schedule, when the effort is over budget).

TIP

Many acquirers don't use an independent quality assurance (QA) function to objectively evaluate process and product quality. In these situations, using objective criteria to evaluate quality and allowing for escalation of issues without retribution become even more critical.

GP 2.10 REVIEW STATUS WITH HIGHER LEVEL MANAGEMENT

Review the activities, status, and results of the process with higher level management and resolve issues.

The purpose of this generic practice is to provide higher level management with the appropriate visibility into the process.

Higher level management includes those levels of management in the organization above the immediate level of management responsible for the process. In particular, higher level management can include senior management. These reviews are for managers who provide the policy and overall guidance for the process and not for those who perform the direct day-to-day monitoring and controlling of the process.

Different managers have different needs for information about the process. These reviews help ensure that informed decisions on the planning and performing of the process can be made. Therefore, these reviews are expected to be both periodic and event driven.

HINT

Some acquisition projects have multiple reporting paths. Make explicit who is considered "higher level management."

HINT

Not every process area will be included in each review with senior management. Establish a strategic rhythm for reviews that includes both examination of high-risk areas and regular health checks on process execution.

Proposed changes to commitments to be made external to the organization (e.g., changes to supplier agreements) are typically reviewed with higher level management to obtain their agreement with the proposed changes.

GG 3 INSTITUTIONALIZE A DEFINED PROCESS

The process is institutionalized as a defined process.

GP 3.1 ESTABLISH A DEFINED PROCESS

Establish and maintain the description of a defined process.

The purpose of this generic practice is to establish and maintain a description of the process that is tailored from the organization's set of standard processes to address the needs of a specific instantiation. The organization should have standard processes that cover the process area, as well as have guidelines for tailoring these standard processes to meet the needs of a project or organizational function. With a defined process, variability in how the processes are performed across the organization is reduced and process assets, data, and learning can be effectively shared.

Refer to the Integrated Project Management process area for more information about establishing the project's defined process.

Refer to the Organizational Process Definition process area for more information about establishing standard processes and establishing tailoring criteria and guidelines.

The descriptions of the defined processes provide the basis for planning, performing, and managing the activities, work products, and services associated with the process.

Subpractices

1. Select from the organization's set of standard processes those processes that cover the process area and best meet the needs of the project or organizational function.
2. Establish the defined process by tailoring the selected processes according to the organization's tailoring guidelines.
3. Ensure that the organization's process objectives are appropriately addressed in the defined process.
4. Document the defined process and the records of the tailoring.
5. Revise the description of the defined process as necessary.

GP 3.2 COLLECT PROCESS RELATED EXPERIENCES

Collect process related experiences derived from planning and performing the process to support the future use and improvement of the organization's processes and process assets.

The purpose of this generic practice is to collect process related experiences, including information and artifacts derived from planning and performing the process. Examples of process related experiences include work products, measures, measurement results, lessons learned, and process improvement suggestions. The information and artifacts are collected so that they can be included in the organizational process assets and made available to those who are (or who will be) planning and performing the same or similar processes. The information and artifacts are stored in the organization's measurement repository and the organization's process asset library.

HINT

Periodically review whether the information provided to the organization is still relevant and useful, and adjust your collection practices accordingly. Often, metrics used and measurements gathered will change as the organization's proficiency in quantitative management increases.

> Examples of relevant information include the effort expended for the various activities, defects injected or removed in a particular activity, and lessons learned.

Refer to the Integrated Project Management process area for more information about contributing to organizational process assets.

Refer to the Organizational Process Definition process area for more information about establishing organizational process assets.

Subpractices

1. Store process and product measures in the organization's measurement repository.

   The process and product measures are primarily those measures that are defined in the common set of measures for the organization's set of standard processes.

2. Submit documentation for inclusion in the organization's process asset library.

3. Document lessons learned from the process for inclusion in the organization's process asset library.

4. Propose improvements to the organizational process assets.

Applying Generic Practices

Generic practices are components that can be applied to all process areas. Think of generic practices as reminders. They serve the purpose of reminding you to do things right and are expected model components.

For example, consider the generic practice, "Establish and maintain the plan for performing the process" (GP 2.2). When applied to the Project Planning process area, this generic practice reminds you to plan the activities involved in creating the plan for the project. When applied to the Organizational Training process area, this same generic practice reminds you to plan the activities involved in developing the skills and knowledge of people in the organization.

Process Areas that Support Generic Practices

While generic goals and generic practices are the model components that directly address the institutionalization of a process across the organization, many process areas likewise address institutionalization by supporting the implementation of the generic practices. Knowing these relationships will help you effectively implement the generic practices.

Such process areas contain one or more specific practices that when implemented can also fully implement a generic practice or generate a work product that is used in the implementation of a generic practice.

An example is the Configuration Management process area and GP 2.6, "Place selected work products of the process under appropriate levels of control." To implement the generic practice for one or more process areas, you might choose to implement the Configuration Management process area, all or in part, to implement the generic practice.

Another example is the Organizational Process Definition process area and GP 3.1, "Establish and maintain the description of a defined process." To implement this generic practice for one or more process areas, you should first implement the Organizational Process Definition process area, all or in part, to establish the organizational process assets that are needed to implement the generic practice.

Table 7.2 describes (1) the process areas that support the implementation of generic practices and (2) the recursive relationships between generic practices and their closely related process areas. Both types of relationships are important to remember during process improvement to take advantage of the natural synergies that exist between the generic practices and their related process areas.

Given the dependencies that generic practices have on these process areas, and given the more holistic view that many of these process areas provide, these process areas are often implemented early, in whole or in part, before or concurrent with implementing the associated generic practices.

TABLE 7.2 Generic Practice and Process Area Relationships

Generic Practice	Roles of Process Areas in Implementation of the Generic Practice	How the Generic Practice Recursively Applies to its Related Process Area(s)[1]
GP 2.2 Plan the Process	**Project Planning:** The project planning process can implement GP 2.2 in full for all project related process areas (except for Project Planning itself).	GP 2.2 applied to the project planning process can be characterized as "plan the plan" and covers planning project planning activities.
GP 2.3 Provide Resources GP 2.4 Assign Responsibility	**Project Planning:** The part of the project planning process that implements Project Planning SP 2.4, "Plan the Project's Resources," supports the implementation of GP 2.3 and GP 2.4 for all project related process areas (except perhaps initially for Project Planning itself) by identifying needed processes, roles, and responsibilities to ensure the proper staffing, facilities, equipment, and other assets needed by the project are secured.	
GP 2.5 Train People	**Organizational Training:** The organizational training process supports the implementation of GP 2.5 as applied to all process areas by making the training that addresses strategic or organization-wide training needs available to those who will perform or support the process. **Project Planning:** The part of the project planning process that implements Project Planning SP 2.5, "Plan Needed Knowledge and Skills," and the organizational training process, supports the implementation of GP 2.5 in full for all project related process areas.	GP 2.5 applied to the organizational training process covers training for performing the organizational training activities, which addresses the skills required to manage, create, and accomplish the training.

Continues

1. When the relationship between a generic practice and a process area is less direct, the risk of confusion is reduced; therefore, we do not describe all recursive relationships in the table (e.g., for generic practices 2.3, 2.4, and 2.10).

TABLE 7.2 Generic Practice and Process Area Relationships *(Continued)*

Generic Practice	Roles of Process Areas in Implementation of the Generic Practice	How the Generic Practice Recursively Applies to its Related Process Area(s)
GP 2.6 Control Work Products	**Configuration Management:** The configuration management process can implement GP 2.6 in full for all project related process areas as well as some of the organizational process areas.	GP 2.6 applied to the configuration management process covers change and version control for the work products produced by configuration management activities.
GP 2.7 Identify and Involve Relevant Stakeholders	**Project Planning:** The part of the project planning process that implements Project Planning SP 2.6, "Plan Stakeholder Involvement," can implement the stakeholder identification part (first two subpractices) of GP 2.7 in full for all project related process areas. **Project Monitoring and Control:** The part of the project monitoring and control process that implements Project Monitoring and Control SP 1.5, "Monitor Stakeholder Involvement," can aid in implementing the third subpractice of GP 2.7 for all project related process areas. **Integrated Project Management:** The part of the integrated project management process that implements Integrated Project Management SP 2.1, "Manage Stakeholder Involvement," can aid in implementing the third subpractice of GP 2.7 for all project related process areas.	GP 2.7 applied to the project planning process covers the involvement of relevant stakeholders in project planning activities. GP 2.7 applied to the project monitoring and control process covers the involvement of relevant stakeholders in project monitoring and control activities. GP 2.7 applied to the integrated project management process covers the involvement of relevant stakeholders in integrated project management activities.
GP 2.8 Monitor and Control the Process	**Project Monitoring and Control:** The project monitoring and control process can implement GP 2.8 in full for all project related process areas.	GP 2.8 applied to the project monitoring and control process covers the monitoring and controlling of the project's monitor and control activities.

TABLE 7.2 Generic Practice and Process Area Relationships *(Continued)*

Generic Practice	*Roles of Process Areas in Implementation of the Generic Practice*	*How the Generic Practice Recursively Applies to its Related Process Area(s)*
	Measurement and Analysis: For all processes, not just project related processes, the Measurement and Analysis process area provides general guidance about measuring, analyzing, and recording information that can be used in establishing measures for monitoring performance of the process.	
GP 2.9 Objectively Evaluate Adherence	**Process and Product Quality Assurance:** The process and product quality assurance process can implement GP 2.9 in full for all process areas (except perhaps for Process and Product Quality Assurance itself).	GP 2.9 applied to the process and product quality assurance process covers the objective evaluation of quality assurance activities and selected work products.
GP 2.10 Review Status with Higher Level Management	**Project Monitoring and Control:** The part of the project monitoring and control process that implements Project Monitoring and Control SP 1.6, "Conduct Progress Reviews," and SP 1.7, "Conduct Milestone Reviews," supports the implementation of GP 2.10 for all project related process areas, perhaps in full, depending on higher level management involvement in these reviews.	
GP 3.1 Establish a Defined Process	**Integrated Project Management:** The part of the integrated project management process that implements Integrated Project Management SP 1.1, "Establish the Project's Defined Process," can implement GP 3.1 in full for all project related process areas.	GP 3.1 applied to the integrated project management process covers establishing defined processes for integrated project management activities.

Continues

TABLE 7.2 Generic Practice and Process Area Relationships *(Continued)*

Generic Practice	Roles of Process Areas in Implementation of the Generic Practice	How the Generic Practice Recursively Applies to its Related Process Area(s)
	Organizational Process Definition: For all processes, not just project related processes, the organizational process definition process establishes the organizational process assets needed to implement GP 3.1.	
GP 3.2 Collect Process Related Experiences	**Integrated Project Management:** The part of the integrated project management process that implements Integrated Project Management SP 1.7, "Contribute to Organizational Process Assets," can implement GP 3.2 in part or in full for all project related process areas.	GP 3.2 applied to the integrated project management process covers collecting process related experiences derived from planning and performing integrated project management activities.
	Organizational Process Focus: The part of the organizational process focus process that implements Organizational Process Focus SP 3.4, "Incorporate Experiences into Organizational Process Assets," can implement GP 3.2 in part or in full for all process areas.	
	Organizational Process Definition: For all processes, the organizational process definition process establishes the organizational process assets needed to implement GP 3.2.	

There are also a few situations where the result of applying a generic practice to a particular process area would seem to make a whole process area redundant, but, in fact, it does not. It can be natural to think that applying GP 3.1, "Establish a Defined Process," to the Project Planning and Project Monitoring and Control process areas gives the same effect as the first specific goal of Integrated Project Management, "Use the Project's Defined Process."

Although it is true that there is some overlap, the application of the generic practice to these two process areas provides defined processes covering project planning and project monitoring and control activities. These defined processes do not necessarily cover support activities (e.g., configuration management), other project management processes (e.g., integrated project management), or other processes. In contrast, the project's defined process, provided by the Integrated Project Management process area, covers all appropriate processes.

AGREEMENT MANAGEMENT
A Project Management Process Area at Maturity Level 2

Purpose

The purpose of Agreement Management (AM) is to ensure that the supplier and the acquirer perform according to the terms of the supplier agreement.

> **TIP**
>
> AM helps to prevent problems, such as suppliers that cannot meet requirements, by providing a proactive approach to supplier management and visibility into supplier activities. Well-executed SSAD processes provide significant leverage to success in AM.

Introductory Notes

The Agreement Management process area involves the following activities:

- Executing the supplier agreement
- Monitoring supplier processes
- Accepting the delivery of acquired products
- Managing supplier invoices

The legal nature of many acquirer–supplier agreements makes it imperative that the project management team is acutely aware of the legal implications of actions taken when managing the acquisition of products or services.

The supplier agreement is the basis for managing the relationship with the supplier, including resolving issues. It defines the mechanisms that allow the acquirer to oversee the supplier's activities and evolving products and to verify compliance with supplier agreement requirements. It is also the vehicle for a mutual understanding between the acquirer and supplier. When the supplier's performance, processes, or products fail to satisfy established criteria as outlined in the supplier agreement, the acquirer may take corrective action.

Related Process Areas

Refer to the Acquisition Technical Management process area for more information about evaluating technical solutions.

191

Refer to the Acquisition Validation process area for more information about validating selected products and product components.

Refer to the Measurement and Analysis process area for more information about specifying measures and communicating results.

Refer to the Project Monitoring and Control process area for more information about monitoring the project against the plan and taking corrective action.

Refer to the Solicitation and Supplier Agreement Development process area for more information about establishing supplier agreements.

Specific Goal and Practice Summary

SG 1 Satisfy Supplier Agreements
  SP 1.1   Execute the Supplier Agreement
  SP 1.2   Monitor Selected Supplier Processes
  SP 1.3   Accept the Acquired Product
  SP 1.4   Manage Supplier Invoices

Specific Practices by Goal

SG 1 SATISFY SUPPLIER AGREEMENTS

The terms of the supplier agreement are met by both the acquirer and the supplier.

SP 1.1 EXECUTE THE SUPPLIER AGREEMENT

Perform activities with the supplier as specified in the supplier agreement.

This specific practice covers internal and external communication as well as the use of information by the acquirer and supplier regarding the relationship, performance, results, and impact to the business. The acquirer manages the relationship with the supplier to maintain effective communication on key issues (e.g., changes in the acquirer's business), new supplier products and technologies, and changes in the organizational structure.

Refer to the Project Monitoring and Control process area for more information about monitoring the project against the plan and taking corrective action.

Example Work Products

1. Integrated list of issues
2. Acquisition project progress and performance reports
3. Supplier review materials and reports

> **TIP**
>
> Although the goal of AM is effective performance by both parties to the agreement, acquirers will be successful in satisfying the goal if they perform all of the elements for which they are accountable and take appropriate corrective actions if the supplier fails to meet the terms of the agreement.

> **TIP**
>
> Often, suppliers have "capture teams" that are different from the team actually assigned to perform the work. As a consequence, AM activities may involve different supplier personnel than SSAD activities, which necessitates reestablishing the acquirer–supplier relationship.

4. Action items tracked to closure

5. Records of product and document deliveries

Example Supplier Deliverables

1. Supplier project progress and performance reports

2. Corrective action results for supplier issues

3. Correspondence with the acquirer

Subpractices

1. Monitor supplier project progress and performance (e.g., schedule, effort, cost) as defined in the supplier agreement.

2. Conduct management reviews with the supplier as specified in the supplier agreement.

> Reviews cover both formal and informal reviews and include the following steps:
> - Preparing for the review
> - Ensuring that relevant stakeholders participate
> - Conducting the review
> - Identifying, documenting, and tracking all action items to closure
> - Preparing and distributing to the relevant stakeholders a summary report of the review

TIP

The purpose of a *management review* is to monitor the supplier's progress against the project plans and identify and resolve potentially problematic issues (usually programmatic risks).

X-REF

Reviews for technical risks are covered in ATM.

Management reviews typically include the following:
- Reviewing critical dependencies
- Reviewing project risks involving the supplier
- Reviewing schedule and budget

> *Refer to the Acquisition Technical Management process area for more information about conducting technical reviews.*
>
> *Refer to the Project Monitoring and Control process area for more information about conducting milestone reviews.*

3. Identify issues and determine corrective actions necessary to resolve and track them to closure.

> *Refer to the Manage Corrective Action to Closure specific goal in the Project Monitoring and Control process area for more information about tracking corrective actions to closure.*

> Unresolved issues escalate through the appropriate management chain according to the organization's issue resolution process.

4. Use the results of reviews to improve the supplier's performance and to establish and nurture long-term relationships with preferred suppliers.

5. Monitor risks involving the supplier and take corrective action as necessary.

> Refer to the Project Monitoring and Control process area for more information about monitoring project risks.

SP 1.2 MONITOR SELECTED SUPPLIER PROCESSES

Select, monitor, and analyze supplier processes.

When there must be tight alignment between supplier and acquirer processes, the acquirer should monitor these processes to help prevent interface problems.

Selecting processes for monitoring involves considering the impact of the supplier's processes on the project. On larger projects with significant subcontracts for development of critical components, monitoring key processes is expected. For less critical components, the selection process can determine that monitoring is not appropriate. Between these extremes, the overall risk should be considered when selecting processes to be monitored.

The acquirer should also determine the levels to which the selected supplier processes should be monitored. Monitoring, if not performed with adequate care, can at one extreme be invasive and burdensome, or at the other extreme be uninformative and ineffective. The acquirer decides on the necessary level of monitoring depending on the level of risk if the supplier's process is not performed correctly and the impact the monitoring activity will have (i.e., the value of information obtained and its cost to both parties). Monitoring activities can range from reviewing supplier supplied process data to on-site appraisals of the supplier's processes.

Analyzing selected processes involves taking the data obtained from monitoring the processes and analyzing them to determine whether there are serious issues.

> As an example, the acquirer may need to monitor and analyze selected supplier development processes to ensure that nonfunctional requirements receive appropriate attention.

Example Work Products

1. List of processes selected for monitoring or rationale for non-selection
2. Activity reports

3. Process performance reports
4. Process performance curves
5. Discrepancy reports

Example Supplier Deliverables

1. Supplier process quality assurance reports

Subpractices

1. Identify supplier processes critical to the success of the project.
2. Monitor selected supplier processes for compliance with requirements of the agreement.
3. Analyze results of monitoring selected processes to detect issues as early as possible that may affect the supplier's ability to satisfy requirements of the agreement.

   Trend analysis can rely on internal and external data.

SP 1.3 ACCEPT THE ACQUIRED PRODUCT

Ensure that the supplier agreement is satisfied before accepting the acquired product.

This practice involves ensuring that the acquired product meets all requirements and that customers concur before acceptance of the product. The acquirer ensures that all acceptance criteria have been satisfied and that all discrepancies have been corrected. Requirements for formal deliverable acceptance and how to address non-conforming deliverables are usually defined in the supplier agreement. The acquirer should be prepared to exercise all remedies if the supplier fails to perform.

The acquirer, usually through its authorized supplier agreement administrator, provides the supplier with formal written notice that supplier deliverables have been accepted or rejected.

Typically, an authorized representative of the acquirer assumes ownership of existing identified supplier products or deliverables tendered, or approves services rendered, as partial or complete satisfaction of the supplier agreement.

The acquirer has defined how this product or service will make the transition to operations and support in the transition to operations and support plan. Transition to operations and support activities are monitored by the acquirer.

Refer to the Monitor Transition to Operations and Support specific practice in the Project Monitoring and Control process area for more information about monitoring transition activities.

TIP

Sometimes the operational need is so great that a conditional acceptance is granted before the supplier agreement is fully satisfied. In these cases, the acquirer must proactively manage the "punch list" of outstanding items or discrepancies to ensure that the agreement is fully satisfied.

Refer to the Plan Transition to Operations and Support specific practice in the Project Planning process area for more information about planning for the transition of the accepted product or service.

Example Work Products

1. Stakeholder approval reports
2. Discrepancy reports
3. Product acceptance review report with approval signatures

Example Supplier Deliverables

1. Work products as defined in the supplier agreement
2. Services as defined in the supplier agreement

Subpractices

X-REF

Acceptance procedures, reviews, and tests are also covered in AVAL. Consult that process area's practices for more information about establishing the appropriate environment, procedures, and criteria for validation (and, therefore, for accepting the acquired product).

1. Review the validation results, reports, logs, and issues for the acquired product.

   Refer to the Acquisition Validation process area for more information about validating selected products and product components.

2. Review supplier verification results, reports, logs, and issues for the acquired product.

3. Confirm that all contractual requirements for the acquired product are satisfied.

   This subpractice can include confirming that appropriate license, warranty, ownership, usage, and support or maintenance agreements are in place and all supporting materials are received.

HINT

Be sure to address proprietary issues related to the acquired product before accepting it.

4. Confirm that all discrepancies have been corrected and all acceptance criteria have been satisfied.

5. Communicate to relevant stakeholders that the supplier agreement has been satisfied.

   The acquirer, usually through its authorized supplier agreement or contract administrator, provides the supplier with formal written notice that the supplier agreement has been satisfied so the supplier can be paid and the supplier agreement closed.

6. Communicate to relevant stakeholders the product's readiness for transition to operations and support.

SP 1.4 MANAGE SUPPLIER INVOICES

Manage invoices submitted by the supplier.

The intent of this practice is to ensure that payment terms defined in the supplier agreement are met and that supplier compensation is linked to supplier progress, as defined in the supplier agreement.

This practice covers invoices for any type of charge (e.g., one-time, monthly, deliverable-based, pass-through). It covers invoice errors or issues, changes to invoices, billing errors, and withholding disputed charges consistent with the terms and conditions of the supplier agreement. The acquirer should also ensure that appropriate financial and invoice management controls are in place.

When accepting supplier deliverables, final payment should not be made to the supplier until it has been certified that all supplier deliverables meet contractual requirements and all acceptance criteria have been satisfied. When acceptance criteria have not been satisfied, the provisions of the supplier agreement can be exercised.

TIP

This practice may be executed by a support function outside the control of the project team. Even so, slow or missed payments pose a risk to the project and must be on the project's radar screen.

AM

Example Work Products

1. Invoices approved for payment

Example Supplier Deliverables

1. Invoices

Subpractices

1. Receive invoices.
2. Review invoices and related supporting material.

> Examples of areas of review for invoices and related support material include the following:
> - Volumes for variable charges
> - Pass-through expenses
> - Regulatory commitments related to payments
> - Purchases made by the supplier on behalf of the acquirer

3. Resolve errors and manage issues with the supplier as required.
4. Approve invoices.

ACQUISITION REQUIREMENTS DEVELOPMENT
An Acquisition Engineering Process Area at Maturity Level 2

Purpose

The purpose of Acquisition Requirements Development (ARD) is to elicit, develop, and analyze customer and contractual requirements.

X-REF

REQM addresses management of requirements once they have been developed.

Introductory Notes

This process area describes two types of requirements: customer requirements, which address the needs of relevant stakeholders for which one or more products and services will be acquired, and contractual requirements, which are the requirements to be addressed through the acquirer's relationship with suppliers and other appropriate organizations. Both sets of requirements should address needs relevant to later product lifecycle phases (e.g., operation, maintenance, support, disposal) and key quality attributes (e.g., safety, reliability, maintainability).

TIP

Customer needs can prescribe particular solutions (e.g., a particular service-oriented architecture to facilitate interoperability) as well as describe the problem to be solved.

In some acquisitions, the acquirer assumes the role of overall systems engineer, architect, or integrator for the product. In these acquisitions, the Requirements Development process area of CMMI-DEV should be used. Requirements Development in CMMI-DEV includes additional information helpful in these situations, including deriving and analyzing requirements at successively lower levels of product definition (e.g., establishing and maintaining product component requirements).

Requirements are the basis for the selection and design or configuration of the acquired product. The development of requirements includes the following activities:

- Elicitation, analysis, and validation of stakeholder needs, expectations, constraints, and interfaces to establish customer requirements that constitute an understanding of what will satisfy stakeholders

ARD

- Development of the lifecycle requirements of the product (e.g., development, maintenance, transition to operations, decommissioning)
- Establishment of contractual requirements consistent with customer requirements to a level of detail that is sufficient to be included in the solicitation package and supplier agreement
- Development of the operational concept
- Analysis of needs and requirements (for each product lifecycle phase), the operational environment, and factors that reflect overall customer and end-user needs and expectations for quality attributes
- Identification of quality attributes, which are non-functional properties of a product or service (e.g., responsiveness, availability, security) and are critical to customer satisfaction and to meeting the needs of relevant stakeholders (see the definition of "quality attributes" in the glossary)

The requirements included in the solicitation package form the basis for evaluating proposals by suppliers and for further negotiations with suppliers and communication with the customer. The contractual requirements for the supplier are baselined in the supplier agreement.

Requirements are refined throughout the project lifecycle. Design decisions, subsequent corrective actions, and feedback during each phase of the project's lifecycle are analyzed for their impact on contractual requirements.

Requirements analyses aid understanding, defining, and selecting requirements at all levels from competing alternatives. Analyses occur recursively at successively more detailed levels until sufficient detail is available to produce contractual requirements and to further refine these requirements, if necessary, while the supplier builds or configures the product.

Involvement of relevant stakeholders in both requirements development and analyses gives them visibility into the evolution of requirements. Participation continually assures stakeholders that requirements are being properly defined.

X-REF

Requirements validation is addressed in ARD because it is critical to align project and customer expectations.

The Acquisition Requirements Development process area includes three specific goals. The Develop Customer Requirements specific goal addresses eliciting and defining a set of customer requirements. The Develop Contractual Requirements specific goal addresses defining contractual requirements that are based on customer requirements and are included in the solicitation package and supplier agreement. The specific practices of the Analyze and Validate Requirements specific goal support the development of the requirements in the first two specific goals. The specific practices associated with this specific goal cover analyzing and validating requirements with respect to the acquirer's intended environment.

Related Process Areas

Refer to the Acquisition Technical Management process area for more information about evaluating technical solutions.

Refer to the Acquisition Validation process area for more information about validating selected products and product components.

Refer to the Solicitation and Supplier Agreement Development process area for more information about establishing a solicitation package and establishing supplier agreements.

Refer to the Requirements Management process area for more information about managing requirements.

Refer to the Risk Management process area for more information about identifying and analyzing risks.

Specific Goal and Practice Summary

SG 1 Develop Customer Requirements
  SP 1.1 Elicit Stakeholder Needs
  SP 1.2 Develop and Prioritize Customer Requirements
SG 2 Develop Contractual Requirements
  SP 2.1 Establish Contractual Requirements
  SP 2.2 Allocate Contractual Requirements
SG 3 Analyze and Validate Requirements
  SP 3.1 Establish Operational Concepts and Scenarios
  SP 3.2 Analyze Requirements
  SP 3.3 Analyze Requirements to Achieve Balance
  SP 3.4 Validate Requirements

Specific Practices by Goal

SG 1 DEVELOP CUSTOMER REQUIREMENTS

Stakeholder needs, expectations, constraints, and interfaces are collected and translated into customer requirements.

Stakeholders (e.g., customers, end users, suppliers, testers, integrators, maintainers, operators, supplier agreement management staff, manufacturers, logistics support staff) are sources of requirements. Their needs, expectations, constraints, interfaces, operational concepts, and product concepts are analyzed, harmonized, refined, and elaborated for translation into a set of customer requirements.

Frequently, stakeholder needs, expectations, constraints, and interfaces are poorly identified or conflicting. Since these needs, expectations, constraints, and interfaces should be clearly identified

---

TIP

Stakeholder needs are rarely communicated fully in an official document. They are communicated in documentation, conversations, meetings, demonstrations, and so on. Thus this information must be translated into requirements that the project and the customer can agree to.

HINT

Pay particular attention to nonfunctional requirements or other architecturally significant quality attributes or "ilities" (e.g., security, interoperability, maintainability, extendibility).

X-REF

For help in facilitating the discovery of quality attributes, see "Quality Attribute Workshops, Third Edition," at www.sei.cmu.edu/library/abstracts/reports/03tr016.cfm.

HINT

Rarely do customers know exactly what they want. Plan to use an iterative process to uncover the requirements for the product or service to be acquired.

ARD

and understood throughout the project lifecycle, an iterative process is used throughout the life of the project to accomplish this objective. To facilitate the required interaction, relevant stakeholders are frequently involved throughout the project lifecycle to communicate their needs, expectations, and constraints, and to help resolve conflicts. Environmental, legal, and other constraints should be considered when creating and evolving the set of requirements to be used in acquiring products or services.

SP 1.1 ELICIT STAKEHOLDER NEEDS

Elicit stakeholder needs, expectations, constraints, and interfaces for all phases of the product lifecycle.

Eliciting goes beyond collecting needs by proactively identifying additional needs not explicitly provided by stakeholders. Relevant stakeholders who represent all phases of the product lifecycle in the acquirer's intended environment should include business as well as technical functions. Using this approach, needs for all product related lifecycle processes are considered concurrently with concepts for acquired products.

An analysis of business processes is a common source of stakeholder needs, expectations, constraints, and interfaces. Additional needs typically address project lifecycle activities and their impact on the product.

> Examples of techniques to elicit needs from stakeholders include the following:
> - Questionnaires and interviews
> - Scenarios (operational, sustainment, and development) obtained from end users and other relevant stakeholders
> - Operational walkthroughs and end-user task analyses
> - Quality attribute elicitation workshops with stakeholders
> - Prototypes and models
> - Observation of existing products, environments, and workflow patterns
> - Technology demonstrations
> - Interim project reviews
> - Brainstorming
> - Quality Function Deployment
>
> *Continues*

TIP

In the case of acquiring product lines or product families, SP 1.1 is sometimes implemented across the product line or product family. A special infrastructure project may establish core assets used in developing each product in the family. In such an organization, requirements come from the organization, the individual acquisition programs, and the core asset development project.

X-REF

For more information on acquiring products and services in a product line environment, see "Acquisition Organizations and Product Lines" at www.sei.cmu.edu/productlines/start/acquisition/index.cfm.

HINT

Ask what the product must do and how it will behave. Also determine what is required to produce it (if it is a physical product), license it, install it, train end users, maintain the product, migrate to new versions, support its use, retire it, and dispose of it.

Continued

- Market surveys
- Extraction from sources such as business process documents, standards, or specifications
- Use cases
- Business case analyses
- Reverse engineering (for legacy products)
- Customer or end user satisfaction surveys

Examples of sources of requirements that might not be identified by the customer include the following:

- Government regulations
- Policies and standards
- Technology
- Legacy products or product components (for reuse)

HINT

Never underestimate the value of reviewing other sources of requirements. A large number of acquisition projects incur cost and schedule impacts because one or more sources of requirements were not considered.

Example Work Products

1. Stakeholder needs, expectations, constraints, and interfaces

Subpractices

1. Engage relevant stakeholders using methods for eliciting needs, expectations, constraints, and external interfaces.

SP 1.2 *Develop and Prioritize Customer Requirements*

Transform stakeholder needs, expectations, constraints, and interfaces into prioritized customer requirements.

The customer typically describes requirements as capabilities expressed in broad operational terms concerned with achieving a desired effect under specified standards and regulations. Customer requirements can also include needs, expectations, constraints, and interfaces with regard to verification and validation. Inputs from the customer and other stakeholders should be aligned to the acquisition strategy. Missing information should be obtained and conflicts should be resolved as customer requirements are developed and prioritized.

Customer requirements can also exist as an output of another activity such as a previous project that delivered the initial capability; or a possible earlier customer or system-of-systems office related activity establishing architectural principles, interoperability standards, and common design constraints.

HINT

Significant changes to requirements may occur during different phases in the project lifecycle. It may be useful to think about your acquisition strategy differently (e.g., evolutionary or incremental approaches), especially if the project lifecycle is lengthy.

X-REF

The acquisition strategy is described in detail in SP 1.1 of the Project Planning process area.

ARD

> Examples of factors to consider when expressing customer requirements include the following:
> - Key characteristics of the desired capability with appropriate parameters and measures
> - Obstacles to overcome to achieve the capability
> - Competitive gap between the existing and the desired capability
> - Supportability of the desired capability
> - Level of detail of customer requirements that does not prejudice decisions in favor of a particular means of implementation but are specific enough to evaluate alternative approaches to implement the capability

Example Work Products

1. Prioritized customer requirements
2. Customer constraints on the conduct of verification
3. Customer constraints on the conduct of validation

Subpractices

1. Translate stakeholder needs, expectations, constraints, and interfaces into documented customer requirements.
2. Establish and maintain a prioritization of customer functional and quality attribute requirements.

   Having prioritized customer requirements guides the acquirer in determining project scope and which requirements and requirements changes to include in supplier agreements. This prioritization ensures that functional and quality attribute requirements critical to the customer and other relevant stakeholders are addressed quickly. Determining priorities and resolving conflicts among them can be addressed when eliciting stakeholder needs, as described in the previous specific practice.

3. Define constraints for verification and validation.

TIP

The relationships among customer and contractual requirements should be investigated and recorded (see REQM SP 1.4).

SG 2 DEVELOP CONTRACTUAL REQUIREMENTS

Customer requirements are refined and elaborated into contractual requirements.

Customer requirements are analyzed in conjunction with the development of the operational concept to derive more detailed and precise sets of requirements, called contractual requirements, to be included in the solicitation package for potential suppliers and eventually in the supplier agreement. The level of detail of contractual requirements is based on the acquisition strategy and project characteristics.

Contractual requirements arise from constraints, consideration of issues implied but not explicitly stated in the customer requirements baseline, and factors introduced by design constraints and supplier capabilities. Contractual requirements include both requirements documented in contracts between an acquirer and supplier and requirements addressed through formal agreements between the acquirer and other organizations (e.g., partners, subcontractors, government agencies, internal organizational units). (See the definition of "contractual requirements" in the glossary.) Requirements are reexamined throughout the project lifecycle.

The requirements are allocated to supplier deliverables. The traceability across levels of requirements and supplier deliverables (and planned supplier delivery increments) is documented.

Refer to the Requirements Management process area for more information about maintaining bidirectional traceability of requirements.

SP 2.1 ESTABLISH CONTRACTUAL REQUIREMENTS

Establish and maintain contractual requirements that are based on the customer requirements.

Customer requirements can be expressed in the customer's terms and can be nontechnical descriptions. Contractual requirements are the expression of these requirements in technical terms that can be used for design decisions.

In addition to technical requirements (e.g., requirements specifying interfaces with other products or applications, functional and operationally related quality attribute requirements and their validation, technical performance measures, verification requirements such as product acceptance criteria), contractual requirements cover nontechnical stakeholder needs, expectations, constraints, and interfaces.

> **TIP**
>
> Translating requirements (i.e., from customer to contractual) introduces opportunities for misinterpretation and risk. Spend extra time ensuring that the contractual requirements accurately reflect the customer need.

Examples of nontechnical requirements include the following:
- Frequency and format of supplier reviews
- Supplier reports and other communication
- Availability of support to meet levels of the business process or product performance
- Warranty of products provided by a supplier
- Logistics support that sustains both short- and long-term readiness
- Minimal total lifecycle cost to own and operate (i.e., minimal total ownership cost)

Continues

Continued

- Maintenance concepts that optimize readiness while drawing on both acquirer and supplier sources
- Data management and configuration management that facilitates cost effective product support throughout the product's use by the acquirer

The modification of requirements due to approved requirement changes is covered by the *maintain* aspect of this specific practice; whereas, the administration of requirement changes is covered by the Requirements Management process area.

Refer to the Requirements Management process area for more information about managing requirements.

Example Work Products

1. External interface requirements
2. Prioritized contractual requirements

Subpractices

1. Develop functional and quality attribute requirements necessary for the determination of alternative solutions and the development of the product by the supplier.

   Priorities can be assigned to product requirements to provide a basis for future requirements tradeoffs should such tradeoffs become necessary. Acquirers may assign priorities using categories such as Essential, Important, or Desirable.

2. Develop requirements for the interfaces between the acquired product and other products in the intended environment.

   Requirements for interfaces are defined in terms of origination, destination, stimulus, data characteristics for software, and electrical and mechanical characteristics for hardware.

3. Develop design considerations and constraints necessary for supplier activities that include: determination of alternative solutions, development and evaluation of architectures, and the development of the product.

   Design considerations and constraints address the quality attributes and technical performance that are critical to the success of the product in its intended operational environment. They account for customer requirements relative to product interoperability, implications from the use of commercial off-the-shelf (COTS) products, safety, security, durability, and other mission critical concerns.

   To achieve high levels of reuse and interoperability, acquirers can establish common design constraints for products or product families that can be deployed in one or more domains. Alternatively, acquirers

---

TIP

Identifying the interfaces for which requirements will be developed is not a one-time event, but rather continues for as long as new interfaces are established.

HINT

If multiple systems are being acquired to provide the needed capability, recognize that the interfaces may change as these systems evolve.

TIP

Previous acquisitions may have had somewhat different needs to fulfill, so requirements and test cases to be reused may need to be analyzed and possibly modified for the current acquisition.

can accelerate the development of technical requirements and design constraints by reusing shared or common constraints or requirements and their associated test cases from previous acquisitions or leverage the supplier's previous product developments.

Common design constraints can also be established and maintained by a customer organization or system-of-systems office for a group of acquisitions collectively intended to establish a major capability (e.g., for systems-of-systems, product lines, standard services).

4. Develop requirements for verification and validation of the product to be developed by the supplier.

   Requirements for verification and validation typically include types and coverage of testing and review to be carried out in the supplier's and acquirer's environments.

Testing requirements can include mirroring the production environment of the acquirer, the type of test data to be used, and simulated testing of interfaces with other products.

TIP

If the satisfaction of a requirement cannot be ensured through some verification process, the requirement should be restated or eliminated.

ARD

5. Establish and maintain relationships among the requirements under consideration during change management and requirements allocation.

   Relationships between requirements can affect evaluating the impact of requirements changes. Expected requirements volatility is a key factor in anticipating scope changes and supporting the acquirer's selection of the appropriate acquisition type.

6. Identify nontechnical requirements.

   Contractual requirements consist of both technical and nontechnical requirements. Examples of nontechnical requirements are listed in the example box in this specific practice.

7. Establish and maintain a prioritization of contractual requirements.

   Priority can be based on a combination of several factors that include customer desires, costs, timeframe for when the capabilities are needed, and length of time to satisfy a particular requirement.

   When cost estimates can be determined for contractual requirements, their priority and costs can be used to guide contract and budget negotiations and to determine which changes should be made to the contract.

   Priority can also help when developing a release strategy (e.g., first release only addresses high priority requirements; lower priority requirements are deferred to a later release or maintenance phase).

Refer to the Project Planning process area for more information about establishing the acquisition strategy and estimating effort and cost.

TIP

Sometimes a seemingly insignificant requirements change can greatly improve the merits of a COTS-based solution, especially with regard to cost and schedule risks. Conversely, the use of a COTS product may constrain the overall solution's performance and the support that can be offered later in the product's life. A relationship with a vendor may need to be maintained.

X-REF

See www.sei.cmu.edu/ acquisition/tools/methods/ cotsintro.cfm for more information about using COTS products.

TIP

Sometimes a higher-level requirement specifies performance that is satisfied by multiple supplier deliverables or even across multiple supplier teams.

TIP

The allocation of a higher-level requirement to supplier deliverables is not necessarily fixed. Often, a provisional allocation of a higher-level requirement to a supplier is made, but is later revised to account for the unique or emerging capabilities of individual suppliers, teams, or new COTS products.

HINT

Pay close attention to integration issues when you allocate contractual requirements to multiple suppliers. You may inadvertently end up filling the role of product integrator.

SP 2.2 ALLOCATE CONTRACTUAL REQUIREMENTS

Allocate contractual requirements to supplier deliverables.

Contractual requirements are allocated, as appropriate, to supplier deliverables. The requirements for each supplier deliverable are documented. In some cases, technical requirements are allocated to third-party products that are used by the supplier (e.g., COTS products).

Example Work Products

1. Requirement allocation sheets

Subpractices

1. Allocate requirements to supplier deliverables.

   In the case of an evolutionary acquisition lifecycle, the requirements for the initial capability can also be allocated to suppliers' initial iterations or increments based on stakeholder priorities, technology issues, supplier capabilities, and acquirer project objectives.

2. Allocate design constraints to supplier deliverables.

3. Document relationships among allocated requirements and design constraints.

   Relationships include dependencies (i.e., a change in one requirement can affect other requirements).

4. Allocate requirements to suppliers.

   In situations where multiple suppliers are involved in developing the technical solution, different products or product components may be allocated to different suppliers.

5. Develop an approach to address requirements that by their nature are shared among multiple stakeholders (e.g., the acquirer, multiple suppliers, customers, end users).

   Some requirements (in particular, for some quality attribute requirements) should be shared among multiple stakeholders and maintained through the life of the product (e.g., security requirements often cannot be allocated to a single supplier). An approach that addresses such requirements should be devised and appropriately incorporated in customer and supplier agreements.

Refer to the Solicitation and Supplier Agreement Development process area for more information about establishing supplier agreements.

SG 3   *ANALYZE AND VALIDATE REQUIREMENTS*

Requirements are analyzed and validated.

Analyses are performed to determine the impact the intended operational environment will have on the ability to satisfy stakeholder needs, expectations, constraints, and interfaces. Considerations such as feasibility, mission needs, cost constraints, potential market size, and acquisition strategy should all be taken into account, depending on the product context.

The objectives of these analyses are (1) to determine candidate requirements for product concepts that will satisfy stakeholder needs, expectations, constraints, and interfaces and (2) to translate these concepts into requirements. In parallel with these activities, the parameters to be used to evaluate the effectiveness of the product are determined based on customer input and the preliminary product concept.

Requirements are validated to increase the probability that the resulting product will perform as intended in the acquirer's intended environment.

SP 3.1   *ESTABLISH OPERATIONAL CONCEPTS AND SCENARIOS*

Establish and maintain operational concepts and associated scenarios.

Operational concepts or concepts of operation are overall descriptions of the problems to be solved in operational terms and the ways in which the products to be acquired are intended to be used or operated, deployed, supported (including maintenance and sustainment), and disposed. The acquirer explicitly accounts for design constraints.

> For example, the operational concept for a satellite based communications product is quite different from one based on landlines.

In contrast, a scenario is a description of a sequence of events that might occur in the use, transition, or sustainment of the product to be acquired and makes explicit some stakeholder functionality and quality attribute needs. Typically, scenarios are derived from business process descriptions and operational concepts.

TIP

The purpose of requirements validation is to ensure that you have a clear understanding of what the customer wants and needs. Often, this understanding evolves over time and requires a series of requirements validation activities.

TIP

Requirements analyses examine requirements from different perspectives (e.g., feasibility, cost, risk) and using different abstractions (e.g., functional, data flow, entity relationship, state diagrams, temporal).

HINT

Identify technical performance measures and other measures that help in assessing or predicting performance, usability, cost, schedule, risk, and other aspects of the product. Use them to state contractual requirements, establish quality objectives, evaluate progress, manage risk, and conduct trade studies. They provide a data-driven approach to engineering the product.

X-REF

Technical performance measures are covered in more detail in the Measurement and Analysis process area.

X-REF

For more information about technical performance parameters, see "Using CMMI to Improve Earned Value Management" at www.sei. cmu.edu/library/abstracts/ reports/02tn016.cfm.

ARD

Operational concepts and scenarios can assist in the elicitation of needs and the analysis and refinement of requirements. Operational concepts and scenarios can be further refined as solution decisions are made and more detailed requirements are developed. They are evolved to facilitate the validation of technical solutions delivered by the supplier.

Example Work Products

1. Operational, maintenance, support, and disposal concepts
2. Use cases, user stories
3. New requirements

Subpractices

1. Develop operational concepts and scenarios that include operations, installation, maintenance, support, and disposal as appropriate.
   Augment scenarios with quality attribute considerations for the functions (or other logical entities) described in the scenario.
2. Define the environment in which the product will operate, including boundaries and constraints.
3. Review operational concepts and scenarios to refine and discover requirements.
   Operational concept and scenario development is an iterative process. Reviews should be held periodically to ensure that the operational concepts and scenarios agree with the requirements. The review can be in the form of a walkthrough.
4. Develop a detailed operational concept, as candidate solutions are identified and product and product component solutions are selected by the supplier, that defines the interaction of the product, the end user, and the environment, and that satisfies operational, maintenance, support, and disposal needs.

SP 3.2 ANALYZE REQUIREMENTS

Analyze requirements to ensure they are necessary and sufficient.

As contractual requirements are defined, their relationship to customer requirements should be understood. In light of the operational concepts and scenarios, the contractual requirements are analyzed to determine whether they are necessary and sufficient to meet customer requirements. The analyzed requirements then provide the basis for more detailed and precise requirements throughout the project lifecycle.

Also, which key requirements will be used to track technical progress is determined. For instance, the weight of a product or size of a software product can be monitored through development based on its risk or its criticality to the customer or end user.

Refer to the Acquisition Technical Management process area for more information about conducting technical reviews.

Example Work Products

1. Requirements defects reports
2. Proposed requirements changes to resolve defects
3. Key requirements
4. Technical performance measures

Subpractices

1. Analyze stakeholder needs, expectations, constraints, and external interfaces to organize into related subjects and remove conflicts.
2. Analyze requirements to determine whether they satisfy higher level requirements.
3. Analyze requirements to ensure that they are complete, feasible, realizable, and verifiable.
4. Analyze and propose the allocation of requirements.
5. Identify key requirements that have a strong influence on cost, schedule, performance, or risk.

   These key requirements often reflect cross-cutting (i.e., system-level) concerns and often address quality attributes that will be a major driver to a supplier's architecture definition and evaluation activities. A clear understanding of such quality attributes (also known as "architecturally significant quality attributes") and their importance based on mission or business needs is essential to an effective analysis of requirements and to effective technical performance measurement.
6. Identify technical performance measures to be tracked during the acquisition.

   Technical performance measures are precisely defined measures based on a product requirement, product capability, or some combination of requirements and capabilities. Technical performance measures are chosen to monitor requirements and capabilities that are considered key factors in a product's performance. Data for technical performance measures are provided by the supplier as specified in the supplier agreement.

   Refer to the Measurement and Analysis process area for more information about specifying measures.

> **HINT**
>
> As conflicts are removed, inform the relevant stakeholders of changes that affect the requirements they provided.

ARD

7. Analyze operational concepts and scenarios to refine customer needs, constraints, and interfaces and to discover new requirements.
   This analysis can result in more detailed operational concepts and scenarios as well as support the derivation of new requirements.

SP 3.3 ANALYZE REQUIREMENTS TO ACHIEVE BALANCE

Analyze requirements to balance stakeholder needs and constraints.

Stakeholder needs and constraints can address such things as cost, schedule, product or project performance, functionality, reusable components, maintainability, or risk.

Requirements are analyzed to determine whether they reflect an appropriate balance among cost, schedule, performance, and other factors of interest to relevant stakeholders. Models and simulations can be used to estimate the impacts that requirements will have on these factors. By involving stakeholders from different phases of the product's lifecycle in analyzing these impacts, risks can be determined. If the risks are considered unacceptable, the requirements can be revised or reprioritized to improve the balance of cost, schedule, and performance.

Example Work Products

1. Assessment of risks related to requirements
2. Proposed requirements changes

Subpractices

1. Use proven models, simulations, and prototyping to analyze the balance of stakeholder needs and constraints.
   Results of analyses can be used to reduce the cost of the product and the risk in acquiring and using the product.
2. Perform a risk assessment on requirements and design constraints.

   Refer to the Risk Management process area for more information about identifying and analyzing risks.

3. Examine product lifecycle concepts for impacts of requirements on risks.
4. Perform a cost benefit analysis to assess impact of the requirements on the overall acquisition strategy and acquisition project costs and risks.
   This assessment of impact often focuses on an evaluation of requirements addressing architecturally significant quality attributes.

As an example, a combination of tight response time requirements and high reliability requirements could prove expensive to implement. Once the possible impacts are better understood, the requirements can be adjusted to achieve a better balance among cost, schedule, performance, and risk; and thus enable a more affordable capability to be acquired.

SP 3.4 VALIDATE REQUIREMENTS

Validate requirements to ensure the resulting product performs as intended in the end user's environment.

Requirements validation is performed early in the acquisition with end users or their representatives to gain confidence that the requirements are capable of guiding a development that results in successful final validation. This activity should be integrated with risk management activities. Mature organizations typically perform requirements validation in a more sophisticated way using multiple techniques and broaden the basis of the validation to include other stakeholder needs and expectations. These organizations typically perform analyses, prototyping, and simulations to ensure that requirements will satisfy stakeholder needs and expectations.

Examples of techniques used for requirements validation include the following:
- Analysis
- Simulations
- Prototyping
- Demonstrations

> **TIP**
>
> *Requirements validation* in this SP focuses on the adequacy and completeness of the requirements. *Product and service validation* in AVAL focuses on predicting at multiple points in development how well the product or service will satisfy user needs.

Example Work Products

1. Records of analysis methods and results

Example Supplier Deliverables

1. Requirements and validation methods (e.g., prototypes, simulations)

Subpractices

1. Analyze the requirements to determine the risk that the resulting product will not perform appropriately in its intended-use environment.

2. Explore the adequacy and completeness of requirements by developing product representations (e.g., prototypes, simulations,

models, scenarios, storyboards) and by obtaining feedback about them from relevant stakeholders.

Refer to the Acquisition Validation process area for more information about preparing for validation and validating selected products and product components.

3. Assess product and product component solutions as they are developed by the supplier in the context of the validation environment to identify issues and expose unstated needs and customer requirements.

ACQUISITION TECHNICAL MANAGEMENT
An Acquisition Engineering Process Area at Maturity Level 3

Purpose

The purpose of Acquisition Technical Management (ATM) is to evaluate the supplier's technical solution and to manage selected interfaces of that solution.

Introductory Notes

The Acquisition Technical Management process area focuses on the following:

- Conducting technical reviews of the supplier's technical solution
- Analyzing the development and implementation of the supplier's technical solution to confirm technical progress criteria or contractual requirements are satisfied
- Managing selected interfaces
- Typically, these activities interactively support one another to gauge technical progress and allow effective management of project technical risks. Different levels of detailed analysis, depending on the development progress and insight required, may be needed to conduct technical reviews to the acquirer's satisfaction. Prototypes, simulations, and technology demonstrations created by the supplier can be used to help gauge technical progress, gauge readiness for technical reviews, assess technical risks, and gain knowledge needed to manage selected interfaces.

In some acquisitions, the acquirer assumes the role of overall systems engineer, architect, or integrator for the product. In these acquisitions, the Technical Solution process area of CMMI-DEV should also be used. Technical Solution in CMMI-DEV includes additional information about designing, developing, and implementing solutions, including the design approaches, design concepts, and

TIP

The focus of ATM is on the various suppliers' products as they evolve into a usable solution; the focus of AVER is on the acquirer's work products.

TIP

Many problems encountered in the integration of product or service components or the product or service transition to operations are caused by interface incompatibilities. Thus ATM covers interface management.

ATM

alternative solutions for which an acquirer can have varying degrees of responsibility.

Acquisition Technical Management activities involve measuring technical progress and the effectiveness of plans and requirements. Activities include the ones associated with technical performance measurement and the conduct of technical reviews. A structured review process should demonstrate and confirm completion of required accomplishments and exit criteria as defined in project planning and technical plans (e.g., the systems engineering management plan). Acquisition Technical Management activities discover deficiencies or anomalies that often result in corrective action.

Acquisition Technical Management should be performed with other technical and agreement management processes, such as requirements management, risk management, configuration management, data management, and agreement management.

For acquisition of product lines and standard services, the practices described in this process area (as well as Acquisition Requirements Development practices) can also be applied to identify and acquire core assets used in developing, acquiring, or customizing products or service systems. (See the definition of "product line" in the glossary.)

When the supplier is using an Agile method, end users or their proxies are typically involved in the supplier's development processes. In such a situation, the acquirer also needs to be involved to ensure that needed changes to requirements and supplier agreements are acceptable given the constraints of the acquisition, and also to incorporate the changes into the supplier agreements.

Refer to the Plan Stakeholder Involvement specific practice in the Project Planning process area for more information about supporting the use of Agile methods.

Related Process Areas

Refer to the Agreement Management process area for more information about satisfying supplier agreements.

Refer to the Acquisition Requirements Development process area for more information about allocating contractual requirements and establishing operational concepts and scenarios.

Refer to the Configuration Management process area for more information about controlling configuration items.

X-REF

ATM is driven by the contractual requirements defined by ARD, managed by REQM, and established contractually in SSAD. The technical management in ATM has to coordinate with the supplier agreement management in AM. The processes associated with these process areas interact significantly to accomplish their purposes.

Refer to the Decision Analysis and Resolution process area for more information about establishing evaluation criteria and selecting alternative solutions.

Refer to the Plan Data Management specific practice in the Project Planning process area for more information about managing data.

Refer to the Requirements Management process area for more information about managing requirements.

Refer to the Risk Management process area for more information about mitigating risks.

Specific Goal and Practice Summary

SG 1 Evaluate Technical Solutions
    SP 1.1   Select Technical Solutions for Analysis
    SP 1.2   Analyze Selected Technical Solutions
    SP 1.3   Conduct Technical Reviews
SG 2 Perform Interface Management
    SP 2.1   Select Interfaces to Manage
    SP 2.2   Manage Selected Interfaces

Specific Practices by Goal

SG 1   EVALUATE TECHNICAL SOLUTIONS

Supplier technical solutions are evaluated to confirm that contractual requirements continue to be met.

Technical reviews (e.g., architectural evaluations) are performed throughout the project lifecycle to gain confidence that the requirements, architecture, and supplier technical solutions are capable of guiding a development that results in a product or service that provides the required capability. This activity should be integrated with risk management activities. Mature organizations typically perform technical reviews using different proven techniques depending on the type of review. They broaden the basis of the review to include other stakeholder needs, expectations, and constraints.

Refer to the Establish the Acquisition Strategy specific practice in the Project Planning process area for more information about specifying technical performance measures and their threshold values.

This specific goal focuses on the following:

- Selecting supplier technical solutions (i.e., preliminary designs, detailed designs, design implementations, delivered increments of component functionality) based on sound decision-making criteria

TIP

SG 1 and SG 2 of ATM apply at any phase in the lifecycle of a product or service if a supplier is delivering a technical solution to meet contractual requirements in a supplier agreement.

TIP

It is best to evaluate a range of candidate solutions. Input from stakeholders with diverse skills and backgrounds can help teams identify and address assumptions, constraints, and biases that may be exhibited in the supplier's candidate designs. Also, consider the "ilities" addressed in the contractual requirements (e.g., usability, reliability, maintainability, interoperability, security).

ATM

X-REF

DAR supports the selection of supplier technical solutions for analysis.

TIP

When you consider the successful products or services you have acquired, ask what made them successful. Was it features, usability, cost, customer support, response time, reliability, or something else? These characteristics were achieved through careful evaluation of technical solutions.

TIP

Complexity is a "double-edged sword." Sometimes today's high-performance solution becomes tomorrow's high-maintenance challenge.

HINT

When evaluating a supplier's alternative solution, treat its components together, not individually. For example, do not rush to evaluate a promising COTS component or new technology without considering the impacts and risks of its integration with the rest of the solution.

HINT

Consider the entire life of the product when evaluating a technical solution to ensure that it will have the desired versatility and market endurance.

- Analyzing selected supplier technical solutions
- Conducting technical reviews using results of the analysis

SP 1.1 SELECT TECHNICAL SOLUTIONS FOR ANALYSIS

Select supplier technical solutions to be analyzed and analysis methods to be used.

The supplier technical solutions are typically in one of the following three stages:

- Candidate solutions or preliminary designs (includes consideration of design approaches, design concepts, architectures, architectural styles and patterns, product partitions, major interfaces, system states and modes) that potentially satisfy an appropriate set of allocated functional and quality attribute requirements
- Detailed designs for selected solutions (i.e., containing all the information needed to manufacture, code, or otherwise implement the design as a product or product component)
- Implemented designs (i.e., the product or service)

Depending on where in the acquisition lifecycle the highest risks occur, the acquirer selects supplier technical solutions for analysis to reduce those risks. Analysis methods are selected based on the type of technical solution being analyzed and the nature of the risk.

For example, in the design phases of the supplier technical solution, quality attribute models, simulations, prototypes, or pilots can be used to provide additional information about the properties of the potential design solutions to aid in their evaluation and selection. Simulations can be particularly useful for systems-of-systems.

For example, in the implementation phase of the supplier technical solution, the acquirer can examine a product to determine if it is ready for production and if the supplier has accomplished adequate production planning. The analysis would determine if production or production preparations incur unacceptable risks that might compromise cost, schedule, performance, or other established objectives. The acquirer might evaluate the full, production configured product to determine if it correctly and completely implements all contractual requirements. The acquirer could also determine whether the traceability of the final contractual requirements to the final production configured product has been maintained.

The acquirer may also want to select interfaces for analysis to help decide which interfaces require acquirer management. (See specific goal 2 of this process area.)

Example Work Products

1. Criteria used to select supplier technical solutions for analysis
2. Lists of supplier technical solutions selected for analysis
3. Analysis methods for each selected supplier solution

Example Supplier Deliverables

1. List of supplier deliverables

Subpractices

1. Develop criteria for determining which supplier technical solutions to analyze.

    Refer to the Decision Analysis and Resolution process area for more information about establishing evaluation criteria.

2. Identify supplier technical solutions for analysis.

Supplier technical solutions that are typically analyzed by the acquirer include the following:

- Supplier derived product and product component requirements, architectures, and designs
- Product interface descriptions
- Products and product components
- Operations manuals
- Plans for training the operations staff

---

3. Identify the functional and quality attribute requirements to be satisfied by each selected technical solution.
    A traceability matrix is a useful tool for identifying requirements for each selected technical solution, as it typically includes information that relates requirements to work products. When identifying requirements for each selected technical solution, consult the appropriate traceability matrix.

    Refer to the Maintain Bidirectional Traceability of Requirements specific practice in the Requirements Management process area for more information about tracing requirements to work products.

4. Identify the analysis methods to be used for each selected technical solution.

TIP

Criteria for selection can include the impact of the technical solution on cost, schedule, performance, and risk. How these criteria are defined in detail, however, depends on the requirements.

TIP

Screening criteria may involve setting thresholds for selected quality attributes (e.g., response time) that must be met by technical solutions.

HINT

Explore the use of COTS products (or open source or new technology) by the supplier early in technical evaluations. To use COTS solutions effectively, you may need to consider changes to requirements. Fully understand the tradeoffs entailed in such requirements and designs early, before committing to (and putting under contract) a particular development approach.

ATM

X-REF

For more information regarding principles, methods, and techniques for creating systems from COTS products, see the SEI website at www.sei.cmu.edu/ acquisition/tools/methods/ cotsintro.cfm.

> Examples of techniques used for analysis include the following:
> - Simulations
> - Prototyping
> - Architecture evaluation
> - Demonstrations

5. Include analysis methods and review activities in the project plan.

Refer to the Project Planning process area for more information about establishing and maintaining plans that define project activities.

SP 1.2 ANALYZE SELECTED TECHNICAL SOLUTIONS

Analyze selected supplier technical solutions.

Depending on the type of technical solution being analyzed (i.e., preliminary design, detailed design, design implementation of components or their interfaces), the results of the analysis are provided to the technical review described in the next specific practice.

The acquirer should select a supplier's design to analyze by exploring the adequacy and completeness of that design by reviewing product representations (e.g., prototypes, simulations, models, scenarios, storyboards) and by obtaining feedback about them from relevant stakeholders.

> For example, the acquirer should assess the design as it matures in the context of the requirements to identify issues and expose unstated needs and customer requirements.

The acquirer should confirm the following:

- The selected design adheres to applicable design standards and criteria.
- The design adheres to allocated functional and quality attribute requirements.
- The resulting product will perform appropriately in its intended-use environment.

During design implementation, the supplier implements the design reviewed and analyzed by the acquirer by developing product components, integrating those components, conducting unit and integration testing of the product, and developing end-user documentation.

HINT

To gain the insight needed to fully evaluate supplier solutions, you may need to refine operational concepts and scenarios so that you understand the implications of each alternative solution. Also, you may need to develop scenarios for other phases of the product lifecycle.

X-REF

ARD SP 3.1 establishes and maintains the operational concepts and scenarios.

HINT

A design is a document used by stakeholders over the life of the product; thus it must communicate clearly and accommodate change. Consider these issues when selecting criteria to be used in evaluating the value of a design.

A successful analysis of the supplier's implementation is predicated on the acquirer's determination that the requirements are fully met in the final production configuration, that the production capability forms a satisfactory basis for proceeding into pilots or full-rate production, and that the product is ready to be brought into the acquirer environment for further integration and acceptance testing.

Examples of success criteria for the analysis of the supplier's detailed design prior to its transition to design implementation include the following:

- The product baseline enables hardware fabrication and software coding to proceed with proper configuration management.
- Adequate production processes and measures are in place for the project to succeed.
- Risks are managed effectively.
- The detailed design is producible within the production budget.

The acquirer can require delivery of verification results from the supplier of the technical solution, as applicable. The suppliers can conduct verifications in an iterative fashion, concurrently with the acquirer's technical analyses, or the supplier can be required to conduct follow-on verifications of technical solutions.

Typical expectations for verification addressed by the supplier agreement include the following:

- List of deliverables and other work products that must be verified by the supplier
- Applicable standards, procedures, methods, tools
- Criteria for verification of supplier work products
- Measurements to be collected and provided by the supplier with regard to verification activities
- Reviews of supplier verification results and corrective actions with the acquirer

---

Examples of considerations for follow-on verifications of technical solutions include the following:

- During the production stage of the project, there are changes in either materials or manufacturing processes.
- Production startup or re-start occurs after a significant shutdown period.
- Production starts up with a new supplier.
- A manufacturing site has relocated.

ATM

TIP

Installers, operators, end users, and maintainers may have different documentation needs that may be addressed in different documents.

TIP

Documentation assists product maintenance and support later in the life of the product.

TIP

Documentation can be treated as a type of product component for which a solution may be selected, designed, and implemented. Design and implementation methods and standards have been developed for documentation.

HINT

It is not enough to consider product functionality and behavior in the intended operational environment when evaluating a solution. Ask questions about other phases in the life of the product, including whether the solution can be manufactured; whether it is easy to test, install, repair, migrate to new versions or platforms, and support; and what the costs and legal implications will be.

HINT

No solution will rank best on every criterion used. Instead, analyze a solution's ability to provide a balanced approach to cost, schedule, performance, and risks across the product lifecycle.

The acquirer should also confirm that sufficient end-user documentation has been developed and is in alignment with the tested implementation. The supplier can develop preliminary versions of the installation, operations, and maintenance documentation in early phases of the project lifecycle for review by acquirer and relevant stakeholders.

Example Work Products

1. Record of analysis
2. Results of analysis

Example Supplier Deliverables

1. Alternative solutions
2. Product architecture
3. Product component designs
4. Architecture evaluations
5. Unit and integration test results
6. Verification results

Subpractices

1. Confirm that the selected technical solution adheres to applicable standards and criteria.
2. Confirm that the selected technical solution adheres to allocated functional and quality attribute requirements.
3. Use analysis results to compare actual performance measurements to specified thresholds of technical performance measures.

   Refer to the Measurement and Analysis process area for more information about analyzing measurement data.

4. Conduct technical interchange meetings as necessary.
   Technical interchange meetings are scheduled meetings between the supplier and acquirer to discuss technical progress. These meetings are less formal than the event-driven technical reviews in the next specific practice. One of the purposes of these meetings is to discuss and understand issues encountered during acquirer analyses or provided results of supplier verification activities.
5. Confirm that the selected technical solution is sufficiently analyzed and meets entrance criteria to begin technical review.

6. Review critical verification results and data from verifications conducted by the supplier.

SP 1.3 CONDUCT TECHNICAL REVIEWS

Conduct technical reviews with the supplier as defined in the supplier agreement.

Technical reviews are used by the acquirer to confirm that products and services being developed or produced by suppliers meet end user needs and requirements.

Technical reviews should have the following characteristics:

- Are conducted when the technical solution under development satisfies review entry criteria (i.e., event driven, not schedule driven)
- At a minimum, are conducted at the transition from one acquisition phase to the next and at major transition points of technical effort
- Have their processes and requirements addressed in and required by the supplier agreement

> Typically, the project's technical plan (e.g., the systems engineering management plan) documents the timing, conduct, entrance criteria, and success or exit criteria used for technical reviews.

Refer to the Project Planning process area for more information about establishing and maintaining plans that define project activities.

> Technical reviews typically include the following activities:
> - Reviewing the supplier's technical activities and verifying that the supplier's interpretation and implementation of requirements are consistent with the acquirer's interpretation
> - Ensuring that technical commitments are being met and that technical issues are communicated and resolved in a timely manner
> - Obtaining technical information about the supplier's products
> - Providing the supplier with insight into customer and end user expectations and requirements regarding functionality and quality attributes
> - Providing appropriate technical information and support to the supplier

> Examples of technical reviews that can be conducted include the following:
> - Initial Technical Review (ITR)
> - Alternative System Review (ASR)

Continues

HINT

Following the evaluation, you may conclude that the selection criteria were not complete or detailed enough to adequately assess the ability of the solution to meet the entrance criteria for the technical review. If so, you may need to iterate through SP 1.1 and 1.2.

TIP

The purpose of a *technical review* is to review the supplier's technical progress and identify and resolve issues.

ATM

Continued

- Integrated Baseline Review (IBR)
- Technology Readiness Assessment (TRA)
- System Requirements Review (SRR)
- System Functional Review (SFR)
- Preliminary Design Review (PDR)
- Critical Design Review (CDR)
- Test Readiness Review (TRR)
- System Verification Review (SVR)
- Production Readiness Review (PRR)
- Operational Test Readiness Review (OTRR)
- Physical Configuration Audit (PCA)

Example Work Products

1. Review schedule
2. Entry and exit criteria
3. Review results
4. Documented issues (e.g., issues with customer requirements, product and product component requirements, product architecture, product design)

Example Supplier Deliverables

1. Progress reports and process, product, and service level measurements
2. Technical performance measurements
3. Review materials and reports
4. Action items tracked to closure
5. Documentation of product and document deliveries

Subpractices

1. Identify participants for the technical review.
2. Conduct the technical review.
3. Analyze and record results of the review.
4. Use the results of technical reviews to improve the supplier's technical solution.

    The results of some reviews may require changes to the supplier agreement.

    Refer to the Solicitation and Supplier Agreement Development process area for more information about preparing a solicitation package,

*selecting one or more suppliers to deliver the product or service, and
establishing and maintaining the supplier agreement.*

SG 2 PERFORM INTERFACE MANAGEMENT

Selected interfaces are managed.

Many integration and transition problems arise from unknown or
uncontrolled aspects of both internal and external interfaces. Effective management of interface requirements, specifications, and
designs helps to ensure implemented interfaces are complete and
compatible.

The supplier is responsible for managing the interfaces of the
product or service it is developing. However, the acquirer identifies interfaces that it will manage as well (particularly external
interfaces).

SP 2.1 SELECT INTERFACES TO MANAGE

Select interfaces to manage.

The interfaces considered for selection include all interfaces with
other products and services in the operations and support environment as well as environments for verification and validation and services that support those environments. The acquirer should review
all supplier interface data for completeness to substantiate the complete coverage of all interfaces when making the selection.

Example Work Products

1. Criteria to be used in selecting acquirer managed interfaces
2. Categories of interfaces
3. List of interfaces per category

Example Supplier Deliverables

1. Interface description documents
2. Categories of interfaces
3. List of interfaces per category
4. Mapping of interfaces to product components and the product integration environment
5. Interface design specifications

TIP

Overlooked or incompletely
described interfaces are risks
to be identified and managed
(RSKM). The realization of
these risks may lead to safety
recalls and can prove very
costly.

HINT

Manage interfaces early in the
project to help prevent
inconsistencies from arising.

HINT

Where possible, reach early
agreement with the supplier on
interface design. For some
external interfaces, agreement
must also be reached by the
acquirers or owners of the
other interfacing products or
services. Lack of agreement
leads to wasted time, as
assumptions made by the
teams on each side of an
interface must be validated.
Project costs may increase and
the schedule may slip.

TIP

You can use a formal
evaluation (DAR) process to
select the interfaces to manage.
Criteria for selection can
include the impact of the
interface on cost, schedule,
performance, and risk.

ATM

TIP

Interface control documents define interfaces in terms of data items passed, protocols used for interaction, and so on. These documents are particularly useful in controlling products and product components being built by different teams.

X-REF

Requirements for the interfaces are developed in ARD. The acquirer should pay special attention to those interfaces that were particularly important to the stakeholders.

X-REF

It may be prudent to mitigate risks by establishing teams across related acquisition programs when the final capabilities require effective interfaces between or within programs. IPM SP 1.6 provides guidance for such teams.

TIP

Interface management may sometimes follow a formal evaluation (DAR) process: Establish criteria for correctness of an interface (based in part on interface requirements), evaluate alternatives, and so on.

6. Interface control documents
7. Interface specification criteria

Subpractices

1. Select the criteria to be used for determining which interfaces the acquirer should manage.

   Refer to the Decision Analysis and Resolution process area for more information about establishing evaluation criteria.

2. Identify interfaces that are candidates for acquirer management.

> Example criteria for interfaces that typically are the focus of the acquirer's management include the following:
> - The interface spans organizational boundaries.
> - The interface is mission critical.
> - The interface is difficult or complex to manage.
> - Capability, interoperability, efficiency, or other key quality attribute issues are associated with the interface.
> - The interface affects multiple acquisition projects.

3. Review identified interfaces against the selection criteria.
4. Include acquirer managed interfaces in the project plan.

SP 2.2 MANAGE SELECTED INTERFACES

Manage selected interfaces.

Managing interfaces includes the maintenance of the consistency of the interfaces throughout the life of the product, compliance with architectural decisions and constraints, and the resolution of conflict, noncompliance, and change issues. In a system-of-systems environment, the management of interfaces between products or services acquired from suppliers and other systems within the system of systems is critical for success of the project.

Interface changes are documented, maintained, and readily accessible.

Refer to the Acquisition Requirements Development process area for more information about validating requirements.

Refer to the Configuration Management process area for more information about tracking and controlling changes.

Refer to the Requirements Management process area for more information about managing requirements changes.

Example Work Products

1. Table of relationships among the supplier's product or service and the external environment
2. Updated interface description or agreement

Example Supplier Deliverables

1. Table of relationships among the product components and the external environment (e.g., main power supply, fastening product, computer bus system)
2. Reports from interface control working group meetings
3. Action items for updating interfaces
4. Application program interface (API)

Subpractices

1. Review and analyze selected interface definitions and designs.
2. Confirm that interface descriptions adhere to allocated requirements.
3. Confirm the compatibility of selected interfaces throughout the life of the product or service.

   Confirm that interface descriptions adhere to applicable standards, criteria, and interface requirements between the supplier's product and acquirer's intended environment.
4. Verify that interfaces have been sufficiently tested by the supplier.
5. Verify that issues identified during testing have been resolved appropriately, with product revisions, if necessary.
6. Resolve conflict, noncompliance, and change issues for the selected interfaces.
7. Periodically review the adequacy of interface descriptions.

   Once established, interface descriptions should be periodically reviewed to ensure there is no deviation between existing descriptions and the products being developed, processed, produced, or bought.

   The interface descriptions should be reviewed with relevant stakeholders to avoid misinterpretations, reduce delays, and prevent the development of interfaces that do not work properly.

ACQUISITION VALIDATION

An Acquisition Engineering Process Area at Maturity Level 3

Purpose

The purpose of Acquisition Validation (AVAL) is to demonstrate that an acquired product or service fulfills its intended use when placed in its intended environment.

Introductory Notes

Validation demonstrates that the acquired product or service, as provided, fulfills its intended use. In other words, validation ensures that the acquired product or service meets stakeholders' needs and customer requirements.

Validation activities are performed early (concept/explorations phases) and incrementally throughout the project lifecycle (including transition to operations and sustainment). These activities can be applied to all aspects of the product and its components in any of their intended environments, such as operations, training, manufacturing, maintenance, and support services. (Throughout the process areas, where the terms "product" and "product component" are used, their intended meanings also encompass services, service systems, and their components.)

The product or product components that are selected to be validated by the acquirer vary depending on project attributes. Methods used to conduct validation also can be applied to selected acquirer work products (e.g., customer requirements) and supplier deliverables (e.g., prototypes, simulations, demonstrations). Method selection is based on which methods best predict how well the acquired product or service will satisfy stakeholder needs.

Whenever possible, validation should be conducted using the product or product component operating in its intended environment. Either the entire environment or part of it can be used.

TIP

Validation is a series of evaluations in which end users, the product, and other elements of the *intended environment* interact to determine whether the product will fulfill its *intended use*. Results may increase confidence in the product or identify issues to be resolved. In contrast with AVER, both the supplier and the acquirer may ensure the utility of the systems in the field.

TIP

Validation can be applied to all aspects of the product or service in any of its intended environments (e.g., operations, training, manufacturing, maintenance, disposal).

HINT

Use well-verified work products in validation; otherwise, you may lose time to disruptions or rediscovery of requirements. Conversely, validation helps you uncover missing requirements.

AVAL

When validation issues are identified, these issues are referred to processes associated with the Acquisition Requirements Development or Project Monitoring and Control process areas for resolution.

The specific practices of this process area build on each other in the following way:

- The Select Products for Validation specific practice enables the identification of the product or product component to be validated and methods to be used to perform the validation.
- The Establish the Validation Environment specific practice enables the determination of the environment to be used to carry out the validation.
- The Establish Validation Procedures and Criteria specific practice enables the development of validation procedures and criteria that are aligned with the characteristics of selected products, customer constraints on validation, methods, and the validation environment.
- The Perform Validation specific practice enables the validation to be conducted according to methods, procedures, and criteria.
- The Analyze Validation Results specific practice enables the analysis of validation results against criteria.

Related Process Areas

Refer to the Agreement Management process area for more information about accepting the acquired product.

Refer to the Acquisition Requirements Development process area for more information about validating requirements.

Refer to the Acquisition Technical Management process area for more information about evaluating the supplier's technical solution and managing selected interfaces of that solution.

Specific Goal and Practice Summary

SG 1 Prepare for Validation
    SP 1.1   Select Products for Validation
    SP 1.2   Establish the Validation Environment
    SP 1.3   Establish Validation Procedures and Criteria
SG 2 Validate Selected Products and Product Components
    SP 2.1   Perform Validation
    SP 2.2   Analyze Validation Results

Specific Practices by Goal

SG 1   PREPARE FOR VALIDATION

Preparation for validation is conducted.

Validation preparation activities include selecting products and product components for validation and establishing and maintaining the validation environment, procedures, and criteria. Items selected for validation may include only the product or it may include appropriate levels of product components used to build the product. Any product or product component may be subject to validation, including replacement, maintenance, and training products, to name a few.

The environment required to validate the product or product component is prepared. The environment can be purchased or can be specified, designed, and built. Environments used for verification can be considered in collaboration with the validation environment to reduce cost and improve efficiency or productivity.

Expectations for validation, which are typically included in the supplier agreement, include the following:

- List of acquired products to be validated by the acquirer before formal acceptance
- List of products to be validated with customers, end users, or other relevant stakeholders by the supplier and applicable validation standards, procedures, methods, tools, and criteria, if any
- Measurements to be collected and provided by the supplier with regard to validation activities
- Supplier roles to be taken in product and product component validation
- Validation environments to be used by the acquirer
- Validation procedures to be developed and criteria to be used for validation

---

SP 1.1 SELECT PRODUCTS FOR VALIDATION

Select products and product components to be validated and validation methods to be used.

Products and product components are selected for validation based on their relationship to end-user needs. For each product or product component, the scope of the validation (e.g., operational behavior, maintenance, training, user interface) should be determined.

HINT

Any product, product component, or service can benefit from validation. What you select to validate should depend on the issues relating to user needs that pose the highest risk to project success and available resources.

TIP

Integration tests can address validation-type activities (with an end user present to evaluate the integrated product under different scenarios). Thus, for some product components, product integration, verification, and validation activities may be addressed together. Stakeholders may come from the customer community, other acquisition organizations needing functionality for their systems, and the suppliers covered by the acquisition agreement.

TIP

AVAL activities should be designed to reduce interference with supplier and end-user performed activities and to reduce duplication of the validation efforts.

AVAL

TIP

Validation can be an expensive activity. It takes good judgment to select (and limit) what to validate. Less formal and more frequent "customer use checks" can augment the more formal validation effort.

HINT

When you want or need to validate a product component that
has not yet been built, consider
developing a prototype. The
timely end-user feedback you
get from prototyping may more
than compensate for the
expense of validation.

Examples of products and product components that can be validated
include the following:
- Customer requirements and design constraints
- Acquired products and product components (e.g., system, hardware
  units, software, service documentation)
- User manuals
- Training materials
- Process documentation

Validation methods should be selected early in the life of the
project so they are clearly understood and agreed to by relevant
stakeholders.

Validation methods address the development, maintenance, support,
and training for the product or product components as appropriate.

X-REF

Customer constraints on the
conduct of validation are
described as part of the
development of customer
requirements in ARD SP 1.2.
Design constraints are
described in ARD SG 2 and
SG 3.

Examples of validation methods include the following:
- Discussions with end users, perhaps in the context of a formal review
- Prototype demonstrations
- Functional demonstrations (e.g., system, hardware units, software, ser-
  vice documentation, user interfaces)
- Pilots of training materials
- Tests of products and product components by end users and other rele-
  vant stakeholders
- End-of-cycle or end-of-phase reviews (with customer or end user) for
  incremental or iterative development

TIP

Because validation generally
involves stakeholders external
to the project, it is important
early in the project to identify
and communicate with them
about validation methods so
that appropriate preparations
can begin.

Example Work Products

1. Lists of products and product components selected for validation
2. Validation methods for each product or product component
3. Requirements for performing validation for each product or product
   component
4. Validation constraints for each product or product component

Subpractices

1. Identify the key principles, features, and phases for product or product component validation throughout the life of the project.
2. Determine the customer requirements to be validated.

The product or product component should be maintainable and supportable in its intended operational environment. This specific practice also addresses the actual maintenance, training, and support services that can be delivered with the product.

3. Select the product and product components to be validated.
4. Select the evaluation methods for product or product component validation.
5. Review the validation selection, constraints, and methods with relevant stakeholders.

SP 1.2 ESTABLISH THE VALIDATION ENVIRONMENT

Establish and maintain the environment needed to support validation.

The requirements for the validation environment are driven by the product or service selected, type of work products (e.g., design, prototype, final version), and validation methods. These selections can yield requirements for the purchase or development of equipment, software, or other resources. The validation environment can include the reuse of existing resources. In this case, arrangements should be made for the use of these resources.

Example types of elements in a validation environment include the following:
- Test tools interfaced with the product being validated (e.g., scope, electronic devices, probes)
- Temporary embedded test software
- Recording tools for dump or further analysis and replay
- Simulated subsystems or components (e.g., software, electronics, mechanics)
- Simulated interfaced systems (e.g., a dummy warship for testing a naval radar)
- Real interfaced systems (e.g., aircraft for testing a radar with trajectory tracking facilities)
- Facilities and customer supplied products
- Skilled people to operate or use all the preceding elements
- Dedicated computing or network test environment (e.g., pseudo-operational telecommunications network test bed or facility with actual trunks, switches, and systems established for realistic integration and validation trials)

HINT

How might a "shrink-wrapped" product be validated? You can observe users with a prototype in their operational environment, bring users to a special testing laboratory, or release a beta version for end-user testing and feedback.

HINT

Preparing for and conducting validation requires coordination with many external groups. Obtain commitment from these groups to support the planned validation efforts.

HINT

The product (or prototype) may need special interfaces and functionality to properly interact with elements of the validation environment (e.g., data recording equipment). Develop these requirements and incorporate them with other product requirements.

AVAL

TIP

When validation environments are shared across multiple programs such as ranges or high-fidelity test beds, the acquirer must proactively plan for the use, evolution, and control of these environments.

TIP

Because validation resembles a controlled experiment, and because the validation environment must maintain fidelity with the operational environment, many tools, simulations, computers, networks, and skilled people may need to be involved. Thus validation planning may itself be challenging.

TIP

This practice helps to answer questions such as how you will exercise the product or service prototype to better understand a particular issue (validation procedures) and how you will know whether the performance is acceptable (validation criteria).

X-REF

ARD addresses requirements validation. Requirements validation determines the adequacy and completeness of the requirements.

Early selection of products or product components to be validated, work products to be used in validation, and validation methods is needed to ensure that the validation environment will be available when necessary.

The validation environment should be carefully controlled to provide for replication, results analysis, and revalidation of problem areas.

Example Work Products

1. Validation environment

Subpractices

1. Identify requirements for the validation environment.
2. Identify customer supplied products.
3. Identify validation equipment and tools.
4. Identify validation resources that are available for reuse and modification.
5. Plan the availability of resources in detail.

SP 1.3 ESTABLISH VALIDATION PROCEDURES AND CRITERIA

Establish and maintain procedures and criteria for validation.

Validation procedures and criteria are defined to ensure the product or product component will fulfill its intended use when placed in its intended environment. Acceptance test cases and procedures can be used for validation procedures.

The validation procedures and criteria include validation of maintenance, training, and support services.

These procedures also address the validation of requirements and the acquired product or service throughout the project lifecycle. Typically, formal acceptance testing procedures and criteria are established to ensure the delivered product or service meets stakeholder needs before it is deployed in the intended environment.

The validation procedures and criteria applicable to the supplier are typically referenced in the solicitation package and supplier agreement.

Examples of sources for validation criteria include the following:
- Business process descriptions
- Customer requirements
- Customer acceptance criteria
- Standards

Example Work Products

1. Validation procedures
2. Validation criteria
3. Test and evaluation procedures for maintenance, training, and support

Subpractices

1. Review the requirements to ensure that issues affecting validation of the acquired product or service are identified and resolved.
2. Document the environment, operational scenario, procedures, inputs, outputs, and criteria for the validation of the acquired product or service.
3. Assess the product or service as it matures in the context of the validation environment to identify validation issues.

SG 2   VALIDATE SELECTED PRODUCTS AND PRODUCT COMPONENTS

Selected products and product components are validated to ensure they are suitable for use in their intended operating environment.

The validation methods, procedures, criteria, and the environment are used to validate the selected products and product components and associated maintenance, training, and support services. Validation activities are performed throughout the project lifecycle.

Validation activities are performed by the acquirer, the supplier, or both parties in accordance with the supplier agreement.

SP 2.1 PERFORM VALIDATION

Perform validation on selected products and product components.

To be acceptable to stakeholders, a product or product component must perform as expected in its intended operational environment.

Validation activities are performed and the resulting data are collected according to established methods, procedures, and criteria.

The as-run validation procedures should be documented and the deviations occurring during the execution should be noted as appropriate.

Example Work Products

1. Validation reports
2. Validation results
3. Validation cross reference matrix
4. As-run procedures log
5. Operational demonstrations

HINT

Items validated might be shown as *a table* with columns identifying items to validate, issues to investigate, related requirements and constraints, and validation methods. The table might also list work products to be verified by the supplier (under VER in CMMI-DEV), the work products to be verified by the acquisition organization (under AVER in this model), and the verification methods to be used. Using one table for verification and validation may lead you to discover opportunities to combine verification and validation efforts.

TIP

Validation is not applied solely to discover missing functionality, and it is not limited to the end user's operational environment. Other features, environments, and categories of user needs should be considered.

HINT

The bottom line: You must determine whether the product will perform as expected.

TIP

The validation environment may support the automatic collection of much of the data.

AVAL

HINT

Validation activities are expensive, so it is important to maximize learning during this process. Analyzing the results of validation activities may help you to discover missing requirements, features in the product that delight the customer, lingering issues, and unmitigated risks. In a system-of-systems environment, results may also suggest needed changes in adjacent systems to maximize the capability being delivered.

SP 2.2 ANALYZE VALIDATION RESULTS

Analyze results of validation activities.

The data resulting from validation tests, inspections, demonstrations, or evaluations are analyzed against defined validation criteria. Analysis reports indicate whether needs were met. In the case of deficiencies, these reports document the degree of success or failure and categorize probable causes of failure. The collected test, inspection, or review results are compared with established acceptance criteria to determine whether to proceed or to address requirements or design issues with the supplier.

Analysis reports or as-run validation documentation may also indicate that bad test results are due to a validation procedure problem or a validation environment problem.

Example Work Products

1. Validation deficiency reports
2. Validation issues
3. Procedure change request

Subpractices

1. Compare actual results to expected results.
2. Based on the established validation criteria, identify products and product components that do not perform suitably in their intended operating environments, or identify problems with methods, criteria, or the environment.
3. Analyze validation data for defects.
4. Record results of the analysis and identify issues.
5. Use validation results to compare actual measurements and product performance to the intended use or operational need.
6. Identify, document, and track action items to closure for work products that do not pass their validation.

> Refer to the Project Monitoring and Control process area for more information about managing corrective action to closure.

HINT

If problems with the validation methods, environment, procedures, or criteria arise, you must revisit project activities that correspond to the specific practices of SG 1.

ACQUISITION VERIFICATION

An Acquisition Engineering Process Area at Maturity Level 3

Purpose

The purpose of Acquisition Verification (AVER) is to ensure that selected work products meet their specified requirements.

Introductory Notes

Acquisition verification addresses whether acquirer work products properly reflect specified requirements.

The Acquisition Verification process area involves the following activities:

- Preparing for verification
- Performing verification
- Identifying corrective action

Verification is inherently an incremental process because it occurs throughout the acquisition of the product or service, beginning with verification of requirements and plans, progressing through the verification of evolving work products, and culminating in the verification of the completed product.

The specific practices of this process area build on each other in the following way:

- The Select Work Products for Verification specific practice enables the identification of work products to be verified, methods to be used to perform the verification, and documented requirements to be satisfied by each selected work product.
- The Establish the Verification Environment specific practice enables the selection or creation of the environment to be used to carry out the verification.

TIP

AVER involves ensuring that the evolving work products of the acquisition project meet specified requirements for those products. The work products covered by AVER are those "owned" by the acquisition organization—not those "owned" by the supplier.

X-REF

Managing corrective action to closure is addressed in PMC SG 2.

X-REF

Understand that supplier work product verification activities are governed by the supplier agreement (SSAD), reviewed and evaluated in ATM, but conducted using VER practices in CMMI-DEV. For complex systems that demand access to environments controlled by the acquirer or customer, collaborative approaches to verification may be essential.

AVER

- The Establish Verification Procedures and Criteria specific practice enables the development of verification procedures and criteria that are aligned with selected work products, requirements, methods, and characteristics of the verification environment.
- The Prepare for Peer Reviews, Conduct Peer Reviews, and Analyze Peer Review Data specific practices enable the conduct of peer reviews, an important type of verification that is a proven mechanism for effective defect removal.
- The Perform Verification specific practice enables the conduct of verification according to established methods, procedures, and criteria.
- The Analyze Verification Results specific practice enables analysis of verification results against established criteria.

TIP

Peer reviews also focus on getting the work product "right" and on obtaining the data necessary to prevent defects and improve the process.

Related Process Areas

Refer to the Acquisition Requirements Development process area for more information about developing and analyzing customer and contractual requirements.

Refer to the Acquisition Technical Management process area for more information about evaluating the supplier's technical solution and managing selected interfaces of that solution.

Refer to the Acquisition Validation process area for more information about demonstrating that an acquired product or service fulfills its intended use when placed in its intended environment.

Refer to the Requirements Management process area for more information about managing requirements.

Specific Goal and Practice Summary

SG 1 Prepare for Verification
    SP 1.1   Select Work Products for Verification
    SP 1.2   Establish the Verification Environment
    SP 1.3   Establish Verification Procedures and Criteria
SG 2 Perform Peer Reviews
    SP 2.1   Prepare for Peer Reviews
    SP 2.2   Conduct Peer Reviews
    SP 2.3   Analyze Peer Review Data
SG 3 Verify Selected Work Products
    SP 3.1   Perform Verification
    SP 3.2   Analyze Verification Results

Specific Practices by Goal

SG 1 PREPARE FOR VERIFICATION

Preparation for verification is conducted.

Up-front preparation is necessary to ensure that verification provisions are embedded in contractual requirements, constraints, plans, and schedules. Verification includes the selection, inspection, testing, analysis, and demonstration of acquirer work products.

Verification methods include but are not limited to inspections, peer reviews, audits, walkthroughs, analyses, architecture evaluations, simulations, testing, and demonstrations. Practices related to peer reviews as a verification method are included in specific goal 2.

Preparation for verification includes the definition of support tools, test equipment and software, simulations, prototypes, and facilities.

SP 1.1 SELECT WORK PRODUCTS FOR VERIFICATION

Select work products to be verified and verification methods to be used.

Acquirer work products are selected based on their contribution to meeting project objectives and requirements, and to addressing project risks.

> Typical verification activities include the review of the solicitation package, supplier agreements and plans, requirements documents, design constraints developed by the acquirer, and other acquirer developed work products.

Selection of verification methods typically begins with the definition of requirements to ensure that the requirements are verifiable. Re-verification should be addressed by verification methods to ensure that rework performed on work products does not cause unintended defects.

Example Work Products

1. Lists of work products selected for verification
2. Verification methods for each selected work product

HINT

Don't forget to verify work products that are important to all phases of the product lifecycle.

HINT

Identify which work products put the project at the highest risk. These work products are often the required elements that must be shared with the supplier and confirmed with the customer.

TIP

Reverification is not called out separately in this process area; however, reverification should be considered when planning verification activities. For example, when fixing a requirements defect, the project team will need to inspect (reverify) other acquisition documents, such as systems engineering plans, test plans, transition plans, and so forth, to ensure that the project baselines remain consistent.

AVER

Subpractices

1. Identify acquirer work products for verification.
2. Identify requirements to be satisfied by each selected work product.
   A traceability matrix is a useful tool for identifying requirements for each selected work product, as it typically includes information that relates requirements to work products. When identifying requirements for each selected work product, consult the traceability matrix maintained as part of managing requirements for the project.

   Refer to the Maintain Bidirectional Traceability of Requirements specific practice in the Requirements Management process area for more information about tracing requirements to work products.

3. Identify verification methods available for use.
4. Define verification methods to be used for each selected work product.
5. Identify verification activities and methods to be used in the project plan.

   Refer to the Project Planning process area for more information about developing a project plan.

SP 1.2 ESTABLISH THE VERIFICATION ENVIRONMENT

Establish and maintain the environment needed to support verification.

An environment should be established to enable verification to take place. The type of environment required depends on the work products selected for verification and the verification methods used. A peer review may require little more than a package of materials, reviewers, and a room. A product test can require simulators, emulators, scenario generators, data reduction tools, environmental controls, and interfaces with other systems.

The verification environment can be acquired, developed, reused, modified, or obtained using a combination of these activities, depending on the needs of the project.

Example Work Products

1. Verification environment

Subpractices

1. Identify verification environment requirements.
2. Identify verification resources that are available for reuse or modification.

TIP

By incorporating such a matrix into the project plan (perhaps by reference), resources can be provided and commitments made to perform the appropriate verification activities.

TIP

Some work products and verification methods may require special facilities and tools. These items should be identified and obtained in advance.

TIP

In the case of engineering artifacts (e.g., architectures, designs, implementations), the primary source for verification criteria is likely to be the requirements assigned to the work product being verified. The acquiring organization may need to verify that the customer's environment can actually support the system being acquired from the supplier.

TIP

In peer reviews, a team might meet in a room where the document being peer-reviewed can be displayed. Remote team members might participate using teleconferencing and a web-based collaboration tool.

3. Identify verification equipment and tools.
4. Acquire verification support equipment and an environment (e.g., test equipment, software).

SP 1.3 ESTABLISH VERIFICATION PROCEDURES AND CRITERIA

Establish and maintain verification procedures and criteria for the selected work products.

Verification criteria are defined to ensure that work products meet their requirements.

> Examples of sources for verification criteria include the following:
> • Standards
> • Organizational policies
> • Types of work products
> • Proposals and agreements

Example Work Products

1. Verification procedures
2. Verification criteria

Subpractices

1. Generate a set of comprehensive, integrated verification procedures for work products and commercial off-the-shelf products, as necessary.
2. Develop and refine verification criteria as necessary.
3. Identify the expected results, tolerances allowed, and other criteria for satisfying the requirements.
4. Identify equipment and environmental components needed to support verification.

SG 2 PERFORM PEER REVIEWS

Peer reviews are performed on selected work products.

Peer reviews are an important part of verification and are a proven mechanism for effective defect removal. An important corollary is to develop an understanding of work products and the processes that produced them to help prevent defects and identify opportunities.

Peer reviews are applied to acquirer developed work products. These reviews involve a methodical examination of work products by

TIP

The organization's information technology (IT) or facilities group, or perhaps other projects, might have some of the verification resources that a project needs. In some cases, domain-specific models, simulators, environmental labs, and antenna ranges are common resources used by multiple projects; if so, they may need to be reserved for use and should be verified as adequate for use.

HINT

The bottom line: You should select verification methods, environments, and procedures as early in the project as is practical.

HINT

Often, there isn't a single right result, but rather a range of results that might be acceptable. In such instances, specify how much variability from the expected answer is considered acceptable.

TIP

Peer reviews provide opportunities to learn and share information across the team.

AVER

TIP

The acquisition project uses peer reviews on selected internally generated products (e.g., solicitation documents, systems engineering plans, test plans) to find and remove defects and to ensure compliance with acquisition standards. Many work products produced by the acquisition project set the stage for project success and are critical to supplier performance.

HINT

Use peer reviews not just for contractual artifacts, but also for project management artifacts (e.g., plans), process management artifacts (e.g., process descriptions), and support artifacts (e.g., measure definitions).

HINT

Using a checklist that identifies the classes of defects that commonly occur for a type of work product makes it less likely that defects will be overlooked. Also, some classes of defects might be assigned to different peer review participants.

HINT

To maximize the effectiveness of the peer review, participants need to prepare prior to the meeting.

TIP

The cost of finding a defect late instead of early in the project is often reported as 100:1.

the acquirer's peers to identify defects for removal and to recommend other changes that are needed.

> Example work products to be peer reviewed include the solicitation package and the supplier agreement.

SP 2.1 PREPARE FOR PEER REVIEWS

Prepare for peer reviews of selected work products.

Preparation activities for peer reviews typically include identifying the staff to be invited to participate in the peer review of each work product; identifying key reviewers who should participate in the peer review; preparing and updating materials to be used during peer reviews, such as checklists and review criteria; and scheduling peer reviews.

Example Work Products

1. Peer review schedule
2. Selected work products to be reviewed

Subpractices

1. Determine the type of peer review to be conducted.
2. Establish and maintain checklists to ensure that work products are reviewed consistently.
3. Distribute the work product to be reviewed and related information to participants early enough to enable them to adequately prepare for the peer review.
4. Assign roles for the peer review as appropriate.

SP 2.2 CONDUCT PEER REVIEWS

Conduct peer reviews of selected work products and identify issues resulting from these reviews.

One of the purposes of conducting a peer review is to find and remove defects early. Peer reviews are performed incrementally as work products are being developed. These reviews are structured and are not management reviews.

Example Work Products

1. Peer review results
2. Peer review issues
3. Peer review data

Subpractices

1. Perform the assigned roles in the peer review.
2. Identify and document defects and other issues in the work product.
3. Record results of the peer review, including action items.
4. Collect peer review data.

Refer to the Measurement and Analysis process area for more information about obtaining measurement data.

5. Identify action items and communicate issues to relevant stakeholders.
6. Conduct an additional peer review if needed.

SP 2.3 *ANALYZE PEER REVIEW DATA*

Analyze data about the preparation, conduct, and results of the peer reviews.

Refer to the Measurement and Analysis process area for more information about obtaining measurement data.

Example Work Products

1. Peer review data
2. Peer review action items

Subpractices

1. Record data related to the preparation, conduct, and results of the peer reviews.
2. Analyze the peer review data.

SG 3   *VERIFY SELECTED WORK PRODUCTS*

Selected work products are verified against their specified requirements.

Verification methods, procedures, criteria, and the environment are used to verify selected work products and associated maintenance, training, and support services. Verification activities should be performed throughout the project lifecycle. Practices related to peer reviews as a verification method are included in specific goal 2.

SP 3.1 *PERFORM VERIFICATION*

Perform verification on selected work products.

Verifying work products incrementally promotes early detection of problems and can result in the early removal of defects. The results of verification save the considerable cost of fault isolation and rework associated with troubleshooting problems.

HINT

Train the staff in all of the roles necessary to conduct the peer reviews. These roles can vary from one peer review to the next.

TIP

The analysis can help answer questions about the types of defects being encountered, their severity, the phases in which they are being injected and detected, the peer review "yield" (i.e., the percentage of defects detected), the review rate (pages per hour), and the cost (or hours expended) per defect found.

X-REF

Some acquisition projects conduct "murder boards" on critical acquisition work products such as a Request for Proposal (RFP) or Statement of Work (SOW). A murder board is a comprehensive, line-by-line walkthrough of a document by all relevant stakeholders. For more information on murder boards, see *A Survival Guide for Project Managers* by James Taylor (AMACOM).

AVER

Example Work Products

1. Verification results
2. Verification reports
3. Demonstrations
4. As-run procedures log

Subpractices

1. Perform the verification of selected work products against their requirements.
2. Record the results of verification activities.
3. Identify action items resulting from the verification of work products.
4. Document the "as-run" verification method and deviations from established methods and procedures discovered during its performance.

SP 3.2 ANALYZE VERIFICATION RESULTS

Analyze results of all verification activities.

Actual results should be compared to established verification criteria to determine acceptability.

The results of the analysis of verification results are recorded as evidence that verification was conducted. The acquirer might consult supplier work product verification results and reports to conduct verification activities of acquirer work products.

Refer to the Acquisition Technical Management process area for more information about evaluating the supplier's technical solution and managing selected interfaces of that solution.

For each work product, all available verification results are incrementally analyzed and corrective actions are initiated to ensure that documented requirements have been met. Corrective actions are typically integrated into project monitoring activities. Since a peer review is one of several verification methods, peer review data should be included in this analysis activity to ensure that verification results are analyzed sufficiently.

Analysis reports or "as-run" method documentation may also indicate that bad verification results are due to method problems, criteria problems, or verification environment problems.

HINT

Sometimes the verification procedure cannot be run as defined—for example, if incorrect assumptions were made as to the nature of the work product or verification environment. If so, record any deviations.

TIP

Analysis helps to identify areas (or risks) on which to focus limited resources.

HINT

When piloting a new verification tool, analyze results to help identify ways to adjust the process or tool to increase the effectiveness of verification activities.

TIP

Peer reviews are addressed in SG 2; this specific practice addresses all other forms of verification.

Refer to the Project Monitoring and Control process area for more information about taking corrective action.

Example Work Products

1. Analysis report (e.g., statistics on work product performance, causal analysis of nonconformances, comparison of the behavior between the real product and models, trends)
2. Trouble reports
3. Change requests for verification methods, criteria, and the environment

Example Supplier Deliverables

1. Verification results
2. Verification reports

Subpractices

1. Compare actual results to expected results.
2. Based on the established verification criteria, identify products that do not meet their requirements or identify problems with methods, procedures, criteria, and the verification environment.
3. Analyze the defect data.
4. Record all results of the analysis in a report.
5. Provide information on how defects can be resolved (including verification methods, criteria, and verification environment) and formalize it in a plan.

TIP

The verification criteria established in SP 1.3 play an important role in determining where problems are.

AVER

CAUSAL ANALYSIS AND RESOLUTION
A Support Process Area at Maturity Level 5

Purpose

The purpose of Causal Analysis and Resolution (CAR) is to identify causes of selected outcomes and take action to improve process performance.

Introductory Notes

Causal analysis and resolution improves quality and productivity by preventing the introduction of defects or problems and by identifying and appropriately incorporating the causes of superior process performance.

The Causal Analysis and Resolution process area involves the following activities:

- Identifying and analyzing causes of selected outcomes. The selected outcomes can represent defects and problems that can be prevented from happening in the future or successes that can be implemented in projects or the organization.
- Taking actions to complete the following:
  - Remove causes and prevent the recurrence of those types of defects and problems in the future
  - Proactively analyze data to identify potential problems and prevent them from occurring
  - Incorporate the causes of successes into the process to improve future process performance

Reliance on detecting defects and problems after they have been introduced is not cost-effective. It is more effective to prevent defects and problems by integrating Causal Analysis and Resolution activities into each phase of the project.

Since similar outcomes may have been previously encountered in other projects or in earlier phases or tasks of the current project, Causal Analysis and Resolution activities are mechanisms for communicating lessons learned among projects.

TIP

CAR helps you establish a disciplined approach to analyzing the causes of outcomes, both positive and negative, of your processes. You can analyze defects or defect trends, problems such as schedule overruns or inter-organizational conflicts, and positive outcomes that you want to replicate elsewhere.

HINT

Integrating CAR activities into each project phase will help (1) prevent many defects from being introduced and (2) facilitate repetition of those conditions that enable superior performance, thereby improving the likelihood of project success.

X-REF

Causal analysis is mentioned in an IPM SP 1.5 subpractice (causes of selected issues); in the notes of OPM SP 1.3, (potential areas for improvement); as QPM SP 2.3, "Perform Root Cause Analysis"; and as an example work product in VER SP 3.2, "Analyze Verification Results."

HINT

The SEI has performed many independent assessments of acquisition programs since it was established and has developed acquisition archetypes, or acquisition patterns of failure, based on analyzing trends across multiple programs. For more information on this research, see www.sei.cmu.edu/ acquisition/research/ archetypes.cfm.

HINT

It is impossible to analyze *all* outcomes; instead, focus on those outcomes that are associated with the largest risk or present the greatest opportunity.

TIP

Unlike OPM, CAR is triggered by an in-depth analysis of either defects or problems in your process to prevent negative or promote positive conditions that enable superior performance that you want to replicate across the organization.

TIP

Successful implementation of CAR requires significant management commitment and process maturity to ensure that process data are accurately and consistently recorded, causal analysis meetings are adequately supported, and CAR activities are consistently performed across the organization.

Types of outcomes encountered are analyzed to identify trends. Based on an understanding of the defined process and how it is implemented, root causes of these outcomes and future implications of them are determined.

Since it is impractical to perform causal analysis on all outcomes, targets are selected by tradeoffs on estimated investments and estimated returns of quality, productivity, and cycle time.

Measurement and analysis processes should already be in place. Existing defined measures can be used, though in some instances new measurement definitions, redefinitions, or clarified definitions may be needed to analyze the effects of a process change.

Refer to the Measurement and Analysis process area for more information about aligning measurement and analysis activities and providing measurement results.

Causal Analysis and Resolution activities provide a mechanism for projects to evaluate their processes at the local level and look for improvements that can be implemented.

Causal Analysis and Resolution activities also include the evaluation of acquirer processes that interface with supplier processes as appropriate. A jointly performed causal analysis can lead to such improvement actions as the supplier improving its processes to more effectively execute in the context of the project or the acquirer improving its supplier interfaces.

When improvements are judged to be effective, the information is submitted to the organizational level for potential deployment in the organizational processes.

The specific practices of this process area apply to a process that is selected for quantitative management. Use of the specific practices of this process area can add value in other situations, but the results may not provide the same degree of impact to the organization's quality and process performance objectives.

Related Process Areas

Refer to the Measurement and Analysis process area for more information about aligning measurement and analysis activities and providing measurement results.

Refer to the Organizational Performance Management process area for more information about selecting and implementing improvements for deployment.

Refer to the Quantitative Project Management process area for more information about quantitatively managing the project to achieve the project's established quality and process performance objectives.

Specific Goal and Practice Summary

SG 1 Determine Causes of Selected Outcomes
    SP 1.1   Select Outcomes for Analysis
    SP 1.2   Analyze Causes
SG 2 Address Causes of Selected Outcomes
    SP 2.1   Implement Action Proposals
    SP 2.2   Evaluate the Effect of Implemented Actions
    SP 2.3   Record Causal Analysis Data

Specific Practices by Goal

SG 1   DETERMINE CAUSES OF SELECTED OUTCOMES

Root causes of selected outcomes are systematically determined.

A root cause is an initiating element in a causal chain which leads to an outcome of interest.

SP 1.1 SELECT OUTCOMES FOR ANALYSIS

Select outcomes for analysis.

This activity could be triggered by an event (reactive) or could be planned periodically, such as at the beginning of a new phase or task (proactive).

Example Work Products

1. Data to be used in the initial analysis
2. Initial analysis results data
3. Outcomes selected for further analysis

Subpractices

1. Gather relevant data.

> Examples of relevant data include the following:
> - Defects reported by customers or end users
> - Defects reported by the supplier
> - Productivity measures that are higher than expected
> - Project management problem reports requiring corrective action
> - Process capability problems
> - Earned value measurements by process (e.g., cost performance index)
> - Resource throughput, utilization, or response time measurements
> - Service fulfillment or service satisfaction problems

HINT

Let your data help you determine which outcomes, if addressed, will confer the most benefit to your organization. Process Performance Baselines (PPBs) and Models (PPMs) may help in this determination.

2. Determine which outcomes to analyze further.

    When determining which outcomes to analyze further, consider their source, impact, frequency of occurrence, similarity, the cost of analysis, the time and resources needed, safety considerations, etc.

> Examples of methods for selecting outcomes include the following:
> • Pareto analysis
> • Histograms
> • Box and whisker plots for attributes
> • Failure mode and effects analysis (FMEA)
> • Process capability analysis

3. Formally define the scope of the analysis, including a clear definition of the improvement needed or expected, stakeholders affected, target affected, etc.

    Refer to the Decision Analysis and Resolution process area for more information about analyzing possible decisions using a formal evaluation process that evaluates identified alternatives against established criteria.

SP 1.2 ANALYZE CAUSES

Perform causal analysis of selected outcomes and propose actions to address them.

The purpose of this analysis is to define actions that will address selected outcomes by analyzing relevant outcome data and producing action proposals for implementation.

Example Work Products

1. Root cause analysis results
2. Action proposal

Example Supplier Deliverables

1. Root cause analysis results
2. Recommended action proposals

Subpractices

1. Conduct causal analysis with those who are responsible for performing the task.

    Causal analysis is performed, typically in meetings, with those who understand the selected outcome under study. Those who have the best understanding of the selected outcome are typically those who are responsible for performing the task. The analysis is most effective when applied to real time data, as close as possible to the event which triggered the outcome.

Examples of when to perform causal analysis include the following:

- When a stable subprocess does not meet its specified quality and process performance objectives, or when a subprocess needs to be stabilized
- During the task, if and when problems warrant a causal analysis meeting
- When a work product exhibits an unexpected deviation from its requirements
- When more defects than anticipated escape from earlier phases to the current phase
- When process performance exceeds expectations
- At the start of a new phase or task

Refer to the Quantitative Project Management process area for more information about performing root cause analysis.

2. Analyze selected outcomes to determine their root causes.
   Analysis of process performance baselines and models can aid in the identification of potential root causes.
   Depending on the type and number of outcomes, it can be beneficial to look at the outcomes in several ways to ensure all potential root causes are investigated. Consider looking at individual outcomes as well as grouping the outcomes.

Examples of methods to determine root causes include the following:

- Cause-and-effect (fishbone) diagrams
- Check sheets

---

3. Combine selected outcomes into groups based on their root causes.
   In some cases, outcomes can be influenced by multiple root causes.

Examples of cause groups or categories include the following:

- Inadequate training and skills
- Breakdown of communication
- Not accounting for all details of a task
- Making mistakes in manual procedures (e.g., keyboard entry)
- Process deficiency
- Inadequate resource allocation
- Incomplete, ambiguous, or unclear contractual requirements
- Ineffective management of changes to the supplier agreement

---

TIP

There are secondary benefits to causal analysis meetings. Participants develop an appreciation for how upstream activities affect downstream activities as well as a sense of responsibility and accountability for outcomes that might otherwise remain unanalyzed.

TIP

In their book *Managing the Unexpected: Assuring High Performance in an Age of Complexity*, Weick and Sutcliffe identify "mindfulness" qualities important in high-reliability organizations, including preoccupation with failure and reluctance to simplify. These attributes imply that the organization pays attention to detail when communicating about an individual situation and seeking to understand possible systemic causes to a range of apparently unrelated small problems.

HINT

You develop cause-and-effect diagrams using iterative brainstorming (i.e., the "five whys"). This process may terminate when it reaches root causes outside the experience of the group or beyond the control of its management.

Where appropriate, look for trends or symptoms in or across groupings.

4. Create an action proposal that documents actions to be taken to prevent the future occurrence of similar outcomes or to incorporate best practices into processes.

Process performance models can support cost benefit analysis of action proposals through prediction of impacts and return on investment.

Examples of proposed preventative actions include changes to the following:

- The process in question
- Training
- Tools
- Methods
- Work products

TIP

In his book *The Checklist Manifesto: How to Get Things Right,* Atul Gawande describes the role that properly designed checklists can play in preventing common problems. He discusses his experiences in designing such checklists and identifies the impact they have had in significantly reducing complications and fatalities from surgery.

Examples of incorporating best practices include the following:

- Creating activity checklists, which reinforce training or communications related to common problems and techniques for preventing them
- Changing a process so that error-prone steps do not occur
- Automating all or part of a process
- Reordering process activities
- Adding process steps, such as task kickoff meetings to review common problems as well as actions to prevent them

---

An action proposal usually documents the following:

- Originator of the action proposal
- Description of the outcome to be addressed
- Description of the cause
- Cause category
- Phase identified
- Description of the action
- Time, cost, and other resources required to implement the action proposal
- Expected benefits from implementing the action proposal
- Estimated cost of not fixing the problem
- Action proposal category

SG 2 ADDRESS CAUSES OF SELECTED OUTCOMES

Root causes of selected outcomes are systematically addressed.

Projects operating according to a well-defined process systematically analyze where improvements are needed and implement process changes to address root causes of selected outcomes.

TIP

The focus of this goal is implementing process changes that address root causes of selected outcomes, both positive and negative.

CAR

SP 2.1 IMPLEMENT ACTION PROPOSALS

Implement selected action proposals developed in causal analysis.

Action proposals describe tasks necessary to address root causes of analyzed outcomes to prevent or reduce the occurrence or recurrence of negative outcomes, or incorporate realized successes. Action plans are developed and implemented for selected action proposals. Only changes that prove to be of value should be considered for broad implementation.

Example Work Products

1. Action proposals selected for implementation
2. Action plans

Example Supplier Deliverables

1. Improvement proposals

Subpractices

1. Analyze action proposals and determine their priorities.

> Criteria for prioritizing action proposals include the following:
> - Implications of not addressing the outcome
> - Cost to implement process improvements to address the outcome
> - Expected impact on quality

> Process performance models can be used to help identify interactions among multiple action proposals.

2. Select action proposals to be implemented.

> *Refer to the Decision Analysis and Resolution process area for more information about analyzing possible decisions using a formal evaluation process that evaluates identified alternatives against established criteria.*

3. Create action plans for implementing the selected action proposals.

> Examples of information provided in an action plan include the following:
> - Person responsible for implementation
> - Detailed description of the improvement
> - Description of the affected areas
> - People who are to be kept informed of status
> - Schedule
> - Cost expended
> - Next date that status will be reviewed
> - Rationale for key decisions
> - Description of implementation actions
> - Time and cost required to identify the defect or problem and to correct it
> - Estimated cost of not fixing the problem

4. Implement action plans.

   To implement action plans, the following tasks should be performed:

   - Make assignments.
   - Coordinate the people doing the work.
   - Review the results.
   - Track action items to closure.

   Experiments may be conducted for particularly complex changes.

X-REF

For more information on designing experiments to understand the impact of certain changes, consult good references on Six Sigma and experimental design.

HINT

When a resolution has more general applicability, don't document it in a "lessons learned" document; instead, document it in an improvement proposal.

X-REF

For more information about improvement proposals, see OPF SP 2.4 and OPM SP 2.1.

HINT

Use the measures associated with a process or subprocess (perhaps supplemented by other measures) to evaluate the effect of changes.

> Examples of experiments include the following:
> - Using a temporarily modified process
> - Using a new tool

   Actions may be assigned to members of the causal analysis team, members of the project team, or other members of the organization.

5. Look for similar causes that may exist in other processes and work products and take action as appropriate.

SP 2.2 EVALUATE THE EFFECT OF IMPLEMENTED ACTIONS

Evaluate the effect of implemented actions on process performance.

Refer to the Quantitative Project Management process area for more information about selecting measures and analytic techniques.

Once the changed process is deployed across the project, the effect of changes is evaluated to verify that the process change has improved process performance.

Example Work Products

1. Analysis of process performance and change in process performance

Example Supplier Deliverables

1. Base and derived supplier measurements

Subpractices

1. Measure and analyze the change in process performance of the project's affected processes or subprocesses.

   This subpractice determines whether the selected change has positively influenced process performance and by how much.

   Statistical and other quantitative techniques (e.g., hypothesis testing) can be used to compare the before and after baselines to assess the statistical significance of the change.

2. Determine the impact of the change on achieving the project's quality and process performance objectives.

   This subpractice determines whether the selected change has positively influenced the ability of the project to meet its quality and process performance objectives by understanding how changes in the process performance data have affected the objectives. Process performance models can aid in the evaluation through prediction of impacts and return on investment.

3. Determine and document appropriate actions if the process or subprocess improvements did not result in expected project benefits.

SP 2.3 RECORD CAUSAL ANALYSIS DATA

Record causal analysis and resolution data for use across projects and the organization.

Example Work Products

1. Causal analysis and resolution records
2. Organizational improvement proposals

Subpractices

1. Record causal analysis data and make the data available so that other projects can make appropriate process changes and achieve similar results.

   Record the following:

   - Data on outcomes that were analyzed
   - Rationale for decisions
   - Action proposals from causal analysis meetings

HINT

Collect data to determine whether you are improving project performance relative to your objectives, to identify whether you have prevented selected problems from reoccurring (or have enabled conditions conducive to superior performance to recur), and to provide sufficient context for organizational evaluation of improvement proposals for possible deployment across the organization (OPM SP 2.1 and 2.2).

- Action plans resulting from action proposals
- Cost of analysis and resolution activities
- Measures of changes to the process performance of the defined process resulting from resolutions

2. Submit process improvement proposals for the organization when the implemented actions are effective for the project as appropriate. When improvements are judged to be effective, the information can be submitted to the organizational level for potential inclusion in the organizational processes.

Refer to the Organizational Performance Management process area for more information about selecting improvements.

CONFIGURATION MANAGEMENT
A Support Process Area at Maturity Level 2

Purpose

The purpose of Configuration Management (CM) is to establish and maintain the integrity of work products using configuration identification, configuration control, configuration status accounting, and configuration audits.

Introductory Notes

The Configuration Management process area involves the following activities:

- Identifying the configuration of selected work products that compose baselines at given points in time
- Controlling changes to configuration items
- Building or providing specifications to build work products from the configuration management system
- Maintaining the integrity of baselines
- Providing accurate status and current configuration data to developers, end users, and customers

The work products placed under configuration management include the products that are delivered to the customer, designated internal work products, acquired products, tools, and other items used in creating and describing these work products. (See the definition of "configuration management" in the glossary.)

Acquired products may need to be placed under configuration management by both the supplier and the acquirer. Provisions for conducting configuration management should be established in supplier agreements. Methods to ensure that data are complete and consistent should be established and maintained.

CM

257

The configuration management approach depends on acquisition factors such as acquisition approach, number of suppliers, design responsibility, support concept, and associated costs and risks. In any case, configuration management involves interaction between the acquirer and supplier.

Planning for managing configuration items, including during the transition to operations and support, is addressed as part of project planning and supplier agreement development to avoid unexpected costs for both the acquirer and supplier. Project plans and supplier agreements should make provisions for managing configuration items in and across project teams and the infrastructure required to manage configuration items among the acquirer, supplier, operational users, and other relevant stakeholders.

> For example, there are shared responsibilities between the acquirer and supplier for the technical solution. The acquirer maintains configuration control of the contractual requirements and the supplier performs configuration management for the technical solution (e.g., establish and maintain the product baseline).
>
> In this example, the acquirer retains the authority and responsibility for approving design changes that affect the product's ability to meet contractual requirements. The supplier manages other design changes. The acquirer maintains the right to access configuration data at any level required to implement planned or potential design changes and support options. Configuration management of legacy systems should be addressed on a case-by-case basis as design changes are contemplated.

> Examples of work products that can be placed under configuration management include the following:
> - Hardware and equipment
> - Acquisition strategies
> - Solicitation packages
> - Supplier agreements
> - Supplier deliverables
> - Plans
> - Process descriptions
> - Requirements
> - Tool configurations

Configuration management of work products can be performed at several levels of granularity. Configuration items can be decomposed into configuration components and configuration units. Only the term "configuration item" is used in this process area. Therefore, in these practices, "configuration item" may be interpreted as "configuration component" or "configuration unit" as appropriate. (See the definition of "configuration item" in the glossary.)

Baselines provide a stable basis for the continuing evolution of configuration items.

> An example of an acquirer's baseline is a collection of acquirer work products such as contractual requirements and acceptance criteria that are related to the product baseline managed by the supplier.

Baselines are added to the configuration management system as they are developed. Changes to baselines and the release of work products built from the configuration management system are systematically controlled and monitored via the configuration control, change management, and configuration auditing functions of configuration management.

This process area applies not only to configuration management on projects but also to configuration management of organizational work products such as standards, procedures, reuse libraries, and other shared supporting assets.

Configuration management is focused on the rigorous control of the managerial and technical aspects of work products, including the delivered product or service.

This process area covers the practices for performing the configuration management function and is applicable to all work products that are placed under configuration management.

For acquisition of product lines and standard services, configuration management can involve additional considerations due to the sharing of core assets across acquisitions (and perhaps organizations) and across multiple versions of core assets. In such a case, the configuration management approach and specific responsibilities should be specified in supplier and customer agreements. (See the definition of "product line" in the glossary.)

Related Process Areas

Refer to the Agreement Management process area for more information about accepting the acquired product.

Refer to the Project Monitoring and Control process area for more information about monitoring the project against the plan and managing corrective action to closure.

TIP

Many acquirer-developed work products, such as plans, requirements, and interfaces, are critical to guiding stakeholders through the life of the project. These work products must be maintained to reflect the current project scope and objectives.

CM

HINT

Make explicit decisions about who has the authority in the project to approve baseline changes; document these decisions in project plans.

TIP

Any work product whose integrity should be ensured over a period of time might benefit from CM. For example, multiple acquisition programs may be ongoing and have schedule dependencies with one another. Establishing a cross-program CM approach may facilitate coordination efforts.

Refer to the Project Planning process area for more information about developing a project plan.

Specific Goal and Practice Summary

SG 1 Establish Baselines
    SP 1.1   Identify Configuration Items
    SP 1.2   Establish a Configuration Management System
    SP 1.3   Create or Release Baselines
SG 2 Track and Control Changes
    SP 2.1   Track Change Requests
    SP 2.2   Control Configuration Items
SG 3 Establish Integrity
    SP 3.1   Establish Configuration Management Records
    SP 3.2   Perform Configuration Audits

Specific Practices by Goal

SG 1   ESTABLISH BASELINES

Baselines of identified work products are established.

Specific practices to establish baselines are covered by this specific goal. The specific practices under the Track and Control Changes specific goal serve to maintain the baselines. The specific practices of the Establish Integrity specific goal document and audit the integrity of the baselines.

SP 1.1   IDENTIFY CONFIGURATION ITEMS

Identify configuration items, components, and related work products to be placed under configuration management.

Configuration identification is the selection and specification of the following:

- Products delivered to the customer
- Designated internal work products
- Acquired products
- Tools and other capital assets of the project's work environment
- Other items used in creating and describing these work products

Configuration items can include hardware, equipment, and tangible assets as well as software and documentation. Documentation can include requirements specifications and interface documents. Other documents that serve to identify the configuration of the product or service, such as test results, may also be included.

A "configuration item" is an entity designated for configuration management, which may consist of multiple related work products that form a baseline. This logical grouping provides ease of identification and controlled access. The selection of work products for configuration management should be based on criteria established during planning.

Configuration items can vary widely in complexity, size, and type, from an aircraft to commercial off-the-shelf software to a test meter or a project plan. Any item required for product support and designated for separate procurement is a configuration item. Acquirer work products provided to suppliers such as solicitation packages and technical standards are typically designated as configuration items.

> **HINT**
>
> When developing your project plan, consider configuration items and work products you receive from customers, those you develop internally, and those delivered by suppliers.

Example Work Products

1. Identified configuration items

Subpractices

1. Select configuration items and work products that compose them based on documented criteria.

> **HINT**
>
> Use criteria when selecting configuration items to ensure that the selection process is consistent and thorough.

Example criteria for selecting configuration items at the appropriate work product level include the following:
- Work products that can be used by two or more groups
- Work products that are expected to change over time either because of errors or changes in requirements
- Work products that are dependent on each other (i.e., a change in one mandates a change in the others)
- Work products critical to project success

Examples of acquirer work products and supplier deliverables that may be part of a configuration item include the following:
- Acceptance criteria
- Supplier project progress and performance reports
- Supplier test results
- Process descriptions
- Requirements

> **HINT**
>
> Consider selecting configuration management tools that are compatible with the tools used by your suppliers and other stakeholders to ensure that unique identifiers are consistent.

2. Assign unique identifiers to configuration items.
3. Specify the important characteristics of each configuration item.

> Example characteristics of configuration items include author, document or file type, programming language for software code files, and the purpose the configuration item serves.

4. Specify when each configuration item is placed under configuration management.

> Example criteria for determining when to place work products under configuration management include the following:
> • When the acquirer work product is ready for review and approval
> • Stage of the project lifecycle
> • Degree of control desired on the work product
> • Cost and schedule limitations
> • Stakeholder requirements

5. Identify the owner responsible for each configuration item.
6. Specify relationships among configuration items.
   Incorporating the types of relationships (e.g., parent-child, dependency) that exist among configuration items into the configuration management structure (e.g., configuration management database) assists in managing the effects and impacts of changes.

SP 1.2 ESTABLISH A CONFIGURATION MANAGEMENT SYSTEM

Establish and maintain a configuration management and change management system for controlling work products.

A configuration management system includes the storage media, procedures, and tools for accessing the system. A configuration management system can consist of multiple subsystems with different implementations that are appropriate for each configuration management environment.

A change management system includes the storage media, procedures, and tools for recording and accessing change requests.

The acquirer considers how configuration items are shared between the acquirer and supplier as well as among relevant stakeholders. If the use of an acquirer's configuration management system is extended to a supplier, the acquirer should exercise security and access control procedures. In many cases, leaving acquired configuration items in the physical possession of the supplier and having access to supplier deliverables is an alternative solution. The supplier agreement specifies appropriate acquirer rights to supplier deliverables, in addition to requirements for delivery or access. Supplier work products, whenever they are delivered to the acquirer, are presented in accordance with accepted standards to ensure usability by the acquirer.

Example Work Products

1. Configuration management system with controlled work products
2. Configuration management system access control procedures
3. Change request database

Subpractices

1. Establish a mechanism to manage multiple levels of control.

    The level of control is typically selected based on project objectives, risk, and resources. Control levels can vary in relation to the project lifecycle, type of system under development, and specific project requirements.

    Example levels of control include the following:

    - Uncontrolled: Anyone can make changes.
    - Work-in-progress: Authors control changes.
    - Released: A designated authority authorizes and controls changes and relevant stakeholders are notified when changes are made.

    Levels of control can range from informal control that simply tracks changes made when configuration items are being developed by the acquirer or when supplier work products are delivered or made accessible to the acquirer, to formal configuration control using baselines that can only be changed as part of a formal configuration management process.

2. Provide access control to ensure authorized access to the configuration management system.
3. Store and retrieve configuration items in a configuration management system.
4. Share and transfer configuration items between control levels in the configuration management system.
5. Store and recover archived versions of configuration items.
6. Store, update, and retrieve configuration management records.
7. Create configuration management reports from the configuration management system.
8. Preserve the contents of the configuration management system.

HINT

When dealing with sensitive information during the acquisition process, you must consider taking additional steps to ensure the integrity of the acquisition process and its products.

CM

TIP

Not all configuration items require the same level of control. Some may require more control as they move through the project lifecycle.

TIP

A formal CM process is typically change-request based and requires extensive tracking, review, and approval of all changes.

TIP

Version control is an important part of CM. A variety of ways may be used to identify versions; the standard approach is to use sequential numbering.

HINT

Review the content of reports from the CM system regularly to ensure the integrity of configuration items and work products.

> Examples of preservation functions of the configuration management system include the following:
> - Backup and restoration of configuration management files
> - Archive of configuration management files
> - Recovery from configuration management errors

9. Revise the configuration management structure as necessary.

SP 1.3 CREATE OR RELEASE BASELINES

Create or release baselines for internal use and for delivery to the customer.

A baseline is represented by the assignment of an identifier to a configuration item or a collection of configuration items and associated entities at a distinct point in time. As a product or service evolves, multiple baselines can be used to control development and testing. (See the definition of "baseline" in the glossary.)

Hardware products as well as software and documentation should also be included in baselines for infrastructure related configurations (e.g., software, hardware) and in preparation for system tests that include interfacing hardware and software.

The acquirer reviews and approves the release of product baselines created by the supplier. The acquirer creates baselines for acquirer work products that describe the project, requirements, funding, schedule, and project performance measures and makes a commitment to manage the project to those baselines.

Example Work Products

1. Baselines
2. Description of baselines

Example Supplier Deliverables

1. Product baselines
2. Description of product baselines

Subpractices

1. Obtain authorization from the CCB before creating or releasing baselines of configuration items.
2. Create or release baselines only from configuration items in the configuration management system.
3. Document the set of configuration items that are contained in a baseline.
4. Make the current set of baselines readily available.

SG 2 TRACK AND CONTROL CHANGES

Changes to the work products under configuration management are tracked and controlled.

The specific practices under this specific goal serve to maintain baselines after they are established by specific practices under the Establish Baselines specific goal.

SP 2.1 TRACK CHANGE REQUESTS

Track change requests for configuration items.

Change requests address not only new or changed requirements but also failures and defects in work products.

Change requests can be initiated either by the acquirer or supplier. Changes that affect acquirer work products and supplier deliverables as defined in the supplier agreement are handled through the acquirer's configuration management process.

Change requests are analyzed to determine the impact that the change will have on the work product, related work products, the budget, and the schedule.

Example Work Products

1. Change requests

Example Supplier Deliverables

1. Change requests

Subpractices

1. Initiate and record change requests in the change request database.
2. Analyze the impact of changes and fixes proposed in change requests.

    Changes are evaluated through activities that ensure that they are consistent with all technical and project requirements.

    Changes are evaluated for their impact beyond immediate project or contract requirements. Changes to an item used in multiple products can resolve an immediate issue while causing a problem in other applications.

    The acquirer analyzes the impact that submitted change requests can have on supplier agreements.

    Refer to the Solicitation and Supplier Agreement Development process area for more information about establishing the supplier agreement.

    Changes are evaluated for their impact on release plans.

TIP

Depending on the types of work products and levels of control required, changes may be tracked and controlled by individuals through management forums or through formal CCBs.

TIP

Change requests must be sufficiently detailed to enable their analysis and disposition. Using mechanisms that require certain types of information to be documented when gathering change requests can save time and ensure adequate information.

TIP

The acquirer may need to track change requests to supplier products that are not within the scope of the supplier's contract.

TIP

A database provides a flexible environment for storing and tracking change requests.

CM

3. Categorize and prioritize change requests.

Emergency requests are identified and referred to an emergency authority if appropriate.

Changes are allocated to future baselines.

4. Review change requests to be addressed in the next baseline with relevant stakeholders and get their agreement.

Conduct the change request review with appropriate participants. Record the disposition of each change request and the rationale for the decision, including success criteria, a brief action plan if appropriate, and needs met or unmet by the change. Perform the actions required in the disposition and report results to relevant stakeholders.

5. Track the status of change requests to closure.

Change requests brought into the system should be handled in an efficient and timely manner. Once a change request has been processed, it is critical to close the request with the appropriate approved action as soon as it is practical. Actions left open result in larger than necessary status lists, which in turn result in added costs and confusion.

SP 2.2 CONTROL CONFIGURATION ITEMS

Control changes to configuration items.

Control is maintained over the configuration of the work product baseline. This control includes tracking the configuration of each configuration item, approving a new configuration if necessary, and updating the baseline.

The acquirer decides which configuration items require version control, or more stringent levels of configuration control, and establishes mechanisms to ensure configuration items are controlled. Although the supplier can manage configuration items on the acquirer's behalf, the acquirer is responsible for approval and control of changes to these configuration items.

Example Work Products

1. Revision history of configuration items
2. Archives of baselines

Subpractices

1. Control changes to configuration items throughout the life of the product or service.
2. Obtain appropriate authorization before changed configuration items are entered into the configuration management system.

> For example, authorization can come from the CCB, the project or acquisition manager, or the customer.

3. Check in and check out configuration items in the configuration management system for incorporation of changes in a manner that maintains the correctness and integrity of configuration items.

> Examples of check-in and check-out steps include the following:
> - Confirming that the revisions are authorized
> - Updating the configuration items
> - Archiving the replaced baseline and retrieving the new baseline
> - Commenting on the changes made to the item
> - Tying changes to related work products such as requirements and acceptance criteria

CM

4. Perform reviews to ensure that changes have not caused unintended effects on the baselines (e.g., ensure that changes have not compromised the safety or security of the system).

5. Record changes to configuration items and reasons for changes as appropriate.

   If a proposed change to the work product is accepted, a schedule is identified for incorporating the change into the work product and other affected areas.

   Configuration control mechanisms can be tailored to categories of changes. For example, the approval considerations could be less stringent for component changes that do not affect other components. Changed configuration items are released after review and approval of configuration changes. Changes are not official until they are released.

SG 3   ESTABLISH INTEGRITY

Integrity of baselines is established and maintained.

The integrity of baselines, established by processes associated with the Establish Baselines specific goal, and maintained by processes associated with the Track and Control Changes specific goal, is addressed by the specific practices under this specific goal.

SP 3.1   ESTABLISH CONFIGURATION MANAGEMENT RECORDS

Establish and maintain records describing configuration items.

Example Work Products

1. Revision history of configuration items
2. Change log

3. Change request records
4. Status of configuration items
5. Differences between baselines

Example Supplier Deliverables

1. Revision history of product and supplier deliverables defined in the supplier agreement

Subpractices

1. Record configuration management actions in sufficient detail so the content and status of each configuration item is known and previous versions can be recovered.
2. Ensure that relevant stakeholders have access to and knowledge of the configuration status of configuration items.

> Examples of activities for communicating configuration status include the following:
> • Providing access permissions to authorized end users
> • Making baseline copies readily available to authorized end users
> • Automatically alerting relevant stakeholders when items are checked in or out or changed, or of decisions made regarding change requests

3. Specify the latest version of baselines.
4. Identify the version of configuration items that constitute a particular baseline.
5. Describe differences between successive baselines.
6. Revise the status and history (i.e., changes, other actions) of each configuration item as necessary.

SP 3.2 *PERFORM CONFIGURATION AUDITS*

Perform configuration audits to maintain the integrity of configuration baselines.

Configuration audits confirm that the resulting baselines and documentation conform to a specified standard or requirement. Configuration item related records can exist in multiple databases or configuration management systems. In such instances, configuration audits should extend to these other databases as appropriate to ensure accuracy, consistency, and completeness of configuration item information. (See the definition of "configuration audit" in the glossary.)

HINT

When describing the differences between baselines, be detailed enough so that users of the baselines can differentiate them easily.

Examples of audit types include the following:

- Functional configuration audits (FCAs): Audits conducted to verify that the development of a configuration item has been completed satisfactorily, that the item has achieved the functional and quality attribute characteristics specified in the functional or allocated baseline, and that its operational and support documents are complete and satisfactory.
- Physical configuration audits (PCAs): Audits conducted to verify that a configuration item, as built, conforms to the technical documentation that defines and describes it.
- Configuration management audits: Audits conducted to confirm that configuration management records and configuration items are complete, consistent, and accurate.

HINT

Consider conducting audits prior to the handoff of work products among the customer, acquirer, supplier, and other stakeholders.

Example Work Products

1. Configuration audit results
2. Action items

Example Supplier Deliverables

1. Supplier configuration audit results

Subpractices

1. Assess the integrity of baselines.
2. Confirm that configuration management records correctly identify configuration items.
3. Review the structure and integrity of items in the configuration management system.
4. Confirm the completeness, correctness, and consistency of items in the configuration management system.

   Completeness, correctness, and consistency of the configuration management system's content are based on requirements as stated in the plan and the disposition of approved change requests.
5. Confirm compliance with applicable configuration management standards and procedures.
6. Track action items from the audit to closure.

TIP

Integrity includes both accuracy and completeness.

TIP

An audit is effective only when all action items from the audit are addressed.

CM

DECISION ANALYSIS AND RESOLUTION
A Support Process Area at Maturity Level 3

Purpose

The purpose of Decision Analysis and Resolution (DAR) is to analyze possible decisions using a formal evaluation process that evaluates identified alternatives against established criteria.

TIP

DAR provides organizations with a criteria-based approach to making important decisions objectively.

Introductory Notes

The Decision Analysis and Resolution process area involves establishing guidelines to determine which issues should be subject to a formal evaluation process and applying formal evaluation processes to these issues.

A formal evaluation process is a structured approach to evaluating alternative solutions against established criteria to determine a recommended solution.

A formal evaluation process involves the following actions:

- Establishing the criteria for evaluating alternatives
- Identifying alternative solutions
- Selecting methods for evaluating alternatives
- Evaluating alternative solutions using established criteria and methods
- Selecting recommended solutions from alternatives based on evaluation criteria

Rather than using the phrase "alternative solutions to address issues" each time, in this process area, one of two shorter phrases are used: "alternative solutions" or "alternatives."

A repeatable criteria based decision-making process is especially important, both for making critical decisions that define and guide the acquisition process and later for critical decisions made with the selected supplier. The establishment of a formal process for decision

HINT

Many key acquisition decisions are made early in a project's lifecycle and have a major impact on project outcomes. Start by using formal evaluation methods on these key decisions before applying them to selected day-to-day decisions. An effective source selection process and well-thought-out lifecycle milestone decisions are results of classic DAR activities.

TIP

DAR takes the blame out of decision making. A bad decision is made when all of the necessary information that might influence the decision was not considered and relevant stakeholders were not consulted.

DAR

HINT

Maintain the rationale for key decisions that drive the acquisition strategy to make early project thinking available to team members and stakeholders who join the project later.

X-REF

For information on how to create an acquisition strategy, see "Techniques for Developing an Acquisition Strategy by Profiling Software Risks" at www.sei.cmu.edu/library/abstracts/reports/06tr002.cfm.

TIP

Examples of nontechnical issues include staffing profiles for the acquisition project team over time and the mix of skills required to ensure project success.

TIP

Tools such as the Analytic Hierarchy Process (AHP), Quality Function Deployment (QFD), Pugh Method, Delphi Method, prioritization matrices, cause-and-effect diagrams, decision trees, weighted-criteria spreadsheets, and simulations can be used to incorporate weights in decision making.

making provides the acquirer with documentation of decision rationale. Such documentation allows criteria for critical decisions to be revisited when changes or technology insertion decisions that affect requirements or other critical project parameters are considered. A formal process also supports the communication of decisions between the acquirer and supplier.

A formal evaluation process reduces the subjective nature of a decision and provides a higher probability of selecting a solution that meets multiple demands of relevant stakeholders.

While the primary application of this process area is to technical concerns, formal evaluation processes can be applied to many nontechnical issues, particularly when a project is being planned. Issues that have multiple alternative solutions and evaluation criteria lend themselves to a formal evaluation process.

Guidelines are created for deciding when to use formal evaluation processes to address unplanned issues. Guidelines often suggest using formal evaluation processes when issues are associated with medium-to-high-impact risks or when issues affect the ability to achieve project objectives.

Defining an issue well helps to define the scope of alternatives to be considered. The right scope (i.e., not too broad, not too narrow) will aid in making an appropriate decision for resolving the defined issue.

Formal evaluation processes can vary in formality, type of criteria, and methods employed. Less formal decisions can be analyzed in a few hours, use few criteria (e.g., effectiveness, cost to implement), and result in a one- or two-page report. More formal decisions can require separate plans, months of effort, meetings to develop and approve criteria, simulations, prototypes, piloting, and extensive documentation.

Both numeric and non-numeric criteria can be used in a formal evaluation process. Numeric criteria use weights to reflect the relative importance of criteria. Non-numeric criteria use a subjective ranking scale (e.g., high, medium, low). More formal decisions can require a full trade study.

A formal evaluation process identifies and evaluates alternative solutions. The eventual selection of a solution can involve iterative activities of identification and evaluation. Portions of identified alternatives can be combined, emerging technologies can change alternatives, and the business situation of suppliers can change during the evaluation period.

A recommended alternative is accompanied by documentation of selected methods, criteria, alternatives, and rationale for the recommendation. The documentation is distributed to relevant stakeholders; it provides a record of the formal evaluation process and rationale, which are useful to other projects that encounter a similar issue.

While some of the decisions made throughout the life of the project involve the use of a formal evaluation process, others do not. As mentioned earlier, guidelines should be established to determine which issues should be subject to a formal evaluation process.

Related Process Areas

Refer to the Integrated Project Management process area for more information about establishing the project's defined process.

Refer to the Risk Management process area for more information about identifying and analyzing risks and mitigating risks.

DAR

Specific Goal and Practice Summary

SG 1 Evaluate Alternatives
- SP 1.1 Establish Guidelines for Decision Analysis
- SP 1.2 Establish Evaluation Criteria
- SP 1.3 Identify Alternative Solutions
- SP 1.4 Select Evaluation Methods
- SP 1.5 Evaluate Alternative Solutions
- SP 1.6 Select Solutions

Specific Practices by Goal

SG 1   EVALUATE ALTERNATIVES

Decisions are based on an evaluation of alternatives using established criteria.

Issues requiring a formal evaluation process can be identified at any time. The objective should be to identify issues as early as possible to maximize the time available to resolve them.

SP 1.1 ESTABLISH GUIDELINES FOR DECISION ANALYSIS

Establish and maintain guidelines to determine which issues are subject to a formal evaluation process.

Not every decision is significant enough to require a formal evaluation process. The choice between the trivial and the truly important is unclear without explicit guidance. Whether a decision is significant or not is dependent on the project and circumstances and is determined by established guidelines.

> Typical guidelines for determining when to require a formal evaluation process include the following:
> - When the decision will have a significant adverse effect on cost, quality, resources, or schedule
> - When legal or supplier agreement issues must be resolved
> - When challenging or competing quality attribute requirements could significantly affect the success of the acquisition strategy or the acquirer project
> - When a decision is directly related to issues that have medium-to-high-impact risk
> - When a decision is related to changing work products under configuration management
> - When a decision would cause schedule delays over a certain percentage or amount of time
> - When a decision affects the ability of the project to achieve its objectives
> - When the costs of the formal evaluation process are reasonable when compared to the decision's impact
> - When a legal obligation exists during a solicitation

Refer to the Risk Management process area for more information about evaluating, categorizing, and prioritizing risks.

> Examples of activities for which you may use a formal evaluation process include the following:
> - Making decisions to trade off cost, schedule, and performance requirements during an acquisition
> - Selecting, terminating, or renewing suppliers
> - Selecting training for project staff
> - Selecting a testing environment to be used for product validation
> - Determining the items to be selected for reuse in related projects
> - Selecting an approach for ongoing support (e.g., disaster recovery, service levels)

Example Work Products

1. Guidelines for when to apply a formal evaluation process

Subpractices

1. Establish guidelines for when to use a formal evaluation process.
2. Incorporate the use of guidelines into the defined process as appropriate.

> Refer to the Integrated Project Management process area for more information about establishing the project's defined process.

SP 1.2 ESTABLISH EVALUATION CRITERIA

Establish and maintain criteria for evaluating alternatives and the relative ranking of these criteria.

Evaluation criteria provide the basis for evaluating alternative solutions. Criteria are ranked so that the highest ranked criteria exert the most influence on the evaluation.

This process area is referenced by many other process areas in the model, and many contexts in which a formal evaluation process can be used. Therefore, in some situations you may find that criteria have already been defined as part of another process. This specific practice does not suggest that a second development of criteria be conducted.

A well-defined statement of the issue to be addressed and the decision to be made focuses the analysis to be performed. Such a statement also aids in defining evaluation criteria that minimize the possibility that decisions will be second guessed or that the reason for making the decision will be forgotten. Decisions based on criteria that are explicitly defined and established remove barriers to stakeholder buy-in.

Example Work Products

1. Documented evaluation criteria
2. Rankings of criteria importance

Subpractices

1. Define the criteria for evaluating alternative solutions.
   Criteria should be traceable to requirements, scenarios, business case assumptions, business objectives, or other documented sources.

> Types of criteria to consider include the following:
> - Technology limitations
> - Environmental impact
> - Risks
> - Business value
> - Impact on priorities
> - Total ownership and lifecycle costs

2. Define the range and scale for ranking the evaluation criteria.

   Scales of relative importance for evaluation criteria can be established with non-numeric values or with formulas that relate the evaluation parameter to a numeric weight.

3. Rank the criteria.

   The criteria are ranked according to the defined range and scale to reflect the needs, objectives, and priorities of the relevant stakeholders.

4. Assess the criteria and their relative importance.

5. Evolve the evaluation criteria to improve their validity.

6. Document the rationale for the selection and rejection of evaluation criteria.

   Documentation of selection criteria and rationale may be needed to justify solutions or for future reference and use.

SP 1.3 IDENTIFY ALTERNATIVE SOLUTIONS

Identify alternative solutions to address issues.

A wider range of alternatives can surface by soliciting as many stakeholders as practical for input. Input from stakeholders with diverse skills and backgrounds can help teams identify and address assumptions, constraints, and biases. Brainstorming sessions can stimulate innovative alternatives through rapid interaction and feedback.

Sufficient candidate solutions may not be furnished for analysis. As the analysis proceeds, other alternatives should be added to the list of potential candidate solutions. The generation and consideration of multiple alternatives early in a decision analysis and resolution process increases the likelihood that an acceptable decision will be made and that consequences of the decision will be understood.

Example Work Products

1. Identified alternatives

Example Supplier Deliverables

1. Supplier identified alternatives, if any

Subpractices

1. Perform a literature search.

   A literature search can uncover what others have done both inside and outside the organization. Such a search can provide a deeper understanding of the problem, alternatives to consider, barriers to implementation, existing trade studies, and lessons learned from similar decisions.

> **HINT**
>
> When you are evaluating competing designs proposed by your suppliers, make sure you solicit alternatives that may be more innovative and less obvious. Consider commissioning a special study by a team with a lower stake in the selection outcome to help ensure that a wide range of alternatives are identified.

2. Identify alternatives for consideration in addition to the alternatives that may be provided with the issue.

> Evaluation criteria are an effective starting point for identifying alternatives. Evaluation criteria identify priorities of relevant stakeholders and the importance of technical, logistical, or other challenges.

> Combining key attributes of existing alternatives can generate additional and sometimes stronger alternatives.

> Solicit alternatives from relevant stakeholders. Brainstorming sessions, interviews, and working groups can be used effectively to uncover alternatives.

3. Document proposed alternatives.

SP 1.4 SELECT EVALUATION METHODS

Select evaluation methods.

Methods for evaluating alternative solutions against established criteria can range from simulations to the use of probabilistic models and decision theory. These methods should be carefully selected. The level of detail of a method should be commensurate with cost, schedule, performance, and risk impacts.

> **HINT**
>
> Make sure the method chosen is appropriate for the decision. A complex and time-consuming approach may be overkill for a simple binary decision.

While many problems may require only one evaluation method, some problems may require multiple methods. For example, simulations may augment a trade study to determine which design alternative best meets a given criterion.

Suppliers competing to develop a technical solution for the acquirer may be directly evaluated in a final competition that involves a performance or functional demonstration of proposed solutions.

Example Work Products

1. Selected evaluation methods

Subpractices

1. Select methods based on the purpose for analyzing a decision and on the availability of the information used to support the method.

Typical evaluation methods include the following:
- Benchmarking studies
- Cost studies
- Business opportunity studies
- Surveys
- Extrapolations based on field experience and prototypes
- User review and comment
- Judgment provided by an expert or group of experts (e.g., Delphi method)

---

2. Select evaluation methods based on their ability to focus on the issues at hand without being overly influenced by side issues.

   Results of simulations can be skewed by random activities in the solution that are not directly related to the issues at hand.

3. Determine the measures needed to support the evaluation method.

   Consider the impact on cost, schedule, performance, and risks.

SP 1.5 EVALUATE ALTERNATIVE SOLUTIONS

Evaluate alternative solutions using established criteria and methods.

Evaluating alternative solutions involves analysis, discussion, and review. Iterative cycles of analysis are sometimes necessary. Supporting analyses, experimentation, prototyping, piloting, or simulations may be needed to substantiate scoring and conclusions.

Often, the relative importance of criteria is imprecise and the total effect on a solution is not apparent until after the analysis is performed. In cases where the resulting scores differ by relatively small amounts, the best selection among alternative solutions may not be clear. Challenges to criteria and assumptions should be encouraged.

Example Work Products

1. Evaluation results

Subpractices

1. Evaluate proposed alternative solutions using the established evaluation criteria and selected methods.

2. Evaluate assumptions related to the evaluation criteria and the evidence that supports the assumptions.

3. Evaluate whether uncertainty in the values for alternative solutions affects the evaluation and address these uncertainties as appropriate.

   For instance, if the score varies between two values, is the difference significant enough to make a difference in the final solution set? Does the variation in score represent a high-impact risk? To address these concerns, simulations may be run, further studies may be performed, or evaluation criteria may be modified, among other things.

4. Perform simulations, modeling, prototypes, and pilots as necessary to exercise the evaluation criteria, methods, and alternative solutions.

   Untested criteria, their relative importance, and supporting data or functions can cause the validity of solutions to be questioned. Criteria and their relative priorities and scales can be tested with trial runs against a set of alternatives. These trial runs of a select set of criteria

---

TIP

Evaluation criteria for a competitive source selection should be part of the solicitation package so that all stakeholders understand the relative importance of solicitation requirements.

X-REF

Refer to SP 1.2 of SSAD for more information on establishing evaluation criteria for use in selecting suppliers.

allow for the evaluation of the cumulative impact of criteria on a solution. If trials reveal problems, different criteria or alternatives might be considered to avoid biases.

5. Consider new alternative solutions, criteria, or methods if proposed alternatives do not test well; repeat evaluations until alternatives do test well.

   Document the rationale for the addition of new alternatives or methods and changes to criteria, as well as the results of interim evaluations. Determine the scores for each alternative based on criteria evaluations and scoring methods previously determined.

6. Document the results of the evaluation.

   Document the rationale for the addition of new alternatives or methods and changes to criteria, as well as the results of interim evaluations.

SP 1.6 SELECT SOLUTIONS

Select solutions from alternatives based on evaluation criteria.

Selecting solutions involves weighing results from the evaluation of alternatives. Risks associated with the implementation of solutions should be assessed.

Example Work Products

1. Recommended solutions to address significant issues

Subpractices

1. Assess the risks associated with implementing the recommended solution.

   Refer to the Risk Management process area for more information about identifying and analyzing risks and mitigating risks.

   Decisions must often be made with incomplete information. There can be substantial risk associated with the decision because of having incomplete information.

   When decisions must be made according to a specific schedule, time and resources may not be available for gathering complete information. Consequently, risky decisions made with incomplete information can require re-analysis later. Identified risks should be monitored.

2. Document and communicate to relevant stakeholders the results and rationale for the recommended solution.

   It is important to record both why a solution is selected and why another solution was rejected.

TIP

Selecting a solution always requires humans to make decisions. These decisions are informed by the results of evaluations. Other considerations (such as risk or external constraints) may cause a project to select solutions that score lower based on the chosen criteria. If this is the case, the rationale for the selection becomes even more critical to maintain.

DAR

INTEGRATED PROJECT MANAGEMENT
A Project Management Process Area at Maturity Level 3

Purpose

The purpose of Integrated Project Management (IPM) is to establish and manage the project and the involvement of relevant stakeholders according to an integrated and defined process that is tailored from the organization's set of standard processes.

X-REF

IPM matures the project management activities described in PP and PMC so that they address the organizational requirements for projects described in OPF and OPD.

Introductory Notes

Integrated Project Management involves the following activities:

- Establishing the project's defined process at project startup by tailoring the organization's set of standard processes
- Managing the project using the project's defined process
- Establishing the work environment for the project based on the organization's work environment standards
- Establishing teams that are tasked to accomplish project objectives
- Using and contributing to organizational process assets
- Enabling relevant stakeholders' concerns to be identified, considered, and, when appropriate, addressed during the project
- Ensuring that relevant stakeholders (1) perform their tasks in a coordinated and timely manner; (2) address project requirements, plans, objectives, problems, and risks; (3) fulfill their commitments; and (4) identify, track, and resolve coordination issues

The integrated and defined process that is tailored from the organization's set of standard processes is called the project's defined process. (See the definition of "project" in the glossary.)

Managing the project's effort, cost, schedule, staffing, risks, and other factors is tied to the tasks of the project's defined process. The implementation and management of the project's defined process are typically described in the project plan. Certain activities may be covered

IPM

281

TIP

Using IPM to guide project management activities enables project plans to be consistent with project activities because both are derived from standard processes created by the organization. Further, plans tend to be more reliable and are developed more quickly, and new projects learn more quickly.

TIP

It is also easier to share resources (e.g., training and software tools) and to "load-balance" staff members across projects.

TIP

A proactive approach to integrating plans and coordinating development efforts with relevant stakeholders outside the project is a key activity. This is particularly important when multiple projects must work together to provide needed capabilities.

in other plans that affect the project, such as the quality assurance plan, risk management strategy, and the configuration management plan.

Since the defined process for each project is tailored from the organization's set of standard processes, variability among projects is typically reduced and projects can easily share process assets, data, and lessons learned.

> This process area also addresses the coordination of all activities associated with the project such as the following:
> - Development activities (e.g., requirements development, design, verification)
> - Service activities (e.g., delivery, help desk, operations, customer contact)
> - Acquisition activities (e.g., solicitation, agreement monitoring, transition to operations)
> - Support activities (e.g., configuration management, documentation, marketing, training)

The working interfaces and interactions among relevant stakeholders internal and external to the project are planned and managed to ensure the quality and integrity of the overall endeavor. Relevant stakeholders participate as appropriate in defining the project's defined process and the project plan. Reviews and exchanges are regularly conducted with relevant stakeholders to ensure that coordination issues receive appropriate attention and everyone involved with the project is appropriately aware of status, plans, and activities. (See the definition of "relevant stakeholder" in the glossary.) In defining the project's defined process, formal interfaces are created as necessary to ensure that appropriate coordination and collaboration occurs.

The acquirer should involve and integrate all relevant acquisition, technical, support, and operational stakeholders. Depending on the scope and risk of the project, coordination efforts with the supplier can be significant.

Formal interfaces among relevant stakeholders take the form of memoranda of understanding, memoranda of agreement, contractual commitments, associated supplier agreements, and similar documents, depending on the nature of the interfaces and involved stakeholders.

This process area applies in any organizational structure, including projects that are structured as line organizations, matrix organizations, or teams. The terminology should be appropriately interpreted for the organizational structure in place.

Related Process Areas

Refer to the Agreement Management process area for more information about ensuring that the supplier and the acquirer perform according to the terms of the supplier agreement.

Refer to the Measurement and Analysis process area for more information about aligning measurement and analysis activities and providing measurement results.

Refer to the Organizational Process Definition process area for more information about establishing and maintaining a usable set of organizational process assets, work environment standards, and rules and guidelines for teams.

Refer to the Project Monitoring and Control process area for more information about monitoring the project against the plan.

Refer to the Project Planning process area for more information about developing a project plan.

Specific Goal and Practice Summary

SG 1 Use the Project's Defined Process
- SP 1.1   Establish the Project's Defined Process
- SP 1.2   Use Organizational Process Assets for Planning Project Activities
- SP 1.3   Establish the Project's Work Environment
- SP 1.4   Integrate Plans
- SP 1.5   Manage the Project Using Integrated Plans
- SP 1.6   Establish Teams
- SP 1.7   Contribute to Organizational Process Assets

SG 2 Coordinate and Collaborate with Relevant Stakeholders
- SP 2.1   Manage Stakeholder Involvement
- SP 2.2   Manage Dependencies
- SP 2.3   Resolve Coordination Issues

> **TIP**
>
> Establishing teams is an expected activity for conducting successful acquisitions. These teams often require participation beyond the project and may include both customers and suppliers.

IPM

Specific Practices by Goal

SG 1   USE THE PROJECT'S DEFINED PROCESS

The project is conducted using a defined process tailored from the organization's set of standard processes.

The project's defined process includes those processes from the organization's set of standard processes that address all processes necessary to acquire, develop, maintain, or deliver the product.

The product related lifecycle processes, such as manufacturing and support processes, are developed concurrently with the product.

> **TIP**
>
> All projects that use IPM rely on the organization's set of standard processes as a basis to begin planning all project activities.

TIP

Establishing the right team structure aids in planning, coordinating, and managing risk. Acquisition projects sometimes choose a single, top-level, integrated team that remains in place for the duration of the acquisition project, but the rest of the project work is performed within traditional organizational boundaries. Such an approach can improve efficiency and be pursued if the product architecture aligns well with existing organizational boundaries.

SP 1.1 *ESTABLISH THE PROJECT'S DEFINED PROCESS*

Establish and maintain the project's defined process from project startup through the life of the project.

Refer to the Organizational Process Definition process area for more information about establishing organizational process assets and establishing the organization's measurement repository.

Refer to the Organizational Process Focus process area for more information about deploying organizational process assets and deploying standard processes.

The project's defined process consists of defined processes that form an integrated, coherent lifecycle for the project.

The project's defined process logically sequences acquirer activities and supplier deliverables (as identified in the supplier agreement) to deliver a product that meets the requirements. The acquirer may require the supplier to align selected processes with the acquirer's defined process.

The project's defined process should satisfy the project's contractual requirements, operational needs, opportunities, and constraints. It is designed to provide a best fit for project needs.

A project's defined process is based on the following factors:

- Stakeholder requirements
- Commitments
- Organizational process needs and objectives
- The organization's set of standard processes and tailoring guidelines
- The operational environment
- The business environment

Establishing the project's defined process at project startup helps to ensure that project staff and relevant stakeholders implement a set of activities needed to efficiently establish an initial set of requirements and plans for the project. As the project progresses, the description of the project's defined process is elaborated and revised to better meet project requirements and the organization's process needs and objectives. Also, as the organization's set of standard processes changes, the project's defined process may need to be revised.

The project's defined process is driven by the acquisition strategy. The acquirer's defined process is affected, for example, by whether the acquisition strategy is to introduce new technology to the organization or to consolidate acquired products or services in use by the acquirer.

Example Work Products

1. The project's defined process

Example Supplier Deliverables

1. Tailored supplier processes that interface with the acquirer's defined process

Subpractices

1. Select a lifecycle model from the ones available in organizational process assets.

> **Examples of project characteristics that could affect the selection of lifecycle models include the following:**
> - Size or complexity of the project
> - Acquisition strategy
> - Experience and familiarity of staff with implementing the process
> - Constraints such as cycle time and acceptable defect levels
> - Clarity of requirements
> - Customer expectations

X-REF

IPM depends strongly on OPD. It is impossible to fully implement the specific practices in IPM without having in place the organizational infrastructure described in OPD.

2. Select standard processes from the organization's set of standard processes that best fit the needs of the project.

3. Tailor the organization's set of standard processes and other organizational process assets according to tailoring guidelines to produce the project's defined process.

   Sometimes the available lifecycle models and standard processes are inadequate to meet project needs. In such circumstances, the project should seek approval to deviate from what is required by the organization. Waivers are provided for this purpose.

   Tailoring can include adapting the organization's common measures and specifying additional measures to meet the information needs of the project.

4. Use other artifacts from the organization's process asset library as appropriate.

> **Other artifacts can include the following:**
> - Lessons learned documents
> - Templates
> - Example documents
> - Estimating models

HINT

Tailor the organization's set of standard processes to address the project's specific needs and situation. Some questions to ask to determine specific needs include the following: Are stringent quality, safety, and security requirements in place? Are the customer's needs still evolving? Is the team working with a new customer, a new acquisition strategy, or a new supplier? Are there stringent schedule constraints?

IPM

HINT

Maintain the process asset library to keep it current. Otherwise, it could become the dumping ground for all project information and quickly become unusable.

5. Document the project's defined process.

6. Conduct peer reviews of the project's defined process.

> *Refer to the Acquisition Verification process area for more information about performing peer reviews.*

7. Revise the project's defined process as necessary.

SP 1.2 USE ORGANIZATIONAL PROCESS ASSETS FOR PLANNING PROJECT ACTIVITIES

Use organizational process assets and the measurement repository for estimating and planning project activities.

Refer to the Organizational Process Definition process area for more information about establishing organizational process assets.

When available, use results of previous planning and execution activities as predictors of the relative scope and risk of the effort being estimated.

Example Work Products

1. Project estimates
2. Project plans

Subpractices

1. Use the tasks and work products of the project's defined process as a basis for estimating and planning project activities.

   An understanding of the relationships among tasks and work products of the project's defined process, and of the roles to be performed by relevant stakeholders, is a basis for developing a realistic plan.

2. Use the organization's measurement repository in estimating the project's planning parameters.

> This estimate typically includes the following:
> - Appropriate historical data from this project or similar projects
> - Similarities and differences between the current project and those projects whose historical data will be used
> - Validated historical data
> - Reasoning, assumptions, and rationale used to select the historical data

SP 1.3 ESTABLISH THE PROJECT'S WORK ENVIRONMENT

Establish and maintain the project's work environment based on the organization's work environment standards.

An appropriate work environment for a project comprises an infrastructure of facilities, tools, and equipment that people need to perform their jobs effectively in support of business and project objectives. The work environment and its components are maintained at a level of work environment performance and reliability indicated by organizational work environment standards. As required, the project's work environment or some of its components can be developed internally or acquired from external sources.

The supplier's work environment should be compatible with the acquirer's work environment to enable efficient and effective transfer of work products.

The work environment might encompass environments for both verification and validation or these environments might be separate.

Refer to the Establish Work Environment Standards specific practice in the Organizational Process Definition process area for more information about work environment standards.

Example Work Products

1. Equipment and tools for the project
2. Installation, operation, and maintenance manuals for the project work environment
3. User surveys and results
4. Use, performance, and maintenance records
5. Support services for the project's work environment

Subpractices

1. Plan, design, and install a work environment for the project.
   The critical aspects of the project work environment are, like any other product, requirements driven. Functionality and quality attributes of the work environment are explored with the same rigor as is done for any other product development project.

It may be necessary to make tradeoffs among quality attributes, costs, and risks. The following are examples of each:

- Quality attribute considerations can include timely communication, safety, security, and maintainability.
- Costs can include capital outlays, training, a support structure, disassembly and disposal of existing environments, and the operation and maintenance of the environment.
- Risks can include workflow and project disruptions.

TIP

Often, the project's work environment contains components that are common to the organization's overall work environment. Many of these components may be provided by an IT or facilities group.

IPM

TIP

A facilities group can use input from the project to create the work environment.

> Examples of equipment and tools include the following:
> - Office software
> - Decision support software
> - Project management tools
> - Test and evaluation equipment
> - Requirements management tools and design tools
> - Configuration management tools

2. Provide ongoing maintenance and operational support for the project's work environment.

   Maintenance and support of the work environment can be accomplished either with capabilities found inside the organization or hired from outside the organization.

> Examples of maintenance and support approaches include the following:
> - Hiring people to perform maintenance and support
> - Training people to perform maintenance and support
> - Contracting maintenance and support
> - Developing expert users for selected tools

3. Maintain the qualification of components of the project's work environment.

   Components include software, databases, hardware, tools, test equipment, and appropriate documentation. Qualification of software includes appropriate certifications. Hardware and test equipment qualification includes calibration and adjustment records and traceability to calibration standards.

4. Periodically review how well the work environment is meeting project needs and supporting collaboration, and take action as appropriate.

SP 1.4 INTEGRATE PLANS

Integrate the project plan and other plans that affect the project to describe the project's defined process.

Refer to the Organizational Process Definition process area for more information about establishing organizational process assets and, in particular, establishing the organization's measurement repository.

Refer to the Organizational Process Focus process area for more information about establishing organizational process needs and determining process improvement opportunities.

TIP

One of the main differences between IPM and PP is that IPM is more proactive in coordinating with relevant stakeholders, both internal (different teams) and external (organizational functions, support groups, customers, and suppliers) to the project, and is concerned with the integration of plans.

Refer to the Project Planning process area for more information about developing a project plan.

This specific practice extends the specific practices for establishing and maintaining a project plan to address additional planning activities such as incorporating the project's defined process, coordinating with relevant stakeholders, using organizational process assets, incorporating plans for peer reviews, and establishing objective entry and exit criteria for tasks.

The development of the project plan should account for current and projected needs, objectives, and requirements of the organization, customer, suppliers, and end users as appropriate.

> **TIP**
>
> To formulate estimates, data should be available from the organization's measurement repository. Additionally, templates, examples, and lessons-learned documents should be available from the organization's process asset library.

Example Work Products

1. Integrated plans

Example Supplier Deliverables

1. Supplier plans

Subpractices

1. Integrate other plans that affect the project with the project plan.

> Other plans that affect the project plan can include the following:
> - Quality assurance plans
> - Risk management strategy
> - Verification and validation plans
> - Transition to operations and support plans
> - Configuration management plans
> - Documentation plans
> - Staff training plans

2. Incorporate into the project plan the definitions of measures and measurement activities for managing the project.

> Examples of measures that would be incorporated include the following:
> - Organization's common set of measures
> - Additional project specific measures

Refer to the Measurement and Analysis process area for more information about developing and sustaining a measurement capability used to support management information needs.

3. Identify and analyze product and project interface risks.

   Refer to the Risk Management process area for more information about identifying and analyzing risks.

4. Schedule tasks in a sequence that accounts for critical development and delivery factors and project risks.

> **Examples of factors considered in scheduling include the following:**
> - **Size and complexity of tasks**
> - **Needs of the customer and end users**
> - **Availability of critical resources**
> - **Availability of key staff**

5. Incorporate plans for performing peer reviews on work products of the project's defined process.
6. Incorporate the training needed to perform the project's defined process in the project's training plans.
   This task typically includes negotiating with the organizational training group on the support they will provide.
7. Establish objective entry and exit criteria to authorize the initiation and completion of tasks described in the work breakdown structure (WBS).

   Refer to the Project Planning process area for more information about estimating the scope of the project.

8. Ensure that the project plan is appropriately compatible with the plans of relevant stakeholders.
   Typically the plan and changes to the plan will be reviewed for compatibility.
9. Identify how conflicts will be resolved that arise among relevant stakeholders.

   Refer to the Agreement Management process area for more information about ensuring that the supplier and the acquirer perform their work according to the terms of the supplier agreement.

TIP

The prior specific practices established the plan; this specific practice implements and manages the project against that plan.

SP 1.5 MANAGE THE PROJECT USING INTEGRATED PLANS

Manage the project using the project plan, other plans that affect the project, and the project's defined process.

Refer to the Organizational Process Definition process area for more information about establishing organizational process assets.

Refer to the Organizational Process Focus process area for more information about establishing organizational process needs, deploying organizational process assets, and deploying standard processes.

Refer to the Project Monitoring and Control process area for more information about providing an understanding of the project's progress so that appropriate corrective actions can be taken when the project's performance deviates significantly from the plan.

Refer to the Risk Management process area for more information about identifying and analyzing risks and mitigating risks.

Example Work Products

1. Work products created by performing the project's defined process
2. Collected measures (i.e., actuals) and status records or reports
3. Revised requirements, plans, and commitments
4. Integrated plans

Example Supplier Deliverables

1. Supplier project progress and performance reports

Subpractices

1. Implement the project's defined process using the organization's process asset library.

This task typically includes the following activities:

- Incorporating artifacts from the organization's process asset library into the project as appropriate
- Using lessons learned from the organization's process asset library to manage the project

---

2. Monitor and control the project's activities and work products using the project's defined process, project plan, and other plans that affect the project.

This task typically includes the following activities:

- Using the defined entry and exit criteria to authorize the initiation and determine the completion of tasks
- Monitoring activities that could significantly affect actual values of the project's planning parameters

Continues

TIP

The organization's process improvement plan might also affect the project.

IPM

Continued

- Tracking project planning parameters using measurable thresholds that will trigger investigation and appropriate actions
- Monitoring product and project interface risks
- Managing external and internal commitments based on plans for tasks and work products of the project's defined process

> An understanding of the relationships among tasks and work products of the project's defined process and of the roles to be performed by relevant stakeholders, along with well-defined control mechanisms (e.g., peer reviews), achieves better visibility into project performance and better control of the project.

3. Obtain and analyze selected measurements to manage the project and support organization needs.

   Refer to the Measurement and Analysis process area for more information about obtaining measurement data and analyzing measurement data.

4. Periodically review and align the project's performance with current and anticipated needs, objectives, and requirements of the organization, customer, and end users as appropriate.
   This review includes alignment with organizational process needs and objectives.

Examples of actions that achieve alignment include the following:
- Changing the schedule with appropriate adjustments to other planning parameters and project risks
- Changing requirements or commitments in response to a change in market opportunities or customer and end-user needs
- Terminating the project

5. Address causes of selected issues that can affect project objectives.
   Issues that require corrective action are determined and analyzed as in the Analyze Issues and Take Corrective Actions specific practices of the Project Monitoring and Control process area. As appropriate, the project may periodically review issues previously encountered on other projects or in earlier phases of the project, and conduct causal analysis of selected issues to determine how to prevent recurrence for issues which can significantly affect project objectives. Project process changes implemented as a result of causal analysis activities should be evaluated for effectiveness to ensure that the process change has prevented recurrence and improved performance.

SP 1.6 ESTABLISH TEAMS

Establish and maintain teams.

The project is managed using teams that reflect the organizational rules and guidelines for team structuring, formation, and operation. (See the definition of "team" in the glossary.)

The project's shared vision is established prior to establishing the team structure, which can be based on the WBS. For small organizations, the whole organization and relevant external stakeholders can be treated as a team.

Refer to the Establish Rules and Guidelines for Teams specific practice in the Organizational Process Definition process area for more information about establishing and maintaining organizational rules and guidelines for the structure, formation, and operation of teams.

One of the best ways to ensure coordination and collaboration with relevant stakeholders is to include them on the team. For projects in a system of systems framework, the most important team may be with stakeholders representing other systems.

Example Work Products

1. Documented shared vision
2. List of members assigned to each team
3. Team charters
4. Periodic team status reports

Subpractices

1. Establish and maintain the project's shared vision.

   When creating a shared vision, it is critical to understand the interfaces between the project and stakeholders external to the project. The vision should be shared among relevant stakeholders to obtain their agreement and commitment.

2. Establish and maintain the team structure.

   The project WBS, cost, schedule, project risks, resources, interfaces, the project's defined process, and organizational guidelines are evaluated to establish an appropriate team structure, including team responsibilities, authorities, and interrelationships.

3. Establish and maintain each team.

   Establishing and maintaining teams encompasses choosing team leaders and team members and establishing team charters for each team. It also involves providing resources required to accomplish tasks assigned to the team.

TIP

This specific practice is included to ensure that integrated teams are used for the purposes of addressing integration issues. Often, these challenges occur across boundaries with customers, suppliers, and other critical acquisition efforts.

HINT

When a supplier is integrated into the project team, pick the best process for the situation and make sure it is covered in the supplier agreement.

HINT

Achieve the right allocation of requirements to each integrated team in the team structure before teams are formed—deciding which requirements to allocate to which team determines how the teams are staffed.

TIP

It may be useful to "sunset" a team once the specific needs of the team are satisfied. It may also be useful to create new teams at various points in the acquisition lifecycle to meet new acquisition challenges that arise during this process.

IPM

4. Periodically evaluate the team structure and composition.

   Teams should be monitored to detect misalignment of work across different teams, mismanaged interfaces, and mismatches of tasks to team members. Take corrective action when team or project performance does not meet expectations.

SP 1.7 CONTRIBUTE TO ORGANIZATIONAL PROCESS ASSETS

Contribute process related experiences to organizational process assets.

Refer to the Organizational Process Definition process area for more information about establishing organizational process assets, establishing the organization's measurement repository, and establishing the organization's process asset library.

Refer to the Organizational Process Focus process area for more information about incorporating experiences into organizational process assets.

This specific practice addresses contributing information from processes in the project's defined process to organizational process assets.

Example Work Products

1. Proposed improvements to organizational process assets
2. Actual process and product measures collected from the project
3. Documentation (e.g., exemplary process descriptions, plans, training modules, checklists, lessons learned)
4. Process artifacts associated with tailoring and implementing the organization's set of standard processes on the project

Subpractices

1. Propose improvements to the organizational process assets.
2. Store process and product measures in the organization's measurement repository.

   Refer to the Measurement and Analysis process area for more information about obtaining measurement data.

   Refer to the Project Monitoring and Control process area for more information about monitoring project planning parameters.

   Refer to the Project Planning process area for more information about planning data management.

3. Submit documentation for possible inclusion in the organization's process asset library.

> Examples of documentation include the following:
> - Exemplary process descriptions
> - Training modules
> - Exemplary plans
> - Checklists and templates
> - Tool configurations

4. Document lessons learned from the project for inclusion in the organization's process asset library.

5. Provide process artifacts associated with tailoring and implementing the organization's set of standard processes in support of the organization's process monitoring activities.

> *Refer to the Monitor the Implementation specific practice in the Organizational Process Focus process area for more information about the organization's activities to understand the extent of deployment of standard processes on new and existing projects.*

SG 2 COORDINATE AND COLLABORATE WITH RELEVANT STAKEHOLDERS

Coordination and collaboration between the project and relevant stakeholders are conducted.

SP 2.1 MANAGE STAKEHOLDER INVOLVEMENT

Manage the involvement of relevant stakeholders in the project.

Stakeholder involvement is managed according to the project's integrated plan and defined process.

The supplier agreement provides the basis for managing supplier involvement in the project. Supplier agreements (e.g., interagency and intercompany agreements, memoranda of understanding, memoranda of agreement) that the acquirer makes with stakeholder organizations, which can be product or service providers or recipients, provide the basis for their involvement.

These agreements are particularly important when the acquirer's project produces a system that will be integrated into a larger system of systems.

Refer to the Project Planning process area for more information about planning stakeholder involvement and obtaining plan commitment.

X-REF

Relevant stakeholders are identified in GP 2.7 and PP SP 2.6.

IPM

Example Work Products

1. Agendas and schedules for collaborative activities
2. Recommendations for resolving relevant stakeholder issues
3. Documented issues

Subpractices

1. Coordinate with relevant stakeholders who should participate in project activities.

   The relevant stakeholders should already be identified in the project plan.

2. Ensure work products that are produced to satisfy commitments meet the requirements of the recipients.

   The work products produced to satisfy commitments can be services.

3. Develop recommendations and coordinate actions to resolve misunderstandings and problems with requirements.

SP 2.2 MANAGE DEPENDENCIES

Participate with relevant stakeholders to identify, negotiate, and track critical dependencies.

Example Work Products

1. Defects, issues, and action items resulting from reviews with relevant stakeholders
2. Critical dependencies
3. Commitments to address critical dependencies
4. Status of critical dependencies

Example Supplier Deliverables

1. Status of critical dependencies

Subpractices

1. Conduct reviews with relevant stakeholders.

   It is particularly important that acquirers or owners of systems that interact with the project in a system of systems be involved in these reviews to manage critical dependencies these types of systems create.

2. Identify each critical dependency.
3. Establish need dates and plan dates for each critical dependency based on the project schedule.
4. Review and get agreement on commitments to address each critical dependency with those who are responsible for providing or receiving the work product.

TIP

These commitments may be external commitments that the project staff is addressing.

TIP

Too often, project members assume that critical dependencies identified at the beginning of a project will not change or are someone else's responsibility.

TIP

When time and money are limited, the integration, coordination, and collaboration activities become even more critical. Coordination helps to ensure that all involved parties contribute to the product in a timely way to minimize rework and delays.

X-REF

You can facilitate coordination on critical dependencies by determining need dates and plan dates for each critical dependency and then establishing and managing commitments as described in these subpractices and in PP and PMC.

5. Document critical dependencies and commitments.

   The acquirer documents supplier commitments to meet critical dependencies in the supplier agreement. Supplier dependencies and acquirer dependencies are documented in an integrated plan.

6. Track the critical dependencies and commitments and take corrective action as appropriate.

   Refer to the Project Monitoring and Control process area for more information about monitoring commitments.

Tracking critical dependencies typically includes the following:

- Evaluating the effects of late and early completion for impacts on future activities and milestones
- Resolving actual and potential problems with responsible parties whenever possible
- Escalating to the appropriate party the actual and potential problems not resolvable by the responsible individual or group

---

SP 2.3 RESOLVE COORDINATION ISSUES

Resolve issues with relevant stakeholders.

Examples of coordination issues include the following:

- Incomplete customer requirements
- Unresolved defects
- Late critical dependencies and commitments
- Product level problems
- Unavailable critical resources or staff

Example Work Products

1. Relevant stakeholder coordination issues
2. Status of relevant stakeholder coordination issues

Subpractices

1. Identify and document issues.
2. Communicate issues to relevant stakeholders.
3. Resolve issues with relevant stakeholders.
4. Escalate to appropriate managers the issues not resolvable with relevant stakeholders.
5. Track issues to closure.
6. Communicate with relevant stakeholders on the status and resolution of issues.

TIP

Coordination issues are typically resolved at the project level. However, because stakeholders may be external to the project, issues may need to be escalated to the appropriate level of management to be resolved.

IPM

TIP

This specific practice is critical if teams are to perform in a manner that is consistent with the project's shared vision.

MEASUREMENT AND ANALYSIS
A Support Process Area at Maturity Level 2

Purpose

The purpose of Measurement and Analysis (MA) is to develop and sustain a measurement capability used to support management information needs.

Introductory Notes

The Measurement and Analysis process area involves the following activities:

- Specifying objectives of measurement and analysis so that they are aligned with identified information needs and project, organizational, or business objectives
- Specifying measures, analysis techniques, and mechanisms for data collection, data storage, reporting, and feedback
- Implementing the analysis techniques and mechanisms for data collection, data reporting, and feedback
- Providing objective results that can be used in making informed decisions and taking appropriate corrective action

The integration of measurement and analysis activities into the processes of the project supports the following:

- Objective planning and estimating
- Tracking actual progress and performance against established plans and objectives
- Identifying and resolving process related issues
- Providing a basis for incorporating measurement into additional processes in the future

MA

TIP

Measurement involves everyone. A centralized group, such as a process group or a measurement group, may provide help in defining the measures to be employed, the analyses to be performed, and the reporting content and charts to be used.

X-REF

Refer to SP 1.4 in OPD for more information about the organization's measurement repository.

TIP

The supplier agreement should specify any measurement and analysis activities that the supplier is expected to perform. Refer to SSAD, AM, and ATM for more information about supplier activities.

The staff required to implement a measurement capability may or may not be employed in a separate organization-wide program. Measurement capability may be integrated into individual projects or other organizational functions (e.g., quality assurance).

The initial focus for measurement activities is at the project level. However, a measurement capability can prove useful for addressing organization- and enterprise-wide information needs. To support this capability, measurement activities should support information needs at multiple levels, including the business, organizational unit, and project to minimize re-work as the organization matures.

Projects can store project specific data and results in a project specific repository, but when data are to be used widely or are to be analyzed in support of determining data trends or benchmarks, data may reside in the organization's measurement repository.

Measurement and analysis of product components provided by suppliers is essential for effective management of the quality and costs of the project. It is possible, with careful management of supplier agreements, to provide insight into data that support supplier performance analysis.

The acquirer specifies measures that enable it to gauge its own progress and output, supplier progress and output as per contractual requirements, and the status of the evolving products acquired. An acquirer establishes measurement objectives for its activities and work products and supplier activities and deliverables. Measurement objectives are derived from information needs that come from project, organizational, or business objectives. In this process area, when the term "objectives" is used without the "measurement" qualifier, it indicates either project, organizational, or business objectives.

Measurement objectives are used to define measures as well as collection, analysis, storage, and usage procedures for measures. These measures are specified in the project plan. Measures for the supplier, data collection processes and timing, expected analysis, and required storage should be specified in the supplier agreement.

In projects where multiple products are acquired to deliver a capability to the end user or where there are relationships with other projects to acquire joint capabilities, additional measures can be identified to track and achieve interoperability for programmatic, technical, and operational interfaces.

Related Process Areas

Refer to the Solicitation and Supplier Agreement Development process area for more information about establishing a solicitation package and establishing the supplier agreement.

Refer to the Configuration Management process area for more information about establishing and maintaining the integrity of work products using configuration identification, configuration control, configuration status accounting, and configuration audits.

Refer to the Organizational Process Definition process area for more information about establishing the organization's measurement repository.

Refer to the Project Monitoring and Control process area for more information about monitoring project planning parameters.

Refer to the Project Planning process area for more information about establishing estimates.

Refer to the Quantitative Project Management process area for more information about quantitatively managing the project.

Refer to the Requirements Management process area for more information about maintaining bidirectional traceability of requirements.

Specific Goal and Practice Summary

SG 1 Align Measurement and Analysis Activities
      SP 1.1   Establish Measurement Objectives
      SP 1.2   Specify Measures
      SP 1.3   Specify Data Collection and Storage Procedures
      SP 1.4   Specify Analysis Procedures
SG 2 Provide Measurement Results
      SP 2.1   Obtain Measurement Data
      SP 2.2   Analyze Measurement Data
      SP 2.3   Store Data and Results
      SP 2.4   Communicate Results

Specific Practices by Goal

SG 1   ALIGN MEASUREMENT AND ANALYSIS ACTIVITIES

Measurement objectives and activities are aligned with identified information needs and objectives.

The specific practices under this specific goal can be addressed concurrently or in any order.

When establishing measurement objectives, experts often think ahead about necessary criteria for specifying measures and analysis procedures. They also think concurrently about the constraints imposed by data collection and storage procedures.

Often it is important to specify the essential analyses to be conducted before attending to details of measurement specification, data collection, or storage.

TIP

When starting a measurement program, an iterative process is usually helpful, because you often do not know all of your objectives. On long-duration acquisition projects, needed measurement activities may change significantly over the life of the project.

MA

SP 1.1 ESTABLISH MEASUREMENT OBJECTIVES

Establish and maintain measurement objectives derived from identified information needs and objectives.

Measurement objectives document the purposes for which measurement and analysis are done and specify the kinds of actions that can be taken based on results of data analyses. Measurement objectives can also identify the change in behavior desired as a result of implementing a measurement and analysis activity.

Measurement objectives focus on acquirer performance, supplier performance, and understanding the effects of their performance on customer operational and financial performance. Measurement objectives for the supplier enable defining and tracking service level expectations documented in the supplier agreement.

Measurement objectives are derived from information needs that are needed to do the following:

- Maintain alignment to project objectives and provide results that keep a project on track to its successful conclusion
- Support the organization's ability to establish an infrastructure that reinforces and grows acquirer capabilities, including processes, people, and technologies as appropriate
- Support the enterprise's ability to monitor and manage its financial results and customer expectations as appropriate

Measurement objectives may be constrained by existing processes, available resources, or other measurement considerations. Judgments may need to be made about whether the value of the result is commensurate with resources devoted to doing the work.

Modifications to identified information needs and objectives can, in turn, be indicated as a consequence of the process and results of measurement and analysis.

Sources of information needs and objectives can include the following:
- Supplier agreements and contractual requirements (e.g., service levels)
- Customer expectations
- Project plans
- Project performance monitoring
- Interviews with managers and others who have information needs
- Established management objectives

Continues

Continued

- Strategic plans
- Business plans
- Formal requirements or contractual obligations
- Recurring or other troublesome management or technical problems
- Experiences of other projects or organizational entities
- External industry benchmarks
- Process improvement plans

Example measurement objectives include the following:
- Provide insight into schedule fluctuations and progress
- Provide insight into actual size compared to plan
- Identify unplanned growth
- Evaluate the effectiveness of defect detection throughout the product development lifecycle
- Determine the cost of correcting defects
- Provide insight into actual costs compared to plan
- Evaluate supplier progress against the plan
- Evaluate the effectiveness of mitigating information system vulnerabilities

Refer to the Project Monitoring and Control process area for more information about monitoring project planning parameters.

Refer to the Project Planning process area for more information about establishing estimates.

Refer to the Requirements Management process area for more information about maintaining bidirectional traceability of requirements.

Example Work Products

1. Measurement objectives

Subpractices

1. Document information needs and objectives.
2. Prioritize information needs and objectives.

    It can be neither possible nor desirable to subject all initially identified information needs to measurement and analysis. Priorities may also need to be set within the limits of available resources.

3. Document, review, and update measurement objectives.

    Carefully consider the purposes and intended uses of measurement and analysis.

The measurement objectives are documented, reviewed by management and other relevant stakeholders, and updated as necessary. Doing so enables traceability to subsequent measurement and analysis activities, and helps to ensure that analyses will properly address identified information needs and objectives.

It is important that users of measurement and analysis results be involved in setting measurement objectives and deciding on plans of action. It may also be appropriate to involve those who provide the measurement data.

4. Provide feedback for refining and clarifying information needs and objectives as necessary.

Identified information needs and objectives can be refined and clarified as a result of setting measurement objectives. Initial descriptions of information needs may be ambiguous. Conflicts can arise between existing needs and objectives. Precise targets on an already existing measure may be unrealistic.

5. Maintain traceability of measurement objectives to identified information needs and objectives.

There should always be a good answer to the question, "Why are we measuring this?"

Of course, measurement objectives can also change to reflect evolving information needs and objectives.

6. Review appropriate measurement objectives with potential suppliers throughout the solicitation, obtaining their feedback and commitment.

Refer to the Solicitation and Supplier Agreement Development process area for more information about preparing for solicitation and supplier agreement development.

SP 1.2 SPECIFY MEASURES

Specify measures to address measurement objectives.

Measurement objectives are refined into precise, quantifiable measures.

Measurement of project and organizational work can typically be traced to one or more measurement information categories. These categories include the following: schedule and progress, effort and cost, size and stability, and quality.

Measures can be either *base* or *derived*. Data for base measures are obtained by direct measurement. Data for derived measures come from other data, typically by combining two or more base measures.

Derived measures typically are expressed as ratios, composite indices, or other aggregate summary measures. They are often more quantitatively reliable and meaningfully interpretable than the base measures used to generate them.

Base measures enable the creation of many derived measures or indicators from the same standard data sources. In addition, there are direct relationships among information needs, measurement objectives, measurement categories, base measures, and derived measures. This direct relationship is depicted using some common examples in Table 8.1.

TABLE 8.1 Example Measurement Relationships

Example Project, Organizational, or Business Objectives	Information Need	Measurement Objective	Measurement Information Categories	Example Base Measures	Example Derived Measures
Shorten time to delivery Be first to market the product	What is the estimated delivery time?	Provide insight into schedule fluctuations and progress	Schedule and progress	Estimated and actual start and end dates by task Estimated and actual start and end dates of acquisition tasks	Milestone performance Percentage of project on time Schedule estimation accuracy
Increase market share by reducing costs of products and services	How accurate are the size and cost estimates?	Provide insight into actual size and costs compared to plan	Size and effort Effort and cost	Estimated and actual effort and size Estimated and actual cost	Productivity Cost performance Cost variance
Deliver specified functionality	Has scope or project size grown?	Provide insight into actual size compared to plan, identify unplanned growth	Size and stability	Requirements count Function point count Lines of code count	Requirements volatility Size estimation accuracy Estimated vs. actual function points Amount of new, modified, and reused code

Continues

MA

TABLE 8.1 Example Measurement Relationships *(Continued)*

Example Project, Organizational, or Business Objectives	*Information Need*	*Measurement Objective*	*Measurement Information Categories*	*Example Base Measures*	*Example Derived Measures*
Reduce defects in products delivered to the customer by 10% without affecting cost	Where are defects being inserted and detected prior to delivery?	Evaluate the effectiveness of defect detection throughout the product lifecycle	Quality	Number of defects inserted and detected by lifecycle phase Product size	Defect containment by lifecycle phase Defect density
	What is the cost of rework?	Determine the cost of correcting defects	Cost	Number of defects inserted and detected by lifecycle phase Effort hours to correct defects Labor rates	Rework costs
Reduce information systems vulnerabilities	What is the magnitude of open system vulnerabilities?	Evaluate the effectiveness of mitigating system vulnerabilities	Information assurance	Number of system vulnerabilities identified and number of system vulnerabilities mitigated	Percentage of system vulnerabilities mitigated

As a part of their measurement and analysis activities, projects can also consider the use of Earned Value Management (EVM) for measures related to cost and schedule [EIA 2002b]. EVM is a method for objectively measuring cost and schedule progress and for predicting estimated total costs and target completion dates based on past and current cost and schedule performance trends.

Typical EVM data include the planned cost of accomplishing specific and measurable tasks, the actual cost of completing tasks, and earned value, which is the planned cost of the work actually completed for each task. Using these base measures or similar ones, the project can calculate derived measures such as schedule and cost variance and more complex measures. These derived measures include schedule and cost performance indices. EVM derived measures can assist with estimating the cost for completion and additional resources that may be required.

To manage projects, an acquirer uses supplier data (i.e., base measures) and supplier reported derived measures in addition to measures of acquirer progress and output. Supplier measures required by the acquirer allow the acquirer to comprehensively address measurement objectives and to comprehensively determine the progress of the project. In some cases, these supplier measures will augment acquirer measures (e.g., supplier's schedule performance index and size estimation accuracy).

In most cases, supplier measures are the primary source of data, especially with regard to the development of the acquired product or service. For instance, measurement and analysis of the product or product components provided by a supplier through technical performance measures is essential for effective management. Technical performance measures are precisely defined measures based on a product requirement, product capability, or some combination of requirements and capabilities.

It is important to use measures to track high-risk items to closure and to help determine risk mitigation and corrective actions. These supplier measures should be defined in the supplier agreement, including a supplier's measurement collection requirements and measurement reports to be provided to the acquirer.

Example Work Products

1. Specifications of base and derived measures
2. Acceptance criteria for supplier measures

Subpractices

1. Identify candidate measures based on documented measurement objectives.

    Measurement objectives are refined into measures. Identified candidate measures are categorized and specified by name and unit of measure.

2. Maintain traceability of measures to measurement objectives.

    Interdependencies among candidate measures are identified to enable later data validation and candidate analyses in support of measurement objectives.

3. Identify existing measures that already address measurement objectives.

    Specifications for measures may already exist, perhaps established for other purposes earlier or elsewhere in the organization.

4. Specify operational definitions for measures.

    Operational definitions are stated in precise and unambiguous terms. They address two important criteria:

    • Communication: What has been measured, how was it measured, what are the units of measure, and what has been included or excluded?

TIP

The project must determine when an integrated answer is needed with the supplier, and when it must deliver an independent analysis as part of its acquisition responsibilities.

TIP

An example of a derived measure that is typically expressed as a ratio is a productivity measure (e.g., proposal pages read per hour). An example of a derived measure that is typically expressed as a composite index is a process capability index (e.g., C_{pk}, which indicates how well centered and tightly distributed a stable process is relative to selected specification limits).

X-REF

Operational definitions play a key role in the effective specification of measures. Activities in ARD may be of assistance in determining many of these definitions.

MA

- Repeatability: Can the measurement be repeated, given the same definition, to get the same results?

5. Prioritize, review, and update measures.

Proposed specifications of measures are reviewed for their appropriateness with potential end users and other relevant stakeholders. Priorities are set or changed, and specifications of measures are updated as necessary.

6. Specify acceptance criteria based on operational definitions for measures that come from suppliers to the acquirer in a way that enables their intended use.

Measures may be provided by the supplier as detailed measurement data or measurement reports. Measures that come from suppliers should be associated with the acquirer's acceptance criteria for supplier measures. Acceptance criteria may be captured in measurement specifications or by checklists.

Acceptance criteria should be defined in a way that enables the intended use of supplier measures, such as potential aggregation and analysis. These criteria should include criteria associated with the collection and transfer mechanisms and procedures that are performed by the supplier. Consider all characteristics about supplier measures that can affect their use, such as differences in financial calendars used by different suppliers.

SP 1.3 SPECIFY DATA COLLECTION AND STORAGE PROCEDURES

Specify how measurement data are obtained and stored.

Explicit specification of collection methods helps to ensure that the right data are collected properly. This specification can also help further clarify information needs and measurement objectives.

Proper attention to storage and retrieval procedures helps to ensure that data are available and accessible for future use.

The supplier agreement specifies the measurement data the supplier must provide to the acquirer, in what format they must be provided to the acquirer, how the measurement data will be collected and stored by the supplier (e.g., retention period of data), how and how often they will be transferred to the acquirer, and who has access to data. Some supplier data may be considered proprietary by the supplier and may need to be protected as such by the acquirer. Also consider that some acquirer measurement data (e.g., total project cost data) may be proprietary and should not be shared with suppliers. An acquirer should plan for the collection, storage, and access control of sensitive data.

The acquirer should ensure that appropriate mechanisms are in place to obtain measurement data from the supplier in a consistent

X-REF

For additional information on specifying measures, see the SEI's Measurement and Analysis website (www.sei.cmu.edu/measurement/index.cfm), the Practical Software and Systems Measurement website (www.psmsc.com), and the iSixSigma website (www.isixsigma.com).

TIP

Ensuring appropriate accessibility of data and maintenance of data integrity are two key concerns related to data storage and retrieval. Both concerns are magnified when there are multiple suppliers or complex interactions among customers, acquirers, and suppliers.

way. It is critical for the acquirer to insist in the supplier agreement on accurate data collection by the supplier for the acquirer's measurement and analysis.

Example Work Products

1. Data collection and storage procedures
2. Data collection tools

Example Supplier Deliverables

1. Recommendations for data collection and storage procedures

Subpractices

1. Identify existing sources of data that are generated from current work products, processes, or transactions.
2. Identify measures for which data are needed but are not currently available.
3. Specify how to collect and store the data for each required measure.

    Explicit specifications are made of what, how, where, and when data will be collected and stored to ensure its validity and to support later use for analysis and documentation purposes.

Questions to be considered typically include the following:

- Have required data collection requirements and applicable procedures been specified in supplier agreement standards and related documents?
- Have the frequency of collection and the points in the process where measurements will be made been determined?
- Has the timeline that is required to move measurement results from points of collection to repositories, other databases, or end users been established?
- Who is responsible for obtaining data?
- Who is responsible for data storage, retrieval, and security?
- Have necessary supporting tools been developed or acquired?

---

4. Create data collection mechanisms and process guidance.

    Data collection and storage mechanisms are well integrated with other normal work processes. Data collection mechanisms can include manual or automated forms and templates. Clear, concise guidance on correct procedures is available to those who are responsible for doing the work. Training is provided as needed to clarify processes required for the collection of complete and accurate data and to minimize the burden on those who provide and record data.

MA

Create mechanisms to transfer data and process guidance from the supplier to the acquirer as appropriate. Data collection from a supplier can be integrated with periodic monitoring and review of supplier activities. Applicable standard report formats and tools to be used for reporting by the supplier should be specified in the supplier agreement.

5. Support automatic collection of data as appropriate and feasible.

6. Prioritize, review, and update data collection and storage procedures. Proposed procedures are reviewed for their appropriateness and feasibility with those who are responsible for providing, collecting, and storing data. They also may have useful insights about how to improve existing processes or may be able to suggest other useful measures or analyses.

Review data collection and storage procedures with potential suppliers throughout the solicitation. Update data collection and storage procedures, as appropriate, and obtain supplier commitment to collect and store measurement data and reference procedures in the supplier agreement.

7. Update measures and measurement objectives as necessary.

SP 1.4 SPECIFY ANALYSIS PROCEDURES

Specify how measurement data are analyzed and communicated.

Specifying analysis procedures in advance ensures that appropriate analyses will be conducted and reported to address documented measurement objectives (and thereby the information needs and objectives on which they are based). This approach also provides a check that necessary data will, in fact, be collected. Analysis procedures should account for the quality (e.g., age, reliability) of all data that enter into an analysis (whether from the project, organization's measurement repository, or other source). The quality of data should be considered to help select the appropriate analysis procedure and evaluate the results of the analysis.

The supplier agreement defines the required data analysis and the definition and examples of measures the supplier must provide to the acquirer.

Example Work Products

1. Analysis specifications and procedures

2. Data analysis tools

TIP

In today's environment, automation is often used. Further, some organizations use multiple tools and databases to address their measurement needs. In such a case, you must carefully manage the compatibility among these tools and databases.

TIP

Often, someone can manipulate data to provide the picture he or she wants to convey. By specifying the analysis procedures in advance, you can minimize this type of abuse.

Example Supplier Deliverables

1. Recommendations for analysis specification and procedures

Subpractices

1. Specify and prioritize the analyses to be conducted and the reports to be prepared.

   Early on, pay attention to the analyses to be conducted and to the manner in which results will be reported. These analyses and reports should meet the following criteria:

   - The analyses explicitly address the documented measurement objectives.
   - Presentation of results is clearly understandable by the audiences to whom the results are addressed.

   Priorities may have to be set for available resources.

   Establish and maintain a description of the analysis approach for data elements, a description of reports that must be provided by the supplier, and a reference to analysis specifications and procedures in the supplier agreement.

2. Select appropriate data analysis methods and tools.

Issues to be considered typically include the following:

- Choice of visual display and other presentation techniques (e.g., pie charts, bar charts, histograms, radar charts, line graphs, scatter plots, tables)
- Choice of appropriate descriptive statistics (e.g., arithmetic mean, median, mode)
- Decisions about statistical sampling criteria when it is impossible or unnecessary to examine every data element
- Decisions about how to handle analysis in the presence of missing data elements
- Selection of appropriate analysis tools

Descriptive statistics are typically used in data analysis to do the following:

- Examine distributions of specified measures (e.g., central tendency, extent of variation, data points exhibiting unusual variation)
- Examine interrelationships among specified measures (e.g., comparisons of defects by phase of the product's lifecycle, comparisons of defects by product component)
- Display changes over time

MA

Refer to the Select Measures and Analytic Techniques specific practice and Monitor the Performance of Selected Subprocesses specific practice in the Quantitative Project Management process area for more information about the appropriate use of statistical techniques and understanding variation.

3. Specify administrative procedures for analyzing data and communicating results.

Data collected from a supplier are subject to validity checks that can be achieved by periodic audits of the supplier's execution of data collection and analysis procedures for acquirer required measures. The acquirer's option to perform validity checks of measurement data collected by the supplier and the supplier's execution of required analysis procedures must be defined in the supplier agreement.

TIP

The people responsible for analyzing the data and presenting the results should include those whose activities generated the measurement data or their management whenever possible. In addition, a process group, QA group, or measurement experts should provide support for these data-related activities.

Issues to be considered typically include the following:
- Identifying the persons and groups responsible for analyzing the data and presenting the results
- Determining the timeline to analyze the data and present the results
- Determining the venues for communicating the results (e.g., progress reports, transmittal memos, written reports, staff meetings)

4. Review and update the proposed content and format of specified analyses and reports.

All of the proposed content and format are subject to review and revision, including analytic methods and tools, administrative procedures, and priorities. Relevant stakeholders consulted should include end users, sponsors, data analysts, and data providers.
Review specified analyses and reports with suppliers and identify their commitment to support the analysis, and review recommendations they may provide related to the analysis of measurement data.

5. Update measures and measurement objectives as necessary.

Just as measurement needs drive data analysis, clarification of analysis criteria can affect measurement. Specifications for some measures may be refined further based on specifications established for data analysis procedures. Other measures may prove unnecessary or a need for additional measures may be recognized.

X-REF

Refer to SP 1.1 when refining your measurement objectives.

6. Specify criteria for evaluating the utility of analysis results and for evaluating the conduct of measurement and analysis activities.

Criteria for evaluating the utility of the analysis might address the extent to which the following apply:

- The results are provided in a timely manner, understandable, and used for decision making.
- The work does not cost more to perform than is justified by the benefits it provides.

Criteria for evaluating the conduct of the measurement and analysis might include the extent to which the following apply:

- The amount of missing data or the number of flagged inconsistencies is beyond specified thresholds.
- There is selection bias in sampling (e.g., only satisfied end users are surveyed to evaluate end-user satisfaction, only unsuccessful projects are evaluated to determine overall productivity).
- Measurement data are repeatable (e.g., statistically reliable).
- Statistical assumptions have been satisfied (e.g., about the distribution of data, about appropriate measurement scales).

TIP

The criteria are divided into two lists. The first comprises criteria that any organization can use. The second is a bit more sophisticated and might be used by organizations once they establish their measurement program.

SG 2 PROVIDE MEASUREMENT RESULTS

Measurement results, which address identified information needs and objectives, are provided.

The primary reason for conducting measurement and analysis is to address identified information needs derived from project, organizational, and business objectives. Measurement results based on objective evidence can help to monitor progress and performance, fulfill obligations documented in a supplier agreement, make informed management and technical decisions, and enable corrective actions to be taken.

TIP

MA provides the foundation for the behavior required in high maturity organizations. By the time organizations reach maturity level 4, management and staff members will use measurement results as part of their daily work.

SP 2.1 OBTAIN MEASUREMENT DATA

Obtain specified measurement data.

The data necessary for analysis are obtained and checked for completeness and integrity.

Example Work Products

1. Base and derived measurement data sets
2. Results of data integrity tests

MA

Example Supplier Deliverables

1. Base and derived supplier measurement data sets
2. Results of data integrity tests of supplier measurement data

Subpractices

1. Obtain data for base measures.

   Data are collected as necessary for previously used and newly specified base measures. Existing data are gathered from project records or elsewhere in the organization.

   Data are obtained from the supplier for base measures as defined in the supplier agreement.

2. Generate data for derived measures.

   Values are newly calculated for all derived measures.

   Derived measures are obtained from the supplier as defined in the supplier agreement.

3. Perform data integrity checks as close to the source of data as possible.

   All measurements are subject to error in specifying or recording data. It is always better to identify these errors and sources of missing data early in the measurement and analysis cycle.

   Checks can include scans for missing data, out-of-bounds data values, and unusual patterns and correlation across measures. It is particularly important to do the following:

   - Test and correct for inconsistency of classifications made by human judgment (i.e., to determine how frequently people make differing classification decisions based on the same information, otherwise known as "inter-coder reliability").

   - Empirically examine the relationships among measures that are used to calculate additional derived measures. Doing so can ensure that important distinctions are not overlooked and that derived measures convey their intended meanings (otherwise known as "criterion validity").

   Use acceptance criteria to verify the results of data integrity tests conducted by the supplier and to verify the integrity of supplier data. Follow up with suppliers if data are not available or data integrity checks indicate potential errors in data.

   Refer to the Agreement Management process area for more information about ensuring that the supplier and the acquirer perform according to the terms of the supplier agreement.

TIP

If too much time has passed, it may be inefficient or even impossible to verify the integrity of a measure or to identify the source of missing data.

SP 2.2 ANALYZE MEASUREMENT DATA

Analyze and interpret measurement data.

Measurement data are analyzed as planned, additional analyses are conducted as necessary, results are reviewed with relevant stakeholders, and necessary revisions for future analyses are noted.

Example Work Products

1. Analysis results and draft reports

Example Supplier Deliverables

1. Responses to analysis results and draft reports

Subpractices

1. Conduct initial analyses, interpret results, and draw preliminary conclusions.

    The results of data analyses are rarely self-evident. Criteria for interpreting results and drawing conclusions should be stated explicitly. Discuss results and preliminary conclusions with suppliers as appropriate.

2. Conduct additional measurement and analysis as necessary and prepare results for presentation.

    Results of planned analyses can suggest (or require) additional, unanticipated analyses. In addition, these analyses can identify needs to refine existing measures, to calculate additional derived measures, or even to collect data for additional base measures to properly complete the planned analysis. Similarly, preparing initial results for presentation can identify the need for additional, unanticipated analyses. Coordinate additional analyses with suppliers as appropriate.

3. Review initial results with relevant stakeholders.

    It may be appropriate to review initial interpretations of results and the way in which these results are presented before disseminating and communicating them widely.

    Relevant stakeholders with whom reviews may be conducted include intended end users, sponsors, data analysts, and data providers.

    Review initial results related to supplier progress or output with suppliers and determine if revisions are appropriate based on their response.

4. Refine criteria for future analyses.

    Lessons that can improve future efforts are often learned from conducting data analyses and preparing results. Similarly, ways to improve measurement specifications and data collection procedures can become apparent as can ideas for refining identified information needs and objectives.

    Update data acceptance criteria for supplier measures as appropriate.

> **TIP**
>
> All too frequently, someone may misinterpret analyses or draw incorrect conclusions. By specifying criteria for interpreting results in advance, you can reduce these risks.

> **TIP**
>
> Measurement and analysis is a learning process. You will typically go through many cycles before the measures and analyses are fine-tuned. Recognize that equivalent learning may also be occurring on the supplier side.

MA

SP 2.3 STORE DATA AND RESULTS

Manage and store measurement data, measurement specifications, and analysis results.

Storing measurement related information enables its timely and cost-effective use as historical data and results. The information also is needed to provide sufficient context for interpretation of data, measurement criteria, and analysis results.

Information stored typically includes the following:
• Data acceptance criteria for supplier data
• Measurement plans
• Specifications of measures
• Sets of data that were collected
• Analysis reports and presentations
• Retention period for data stored

Stored information contains or refers to other information needed to understand and interpret the measures and to assess them for reasonableness and applicability (e.g., measurement specifications used on different projects when comparing across projects).

Typically, data sets for derived measures can be recalculated and need not be stored. However, it may be appropriate to store summaries based on derived measures (e.g., charts, tables of results, report text).

Interim analysis results need not be stored separately if they can be efficiently reconstructed.

Projects can choose to store project specific data and results in a project specific repository. When data are shared across projects, the data can reside in the organization's measurement repository.

Refer to the Configuration Management process area for more information about establishing a configuration management system.

Refer to the Establish the Organization's Measurement Repository specific practice in the Organizational Process Definition process area for more information about establishing the organization's measurement repository.

Example Work Products

1. Stored data inventory

Subpractices

1. Review data to ensure their completeness, integrity, accuracy, and currency.
2. Store data according to data storage procedures.
3. Make stored contents available for use only to appropriate groups and staff members.

   The acquirer protects measurement data provided by the supplier according to the supplier agreement. The supplier agreement might specify that the acquirer must restrict access to a supplier's measurement data to acquirer staff only.

HINT

Understand what to store, what can be recalculated or reconstructed, and what to discard.

4. Prevent stored information from being used inappropriately.

> Examples of ways to prevent the inappropriate use of data and related information include controlling access to data and educating people on the appropriate use of data.

> Examples of the inappropriate use of data include the following:
> - Disclosure of information provided in confidence
> - Faulty interpretations based on incomplete, out-of-context, or otherwise misleading information
> - Measures used to improperly evaluate the performance of people or to rank projects
> - Impugning the integrity of individuals

TIP

Inappropriate use of data will seriously undermine the credibility of your MA implementation. It may also threaten effective collaboration with customers and suppliers.

SP 2.4 COMMUNICATE RESULTS

Communicate results of measurement and analysis activities to all relevant stakeholders.

The results of the measurement and analysis process are communicated to relevant stakeholders in a timely and usable fashion to support decision making and assist in taking corrective action.

Relevant stakeholders include intended end users, sponsors, data analysts, and data providers.

Relevant stakeholders also include suppliers.

TIP

An indicator of a mature organization is the daily use of measurement data by both staff members and management to guide their activities. This approach requires effective communication of measurement data and the results of analyses.

Example Work Products

1. Delivered reports and related analysis results
2. Contextual information or guidance to help interpret analysis results

Subpractices

1. Keep relevant stakeholders informed of measurement results in a timely manner.

   To the extent possible and as part of the normal way they do business, users of measurement results are kept personally involved in setting objectives and deciding on plans of action for measurement and analysis. Users are regularly kept informed of progress and interim results.

   Refer to the Project Monitoring and Control process area for more information about conducting progress reviews.

2. Assist relevant stakeholders in understanding results.

   Results are communicated in a clear and concise manner appropriate to relevant stakeholders. Results are understandable, easily interpretable, and clearly tied to identified information needs and objectives.

MA

TIP

As organizations mature, management and staff members should become more comfortable with measurement, be more likely to interpret the analyses correctly, and be able to ask the right questions to help them draw the right conclusions.

The acquirer establishes and maintains a standard format for communicating measurement data to relevant stakeholders.

The data analyzed are often not self-evident to practitioners who are not measurement experts. The communication of results should be clear about the following:

- How and why base and derived measures were specified
- How data were obtained
- How to interpret results based on the data analysis methods used
- How results address information needs

Examples of actions taken to help others to understand results include the following:

- Discussing the results with relevant stakeholders
- Providing background and explanation in a document
- Briefing users on results
- Providing training on the appropriate use and understanding of measurement results

---

ORGANIZATIONAL PROCESS DEFINITION
A Process Management Process Area at Maturity Level 3

Purpose

The purpose of Organizational Process Definition (OPD) is to establish and maintain a usable set of organizational process assets, work environment standards, and rules and guidelines for teams.

Introductory Notes

Organizational process assets enable consistent process execution across the organization and provide a basis for cumulative, long-term benefits to the organization. (See the definition of "organizational process assets" in the glossary.)

The organization's process asset library supports organizational learning and process improvement by allowing the sharing of best practices and lessons learned across the organization. (See the definition of "organizational process assets" in the glossary.)

The acquirer's organizational process assets also include acquisition guidance and practices established for use across acquisition projects and which refer to applicable statutes and regulations.

The organization's set of standard processes also describes standard interactions with suppliers. Supplier interactions are characterized by the following typical items: deliverables expected from suppliers, acceptance criteria applicable to those deliverables, standards (e.g., architecture and technology standards), and standard milestone and progress reviews.

The organization's "set of standard processes" is tailored by projects to create their defined processes. Other organizational process assets are used to support tailoring and implementing defined processes. Work environment standards are used to guide the creation of project work environments. Rules and guidelines for teams are used to aid in their structuring, formation, and operation.

TIP

Acquisition organizations come in a variety of configurations. For some larger acquisition programs, responsibility for the organizational elements of the model may rest within the program, which gives guidance to the projects within it. In others, a collection of programs may be gathered under a specific organizational executive. Given this diversity, it is difficult to provide specific guidance on the location of the various model elements associated with the "process management" category.

TIP

OPD contains specific practices that capture the organization's requirements, standards, and guidelines that are to be used by all projects across the organization.

HINT

With any library, a key challenge is to enable staff members to locate information quickly. Therefore, it is necessary to catalog, maintain, and archive information.

OPD

A "standard process" is composed of other processes (i.e., subprocesses) or process elements. A "process element" is the fundamental (i.e., atomic) unit of process definition that describes activities and tasks to consistently perform work. The process architecture provides rules for connecting the process elements of a standard process. The organization's set of standard processes can include multiple process architectures.

(See the definitions of "standard process," "process architecture," "subprocess," and "process element" in the glossary.)

TIP

CMMI models try to capture the "what" and not the "how." However, notes and examples are provided to give you some tips on the interpretation and implementation of the concepts.

Organizational process assets can be organized in many ways, depending on the implementation of the Organizational Process Definition process area. Examples include the following:

- Descriptions of lifecycle models can be part of the organization's set of standard processes or they can be documented separately.
- The organization's set of standard processes can be stored in the organization's process asset library or it can be stored separately.
- A single repository can contain both measurements and process related documentation, or they can be stored separately.

Related Process Areas

Refer to the Organizational Process Focus process area for more information about deploying organizational process assets.

Specific Goal and Practice Summary

SG 1 Establish Organizational Process Assets
- SP 1.1   Establish Standard Processes
- SP 1.2   Establish Lifecycle Model Descriptions
- SP 1.3   Establish Tailoring Criteria and Guidelines
- SP 1.4   Establish the Organization's Measurement Repository
- SP 1.5   Establish the Organization's Process Asset Library
- SP 1.6   Establish Work Environment Standards
- SP 1.7   Establish Rules and Guidelines for Teams

TIP

Organizational process assets support a fundamental change in behavior. Projects no longer create their processes from scratch but instead use the best practices of the organization, thereby improving quality and saving time and money.

Specific Practices by Goal

SG 1   ESTABLISH ORGANIZATIONAL PROCESS ASSETS

A set of organizational process assets is established and maintained.

SP 1.1 ESTABLISH STANDARD PROCESSES

Establish and maintain the organization's set of standard processes.

Standard processes can be defined at multiple levels in an enterprise and they can be related hierarchically. For example, an enterprise can have a set of standard processes that is tailored by individual organizations (e.g., a division, a site) in the enterprise to establish their set of standard processes. The set of standard processes can also be tailored for each of the organization's business areas, product lines, or standard services. Thus the *organization's set of standard processes* can refer to the standard processes established at the organization level and standard processes that may be established at lower levels, although some organizations may have only one level of standard processes. (See the definitions of "standard process" and "organization's set of standard processes" in the glossary.)

Multiple standard processes may be needed to address the needs of different application domains, lifecycle models, methodologies, and tools. The organization's set of standard processes contains process elements (e.g., a work product size estimating element) that may be interconnected according to one or more process architectures that describe relationships among process elements.

The organization's set of standard processes typically includes technical, management, administrative, support, and organizational processes.

Basing standard processes on industry standards and widely accepted models, with common terminology and lexicon, enables seamless interactions between the acquirer and supplier. In a multi-supplier environment, this seamless interaction is most important for acquirer standard processes that directly interface with supplier processes. Also, there can be cost and coordination benefits from having suppliers work together to develop or reconcile common support processes that are aligned with acquirer processes.

The level of detail required for standard processes depends on the flexibility needed by an enterprise, for instance, based on differences in business context, project types, and application domains.

The organization's set of standard processes should collectively cover all processes needed by the organization and projects, including those processes addressed by the process areas at maturity level 2.

Example Work Products

1. Organization's set of standard processes

> **TIP**
>
> Standard processes define the key activities performed in an organization. Examples of standard acquisition processes include source selection, contract negotiations, planning, and both technical and business reviews.

> **TIP**
>
> The organization's set of standard processes can include processes that are not directly addressed by CMMI, such as project acquisition strategy approval, financial management, and progress reporting to higher management or customers.

> **TIP**
>
> Often, organizations look at the exemplar processes from their successful acquisition projects or from other organizations as starting points to populate the organization's set of standard processes.

OPD

Subpractices

TIP

The objective is to decompose and define the process so that it can be performed consistently across projects, yet allow enough flexibility to meet the unique requirements of each project.

1. Decompose each standard process into constituent process elements to the detail needed to understand and describe the process.

   Each process element covers a closely related set of activities. The descriptions of process elements may be templates to be filled in, fragments to be completed, abstractions to be refined, or complete descriptions to be tailored or used unmodified. These elements are described in such detail that the process, when fully defined, can be consistently performed by appropriately trained and skilled people.

Examples of process elements include the following:
- Templates for supplier deliverables
- Common lexicon for directly interfacing acquirer and supplier processes
- Templates for standard supplier agreements
- Description of methods for verifying supplier estimates
- Description of standard acquisition approaches related to teaming with suppliers
- Description of methods for prequalifying suppliers as preferred suppliers
- Description of standard acceptance criteria
- Description of standard decision making and issue resolution
- Template for conducting management reviews
- Templates or task flows embedded in workflow tools

---

2. Specify the critical attributes of each process element.

Examples of critical attributes include the following:
- Process roles
- Applicable standards
- Applicable procedures, methods, tools, and resources
- Process performance objectives
- Entry criteria
- Inputs
- Verification points (e.g., peer reviews)
- Outputs
- Interfaces
- Exit criteria
- Product and process measures

---

3. Specify relationships among process elements.

> Examples of relationships include the following:
> • Order of the process elements
> • Interfaces among process elements
> • Interfaces with external processes
> • Interdependencies among process elements

The rules for describing relationships among process elements are referred to as the "process architecture." The process architecture covers essential requirements and guidelines. Detailed specifications of these relationships are covered in descriptions of defined processes that are tailored from the organization's set of standard processes.

4. Ensure that the organization's set of standard processes adheres to applicable policies, standards, and models.
   Adherence to applicable process standards and models is typically demonstrated by developing a mapping from the organization's set of standard processes to relevant process standards and models. This mapping is a useful input to future appraisals.

5. Ensure that the organization's set of standard processes satisfies process needs and objectives of the organization.

   Refer to the Organizational Process Focus process area for more information about establishing organizational process needs.

6. Ensure that there is appropriate integration among processes that are included in the organization's set of standard processes.

7. Document the organization's set of standard processes.

8. Conduct peer reviews on the organization's set of standard processes.
   The acquirer's review of its standard processes can include the participation of suppliers for those processes and process elements that define standard interactions with suppliers.

   Refer to the Acquisition Verification process area for more information about performing peer reviews.

9. Revise the organization's set of standard processes as necessary.

> Examples of when the organization's set of standard processes may need to be revised include the following:
> • When improvements to the process are identified
> • When causal analysis and resolution data indicate that a process change is needed
> • When process improvement proposals are selected for deployment across the organization
> • When the organization's process needs and objectives are updated

HINT
Your initial focus should be on standardizing what you already do well.

HINT
Break down stovepipes: When capabilities residing in different organizations are routinely needed to understand tradeoffs and resolve system-level problems, consider establishing a standard end-to-end process for performing joint work. To improve workflow, consider process integration between acquisition and supplier elements where appropriate.

OPD

SP 1.2 ESTABLISH LIFECYCLE MODEL DESCRIPTIONS

Establish and maintain descriptions of lifecycle models approved for use in the organization.

Lifecycle models can be developed for a variety of customers or in a variety of situations, since one lifecycle model may not be appropriate for all situations. Lifecycle models are often used to define phases of the project. Also, the organization can define different lifecycle models for each type of product and service it delivers.

Lifecycle models describe acquisition lifecycles, depending on the acquisition strategy chosen. The acquisition lifecycle typically begins with the pre-award phase of a supplier agreement, continues through the phases of awarding and managing the supplier agreement, and ends when the supplier agreement period of performance ends, usually with the acceptance and completion of the warranty for the acquired product and the transition of the product to the support organization.

Example Work Products

1. Descriptions of lifecycle models

Subpractices

1. Select lifecycle models based on the needs of projects and the organization.
2. Document descriptions of lifecycle models.
   Lifecycle models can be documented as part of the organization's standard process descriptions or they can be documented separately.
3. Conduct peer reviews on lifecycle models.
   The acquirer's review of lifecycle models should include the participation of suppliers for those processes and process elements that define expectations and constraints for suppliers.

   Refer to the Acquisition Verification process area for more information about performing peer reviews.

4. Revise the descriptions of lifecycle models as necessary.

SP 1.3 ESTABLISH TAILORING CRITERIA AND GUIDELINES

Establish and maintain tailoring criteria and guidelines for the organization's set of standard processes.

Tailoring criteria and guidelines describe the following:

- How the organization's set of standard processes and organizational process assets are used to create defined processes

TIP

When managing a project, it is helpful to have a standard description for the phases that the project moves through (i.e., project lifecycle model) to organize and assess the adequacy of project activities and to monitor progress.

TIP

It helps to provide guidance about which lifecycle models work best with which types of projects. This guidance may be found in organizations' process asset libraries based on their previous experiences.

TIP

Tailoring allows projects to adapt the organization's set of standard processes and other assets to meet their needs. The challenge is to provide guidance that has sufficient flexibility to meet the unique needs of each project while simultaneously ensuring meaningful consistency.

- Requirements that must be satisfied by defined processes (e.g., the subset of organizational process assets that are essential for any defined process)
- Options that can be exercised and criteria for selecting among options
- Procedures that must be followed in performing and documenting process tailoring

---

Examples of reasons for tailoring include the following:
- Adapting the process for a new supplier
- Accommodating supplier characteristics such as the number of projects executed for the acquirer and the supplier's process maturity
- Following the acquisition strategy
- Elaborating the process description so that the resulting defined process can be performed
- Customizing the process for an application or class of similar applications

---

Flexibility in tailoring and defining processes is balanced with ensuring appropriate consistency of processes across the organization. Flexibility is needed to address contextual variables such as the domain; the nature of the customer; cost, schedule, and quality tradeoffs; the technical difficulty of the work; and the experience of the people implementing the process. Consistency across the organization is needed so that organizational standards, objectives, and strategies are appropriately addressed, and process data and lessons learned can be shared.

Tailoring is a critical activity that allows controlled changes to processes due to the specific needs of a project or a part of the organization. Processes and process elements that are directly related to critical business objectives should usually be defined as mandatory, but processes and process elements that are less critical or only indirectly affect business objectives may allow for more tailoring.

The amount of tailoring could also depend on the project's lifecycle model, the supplier, or the acquirer-supplier relationship.

Tailoring criteria and guidelines can allow for using a standard process "as is," with no tailoring.

TIP

Finding this balance usually takes time, as the organization gains experience from using these assets.

Example Work Products

1. Tailoring guidelines for the organization's set of standard processes

OPD

Subpractices

1. Specify selection criteria and procedures for tailoring the organization's set of standard processes.

    To fully leverage the supplier's process capability, the acquirer can choose to minimize the tailoring of the supplier's standard processes. Depending on the interfaces of the acquirer's processes with the supplier's processes, the acquirer's standard processes can be tailored to allow the supplier to execute its standard processes.

Examples of criteria and procedures include the following:
- Criteria for selecting an acquisition strategy and suppliers
- Criteria for selecting acquirer processes based on supplier process tailoring such as adding or combining testing cycles
- Criteria for selecting lifecycle models from the ones approved by the organization
- Criteria for selecting process elements from the organization's set of standard processes
- Procedures for tailoring selected lifecycle models and process elements to accommodate process characteristics and needs
- Procedures for adapting the organization's common measures to address information needs

---

Examples of tailoring include the following:
- Modifying a lifecycle model
- Combining elements of different lifecycle models
- Modifying process elements
- Replacing process elements
- Reordering process elements

HINT

Streamline the waiver process to enable new projects to establish their defined process quickly and to avoid stalling.

TIP

Both the tailoring process and guidelines may be documented as part of the organization's set of standard processes.

2. Specify the standards used for documenting defined processes.
3. Specify the procedures used for submitting and obtaining approval of waivers from the organization's set of standard processes.
4. Document tailoring guidelines for the organization's set of standard processes.
5. Conduct peer reviews on the tailoring guidelines.

    Refer to the Acquisition Verification process area for more information about performing peer reviews.

6. Revise tailoring guidelines as necessary.

SP 1.4 ESTABLISH THE ORGANIZATION'S MEASUREMENT REPOSITORY

Establish and maintain the organization's measurement repository.

Refer to the Use Organizational Process Assets for Planning Project Activities specific practice in the Integrated Project Management process area for more information about the use of the organization's measurement repository in planning project activities.

The repository contains both product and process measures that are related to the organization's set of standard processes. It also contains or refers to information needed to understand and interpret measures and to assess them for reasonableness and applicability. For example, the definitions of measures are used to compare similar measures from different processes.

Standard measures that must be collected from the supplier are included as requirements in standard supplier agreements and can appear in the organization's measurement repository.

Example Work Products

1. Definition of the common set of product and process measures for the organization's set of standard processes
2. Design of the organization's measurement repository
3. Organization's measurement repository (i.e., the repository structure, support environment)
4. Organization's measurement data

Subpractices

1. Determine the organization's needs for storing, retrieving, and analyzing measurements.
2. Define a common set of process and product measures for the organization's set of standard processes.

    Measures in the common set are selected for their ability to provide visibility into processes critical to achieving business objectives and to focus on process elements significantly impacting cost, schedule, and performance within a project and across the organization. The common set of measures can vary for different standard processes. Measures defined include the ones related to agreement management, some of which may need to be collected from suppliers.

    Operational definitions for measures specify procedures for collecting valid data and the point in the process where data will be collected.

3. Design and implement the measurement repository.

    Functions of the measurement repository include the following:

    • Supporting effective comparison and interpretation of measurement data among projects

---

TIP

The organization's measurement repository is a critical resource that helps new projects plan by providing answers to questions about similar projects undertaken in the past (e.g., How long did it take? How much effort was expended? What was the resultant quality?).

TIP

Although this practice concentrates on establishing and maintaining a repository, the real value becomes evident when the people in the organization begin to use the data in the repository when they establish defined processes and plans.

TIP

These measures change over time and, therefore, should be reviewed periodically.

X-REF

Measurement and analysis practices (see MA) are a prerequisite to establishing the organization's measurement repository.

OPD

- Providing sufficient context to allow a new project to quickly identify and access data in the repository for similar projects
- Enabling projects to improve the accuracy of their estimates by using their own and other projects' historical data
- Aiding in the understanding of process performance
- Supporting potential statistical management of processes or subprocesses, as needed

4. Specify procedures for storing, updating, and retrieving measures.

   Refer to the Measurement and Analysis process area for more information about specifying data collection and storage procedures.

5. Conduct peer reviews on definitions of the common set of measures and procedures for storing, updating, and retrieving measures.

   Refer to the Acquisition Verification process area for more information about performing peer reviews.

6. Enter specified measures into the repository.

   Refer to the Measurement and Analysis process area for more information about specifying measures.

7. Make the contents of the measurement repository available for use by the organization and projects as appropriate.

8. Revise the measurement repository, the common set of measures, and procedures as the organization's needs change.

Examples of when the common set of measures may need to be revised include the following:

- New processes are added
- Processes are revised and new measures are needed
- Finer granularity of data is required
- Greater visibility into the process is required
- Measures are retired

SP 1.5 *ESTABLISH THE ORGANIZATION'S PROCESS ASSET LIBRARY*

Establish and maintain the organization's process asset library.

Examples of items to be stored in the organization's process asset library include the following:

- Organizational policies
- Process descriptions

Continues

Continued

- Procedures (e.g., estimating procedure)
- Development plans
- Acquisition plans
- Quality assurance plans
- Training materials
- Process aids (e.g., checklists)
- Lessons learned reports

Example Work Products

1. Design of the organization's process asset library
2. The organization's process asset library
3. Selected items to be included in the organization's process asset library
4. The catalog of items in the organization's process asset library

Subpractices

1. Design and implement the organization's process asset library, including the library structure and support environment.
2. Specify criteria for including items in the library.
   Items are selected based primarily on their relationship to the organization's set of standard processes.
3. Specify procedures for storing, updating, and retrieving items.
4. Enter selected items into the library and catalog them for easy reference and retrieval.
5. Make items available for use by projects.
6. Periodically review the use of each item.
7. Revise the organization's process asset library as necessary.

Examples of when the library may need to be revised include the following:

- New items are added
- Items are retired
- Current versions of items are changed

HINT

Think about why you are storing this information and how often it will be retrieved.

TIP

A major objective of the process asset library is to ensure that information is easy to locate and use.

TIP

Library maintenance can quickly become an issue if all documents from every project are stored in the library.

TIP

Some organizations regularly review their process asset library contents every 12 to 18 months to decide what to discard or archive.

OPD

TIP

Work environment standards must make sense for your organization given its line of business, the degree of collaboration to be supported, and other factors.

HINT

If your organization has a shared vision, your work environment must support it.

TIP

Typically, projects have additional requirements for their work environment. This specific practice establishes the standards to be addressed across the organization.

TIP

Specific practice 1.7 is included in this process area to address the use of integrated teams, as these groups are more likely to be needed to meet the complex needs of the acquisition organization in its interactions with other acquisition organizations, supplier organizations, and customer organizations.

TIP

This specific practice establishes organizational rules and guidelines so that projects do not get "bogged down" when establishing their team structure, integrated teams in that structure, and adequate collaboration among interfacing teams.

SP 1.6 ESTABLISH WORK ENVIRONMENT STANDARDS

Establish and maintain work environment standards.

Work environment standards allow the organization and projects to benefit from common tools, training, and maintenance, as well as cost savings from volume purchases. Work environment standards address the needs of all stakeholders and consider productivity, cost, availability, security, and workplace health, safety, and ergonomic factors. Work environment standards can include guidelines for tailoring and the use of waivers that allow adaptation of the project's work environment to meet needs.

Examples of work environment standards include the following:
- Procedures for the operation, safety, and security of the work environment
- Standard workstation hardware and software
- Standard application software and tailoring guidelines for it
- Standard production and calibration equipment
- Process for requesting and approving tailoring or waivers

Example Work Products

1. Work environment standards

Subpractices

1. Evaluate commercially available work environment standards appropriate for the organization.
2. Adopt existing work environment standards and develop new ones to fill gaps based on the organization's process needs and objectives.

SP 1.7 ESTABLISH RULES AND GUIDELINES FOR TEAMS

Establish and maintain organizational rules and guidelines for the structure, formation, and operation of teams.

In an acquisition organization, teams are useful not just in the acquirer's organization but between the acquirer and supplier and among the acquirer, supplier, and other relevant stakeholders as appropriate. Teams can be especially important in a system of systems environment.

Operating rules and guidelines for teams define and control how teams are created and how they interact to accomplish objectives. Team members should understand the standards for work and participate according to those standards.

When establishing rules and guidelines for teams, ensure they comply with all local and national regulations or laws that can affect the use of teams.

Structuring teams involves defining the number of teams, the type of each team, and how each team relates to the others in the structure. Forming teams involves chartering each team, assigning team members and team leaders, and providing resources to each team to accomplish work.

Example Work Products

1. Rules and guidelines for structuring and forming teams
2. Operating rules for teams

Subpractices

1. Establish and maintain empowerment mechanisms to enable timely decision making.
   In a successful teaming environment, clear channels of responsibility and authority are established by documenting and deploying organizational guidelines that clearly define the empowerment of teams.

2. Establish and maintain rules and guidelines for structuring and forming teams.

> Organizational process assets can help the project to structure and implement teams. Such assets can include the following:
> - Guidelines for establishing lines of communication, authority, and escalation
> - Team structure guidelines
> - Team formation guidelines
> - Team authority and responsibility guidelines
> - Team leader selection criteria

3. Define the expectations, rules, and guidelines that guide how teams work collectively.

TIP
Teams cannot operate at a high performance level if they must consult management to obtain approval of every action or decision.

TIP
This specific practice also addresses issue resolution.

TIP
The authority initially given to a newly formed team may be expanded later as project phases are completed and as the team demonstrates mature use of the authority granted to it. The rules and guidelines for the degree of empowerment should support making such adjustments.

OPD

X-REF

For more information on establishing integrated teams, see IPM SP 1.6.

These rules and guidelines establish organizational practices for consistency across teams and can include the following:

- How interfaces among teams are established and maintained
- How assignments are accepted and transferred
- How resources and inputs are accessed
- How work gets done
- Who checks, reviews, and approves work
- How work is approved
- How work is delivered and communicated
- Who reports to whom
- What the reporting requirements (e.g., cost, schedule, performance status), measures, and methods are
- Which progress reporting measures and methods are used

ORGANIZATIONAL PROCESS FOCUS
A Process Management Process Area at Maturity Level 3

Purpose

The purpose of Organizational Process Focus (OPF) is to plan, implement, and deploy organizational process improvements based on a thorough understanding of current strengths and weaknesses of the organization's processes and process assets.

Introductory Notes

The organization's processes include all processes used by the organization and its projects. Candidate improvements to the organization's processes and process assets are obtained from various sources, including the measurement of processes, lessons learned in implementing processes, results of process appraisals, results of product and service evaluation activities, results of customer satisfaction evaluations, results of benchmarking against other organizations' processes, and recommendations from other improvement initiatives in the organization.

Process improvement occurs in the context of the organization's needs and is used to address the organization's objectives. The organization encourages participation in process improvement activities by those who perform the process. The responsibility for facilitating and managing the organization's process improvement activities, including coordinating the participation of others, is typically assigned to a process group. The organization provides the long-term commitment and resources required to sponsor this group and to ensure the effective and timely deployment of improvements.

The acquirer encourages supplier participation in process improvement activities.

Careful planning is required to ensure that process improvement efforts across the organization are adequately managed and implemented. Results of the organization's process improvement planning are documented in a process improvement plan.

> **TIP**
>
> The many organizational approaches possible for structuring acquisition offices and positioning process improvement programs within them makes this process area vitally important for pursuing CMMI-ACQ beyond the basic acquisition best practices found in the CMMI-ACQ Primer at www.sei.cmu.edu/library/abstracts/reports/08tr010.cfm.

> **TIP**
>
> In some cases, organizational process improvement may be best managed at a site where multiple acquisition projects are operating. In other cases, process improvement efforts may be dispersed across regions or the globe, with needed commitment to process discipline imposed by a central office, such as the office of the company CIO.

TIP

When multiple organizations are involved in the success of the development of the product or service (e.g., acquirers and suppliers), coordinating and potentially sharing appraisal efforts deserves consideration.

HINT

Run your process improvement program like a project or a series of projects. Use CMMI practices to help you plan, implement, and manage your process improvement activities.

TIP

With any type of change, an investment is required. These activities may require weeks, months, or even years to complete. One challenge is to demonstrate improvements the organization can see quickly.

The "organization's process improvement plan" addresses appraisal planning, process action planning, pilot planning, and deployment planning. Appraisal plans describe the appraisal timeline and schedule, the scope of the appraisal, resources required to perform the appraisal, the reference model against which the appraisal will be performed, and logistics for the appraisal.

Process action plans usually result from appraisals and document how improvements targeting weaknesses uncovered by an appraisal will be implemented. Sometimes the improvement described in the process action plan should be tested on a small group before deploying it across the organization. In these cases, a pilot plan is generated.

When the improvement is to be deployed, a deployment plan is created. This plan describes when and how the improvement will be deployed across the organization.

Organizational process assets are used to describe, implement, and improve the organization's processes. (See the definition of "organizational process assets" in the glossary.)

Related Process Areas

Refer to the Organizational Process Definition process area for more information about establishing organizational process assets.

Specific Goal and Practice Summary

SG 1 Determine Process Improvement Opportunities
    SP 1.1   Establish Organizational Process Needs
    SP 1.2   Appraise the Organization's Processes
    SP 1.3   Identify the Organization's Process Improvements
SG 2 Plan and Implement Process Actions
    SP 2.1   Establish Process Action Plans
    SP 2.2   Implement Process Action Plans
SG 3 Deploy Organizational Process Assets and Incorporate Experiences
    SP 3.1   Deploy Organizational Process Assets
    SP 3.2   Deploy Standard Processes
    SP 3.3   Monitor the Implementation
    SP 3.4   Incorporate Experiences into Organizational Process Assets

Specific Practices by Goal

TIP

Project participation is essential to any process improvement effort. Because acquisition success depends on both acquirers and suppliers, coordinated approaches can produce a powerful synergy.

SG 1   DETERMINE PROCESS IMPROVEMENT OPPORTUNITIES

Strengths, weaknesses, and improvement opportunities for the organization's processes are identified periodically and as needed.

Strengths, weaknesses, and improvement opportunities can be determined relative to a process standard or model such as a CMMI model or ISO standard. Process improvements should be selected to address the organization's needs.

Process improvement opportunities can arise as a result of changing business objectives, legal and regulatory requirements, and results of benchmarking studies.

TIP

Although CMMI describes many of the processes that are critical to success, it does not cover everything. Within your organization, you may need to improve processes such as portfolio management, which might not be discussed in CMMI.

SP 1.1 ESTABLISH ORGANIZATIONAL PROCESS NEEDS

Establish and maintain the description of process needs and objectives for the organization.

The organization's processes operate in a business context that should be understood. The organization's business objectives, needs, and constraints determine the needs and objectives for the organization's processes. Typically, issues related to customer satisfaction, finance, technology, quality, human resources, and marketing are important process considerations.

TIP

Process improvement must relate directly to the organization's business objectives.

> The organization's process needs and objectives cover aspects that include the following:
> - Characteristics of processes
> - Process performance objectives, such as time-to-market and delivered quality
> - Process effectiveness

Issues related to the organization's acquisition management needs are important process considerations.

Example Work Products

1. The organization's process needs and objectives

Subpractices

1. Identify policies, standards, and business objectives that are applicable to the organization's processes.

> Examples of standards include the following:
> - ISO/IEC 12207:2008 Systems and Software Engineering – Software Life Cycle Processes [ISO 2008a]
> - ISO/IEC 15288:2008 Systems and Software Engineering – System Life Cycle Processes [ISO 2008b]
>
> *Continues*

TIP

Especially in the early phases of process improvement, the process group must visibly demonstrate return on the organization's investment in process improvement.

Continued

- ISO/IEC 27001:2005 Information technology – Security techniques – Information Security Management Systems – Requirements [ISO/IEC 2005]
- ISO/IEC 14764:2006 Software Engineering – Software Life Cycle Processes – Maintenance [ISO 2006b]
- ISO/IEC 20000 Information Technology – Service Management [ISO 2005b]
- Assurance Focus for CMMI [DHS 2009]
- NDIA Engineering for System Assurance Guidebook [NDIA 2008]
- Resiliency Management Model [SEI 2010c]

2. Examine relevant process standards and models for best practices.
3. Determine the organization's process performance objectives.
   Process performance objectives can be expressed in quantitative or qualitative terms.

   Refer to the Measurement and Analysis process area for more information about establishing measurement objectives.

   Refer to the Organizational Process Performance process area for more information about establishing quality and process performance objectives.

TIP

Examples of process performance objectives include reducing defects identified by the end user in the field by 20 percent per year (quantitative) and increasing customer satisfaction (qualitative).

Examples of process performance objectives include the following:
- Reduce defect insertion rate by a certain percentage
- Achieve a certain cycle time for a given activity
- Improve productivity by a given percentage
- Simplify the requirements approval workflow
- Improve quality of products delivered to customer

4. Define essential characteristics of the organization's processes.
   Essential characteristics of the organization's processes are determined based on the following:
   - Processes currently being used in the organization
   - Standards imposed by the organization
   - Standards commonly imposed by customers of the organization

Examples of process characteristics include the following:
- Level of detail
- Process notation
- Granularity

5. Document the organization's process needs and objectives.

6. Revise the organization's process needs and objectives as needed.

SP 1.2 APPRAISE THE ORGANIZATION'S PROCESSES

Appraise the organization's processes periodically and as needed to maintain an understanding of their strengths and weaknesses.

Process appraisals can be performed for the following reasons:
- To identify processes to be improved
- To confirm progress and make the benefits of process improvement visible
- To satisfy the needs of a customer-supplier relationship
- To motivate and facilitate buy-in

The buy-in gained during a process appraisal can be eroded significantly if it is not followed by an appraisal based action plan.

Example Work Products

1. Plans for the organization's process appraisals
2. Appraisal findings that address strengths and weaknesses of the organization's processes
3. Improvement recommendations for the organization's processes

Subpractices

1. Obtain sponsorship of the process appraisal from senior management.

   Senior management sponsorship includes the commitment to have the organization's managers and staff participate in the process appraisal and to provide resources and funding to analyze and communicate findings of the appraisal.

2. Define the scope of the process appraisal.

   Process appraisals can be performed on the entire organization or can be performed on a smaller part of an organization such as a single project or business area.

   The scope of the process appraisal addresses the following:

   - Definition of the organization (e.g., sites, business areas) to be covered by the appraisal
   - Identification of the project and support functions that will represent the organization in the appraisal
   - Processes to be appraised

OPF

HINT

Select the appraisal method that matches the purpose and information needed. To guide your selection, determine the amount of information needed and the importance of its accuracy.

TIP

Remember that these appraisals focus on the acquisition organization seeking to improve its own process performance.

X-REF

Using appraisals as part of managing supplier activities is covered in SSAD and AM. Another useful resource for understanding how to interpret appraisals effectively is the guidebook "Understanding and Leveraging a Supplier's CMMI Efforts: A Guidebook for Acquirers," found at www.sei.cmu.edu/library/abstracts/reports/07tr004.cfm.

TIP

The commitment of resources to the appraisal must be visible throughout the organization.

3. Determine the method and criteria to be used for the process appraisal.

> Process appraisals can occur in many forms. They should address the needs and objectives of the organization, which can change over time. For example, the appraisal can be based on a process model, such as a CMMI model, or on a national or international standard, such as ISO 9001 [ISO 2008c]. Appraisals can also be based on a benchmark comparison with other organizations in which practices that can contribute to improved organizational performance are identified. The characteristics of the appraisal method may vary, including time and effort, makeup of the appraisal team, and the method and depth of investigation.

4. Plan, schedule, and prepare for the process appraisal.

5. Conduct the process appraisal.

6. Document and deliver the appraisal's activities and findings.

SP 1.3 IDENTIFY THE ORGANIZATION'S PROCESS IMPROVEMENTS

Identify improvements to the organization's processes and process assets.

Example Work Products

1. Analysis of candidate process improvements
2. Identification of improvements for the organization's processes

Subpractices

1. Determine candidate process improvements.

> Candidate process improvements are typically determined by doing the following:
> - Measuring processes and analyzing measurement results
> - Reviewing processes for effectiveness and suitability
> - Assessing customer satisfaction
> - Reviewing lessons learned from tailoring the organization's set of standard processes
> - Reviewing lessons learned from implementing processes
> - Reviewing process improvement proposals submitted by the organization's managers, staff, and other relevant stakeholders
> - Soliciting inputs on process improvements from senior management and other leaders in the organization
> - Examining results of process appraisals and other process related reviews
> - Reviewing results of other organizational improvement initiatives

> Candidate process improvements are also determined by doing the following:
> - Reviewing process improvement proposals submitted by the organization's suppliers
> - Obtaining feedback from suppliers on acquirer processes and supplier-acquirer interface points

2. Prioritize candidate process improvements.

   Criteria for prioritization are as follows:

   - Consider the estimated cost and effort to implement the process improvements.
   - Evaluate the expected improvement against the organization's improvement objectives and priorities.
   - Determine the potential barriers to the process improvements and develop strategies for overcoming these barriers.

HINT

Choose improvements that are visible to the organization, have a defined scope, and can be addressed successfully by available resources. If you try to do too much too quickly, the over-extension may result in failure and cause the improvement program as a whole to be questioned.

> Examples of techniques to help determine and prioritize possible improvements to be implemented include the following:
> - A cost benefit analysis that compares the estimated cost and effort to implement the process improvements and their associated benefits
> - A gap analysis that compares current conditions in the organization with optimal conditions
> - Force field analysis of potential improvements to identify potential barriers and strategies for overcoming those barriers
> - Cause-and-effect analyses to provide information on the potential effects of different improvements that can then be compared

3. Identify and document the process improvements to be implemented.
4. Revise the list of planned process improvements to keep it current.

SG 2 PLAN AND IMPLEMENT PROCESS ACTIONS

Process actions that address improvements to the organization's processes and process assets are planned and implemented.

The successful implementation of improvements requires participation in process action planning and implementation by process owners, those who perform the process, and support organizations.

X-REF

Organizational process assets are those created by the activities in OPD.

TIP

Most of the acquisition organization should be involved in these activities.

SP 2.1 ESTABLISH PROCESS ACTION PLANS

Establish and maintain process action plans to address improvements to the organization's processes and process assets.

Establishing and maintaining process action plans typically involves the following roles:

- Management steering committees that set strategies and oversee process improvement activities
- Process groups that facilitate and manage process improvement activities
- Process action teams that define and implement process actions
- Process owners that manage deployment
- Practitioners that perform the process

Stakeholder involvement helps to obtain buy-in on process improvements and increases the likelihood of effective deployment.

Process action plans are detailed implementation plans. These plans differ from the organization's process improvement plan by targeting improvements that were defined to address weaknesses and that were usually uncovered by appraisals.

Suppliers can be involved in developing process action plans if the processes that define interfaces between the acquirer and supplier are targeted for improvement.

Example Work Products

1. The organization's approved process action plans

Subpractices

1. Identify strategies, approaches, and actions to address identified process improvements.
   New, unproven, and major changes are piloted before they are incorporated into normal use.
2. Establish process action teams to implement actions.
   The teams and people performing the process improvement actions are called "process action teams." Process action teams typically include process owners and those who perform the process.
   Process action teams can also include supplier representatives when suppliers interact with the acquirer process to be improved or provide supplemental resources to the acquirer to perform an acquirer process.
3. Document process action plans.

TIP

Depending on the magnitude of the improvement, a process action plan may look similar to a project plan. If the improvement is small, the plan may look similar to a plan for a routine maintenance activity.

X-REF

Piloting guidance can be found in OPM and can be useful even if the thorough quantitative information expected by OPM is not yet available.

> Process action plans typically cover the following:
> - Process improvement infrastructure
> - Process improvement objectives
> - Process improvements to be addressed
> - Procedures for planning and tracking process actions
> - Strategies for piloting and implementing process actions
> - Responsibility and authority for implementing process actions
> - Resources, schedules, and assignments for implementing process actions
> - Methods for determining the effectiveness of process actions
> - Risks associated with process action plans

4. Review and negotiate process action plans with relevant stakeholders.

5. Revise process action plans as necessary.

SP 2.2 IMPLEMENT PROCESS ACTION PLANS

Implement process action plans.

Example Work Products

1. Commitments among process action teams
2. Status and results of implementing process action plans
3. Plans for pilots

Subpractices

1. Make process action plans readily available to relevant stakeholders.

2. Negotiate and document commitments among process action teams and revise their process action plans as necessary.

3. Track progress and commitments against process action plans.

4. Conduct joint reviews with process action teams and relevant stakeholders to monitor the progress and results of process actions.

5. Plan pilots needed to test selected process improvements.

6. Review the activities and work products of process action teams.

7. Identify, document, and track to closure issues encountered when implementing process action plans.

8. Ensure that results of implementing process action plans satisfy the organization's process improvement objectives.

TIP

Depending on the size of the organization and the extent of the change, the implementation activity may take days, weeks, months, or even years. Legacy acquisition programs may need to tailor changes to recognize existing agreements with customers and suppliers or with other acquisition offices in a system-of-systems environment.

SG 3 DEPLOY ORGANIZATIONAL PROCESS ASSETS AND INCORPORATE EXPERIENCES

Organizational process assets are deployed across the organization and process related experiences are incorporated into organizational process assets.

The specific practices under this specific goal describe ongoing activities. New opportunities to benefit from organizational process assets and changes to them can arise throughout the life of each project. Deployment of standard processes and other organizational process assets should be continually supported in the organization, particularly for new projects at startup.

SP 3.1 DEPLOY ORGANIZATIONAL PROCESS ASSETS

Deploy organizational process assets across the organization.

HINT

Be sure to think about retiring the assets and work products that the change replaces. This activity is particularly important when acquisition organizations are dispersed regionally or globally.

Deploying organizational process assets or changes to them should be performed in an orderly manner. Some organizational process assets or changes to them may not be appropriate for use in some parts of the organization (e.g., because of stakeholder requirements or the current lifecycle phase being implemented). It is therefore important that those who are or will be executing the process, as well as other organization functions (e.g., training, quality assurance), be involved in deployment as necessary.

Refer to the Organizational Process Definition process area for more information about establishing organizational process assets.

Example Work Products

1. Plans for deploying organizational process assets and changes to them across the organization
2. Training materials for deploying organizational process assets and changes to them
3. Documentation of changes to organizational process assets
4. Support materials for deploying organizational process assets and changes to them

Subpractices

1. Deploy organizational process assets across the organization.

Typical activities performed as a part of the deployment of process assets include the following:

- Identifying organizational process assets that should be adopted by those who perform the process

Continues

Continued

- Determining how organizational process assets are made available (e.g., via a website)
- Identifying how changes to organizational process assets are communicated
- Identifying resources (e.g., methods, tools) needed to support the use of organizational process assets
- Planning the deployment
- Assisting those who use organizational process assets
- Ensuring that training is available for those who use organizational process assets

Refer to the Organizational Training process area for more information about establishing an organizational training capability.

2. Document changes to organizational process assets.

   Documenting changes to organizational process assets serves two main purposes:

   - To enable the communication of changes
   - To understand the relationship of changes in the organizational process assets to changes in process performance and results

3. Deploy changes that were made to organizational process assets across the organization.

Typical activities performed as a part of deploying changes include the following:

- Determining which changes are appropriate for those who perform the process
- Planning the deployment
- Arranging for the support needed for the successful transition of changes

4. Provide guidance and consultation on the use of organizational process assets.

SP 3.2 Deploy Standard Processes

Deploy the organization's set of standard processes to projects at their startup and deploy changes to them as appropriate throughout the life of each project.

It is important that new projects use proven and effective processes to perform critical early activities (e.g., project planning, receiving requirements, obtaining resources).

Projects should also periodically update their defined processes to incorporate the latest changes made to the organization's set of

HINT
Project start-up is the first and least expensive opportunity to get things right. Consider using experienced teams to help guide a project through high-risk areas by selecting from and tailoring the organization's set of standard processes to mitigate project risk.

standard processes when it will benefit them. This periodic update helps to ensure that all project activities derive the full benefit of what other projects have learned.

Refer to the Organizational Process Definition process area for more information about establishing standard processes and establishing tailoring criteria and guidelines.

Example Work Products

1. The organization's list of projects and the status of process deployment on each (i.e., existing and planned projects)
2. Guidelines for deploying the organization's set of standard processes on new projects
3. Records of tailoring and implementing the organization's set of standard processes

Subpractices

1. Identify projects in the organization that are starting up.
2. Identify active projects that would benefit from implementing the organization's current set of standard processes.
3. Establish plans to implement the organization's current set of standard processes on the identified projects.
4. Assist projects in tailoring the organization's set of standard processes to meet their needs.

   Refer to the Integrated Project Management process area for more information about establishing the project's defined process.

5. Maintain records of tailoring and implementing processes on the identified projects.
6. Ensure that the defined processes resulting from process tailoring are incorporated into plans for process compliance audits.
   Process compliance audits are objective evaluations of project activities against the project's defined process.
7. As the organization's set of standard processes is updated, identify which projects should implement the changes.

SP 3.3 MONITOR THE IMPLEMENTATION

Monitor the implementation of the organization's set of standard processes and use of process assets on all projects.

By monitoring implementation, the organization ensures that the organization's set of standard processes and other process assets are

HINT
It is important not to limit improvement activities to just a few projects in your portfolio. Even legacy or small projects will benefit from the planned adoption of better processes.

appropriately deployed to all projects. Monitoring implementation also helps the organization to develop an understanding of the organizational process assets being used and where they are used in the organization. Monitoring also helps to establish a broader context for interpreting and using process and product measures, lessons learned, and improvement information obtained from projects.

Example Work Products

1. Results of monitoring process implementation on projects
2. Status and results of process compliance audits
3. Results of reviewing selected process artifacts created as part of process tailoring and implementation

Subpractices

1. Monitor the projects' use of organizational process assets and changes to them.
2. Review selected process artifacts created during the life of each project.

    Reviewing selected process artifacts created during the life of a project ensures that all projects are making appropriate use of the organization's set of standard processes.

3. Review results of process compliance audits to determine how well the organization's set of standard processes has been deployed.

    Refer to the Process and Product Quality Assurance process area for more information about objectively evaluating processes.

4. Identify, document, and track to closure issues related to implementing the organization's set of standard processes.

SP 3.4 *INCORPORATE EXPERIENCES INTO ORGANIZATIONAL PROCESS ASSETS*

Incorporate process related experiences derived from planning and performing the process into organizational process assets.

Example Work Products

1. Process improvement proposals
2. Process lessons learned
3. Measurements of organizational process assets
4. Improvement recommendations for organizational process assets
5. Records of the organization's process improvement activities
6. Information on organizational process assets and improvements to them

> **X-REF**
>
> Practices in IPM, OPF, and OPD are tightly intertwined. OPD defines the organizational assets; OPF manages them, deploys them across the organization, and collects feedback; IPM uses the assets on the project and provides feedback to the organization.

Subpractices

TIP

Some feedback may be collected as part of quality assurance (QA) activities.

X-REF

Lessons learned are usually made available through the library established in OPD.

1. Conduct periodic reviews of the effectiveness and suitability of the organization's set of standard processes and related organizational process assets relative to the process needs and objectives derived from the organization's business objectives.

2. Obtain feedback about the use of organizational process assets.

3. Derive lessons learned from defining, piloting, implementing, and deploying organizational process assets.

4. Make lessons learned available to people in the organization as appropriate.

   Actions may be necessary to ensure that lessons learned are used appropriately.

> Examples of the inappropriate use of lessons learned include the following:
> - Evaluating the performance of people
> - Judging process performance or results

> Examples of ways to prevent the inappropriate use of lessons learned include the following:
> - Controlling access to lessons learned
> - Educating people about the appropriate use of lessons learned

X-REF

Common sets of measures are usually kept in the organization's measurement repository, established in OPD.

5. Analyze measurement data obtained from the use of the organization's common set of measures.

   Refer to the Measurement and Analysis process area for more information about analyzing measurement data.

   Refer to the Organizational Process Definition process area for more information about establishing the organization's measurement repository.

TIP

We use the word *appraise* here more in line with *Webster's* definition of the word, rather than the *appraisal* term used in CMMI.

6. Appraise processes, methods, and tools in use in the organization and develop recommendations for improving organizational process assets.

> This appraisal typically includes the following:
> - Determining which processes, methods, and tools are of potential use to other parts of the organization
> - Appraising the quality and effectiveness of organizational process assets

Continues

Continued
- Identifying candidate improvements to organizational process assets
- Determining compliance with the organization's set of standard processes and tailoring guidelines

7. Make the best of the organization's processes, methods, and tools available to people in the organization as appropriate.
8. Manage process improvement proposals.
    Process improvement proposals can address both process and technology improvements.

The activities for managing process improvement proposals typically include the following:
- Soliciting process improvement proposals
- Collecting process improvement proposals
- Reviewing process improvement proposals
- Selecting the process improvement proposals to be implemented
- Tracking the implementation of process improvement proposals

    Process improvement proposals are documented as process change requests or problem reports as appropriate.
    Some process improvement proposals can be incorporated into the organization's process action plans.
9. Establish and maintain records of the organization's process improvement activities.

ORGANIZATIONAL PERFORMANCE MANAGEMENT
A Process Management Process Area at Maturity Level 5

Purpose

The purpose of Organizational Performance Management (OPM) is to proactively manage the organization's performance to meet its business objectives.

Introductory Notes

The Organizational Performance Management process area enables the organization to manage organizational performance by iteratively analyzing aggregated project data, identifying gaps in performance against the business objectives, and selecting and deploying improvements to close the gaps.

In this process area, the term "improvement" includes all incremental and innovative process and technology improvements, including those improvements made to project work environments. "Improvement" refers to all ideas that would change the organization's processes, technologies, and performance to better meet the organization's business objectives and associated quality and process performance objectives.

Business objectives that this process area might address include the following:

- Improved product quality (e.g., functionality, quality attributes)
- Increased productivity
- Increased process efficiency and effectiveness
- Increased consistency in meeting budget and schedule
- Decreased cycle time
- Greater customer and end-user satisfaction
- Shorter development or production time to change functionality, add new features, or adapt to new technologies

- Improved performance of a supply chain involving multiple suppliers
- Improved use of resources across the organization

The organization analyzes product and process performance data from the projects to determine if it is capable of meeting the quality and process performance objectives. Process performance baselines and process performance models, developed using Organizational Process Performance processes, are used as part of the analysis. Causal Analysis and Resolution processes can also be used to identify potential areas of improvement or specific improvement proposals.

The organization identifies and proactively solicits incremental and innovative improvements from within the organization and from external sources such as academia, competitive intelligence, and successful improvements implemented elsewhere.

Realization of the improvements and their effects on the quality and process performance objectives depends on being able to effectively identify, evaluate, implement, and deploy improvements to the organization's processes and technologies.

Realization of the improvements and beneficial effects also depends on engaging the workforce in identifying and evaluating possible improvements and maintaining a focus on long-term planning that includes the identification of innovations.

Improvements can be identified and executed by the acquirer or the supplier. The acquirer encourages all suppliers to participate in the acquirer's process and technology improvement activities. Some selected improvements can be deployed across acquirer and supplier organizations.

The acquirer and suppliers may share the costs and benefits of improvements. Acquirers may increase the incentive for suppliers to participate in improvement efforts across the supply chain by allowing suppliers to appropriate the entire value derived from a contributed improvement for an initial period (e.g., 6 to 18 months). Over time, the supplier may be expected to share a proportion of those savings with the acquirer (e.g., through cost reductions to the acquirer). Acquirer and supplier expectations related to participation in process and technology improvement activities, and the sharing of associated costs and benefits, should be documented in the supplier agreement.

Improvement proposals are evaluated and validated for their effectiveness in the target environment. Based on this evaluation, improvements are prioritized and selected for deployment to new and ongoing projects. Deployment is managed in accordance with the deployment plan and performance data are analyzed using statistical and other quantitative techniques to determine the effects of the improvement on quality and process performance objectives.

This improvement cycle continually optimizes organizational processes based on quality and process performance objectives. Business objectives are periodically reviewed to ensure they are current and quality and process performance objectives are updated as appropriate.

The Organizational Process Focus process area includes no assumptions about the quantitative basis for identifying improvements, nor their expected results. This process area extends the Organizational Process Focus practices by focusing on process improvement based on a quantitative understanding of the organization's set of standard processes and technologies and their expected quality and process performance.

The specific practices of this process area apply to organizations whose projects are quantitatively managed. Use of the specific practices of this process area can add value in other situations, but the results may not provide the same degree of impact to the organization's quality and process performance objectives.

Related Process Areas

Refer to the Causal Analysis and Resolution process area for more information about identifying causes of selected outcomes and taking action to improve process performance.

Refer to the Decision Analysis and Resolution process area for more information about analyzing possible decisions using a formal evaluation process that evaluates identified alternatives against established criteria.

Refer to the Measurement and Analysis process area for more information about aligning measurement and analysis activities and providing measurement results.

Refer to the Organizational Process Focus process area for more information about planning, implementing, and deploying organizational process improvements based on a thorough understanding of current strengths and weaknesses of the organization's processes and process assets.

Refer to the Organizational Process Performance process area for more information about establishing quality and process performance objectives and establishing process performance baselines and models.

Refer to the Organizational Training process area for more information about providing training.

OPM

HINT
Although many changes may individually have merit, the organization can devote only so much attention and resources to performance improvement. Some kind of evaluation and ranking leading to a selection is necessary.

HINT
OPF may provide sufficient assistance to your initial process improvement efforts. Implement OPM once the organization has established assets (OPP) that enable quantitative project management (QPM) and has developed some facility in the use of statistical and other quantitative techniques in both project and organizational settings.

X-REF
See *The Innovator's Solution: Creating and Sustaining Successful Growth* by Clayton M. Christensen and Michael E. Raynor (Harvard Business Press).

X-REF
See *The Strategy Paradox: Why Committing to Success Leads to Failure (And What to Do About It)* by Michael E. Raynor (Crown Business).

Specific Goal and Practice Summary

SG 1 Manage Business Performance
    SP 1.1   Maintain Business Objectives
    SP 1.2   Analyze Process Performance Data
    SP 1.3   Identify Potential Areas for Improvement
SG 2 Select Improvements
    SP 2.1   Elicit Suggested Improvements
    SP 2.2   Analyze Suggested Improvements
    SP 2.3   Validate Improvements
    SP 2.4   Select and Implement Improvements for Deployment
SG 3 Deploy Improvements
    SP 3.1   Plan the Deployment
    SP 3.2   Manage the Deployment
    SP 3.3   Evaluate Improvement Effects

Specific Practices by Goal

SG 1 MANAGE BUSINESS PERFORMANCE

The organization's business performance is managed using statistical and other quantitative techniques to understand process performance shortfalls, and to identify areas for process improvement.

Managing business performance requires the following:

- Maintaining the organization's business objectives
- Understanding the organization's ability to meet the business objectives
- Continually improving processes related to achieving the business objectives

    The organization uses defined process performance baselines to determine if the current and projected organizational business objectives are being met. Shortfalls in process performance are identified and analyzed to determine potential areas for process improvement.

    The term "shortfall" in OPM refers to the gap between desired business performance (as characterized in business objectives or quality and process performance objectives [QPPOs]) and actual business performance (as characterized in process performance baselines [PPBs]).

Refer to the Organizational Process Performance process area for more information about establishing performance baselines and models.

> **TIP**
>
> These three bullets correspond to SPs 1.1, 1.2, and 1.3–3.3 (i.e., the rest of the PA), respectively.

> **TIP**
>
> In government, nongovernment organizations (NGOs), and nonprofit organizations, the term "business performance" may include both "business performance" and "mission performance."

As the organization improves its process performance or as business strategies change, new business objectives are identified and associated quality and process performance objectives are derived.

Specific goal 2 addresses eliciting and analyzing improvement suggestions that address shortfalls in achieving quality and process performance objectives.

SP 1.1 MAINTAIN BUSINESS OBJECTIVES

Maintain business objectives based on an understanding of business strategies and actual performance results.

Organizational performance data, characterized by process performance baselines, are used to evaluate whether business objectives are realistic and aligned with business strategies. After business objectives have been revised and prioritized by senior management, quality and process performance objectives may need to be created or maintained and re-communicated.

Example Work Products

1. Revised business objectives
2. Revised quality and process performance objectives
3. Senior management approval of revised business objectives and quality and process performance objectives
4. Communication of all revised objectives
5. Updated process performance measures

Subpractices

1. Evaluate business objectives periodically to ensure they are aligned with business strategies.

   Senior management is responsible for understanding the marketplace, establishing business strategies, and establishing business objectives.

   Because business strategies and organizational performance evolve, business objectives should be reviewed periodically to determine whether they should be updated. For example, a business objective might be retired when process performance data show that the business objective is being met consistently over time or when the associated business strategy has changed.

2. Compare business objectives with actual process performance results to ensure they are realistic.

   Business objectives can set the bar too high to motivate real improvement. Using process performance baselines helps balance desires and reality.

OPM

> **TIP**
>
> Without a well-defined and clearly communicated set of objectives for the organization, improvements are less likely to be mutually reinforcing and can even work at cross purposes.

> **TIP**
>
> This practice is the responsibility of senior management and should not be delegated.

> **HINT**
>
> Understanding actual performance is key to establishing realistic objectives with some "stretch" in them (e.g., as in Hoshin planning; see Wikipedia).

> **X-REF**
>
> The business strategy literature is vast, with an early touchstone being Michael Porter's framework for business strategy development (see "Porter five forces analysis" in Wikipedia). The Christensen and Raynor books mentioned earlier are more recent, addressing how to nurture innovations to create sustained growth. Both books summarize many findings from the broader business strategy literature.

If process performance baselines are unavailable, sampling techniques can be used to develop a quantitative basis for comparison in a short period of time.

3. Prioritize business objectives based on documented criteria, such as the ability to win new business, retain existing clients, or accomplish other key business strategies.

4. Maintain quality and process performance objectives to address changes in business objectives.

Business objectives and quality and process performance objectives will typically evolve over time. As existing objectives are achieved, they will be monitored to ensure they continue to be met, while new business objectives and associated quality and process performance objectives are identified and managed.

Refer to the Organizational Process Performance process area for more information about establishing quality and process performance objectives.

5. Revise process performance measures to align with quality and process performance objectives.

Refer to the Organizational Process Performance process area for more information about establishing process performance measures.

SP 1.2 ANALYZE PROCESS PERFORMANCE DATA

Analyze process performance data to determine the organization's ability to meet identified business objectives.

The data that result from applying the process performance measures, which are defined using Organizational Process Performance processes, are analyzed to create process performance baselines that help in understanding the current capability of the organization. Comparing process performance baselines to quality and process performance objectives helps the organization to determine its ability to meet business objectives. This data typically are collected from project level process performance data to enable organizational analysis.

Example Work Products

1. Analysis of current capability vs. business objectives
2. Process performance shortfalls
3. Risks associated with meeting business objectives

Subpractices

1. Periodically compare quality and process performance objectives to current process performance baselines to evaluate the ability of the organization to meet its business objectives.

TIP

Business objectives are refined into QPPOs (e.g., as described in OPP SP 1.1), which then serve as "touch points" between senior management and the organization's performance management and analysis activities as described in the rest of this PA and OPP.

TIP

Is the organization achieving its QPPOs? Where are the shortfalls?

HINT

Poor supplier performance can influence achievement of the QPPOs for the acquisition organization. Make sure you clearly understand the contributions of suppliers to achieving your QPPOs and understand where you have direct *control* of outcomes versus just *influence*. Consider revising your objectives if your ability to meet them depends entirely on external factors.

HINT

Analyses using PPBs, process simulations, and process performance models (PPMs) can assist in evaluating the ability of the organization to meet its business objectives.

For example, if cycle time is a critical business need, many different cycle time measures may be collected by the organization. Overall cycle time performance data should be compared to the business objectives to understand if expected performance will satisfy business objectives.

2. Identify shortfalls where the actual process performance is not satisfying the business objectives.

3. Identify and analyze risks associated with not meeting business objectives.

4. Report results of the process performance and risk analyses to organizational leadership.

SP 1.3 IDENTIFY POTENTIAL AREAS FOR IMPROVEMENT

Identify potential areas for improvement that could contribute to meeting business objectives.

Potential areas for improvement are identified through a proactive analysis to determine areas that could address process performance shortfalls. Causal Analysis and Resolution processes can be used to diagnose and resolve root causes.

The output from this activity is used to evaluate and prioritize potential improvements, and can result in either incremental or innovative improvement suggestions as described in specific goal 2.

Example Work Products

1. Potential areas for improvement

Subpractices

1. Identify potential improvement areas based on the analysis of process performance shortfalls.

    Performance shortfalls include not meeting productivity, cycle time, or customer satisfaction objectives. Examples of areas to consider for improvement include product technology, process technology, staffing and staff development, team structures, supplier selection and management, and other organizational infrastructures.

2. Document the rationale for the potential improvement areas, including references to applicable business objectives and process performance data.

3. Document anticipated costs and benefits associated with addressing potential improvement areas.

4. Communicate the set of potential improvement areas for further evaluation, prioritization, and use.

OPM

TIP

Process performance shortfalls limit the ability of the organization to pursue its chosen business strategies.

TIP

Which areas should the organization target to resolve shortfalls?

HINT

PPBs, process simulations, and PPMs can assist in these analyses.

SG 2   SELECT IMPROVEMENTS

Improvements are proactively identified, evaluated using statistical and other quantitative techniques, and selected for deployment based on their contribution to meeting quality and process performance objectives.

- Improvements to be deployed across the organization are selected from improvement suggestions which have been evaluated for effectiveness in the target deployment environment. These improvement suggestions are elicited and submitted from across the organization to address the improvement areas identified in specific goal 1.
- Evaluations of improvement suggestions are based on the following:
  - A quantitative understanding of the organization's current quality and process performance
  - Satisfaction of the organization's quality and process performance objectives
  - Estimated costs and impacts of developing and deploying the improvements, resources, and funding available for deployment
  - Estimated benefits in quality and process performance resulting from deploying the improvements

SP 2.1   ELICIT SUGGESTED IMPROVEMENTS

Elicit and categorize suggested improvements.

This practice focuses on eliciting suggested improvements and includes categorizing suggested improvements as incremental or innovative.

Incremental improvements generally originate with those who do the work (i.e., users of the process or technology). Incremental improvements can be simple and inexpensive to implement and deploy. Incremental improvement suggestions are analyzed, but, if selected, may not need rigorous validation or piloting. Innovative improvements such as new or redesigned processes are more transformational than incremental improvements.

Innovative improvements often arise out of a systematic search for solutions to particular performance issues or opportunities to improve performance. They are identified by those who are trained and experienced with the maturation of particular technologies or whose job it is to track or directly contribute to increased performance.

Innovations can be found externally by actively monitoring innovations used in other organizations or documented in the research literature. Innovations can also be found by looking internally (e.g., by examining project lessons learned). Innovations are inspired by the need to achieve quality and process performance objectives, the need to improve performance baselines, or the external business environment.

The acquirer should continuously improve its processes and its alignment with its customer and suppliers. The acquirer may look for opportunities to maximize throughput based on the identification of the most limiting resource and, as a result, create a more agile supply chain (e.g., giving higher priority to improvement proposals that promote a supply chain that responds both quickly and cost-effectively).

> An example of an incremental improvement is to establish guidelines for multiple supplier interactions.

Some suggested improvements may be received in the form of a proposal (e.g., an organizational improvement proposal arising from a causal analysis and resolution activity). These suggested improvements will have been analyzed and documented prior to input to Organizational Performance Management processes. When suggested improvements are received as proposals, the proposals are reviewed for completeness and are evaluated as part of the selection process for implementation.

Improvement searches can involve looking outside the organization, deriving innovations from projects using Causal Analysis and Resolution processes, using competitive business intelligence, or analyzing existing organizational performance.

Example Work Products

1. Suggested incremental improvements
2. Suggested innovative improvements

Example Supplier Deliverables

1. Process and technology improvement proposals

Subpractices

1. Elicit suggested improvements.

   These suggestions document potential improvements to processes and technologies. Managers and staff in the organization as well as

HINT

You can collect suggestions using open-ended mechanisms, surveys, or focus groups.

customers, end users, and suppliers can submit suggestions. The organization can also search the academic and technology communities for suggested improvements. Some suggested improvements may have been implemented at the project level before being proposed for the organization.

Examples of sources for improvements include the following:

- Findings and recommendations from process appraisals
- The organization's quality and process performance objectives
- Analysis of data about customer and end-user problems as well as customer and end-user satisfaction
- Results of process and product benchmarking efforts
- Measured effectiveness of process activities
- Measured effectiveness of project work environments
- Examples of improvements that were successfully adopted elsewhere
- Feedback on previous improvements
- Spontaneous ideas from managers and staff
- Improvement proposals from Causal Analysis and Resolution processes resulting from implemented actions with proven effectiveness
- Analysis of data on defect causes
- Analysis of technical performance measures
- Templates for acquirer work products
- Findings and recommendations from joint acquirer and supplier study groups
- Analysis of project and organizational performance compared to quality and productivity objectives

---

Refer to the Organizational Process Focus process area for more information about deploying organizational process assets and incorporating experiences.

2. Identify suggested improvements as incremental or innovative.
3. Investigate innovative improvements that may improve the organization's processes and technologies.

Investigating innovative improvements typically involves the following:

- Maintaining awareness of leading relevant technical work and technology trends
- Searching for commercially available innovative improvements
- Collecting proposals for innovative improvements from the projects and the organization

Continues

Continued

- Reviewing processes and technologies used externally and comparing them to the processes and technologies used in the organization
- Identifying areas where innovative improvements have been used successfully, and reviewing data and documentation of experience using these improvements
- Identifying improvements that integrate new technology into products and project work environments

SP 2.2 ANALYZE SUGGESTED IMPROVEMENTS

Analyze suggested improvements for their possible impact on achieving the organization's quality and process performance objectives.

Suggested improvements are incremental and innovative improvements that are analyzed and possibly selected for validation, implementation, and deployment throughout the organization.

Example Work Products

1. Suggested improvement proposals
2. Selected improvements to be validated

Subpractices

1. Analyze the costs and benefits of suggested improvements.
   Process performance models provide insight into the effect of process changes on process capability and performance.

   Refer to the Organizational Process Performance process area for more information about establishing process performance models.

   Improvement suggestions that have a large cost-to-benefit ratio or that would not improve the organization's processes may be rejected.

   Criteria for evaluating costs and benefits include the following:
   - Contribution toward meeting the organization's quality and process performance objectives
   - Effect on mitigating identified project and organizational risks
   - Ability to respond quickly to changes in project requirements, market situations, and the business environment
   - Effect on related processes and associated assets
   - Cost of defining and collecting data that support the measurement and analysis of the process and technology improvement
   - Expected life span of the improvement

TIP

Elicited improvement suggestions are analyzed (evaluated) for their potential effects.

HINT

When analyzing innovations, it is important to consider their potential contributions to business strategy and growth. For more information, see the Christensen and Raynor books mentioned near the Related Process Areas section.

TIP

These SP 2.2 subpractices exemplify the discipline and rigor that are expected of high maturity organizations. Implementing these subpractices is typically not possible at earlier stages of process improvement.

OPM

TIP

To identify barriers to deployment, it is helpful to understand the organization's attitude toward change and its ability to change. Such knowledge should guide how changes—especially large or complicated ones—are implemented.

2. Identify potential barriers and risks to deploying each suggested improvement.

> Examples of barriers to deploying improvements include the following:
> - Turf guarding and parochial perspectives
> - Unclear or weak business rationale
> - Lack of short-term benefits and visible successes
> - Unclear picture of what is expected from everyone
> - Too many changes at the same time
> - Lack of involvement and support from relevant stakeholders

> Examples of risk factors that affect the deployment of improvements include the following:
> - Compatibility of the improvement with existing processes, values, and skills of potential end users
> - Complexity of the improvement
> - Difficulty implementing the improvement
> - Ability to demonstrate the value of the improvement before widespread deployment
> - Justification for large, up-front investments in areas such as tools and training
> - Inability to overcome "technology drag" where the current implementation is used successfully by a large and mature installed base of end users
> - Additional cost to the customer or supplier
> - Misalignment of customer, acquirer, and supplier improvement priorities

3. Estimate the cost, effort, and schedule required for implementing, verifying, and deploying each suggested improvement.
4. Select suggested improvements for validation and possible implementation and deployment based on the evaluations.

   Refer to the Decision Analysis and Resolution process area for more information about analyzing possible decisions using a formal evaluation process that evaluates identified alternatives against established criteria.

TIP

For selected improvement suggestions, an "improvement proposal" incorporates the results of the SP 2.2 subpractices, including analyses and evaluations, a plan for implementing the improvement, changes needed, a validation method, and success criteria.

5. Document the evaluation results of each selected improvement suggestion in an improvement proposal.
   The proposal should include a problem statement, a plan (including cost and schedule, risk handling, method for evaluating effectiveness in the target environment) for implementing the improvement, and

quantitative success criteria for evaluating actual results of the deployment.

6. Determine the detailed changes needed to implement the improvement and document them in the improvement proposal.

7. Determine the validation method that will be used before broad-scale deployment of the change and document it in the improvement proposal.

   - Determining the validation method includes defining the quantitative success criteria that will be used to evaluate results of the validation.

   - Since innovations, by definition, represent a major change with high impact, most innovative improvements will be piloted. Other validation methods, including modeling and simulation, can be used as appropriate.

8. Document results of the selection process.

Results of the selection process usually include the following:

- The disposition of each suggested improvement
- The rationale for the disposition of each suggested improvement

---

SP 2.3 VALIDATE IMPROVEMENTS

Validate selected improvements.

Selected improvements are validated in accordance with their improvement proposals.

TIP

Selected improvement suggestions are further evaluated through a validation activity.

Examples of validation methods include the following:

- Discussions with stakeholders, perhaps in the context of a formal review
- Prototype demonstrations
- Pilots of suggested improvements
- Modeling and simulation

Pilots can be conducted to evaluate significant changes involving untried, high-risk, or innovative improvements before they are broadly deployed. Not all improvements need the rigor of a pilot. Criteria for selecting improvements for piloting are defined and used. Factors such as risk, transformational nature of change, or number of functional areas affected will determine the need for a pilot of the improvement.

Red-lined or rough-draft process documentation can be made available for use in piloting.

TIP

Another purpose of a pilot is to gauge a change's applicability to other projects.

TIP

A pilot may involve a single project or a group of projects.

Example Work Products

1. Validation plans
2. Validation evaluation reports
3. Documented lessons learned from validation

Example Supplier Deliverables

1. Pilot evaluation reports for pilots executed in the supplier environment
2. Documented lessons learned from pilots executed in the supplier environment

Subpractices

1. Plan the validation.

   Quantitative success criteria documented in the improvement proposal can be useful when planning validation.
   Validation plans for selected improvements to be piloted should include target projects, project characteristics, a schedule for reporting results, and measurement activities.

2. Review and get relevant stakeholder agreement on validation plans.
3. Consult with and assist those who perform the validation.
4. Create a trial implementation, in accordance with the validation plan, for selected improvements to be piloted.
5. Perform each validation in an environment that is similar to the environment present in a broad scale deployment.
6. Track validation against validation plans.
7. Review and document the results of validation.

   Validation results are evaluated using the quantitative criteria defined in the improvement proposal.

Reviewing and documenting results of pilots typically involves the following activities:

- Reviewing pilot results with stakeholders
- Deciding whether to terminate the pilot, rework implementation of the improvement, replan and continue the pilot, or proceed with deployment
- Updating the disposition of improvement proposals associated with the pilot
- Identifying and documenting new improvement proposals as appropriate
- Identifying and documenting lessons learned and problems encountered during the pilot including feedback to the improvement team and changes to the improvement

SP 2.4 SELECT AND IMPLEMENT IMPROVEMENTS FOR DEPLOYMENT

Select and implement improvements for deployment throughout the organization based on an evaluation of costs, benefits, and other factors.

Selection of suggested improvements for deployment is based on cost-to-benefit ratios with regard to quality and process performance objectives, available resources, and the results of improvement proposal evaluation and validation activities.

Refer to the Decision Analysis and Resolution process area for more information about analyzing possible decisions using a formal evaluation process that evaluates identified alternatives against established criteria.

Example Work Products

1. Improvements selected for deployment
2. Updated process documentation and training

Subpractices

1. Prioritize improvements for deployment.

   The priority of an improvement is based on an evaluation of its estimated cost-to-benefit ratio with regard to the quality and process performance objectives as compared to the performance baselines. Return on investment can be used as a basis of comparison.

2. Select improvements to be deployed.

   Selection of improvements to be deployed is based on their priorities, available resources, and results of improvement proposal evaluation and validation activities.

3. Determine how to deploy each improvement.

Examples of where the improvements may be deployed include the following:
- Project specific or common work environments
- Product families
- Organization's projects
- Organizational groups

---

4. Document results of the selection process.

Results of the selection process usually include the following:
- The selection criteria for suggested improvements
- The characteristics of the target projects
- The disposition of each improvement proposal
- The rationale for the disposition of each improvement proposal

---

OPM

> **TIP**
>
> This practice not only selects improvements for deployment, but also prepares the organization for their deployment by reviewing impacts on commitments and skills, and identifying and making changes to training, work environments, and process assets.

> **TIP**
>
> Stability must be balanced with change. You cannot afford to make every promising change; therefore, you must be selective about which changes you deploy across the organization.

> **HINT**
>
> Documenting the results of the selection process can be beneficial if the business environment changes enough for you to reconsider the decision and make a different choice.

5. Review any changes needed to implement the improvements.

Examples of changes needed to deploy an improvement include the following:
- Process descriptions, standards, and procedures
- Work environments
- Education and training
- Skills
- Existing commitments
- Existing activities
- Continuing support to end users
- Organizational culture and characteristics

6. Update the organizational process assets.

Updating the organizational process assets typically includes reviewing them, gaining approval for them, and communicating them.

Refer to the Organizational Process Definition process area for more information about establishing organizational process assets.

SG 3 DEPLOY IMPROVEMENTS

Measurable improvements to the organization's processes and technologies are deployed and evaluated using statistical and other quantitative techniques.

Once improvements are selected for deployment, a plan for deployment is created and executed. The deployment of improvements is managed and the effects of the improvements are measured and evaluated as to how well they contribute to meeting quality and process performance objectives.

SP 3.1 PLAN THE DEPLOYMENT

Establish and maintain plans for deploying selected improvements.

The plans for deploying selected improvements can be included in the plan for organizational performance management, in improvement proposals, or in separate deployment documents.

An acquirer's plans for deploying improvements can include openly sharing most process knowledge and expertise with its suppliers. Any process related knowledge that the acquirer or one of its suppliers possesses is viewed as accessible to virtually any other supplier in the acquirer's supply chain (perhaps with the exception of a direct competitor).

This specific practice complements the Deploy Organizational Process Assets specific practice in the Organizational Process Focus process area and adds the use of quantitative data to guide the deployment and to determine the value of improvements.

Refer to the Organizational Process Focus process area for more information about deploying organizational process assets and incorporating experiences.

Example Work Products

1. Deployment plans for selected improvements

Subpractices

1. Determine how each improvement should be adjusted for deployment.

    Improvements identified in a limited context (e.g., for a single improvement proposal) might need to be modified for a selected portion of the organization.

2. Identify strategies that address the potential barriers to deploying each improvement that were defined in the improvement proposals.

3. Identify the target project population for deployment of the improvement.

    Not all projects are good candidates for all improvements. For example, improvements may be targeted to software only projects, COTS integration projects, or operations and support projects.

4. Establish measures and objectives for determining the value of each improvement with respect to the organization's quality and process performance objectives.

    Measures can be based on the quantitative success criteria documented in the improvement proposal or derived from organizational objectives.

> **TIP**
>
> For example, one strategy could be to deploy sets of related improvements incrementally across the organization so that PPBs and PPMs established in early increments are available for use in later increments.

Examples of measures for determining the value of an improvement include the following:

- Measured improvement in the project's or organization's process performance
- Time to recover the cost of the improvement
- Number and types of project and organizational risks mitigated by the process or technology improvement
- Average time required to respond to changes in project requirements, market situations, and the business environment

Refer to the Measurement and Analysis process area for more information about aligning measurement and analysis activities and providing measurement results.

5. Document the plans for deploying selected improvements.
   The deployment plans should include relevant stakeholders, risk strategies, target projects, measures of success, and schedule.
6. Review and get agreement with relevant stakeholders on the plans for deploying selected improvements.
   Relevant stakeholders include the improvement sponsor, target projects, support organizations, etc.
7. Revise the plans for deploying selected improvements as necessary.

SP 3.2 MANAGE THE DEPLOYMENT

Manage the deployment of selected improvements.

This specific practice can overlap with the Implement Action Proposals specific practice in the Causal Analysis and Resolution process area (e.g., when causal analysis and resolution is used organizationally or across multiple projects).

Example Work Products

1. Updated training materials (to reflect deployed improvements)
2. Documented results of improvement deployment activities
3. Revised improvement measures, objectives, priorities, and deployment plans

Subpractices

1. Monitor the deployment of improvements using deployment plans.
2. Coordinate the deployment of improvements across the organization.

TIP

One of the goals of most organizations is to be nimble and agile. Therefore, it is necessary to learn how to introduce changes quickly and yet correctly.

> Coordinating deployment includes the following activities:
> - Coordinating activities of projects, support groups, and organizational groups for each improvement
> - Coordinating activities for deploying related improvements

3. Deploy improvements in a controlled and disciplined manner.

> Examples of methods for deploying improvements include the following:
> - Deploying improvements incrementally rather than as a single deployment
> - Providing comprehensive consulting to early adopters of improvement in lieu of revised formal training

4. Coordinate the deployment of improvements into the projects' defined processes as appropriate.

   Refer to the Organizational Process Focus process area for more information about deploying organizational process assets and incorporating experiences.

5. Provide consulting as appropriate to support deployment of improvements.

6. Provide updated training materials or develop communication packages to reflect improvements to organizational process assets.

   Refer to the Organizational Training process area for more information about providing training.

> **TIP**
>
> Extensive or complex improvements may require much support, such as training, user support, customer and supplier involvement, or feedback on use of the new or updated process.

7. Confirm that the deployment of all improvements is completed in accordance with the deployment plan.

8. Document and review results of improvement deployment.

> **TIP**
>
> Ensure that any unanticipated consequences have been addressed.

Documenting and reviewing results includes the following:
- Identifying and documenting lessons learned
- Revising improvement measures, objectives, priorities, and deployment plans

---

SP 3.3 EVALUATE IMPROVEMENT EFFECTS

Evaluate the effects of deployed improvements on quality and process performance using statistical and other quantitative techniques.

Refer to the Measurement and Analysis process area for more information about aligning measurement and analysis activities and providing measurement results.

This specific practice can overlap with the Evaluate the Effect of Implemented Actions specific practice in the Causal Analysis and Resolution process area (e.g., when causal analysis and resolution is applied organizationally or across multiple projects).

> **TIP**
>
> This specific practice looks at measurement of the effects of improvements being deployed across the organization. In particular, what is the impact on achieving QPPOs? Is it time to move the "goal post" and introduce new "stretch" QPPOs (see SP 1.1)?

Example Work Products

1. Documented measures of the effects resulting from deployed improvements

Subpractices

1. Measure the results of each improvement as implemented on the target projects, using the measures defined in the deployment plans.

2. Measure and analyze progress toward achieving the organization's quality and process performance objectives using statistical and other quantitative techniques and take corrective action as needed.

   Refer to the Organizational Process Performance process area for more information about establishing quality and process performance objectives and establishing process performance baselines and models.

ORGANIZATIONAL PROCESS PERFORMANCE
A Process Management Process Area at Maturity Level 4

Purpose

The purpose of Organizational Process Performance (OPP) is to establish and maintain a quantitative understanding of the performance of selected processes in the organization's set of standard processes in support of achieving quality and process performance objectives, and to provide process performance data, baselines, and models to quantitatively manage the organization's projects.

HINT

OPP establishes assets for use by projects (QPM and CAR) and the organization (OPM). Consult these PAs to better understand which roles these assets play. This understanding, as well as your business objectives and project needs, will help you design appropriate assets as you implement OPP.

OPP

Introductory Notes

The Organizational Process Performance process area involves the following activities:

- Establishing organizational quantitative quality and process performance objectives based on business objectives (see the definition of "quality and process performance objectives" in the glossary)
- Selecting processes or subprocesses for process performance analyses
- Establishing definitions of the measures to be used in process performance analyses (see the definition of "process performance" in the glossary)
- Establishing process performance baselines and process performance models (see the definitions of "process performance baselines" and "process performance models" in the glossary)

The collection and analysis of the data and creation of the process performance baselines and models can be performed at different levels of the organization, including individual projects or groups of related projects as appropriate based on the needs of the projects and organization.

The common measures for the organization consist of process and product measures that can be used to characterize the actual performance of processes in the organization's individual projects. By

X-REF

OPP and QPM are tightly coupled process areas. Refer to QPM extensively when considering how you should implement OPP. In particular, note the correspondence between OPP SP 1.1 and 1.2 and QPM SP 1.1, 1.3, and 1.4.

X-REF

The CMMI principle that specific practices are agnostic as to who performs them applies here as well. The OPP specific practices, including those establishing Process Performance Baselines (PPBs) and Process Performance Models (PPMs) (SP 1.4 and SP 1.5, respectively), may in some cases provide more benefit when implemented for an individual project.

analyzing the resulting measurements, a distribution or range of results can be established that characterize the expected performance of the process when used on an individual project.

Measuring quality and process performance can involve combining existing measures into additional derived measures to provide more insight into overall efficiency and effectiveness at a project or organization level. The analysis at the organization level can be used to study productivity, improve efficiencies, and increase throughput across projects in the organization.

The expected process performance can be used in establishing the project's quality and process performance objectives and can be used as a baseline against which actual project performance can be compared. This information is used to quantitatively manage the project. Each quantitatively managed project, in turn, provides actual performance results that become a part of organizational process assets that are made available to all projects.

The acquirer can use quality and process performance objectives to define performance and service level expectations for suppliers.

Process performance models are used to represent past and current process performance and to predict future results of the process. For example, the latent defects in the delivered product can be predicted using measurements of work product attributes such as complexity and process attributes such as preparation time for peer reviews.

The same measures of latent defects, analyzed using a supplier's past projects data, can be used to predict the quality of products delivered by that supplier. The acquirer can use supplier process performance models to predict the overall capability of the acquirer to deliver the product.

When the organization has sufficient measures, data, and analytical techniques for critical process, product, and service characteristics, it is able to do the following:

- Identify aspects of processes that could be improved across acquirer-supplier interfaces
- Determine whether processes are behaving consistently or have stable trends (i.e., are predictable)
- Identify processes in which performance is within natural bounds that are consistent across projects and could potentially be aggregated
- Identify processes that show unusual (e.g., sporadic, unpredictable) behavior
- Identify aspects of processes that can be improved in the organization's set of standard processes
- Identify the implementation of a process that performs best

This process area interfaces with and supports the implementation of other high maturity process areas. The assets established and maintained as part of implementing this process area (e.g., the measures to be used to characterize subprocess behavior, process performance baselines, process performance models) are inputs to the quantitative project management, causal analysis and resolution, and organizational performance management processes in support of the analyses described there. Quantitative project management processes provide the quality and process performance data needed to maintain the assets described in this process area.

Related Process Areas

Refer to the Measurement and Analysis process area for more information about specifying measures, obtaining measurement data, and analyzing measurement data.

Refer to the Organizational Performance Management process area for more information about proactively managing the organization's performance to meet its business objectives.

Refer to the Quantitative Project Management process area for more information about quantitatively managing the project to achieve the project's established quality and process performance objectives.

Specific Goal and Practice Summary

SG 1 Establish Performance Baselines and Models
    SP 1.1   Establish Quality and Process Performance Objectives
    SP 1.2   Select Processes
    SP 1.3   Establish Process Performance Measures
    SP 1.4   Analyze Process Performance and Establish Process Performance Baselines
    SP 1.5   Establish Process Performance Models

Specific Practices by Goal

SG 1   ESTABLISH PERFORMANCE BASELINES AND MODELS

Baselines and models, which characterize the expected process performance of the organization's set of standard processes, are established and maintained.

Prior to establishing process performance baselines and models, it is necessary to determine the quality and process performance objectives for those processes (the Establish Quality and Process Performance Objectives specific practice), which processes are suitable to

TIP

Mastering the practices in MA is a prerequisite to effectively implementing OPP and QPM. In particular, it is important to evaluate the effectiveness of your measurement system. Are subprocess measures sufficiently accurate and precise to be useful for your intended purposes? Techniques such as ANOVA Gauge Repeatability and Reproducibility (GR&R) and Fleiss's kappa (see Wikipedia) may help answer these questions.

TIP

Another suitable reference is "Measurement and Analysis Infrastructure Diagnostic: Version 1.0: Method Definition Document," by Mark Kasunic. See www.sei.cmu.edu/library/abstracts/reports/10tr035.cfm.

be measured (the Select Processes specific practice), and which measures are useful for determining process performance (the Establish Process Performance Measures specific practice).

The first three practices of this goal are interrelated and often need to be performed concurrently and iteratively to select quality and process performance objectives, processes, and measures. Often, the selection of one quality and process performance objective, process, or measure will constrain the selection of the others. For example, selecting a quality and process performance objective relating to defects delivered to the customer will almost certainly require selecting the verification processes and defect related measures.

The intent of this goal is to provide projects with the process performance baselines and models they need to perform quantitative project management. Many times these baselines and models are collected or created by the organization, but there are circumstances in which a project may need to create the baselines and models for themselves. These circumstances include projects that are not covered by the organization's baselines and models. For these cases the project follows the practices in this goal to create its baselines and models.

SP 1.1 ESTABLISH QUALITY AND PROCESS PERFORMANCE OBJECTIVES

Establish and maintain the organization's quantitative objectives for quality and process performance, which are traceable to business objectives.

The organization's quality and process performance objectives can be established for different levels in the organizational structure (e.g., business area, product line, function, project) as well as at different levels in the process hierarchy. When establishing quality and process performance objectives, consider the following:

- Traceability to the organization's business objectives
- Past performance of the selected processes or subprocesses in context (e.g., on projects)
- Multiple attributes of process performance (e.g., product quality, productivity, cycle time, response time)
- Inherent variability or natural bounds of the selected processes or subprocesses

The organization's quality and process performance objectives provide focus and direction to the process performance analysis and quantitative project management activities. However, it should be noted that achieving quality and process performance objectives that

---

TIP

By ensuring traceability to business objectives, the organization's quality and process performance objectives (QPPOs) become the mechanism for aligning the activities described in OPP and QPM with the organization's business objectives.

are significantly different from current process capability requires use of techniques found in Causal Analysis and Resolution and Organizational Performance Management.

TIP

Ideally, the QPPOs should be attainable, but perhaps a "stretch" beyond the current PPBs. This comparison can help establish feasible objectives. CAR or OPM can also be invoked to improve process performance.

Example Work Products

1. Organization's quality and process performance objectives

Subpractices

1. Review the organization's business objectives related to quality and process performance.

> Examples of business objectives include the following:
> * Deliver products within budget and on time
> * Improve product quality by a specified percent in a specified timeframe
> * Improve productivity by a specified percent in a specified timeframe
> * Maintain customer satisfaction ratings
> * Improve time-to-market for new product or service releases by a specified percent in a specified timeframe
> * Reduce deferred product functionality by a specified percent in a specified timeframe
> * Reduce the rate of product recalls by a specified percent in a specified timeframe
> * Reduce customer total cost of ownership by a specified percent in a specified timeframe
> * Decrease the cost of maintaining legacy products by a specified percent in a specified timeframe

2. Define the organization's quantitative objectives for quality and process performance.

> QPPOs can be established at multiple levels of an organization. One approach that aligns the whole organization toward achieving the organization's QPPOs and links QPPOs across all levels is Hoshin Kanri or Hoshin Planning (see Wikipedia). Quality and process performance objectives can be established for process or subprocess measurements (e.g., effort, cycle time, defect removal effectiveness) as well as for product measurements (e.g., reliability, defect density) and service measurements (e.g., capacity, response times) as appropriate.

> Examples of quality and process performance objectives include the following:
> * Achieve a specified defect escape rate, productivity, duration, capacity, or cost target

Continues

Continued

- Improve the defect escape rate, productivity, duration, capacity, or cost performance by a specified percent of the process performance baseline in a specified timeframe
- Improve service level agreement performance by a specified percent of the process performance baseline in a specified timeframe

3. Define the priorities of the organization's objectives for quality and process performance.

4. Review, negotiate, and obtain commitment to the organization's quality and process performance objectives and their priorities from relevant stakeholders.

5. Revise the organization's quantitative objectives for quality and process performance as necessary.

Examples of when the organization's quantitative objectives for quality and process performance may need to be revised include the following:
- When the organization's business objectives change
- When the organization's set of standard processes change
- When actual quality and process performance differ significantly from objectives

SP 1.2 SELECT PROCESSES

Select processes or subprocesses in the organization's set of standard processes to be included in the organization's process performance analyses and maintain traceability to business objectives.

Refer to the Organizational Process Definition process area for more information about establishing organizational process assets.

The organization's set of standard processes consists of a set of standard processes that, in turn, are composed of subprocesses.

Typically, it is not possible, useful, or economically justifiable to apply statistical management techniques to all processes or subprocesses of the organization's set of standard processes. Selection of processes or subprocesses is based on the quality and process performance objectives of the organization, which are derived from business objectives as described in the previous specific practice.

Example Work Products

1. List of processes or subprocesses identified for process performance analyses with rationale for their selection including traceability to business objectives

Subpractices

1. Establish the criteria to use when selecting subprocesses.

> Examples of criteria that can be used for the selection of a process or subprocess for the organization's process performance analysis include the following:
> - The process or subprocess is strongly related to key business objectives.
> - The process or subprocess has demonstrated stability in the past.
> - Valid historical data are currently available that are relevant to the process or subprocess.
> - The process or subprocess will generate data with sufficient frequency to allow for statistical management.
> - The process or subprocess is an important contributor to quality and process performance.
> - The process or subprocess is an important predictor of quality and process performance.
> - The process or subprocess is a factor important to understanding the risk associated with achieving the quality and process performance objectives.
> - The quality of the measures and measurements associated with the process or subprocess (e.g., measurement system error) is adequate.
> - Multiple measurable attributes that characterize process or subprocess behavior are available.

2. Select the subprocesses and document the rationale for their selection.

> Example approaches to identifying and evaluating subprocess alternatives as part of a selection include the following:
> - Causal analysis
> - Sensitivity analysis

> *Refer to the Decision Analysis and Resolution process area for more information about analyzing possible decisions using a formal evaluation process that evaluates identified alternatives against established criteria.*

3. Establish and maintain traceability between the selected subprocesses, quality and process performance objectives, and business objectives.

> Examples of ways in which traceability can be expressed include the following:
> - Mapping of subprocesses to quality and process performance objectives
>
> *Continues*

Continued

- Objective flow-down (e.g., Big Y to Vital X, Hoshin planning)
- Balanced scorecard
- Quality Function Deployment (QFD)
- Goal Question Metric
- Documentation for a process performance model

4. Revise the selection as necessary.
   - It may be necessary to revise the selection in the following situations:
     - The predictions made by process performance models result in too much variation to make them useful.
     - The objectives for quality and process performance change.
     - The organization's set of standard processes change.
     - The underlying quality and process performance changes.

SP 1.3 ESTABLISH PROCESS PERFORMANCE MEASURES

Establish and maintain definitions of measures to be included in the organization's process performance analyses.

Refer to the Measurement and Analysis process area for more information about specifying measures.

Example Work Products

1. Definitions of selected measures of process performance with rationale for their selection including traceability to selected processes or subprocesses

Subpractices

1. Select measures that reflect appropriate attributes of the selected processes or subprocesses to provide insight into the organization's quality and process performance.

   It is often helpful to define multiple measures for a process or subprocess to understand the impact of changes to the process and avoid sub-optimization. Also, it is often helpful to establish measures for both product and process attributes for the selected process and subprocess, as well as its inputs, outputs, and resources (including people and the skill they bring) consumed.

   The Goal Question Metric paradigm is an approach that can be used to select measures that provide insight into the organization's quality and process performance objectives. It is often useful to analyze how these quality and process performance objectives can be achieved

---

TIP

A commonly heard objection is that it is not possible to measure certain attributes. In his book *How to Measure Anything: Finding the Value of "Intangibles" in Business,* Doug Hubbard provides strategies for how to proceed in these circumstances.

based on an understanding of process performance provided by the selected measures.

For quality and process performance objectives addressed through acquisition, select process, product, and service level measures that provide insight into the process performance of suppliers and into the quality of their deliverables.

X-REF

The Goal Question Metric (GQM; www.cs.umd.edu/~mvz/handouts/gqm.pdf) is a well-known approach to deriving measures that provide insight into issues of interest. The SEI's variant of GQM is called the Goal Question Indicator Metric (GQIM; www.sei.cmu.edu/training/p06.cfm).

> Examples of criteria used to select measures include the following:
> - Relationship of measures to the organization's quality and process performance objectives
> - Coverage that measures provide over the life of the product or service
> - Visibility that measures provide into process performance
> - Availability of measures
> - Frequency at which observations of the measure can be collected
> - Extent to which measures are controllable by changes to the process or subprocess
> - Extent to which measures represent the end users' view of effective process performance
> - Extent to which measures provide insight that enables the acquirer to manage the project

2. Establish operational definitions for the selected measures.

   Refer to the Measurement and Analysis process area for more information about specifying measures.

3. Incorporate selected measures into the organization's set of common measures.

   Measures expected to be collected and reported by suppliers are incorporated into standard supplier agreement templates and standard service level agreements as appropriate.

   Refer to the Organizational Process Definition process area for more information about establishing organizational process assets.

HINT

To begin systematic collection of these measures from new projects, incorporate them into the organization's set of common measures (OPD SP 1.4).

4. Revise the set of measures as necessary.

   Measures are periodically evaluated for their continued usefulness and ability to indicate process effectiveness.

SP 1.4 ANALYZE PROCESS PERFORMANCE AND ESTABLISH PROCESS PERFORMANCE BASELINES

Analyze the performance of the selected processes, and establish and maintain the process performance baselines.

The selected measures are analyzed to characterize the performance of the selected processes or subprocesses achieved on projects. This charac-

OPP

terization is used to establish and maintain process performance baselines. (See the definition of "process performance baseline" in the glossary.) These baselines are used to determine the expected results of the process or subprocess when used on a project under a given set of circumstances.

Process performance baselines are compared to the organization's quality and process performance objectives to determine if the quality and process performance objectives are being achieved.

TIP

QPPOs should motivate superior performance. QPPOs that set the bar too high may demoralize more than they motivate. What do the performance data say about how well a project can do relative to the QPPOs? There is a need for balance between "desires" and "reality."

The process performance baselines are a measurement of performance for the organization's set of standard processes at various levels of detail. The processes that the process performance baselines can address include the following:

- Sequence of connected processes
- Processes that cover the entire life of the project
- Processes for developing individual work products

There can be several process performance baselines to characterize performance for subgroups of the organization.

Examples of criteria used to categorize subgroups include the following:
- Supplier-acquisition approach
- Agreement type (e.g., fixed price, time and effort)
- Product line or standard service
- Line of business
- Application domain
- Complexity
- Team size
- Work product size
- Process elements from the organization's set of standard processes

---

Tailoring the organization's set of standard processes can significantly affect the comparability of data for inclusion in process performance baselines. Effects of tailoring should be considered in establishing baselines. Depending on the tailoring allowed, separate performance baselines may exist for each type of tailoring.

Refer to the Quantitative Project Management process area for more information about quantitatively managing the project to achieve the project's established quality and process performance objectives.

Example Work Products

1. Analysis of process performance data
2. Baseline data on the organization's process performance

Subpractices

1. Collect the selected measurements for the selected processes and subprocesses.

    The process or subprocess in use when the measurement was taken is recorded to enable its use later.

    Refer to the Measurement and Analysis process area for more information about specifying measurement data collection and storage procedures.

2. Analyze the collected measures to establish a distribution or range of results that characterize the expected performance of selected processes or subprocesses when used on a project.

    This analysis should include the stability of the related process or subprocess, and the impacts of associated factors and context. Related factors include inputs to the process and other attributes that can affect the results obtained. The context includes the business context (e.g., domain) and significant tailoring of the organization's set of standard processes.

    The measurements from stable subprocesses in projects should be used when possible; other data may not be reliable.

3. Establish and maintain the process performance baselines from collected measurements and analyses.

    Refer to the Measurement and Analysis process area for more information about aligning measurement and analysis activities and providing measurement results.

    Process performance baselines are derived by analyzing collected measures to establish a distribution or range of results that characterize the expected performance for selected processes or subprocesses when used on a project in the organization.

4. Review and get agreement with relevant stakeholders about the process performance baselines.

5. Make the process performance information available across the organization in the measurement repository.

    The organization's process performance baselines are used by projects to estimate the natural bounds for process performance.

6. Compare the process performance baselines to associated quality and process performance objectives to determine if those quality and process performance objectives are being achieved.

    These comparisons should use statistical techniques beyond a simple comparison of the mean to gauge the extent of quality and process performance objective achievement. If the quality and process performance objectives are not being achieved, corrective actions should be considered.

HINT

Record sufficient contextual information with a measurement to enable identification of when that information was generated, by whom, and in which PPB it should be included (or which PPB it should be used to regenerate, for a different class of process instances).

TIP

Unless the process is stable, the data from the process may actually comprise a mixture of measurements taken from *different* processes. PPBs developed from such data are limited in their usefulness to projects (e.g., the estimated natural bounds are likely to be far apart).

HINT

Investigate subgrouping when data from multiple projects (and teams) will be incorporated into the same PPB. Even if the process is stable *within* individual projects, its performance *across* projects may vary so much that the resultant single PPB will be too "wide" to be useful.

HINT

Even when organizational PPBs are established, individual projects may still benefit from establishing their own individual PPBs when they have accumulated sufficient data.

OPP

Refer to the Causal Analysis and Resolution process area for more information about determining causes of selected outcomes.

Refer to the Organizational Process Focus process area for more information about planning and implementing process actions.

Refer to the Organizational Performance Management process area for more information about analyzing process performance data and identifying potential areas for improvement.

7. Revise the process performance baselines as necessary.

Examples of when the organization's process performance baselines may need to be revised include the following:
- When processes change
- When the organization's results change
- When the organization's needs change
- When suppliers' processes change
- When suppliers change

SP 1.5 ESTABLISH PROCESS PERFORMANCE MODELS

Establish and maintain process performance models for the organization's set of standard processes.

TIP

Part of mastering any discipline is developing "nuance" for factors that matter in how a situation will unfold, yet realizing every situation is somewhat different. Thus, while PPMs can never be perfectly accurate, they offer a systematic approach to using the data available in a situation and similar situations toward making, scientifically, the best possible judgment or prediction.

HINT

Establish PPMs that provide insight at different points in a project that will help the project assess progress toward achieving its QPPOs (QPM SP 2.2).

High maturity organizations generally establish and maintain a set of process performance models at various levels of detail that cover a range of activities that are common across the organization and address the organization's quality and process performance objectives. (See the definition of "process performance model" in the glossary.) Under some circumstances, projects may need to create their own process performance models.

Process performance models are used to estimate or predict the value of a process performance measure from the values of other process, product, and service measurements. These process performance models typically use process and product measurements collected throughout the life of the project to estimate progress toward achieving quality and process performance objectives that cannot be measured until later in the project's life.

Process performance models are used to estimate or predict when to fund, hold, cancel, migrate, re-engineer, or retire a project. Process performance models allow the acquirer to synchronize processes with customer needs. The organization's process performance baselines provide quantitative data on those aspects of the projects and organization that can approximate the throughput potential of its processes. Focusing on these critical constraints, process performance models allow the acquirer to predict how to best maximize the flow of work through projects and the organization.

Process performance models are used as follows:

- The organization uses them for estimating, analyzing, and predicting the process performance associated with processes in and changes to the organization's set of standard processes.
- The organization uses them to assess the (potential) return on investment for process improvement activities.
- Projects use them for estimating, analyzing, and predicting the process performance of their defined processes.
- Projects use them for selecting processes or subprocesses for use.
- Projects use them for estimating progress toward achieving the project's quality and process performance objectives.

Process performance models are also used to set quality and process performance objectives for suppliers and to provide data that can help suppliers achieve these objectives.

These measures and models are defined to provide insight into and to provide the ability to predict critical process and product characteristics that are relevant to the organization's quality and process performance objectives.

Results of the acquirer's process performance models are shared with suppliers to help ensure the synchronized delivery of products and services.

Examples of process performance models include the following:
- System dynamics models
- Regression models
- Complexity models
- Supply chain models
- Discrete event simulation models
- Monte Carlo simulation models

Refer to the Quantitative Project Management process area for more information about quantitatively managing the project to achieve the project's established quality and process performance objectives.

Example Work Products

1. Process performance models

X-REF

Experiences from using PPMs are described in "Performance Effects of Measurement and Analysis: Perspectives from CMMI High Maturity Organizations and Appraisers" found at www.sei.cmu.edu/library/abstracts/reports/10tr022.cfm.

OPP

TIP

In general, data-driven approaches to judgment and prediction should, over the long term, perform better than human judgment alone. Perhaps the performance of both should be analyzed and contrasted, and then the team should determine how to best use both. Be aware, however, that in situations unlike those experienced before, neither approach is likely to perform well.

TIP

Many books on the limitations of human judgment are available, including an update to a classic text, *Rational Choice in an Uncertain World: The Psychology of Judgment and Decision Making* by Hastie and Dawes. A more recent book is *The Invisible Gorilla: And Other Ways Our Intuitions Deceive Us* by Chabris and Simons.

Example Supplier Deliverables

1. Supplier process performance models

Subpractices

1. Establish process performance models based on the organization's set of standard processes and process performance baselines.
2. Calibrate process performance models based on the past results and current needs.
3. Review process performance models and get agreement with relevant stakeholders.
4. Support the projects' use of process performance models.
5. Revise process performance models as necessary.

Examples of when process performance models may need to be revised include the following:
- When supplier processes that directly interface with acquirer processes change
- When suppliers change
- When processes change
- When the organization's results change
- When the organization's quality and process performance objectives change

---

ORGANIZATIONAL TRAINING

A Process Management Process Area at Maturity Level 3

Purpose

The purpose of Organizational Training (OT) is to develop skills and knowledge of people so they can perform their roles effectively and efficiently.

Introductory Notes

Organizational Training addresses training provided to support the organization's strategic business objectives and to meet the tactical training needs that are common across projects and support groups. Training needs identified by individual projects and support groups to meet their specific needs are handled at the project and support group level and are outside the scope of the Organizational Training process area.

Refer to the Project Planning process area for more information about planning needed knowledge and skills.

An organizational training program involves the following activities:

- Identifying the training needed by the organization
- Obtaining and providing training to address those needs
- Establishing and maintaining a training capability
- Establishing and maintaining training records
- Assessing training effectiveness

Effective training requires the assessment of needs, planning, instructional design, and appropriate training media (e.g., workbooks, computer software), as well as a repository of training process data. As an organizational process, the main components of training include a managed training development program, documented plans, staff with an appropriate mastery of disciplines and other areas of knowledge, and mechanisms for measuring the effectiveness of the training program.

> **TIP**
>
> OT addresses the organization's training needs. The project's training needs are often more specific and are addressed in PP, PMC, and IPM.

OT

> **TIP**
>
> Training data include staff training records, dates of classes, and other training information.

383

Identifying process training needs is based primarily on the skills required to perform the organization's set of standard processes.

Refer to the Organizational Process Definition process area for more information about establishing standard processes.

TIP

CMMI sets expectations on *what* needs to be done, not *how* to do it. Therefore, each organization must decide which type of training is best for any particular situation.

TIP

To deploy these processes effectively across the organization, training is typically required.

TIP

Opportunities for joint training of acquirer and supplier team members should be explored, as they typically improve cross-functional activities.

Certain skills can be effectively and efficiently imparted through vehicles other than classroom training experiences (e.g., informal mentoring). Other skills require more formalized training vehicles, such as in a classroom, by web-based training, through guided self study, or via a formalized on-the-job training program. The formal or informal training vehicles employed for each situation should be based on an assessment of the need for training and the performance gap to be addressed. The term "training" used throughout this process area is used broadly to include all of these learning options.

Success in training is indicated by the availability of opportunities to acquire the skills and knowledge needed to perform new and ongoing enterprise activities.

Skills and knowledge can be technical, organizational, or contextual. Technical skills pertain to the ability to use equipment, tools, materials, data, and processes required by a project or process. Organizational skills pertain to behavior within and according to the staff members' organization structure, role and responsibilities, and general operating principles and methods. Contextual skills are the self-management, communication, and interpersonal abilities needed to successfully perform work in the organizational and social context of the project and support groups.

This process area applies to developing acquirer skills and knowledge so that those acquirers in the organization can perform their roles effectively and efficiently. However, these practices can also apply to developing the supplier skills and knowledge. Topics can include acquirer business practices (e.g., acceptance, invoicing) as well as practices that the acquirer desires to be performed in a particular way (e.g., reflect lean thinking) or a collaborative way (e.g., using an Agile approach).

Related Process Areas

Refer to the Decision Analysis and Resolution process area for more information about analyzing possible decisions using a formal evaluation process that evaluates identified alternatives against established criteria.

Refer to the Organizational Process Definition process area for more information about establishing organizational process assets.

Refer to the Project Planning process area for more information about planning needed knowledge and skills.

Specific Goal and Practice Summary

SG 1 Establish an Organizational Training Capability
  SP 1.1   Establish Strategic Training Needs
  SP 1.2   Determine Which Training Needs Are the Responsibility of the Organization
  SP 1.3   Establish an Organizational Training Tactical Plan
  SP 1.4   Establish a Training Capability
SG 2 Provide Training
  SP 2.1   Deliver Training
  SP 2.2   Establish Training Records
  SP 2.3   Assess Training Effectiveness

Specific Practices by Goal

SG 1   ESTABLISH AN ORGANIZATIONAL TRAINING CAPABILITY

A training capability, which supports the roles in the organization, is established and maintained.

The organization identifies training required to develop the skills and knowledge necessary to perform enterprise activities. Once the needs are identified, a training program addressing those needs is developed.

SP 1.1 ESTABLISH STRATEGIC TRAINING NEEDS

Establish and maintain strategic training needs of the organization.

Strategic training needs address long-term objectives to build a capability by filling significant knowledge gaps, introducing new technologies, or implementing major changes in behavior. Strategic planning typically looks two to five years into the future.

> Examples of sources of strategic training needs include the following:
> - The organization's standard processes
> - The organization's strategic business plan
> - The organization's process improvement plan
> - Enterprise level initiatives
> - Skill assessments
> - Risk analyses
> - Acquisition and supplier management

OT

HINT

Use strategic training to ensure that the organization continues to function as a learning organization, strengthens its core competencies, and remains competitive.

TIP

Small acquisition-specific organizations may choose to use the practices in this process area to address all of their training. If so, the scope and intent of the practices should be expanded appropriately.

Example Work Products

1. Training needs
2. Assessment analysis

Subpractices

1. Analyze the organization's strategic business objectives and process improvement plan to identify potential training needs.
2. Document the strategic training needs of the organization.

Examples of categories of training needs include the following:
- Process analysis and documentation
- Engineering (e.g., requirements analysis, design, testing, configuration management, quality assurance)
- Selection and management of suppliers
- Team building
- Management (e.g., estimating, tracking, risk management)
- Leadership
- Disaster recovery and continuity of operations
- Acquisition management (e.g., solicitation, supplier selection, supplier management)
- Communication and negotiation skills

---

3. Determine the roles and skills needed to perform the organization's set of standard processes.

Roles typically include project manager, architects, business process analysts, and suppliers, especially in process elements that identify interfaces with and expectations from suppliers.

---

4. Document the training needed to perform roles in the organization's set of standard processes.
5. Document the training needed to maintain the safe, secure, and continued operation of the business.
6. Revise the organization's strategic needs and required training as necessary.

SP 1.2 DETERMINE WHICH TRAINING NEEDS ARE THE RESPONSIBILITY OF THE ORGANIZATION

Determine which training needs are the responsibility of the organization and which are left to the individual project or support group.

Refer to the Project Planning process area for more information about planning needed knowledge and skills.

In addition to strategic training needs, organizational training addresses training requirements that are common across projects and support groups. Projects and support groups have the primary responsibility for identifying and addressing their training needs. The organization's training staff is responsible for addressing only common cross-project and support group training needs (e.g., training in work environments common to multiple projects). In some cases, however, the organization's training staff may address additional training needs of projects and support groups, as negotiated with them, in the context of the training resources available and the organization's training priorities.

Example Work Products

1. Common project and support group training needs
2. Training commitments

Subpractices

1. Analyze the training needs identified by projects and support groups.
   Analysis of project and support group needs is intended to identify common training needs that can be most efficiently addressed organization wide. These needs analysis activities are used to anticipate future training needs that are first visible at the project and support group level.
2. Negotiate with projects and support groups on how their training needs will be satisfied.
   The support provided by the organization's training staff depends on the training resources available and the organization's training priorities.

Examples of training appropriately performed by the project or support group include the following:
- Training in the application or service domain of the project
- Training in the unique tools and methods used by the project or support group
- Training in safety, security, and human factors

---

3. Document commitments for providing training support to projects and support groups.

SP 1.3 *ESTABLISH AN ORGANIZATIONAL TRAINING TACTICAL PLAN*

Establish and maintain an organizational training tactical plan.

TIP

For many organizations, this
planning is performed
annually, with a review taking
place each quarter.

The organizational training tactical plan is the plan to deliver the training that is the responsibility of the organization and is necessary for individuals to perform their roles effectively. This plan addresses the near-term execution of training and is adjusted periodically in response to changes (e.g., in needs, in resources) and to evaluations of effectiveness.

Example Work Products

1. Organizational training tactical plan

Subpractices

1. Establish the content of the plan.

> Organizational training tactical plans typically contain the following:
> - Training needs
> - Training topics
> - Schedules based on training activities and their dependencies
> - Methods used for training
> - Requirements and quality standards for training materials
> - Training tasks, roles, and responsibilities
> - Required resources including tools, facilities, environments, staffing, skills, and knowledge

2. Establish commitments to the plan.
   Documented commitments by those who are responsible for implementing and supporting the plan are essential for the plan to be effective.
3. Revise the plan and commitments as necessary.

SP 1.4 *ESTABLISH A TRAINING CAPABILITY*

Establish and maintain a training capability to address organizational training needs.

Refer to the Decision Analysis and Resolution process area for more information about analyzing possible decisions using a formal evaluation process that evaluates identified alternatives against established criteria.

Example Work Products

1. Training materials and supporting artifacts

Subpractices

1. Select appropriate approaches to satisfy organizational training needs.

   Many factors may affect the selection of training approaches, including audience specific knowledge, costs, schedule, and the work environment. Selecting an approach requires consideration of the means to provide skills and knowledge in the most effective way possible given the constraints.

Examples of training approaches include the following:
- Classroom training
- Computer aided instruction
- Guided self-study
- Formal apprenticeship and mentoring programs
- Facilitated videos
- Chalk talks
- Brown bag lunch seminars
- Structured on-the-job training

---

2. Determine whether to develop training materials internally or to acquire them externally.

   Determine the costs and benefits of internal training development and of acquiring training externally.

Example criteria that can be used to determine the most effective mode of knowledge or skill acquisition include the following:
- Applicability to work or process performance objectives
- Availability of time to prepare for project execution
- Applicability to business objectives
- Availability of in-house expertise
- Availability of training from external sources

Examples of external sources of training include the following:
- Customer provided training
- Commercially available training courses
- Academic programs
- Professional conferences
- Seminars

OT

3. Develop or obtain training materials.

Training can be provided by the project, support groups, the organization, or an external organization. The organization's training staff coordinates the acquisition and delivery of training regardless of its source.

> Examples of training materials include the following:
> - Courses
> - Computer-aided instruction
> - Videos

4. Develop or obtain qualified instructors, instructional designers, or mentors.

To ensure that those who develop and deliver internal training have the necessary knowledge and training skills, criteria can be defined to identify, develop, and qualify them. The development of training, including self-study and online training, should involve those who have experience in instructional design. In the case of external training, the organization's training staff can investigate how the training provider determines which instructors will deliver the training. This selection of qualified instructors can also be a factor in selecting or continuing to use a training provider.

5. Describe the training in the organization's training curriculum.

> Examples of the information provided in training descriptions for each course include the following:
> - Topics covered in the training
> - Intended audience
> - Prerequisites and preparation for participating
> - Training objectives
> - Length of the training
> - Lesson plans
> - Completion criteria for the course
> - Criteria for granting training waivers

6. Revise training materials and supporting artifacts as necessary.

> Examples of situations in which training materials and supporting artifacts may need to be revised include the following:
> - Training needs change (e.g., when new technology associated with the training topic is available)
> - An evaluation of the training identifies the need for change (e.g., evaluations of training effectiveness surveys, training program performance assessments, instructor evaluation forms)

SG 2   PROVIDE TRAINING

Training for individuals to perform their roles effectively is provided.

When selecting people to be trained, the following should be considered:

- Background of the target population of training participants
- Prerequisite background to receive training
- Skills and abilities needed by people to perform their roles
- Need for cross-discipline training for all disciplines, including project management
- Need for managers to have training in appropriate organizational processes
- Need for training in basic principles of all appropriate disciplines or services to support staff in quality management, configuration management, and other related support functions
- Need to provide competency development for critical functional areas
- Need to maintain competencies and qualifications of staff to operate and maintain work environments common to multiple projects

SP 2.1   DELIVER TRAINING

Deliver training following the organizational training tactical plan.

Example Work Products

1. Delivered training course

Subpractices

1. Select those who will receive the training necessary to perform their roles effectively.

   The acquirer includes supplier representatives, as appropriate, to ensure selected suppliers can effectively interface with acquirer processes.

   Training is intended to impart knowledge and skills to people performing various roles in the organization. Some people already possess the knowledge and skills required to perform well in their designated roles. Training can be waived for these people, but care should be taken that training waivers are not abused.

2. Schedule the training, including any resources, as necessary (e.g., facilities, instructors).

   Training should be planned and scheduled. Training is provided that has a direct bearing on work performance expectations. Therefore, optimal training occurs in a timely manner with regard to imminent job performance expectations.

> These performance expectations often include the following:
> - Training in the use of specialized tools
> - Training in procedures that are new to the person who will perform them

3. Deliver the training.

    If the training is delivered by a person, then appropriate training professionals (e.g., experienced instructors, mentors) should deliver the training. When possible, training is delivered in settings that closely resemble the actual work environment and includes activities to simulate actual work situations. This approach includes integration of tools, methods, and procedures for competency development. Training is tied to work responsibilities so that on-the-job activities or other outside experiences will reinforce the training within a reasonable time after the training was delivered.

4. Track the delivery of training against the plan.

SP 2.2 ESTABLISH TRAINING RECORDS

Establish and maintain records of organizational training.

This practice applies to the training performed at the organizational level. Establishment and maintenance of training records for project or support group sponsored training is the responsibility of each individual project or support group.

Example Work Products

1. Training records
2. Training updates to the organizational repository

Example Supplier Deliverables

1. Training records as appropriate

Subpractices

1. Keep records of all students who successfully complete each training course or other approved training activity as well as those who are unsuccessful.
2. Keep records of all staff who are waived from training.

    The rationale for granting a waiver should be documented, and both the manager responsible and the manager of the excepted individual should approve the waiver.
3. Keep records of all students who successfully complete their required training.

TIP

To provide consistent and complete information on each employee, the training records may document all training, whether performed at the organization's level or by a project or support group.

X-REF

To ensure that training records are accurate, you may want to use some CM practices.

4. Make training records available to the appropriate people for consideration in assignments.

> Training records may be part of a skills matrix developed by the training organization to provide a summary of the experience and education of people, as well as training sponsored by the organization.

SP 2.3 ASSESS TRAINING EFFECTIVENESS

Assess the effectiveness of the organization's training program.

A process should exist to determine the effectiveness of training (i.e., how well training is meeting the organization's needs).

> **Examples of methods used to assess training effectiveness include the following:**
> - Testing in the training context
> - Post-training surveys of training participants
> - Surveys of manager satisfaction with post-training effects
> - Assessment mechanisms embedded in courseware

TIP

Training effectiveness can change over time. Initially, training may be done using one medium or mode of delivery to train large numbers of people, with another medium or mode of delivery then being employed to train the "stragglers."

Measures can be taken to assess the benefits of training against both the project's and organization's objectives. Particular attention should be paid to the need for various training methods, such as training teams as integral work units. When used, work or process performance objectives should be unambiguous, observable, verifiable, and shared with course participants. The results of the training effectiveness assessment should be used to revise training materials as described in the Establish a Training Capability specific practice.

Example Work Products

1. Training effectiveness surveys
2. Training program performance assessments
3. Instructor evaluation forms
4. Training examinations

Subpractices

1. Assess in-progress or completed projects to determine whether staff knowledge is adequate for performing project tasks.
2. Provide a mechanism for assessing the effectiveness of each training course with respect to established organizational, project, or individual learning (or performance) objectives.
3. Obtain student evaluations of how well training activities met their needs.

OT

PROJECT MONITORING AND CONTROL
A Project Management Process Area at Maturity Level 2

Purpose

The purpose of Project Monitoring and Control (PMC) is to provide an understanding of the project's progress so that appropriate corrective actions can be taken when the project's performance deviates significantly from the plan.

X-REF

PP provides the overall plan and PMC tracks activities against the plan.

Introductory Notes

A project's documented plan is the basis for monitoring activities, communicating status, and taking corrective action. Progress is primarily determined by comparing actual work product and task attributes, effort, cost, and schedule to the plan at prescribed milestones or control levels in the project schedule or WBS. Appropriate visibility of progress enables timely corrective action to be taken when performance deviates significantly from the plan. A deviation is significant if, when left unresolved, it precludes the project from meeting its objectives.

The term "project plan" is used throughout this process area to refer to the overall plan for controlling the project.

Monitoring and control functions are established early in the project as the project's planning is performed and the acquisition strategy is defined. As the acquisition of technology solutions unfolds, monitoring and control activities are essential to ensure that appropriate resources are being applied and that acquirer activities are progressing according to plan.

When actual status deviates significantly from expected values, corrective actions are taken as appropriate. These actions can require replanning, which can include revising the original plan, establishing new agreements, or including additional mitigation activities in the current plan.

If corrective action is required to resolve variances from project plans, these actions should be defined and tracked to closure.

TIP

Initially, as processes based on PMC are introduced, project managers and staff members are reactive. However, as monitoring and control of activities become routine, project managers and staff members begin to anticipate problems and success in advance.

PMC

HINT

Normally, variation will occur. Perform corrective action only when a significant deviation occurs.

X-REF

Some corrective actions may require changes to agreements. These maintenance activities are covered in SSAD SP 3.2.

After one or more suppliers are selected and agreements are established, the role of monitoring and control becomes twofold: (1) the acquirer continues to monitor and control its activities and work products while also (2) monitoring and controlling supplier project progress and performance for impacts to the overall project plan.

The supplier project progress and performance reporting requirements are established in the supplier agreement consistent with the needs of the project.

Related Process Areas

Refer to the Agreement Management process area for more information about ensuring that the supplier and the acquirer perform according to the terms of the supplier agreement.

Refer to the Solicitation and Supplier Agreement Development process area for more information about establishing supplier agreements.

Refer to the Measurement and Analysis process area for more information about providing measurement results.

Refer to the Project Planning process area for more information about establishing and maintaining plans that define project activities.

Specific Goal and Practice Summary

SG 1 Monitor the Project Against the Plan
    SP 1.1   Monitor Project Planning Parameters
    SP 1.2   Monitor Commitments
    SP 1.3   Monitor Project Risks
    SP 1.4   Monitor Data Management
    SP 1.5   Monitor Stakeholder Involvement
    SP 1.6   Conduct Progress Reviews
    SP 1.7   Conduct Milestone Reviews
    SP 1.8   Monitor Transition to Operations and Support
SG 2 Manage Corrective Action to Closure
    SP 2.1   Analyze Issues
    SP 2.2   Take Corrective Action
    SP 2.3   Manage Corrective Actions

Specific Practices by Goal

SG 1   *MONITOR THE PROJECT AGAINST THE PLAN*

Actual project progress and performance are monitored against the project plan.

Monitoring acquirer project progress and performance begins as soon as a plan is established. The acquirer is responsible for monitoring the progress and output of the project. After a supplier is selected and a supplier agreement put in place, the acquirer's monitoring and control activities extend to the supplier and its activities. The acquirer monitors supplier progress, including achievement of requirements established in the supplier agreement and using specified process, product, and service level measures.

SP 1.1 MONITOR PROJECT PLANNING PARAMETERS

Monitor actual values of project planning parameters against the project plan.

Project planning parameters constitute typical indicators of project progress and performance and include attributes of work products and tasks, costs, effort, and schedule. Attributes of the work products and tasks include size, complexity, service level, availability, weight, form, fit, and function. The frequency of monitoring parameters should be considered.

Monitoring typically involves measuring actual values of project planning parameters, comparing actual values to estimates in the plan, and identifying significant deviations. Recording actual values of project planning parameters includes recording associated contextual information to help understand measures. An analysis of the impact that significant deviations have on determining the corrective actions to take is handled in specific goal 2 and its specific practices in this process area.

Example Work Products

1. Records of project performance
2. Records of significant deviations
3. Cost performance reports

Example Supplier Deliverables

1. Supplier project progress and performance reports
2. Records of significant deviations
3. Cost performance reports

Subpractices

1. Monitor progress against the schedule.

> **X-REF**
> These subpractices mirror the specific practices in PP.

PMC

Progress monitoring typically includes the following:
- Periodically measuring the actual completion of activities and milestones
- Comparing actual completion of activities and milestones against the project plan schedule
- Identifying significant deviations from the project plan schedule estimates

2. Monitor the project's costs and expended effort.

> An example of a system for monitoring and updating the project's costs and expended effort is an Earned Value Management System (EVMS) [EIA 2002b].

> Effort and cost monitoring typically includes the following:
> - Periodically measuring the actual effort and costs expended and staff assigned
> - Comparing actual effort, costs, staffing, and training to the project plan budget and estimates
> - Identifying significant deviations from the project plan budget and estimates

3. Monitor the attributes of work products and tasks.

Refer to the Measurement and Analysis process area for more information about developing and sustaining a measurement capability used to support management information needs.

Refer to the Project Planning process area for more information about establishing estimates of work product and task attributes.

> Monitoring the attributes of work products and tasks typically includes the following:
> - Periodically measuring the actual attributes of work products and tasks, such as size, complexity, or service levels (and changes to these attributes)
> - Comparing the actual attributes of work products and tasks (and changes to these attributes) to the project plan estimates
> - Identifying significant deviations from the project plan estimates

Monitoring attributes applies to both acquirer and supplier work products and tasks.

4. Monitor resources provided and used.

Refer to the Project Planning process area for more information about planning the project's resources.

This resource monitoring includes monitoring the availability of resources provided by the supplier for the project.

> Examples of resources include the following:
> - Physical facilities
> - Computers, peripherals, and software

Continues

Continued

- Networks
- Security environment
- Project staff
- Processes

---

5. Monitor the knowledge and skills of project staff.

   Refer to the Project Planning process area for more information about planning needed knowledge and skills.

Monitoring the knowledge and skills of project staff typically includes the following:

- Periodically measuring the acquisition of knowledge and skills by project staff
- Comparing the actual training obtained to that documented in the project plan
- Identifying significant deviations from the project plan estimates

---

   Staff monitoring includes monitoring the skills and knowledge of supplier staff provided for the project.

6. Document significant deviations in project planning parameters. Document significant deviations that apply either to acquirer project execution or to supplier deviations from the project plan.

   Refer to the Solicitation and Supplier Agreement Development process area for more information about establishing supplier agreements.

SP 1.2 MONITOR COMMITMENTS

Monitor commitments against those identified in the project plan.

Resource commitments that result in expenditures (e.g., issued purchase orders and completed supplier deliverables that are accepted) are tracked when the expense is incurred, even prior to formal payment, to ensure that future financial and legal obligations are accounted for as soon as they are incurred. Commitments that do not result in expenditures (e.g., allocation of resources or skill sets) should also be monitored.

   Supplier commitments for the project are also monitored by the acquirer through these practices.

Example Work Products

1. Records of commitment reviews

TIP

Things may happen that prevent appropriate follow-through with commitments, especially in an immature organization. For this reason, it is necessary to monitor commitments and take corrective action when commitments change.

PMC

Subpractices

1. Regularly review commitments (both external and internal).
2. Identify commitments that have not been satisfied or are at significant risk of not being satisfied.
3. Document the results of commitment reviews.

SP 1.3 MONITOR PROJECT RISKS

Monitor risks against those identified in the project plan.

X-REF

Specific practice 1.3 is the handshake with the risks that were identified in PP. This practice is reactive and involves minimal risk management activities. For more complete and proactive handling of project risks, refer to RSKM.

Refer to the Project Planning process area for more information about identifying project risks.

Refer to the Risk Management process area for more information about identifying potential problems before they occur so that risk handling activities can be planned and invoked as needed across the life of the product or project to mitigate adverse impacts on achieving objectives.

The acquirer monitors the overall project risk. Many risks are the sole responsibility of the acquirer and can include information that should not be shared with the supplier (e.g., source selection sensitive, re-competition, internal staffing).

There can also be risks that require careful coordination with suppliers and the establishment of appropriate mechanisms for the escalation of risks and risk status (e.g., feasibility of the technology to meet end-user functionality and quality attribute requirements). Shared risks can require jointly planned mitigations.

Example Work Products

1. Records of project risk monitoring

Example Supplier Deliverables

1. Records of supplier risk monitoring

Subpractices

1. Periodically review the documentation of risks in the context of the project's current status and circumstances.
   This review includes the risks defined in the solicitation package, risks identified by the supplier in their proposal, and risks raised as part of regular supplier status reporting.
2. Revise the documentation of risks as additional information becomes available.

As projects progress (especially projects of long duration or continuous operation), new risks arise. It is important to identify and analyze these new risks. For example, software, equipment, and tools in use can become obsolete; or key staff can gradually lose skills in areas of particular long-term importance to the project and organization.

3. Communicate the risk status to relevant stakeholders.

Examples of risk status include the following:
- A change in the probability that the risk occurs
- A change in risk priority

SP 1.4 MONITOR DATA MANAGEMENT

Monitor the management of project data against the project plan.

Refer to the Plan Data Management specific practice in the Project Planning process area for more information about identifying types of data to be managed and how to plan for their management.

Data management activities should be monitored to ensure that data management requirements are being satisfied. Depending on the results of monitoring and changes in project requirements, situation, or status, it may be necessary to re-plan the project's data management activities.

Example Work Products

1. Records of data management

Example Supplier Deliverables

1. Records of supplier data management

Subpractices

1. Periodically review data management activities against their description in the project plan.
2. Identify and document significant issues and their impacts.

An example of a significant issue is when stakeholders do not have the access to project data they need to fulfill their roles as relevant stake holders.

3. Document results of data management activity reviews.

SP 1.5 MONITOR STAKEHOLDER INVOLVEMENT

Monitor stakeholder involvement against the project plan.

Refer to the Plan Stakeholder Involvement specific practice in the Project Planning process area for more information about identifying relevant stakeholders and planning appropriate involvement with them.

Stakeholder involvement should be monitored to ensure that appropriate interactions occur. Depending on the results of monitoring and changes in project requirements, situation, or status, it may be necessary to re-plan stakeholder involvement.

This monitoring is particularly important in a system of systems environment in which the involvement of owners, acquirers, and customers of other systems in the system of systems is crucial to the success of that system of systems.

This monitoring is also particularly important in an environment in which a supplier is using an Agile method, in which case the sustained involvement of end users or their proxies in the supplier's product development activities can be crucial to developing and validating one or more elements of the overall capability to be provided.

Refer to the Plan Stakeholder Involvement specific practice in the Project Planning process area for more information about supporting the use of Agile methods.

Example Work Products

1. Records of stakeholder involvement

Example Supplier Deliverables

1. Records of supplier involvement

Subpractices

1. Periodically review the status of stakeholder involvement.
2. Identify and document significant issues and their impacts.
3. Document the results of stakeholder involvement status reviews.

SP 1.6 CONDUCT PROGRESS REVIEWS

Periodically review the project's progress, performance, and issues.

A "project's progress" is the project's status as viewed at a particular time when the project activities performed so far and their results and impacts are reviewed with relevant stakeholders (especially project representatives and project management) to determine whether there are significant issues or performance shortfalls to be addressed.

Progress reviews are project reviews to keep relevant stakeholders informed. These project reviews can be informal and may not be specified explicitly in project plans.

TIP
Progress reviews are held regularly (e.g., weekly, monthly, or quarterly).

Refer to the Agreement Management process area for more information about monitoring selected supplier processes.

Refer to the Solicitation and Supplier Agreement Development process area for more information about monitoring selected supplier processes.

Example Work Products

1. Documented project review results

Example Supplier Deliverables

1. Supplier project progress and performance reports
2. Supplier review materials and reports
3. Documentation of product and document deliveries

Subpractices

1. Regularly communicate status on assigned activities and work products to relevant stakeholders.

   Managers, staff, customers, end users, suppliers, and other relevant stakeholders are included in reviews as appropriate.

2. Review the results of collecting and analyzing measures for controlling the project.

Examples of classes of commonly used acquirer measures include the following:

- Requirements volatility
- Return on investment
- Cost performance index
- Number of defects per phase and by severity of defects
- Schedule performance index
- Customer satisfaction trends
- Supplier performance and relationship trends

Refer to the Measurement and Analysis process area for more information about aligning measurement and analysis activities and providing measurement results.

3. Identify and document significant issues and deviations from the plan.

This activity includes identifying and documenting both acquirer and supplier issues and deviations.

4. Document change requests and problems identified in work products and processes.

   Refer to the Configuration Management process area for more information about tracking and controlling changes.

5. Document the results of reviews.
6. Track change requests and problem reports to closure.

SP 1.7 CONDUCT MILESTONE REVIEWS

Review the project's accomplishments and results at selected project milestones.

Refer to the Establish the Budget and Schedule specific practice in the Project Planning process area for more information about identifying major milestones.

Milestones are pre-planned events or points in time at which a thorough review of status is conducted to understand how well stakeholder requirements are being met. (If the project includes a developmental milestone, then the review is conducted to ensure that the assumptions and requirements associated with that milestone are being met.) Milestones can be associated with the overall project or a particular service type or instance. Milestones can thus be event based or calendar based.

Milestone reviews are planned during project planning and are typically formal reviews.

Progress reviews and milestone reviews need not be held separately. A single review can address the intent of both. For example, a single pre-planned review can evaluate progress, issues, and performance up through a planned time period (or milestone) against the plan's expectations.

Depending on the project, "project startup" and "project closeout" could be phases covered by milestone reviews.

Example Work Products

1. Documented milestone review results

Example Supplier Deliverables

1. Documented measurement results
2. Measurement analysis reports

TIP

Milestones are major events in a project. If you are using a project lifecycle model, milestones may be predetermined. Many professional organizations recommend iterative planning and managing at the "inchstone" level for near-term tasks to avoid surprises at the official milestone event.

Subpractices

1. Conduct milestone reviews with relevant stakeholders at meaningful points in the project's schedule, such as the completion of selected phases.

   Managers, staff, customers, end users, suppliers, and other relevant stakeholders are included in milestone reviews as appropriate. Conduct milestone reviews with the supplier as specified in the supplier agreement.

   Refer to the Acquisition Technical Management process area for more information about conducting technical reviews.

   Refer to the Establish the Supplier Agreement specific practice in the Solicitation and Supplier Agreement Development process area for more information about establishing review requirements in the supplier agreement.

2. Review commitments, the plan, status, and risks of the project.

3. Identify and document significant issues and their impacts.

4. Document results of the review, action items, and decisions.

5. Track action items to closure.

SP 1.8 *MONITOR TRANSITION TO OPERATIONS AND SUPPORT*

Monitor transition to operations and support.

The acquirer monitors and controls the transition of the accepted product or service against the plan for transition to operations and support.

Refer to the Plan Transition to Operations and Support specific practice in the Project Planning process area for more information about planning for the transition of the product or service to operations and support.

Typically, the supplier has a role in integrating and packaging products and prepares for the transition to operations and support, including support for business user acceptance; the acquirer monitors these supplier activities. These expectations of the supplier and the acceptance criteria for transition to operations and support are included in the solicitation package and then the supplier agreement.

Example Work Products

1. Transition readiness report
2. Records of transition to support reviews
3. Transition analysis report

> **TIP**
>
> A successful transition involves executing an effective plan for the appropriate facilities, training, use, maintenance, and support of the acquired capability.

> **TIP**
>
> Sometimes the acquisition organization may be expected to perform specific transition activities itself. In still other cases, it may need to acquire a service supplier to support the capability provided to the customer.

PMC

Example Supplier Deliverables

1. Training materials and supporting artifacts
2. Site readiness report
3. Verification reports
4. Training records
5. Operational readiness reports
6. Test results
7. Pilot results

Subpractices

1. Monitor the operations and support organization's capability and facilities designated to receive, store, use, and maintain acquired products.

    The acquirer makes adequate provisions through the supplier agreement or in-house operations and support organizations to operate the acquired product. Typically, the acquirer uses verification practices to confirm that the organization, physical environment, and operations and support resources are equipped to execute operations and support activities.

    The acquirer also reviews operations and support organizations designated to take responsibility for the operation of the product and to ensure that resources identified and budgeted are available when needed. The designated operations and support organizations demonstrate their readiness (i.e., capability, capacity) to accept responsibility for the product and to ensure uninterrupted support. Typically, a demonstration involves execution of all the activities of operations (e.g., a pilot).

2. Monitor the delivery of training for those who are involved in receiving, storing, using, and maintaining acquired products.

    Typically, the supplier develops training resources for the product. Training materials and resources are specified in the supplier agreement to meet the needs of various audiences (e.g., operations and support staff, end users). The acquirer verifies that training is provided at the appropriate time to the appropriate audience and determines whether the training capability provided is adequate.

3. Review pilot results, if any, and operational readiness reports for the acquired product.

    Determine readiness of the product and involved stakeholders, such as the operations and support organizations, for the transition of responsibility. The acquirer typically uses transition readiness criteria and verification and validation practices to determine if the supplier delivered products meet specified requirements. The criteria also address the readiness of the product for maintenance over the intended product lifecycle.

4. Review and analyze the results of transition activities.

The acquirer reviews and analyzes the results of transition activities and determines whether corrective actions must be completed before responsibility is transferred to the operational and support organizations.

Example reports and logs used by the acquirer include the following:

- Transition activity reports, including quality measures collected during the pilot and the warranty period
- Problem tracking reports, detailing resolution time, escalation, and root cause analysis
- Change management reports
- Configuration management records
- Operation logs to determine that sufficient information is stored to support reconstruction
- Security reports
- Actual operations and support costs compared to estimates

SG 2   MANAGE CORRECTIVE ACTION TO CLOSURE

Corrective actions are managed to closure when the project's performance or results deviate significantly from the plan.

When the acquirer determines (e.g., through its monitoring of measurement data) that supplier progress does not appear to be sufficient to meet a service level defined in the supplier agreement, then the acquirer initiates and manages corrective action with the supplier.

If the supplier does not comply appropriately with the acquirer's initiation of corrective action, the acquirer escalates and resolves this issue as a supplier agreement issue.

SP 2.1 ANALYZE ISSUES

Collect and analyze issues and determine corrective actions to address them.

Corrective action is taken for both acquirer deviations and when supplier execution does not align with project planning (e.g., milestones and work product date slippages).

Many issues and corrective actions are the sole responsibility of the acquirer and can include information that should not be shared with the supplier (e.g., source selection sensitive, re-competition, internal staffing).

Example Work Products

1. List of issues requiring corrective actions

Example Supplier Deliverables

1. List of supplier issues needing corrective action by the acquirer

Subpractices

1. Gather issues for analysis.

    Issues are collected from reviews and the execution of other processes.

Examples of issues to be gathered include the following:
- Issues discovered when performing technical reviews, verification, and validation
- Significant deviations in project planning parameters from estimates in the project plan
- Commitments (either internal or external) that have not been satisfied
- Significant changes in risk status
- Data access, collection, privacy, or security issues
- Stakeholder representation or involvement issues
- Product, tool, or environment transition assumptions (or other customer or supplier commitments) that have not been achieved

---

2. Analyze issues to determine the need for corrective action.

    Refer to the Establish the Budget and Schedule specific practice in the Project Planning process area for more information about corrective action criteria.

    Corrective action is required when the issue, if left unresolved, may prevent the project from meeting its objectives.

SP 2.2 *Take Corrective Action*

Take corrective action on identified issues.

Some corrective actions can be assigned to a supplier. The acquirer oversees corrective actions assigned to the supplier as appropriate.

Example Work Products

1. Corrective action plans

Example Supplier Deliverables

1. Corrective action plans for supplier issues

TIP

In some cases, the corrective action can be to monitor the situation. A corrective action does not always result in a complete solution to the problem.

Subpractices

1. Determine and document the appropriate actions needed to address identified issues.

   Refer to the Project Planning process area for more information about developing a project plan.

Examples of potential actions include the following:
- Modifying the statement of work
- Modifying requirements
- Revising estimates and plans
- Renegotiating commitments
- Adding resources
- Changing processes
- Revising project risks

---

2. Review and get agreement with relevant stakeholders on the actions to be taken.
3. Negotiate changes to internal and external commitments.

SP 2.3 MANAGE CORRECTIVE ACTIONS

Manage corrective actions to closure.

Example Work Products

1. Corrective action results

Example Supplier Deliverables

1. Corrective action results for supplier issues

Subpractices

1. Monitor corrective actions for their completion.
2. Analyze results of corrective actions to determine the effectiveness of the corrective actions.
3. Determine and document appropriate actions to correct deviations from planned results from performing corrective actions.
   Lessons learned as a result of taking corrective action can be inputs to planning and risk management processes.

TIP

When managing multiple suppliers, the acquirer may need to adjudicate the assignment of actions between the suppliers and itself. Consider including contractual language to set the expectations for suppliers when participating in issue allocation and resolution of issues. Such preparation becomes particularly important near the end of the project when funding is low and suppliers are eager to close out the contract.

PMC

PROJECT PLANNING
A Project Management Process Area at Maturity Level 2

Purpose

The purpose of Project Planning (PP) is to establish and maintain plans that define project activities.

Introductory Notes

One of the keys to effectively managing a project is project planning. The Project Planning process area involves the following activities:

- Developing the project plan
- Interacting with relevant stakeholders appropriately
- Getting commitment to the plan
- Maintaining the plan

Planning begins with requirements that define the product and project.

Project planning is based on the acquisition strategy, which is a guide for directing and controlling the project and a framework for integrating activities essential to acquiring an operational product or service. The acquisition strategy outlines acquisition objectives and constraints, availability of assets and technologies, consideration of acquisition methods, potential supplier agreement types and terms, accommodation of end-user considerations, considerations of risk, and support for the project throughout the project lifecycle.

Planning includes estimating the attributes of work products and tasks, determining the resources needed, negotiating commitments, producing a schedule, and identifying and analyzing project risks. Iterating through these activities may be necessary to establish the project plan. The project plan provides the basis for performing and controlling project activities that address commitments with the project's customer. (See the definition of "project" in the glossary.)

TIP

In planning, you determine the requirements to be fulfilled, the tasks to be performed, and the resources and coordination required. You then document all of this information so that you can obtain the needed resources and commitments.

TIP

The plan is a declaration that the work has been rationally thought through and requests for resources are credible. If you ask management to commit resources, they want to know it is worth the investment. A project plan helps you to convince them.

TIP

Before committing resources to an acquisition project, management needs a clear plan.

X-REF

PMC addresses tracking of project activities in the plan.

PP

411

Project Planning involves the development and maintenance of plans for all acquirer processes, including plans required for effective acquirer-supplier interaction. Once the supplier agreement is signed and schedule, costs, and resources from the supplier are established, the acquirer takes the supplier estimations for the project into account at an appropriate level of detail in its project plan.

Project planning includes establishing and maintaining a plan for the orderly, smooth transition of the acquired product from a supplier to its use by the acquirer or its customers. In addition, if an existing product is to be replaced as part of the acquisition, the acquirer may be required to consider the disposal of the existing product as part of the planning for acquiring the new product. All transition activities are included in the project plan and provisions for accommodating such specialized requirements are also included.

All relevant stakeholders should be involved in the planning process from all lifecycle phases to ensure all technical and support activities are adequately addressed in project plans.

The project plan is usually revised as the project progresses to address changes in requirements and commitments, inaccurate estimates, corrective actions, and process changes. Specific practices describing both planning and replanning are contained in this process area.

Changes to the supplier agreement can also affect the project's planning estimates, budget, schedules, risks, project work tasks, commitments, and resources.

The term "project plan" is used throughout this process area to refer to the overall plan for controlling the project. The project plan can be a stand-alone document or be distributed across multiple documents. In either case, a coherent picture of who does what should be included. Likewise, monitoring and control can be centralized or distributed, as long as at the project level a coherent picture of project status can be maintained.

Related Process Areas

Refer to the Acquisition Requirements Development process area for more information about developing and analyzing customer and contractual requirements.

Refer to the Acquisition Technical Management process area for more information about evaluating the supplier's technical solution and managing selected interfaces of that solution.

Refer to the Solicitation and Supplier Agreement Development process area for more information about establishing supplier agreements.

Refer to the Measurement and Analysis process area for more information about specifying measures.

Refer to the Requirements Management process area for more information about managing requirements.

Refer to the Risk Management process area for more information about identifying and analyzing risks and mitigating risks.

Specific Goal and Practice Summary

SG 1 Establish Estimates
    SP 1.1   Establish the Acquisition Strategy
    SP 1.2   Estimate the Scope of the Project
    SP 1.3   Establish Estimates of Work Product and Task Attributes
    SP 1.4   Define Project Lifecycle Phases
    SP 1.5   Estimate Effort and Cost

SG 2 Develop a Project Plan
    SP 2.1   Establish the Budget and Schedule
    SP 2.2   Identify Project Risks
    SP 2.3   Plan Data Management
    SP 2.4   Plan the Project's Resources
    SP 2.5   Plan Needed Knowledge and Skills
    SP 2.6   Plan Stakeholder Involvement
    SP 2.7   Plan Transition to Operations and Support
    SP 2.8   Establish the Project Plan

SG 3 Obtain Commitment to the Plan
    SP 3.1   Review Plans That Affect the Project
    SP 3.2   Reconcile Work and Resource Levels
    SP 3.3   Obtain Plan Commitment

Specific Practices by Goal

SG 1   ESTABLISH ESTIMATES

Estimates of project planning parameters are established and maintained.

Project planning parameters include all information needed by the project to perform necessary planning, organizing, staffing, directing, coordinating, reporting, and budgeting.

The acquirer develops estimates for project work based on the acquisition strategy, including high-level estimates for the work to be done by suppliers. Initial estimates can be revised based on supplier estimates in response to the solicitation package.

Estimates of planning parameters should have a sound basis to instill confidence that plans based on these estimates are capable of supporting project objectives.

> **X-REF**
>
> Specific goal 1 focuses on providing estimates of project planning parameters; actual values are monitored in PMC SP 1.1.

> **TIP**
>
> Project planning parameters are a key to managing a project. Planning parameters primarily include size, effort, and cost.

PP

> Factors to consider when estimating these parameters include the following:
> - The acquisition strategy
> - Project requirements, including product requirements, requirements imposed by the organization, requirements imposed by the customer, and other requirements that affect the project
> - The scope of the project
> - Identified tasks and work products
> - The technical approach
> - The selected project lifecycle model (e.g., waterfall, incremental, spiral)
> - Attributes of work products and tasks (e.g., size, complexity)
> - The schedule
> - Models or historical data used for converting attributes of work products and tasks into labor hours and costs
> - The methodology (e.g., models, data, algorithms) used to determine needed material, skills, labor hours, and cost

The acquisition strategy is a key factor when estimating the project.

Documentation of the estimating rationale and supporting data is needed for stakeholder review and commitment to the plan and for maintenance of the plan as the project progresses.

SP 1.1 ESTABLISH THE ACQUISITION STRATEGY

Establish and maintain the acquisition strategy.

The acquisition strategy is the business and technical management framework for planning, executing, and managing agreements for a project. The acquisition strategy relates to the objectives for the acquisition, the constraints, availability of resources and technologies, consideration of acquisition methods, potential supplier agreement types, terms and conditions, accommodation of business considerations, considerations of risk, and support for the acquired product over its lifecycle. The acquisition strategy reflects the entire scope of the project. It encompasses the work to be performed by the acquirer and the supplier, or in some cases multiple suppliers, for the full lifecycle of the product.

The acquisition strategy results from a thorough understanding of both the acquisition project and the general acquisition environment. The acquirer accounts for the potential value or benefit of the acquisition in the light of potential risks, considers constraints, and takes into account experiences with different types of suppliers, agreements, and terms. A well-developed strategy minimizes the time and cost required to satisfy approved capability needs, and maximizes affordability throughout the project lifecycle.

The acquisition strategy is the basis for formulating solicitation packages, supplier agreements, and project plans. The strategy evolves over time and should continuously reflect the current status and desired end point of the project.

X-REF

See "Techniques for Developing an Acquisition Strategy by Profiling Software Risks" (CMU/SEI-2006-TR-002) for guidance on how to use a risk-based approach to develop an acquisition strategy for a software-intensive system.

Example Work Products

1. Acquisition strategy

Subpractices

1. Identify the capabilities and objectives the acquisition is intended to satisfy or provide.

   The capabilities describe what the organization intends to acquire. Typically, the capabilities included in the acquisition strategy highlight product characteristics driven by interoperability or families of products. The acquisition strategy also identifies dependencies on planned or existing capabilities of other projects or products.

   Refer to the Acquisition Requirements Development process area for more information about developing and analyzing customer and contractual requirements.

   The acquirer defines objectives in terms of cost, schedule, and performance. Performance related objectives are stated in terms of key process, product, and service level measures and technical performance measures as defined in requirements. These measures reflect customer expectations and threshold values representing acceptable limits for key quality attributes (addressing, e.g., responsiveness, safety, reliability, and maintainability) that, in the customer's judgment, provide the needed capability. While the number and specificity of measures can change over the duration of an acquisition, the acquirer typically focuses on the minimum number of measures that, if thresholds are not met, will require a re-evaluation of the project.

   The acquisition strategy establishes the milestone decision points and acquisition phases planned for the project. It prescribes the accomplishments for each phase and identifies the critical events affecting project management. Schedule parameters include, at a minimum, the projected dates for project initiation, other major decision points, and initial operational capability.

> Examples of cost parameters include the following:
> - Research, development, test, and evaluation costs
> - Acquisition costs
> - Acquisition related operations, support, and disposal costs
> - Total product quantity (to include both fully configured development and production units)

TIP

The type of acquisition varies according to the nature of products and services that are available to satisfy the project's needs and requirements (including COTS products).

TIP

The acquisition approach and the supplier's development approach are complementary but not always the same. For example, the acquisition approach can be single step, whereas the supplier may use an incremental approach in developing the solution.

2. Identify the acquisition approach.

   The acquirer defines the approach the project will use to achieve full capability, e.g., whether evolutionary or single step, and includes a brief rationale to justify the choice. When a project uses an evolutionary acquisition approach, the acquisition strategy describes the initial capability and how it will be funded, developed, tested, produced, and supported. The acquisition strategy previews similar planning for subsequent increments and identifies the approach to integrate or retrofit earlier increments with later increments.

> Examples of considerations for the acquisition approach include the following:
> - Actions a project team can take on its own if the acquiring organization has an acquisition, contracting, or purchasing department
> - Who will prepare objective estimates and if these estimates are needed as evaluation criteria
> - Managing multiple suppliers
> - Anticipated lead times from potential suppliers to acquire items

3. Document business considerations.

   Business considerations include the type of competition planned for all phases of the acquisition or an explanation of why competition is not practicable or not in the best interests of the acquirer. Also included are considerations for establishing or maintaining access to competitive suppliers for critical products or product components. Availability and suitability of commercial items and the extent to which interfaces for these items have broad market acceptance, standards, organization support, and stability are other business considerations. Also included are considerations for both international and domestic sources that can meet the required need as primary sources of supply consistent with organizational policies and regulations.

> Other examples of business considerations for an acquisition strategy include the following:
> - Product and technology areas critical to satisfying or providing the desired capabilities
> - Data rights
>
> *Continues*

Continued

- Product line considerations
- Socio-economic constraints
- Safety and health issues
- Security issues (physical and information technology)
- Other business oriented product quality attributes that can be market differentiators or mission critical (e.g., product responsiveness, platform openness, availability, sustainability)

4. Identify major risks and which risks will be addressed jointly with the supplier.

Major acquisition risks, whether primarily managed by the acquirer or supplier, should be identified and assessed by the acquirer. The acquisition strategy identifies major risks, which risks are to be shared with the supplier, and which are retained by the acquirer.

Refer to the Risk Management process area for more information about establishing a risk management strategy.

5. Identify the preferred type of supplier.

The acquirer identifies standardized acquisition documents (e.g., standard supplier agreements), if any. The acquirer also determines the preferred type of supplier agreement (e.g., firm fixed-price; fixed-price incentive, firm target; cost plus incentive fee; cost plus award fee) and the reasons it is suitable, including considerations of risk and reasonable risk sharing by the acquirer and supplier.
The acquisition strategy explains the planned incentive structure for the acquisition and how it encourages the supplier to provide the product or service at or below the established cost objectives and satisfy the schedule and key measurement objectives. Considerations should be given to using incentives to reduce primary project risks. If more than one incentive is planned for a supplier agreement, the acquisition strategy explains how the incentives complement one other and do not interfere with one another. The acquisition strategy identifies unusual terms and conditions of the planned supplier agreement and all existing or contemplated deviations to an organization's terms and conditions, if any.

6. Identify the product support strategy.

The acquirer develops a product support strategy for lifecycle sustainment and continuous improvement of product affordability, reliability, and supportability, while sustaining readiness. The support strategy addresses how the acquirer will maintain oversight of the fielded product and ensure satisfaction of support related quality attributes.
If support is going to be performed by an organization different from the supplier, a sufficient overlap period should be defined to ensure smooth transition.

PP

The acquirer's sustainment organization or supplier typically participates in the development of the product support strategy.

7. Review and obtain agreement with senior management on the acquisition strategy.

   The development of the acquisition strategy for a project typically requires senior management sponsorship. Appropriate senior management should approve the acquisition strategy before initiating a project.

SP 1.2 ESTIMATE THE SCOPE OF THE PROJECT

Establish a top-level work breakdown structure (WBS) to estimate the scope of the project.

The acquirer establishes the objectives of the project in the acquisition strategy. An initial set of requirements and project objectives form the basis for establishing the WBS or for selecting a standard WBS from organizational process assets. To ensure the full scope of the project is estimated, the WBS includes activities performed by the acquirer as well as milestones and deliverables for suppliers.

The acquisition strategy drives a key decision in this practice, specifically how much work, and what work, to give to a supplier. The acquirer develops a WBS that clearly identifies the project work performed by the acquirer and the project work performed by the supplier. The supplier work identified in the WBS becomes the foundation for the statement of work defined in the Solicitation and Supplier Agreement Development process area. The WBS identifies deliverables from the supplier and work products developed by the acquirer.

The WBS evolves with the project. A top-level WBS can serve to structure initial estimating. The development of a WBS divides the overall project into an interconnected set of manageable components.

Typically, the WBS is a product, work product, or task oriented structure that provides a scheme for identifying and organizing the logical units of work to be managed, which are called "work packages." The WBS provides a reference and organizational mechanism for assigning effort, schedule, and responsibility and is used as the underlying framework to plan, organize, and control the work done on the project.

Some projects use the term "contract WBS" to refer to the portion of the WBS placed under contract (possibly the entire WBS). Not all projects have a contract WBS (e.g., internally funded development).

HINT

For some acquisition programs, the acquisition strategy is created by a project team whose formation precedes the creation of the final acquisition project team.

HINT

To develop estimates, decompose the project into smaller work items (the WBS), estimate the resources needed by each item, and then roll these elements up. This activity will result in more accurate estimates.

TIP

Interaction and iteration among planning, requirements definition, and design are often necessary. A project can learn a lot from each iteration and can use this knowledge to update the plan, requirements, and design for the next iteration.

Example Work Products

1. Task descriptions
2. Work package descriptions
3. WBS

Subpractices

1. Develop a WBS based on the product architecture.

    The WBS provides a scheme for organizing the project's work. The WBS should permit the identification of the following items:

    - Risks and their mitigation tasks
    - Tasks for deliverables and supporting activities
    - Tasks for skill and knowledge acquisition
    - Tasks for the development of needed support plans, such as configuration management, quality assurance, and verification plans
    - Tasks for the integration and management of nondevelopmental items

2. Define the work packages in sufficient detail so that estimates of project tasks, responsibilities, and schedule can be specified.

    The top-level WBS is intended to help gauge the project work effort for tasks and organizational roles and responsibilities. The amount of detail in the WBS at this level helps in developing realistic schedules, thereby minimizing the need for management reserve.

3. Identify products and product components to be externally acquired.
4. Identify work products to be reused.

SP 1.3 ESTABLISH ESTIMATES OF WORK PRODUCT AND TASK ATTRIBUTES

Establish and maintain estimates of work product and task attributes.

Size is the primary input to many models used to estimate effort, cost, and schedule. Models can also be based on other attributes such as service level, connectivity, complexity, availability, and structure.

Estimation methods include using historical acquirer and supplier data and standard estimating models to compare projects of similar complexity. Where historical size data are not available, develop an estimate based on the understanding of the design of similar products.

Estimation models can be built based on historical data as part of organizational process performance, and estimates for any project can be validated using these models.

Refer to the Organizational Process Performance process area for more information about establishing process performance models.

HINT

Use the WBS to help you define the product architecture.

HINT

You may select different suppliers to deliver different architectural components. In such a case, make sure you account for the integration activities.

TIP

The level of detail often depends on the level and completeness of the requirements. Often, the work packages and estimates evolve as the requirements evolve.

HINT

Consider establishing a management reserve commensurate to the overall uncertainty that allows for the efficient allocation of resources to address the uncertainty of estimates.

HINT

Learn to quantify the resources needed for particular tasks by associating size measures with each type of work product and building historical data. By collecting historical data from projects, you can learn how measured size relates to the resources consumed by tasks. This knowledge can then be used when planning the next project.

PP

X-REF

For more information on tools and methods used for cost estimating, see www. cssc.usc.edu.

Examples of attributes to estimate include the following:

- Number of logic gates for integrated circuits
- Number of parts (e.g., printed circuit boards, components, mechanical parts)
- Physical constraints (e.g., weight, volume)
- Number of pages
- Number of inputs and outputs
- Number of technical risk items
- Number of functions
- Function points
- Source lines of code
- Amount of code to be reused versus created
- Number of classes and objects
- Number and complexity of requirements
- Number and complexity of interfaces
- Volume of data
- Maturity of the technology specified in the technical solution
- Amount and complexity of the work potentially assigned to suppliers
- Number of locations where the product is to be installed
- Experience of project participants
- Team velocity or productivity
- Geographic dispersal of project members
- Proximity of customers, end users, and suppliers

HINT

Consider providing guidelines on how to estimate the difficulty or complexity of a task. This step may improve estimation accuracy, especially when size measures are not available.

The estimates should be consistent with project requirements to determine the project's effort, cost, and schedule. A relative level of difficulty or complexity should be assigned for each size attribute.

Example Work Products

1. Size and complexity of tasks and work products
2. Estimating models
3. Attribute estimates
4. Technical approach

Subpractices

1. Determine the technical approach for the project.

   The technical approach defines a top-level strategy for development of the product. It includes decisions on architectural features, such as distributed or client/server; state-of-the-art or established technologies to be applied, such as robotics, composite materials, or artificial intelligence; and the functionality and quality attributes expected in the final products, such as safety, security, and ergonomics.

The technical approach provides a basis for interoperability and supportability of the technical solution developed by the supplier. The technical approach is often developed as part of and included in the acquisition strategy.

2. Use appropriate methods to determine the attributes of the work products and tasks to be used to estimate resource requirements.

   Methods for determining size and complexity should be based on validated models or historical data.

   The methods for determining attributes evolve as the understanding of the relationship of product characteristics to attributes increases.

X-REF

Mature organizations maintain historical data to help projects establish reasonable estimates (see MA SP 1.5 and IPM SP 1.2).

Examples of attributes include the following:
- Maturity of the technology specified in the technical solution
- Amount and complexity of the work potentially assigned to suppliers
- Number of locations where the product is to be installed

---

3. Estimate the attributes of work products and tasks.

Examples of work products for which size estimates are made include the following:
- Deliverable and nondeliverable work products
- Documents and files
- Operational and support hardware, firmware, and software

SP 1.4 DEFINE PROJECT LIFECYCLE PHASES

Define project lifecycle phases on which to scope the planning effort.

The determination of a project's lifecycle phases provides for planned periods of evaluation and decision making. These periods are normally defined to support logical decision points at which the appropriateness of continued reliance on the project plan and strategy is determined and significant commitments are made concerning resources. Such points provide planned events at which project course corrections and determinations of future scope and cost can be made.

Understanding the project lifecycle is crucial in determining the scope of the planning effort and the timing of initial planning, as well as the timing and criteria (critical milestones) for replanning.

Depending on the nature of the project, explicit phases for "project startup" and "project close-out" can be included in the lifecycle.

Project lifecycle phases should be defined depending on the scope of requirements, estimates for project resources, and the nature of the project.

TIP

For example, in a single-step acquisition, at the end of the requirements analysis phase, the requirements are evaluated to assess their consistency, completeness, and feasibility, and to decide whether the project is ready (from a technical and risk perspective) to commit resources for suppliers to begin the design phase.

PP

The acquirer includes the entire project lifecycle (i.e., from end user needs through initial and subsequent upgrades) when planning lifecycle phases and refines the acquisition strategy as appropriate. The acquirer considers all supplier agreements in the context of the acquisition so that an integrated approach results. A complex project can involve managing multiple supplier agreements simultaneously or in sequence. In such cases, any acquisition lifecycle can end during any phase of the project lifecycle. Depending on the acquisition strategy, there can be intermediate phases for the creation of prototypes, increments of capability, or spiral model cycles.

Refer to the Establish Lifecycle Model Descriptions specific practice in the Organizational Process Definition process area for more information about acquisition lifecycles.

During establishment of the supplier agreement, the acquirer works with the supplier to understand supplier lifecycle models and processes, especially those models and processes that interact directly with acquirer processes. Agreement on the lifecycle models and processes to be used during the project enables seamless interactions between supplier and acquirer, resulting in a successful acquirer-supplier relationship.

Example Work Products

1. Project lifecycle phases

SP 1.5 ESTIMATE EFFORT AND COST

Estimate the project's effort and cost for work products and tasks based on estimation rationale.

Estimates of effort and cost are generally based on results of analysis using models or historical data applied to size, activities, and other planning parameters. Confidence in these estimates is based on rationale for the selected model and the nature of the data. There can be occasions when available historical data do not apply, such as when efforts are unprecedented or when the type of task does not fit available models. For example, an effort can be considered unprecedented if the organization has no experience with such a product or task.

Unprecedented efforts are more risky, require more research to develop reasonable bases of estimate, and require more management reserve. The uniqueness of the project should be documented when using these models to ensure a common understanding of any assumptions made in the initial planning phases.

Estimates address all processes and activities performed by the project for the project lifecycle, including an estimate of effort and cost for supplier work. The project estimate includes detailed estimates for activities performed by the acquirer and its stakeholders. The acquirer should include members of their technical community (e.g., systems, hardware, software engineers) to ensure all technical considerations have been accounted for in the estimates. As the project evolves, these estimates can be revised based on changed conditions (e.g., new circumstances encountered during execution of the supplier agreement).

In addition to creating an estimate for the project work products, the acquirer is encouraged to have its estimate and WBS reviewed by individuals external to the project to ensure that the project estimation and WBS can be validated.

> **TIP**
>
> Differences between the acquirer's estimate and the supplier's estimate should be analyzed to uncover risks that may demand management attention.

Example Work Products

1. Estimation rationale
2. Project effort estimates
3. Project cost estimates

Subpractices

1. Collect models or historical data to be used to transform the attributes of work products and tasks into estimates of labor hours and costs.

   Effort estimation at the work product and task level needs to be established for acquirer work. Effort estimation for supplier deliverables and processes should be established as well.

   Many parametric models have been developed to help estimate cost and schedule. The use of these models as the sole source of estimation is not recommended because these models are based on historical project data that may or may not be pertinent to the project. Multiple models and methods can be used to ensure a high level of confidence in the estimate.

   Historical data should include the cost, effort, and schedule data from previously executed projects and appropriate scaling data to account for differing sizes and complexity.

> **HINT**
>
> If you are using only one parametric model, make sure it is calibrated to your project's characteristics.

2. Include supporting infrastructure needs when estimating effort and cost.

   The supporting infrastructure includes resources needed from a development and sustainment perspective for the product.

   Consider the infrastructure resource needs in the development environment, the test environment, the production environment, the operational environment, or any appropriate combination of these environments when estimating effort and cost.

> **TIP**
>
> Scaling can be reliable when applied from experiences similar to the one at hand. However, increased complexity usually adds more interactions with other acquisition projects or legacy capabilities, which in turn requires additional coordination effort.

PP

Examples of supporting infrastructure typically provided by the supplier include the following:

- Critical computing resources in the host and testing environment (e.g., memory, disk, network capability)
- Test equipment

---

3. Estimate effort and cost using models, historical data, or a combination of both.

Examples of effort and cost inputs used for estimating typically include the following:

- Facilities needed (e.g., office and meeting space and workstations)
- Estimates for the development of requirements
- Costs of acquired work products
- Travel
- Estimates provided by an expert or group of experts (e.g., Delphi Method)
- Risks, including the extent to which the effort is unprecedented
- Critical competencies and roles needed to perform the work
- WBS
- Selected project lifecycle model and processes
- Lifecycle cost estimates
- Skill levels of managers and staff needed to perform the work
- Knowledge, skill, and training needs
- Direct labor and overhead
- Service agreements for call centers and warranty work
- Level of security required for tasks, work products, hardware, software, staff, and work environment

---

The amount of supplier work for a project largely determines the amount of acquirer work required to manage the project and the supplier. Effort for the acquirer includes (1) effort associated with defining the scope of the project; (2) effort associated with the development of the solicitation and supplier agreement; agreement and technical management; project planning, monitoring, and control; acquisition requirements development, verification, and validation; configuration management; measurement and analysis; process and product quality assurance; requirements management; and risk management; (3) operating and maintenance effort associated with the sustainment of the solution; and (4) disposal effort.

SG 2 DEVELOP A PROJECT PLAN

A project plan is established and maintained as the basis for managing the project.

A project plan is a formal, approved document used to manage and control the execution of the project. It is based on project requirements and established estimates.

The project plan should consider all phases of the project lifecycle. Project planning should ensure that all plans affecting the project are consistent with the overall project plan.

SP 2.1 ESTABLISH THE BUDGET AND SCHEDULE

Establish and maintain the project's budget and schedule.

The project's budget and schedule are based on developed estimates and ensure that budget allocation, task complexity, and task dependencies are appropriately addressed.

The project's budget and schedule (including the lifecycle related activities of the acquirer), the supplier's efforts, and efforts of supporting organizations and other stakeholders (including any supplier that supports the acquirer) are established, tracked, and maintained for the duration of the project. In addition to creating a schedule for project work products, the acquirer should have the schedule reviewed by individuals external to the project to ensure that the project schedule can be validated.

Event driven, resource-limited schedules have proven to be effective in dealing with project risk. Identifying accomplishments to be demonstrated before initiation of an event provides some flexibility in the timing of the event, a common understanding of what is expected, a better vision of the state of the project, and a more accurate status of the project's tasks.

Example Work Products

1. Project schedules
2. Schedule dependencies
3. Project budget

Subpractices

1. Identify major milestones.
   Milestones are pre-planned events or points in time at which a thorough review of status is conducted to understand how well stakeholder requirements are being met. (If the project includes a

Sometimes, each project phase may have a more detailed and focused plan of its own, in addition to the overall project plan. Also, a detailed plan typically is provided for each increment or iteration when using an evolutionary acquisition approach and will focus on particular requirements issues, design issues, or other risks.

TIP

Plans that may affect the project plan include configuration management plans, plans for interfacing acquisition projects, the system's support plan, the organization's process improvement plan, and the organization's training plan.

HINT

If the budget is dictated by others and doesn't cover your estimated resource needs, replan to ensure that the project will be within budget. Likewise, if the schedule is dictated by others and isn't consistent with your plan, replan to ensure that the project will be able to deliver the product on time (perhaps with fewer features).

TIP

In an event-driven schedule, tasks can be initiated only after certain criteria are met.

X-REF

Defining event-based milestones and monitoring their completion (PMC SP 1.1 subpractice 1) provides visibility into the project's progress.

developmental milestone, then the review is conducted to ensure that the assumptions and requirements associated with that milestone are being met.) Milestones can be associated with the overall project or a particular service type or instance. Milestones can thus be event based or calendar based. If calendar based, once agreed, milestone dates are often difficult to change.

2. Identify schedule assumptions.

When schedules are initially developed, it is common to make assumptions about the duration of certain activities. These assumptions are frequently made on items for which little if any estimation data are available. Identifying these assumptions provides insight into the level of confidence (i.e., uncertainties) in the overall schedule.

3. Identify constraints.

Factors that limit the flexibility of management options should be identified as early as possible. The examination of the attributes of work products and tasks often bring these issues to the surface. Such attributes can include task duration, resources, inputs, and outputs.

Since key characteristics of pre-qualified or other potential suppliers are elements of project success, the acquirer considers these characteristics (e.g., technical and financial capability, management and delivery processes, production capacity, business type and size) in identifying constraints for the project.

4. Identify task dependencies.

Frequently, the tasks for a project or service can be accomplished in some ordered sequence that minimizes the duration. This sequencing involves the identification of predecessor and successor tasks to determine optimal ordering.

Examples of tools and inputs that can help determine optimal ordering of task activities include the following:
- Critical chain method
- Critical Path Method (CPM)
- Program Evaluation and Review Technique (PERT)
- Resource limited scheduling
- Customer priorities
- End-user value

5. Establish and maintain the budget and schedule.

An example of a system used for documenting the costs and schedule of a project is an EVMS [EIA 2002].

Establishing and maintaining the project's budget and schedule typically includes the following:

- Determining the approach to incorporating supplier schedules at an appropriate level of detail
- Defining the committed or expected availability of resources and facilities
- Determining the time phasing of activities
- Determining a breakout of subordinate schedules
- Defining dependencies among activities (predecessor or successor relationships)
- Defining schedule activities and milestones to support project monitoring and control
- Identifying milestones, releases, or increments for the delivery of products to the customer
- Defining activities of appropriate duration
- Defining milestones of appropriate time separation
- Defining a management reserve based on the confidence level in meeting the schedule and budget
- Using appropriate historical data to verify the schedule
- Defining incremental funding requirements
- Documenting project assumptions and rationale

6. Establish corrective action criteria.

Criteria are established for determining what constitutes a significant deviation from the project plan. A basis for gauging issues and problems is necessary to determine when corrective action should be taken. Corrective actions can lead to replanning, which may include revising the original plan, establishing new agreements, or including mitigation activities in the current plan. The project plan defines when (e.g., under what circumstances, with what frequency) the criteria will be applied and by whom.

SP 2.2 *IDENTIFY PROJECT RISKS*

Identify and analyze project risks.

Refer to the Monitor Project Risks specific practice in the Project Monitoring and Control process area for more information about risk monitoring activities.

Refer to the Risk Management process area for more information about identifying potential problems before they occur so that risk handling activities can be planned and invoked as needed across the life of the product or project to mitigate adverse impacts on achieving objectives.

HINT

Establish corrective action criteria early in the project to ensure that issues are addressed appropriately and consistently.

TIP

Risk management is a key to project success.

HINT

Once suppliers are selected, the acquisition project should define how risks will be continuously identified, managed, and escalated by all stakeholders. Don't rely on the supplier to do all the work; many risks fall under the purview of the acquirer and must be identified, analyzed, and mitigated by the acquisition project team.

PP

Risks are identified or discovered and analyzed to support project planning. This specific practice should be extended to all plans that affect the project to ensure that appropriate interfacing is taking place among all relevant stakeholders on identified risks.

Project planning risk identification and analysis typically include the following:

- Identifying risks
- Analyzing risks to determine the impact, probability of occurrence, and time frame in which problems are likely to occur
- Prioritizing risks

Risks are identified from multiple perspectives (e.g., acquisition, technical, management, operational, supplier agreement, industry, support, end user) to ensure all project risks are considered comprehensively in planning activities. Applicable regulatory and statutory requirements with respect to safety and security should be considered while identifying risks.

The acquisition strategy and the risks identified in other project planning activities form the basis for some of the criteria used in evaluation practices in the Solicitation and Supplier Agreement Development process area. As the project evolves, risks can be revised based on changed conditions.

Example Work Products

1. Identified risks
2. Risk impacts and probability of occurrence
3. Risk priorities

Subpractices

1. Identify risks.

   The identification of risks involves the identification of potential issues, hazards, threats, vulnerabilities, and so on that could negatively affect work efforts and plans. Risks should be identified and described understandably before they can be analyzed and managed properly. When identifying risks, it is a good idea to use a standard method for defining risks. Risk identification and analysis tools can be used to help identify possible problems.

Examples of risk identification and analysis tools include the following:

- Risk taxonomies
- Risk assessments

Continues

Continued

- Checklists
- Structured interviews
- Brainstorming
- Process, project, and product performance models
- Cost models
- Network analysis
- Quality factor analysis

Numerous risks are associated with acquiring products through suppliers (e.g., the stability of the supplier, the ability to maintain sufficient insight into the progress of their work, the supplier's capability to meet product requirements, the skills and availability of supplier resources to meet commitments).

The process, product, and service level measures and associated thresholds should be analyzed to identify instances where thresholds are at risk of not being met. These project measures are key indicators of project risk.

2. Document risks.
3. Review and obtain agreement with relevant stakeholders on the completeness and correctness of documented risks.
4. Revise risks as appropriate.

Examples of when identified risks may need to be revised include the following:

- When new risks are identified
- When risks become problems
- When risks are retired
- When project circumstances change significantly

TIP

Risk identification and analysis tools help to identify risks more completely and rapidly, enable the team to analyze them more consistently, and allow lessons learned on previous projects to be applied to new projects.

TIP

Managing risk can be considered a "team sport." It may be prudent to manage some risks in tandem with suppliers, gain insight into suppliers' handling of their unique risks, and manage specific acquisition risks independently.

TIP

This specific practice helps to answer questions such as which data the project should collect, distribute, deliver, and archive; how and when it should handle these tasks; who should be able to access the data; and how data will be stored to address the need for privacy and security, yet give access to those who need it.

SP 2.3 PLAN DATA MANAGEMENT

Plan for the management of project data.

Data are forms of documentation required to support a project in all of its areas (e.g., administration, engineering, configuration management, finance, logistics, quality, safety, manufacturing, procurement). The data can take any form (e.g., reports, manuals, notebooks, charts, drawings, specifications, files, correspondence). The data can exist in any medium (e.g., printed or drawn on various materials, photographs, electronic, multimedia).

PP

Data can be deliverable (e.g., items identified by a project's contract data requirements) or data can be nondeliverable (e.g., informal data, trade studies, analyses, internal meeting minutes, internal design review documentation, lessons learned, action items). Distribution can take many forms, including electronic transmission.

Data requirements for the project should be established for both data items to be created and their content and form, based on a common or standard set of data requirements. Uniform content and format requirements for data items facilitate understanding of data content and help with consistent management of data resources.

The reason for collecting each document should be clear. This task includes the analysis and verification of project deliverables and nondeliverables, data requirements, and customer supplied data. Often, data are collected with no clear understanding of how they will be used. Data are costly and should be collected only when needed.

Project data include both acquirer and supplier created data. The acquirer identifies the minimal data required to cost-effectively operate, maintain, and improve the acquired product and to foster source-of-support competition throughout the product's lifecycle in the acquirer's intended environment. Data should be available in a format that is compatible with the intended end user's environment and a quality assurance program should be implemented to guarantee the accuracy and completeness of data.

The acquirer considers how data will be shared between acquirer and supplier as well as across relevant stakeholders. In many cases, leaving acquirer data in the physical possession of the supplier and having access to supplier data is the preferred solution. In addition to data access, the requirement for acquirer use, reproduction, manipulation, alteration, or transfer of possession of data should be part of the data management plan. The supplier agreement specifies appropriate acquirer rights to the data acquired, in addition to requirements for delivery or access.

Data, when delivered to the acquirer, are formatted according to accepted data standards to ensure their usability by the acquirer. Planning for managing data, including during transition to operations and support, is addressed as part of project planning to avoid unexpected costs to procure, reformat, and deliver data. Plans for managing data in project teams and the infrastructure required to manage data between the supplier, operational users, and other relevant stakeholders are included.

Project data and plans requiring version control or more stringent levels of configuration control are determined and mechanisms established to ensure project data are controlled. The implications of controlling access to classified and sensitive data (e.g., proprietary, export controlled, source selection sensitive) and other access controlled data also should be considered.

Example Work Products

1. Data management plan
2. Master list of managed data
3. Data content and format description
4. Lists of data requirements for acquirers and suppliers
5. Privacy requirements
6. Security requirements
7. Security procedures
8. Mechanisms for data retrieval, reproduction, and distribution
9. Schedule for the collection of project data
10. List of project data to be collected

TIP

The data management plan defines the data necessary for the project, including who owns the data, where the data are stored, and how the data are used. It may even specify what happens to the data after the project terminates.

Subpractices

1. Establish requirements and procedures to ensure privacy and the security of data.

   Not everyone will have the need or clearance necessary to access project data. Procedures should be established to identify who has access to which data as well as when they have access to which data. Security and access control are critical when the acquirer provides data access to the supplier. Security and access control includes access lists of authorized supplier staff and non-disclosure agreements between the acquirer and supplier.

TIP

Data privacy and security issues should be considered, but may not be applicable concerns for certain types of projects.

> For example, when the supplier performs work for the acquirer off-site (e.g., off-shore development center), the acquirer should consider additional security measures such as a firewall between acquirer and supplier networks and restricted access to the acquirer's work place.

2. Establish a mechanism to archive data and to access archived data.

   Accessed information should be in an understandable form (e.g., electronic or computer output from a database) or represented as originally generated.

   The data management plan is ideally supported by an integrated data system that meets the needs of both initial acquisition and support communities. Integrating acquisition and sustainment data

PP

systems into a total lifecycle integrated data environment provides the capability needed to plan effectively for sustainment and to facilitate technology insertion for affordability improvements during re-procurement and post-production support, while ensuring that acquisition planners have accurate information about total lifecycle costs.

3. Determine the project data to be identified, collected, and distributed.

4. Determine the requirements for providing access to and distribution of data to relevant stakeholders.

    A review of other elements of the project plan can help to determine who requires access to or receipt of project data as well as which data are involved.

5. Decide which project data and plans require version control or other levels of configuration control and establish mechanisms to ensure project data are controlled.

SP 2.4 PLAN THE PROJECT'S RESOURCES

Plan for resources to perform the project.

Defining project resources (e.g., labor, equipment, materials, methods) and quantities needed to perform project activities builds on initial estimates and provides additional information that can be applied to expand the WBS used to manage the project.

The top-level WBS developed earlier as an estimation mechanism is typically expanded by decomposing these top levels into work packages that represent single work units that can be separately assigned, performed, and tracked. This subdivision is done to distribute management responsibility and provide better management control.

Each work package in the WBS should be assigned a unique identifier (e.g., number) to permit tracking. A WBS can be based on requirements, activities, work products, services, or a combination of these items. A dictionary that describes the work for each work package in the WBS should accompany the work breakdown structure.

The resource plan should include planning for staff with appropriate training and experience to evaluate supplier proposals and participate in negotiations with suppliers. The resource plan identifies the project resources expected from the supplier, including critical facilities or equipment needed to support the work. The resource plan can be revised based on the supplier agreement or changes in conditions during project execution.

X-REF

Measurement data represent a subset of project data. See MA SPs 1.3 and 2.3 for more information on collecting, storing, and controlling access to measurement data.

TIP

This practice addresses *all* resources, not just personnel.

TIP

The WBS established in SP 1.2 is expanded to help identify roles as well as staffing, process, facility, and tool requirements; to assign work; to obtain commitment to perform the work; and to track the work to completion. Automated tools can help you with these activities.

Example Work Products

1. Work packages
2. WBS task dictionary
3. Staffing requirements based on project size and scope
4. Critical facilities and equipment list
5. Process and workflow definitions and diagrams
6. Project administration requirements list
7. Status reports

Subpractices

1. Determine process requirements.

   The processes used to manage a project are identified, defined, and coordinated with all relevant stakeholders to ensure efficient operations during project execution.

   The acquirer determines how its processes interact with supplier processes to enable seamless execution of the project and successful acquirer-supplier relationships. Considerations include the use of a common process across multiple suppliers and the acquirer or the use of unique but compatible processes. At least, processes should be compatible across interfaces.

2. Determine communication requirements.

   These requirements address the kinds of mechanisms to be used for communicating with customers, end users, project staff, and other relevant stakeholders.

> **X-REF**
>
> At maturity level 3, the organization is typically the main source of process requirements, standard processes, and process assets that aid in their use (see OPF SP 2.3 and OPD).

3. Determine staffing requirements.

   The staffing of a project depends on the decomposition of project requirements into tasks, roles, and responsibilities for accomplishing project requirements as laid out in the work packages of the WBS.

   Staffing requirements should consider the knowledge and skills required for each identified position as defined in the Plan Needed Knowledge and Skills specific practice.

   The acquirer determines its staffing requirements, including staffing for solicitation and supplier agreement management activities and staffing expected by the supplier to complete its portion of the work as defined in the WBS.

4. Determine facility, equipment, and component requirements.

   Most projects are unique in some way and require a set of unique assets to accomplish project objectives. The determination and acquisition of these assets in a timely manner are crucial to project success.

   It is best to identify lead-time items early to determine how they will be addressed. Even when required assets are not unique, compiling a list of all facilities, equipment, and parts (e.g., number of computers for the

PP

staff working on the project, software applications, office space) provides insight into aspects of the scope of an effort that are often overlooked. The acquirer considers what it may need to provide for acceptance of supplier deliverables and for transition and support of the acquired product.

The acquirer should also identify and ensure that facilities or equipment to be provided to the supplier for project work are accounted for in the project plan.

5. Determine other continuing resource requirements.

   Beyond determining processes, reporting templates, staffing, facilities, and equipment, there may be a continuing need for other types of resources to effectively carry out project activities, including the following:

   *   Access to intellectual property
   *   Access to transportation (for people and equipment)
   *   Consumables (e.g., electricity, office supplies)

   The requirements for such resources are derived from the requirements found in (existing and future) agreements (e.g., customer agreements, service agreements, supplier agreements), the project's strategic approach, and the need to manage and maintain the project's operations for a period of time.

SP 2.5 PLAN NEEDED KNOWLEDGE AND SKILLS

Plan for knowledge and skills needed to perform the project.

Refer to the Organizational Training process area for more information about developing skills and knowledge of people so they can perform their roles effectively and efficiently.

Knowledge delivery to projects involves training project staff and acquiring knowledge from outside sources.

Staffing requirements are dependent on the knowledge and skills available to support the execution of the project.

The acquirer plans for knowledge and skills required by the project team to perform their tasks. Knowledge and skill requirements can be derived from project risk.

> For example, if the acquirer is purchasing a software-intensive product, it ensures that acquisition staff assigned to the project have expertise in systems and software engineering or provides training for the project team in these areas.

Orientation and training in acquirer processes and the domain knowledge required to execute the project are also required. The acquirer also plans for knowledge and skills needed from the supplier.

TIP

This practice addresses the training that is specific to the project.

TIP

At maturity level 2, the organization may not be capable of providing much training for its projects. Each project might address all of its knowledge and skill needs. At maturity level 3, the organization takes responsibility for addressing common training needs (e.g., training in the organization's set of standard processes).

> For example, the acquirer can provide role descriptions and skill profiles to the supplier as part of the solicitation package.

Planning for needed knowledge and skills includes ensuring that appropriate training is planned for staff involved in receiving, storing, using, and supporting the transitioned product. Also included is ensuring that costs and funding sources to pay for training are available and lead times to obtain the funding are identified.

Example Work Products

1. Inventory of skill needs
2. Staffing and new hire plans
3. Databases (e.g., skills, training)
4. Training plans

Subpractices

1. Identify the knowledge and skills needed to perform the project.
2. Assess the knowledge and skills available.
3. Select mechanisms for providing needed knowledge and skills.

> Example mechanisms include the following:
> - In-house training (both organizational and project)
> - External training
> - Staffing and new hires
> - External skill acquisition

> The choice of in-house training or outsourced training for needed knowledge and skills is determined by the availability of training expertise, the project's schedule, and business objectives.

4. Incorporate selected mechanisms into the project plan.

SP 2.6 PLAN STAKEHOLDER INVOLVEMENT

Plan the involvement of identified stakeholders.

Stakeholders are identified from all phases of the project lifecycle by identifying the people and functions that should be represented in the project and describing their relevance and the degree of interaction for project activities. A two-dimensional matrix with stakeholders along one axis and project activities along the other axis is a convenient format for accomplishing this identification. Relevance of the stakeholder to the activity in a particular project phase and the

TIP

Either the project or the organization can maintain these example work products.

HINT

Consider all knowledge and skills required for the project, not just the technical aspects.

TIP

If a skill is needed for the current project, but is not expected to be needed for future projects, external skills acquisition may be the best choice. In contrast, if the skill needed for the project is expected to continue, training existing employees or hiring a new employee should be explored.

X-REF

Identifying and involving relevant stakeholders is also addressed in PMC SP 1.5, IPM, and GP 2.7.

PP

amount of interaction expected would be shown at the intersection of the project phase activity axis and the stakeholder axis.

Stakeholders can include operational users and project participants as well as potential suppliers. When acquiring products that must interoperate with other products, the acquirer plans the involvement of relevant stakeholders from other projects or communities to ensure the delivered product can perform as required in its intended environment. Such planning often includes steps for establishing and maintaining supplier agreements with these stakeholders (e.g., interagency and intercompany agreements, memoranda of understanding, memoranda of agreement).

For inputs of stakeholders to be useful, careful selection of relevant stakeholders is necessary. For each major activity, identify stakeholders who are affected by the activity and those who have expertise that is needed to conduct the activity. This list of relevant stakeholders will probably change as the project moves through phases of the project lifecycle. It is important, however, to ensure that relevant stakeholders in the latter phases of the lifecycle have early input to requirements and design decisions that affect them.

Sometimes the supplier will be using an Agile method. The phrase "Agile method" is shorthand for any development or management method that adheres to the *Manifesto for Agile Development* [Beck 2001]. More guidance on the use of Agile methods can be found in CMMI-DEV Section 5.0 Interpreting CMMI When Using Agile Approaches and in the SEI technical notes *CMMI or Agile: Why Not Embrace Both!* [Glazer 2008] and *Considerations for Using Agile in DoD Acquisition* [Lapham 2010].

When the supplier is using an Agile method, the risk is shared with the acquirer and end users for the product being developed. To be effective, the end user or their proxy, acquirer, and supplier will need to operate as a team that crosses organizational and contractual boundaries. The results of the acquirer's stakeholder involvement planning can be incorporated in a team charter that defines roles and responsibilities for the three parties. For example, the team charter can specify who has responsibility for making changes to project scope and requirements and how such changes will be made and managed.

HINT

For each project phase, identify all stakeholders important to the success of that phase and their roles (e.g., implementer, reviewer, consultant). Arrange this information into a matrix to aid in communication, obtain the stakeholders' commitment (SP 3.3), and monitor status (PMC SP 1.5).

TIP

Not all stakeholders identified will be relevant stakeholders. Only a limited number of stakeholders are selected for interaction with the project as work progresses.

Examples of the type of material that should be included in a plan for stakeholder interaction include the following:

- Roles and responsibilities of relevant stakeholders with respect to the project, by project lifecycle phase
- Relative importance of the stakeholder to the success of the project by project lifecycle phase

Continues

Continued

- List of all relevant stakeholders
- Rationale for stakeholder involvement
- Relationships among stakeholders
- Resources (e.g., training, materials, time, funding) needed to ensure stakeholder interaction
- Schedule for the phasing of stakeholder interaction

Implementing this specific practice relies on shared or exchanged information with the previous Plan Needed Knowledge and Skills specific practice.

Example Work Products

1. Stakeholder involvement plan

SP 2.7 PLAN TRANSITION TO OPERATIONS AND SUPPORT

Plan transition to operations and support.

Planning for transition should be considered part of initial planning for the project.

Transition and support plans include the approach for introducing and maintaining readiness, sustainment, and the operational capability of the products delivered by the supplier. Plans for transition to operations and support include assignment of responsibility for transition to operations and support of the product, as well as all activities needed to manage the transition and to support the product in its intended environment (e.g., definition of transition readiness criteria agreed to by relevant stakeholders). These plans can include reasonable accommodations for potential risks and for the evolution of acquired products and their eventual removal from operational use.

> **TIP**
>
> A successful transition involves planning for the appropriate facilities, training, use, maintenance, and support.

> **TIP**
>
> Acquirers should not overlook a supplier's responsibilities for ongoing maintenance and support. Long-term support needs should be considered when establishing the supplier agreement.

Transition to operations and support plans typically include the following:
- Processes and procedures for the transition to operations and support
- Evaluation methods and acceptance criteria for ensuring the transition of the product to operations and support
- Readiness criteria for the product
- Readiness criteria for the operations organization
- Readiness criteria for the product support organization
- Expectations for supplier execution of the transition
- Warranty expectations for the acquired product

Continues

PP

> *Continued*
>
> • Identification of the maintenance organization
> • Transition of intellectual property or other acquirer assets to the acquirer's designated repository
> • Resolution steps if any problems are encountered

If support is to be provided by an organization different from the supplier, a sufficient overlap period should be included in the plan.

> Typically, the acquirer develops initial transition and support plans and then reviews and approves more detailed transition and support plans.

Refer to the Agreement Management process area for more information about accepting the acquired product.

Refer to the Acquisition Technical Management process area for more information about evaluating technical solutions.

Example Work Products

1. Transition to operations and support plans

Subpractices

1. Determine the transition scope and objectives.
2. Determine transition requirements and criteria.
3. Determine transition responsibilities and resources to include post-transition support enhancements and lifecycle considerations.
4. Determine configuration management needs of the transition.
5. Determine training needs for operations and support.

SP 2.8 ESTABLISH THE PROJECT PLAN

Establish and maintain the overall project plan.

A documented plan that addresses all relevant planning items is necessary to achieve the mutual understanding and commitment of individuals, groups, and organizations that execute or support the plans.

The plan generated for the project defines all aspects of the effort, tying together the following in a logical manner:

• Project lifecycle considerations
• Project tasks

TIP

How related plans are documented is up to the project. Sometimes it makes sense to include all plans in one document; sometimes it doesn't. Whichever documentation approach is used, all the plans must be consistent and be consistently updated.

TIP

A well-written plan includes estimates of the resources needed to complete the project successfully. When the estimates exceed the resources available, the situation must be reconciled so that all relevant stakeholders can commit to a feasible plan (SP 3.3).

- Budgets and schedules
- Milestones
- Data management
- Risk identification
- Resource and skill requirements
- Stakeholder identification and interaction
- Infrastructure considerations

Infrastructure considerations include responsibility and authority relationships for project staff, management, and support organizations.

The project plan can include multiple plans such as staffing plans, stakeholder involvement plans, measurement and analysis plans, monitoring and control plans, solicitation plans, agreement management plans, risk mitigation plans, transition plans, quality assurance plans, and configuration management plans. Regardless of form, the plan or plans should address the acquisition strategy as well as the cradle-to-grave considerations for the project and product to be acquired.

> Examples of plans that have been used in the U.S. Department of Defense community include the following:
>
> - Integrated Master Plan—an event driven plan that documents significant accomplishments with pass/fail criteria for both business and technical elements of the project and that ties each accomplishment to a key project event.
> - Integrated Master Schedule—an integrated and networked multi-layered schedule of project tasks required to complete the work effort documented in a related Integrated Master Plan.
> - Systems Engineering Management Plan—a plan that details the integrated technical effort across the project.
> - Systems Engineering Master Schedule—an event based schedule that contains a compilation of key technical accomplishments, each with measurable criteria, requiring successful completion to pass identified events.
> - Systems Engineering Detailed Schedule—a detailed, time dependent, task oriented schedule that associates dates and milestones with the Systems Engineering Master Schedule.

TIP

The plan document should be updated to reflect the project's status as requirements and the project environment change.

TIP

A documented plan communicates resources needed, expectations, and commitments; contains a game plan for relevant stakeholders, including the project team (SP 3.3); documents the commitment to management and other providers of resources; and serves as the basis for managing the project.

HINT

Most project plans change over time as requirements become better understood, so plan how and when you will update the plan.

Example Work Products

1. Overall project plan

SG 3 OBTAIN COMMITMENT TO THE PLAN

Commitments to the project plan are established and maintained.

To be effective, plans require commitment by those who are responsible for implementing and supporting the plan.

Refer to the Solicitation and Supplier Agreement Development process area for more information about establishing the supplier agreement.

SP 3.1 REVIEW PLANS THAT AFFECT THE PROJECT

Review all plans that affect the project to understand project commitments.

TIP

Before making a commitment, a project member analyzes what it will take to meet the commitment. Project members who make commitments should continually evaluate their ability to meet their commitments, communicate immediately to those affected when they cannot meet their commitments, and mitigate the impacts of their inability to meet their commitments.

X-REF

Commitments are a recurring theme in CMMI. Requirements are committed to in REQM. Commitments are documented and reconciled in PP, monitored in PMC, and addressed more thoroughly in IPM.

HINT

Beware of commitments that are not given freely. A favorite quote that applies is "How bad do you want it? That is how bad you will get it!" If you do not allow commitments to be made freely, staff members most likely will try to provide the commitment you want to hear instead of giving a well-thought-out, accurate answer to your request.

Plans developed in other process areas typically contain information similar to that called for in the overall project plan. These plans can provide additional detailed guidance and should be compatible with and support the overall project plan to indicate who has the authority, responsibility, accountability, and control. All plans that affect the project should be reviewed to ensure they contain a common understanding of the scope, objectives, roles, and relationships that are required for the project to be successful. Many of these plans are described by the Plan the Process generic practice.

The project can have a hierarchy of plans (e.g., risk mitigation plans, transition plans, quality assurance plans, configuration management plans). In addition, stakeholder plans (e.g., operational, test, support, supplier plans) should be reviewed to ensure consistency among all project participants. Acquirer review of plans should include reviewing cross-supplier dependencies.

Example Work Products

1. Record of the reviews of plans that affect the project

SP 3.2 RECONCILE WORK AND RESOURCE LEVELS

Adjust the project plan to reconcile available and estimated resources.

To establish a project that is feasible, obtain commitment from relevant stakeholders and reconcile differences between estimates and available resources. Reconciliation is typically accomplished by modifying or deferring requirements, negotiating more resources, finding ways to increase productivity, outsourcing, adjusting the staff skill mix, or revising all plans that affect the project or its schedules.

During supplier selection and negotiation of the supplier agreement, the acquirer reconciles overall project work and resource levels based on proposals from the supplier. Following completion of the supplier agreement, the acquirer incorporates supplier plans at an appropriate level of detail into the project plan to support the alignment of plans. For example, an acquirer can incorporate major supplier milestones, deliverables, and reviews.

Example Work Products

1. Revised methods and corresponding estimating parameters (e.g., better tools, the use of off-the-shelf components)
2. Renegotiated budgets
3. Revised schedules
4. Revised requirements list
5. Renegotiated stakeholder agreements

SP 3.3 OBTAIN PLAN COMMITMENT

Obtain commitment from relevant stakeholders responsible for performing and supporting plan execution.

Obtaining commitment involves interaction among all relevant stakeholders, both internal and external to the project. The individual or group making a commitment should have confidence that the work can be performed within cost, schedule, and performance constraints. Often, a provisional commitment is adequate to allow the effort to begin and to permit research to be performed to increase confidence to the appropriate level needed to obtain a full commitment.

Example Work Products

1. Documented requests for commitments
2. Documented commitments

Subpractices

1. Identify needed support and negotiate commitments with relevant stakeholders.

   The WBS can be used as a checklist for ensuring that commitments are obtained for all tasks.

   The plan for stakeholder interaction should identify all parties from whom commitment should be obtained.

2. Document all organizational commitments, both full and provisional, ensuring the appropriate level of signatories.

   Commitments should be documented to ensure a consistent mutual understanding and for project tracking and maintenance. Provisional commitments should be accompanied by a description of risks associated with the relationship.

PP

TIP

A commitment not documented is a commitment not made. When it comes to commitments, memory is imperfect and, therefore, unreliable.

TIP

Senior management must be informed of external commitments (especially those with customers, end users, and suppliers), as they can expose the organization to unnecessary risk.

X-REF

For more information on managing commitments, dependencies, and coordination issues among relevant stakeholders, see IPM SG 2. For more information on identifying and managing interfaces, see ATM SG 2.

3. Review internal commitments with senior management as appropriate.

4. Review external commitments with senior management as appropriate.
   Management can have the necessary insight and authority to reduce risks associated with external commitments.

5. Identify commitments regarding interfaces between project elements and other projects and organizational units so that these commitments can be monitored.
   Well-defined interface specifications form the basis for commitments.

PROCESS AND PRODUCT QUALITY ASSURANCE
A Support Process Area at Maturity Level 2

Purpose

The purpose of Process and Product Quality Assurance (PPQA) is to provide staff and management with objective insight into processes and associated work products.

Introductory Notes

The Process and Product Quality Assurance process area involves the following activities:

- Objectively evaluating performed processes and work products against applicable process descriptions, standards, and procedures
- Identifying and documenting noncompliance issues
- Providing feedback to project staff and managers on the results of quality assurance activities
- Ensuring that noncompliance issues are addressed

The Process and Product Quality Assurance process area supports the delivery of high-quality products by providing project staff and managers at all levels with appropriate visibility into, and feedback on, processes and associated work products throughout the life of the project.

The practices in the Process and Product Quality Assurance process area ensure that planned processes are implemented, while the practices in the Acquisition Verification process area ensure that specified requirements are satisfied. These two process areas can on occasion address the same work product but from different perspectives. Projects should take advantage of the overlap to minimize duplication of effort while taking care to maintain separate perspectives.

Objectivity in process and product quality assurance evaluations is critical to the success of the project. (See the definition of "objectively evaluate" in the glossary.) Objectivity is achieved by both independence and the use of criteria. A combination of methods providing evaluations against criteria by those who do not produce the work product is often used. Less formal methods can be used to provide broad day-to-day coverage. More formal methods can be used periodically to assure objectivity.

Examples of ways to perform objective evaluations include the following:
- Formal audits by organizationally separate quality assurance organizations
- Peer reviews, which can be performed at various levels of formality
- In-depth review of work at the place it is performed (i.e., desk audits)
- Distributed review and comment of work products
- Process checks built into the processes such as a fail-safe for processes when they are done incorrectly (e.g., Poka-Yoke)

Traditionally, a quality assurance group that is independent of the project provides objectivity. However, another approach may be appropriate in some organizations to implement the process and product quality assurance role without that kind of independence.

For example, in an organization with an open, quality oriented culture, the process and product quality assurance role can be performed, partially or completely, by peers and the quality assurance function can be embedded in the process. For small organizations, this embedded approach might be the most feasible approach.

If quality assurance is embedded in the process, several issues should be addressed to ensure objectivity. Everyone performing quality assurance activities should be trained in quality assurance. Those who perform quality assurance activities for a work product should be separate from those who are directly involved in developing or maintaining the work product. An independent reporting channel to the appropriate level of organizational management should be available so that noncompliance issues can be escalated as necessary.

> For example, when implementing peer reviews as an objective evaluation method, the following issues should be addressed:
>
> - Members are trained and roles are assigned for people attending the peer reviews.
> - A member of the peer review who did not produce this work product is assigned to perform the quality assurance role.
> - Checklists based on process descriptions, standards, and procedures are available to support the quality assurance activity.
> - Noncompliance issues are recorded as part of the peer review report and are tracked and escalated outside the project when necessary.

TIP

Acquisition project leadership must create an environment in which team members are encouraged to identify and fix process and product defects.

Quality assurance should begin in the early phases of a project to establish plans, processes, standards, and procedures that will add value to the project and satisfy the requirements of the project and organizational policies. Those who perform quality assurance activities participate in establishing plans, processes, standards, and procedures to ensure that they fit project needs and that they will be usable for performing quality assurance evaluations. In addition, processes and associated work products to be evaluated during the project are designated. This designation can be based on sampling or on objective criteria that are consistent with organizational policies, project requirements, and project needs.

HINT

Establish your quality assurance approach early in the project and continually focus on identifying constraints that may keep you from achieving project objectives.

When noncompliance issues are identified, they are first addressed in the project and resolved there if possible. Noncompliance issues that cannot be resolved in the project are escalated to an appropriate level of management for resolution.

HINT

Use a risk-based approach when designating which processes and work products to evaluate.

This process area applies to evaluations of project activities and work products, and to organizational (e.g., process group, organizational training) activities and work products. For organizational activities and work products, the term "project" should be appropriately interpreted.

TIP

Limit the appraisal scope to those supplier processes that are most critical to the current phase of the project. Use Class B or Class C (nonbenchmarking) methods to help identify and mitigate project risk.

Related Process Areas

Refer to the Acquisition Verification process area for more information about ensuring that selected work products meet their specified requirements.

X-REF

For more information about interpreting your suppliers' CMMI achievements, see "Understanding and Leveraging a Supplier's CMMI Efforts: A Guidebook for Acquirers" at www.sei.cmu.edu/library/abstracts/reports/07tr004.cfm.

Specific Goal and Practice Summary

SG 1 Objectively Evaluate Processes and Work Products
    SP 1.1 Objectively Evaluate Processes
    SP 1.2 Objectively Evaluate Work Products

SG 2 Provide Objective Insight
    SP 2.1 Communicate and Resolve Noncompliance Issues
    SP 2.2 Establish Records

Specific Practices by Goal

SG 1   OBJECTIVELY EVALUATE PROCESSES AND WORK PRODUCTS

Adherence of the performed process and associated work products to applicable process descriptions, standards, and procedures is objectively evaluated.

SP 1.1 OBJECTIVELY EVALUATE PROCESSES

Objectively evaluate selected performed processes against applicable process descriptions, standards, and procedures.

Objectivity in quality assurance evaluations is critical to the success of the project. A description of the quality assurance reporting chain and how it ensures objectivity should be defined.

Example Work Products

1. Evaluation reports
2. Noncompliance reports
3. Corrective actions

Subpractices

1. Promote an environment (created as part of project management) that encourages staff participation in identifying and reporting quality issues.
2. Establish and maintain clearly stated criteria for evaluations.
   The intent of this subpractice is to provide criteria, based on business needs, such as the following:
   - What will be evaluated
   - When or how often a process will be evaluated
   - How the evaluation will be conducted
   - Who must be involved in the evaluation
3. Use the stated criteria to evaluate selected performed processes for adherence to process descriptions, standards, and procedures.
4. Identify each noncompliance found during the evaluation.
5. Identify lessons learned that could improve processes.

SP 1.2 OBJECTIVELY EVALUATE WORK PRODUCTS

Objectively evaluate selected work products against applicable process descriptions, standards, and procedures.

Example Work Products

1. Evaluation reports
2. Noncompliance reports
3. Corrective actions

Subpractices

1. Select work products to be evaluated based on documented sampling criteria if sampling is used.

   Work products can include services produced by a process whether the recipient of the service is internal or external to the project or organization.

2. Establish and maintain clearly stated criteria for the evaluation of selected work products.

   The intent of this subpractice is to provide criteria, based on business needs, such as the following:

   - What will be evaluated during the evaluation of a work product
   - When or how often a work product will be evaluated
   - How the evaluation will be conducted
   - Who must be involved in the evaluation

3. Use the stated criteria during evaluations of selected work products.
4. Evaluate selected work products at selected times.

Examples of when work products can be evaluated against process descriptions, standards, or procedures include the following:

- Before delivery to the customer
- During delivery to the customer
- Incrementally, when it is appropriate

---

5. Identify each case of noncompliance found during evaluations.
6. Identify lessons learned that could improve processes.

SG 2   PROVIDE OBJECTIVE INSIGHT

Noncompliance issues are objectively tracked and communicated, and resolution is ensured.

SP 2.1 COMMUNICATE AND RESOLVE NONCOMPLIANCE ISSUES

Communicate quality issues and ensure the resolution of noncompliance issues with the staff and managers.

Noncompliance issues are problems identified in evaluations that reflect a lack of adherence to applicable standards, process descriptions,

---

HINT

Resist the temptation to put total attention on the suppliers' work products and not give "due diligence" to evaluating your own (acquirer) work products. Both must be of high quality to ensure program success.

HINT

You can embed objective evaluations of work products within some of the verification activities—particularly peer reviews—although doing so requires care. (See the introductory notes for more information.)

TIP

Subpractices 4 through 6 recommend evaluation of work products at different times and from different perspectives. The important point is that you think broadly about which steps will give you the best objective insight during your project.

HINT

Your quality assurance activities can benefit other projects in your organization. For this reason, you should share your results more broadly, outside your project team.

or procedures. The status of noncompliance issues provides an indication of quality trends. Quality issues include noncompliance issues and trend analysis results.

When noncompliance issues cannot be resolved in the project, use established escalation mechanisms to ensure that the appropriate level of management can resolve the issue. Track noncompliance issues to resolution.

Example Work Products

1. Corrective action reports
2. Evaluation reports
3. Quality trends

Subpractices

1. Resolve each noncompliance with the appropriate members of the staff if possible.
2. Document noncompliance issues when they cannot be resolved in the project.

Examples of ways to resolve noncompliance in the project include the following:

- Fixing the noncompliance
- Changing the process descriptions, standards, or procedures that were violated
- Obtaining a waiver to cover the noncompliance

---

3. Escalate noncompliance issues that cannot be resolved in the project to the appropriate level of management designated to receive and act on noncompliance issues.
4. Analyze noncompliance issues to see if there are quality trends that can be identified and addressed.
5. Ensure that relevant stakeholders are aware of results of evaluations and quality trends in a timely manner.
6. Periodically review open noncompliance issues and trends with the manager designated to receive and act on noncompliance issues.
7. Track noncompliance issues to resolution.

SP 2.2 ESTABLISH RECORDS

Establish and maintain records of quality assurance activities.

Example Work Products

1. Evaluation logs
2. Quality assurance reports
3. Status reports of corrective actions
4. Reports of quality trends

Subpractices

1. Record process and product quality assurance activities in sufficient detail so that status and results are known.
2. Revise the status and history of quality assurance activities as necessary.

QUANTITATIVE PROJECT MANAGEMENT
A Project Management Process Area at Maturity Level 4

Purpose

The purpose of Quantitative Project Management (QPM) is to quantitatively manage the project to achieve the project's established quality and process performance objectives.

Introductory Notes

The Quantitative Project Management process area involves the following activities:

- Establishing and maintaining the project's quality and process performance objectives
- Composing a defined process for the project to help to achieve the project's quality and process performance objectives
- Selecting subprocesses and attributes critical to understanding performance and that help to achieve the project's quality and process performance objectives
- Selecting measures and analytic techniques to be used in quantitative management
- Monitoring the performance of selected subprocesses using statistical and other quantitative techniques
- Managing the project using statistical and other quantitative techniques to determine whether or not the project's objectives for quality and process performance are being satisfied
- Performing root cause analysis of selected issues to address deficiencies in achieving the project's quality and process performance objectives

Organizational process assets used to achieve high maturity, including quality and process performance objectives, selected processes, measures, baselines, and models, are established using organizational process

X-REF

QPM and OPP are tightly coupled process areas; each produces work products used by the other. Refer to OPP extensively when considering how to implement QPM.

performance processes and used in quantitative project management processes. The project can use organizational process performance processes to define additional objectives, measures, baselines, and models as needed to effectively analyze and manage performance. The measures, measurements, and other data resulting from quantitative project management processes are incorporated into the organizational process assets. In this way, the organization and its projects derive benefit from assets improved through use.

The project's defined process is a set of interrelated subprocesses that form an integrated and coherent process for the project. The Integrated Project Management practices describe establishing the project's defined process by selecting and tailoring processes from the organization's set of standard processes. (See the definition of "defined process" in the glossary.)

Quantitative Project Management practices, unlike Integrated Project Management practices, help you to develop a quantitative understanding of the expected performance of processes or subprocesses. This understanding is used as a basis for establishing the project's defined process by evaluating alternative processes or subprocesses for the project and selecting the ones that will best achieve the quality and process performance objectives.

HINT

Take advantage of the quantitative insights a high maturity supplier brings to the relationship. But be realistic: Don't expect your lower maturity suppliers to have the same understanding of the value of managing quantitatively.

Establishing effective relationships with suppliers is also important to the successful implementation of this process area. Establishing effective relationships can involve establishing quality and process performance objectives for suppliers, determining the measures and analytic techniques to be used to gain insight into supplier progress and performance, and monitoring progress toward achieving those objectives.

The acquirer uses statistical and other quantitative techniques to both manage its work and to gain insight into supplier work and work products.

An essential element of quantitative management is having confidence in predictions (i.e., the ability to accurately predict the extent to which the project can fulfill its quality and process performance objectives). Subprocesses to be managed through the use of statistical and other quantitative techniques are chosen based on the needs for predictable process performance.

Another essential element of quantitative management is understanding the nature and extent of the variation experienced in process performance and recognizing when the project's actual performance may not be adequate to achieve the project's quality and process performance objectives.

Thus, quantitative management includes statistical thinking and the correct use of a variety of statistical techniques. (See the definition of "quantitative management" in the glossary.)

Statistical and other quantitative techniques are used to develop an understanding of the actual performance or to predict the performance of processes. Such techniques can be applied at multiple levels, from a focus on individual subprocesses to analyses that span lifecycle phases, projects, and support functions. Non-statistical techniques provide a less rigorous but still useful set of approaches that together with statistical techniques help the project to understand whether or not quality and process performance objectives are being satisfied and to identify any needed corrective actions.

This process area applies to managing a project. Applying these concepts to managing other groups and functions can help to link different aspects of performance in the organization to provide a basis for balancing and reconciling competing priorities to address a broader set of business objectives.

Examples of other groups and functions that could benefit from using this process area include the following:

- Quality assurance or quality control functions
- Process definition and improvement
- Internal research and development functions
- Risk identification and management functions
- Technology scouting functions
- Market research
- Customer satisfaction assessment
- Problem tracking and reporting

TIP

Here "statistical thinking" refers to the use of statistical techniques as tools in appropriate ways to assess the variation in the performance of a process, to investigate its causes, and to recognize from the data when the process is not performing as it should. (See the definition of "statistical techniques" in the glossary.)

TIP

A related term is "statistical and other quantitative techniques." (See its definition in the glossary.) High maturity organizations and projects leverage an understanding of which factors matter in an unfolding situation to control its future course. Statistical and other quantitative techniques provide the insight needed to accomplish this feat, thus helping "steer" the project toward achieving its objectives.

Related Process Areas

Refer to the Solicitation and Supplier Agreement Development process area for more information about establishing supplier agreements.

Refer to the Causal Analysis and Resolution process area for more information about identifying causes of selected outcomes and taking action to improve process performance.

Refer to the Integrated Project Management process area for more information about establishing the project's defined process.

Refer to the Measurement and Analysis process area for more information about aligning measurement and analysis activities and providing measurement results.

X-REF

See *How to Measure Anything: Finding the Value of "Intangibles" in Business* by Douglas W. Hubbard (John Wiley & Sons, Inc.).

X-REF

See *Moving Up the CMMI Capability and Maturity Levels Using Simulation* by David M. Raffo and Wayne Wakeland (www.sei.cmu.edu/reports/08tr002.pdf).

X-REF

See *Understanding Variation: The Key to Managing Chaos*, second edition, by Donald J. Wheeler (SPC Press, Inc.).

Refer to the Organizational Process Definition process area for more information about establishing organizational process assets.

Refer to the Organizational Performance Management process area for more information about proactively managing the organization's performance to meet its business objectives.

Refer to the Organizational Process Performance process area for more information about establishing and maintaining a quantitative understanding of the performance of selected processes in the organization's set of standard processes in support of achieving quality and process performance objectives, and providing process performance data, baselines, and models to quantitatively manage the organization's projects.

Refer to the Project Monitoring and Control process area for more information about providing an understanding of the project's progress so that appropriate corrective actions can be taken when the project's performance deviates significantly from the plan.

Specific Goal and Practice Summary

SG 1 Prepare for Quantitative Management
    SP 1.1   Establish the Project's Objectives
    SP 1.2   Compose the Defined Process
    SP 1.3   Select Subprocesses and Attributes
    SP 1.4   Select Measures and Analytic Techniques
SG 2 Quantitatively Manage the Project
    SP 2.1   Monitor the Performance of Selected Subprocesses
    SP 2.2   Manage Project Performance
    SP 2.3   Perform Root Cause Analysis

Specific Practices by Goal

SG 1 PREPARE FOR QUANTITATIVE MANAGEMENT

Preparation for quantitative management is conducted.

Preparation activities include establishing quantitative objectives for the project, composing a defined process for the project that can help to achieve those objectives, selecting subprocesses and attributes critical to understanding performance and achieving the objectives, and selecting measures and analytic techniques that support quantitative management.

These activities may need to be repeated when needs and priorities change, when there is an improved understanding of process performance, or as part of risk mitigation or corrective action.

HINT

You can perform SPs 1.1 through 1.4 concurrently and iteratively.

SP 1.1 ESTABLISH THE PROJECT'S OBJECTIVES

Establish and maintain the project's quality and process performance objectives.

When establishing the project's quality and process performance objectives, think about the processes that will be included in the project's defined process and what the historical data indicate regarding their process performance. These considerations, along with others such as technical capability, will help in establishing realistic objectives for the project.

The project's objectives for quality and process performance are established and negotiated at an appropriate level of detail (e.g., for individual product components, subprocesses, project teams) to permit an overall evaluation of the objectives and risks at the project level. As the project progresses, project objectives can be updated as the project's actual performance becomes known and more predictable, and to reflect changing needs and priorities of relevant stakeholders.

The acquirer establishes the project's quality and process performance objectives based on objectives of the organization, the customer, and other relevant stakeholders. The acquirer can also establish quality and process performance objectives for supplier deliverables. These quantitative quality and process performance objectives for the supplier are documented in the supplier agreement. The acquirer typically expects the supplier to execute its processes and apply its process performance models toward achieving these objectives.

Example Work Products

1. The project's quality and process performance objectives
2. Assessment of the risk of not achieving the project's objectives

Subpractices

1. Review the organization's objectives for quality and process performance.

   This review ensures that project staff understand the broader business context in which the project operates. The project's objectives for quality and process performance are developed in the context of these overarching organizational objectives.

   Refer to the Organizational Process Performance process area for more information about establishing quality and process performance objectives.

TIP

Generally, these objectives are established early during project planning as customer requirements relating to product quality, service quality, and process performance are being established and analyzed.

HINT

Once a supplier or set of suppliers is selected, revisit these objectives. Teaming with suppliers that have quantitatively managed processes may present opportunities to optimize those processes across organizational boundaries.

X-REF

Quality and process performance objectives (QPPOs) should satisfy certain criteria, such as "SMART criteria." In this context, SMART is an acronym standing for "specific, measurable, attainable, relevant, and time bound" (see Wikipedia for more information).

HINT

Supplier QPPOs that are "specified" prior to contract award will need to be revised once the selected supplier's process performance baselines (PPBs) are established.

TIP

The project's QPPOs should be based, in part, on those of the organization. This approach helps to ensure that the project's QPPOs are aligned with those of the organization, while recognizing unique project or customer needs.

2. Identify the quality and process performance needs and priorities of the customer, suppliers, end users, and other relevant stakeholders. Typically, the identification of relevant stakeholders' needs will begin early (e.g., during development of the acquisition strategy). Needs are further elicited, analyzed, refined, prioritized, and balanced during acquisition requirements development.

Examples of quality and process performance attributes for which needs and priorities might be identified include the following:

- Duration
- Predictability
- Reliability
- Maintainability
- Usability
- Timeliness
- Functionality
- Accuracy

---

3. Define and document measurable quality and process performance objectives for the project.

Defining and documenting objectives for the project involve the following:

- Incorporating appropriate organizational quality and process performance objectives
- Writing objectives that reflect the quality and process performance needs and priorities of the customer, end users, and other relevant stakeholders
- Determining how each objective will be achieved
- Reviewing the objectives to ensure they are sufficiently specific, measurable, attainable, relevant, and time-bound

---

Examples of measurable quality attributes include the following:

- Mean time between failures
- Number and severity of customer complaints concerning the provided service
- Critical resource utilization
- Number and severity of defects in the released product

Examples of measurable process performance attributes include the following:
- Cycle time
- Percentage of rework time
- Percentage of defects removed by product verification activities (perhaps by type of verification, such as peer reviews and testing)
- Defect escape rates

4. Derive interim objectives to monitor progress toward achieving the project's objectives.

   Interim objectives can be established for attributes of selected lifecycle phases, milestones, work products, and subprocesses.

   Since process performance models characterize relationships among product and process attributes, these models can be used to help derive interim objectives that guide the project toward achieving its objectives.

5. Determine the risk of not achieving the project's quality and process performance objectives.

   The risk is a function of the established objectives, the product architecture, the project's defined process, availability of needed knowledge and skills, etc. Process performance baselines and models can be used to evaluate the likelihood of achieving a set of objectives and provide guidance in negotiating objectives and commitments. The assessment of risk can involve various project stakeholders and can be conducted as part of the conflict resolution described in the next subpractice.

6. Resolve conflicts among the project's quality and process performance objectives (e.g., if one objective cannot be achieved without compromising another).

   Process performance models can help to identify conflicts and help to ensure that the resolution of conflicts does not introduce new conflicts or risks.

   Resolving conflicts involves the following activities:

   - Setting relative priorities for objectives
   - Considering alternative objectives in light of long-term business strategies as well as short-term needs
   - Involving the customer, end users, senior management, project management, and other relevant stakeholders in tradeoff decisions
   - Revising objectives as necessary to reflect results of conflict resolution

7. Establish traceability to the project's quality and process performance objectives from their sources.

Examples of sources of objectives include the following:

- Requirements
- The organization's quality and process performance objectives
- The customer's quality and process performance objectives
- Business objectives
- Discussions with customers and potential customers
- Market surveys
- Product architecture

An example of a method to identify and trace these needs and priorities is Quality Function Deployment (QFD).

---

8. Define and negotiate quality and process performance objectives for suppliers.

   Refer to the Solicitation and Supplier Agreement Development process area for more information about establishing supplier agreements.

9. Revise the project's quality and process performance objectives as necessary.

SP 1.2 COMPOSE THE DEFINED PROCESS

Using statistical and other quantitative techniques, compose a defined process that enables the project to achieve its quality and process performance objectives.

Refer to the Integrated Project Management process area for more information about establishing the project's defined process.

Refer to the Organizational Process Definition process area for more information about establishing organizational process assets.

Refer to the Organizational Process Performance process area for more information about establishing performance baselines and models.

Composing the project's defined process goes beyond the process selection and tailoring described in the Integrated Project Management process area. It involves identifying alternatives to one or more processes or subprocesses, performing quantitative analysis of performance, and selecting the alternatives that are best able to help the project to achieve its quality and process performance objectives.

These subprocesses can include activities used for interacting with a supplier (e.g., negotiating a supplier agreement, conducting supplier reviews).

TIP

Some organizations may not need alternative subprocesses (e.g., because the projects are sufficiently similar to one another). In such cases, some alternatives remain to be explored (e.g., one can adjust the level or depth of intensity with which a subprocess is applied; see subpractice 2).

TIP

PPBs and process performance models (PPMs) can help the project evaluate alternatives to determine which alternatives best help it achieve its QPPOs.

Example Work Products

1. Criteria used to evaluate alternatives for the project
2. Alternative subprocesses
3. Subprocesses to be included in the project's defined process
4. Assessment of risk of not achieving the project's objectives

Subpractices

1. Establish the criteria to use in evaluating process alternatives for the project.

Criteria can be based on the following:
- Quality and process performance objectives
- Availability of process performance data and the relevance of the data to evaluating an alternative
- Familiarity with an alternative or with alternatives similar in composition
- Existence of process performance models that can be used in evaluating an alternative
- Product line standards
- Standard services and service levels
- Project lifecycle models
- Stakeholder requirements
- Laws and regulations

---

2. Identify alternative processes and subprocesses for the project.

   Identifying alternatives can include one or more of the following:

   - Analyzing organizational process performance baselines to identify candidate subprocesses that would help achieve the project's quality and process performance objectives
   - Identifying subprocesses from the organization's set of standard processes as well as tailored processes in the process asset library that can help to achieve the objectives
   - Identifying processes from external sources (e.g., such as other organizations, professional conferences, academic research)
   - Adjusting the level or depth of intensity with which a subprocess is applied (as described in further detail in a subpractice that follows)

   Adjusting the level or depth of intensity with which the subprocesses are applied can involve the following choices:

   - Number and type of peer reviews to be held and when
   - Amount of effort or calendar time devoted to particular tasks

- Number and selection of people involved
- Skill level requirements for performing specific tasks
- Selective application of specialized construction or verification techniques
- Reuse decisions and associated risk mitigation strategies
- The product and process attributes to be measured
- Sampling rate for management data

Refer to the Integrated Project Management process area for more information about using organizational process assets for planning project activities.

3. Analyze the interaction of alternative subprocesses to understand relationships among the subprocesses, including their attributes.
   An analysis of the interaction will provide insight into the relative strengths and weaknesses of particular alternatives. This analysis can be supported by a calibration of the organization's process performance models with process performance data (e.g., as characterized in process performance baselines).
   Additional modeling may be needed if existing process performance models cannot address significant relationships among the alternative subprocesses under consideration and there is high risk of not achieving objectives.

4. Evaluate alternative subprocesses against the criteria.
   Use historical data, process performance baselines, and process performance models as appropriate to assist in evaluating alternatives against the criteria. These evaluations can include use of a sensitivity analysis particularly in high risk situations.

   Refer to the Decision Analysis and Resolution process area for more information about evaluating alternatives.

5. Select the alternative subprocesses that best meet the criteria.
   It may be necessary to iterate through the activities described in the previous subpractices several times before confidence is achieved that the best available alternatives have been identified.

6. Evaluate the risk of not achieving the project's quality and process performance objectives.
   An analysis of risk associated with the selected alternative defined process can lead to identifying new alternatives to be evaluated, as well as areas requiring more management attention.

   Refer to the Risk Management process area for more information about identifying and analyzing risks.

HINT

When project subprocesses interact with supplier or end-user subprocesses, the dynamics may not always be obvious. Use process simulation in concert with PPMs to uncover hidden behavior and unintended consequences.

X-REF

Systems thinking may be used to evaluate the underlying dynamics of common patterns of failure; see "Acquisition Archetypes: Changing Counterproductive Behaviors in Real Acquisitions" at www.sei.cmu.edu/acquisition/research/archetypes.cfm.

X-REF

For more information about process simulation, see the Raffo and Wakeland report mentioned earlier.

SP 1.3 SELECT SUBPROCESSES AND ATTRIBUTES

Select subprocesses and attributes critical to evaluating performance and that help to achieve the project's quality and process performance objectives.

Some subprocesses are critical because their performance significantly influences or contributes to achieving the project's objectives. These subprocesses may be good candidates for monitoring and control using statistical and other quantitative techniques as described in the first specific practice of the second specific goal.

Also, some attributes of these subprocesses can serve as leading indicators of the process performance to expect of subprocesses that are further downstream and can be used to assess the risk of not achieving the project's objectives (e.g., by using process performance models).

Subprocesses and attributes that play such critical roles may have already been identified as part of the analyses described in the previous specific practice.

For small projects, and other circumstances in which subprocess data may not be generated frequently enough in the project to support a sufficiently sensitive statistical inference, it may still be possible to understand performance by examining process performance across similar iterations, teams, or projects.

Example Work Products

1. Criteria used to select subprocesses that are key contributors to achieving the project's objectives
2. Selected subprocesses
3. Attributes of selected subprocesses that help in predicting future project performance

Subpractices

1. Analyze how subprocesses, their attributes, other factors, and project performance results relate to each other.

   A root cause analysis, sensitivity analysis, or process performance model can help to identify the subprocesses and attributes that most contribute to achieving particular performance results (and variation in performance results) or that are useful indicators of future achievement of performance results.

   Refer to the Causal Analysis and Resolution process area for more information about determining causes of selected outcomes.

2. Identify criteria to be used in selecting subprocesses that are key contributors to achieving the project's quality and process performance objectives.

TIP

The focus of SP 1.2 is on determining which process will best help the organization achieve QPPOs. In SP 1.3, the focus shifts to identifying those critical subprocesses within that process that need to be performed correctly and consistently (that need to be "mastered") so that project performance will not suffer; in addition, the focus is on identifying those attributes that give an early indication (or "signal") that the project has gone "off course."

HINT

Learn which knobs you can turn at different points within a project to desirably affect project performance and achievement of outcomes. Such learning goes on at the organizational level (OPP SPs 1.2 and 1.5) and continues within individual projects.

HINT

Avoid subprocesses that are beyond the acquisition team's ability to control. Subprocesses that are enacted by a supplier or end user are important to track, for example, but difficult to quantitatively manage using statistical process control techniques because the processes fall outside the acquirer's control.

TIP

The project's selection of sub-processes and attributes is based, in part, on those selected by the organization (OPP SP 1.2).

> Examples of criteria used to select subprocesses include the following:
> - There is a strong correlation with performance results that are addressed in the project's objectives.
> - Stable performance of the subprocess is important.
> - Poor subprocess performance is associated with major risks to the project.
> - One or more attributes of the subprocess serve as key inputs to process performance models used in the project.
> - The subprocess will be executed frequently enough to provide sufficient data for analysis.

3. Select subprocesses using the identified criteria.

   Historical data, process performance models, and process performance baselines can help in evaluating candidate subprocesses against selection criteria.

   Refer to the Decision Analysis and Resolution process area for more information about evaluating alternatives.

4. Identify product and process attributes to be monitored.

   These attributes may have been identified as part of performing the previous subpractices.

   Attributes that provide insight into current or future subprocess performance are candidates for monitoring, whether or not the associated subprocesses are under the control of the project. Also, some of these same attributes may serve other roles (e.g., to help in monitoring project progress and performance as described in Project Monitoring and Control [PMC]).

TIP

This practice has a dynamic aspect to it. While many measures and analytic techniques can be identified in advance, and thus the project team(s) may be prepared to apply these elements and interpret their results, specific situations may arise during the project that require more in-depth analysis to diagnose the situation and evaluate potential resolutions (e.g., see SP 2.3). Access to special expertise in analytic techniques may be needed in these circumstances.

> Examples of product and process attributes include the following:
> - Effort consumed to perform the subprocess
> - The rate at which the subprocess is performed
> - Cycle time for process elements that make up the subprocess
> - Resource or materials consumed as input to the subprocess
> - Skill level of the staff member performing the subprocess
> - Quality of the work environment used to perform the subprocess
> - Volume of outputs of the subprocess (e.g., intermediate work products)
> - Quality attributes of outputs of the subprocess (e.g., reliability, testability)

SP 1.4 SELECT MEASURES AND ANALYTIC TECHNIQUES

Select measures and analytic techniques to be used in quantitative management.

Refer to the Measurement and Analysis process area for more information about aligning measurement and analysis activities and providing measurement results.

Example Work Products

1. Definitions of measures and analytic techniques to be used in quantitative management
2. Traceability of measures back to the project's quality and process performance objectives
3. Quality and process performance objectives for selected subprocesses and their attributes
4. Process performance baselines and models for use by the project

Subpractices

1. Identify common measures from the organizational process assets that support quantitative management.

   Refer to the Organizational Process Definition process area for more information about establishing organizational process assets.

   Refer to the Organizational Process Performance process area for more information about establishing performance baselines and models.

   Product lines, standard services, and service levels or other stratification criteria can categorize common measures.

2. Identify additional measures that may be needed to cover critical product and process attributes of the selected subprocesses.
   In some cases, measures can be research oriented. Such measures should be explicitly identified.

3. Identify the measures to be used in managing subprocesses.
   When selecting measures, keep the following considerations in mind:

   - Measures that aggregate data from multiple sources (e.g., different processes, input sources, environments) or over time (e.g., at a phase level) can mask underlying problems, making problem identification and resolution difficult.

   - For short-term projects, it may be necessary to aggregate data across similar instances of a process to enable analysis of its process performance while continuing to use the unaggregated data in support of individual projects.

   - Selection should not be limited to progress or performance measures only. "Analysis measures" (e.g., inspection preparation rates, staff member skill levels, path coverage in testing) may provide better insight into process performance.

4. Specify the operational definitions of measures, their collection points in subprocesses, and how the integrity of measures will be determined.

5. Analyze the relationship of identified measures to the project quality and process performance objectives and derive subprocess quality and process performance objectives that state targets

TIP

For example, the identification of measures to support monitoring of selected subprocesses (SP 2.1) is based on the attributes selected (SP 1.3) and on the measures established by the organization to be included in its process performance analyses (OPP SP 1.3).

X-REF

Much of the material found in the remaining subpractices (2 through 9) represents a direct application of MA SG 1, Align Measurement and Analysis Activities.

TIP

Additional measures may be needed, for example, to address unique customer requirements or supplier approaches.

(e.g., thresholds, ranges) to be met for each measured attribute of each selected subprocess.

TIP

See the definitions of "statistical and other quantitative techniques" and "statistical techniques" in the glossary.

Examples of derived subprocess quality and process performance objectives include the following:
- Maintain a code review rate between 75 to 100 lines of code per hour
- Keep requirements gathering sessions to under three hours
- Keep test rate over a specified number of test cases per day
- Maintain rework levels below a specified percent
- Maintain productivity in generating use cases per day
- Keep design complexity (fan-out rate) below a specified threshold

---

6. Identify the statistical and other quantitative techniques to be used in quantitative management.

In quantitative management, the process performance of selected subprocesses is analyzed using statistical and other quantitative techniques that help to characterize subprocess variation, identify when statistically unexpected behavior occurs, recognize when variation is excessive, and investigate why. Examples of statistical techniques that can be used in the analysis of process performance include statistical process control charts, regression analysis, analysis of variance, and time series analysis. The project can benefit from analyzing the performance of subprocesses not selected for their impact on project performance. Statistical and other quantitative techniques can be identified to address these subprocesses as well.

Statistical and other quantitative techniques sometimes involve the use of graphical displays that help visualize associations among the data and results of analyses. Such graphical displays can help visualize process performance and variation over time (i.e., trends), identify problems or opportunities, and evaluate the effects of particular factors.

Examples of graphical displays include the following:
- Scatterplots
- Histograms
- Box and whiskers plots
- Run charts
- Ishikawa diagrams

Examples of other techniques used to analyze process performance include the following:
- Tally sheets
- Classification schemas (e.g., Orthogonal Defect Classification)

---

7. Determine what process performance baselines and models may be needed to support identified analyses.

   In some situations, the set of baselines and models provided as described in Organizational Process Performance may be inadequate to support quantitative project management. This situation can happen when the objectives, processes, stakeholders, skill levels, or environment for the project are different from other projects for which baselines and models were established.

   As the project progresses, data from the project can serve as a more representative data set for establishing missing or a project specific set of process performance baselines and models.

   Hypothesis testing comparing project data to prior historical data can confirm the need to establish additional baselines and models specific to the project.

8. Instrument the organizational or project support environment to support collection, derivation, and analysis of measures.

   This instrumentation is based on the following:

   • Description of the organization's set of standard processes
   • Description of the project's defined process
   • Capabilities of the organizational or project support environment

9. Revise measures and statistical analysis techniques as necessary.

SG 2   QUANTITATIVELY MANAGE THE PROJECT

The project is quantitatively managed.

Quantitatively managing the project involves the use of statistical and other quantitative techniques to do the following:

• Monitor the selected subprocesses using statistical and other quantitative techniques
• Determine whether or not the project's quality and process performance objectives are being satisfied
• Perform root cause analysis of selected issues to address deficiencies

SP 2.1 MONITOR THE PERFORMANCE OF SELECTED SUBPROCESSES

Monitor the performance of selected subprocesses using statistical and other quantitative techniques.

The intent of this specific practice is to use statistical and other quantitative techniques to analyze variation in subprocess performance and to determine actions necessary to achieve each subprocess's quality and process performance objectives.

QPM

TIP

We prepare for quantitative management in SG 1. We perform quantitative management in SG 2. Under some circumstances, it may be necessary to revisit the practices under SG 1 (e.g., to address changes to QPPOs or select a superior subprocess alternative).

HINT

These three bullets correspond to SPs 2.1-2.3.

TIP

The subprocesses being monitored are, of course, those selected in SP 1.3.

Example Work Products

1. Natural bounds of process performance for each selected subprocess attribute
2. The actions needed to address deficiencies in the process stability or capability of each selected subprocess

Example Supplier Deliverables

1. Actions needed to address deficiencies in supplier process performance or the quality of deliverables

Subpractices

1. Collect data, as defined by the selected measures, on the subprocesses as they execute.
2. Monitor the variation and stability of the selected subprocesses and address deficiencies.

   This analysis involves evaluating measurements in relation to the natural bounds calculated for each selected measure and identifying outliers or other signals of potential non-random behavior, determining their causes, and preventing or mitigating the effects of their recurrence (i.e., addressing special causes of variation).

   During such analysis, be sensitive to the sufficiency of the data and to shifts in process performance that can affect the ability to achieve or maintain process stability.

   Analytic techniques for identifying outliers or signals include statistical process control charts, prediction intervals, and analysis of variance. Some of these techniques involve graphical displays.

   Other deficiencies in process performance to consider include when variation is too large to have confidence that the subprocess is stable, or too great to assess its capability (next subpractice) of achieving the objectives established for each selected attribute.

3. Monitor the capability and performance of the selected subprocesses and address deficiencies.

   The intent of this subpractice is to identify what actions to take to help the subprocess achieve its quality and process performance objectives. Be sure that the subprocess performance is stable relative to the selected measures (previous subpractice) before comparing its capability to its quality and process performance objectives.

> Examples of actions that can be taken when the performance of a selected subprocess fails to satisfy its objectives include the following:
> • Improving the implementation of the existing subprocess to reduce its variation or improve its performance (i.e., addressing common causes of variation)
>
> *Continues*

TIP

This subpractice addresses the question, "Is the subprocess stable?"

HINT

When the subprocess variation is too large, investigate process and measurement fidelity. Also, investigate what is happening "upstream" and at a lower level of granularity. You may need to restratify your data (e.g., to match input types) or disaggregate the measure (so it is no longer reporting totals) to achieve adequate control.

X-REF

See Example 7.1 in *Measuring the Software Process: Statistical Process Control for Software Process Improvement,* by William A. Florac and Anita D. Carleton (Addison-Wesley).

TIP

This subpractice addresses the question, "Is the subprocess capable?"

HINT

Regularly compare the natural bounds for the subprocess ("voice of the process") against the associated QPPOs ("voice of the customer") and take corrective action as appropriate.

Continued

- Identifying and implementing an alternative subprocess through identifying and adopting new process elements, subprocesses, and technologies that may help better align with objectives
- Identifying risks and risk mitigation strategies for each deficiency in subprocess capability
- Renegotiating or re-deriving objectives for each selected attribute of a subprocess so that they can be met by the subprocess

Some actions can involve the use of root cause analysis, which is further described in SP 2.3.

Refer to the Project Monitoring and Control process area for more information about managing corrective action to closure.

SP 2.2 MANAGE PROJECT PERFORMANCE

Manage the project using statistical and other quantitative techniques to determine whether or not the project's objectives for quality and process performance will be satisfied.

Refer to the Measurement and Analysis process area for more information about aligning measurement and analysis activities and providing measurement results.

Refer to the Organizational Performance Management process area for more information about managing business performance.

This specific practice is project focused and uses multiple inputs to predict if the project's quality and process performance objectives will be satisfied. Based on this prediction, risks associated with not meeting the project's quality and process performance objectives are identified and managed, and actions to address deficiencies are defined as appropriate.

Key inputs to this analysis include the individual subprocess stability and capability data derived from the previous specific practice, as well as performance data from monitoring other subprocesses, risks, and suppliers' progress.

Example Work Products

1. Predictions of results to be achieved relative to the project's quality and process performance objectives
2. Graphical displays and data tabulations for other subprocesses, which support quantitative management
3. Assessment of risks of not achieving the project's quality and process performance objectives
4. Actions needed to address deficiencies in achieving project objectives

TIP

Sometimes you can change QPPOs associated with a particular subprocess by investigating whether other subprocesses can give up some needed slack (or by differentiating which type or size of work products the subprocess is applied to).

QPM

TIP

Expand your process improvement toolkit to include techniques such as Six Sigma or Theory of Constraints when managing project performance.

X-REF

For information on how to use Six Sigma with CMMI, see "CMMI and Six Sigma: Partners in Process Improvement" at www.sei.cmu.edu/library/abstracts/books/0321516087.cfm.

X-REF

For more information on using Theory of Constraints and the critical thinking tools, see *Thinking for a Change: Putting the TOC Thinking Processes to Use* by Lisa Scheinkopf (CRC).

Example Supplier Deliverables

1. Supplier process performance data for quality and process performance objectives and expected service levels

Subpractices

1. Periodically review the performance of subprocesses.

    Stability and capability data from monitoring selected subprocesses, as described in SP 2.1, are a key input into understanding the project's overall ability to meet quality and process performance objectives. In addition, subprocesses not selected for their impact on project objectives can still create problems or risks for the project and thus some level of monitoring for these subprocesses may be desired as well. Analytic techniques involving the use of graphical displays can also prove to be useful to understanding subprocess performance.

2. Monitor and analyze suppliers' progress toward achieving their quality and process performance objectives.

3. Periodically review and analyze actual results achieved against established interim objectives.

4. Use process performance models calibrated with project data to assess progress toward achieving the project's quality and process performance objectives.

    Process performance models are used to assess progress toward achieving objectives that cannot be measured until a future phase in the project lifecycle. Objectives can either be interim objectives or overall objectives.

> An example is the use of process performance models to predict the latent defects in work products in future phases or in the delivered product.

    Calibration of process performance models is based on the results obtained from performing the activities described in the previous subpractices and specific practices.

5. Identify and manage risks associated with achieving the project's quality and process performance objectives.

    Refer to the Risk Management process area for more information about identifying and analyzing risks and mitigating risks.

> Example sources of risks include the following:
> - Subprocesses having inadequate performance or capability
> - Suppliers not achieving their quality and process performance objectives
> - Lack of visibility into supplier capability
> - Inaccuracies in the process performance models used for predicting performance
>
> *Continues*

TIP
The organization's PPMs (OPP SP 1.5), when calibrated with project-specific data or PPBs, can help the project determine whether it will be able to achieve its QPPOs.

> *Continued*
> • Deficiencies in predicted process performance (estimated progress)
> • Other identified risks associated with identified deficiencies

6. Determine and implement actions needed to address deficiencies in achieving the project's quality and process performance objectives.

   The intent of this subpractice is to identify and implement the right set of actions, resources, and schedule to place the project back on a path toward achieving its objectives.

> Examples of actions that can be taken to address deficiencies in achieving the project's objectives include the following:
> • Changing quality and process performance objectives so that they are within the expected range of the project's defined process
> • Improving the implementation of the project's defined process
> • Adopting new subprocesses and technologies that have the potential for satisfying objectives and managing associated risks
> • Identifying the risk and risk mitigation strategies for deficiencies
> • Terminating the project

   Some actions can involve the use of root cause analysis, which is addressed in the next specific practice.

   Refer to the Project Monitoring and Control process area for more information about managing corrective action to closure.

   When corrective actions result in changes to attributes or measures related to adjustable factors in a process performance model, the model can be used to predict the effects of the actions. When undertaking critical corrective actions in high risk situations, a process performance model can be created to predict the effects of the change.

SP 2.3 PERFORM ROOT CAUSE ANALYSIS

Perform root cause analysis of selected issues to address deficiencies in achieving the project's quality and process performance objectives.

Issues to address include deficiencies in subprocess stability and capability, and deficiencies in project performance relative to its objectives.

   Root cause analysis of selected issues is best performed shortly after the problem is first identified, while the event is still recent enough to be carefully investigated.

   The formality of and effort required for a root cause analysis can vary greatly and can be determined by such factors as the stakeholders who are involved; the risk or opportunity that is present; the

TIP

The deficiencies mentioned in the specific practice statement are those arising out of the analyses described in SP 2.1 (subprocess performance deficiencies) and SP 2.2 (predicted deficiencies in achieving project QPPOs).

complexity of the situation; the frequency with which the situation could recur; the availability of data, baselines, and models that can be used in the analysis; and how much time has passed since the events triggering the deficiency.

In the case of a subprocess that exhibits too much variation, is performed rarely, and involves different stakeholders, it could take weeks or months to identify root causes.

Likewise, the actions to take can range significantly in terms of effort and time needed to determine, plan, and implement them.

It is often difficult to know how much time is needed unless an initial analysis of the deficiencies is undertaken.

Refer to the Causal Analysis and Resolution process area for more information about identifying causes of selected outcomes and taking action to improve process performance.

Refer to the Measurement and Analysis process area for more information about aligning measurement and analysis activities and providing measurement results.

Example Work Products

1. Subprocess and project performance measurements and analyses (including statistical analyses) recorded in the organization's measurement repository
2. Graphical displays of data used to understand subprocess and project performance and performance trends
3. Identified root causes and potential actions to take

Subpractices

X-REF

Although an Ishikawa diagram (i.e., fishbone diagram) is a popular tool for simple root cause analysis, most deficiencies affecting achievement of the project's QPPOs require more in-depth analysis. In addition to the use of PPBs and PPMs, consider tools such as the *current reality tree* from the Theory of Constraints. For more information, visit the Goldratt Institute at www.goldratt.com/ or consult Wikipedia.

1. Perform root cause analysis, as appropriate, to diagnose process performance deficiencies.

    Process performance baselines and models are used in diagnosing deficiencies; identifying possible solutions; predicting future project and process performance; and evaluating potential actions as appropriate.

    The use of process performance models in predicting future project and process performance is described in a subpractice of the previous specific practice.

2. Identify and analyze potential actions.

3. Implement selected actions.

4. Assess the impact of the actions on subprocess performance.

    This assessment of impact can include an evaluation of the statistical significance of the impacts resulting from the actions taken to improve process performance.

REQUIREMENTS MANAGEMENT
A Project Management Process Area at Maturity Level 2

Purpose

The purpose of Requirements Management (REQM) is to manage requirements of the project's products and product components and to ensure alignment between those requirements and the project's plans and work products.

X-REF

REQM does not address eliciting or developing requirements. For more information on these topics, refer to the ARD process area.

REQM

Introductory Notes

Requirements management processes manage all requirements received or generated by the project, including both technical and nontechnical requirements as well as requirements levied on the project by the organization.

In particular, if the Acquisition Requirements Development process area is implemented, the resulting processes will generate customer and contractual requirements to be managed by requirements management processes. When the Requirements Management and the Acquisition Requirements Development process areas are both implemented, their associated processes can be closely tied and performed concurrently.

Throughout the process areas, where the terms "product" and "product component" are used, their intended meanings also encompass services, service systems, and their components.

The project takes appropriate steps to ensure that the set of approved requirements is managed to support the planning and execution needs of the project. When a project receives requirements from an approved requirements provider, these requirements are reviewed with the requirements provider to resolve issues and prevent misunderstanding before requirements are incorporated into project plans. Once the requirements provider and the requirements receiver reach an agreement, commitment to the requirements is obtained from project participants. The project manages changes to

TIP

REQM addresses *all* customer and contractual *requirements* handled by the project, thereby providing a stable foundation for acquisition activities and for suppliers to perform project planning, development, testing, and delivery activities. Requirements providers may include customers, end users, suppliers, management, regulatory agencies, and standards bodies.

TIP

Nontechnical requirements include requirements related to issues such as cost, schedule, packaging, and delivery, as well as other requirements not associated directly with attributes of the product or service.

requirements as they evolve and identifies inconsistencies that occur among plans, work products, and requirements.

Part of managing requirements is documenting requirements changes and their rationale and maintaining bidirectional traceability between source requirements, all product and product component requirements, and other specified work products. (See the definition of "bidirectional traceability" in the glossary.)

All projects have requirements. In the case of maintenance activities, changes are based on changes to the existing requirements, design, or implementation. The requirements changes, if any, might be documented in change requests from the customer or end users, or they might take the form of new requirements received from the requirements development process. Regardless of their source or form, the maintenance activities that are driven by changes to requirements are managed accordingly.

Related Process Areas

Refer to the Acquisition Requirements Development process area for more information about developing and analyzing customer and contractual requirements.

Refer to the Configuration Management process area for more information about establishing baselines and tracking and controlling changes.

Refer to the Project Monitoring and Control process area for more information about monitoring the project against the plan and managing corrective action to closure.

Refer to the Project Planning process area for more information about establishing and maintaining plans that define project activities.

Refer to the Risk Management process area for more information about identifying and analyzing risks.

Specific Goal and Practice Summary

SG 1 Manage Requirements
- SP 1.1   Understand Requirements
- SP 1.2   Obtain Commitment to Requirements
- SP 1.3   Manage Requirements Changes
- SP 1.4   Maintain Bidirectional Traceability of Requirements
- SP 1.5   Ensure Alignment Between Project Work and Requirements

Specific Practices by Goal

SG 1   MANAGE REQUIREMENTS

Requirements are managed and inconsistencies with project plans and work products are identified.

The project maintains a current and approved set of requirements over the life of the project by doing the following:

- Managing all changes to requirements
- Maintaining relationships among requirements, project plans, and work products
- Ensuring alignment among requirements, project plans, and work products
- Taking corrective action

Refer to the Project Monitoring and Control process area for more information about managing corrective action to closure.

Requirements management typically includes directly managing changes to customer and contractual requirements developed by the acquirer and overseeing the supplier's requirements management process. Requirements changes can result in changes to the supplier agreement.

SP 1.1   UNDERSTAND REQUIREMENTS

Develop an understanding with the requirements providers on the meaning of the requirements.

As the project matures and requirements are derived, all activities or disciplines will receive requirements. To avoid requirements creep, criteria are established to designate appropriate channels or official sources from which to receive requirements. Those who receive requirements conduct analyses of them with the provider to ensure that a compatible, shared understanding is reached on the meaning of requirements. The result of these analyses and dialogs is a set of approved requirements.

Example Work Products

1. Lists of criteria for distinguishing appropriate requirements providers
2. Criteria for evaluation and acceptance of requirements
3. Results of analyses against criteria
4. A set of approved requirements

TIP

Requirements are a vehicle used to communicate expectations to both customers and suppliers. These expectations evolve as the project progresses.

TIP

"Requirements creep" is the tendency for requirements to continually flow into a project (often from multiple sources) and expand the project's scope beyond what was originally planned. "Unfunded requirements" or "mandates" are frequently sources of cost and schedule overruns.

TIP

Requirements may come from many different stakeholders. Sometimes the eventual end-user community is too diverse to work with directly and will identify a surrogate to act as its representative. This additional layer between the acquirer and the end user is a potential source of risk for requirements interpretation issues.

TIP

Examples of agreed-to sets of requirements include an operational requirements document that captures customer needs and a technical requirements document that is provided to suppliers as part of the solicitation package, both with appropriate sign-offs from relevant stakeholders.

REQM

Subpractices

TIP

Having clear lines of communication and authority when dealing with requirements helps to keep "requirements creep" under control.

1. Establish criteria for distinguishing appropriate requirements providers.

2. Establish objective criteria for the evaluation and acceptance of requirements.

    Lack of evaluation and acceptance criteria often results in inadequate verification, costly rework, or customer rejection.

Examples of evaluation and acceptance criteria include the following:
- Clearly and properly stated
- Complete
- Consistent with one another
- Uniquely identified
- Consistent with overall architectural approach and quality attribute priorities (e.g., as defined in the acquisition strategy)
- Appropriate to implement
- Verifiable (i.e., testable)
- Traceable
- Achievable
- Tied to business value
- Identified as a priority for the customer

---

3. Analyze requirements to ensure that established criteria are met.

4. Reach an understanding of requirements with requirements providers so that project participants can commit to them.

SP 1.2 OBTAIN COMMITMENT TO REQUIREMENTS

Obtain commitment to requirements from project participants.

Refer to the Project Monitoring and Control process area for more information about monitoring commitments.

TIP

Maintaining two-way communication through the life of the project is critical to ensuring that a shared understanding of requirements is maintained between the project and the requirements providers.

TIP

Commitments comprise both the resources involved and the schedule for completion.

The previous specific practice dealt with reaching an understanding with requirements providers. This specific practice deals with agreements and commitments among those who carry out activities necessary to implement requirements. Requirements evolve throughout the project. As requirements evolve, this specific practice ensures that project participants commit to the current and approved requirements and the resulting changes in project plans, activities, and work products.

Changes to requirements can lead to changes in supplier agreements. These changes should be agreed on by the acquirer and supplier after appropriate negotiations.

Example Work Products

1. Requirements impact assessments
2. Documented commitments to requirements and requirements changes

Example Supplier Deliverables

1. Supplier requirements impact assessments

Subpractices

1. Assess the impact of requirements on existing commitments.
   The impact on the project participants should be evaluated when the requirements change or at the start of a new requirement.
2. Negotiate and record commitments.
   Changes to existing commitments should be negotiated before project participants commit to a new requirement or requirement change.
   The acquirer negotiates commitments with the customer and supplier before committing to requirement changes.

SP 1.3 MANAGE REQUIREMENTS CHANGES

Manage changes to requirements as they evolve during the project.

Refer to the Configuration Management process area for more information about tracking and controlling changes.

Requirements change for a variety of reasons. As needs change and as work proceeds, changes may have to be made to existing requirements. It is essential to manage these additions and changes efficiently and effectively. To effectively analyze the impact of changes, it is necessary that the source of each requirement is known and the rationale for the change is documented. The project may want to track appropriate measures of requirements volatility to judge whether new or revised approach to change control is necessary.

If contractual requirements defined in the supplier agreement are affected by the changes, the supplier agreement also must be aligned with the changed requirements.

Example Work Products

1. Requirements change requests
2. Requirements change impact reports

HINT

If you expect changes in requirements to occur, make sure your acquisition strategy and supplier agreements include explicit mechanisms for dealing with these changes.

TIP

Project members who make commitments must continually evaluate whether they can meet their commitments, communicate immediately when they realize they cannot meet a commitment, and mitigate the impacts of not being able to meet a commitment.

REQM

TIP

"Requirements volatility" is the rate at which requirements change once implementation begins. Customer requirements and contractual requirements should be assessed for volatility. Customer requirements volatility could affect the acquisition strategy, and contractual requirements volatility will affect the suppliers' ability to achieve progress as planned.

3. Requirements status
4. Requirements database

Example Supplier Deliverables

1. Requirements change requests
2. Requirements change impact reports

Subpractices

1. Document all requirements and requirements changes that are given to or generated by the project.
2. Maintain a requirements change history, including the rationale for changes.

    Maintaining the change history helps to track requirements volatility.
3. Evaluate the impact of requirement changes from the standpoint of relevant stakeholders.

    Requirements changes that affect the architectures of products being acquired can affect many stakeholders.
4. Make requirements and change data available to the project.

SP 1.4 MAINTAIN BIDIRECTIONAL TRACEABILITY OF REQUIREMENTS

Maintain bidirectional traceability among requirements and work products.

The intent of this specific practice is to maintain the bidirectional traceability of requirements. (See the definition of "bidirectional traceability" in the glossary.) When requirements are managed well, traceability can be established from a source requirement to its lower level requirements and from those lower level requirements back to their source requirements. Such bidirectional traceability helps to determine whether all source requirements have been completely addressed and whether all lower level requirements can be traced to a valid source.

Requirements traceability also covers relationships to other entities such as intermediate and final work products, changes in design documentation, and test plans. Traceability can cover horizontal relationships, such as across interfaces, as well as vertical relationships. Traceability is particularly needed when assessing the impact of requirements changes on project activities and work products.

The supplier maintains comprehensive bidirectional traceability to requirements defined in the supplier agreement by the acquirer, and the acquirer verifies that traceability. The acquirer maintains bidirectional traceability between customer requirements and contractual requirements.

Examples of what aspects of traceability to consider include the following:
- Scope of traceability: The boundaries within which traceability is needed
- Definition of traceability: The elements that need logical relationships
- Type of traceability: When horizontal and vertical traceability is needed

Example Work Products

1. Requirements traceability matrix
2. Requirements tracking system

Example Supplier Deliverables

1. Comprehensive requirements traceability matrix managed by the supplier as required by the supplier agreement

Subpractices

1. Maintain requirements traceability to ensure that the source of lower level (i.e., derived) requirements is documented.

    Traceability from customer to contractual requirements is maintained by the acquirer. Traceability from contractual requirements to derived or additional requirements is maintained by the supplier.

2. Maintain requirements traceability from a requirement to its derived requirements and allocation to work products.

    Requirements changes that affect the architectures of products being acquired can affect many stakeholders.

3. Generate a requirements traceability matrix.

    A comprehensive traceability matrix, tracing from customer requirements to contractual requirements is maintained by the acquirer. A comprehensive traceability matrix, tracing from contractual requirements to lower level requirements is maintained by the supplier.

SP 1.5 *ENSURE ALIGNMENT BETWEEN PROJECT WORK AND REQUIREMENTS*

Ensure that project plans and work products remain aligned with requirements.

This specific practice finds inconsistencies between requirements and project plans and work products and initiates corrective actions to resolve them.

Corrective actions taken by the project to resolve inconsistencies can also result in changes to project plans and supplier agreements.

TIP

Maintaining traceability across horizontal relationships can greatly reduce problems encountered in the transition to operations and support activities.

TIP

A traceability matrix can take many forms—for example, a spreadsheet or a database.

TIP

Sometimes the customer requirements baseline differs from the contractual baseline that the suppliers are working on. The acquisition project must maintain both baselines and plan to resolve or negotiate inconsistencies.

REQM

HINT

When a requirement changes, use the traceability matrix to evaluate how that change will affect supplier deliverables and customer needs.

TIP

Especially for large projects, product components are developed in parallel, sometimes by multiple suppliers. In such an environment, it is challenging to keep all work products fully consistent with changes to the requirements.

Example Work Products

1. Documentation of inconsistencies between requirements and project plans and work products, including sources and conditions
2. Corrective actions

Subpractices

1. Review project plans, activities, and work products for consistency with requirements and changes made to them.
2. Identify the source of the inconsistency (if any).
3. Identify any changes that should be made to plans and work products resulting from changes to the requirements baseline.
4. Initiate any necessary corrective actions.

RISK MANAGEMENT
A Project Management Process Area at Maturity Level 3

Purpose

The purpose of Risk Management (RSKM) is to identify potential problems before they occur so that risk handling activities can be planned and invoked as needed across the life of the product or project to mitigate adverse impacts on achieving objectives.

TIP

The practices in RSKM also apply to identifying, evaluating, and maximizing (or realizing) *opportunities*.

Introductory Notes

Risk management is a continuous, forward-looking process that is an important part of project management. Risk management should address issues that could endanger achievement of critical objectives. A continuous risk management approach effectively anticipates and mitigates risks that can have a critical impact on a project.

Effective risk management includes early and aggressive risk identification through collaboration and the involvement of relevant stakeholders as described in the stakeholder involvement plan addressed in the Project Planning process area. Strong leadership among all relevant stakeholders is needed to establish an environment for free and open disclosure and discussion of risk.

Risk management should consider both internal and external, as well as both technical and non-technical, sources of cost, schedule, performance, and other risks. Early and aggressive detection of risk is important because it is typically easier, less costly, and less disruptive to make changes and correct work efforts during the earlier, rather than the later, phases of the project.

When the project identifies and assesses project risks during project planning and manages risks throughout the life of the project, risk identification includes identifying risks associated with the acquisition process and the use of a supplier to perform project work. Initially, the acquisition strategy identifies risks associated with an acquisition. The approach to the acquisition is planned based on

TIP

In a dynamic environment, risk management must be a continuous process of identifying, analyzing, and monitoring risks.

TIP

Without a free and open environment, many risks will remain undisclosed until they surface as problems, when it is often too late to address them. Free and open discussions should involve the following parties:

- Customers and other stakeholders when the acquisition strategy is being formulated
- Potential suppliers when negotiations are taking place
- Suppliers when the supplier agreement is being established and throughout the project

RSKM

479

those risks. As the project progresses to the selection of a supplier, risks specific to the supplier's technical and management approach become important to the success of the acquisition.

These risks refer to the capability of the supplier to meet contractual requirements, including schedules and cost targets. When the project selects a supplier and awards the supplier agreement, the acquirer continues to manage project risks, including risks related to the supplier meeting its contractual requirements. Typically the acquirer does not manage risks being addressed or managed by the supplier.

Industry standards can help when determining how to prevent or mitigate specific risks commonly found in a particular industry. Certain risks can be proactively managed or mitigated by reviewing industry best practices and lessons learned.

Risk management can be divided into the following parts:

- Defining a risk management strategy
- Identifying and analyzing risks
- Handling identified risks, including the implementation of risk mitigation plans as needed

Both the acquirer and supplier should understand project risks and how to modify the risk management strategy and plans as a project progresses through its lifecycle. Managing project risks requires a close partnership between the acquirer and supplier. Both should share appropriate risk management documentation, understand the risks, and develop and execute risk management activities.

The complexity of an acquirer-supplier relationship increases the need for early and aggressive risk identification. For example, acquirer capabilities, supplier experience working with the acquirer, financial stability of the supplier, and availability of well-defined dispute resolution processes all influence the risk of a project.

As represented in the Project Planning and Project Monitoring and Control process areas, organizations initially may focus on risk identification for awareness and react to the realization of these risks as they occur. The Risk Management process area describes an evolution of these specific practices to systematically plan, anticipate, and mitigate risks to proactively minimize their impact on the project.

Although the primary emphasis of the Risk Management process area is on the project, these concepts can also be applied to manage organizational risks.

Related Process Areas

Refer to the Solicitation and Supplier Agreement Development process area for more information about establishing supplier agreements.

Refer to the Decision Analysis and Resolution process area for more information about analyzing possible decisions using a formal evaluation process that evaluates identified alternatives against established criteria.

Refer to the Project Monitoring and Control process area for more information about monitoring project risks.

Refer to the Project Planning process area for more information about identifying project risks and planning stakeholder involvement.

X-REF

PP and PMC contain risk management related practices. See PP SP 2.2, "Identify Project Risks," and PMC SP 1.3, "Monitor Project Risks."

HINT

Relevant stakeholders external to the project bring perspectives and insight into the process of identifying and evaluating risks—especially when the project is contributing to a system of systems. It is important to maintain a dialog on related risks pertaining to other systems within the system of systems.

Specific Goal and Practice Summary

SG 1 Prepare for Risk Management
    SP 1.1   Determine Risk Sources and Categories
    SP 1.2   Define Risk Parameters
    SP 1.3   Establish a Risk Management Strategy
SG 2 Identify and Analyze Risks
    SP 2.1   Identify Risks
    SP 2.2   Evaluate, Categorize, and Prioritize Risks
SG 3 Mitigate Risks
    SP 3.1   Develop Risk Mitigation Plans
    SP 3.2   Implement Risk Mitigation Plans

Specific Practices by Goal

SG 1 *PREPARE FOR RISK MANAGEMENT*

Preparation for risk management is conducted.

Prepare for risk management by establishing and maintaining a strategy for identifying, analyzing, and mitigating risks. Typically, this strategy is documented in a risk management plan. The risk management strategy addresses specific actions and the management approach used to apply and control the risk management program. The strategy typically includes identifying sources of risk, the scheme used to categorize risks, and parameters used to evaluate, bound, and control risks for effective handling.

TIP

If your project uses safety and security analysis methods, incorporate these methods as part of the risk management strategy.

SP 1.1 *DETERMINE RISK SOURCES AND CATEGORIES*

Determine risk sources and categories.

Identifying risk sources provides a basis for systematically examining changing situations over time to uncover circumstances that affect the

RSKM

ability of the project to meet its objectives. Risk sources are both internal and external to the project. As the project progresses, additional sources of risk can be identified. Establishing categories for risks provides a mechanism for collecting and organizing risks as well as ensuring appropriate scrutiny and management attention to risks that can have serious consequences on meeting project objectives.

Acquirers initially identify and categorize risk sources and categories for the project and refine those sources and categories over time (e.g., schedule, cost, sourcing, contract management, supplier execution, technology readiness, human safety, reliability related risks, other issues outside the control of the acquirer). The supplier is also a source of risk (e.g., financial stability of the supplier, the possibility of the supplier's acquisition by another organization).

Example Work Products

1. Risk source lists (external and internal)
2. Risk categories list

Subpractices

1. Determine risk sources.

   Risk sources are fundamental drivers that cause risks in a project or organization. There are many sources of risks, both internal and external to a project. Risk sources identify where risks can originate.

> Typical internal and external risk sources include the following:
> - Uncertain requirements
> - Unprecedented efforts (i.e., estimates unavailable)
> - Infeasible design
> - Competing quality attribute requirements that affect technical solution and design
> - Supplier architectural decisions that affect quality attribute requirements or acquirer's business objectives
> - Unavailable technology
> - Unrealistic schedule estimates or allocation
> - Inadequate staffing and skills
> - Cost or funding issues
> - Uncertain or inadequate subcontractor capability
> - Uncertain or inadequate supplier capability
> - Inadequate communication with actual or potential customers or with their representatives
> - Disruptions to the continuity of operations
> - Regulatory constraints (e.g. security, safety, environment)

Many of these sources of risk are accepted without adequately planning for them. Early identification of both internal and external sources of risk can lead to early identification of risks. Risk mitigation plans can then be implemented early in the project to preclude occurrence of risks or reduce consequences of their occurrence.

2. Determine risk categories.

Risk categories are "bins" used for collecting and organizing risks. Identifying risk categories aids the future consolidation of activities in risk mitigation plans.

TIP

Categories are used to group related risks that can often be addressed by the same mitigation activities, thereby increasing efficiency.

The following factors can be considered when determining risk categories:

- Phases of the project's lifecycle model (e.g., requirements, design, manufacturing, test and evaluation, delivery, disposal)
- Supplier risks (e.g., financial viability of the supplier, the geographic location of supplier resources)
- Product safety, security, and reliability
- Types of processes used
- Types of products used
- Project management risks (e.g., contract risks, budget risks, schedule risks, resource risks)
- Technical performance risks (e.g., quality attribute related risks, supportability risks)

A risk taxonomy can be used to provide a framework for determining risk sources and categories.

TIP

Risks are often grouped by lifecycle phase.

RSKM

SP 1.2 DEFINE RISK PARAMETERS

Define parameters used to analyze and categorize risks and to control the risk management effort.

Parameters for evaluating, categorizing, and prioritizing risks include the following:

- Risk likelihood (i.e., probability of risk occurrence)
- Risk consequence (i.e., impact and severity of risk occurrence)
- Thresholds to trigger management activities

Risk parameters are used to provide common and consistent criteria for comparing risks to be managed. Without these parameters, it is difficult to gauge the severity of an unwanted change caused by a risk and to prioritize the actions required for risk mitigation planning.

Projects should document the parameters used to analyze and categorize risks so that they are available for reference throughout the life of the project because circumstances change over time. Using these parameters, risks can easily be re-categorized and analyzed when changes occur.

X-REF

The risk taxonomies developed at the SEI and mentioned in Barry Boehm and Vic Basili's "Top 10 Software Risks" (www. cebase.org/www/ AboutCebase/News/top-10-defects.html) remain useful even more than a decade after their creation.

TIP

To be effective, risk management must be objective and quantitative. Therefore, you must treat risks consistently with respect to the key parameters. Defining criteria for evaluating risks helps to ensure consistency.

TIP

When you are in the middle of a project, it is easy to lose perspective on the risks involved. Defining thresholds in advance enables a more objective treatment of risks.

TIP

These thresholds may need to be refined later as part of risk mitigation planning.

TIP

Bounds are intended to scope the risk management effort in sensible ways that help the organization conserve project resources.

The project can use techniques such as failure mode and effects analysis (FMEA) to examine risks of potential failures in the acquisition strategy, acquisition, or in selected transition and product support processes. Such techniques can help to provide discipline in working with risk parameters.

Example Work Products

1. Risk evaluation, categorization, and prioritization criteria
2. Risk management requirements (e.g., control and approval levels, reassessment intervals)

Subpractices

1. Define consistent criteria for evaluating and quantifying risk likelihood and severity levels.

   Consistently used criteria (e.g., bounds on likelihood, severity levels) allow impacts of different risks to be commonly understood, to receive the appropriate level of scrutiny, and to obtain the management attention warranted. In managing dissimilar risks (e.g., staff safety versus environmental pollution), it is important to ensure consistency in the end result. (For example, a high-impact risk of environmental pollution is as important as a high-impact risk to staff safety.) One way of providing a common basis for comparing dissimilar risks is assigning dollar values to risks (e.g., through a process of risk monetization).

2. Define thresholds for each risk category.

   For each risk category, thresholds can be established to determine acceptability or unacceptability of risks, prioritization of risks, or triggers for management action.

   Examples of thresholds include the following:
   - Project-wide thresholds could be established to involve senior management when product costs exceed 10 percent of the target cost or when cost performance indices (CPIs) fall below 0.95.
   - Schedule thresholds could be established to involve senior management when schedule performance indices (SPIs) fall below 0.95.
   - Performance thresholds could be established to involve senior management when specified key items (e.g., processor utilization, average response times) exceed 125 percent of the intended design.

3. Define bounds on the extent to which thresholds are applied against or within a category.

   There are few limits to which risks can be assessed in either a quantitative or qualitative fashion. Definition of bounds (or boundary conditions) can be used to help define the extent of the risk management effort and avoid excessive resource expenditures. Bounds can include the exclusion of a risk source from a category. These bounds can also exclude conditions that occur below a given frequency.

SP 1.3 ESTABLISH A RISK MANAGEMENT STRATEGY

Establish and maintain the strategy to be used for risk management.

A comprehensive risk management strategy addresses items such as the following:

TIP

The risk management strategy documents the results of the first two specific practices.

- The scope of the risk management effort
- Methods and tools to be used for risk identification, risk analysis, risk mitigation, risk monitoring, and communication
- Project specific sources of risks
- How risks are to be organized, categorized, compared, and consolidated
- Parameters used for taking action on identified risks, including likelihood, consequence, and thresholds
- Risk mitigation techniques to be used, such as prototyping, piloting, simulation, alternative designs, or evolutionary development
- The definition of risk measures used to monitor the status of risks
- Time intervals for risk monitoring or reassessment

TIP

Some large acquisition organizations develop a standard risk management strategy template that is then tailored to meet the needs of individual projects.

The risk management strategy should be guided by a common vision of success that describes desired future project outcomes in terms of the product delivered, its cost, and its fitness for the task. The risk management strategy is often documented in a risk management plan for the organization or project. This strategy is reviewed with relevant stakeholders to promote commitment and understanding.

A risk management strategy should be developed early in the project, so that relevant risks are identified and managed proactively. Early identification and assessment of critical risks allows the project to formulate risk handling approaches and adjust project definition and allocation of resources based on critical risks.

TIP

The risk management strategy is often documented as part of a risk management plan, or as a section in the project plan.

TIP

All relevant stakeholders must understand fully the risk management strategy.

Example Work Products

1. Project risk management strategy

SG 2 IDENTIFY AND ANALYZE RISKS

Risks are identified and analyzed to determine their relative importance.

The degree of risk affects the resources assigned to handle the risk and the timing of when appropriate management attention is required.

TIP

Risk identification and analysis is an activity that continues for the duration of the project.

RSKM

Risk analysis entails identifying risks from identified internal and external sources and evaluating each identified risk to determine its likelihood and consequences. Risk categorization, based on an evaluation against established risk categories and criteria developed for the risk management strategy, provides information needed for risk handling. Related risks can be grouped to enable efficient handling and effective use of risk management resources.

SP 2.1 IDENTIFY RISKS

Identify and document risks.

Identifying potential issues, hazards, threats, and vulnerabilities that could negatively affect work efforts or plans is the basis for sound and successful risk management. Risks should be identified and described understandably before they can be analyzed and managed properly. Risks are documented in a concise statement that includes the context, conditions, and consequences of risk occurrence.

Risk identification should be an organized, thorough approach to seek out probable or realistic risks in achieving objectives. To be effective, risk identification should not attempt to address every possible event. Using categories and parameters developed in the risk management strategy and identified sources of risk can provide the discipline and streamlining appropriate for risk identification. Identified risks form a baseline for initiating risk management activities. Risks should be reviewed periodically to reexamine possible sources of risk and changing conditions to uncover sources and risks previously overlooked or nonexistent when the risk management strategy was last updated.

Risk identification focuses on the identification of risks, not the placement of blame. The results of risk identification activities should never be used by management to evaluate the performance of individuals.

Many methods are used for identifying risks. Typical identification methods include the following:

- Examine each element of the project work breakdown structure.
- Conduct a risk assessment using a risk taxonomy.
- Interview subject matter experts.
- Review risk management efforts from similar products.
- Examine lessons learned documents or databases.
- Examine design specifications and agreement requirements.

TIP

"Can a project have no risks?" "Can multiple projects have the same risk lists?" If these questions are asked, someone does not understand risks. Some risks may be product specific, contract specific, or supplier specific.

TIP

The context, conditions, and consequences of a risk statement provide much of the information that is needed later to understand and evaluate the risk.

HINT

Establish a work environment in which risks can be disclosed and discussed openly, without fear of repercussions. (Don't shoot the messenger!)

TIP

Many of the methods used for identifying risks rely on organizational process assets such as a risk taxonomy, risk repository, and lessons learned from past projects. Subject-matter experts may also be utilized for this purpose. Other methods involve reviewing project artifacts such as the project's shared vision, project interfaces, and contractual requirements.

Some risks are identified by examining the supplier's WBS, product, and processes using the categories and parameters developed in the risk management strategy. Risks can be identified in many areas (e.g., requirements, technology, design, testing, vulnerability to threats, life-cycle costs). An examination of the project in these areas can help to develop or refine the acquisition strategy and the risk sharing structure between the acquirer and supplier.

The acquirer considers risks associated with a supplier's capability (e.g., meeting schedule, cost requirements for the project), including potential risks to the acquirer's intellectual capital or security vulnerabilities introduced by using a supplier.

Example Work Products

1. List of identified risks, including the context, conditions, and consequences of risk occurrence

Example Supplier Deliverables

1. List of identified risks, including the context, conditions, and consequences of risk occurrence

Subpractices

1. Identify the risks associated with cost, schedule, and performance.

   Risks associated with cost, schedule, performance, and other business objectives should be examined to understand their effect on project objectives. Risk candidates can be discovered that are outside the scope of project objectives but vital to customer interests. For example, risks in development costs, product acquisition costs, cost of spare (or replacement) products, and product disposition (or disposal) costs have design implications.

   The customer may not have considered the full cost of supporting a fielded product or using a delivered service. The customer should be informed of such risks, but actively managing those risks may not be necessary. Mechanisms for making such decisions should be examined at project and organization levels and put in place if deemed appropriate, especially for risks that affect the project's ability to verify and validate the product.

   In addition to the cost risks identified above, other cost risks can include the ones associated with funding levels, funding estimates, and distributed budgets.

   Schedule risks can include risks associated with planned activities, key events, and milestones.

X-REF

For more information, see *Software Risk Management: Principles and Practices* by Barry Boehm (IEEE Software, 1990); *A Guide to the Project Management Body of Knowledge* (PMBOK Guide), third edition (Project Management Institute, 2004; Chapter 11 deals with risk management); and www.sei.cmu.edu/risk/index.cfm.

TIP

One approach to identifying risks is to consider the cost, schedule, and performance issues associated with each lifecycle phase. Because each phase typically has a clear set of objectives and a completion milestone, a phase is a suitable context for identifying the risks associated with that phase.

HINT

When necessary, explain to customers the implications of their requirements, as they may not be aware of the acquisition risks associated with certain requirements. Clarifying or changing requirements may significantly mitigate risks in a complex acquisition.

TIP

Performance risks may be associated with lifecycle phases, new technology, or desired attributes of the product.

RSKM

Performance risks can include risks associated with the following:
- Requirements
- Analysis and design
- Application of new technology
- Physical size
- Shape
- Weight
- Manufacturing and fabrication
- Product behavior and operation with respect to functionality or quality attributes
- Verification
- Validation
- Performance maintenance attributes

Performance maintenance attributes are those characteristics that enable an in-use product or service to provide required performance, such as maintaining safety and security performance.

There are risks that do not fall into cost, schedule, or performance categories, but can be associated with other aspects of the organization's operation.

Examples of these other risks include risks related to the following:
- Strikes
- Diminishing sources of supply
- Technology cycle time
- Competition

TIP

Environmental risks are often ignored, even though some cost-effective mitigation activities addressing such risks are possible. Failing to mitigate these risks can be a major hazard for system acquisition success.

2. Review environmental elements that can affect the project.
   Risks to a project that frequently are missed include risks supposedly outside the scope of the project (i.e., the project does not control whether they occur but can mitigate their impact). These risks can include weather or natural disasters, political changes, and telecommunications failures.
3. Review all elements of the work breakdown structure as part of identifying risks to help ensure that all aspects of the work effort have been considered.
4. Review all elements of the project plan as part of identifying risks to help ensure that all aspects of the project have been considered.

   Refer to the Project Planning process area for more information about identifying project risks.

5. Document the context, conditions, and potential consequences of each risk.

   Risk statements are typically documented in a standard format that contains the risk context, conditions, and consequences of occurrence. The risk context provides additional information about the risk such as the relative time frame of the risk, the circumstances or conditions surrounding the risk that has brought about the concern, and any doubt or uncertainty.

6. Identify the relevant stakeholders associated with each risk.

TIP

A good risk statement is fact based, actionable, and brief.

TIP

A standard format for documenting risks makes it easier to train personnel on what is needed in risk statements.

SP 2.2 EVALUATE, CATEGORIZE, AND PRIORITIZE RISKS

Evaluate and categorize each identified risk using defined risk categories and parameters, and determine its relative priority.

The evaluation of risks is needed to assign a relative importance to each identified risk and is used in determining when appropriate management attention is required. Often it is useful to aggregate risks based on their interrelationships and develop options at an aggregate level. When an aggregate risk is formed by a roll up of lower level risks, care should be taken to ensure that important lower level risks are not ignored.

Collectively, the activities of risk evaluation, categorization, and prioritization are sometimes called a "risk assessment" or "risk analysis."

The acquirer should conduct a risk assessment before solicitation to evaluate if the project can achieve its technical, schedule, and budget constraints. Technical, schedule, and cost risks should be discussed with potential suppliers before the solicitation is released. Using this approach, critical risks inherent in the project can be identified and addressed in the solicitation.

HINT

Risk management is simplified when you can treat a number of risks as one group from evaluation and mitigation perspectives.

Example Work Products

1. List of risks and their assigned priority

Example Supplier Deliverables

1. List of risks and their assigned priority

Subpractices

1. Evaluate identified risks using defined risk parameters.

   Each risk is evaluated and assigned values according to defined risk parameters, which can include likelihood, consequence (i.e., severity, impact), and thresholds. The assigned risk parameter values can be integrated to produce additional measures, such as risk exposure (i.e., the combination of likelihood and consequence), which can be used to prioritize risks for handling.

TIP

Risk exposure is the result of the combination of the likelihood and the consequence of a risk (expressed quantitatively).

RSKM

Often, a scale with three to five values is used to evaluate both likelihood and consequence.

Likelihood, for example, can be categorized as remote, unlikely, likely, highly likely, or nearly certain.

Example categories for consequence include the following:
- Low
- Medium
- High
- Negligible
- Marginal
- Significant
- Critical
- Catastrophic

Probability values are frequently used to quantify likelihood. Consequences are generally related to cost, schedule, environmental impact, or human measures (e.g., labor hours lost, severity of injury).

Risk evaluation is often a difficult and time consuming task. Specific expertise or group techniques may be needed to assess risks and gain confidence in the prioritization. In addition, priorities can require reevaluation as time progresses. To provide a basis for comparing the impact of the realization of identified risks, consequences of the risks can be monetized.

2. Categorize and group risks according to defined risk categories.
   Risks are categorized into defined risk categories, providing a means to review them according to their source, taxonomy, or project component. Related or equivalent risks can be grouped for efficient handling. The cause-and-effect relationships between related risks are documented.

An acquirer's risk categories can include sourcing, contract management, and supplier execution, in addition to project management, technology, and requirements.

---

3. Prioritize risks for mitigation.
   A relative priority is determined for each risk based on assigned risk parameters. Clear criteria should be used to determine risk priority. Risk prioritization helps to determine the most effective areas to which resources for risks mitigation can be applied with the greatest positive impact on the project.

TIP

Determining values for risk likelihood and consequence is easier and more repeatable if objectives are stated clearly, criteria exist for assigning values, relevant stakeholders are represented appropriately, and personnel have been trained correctly.

TIP

Priority assignment can likewise be a repeatable process.

SG 3   MITIGATE RISKS

Risks are handled and mitigated as appropriate to reduce adverse impacts on achieving objectives.

The steps in handling risks include developing risk handling options, monitoring risks, and performing risk handling activities when defined thresholds are exceeded. Risk mitigation plans are developed and implemented for selected risks to proactively reduce the potential impact of risk occurrence. Risk mitigation planning can also include contingency plans to deal with the impact of selected risks that can occur despite attempts to mitigate them. Risk parameters used to trigger risk handling activities are defined by the risk management strategy.

SP 3.1   DEVELOP RISK MITIGATION PLANS

Develop a risk mitigation plan in accordance with the risk management strategy.

A critical component of risk mitigation planning is developing alternative courses of action, workarounds, and fallback positions, and a recommended course of action for each critical risk. The risk mitigation plan for a given risk includes techniques and methods used to avoid, reduce, and control the probability of risk occurrence; the extent of damage incurred should the risk occur (sometimes called a "contingency plan"); or both. Risks are monitored and when they exceed established thresholds, risk mitigation plans are deployed to return the affected effort to an acceptable risk level. If the risk cannot be mitigated, a contingency plan can be invoked. Both risk mitigation and contingency plans often are generated only for selected risks for which consequences of the risks are high or unacceptable. Other risks may be accepted and simply monitored.

Options for handling risks typically include alternatives such as the following:

- **Risk avoidance:** changing or lowering requirements while still meeting end user needs
- **Risk control:** taking active steps to minimize risks
- **Risk transfer:** reallocating requirements to lower risks
- **Risk monitoring:** watching and periodically reevaluating the risk for changes in assigned risk parameters
- **Risk acceptance:** acknowledging risk but not taking action

---

X-REF

RSKM heavily influences technical management (i.e., to adjust requirements, design, implementation, verification, and validation in light of risks and risk mitigation), project management (i.e., to plan for these activities and monitor thresholds that trigger the deployment of mitigation plans), and supplier agreement management (i.e., to understand how these activities are reflected in the supplier agreement).

TIP

The risk management literature uses the term *contingency plans* in various ways. In CMMI, a risk contingency plan is the part of a risk mitigation plan that addresses which actions to take *after* a risk is realized.

HINT

Reward personnel who prevent crises—not those who allow a crisis to happen and then work heroically to resolve it.

HINT

One way to identify actions that will avoid, reduce, or control a risk is to perform a causal analysis on the sources of the risk. Actions that eliminate or reduce causes may be suitable candidates for inclusion in a risk mitigation plan.

RSKM

TIP

When its associated threshold is exceeded, a risk mitigation plan should return the project to an acceptable risk level.

Often, especially for high-impact risks, more than one approach to handling a risk should be generated.

> For example, in the case of an event that disrupts the continuity of operations, approaches to risk management can include establishing the following:
> - Resource reserves to respond to disruptive events
> - Lists of available backup equipment
> - Backups to key staff
> - Plans for testing emergency response systems
> - Posted procedures for emergencies
> - Disseminated lists of key contacts and information resources for emergencies

In many cases, risks are accepted or watched. Risk acceptance is usually done when the risk is judged too low for formal mitigation or when there appears to be no viable way to reduce the risk. If a risk is accepted, the rationale for this decision should be documented. Risks are watched when there is an objectively defined, verifiable, and documented threshold (e.g., for cost, schedule, performance, risk exposure) that will trigger risk mitigation planning or invoke a contingency plan.

Refer to the Decision Analysis and Resolution process area for more information about evaluating alternatives and selecting solutions.

Thresholds for supplier risks that affect the project (e.g., schedule, quality, risk exposure due to supplier risks) are specified in the supplier agreement along with escalation procedures if thresholds are exceeded.

HINT

You can establish thresholds for different attributes (e.g., cost, schedule, and performance) and trigger different activities (e.g., contingency plan deployment and risk mitigation planning).

Adequate consideration should be given early to technology demonstrations, models, simulations, pilots, and prototypes as part of risk mitigation planning.

Example Work Products

1. Documented handling options for each identified risk
2. Risk mitigation plans
3. Contingency plans
4. List of those who are responsible for tracking and addressing each risk
5. Disaster recovery or continuity plans

Example Supplier Deliverables

1. Documented handling options for each identified risk
2. Risk mitigation plans
3. Contingency plans
4. List of those who are responsible for tracking and addressing each risk
5. Disaster recovery or continuity plans

Subpractices

1. Determine the levels and thresholds that define when a risk becomes unacceptable and triggers the execution of a risk mitigation plan or contingency plan.

    Risk level (derived using a risk model) is a measure combining the uncertainty of reaching an objective with the consequences of failing to reach the objective.

    Risk levels and thresholds that bound planned or acceptable cost, schedule, or performance should be clearly understood and defined to provide a means with which risk can be understood. Proper categorization of risk is essential for ensuring an appropriate priority based on severity and the associated management response. There can be multiple thresholds employed to initiate varying levels of management response. Typically, thresholds for the execution of risk mitigation plans are set to engage before the execution of contingency plans.

2. Identify the person or group responsible for addressing each risk.
3. Determine the costs and benefits of implementing the risk mitigation plan for each risk.

    Risk mitigation activities should be examined for benefits they provide versus resources they will expend. Just like any other design activity, alternative plans may need to be developed and costs and benefits of each alternative assessed. The most appropriate plan is selected for implementation.

4. Develop an overall risk mitigation plan for the project to orchestrate the implementation of individual risk mitigation and contingency plans.

    The complete set of risk mitigation plans may not be affordable. A tradeoff analysis should be performed to prioritize risk mitigation plans for implementation.

5. Develop contingency plans for selected critical risks in the event their impacts are realized.

    Risk mitigation plans are developed and implemented as needed to proactively reduce risks before they become problems. Despite best efforts, some risks can be unavoidable and will become problems that

TIP

Thresholds trigger actions that may affect the work of personnel and relevant stakeholders. The motivation for particular thresholds and the actions they invoke should be well understood by all who will be affected by those events.

TIP

Assigning responsibility for risk mitigation becomes easier when mitigation activities and responsibilities are documented in a plan, such as the project plan.

TIP

Alternative risk mitigation plans may be formally evaluated (using DAR) to choose the best one. Relevant stakeholders may play an important role in such an evaluation (particularly for risks that affect them).

HINT

If you integrate all risk mitigation plans and find that the result is not affordable, trim the list using the priorities assigned in SP 2.2 or reprioritize them using a group-consensus approach (e.g., multivoting within risk categories).

RSKM

affect the project. Contingency plans can be developed for critical risks to describe actions a project can take to deal with the occurrence of this impact. The intent is to define a proactive plan for handling the risk. Either the risk is reduced (mitigation) or addressed (contingency). In either event, the risk is managed.

Some risk management literature may consider contingency plans a synonym or subset of risk mitigation plans. These plans also can be addressed together as risk handling or risk action plans.

SP 3.2 IMPLEMENT RISK MITIGATION PLANS

Monitor the status of each risk periodically and implement the risk mitigation plan as appropriate.

To effectively control and manage risks during the work effort, follow a proactive program to regularly monitor risks and the status and results of risk handling actions. The risk management strategy defines the intervals at which risk status should be revisited. This activity can result in the discovery of new risks or new risk handling options that can require replanning and reassessment. In either event, acceptability thresholds associated with the risk should be compared to the risk status to determine the need for implementing a risk mitigation plan.

The acquirer shares selected risks with the supplier. Risks associated with the acquisition process are tracked and resolved or controlled until mitigated. This monitoring includes risks that can be escalated by the supplier.

Example Work Products

1. Updated lists of risk status
2. Updated assessments of risk likelihood, consequence, and thresholds
3. Updated list of risk handling options
4. Updated list of actions taken to handle risks
5. Risk mitigation plans of risk handling options

Example Supplier Deliverables

1. Updated list of risk status
2. Updated assessments of risk likelihood, consequence, and thresholds
3. Updated list of risk handling options
4. Updated list of actions taken to handle risks
5. Risk mitigation plans

HINT

Monitor both the mitigation activity and the risk itself. Don't assume the risk is mitigated simply because the mitigation plan is executed: Unintended consequences or additional complexity may cause the risk exposure to increase when you expect it to decrease.

TIP

Weekly or monthly updates to risk status are typical.

TIP

Incorporating risk mitigation plans into the project plan enables their status to be assessed periodically as part of the project's regular progress reviews.

Subpractices

1. Monitor risk status.

   After a risk mitigation plan is initiated, the risk is still monitored. Thresholds are assessed to check for the potential execution of a contingency plan.

   A mechanism for monitoring should be employed.

2. Provide a method for tracking open risk handling action items to closure.

   Refer to the Project Monitoring and Control process area for more information about managing corrective action to closure.

3. Invoke selected risk handling options when monitored risks exceed defined thresholds.

   Often, risk handling is only performed for risks judged to be *high* and *medium*. The risk handling strategy for a given risk can include techniques and methods to avoid, reduce, and control the likelihood of the risk or the extent of damage incurred should the risk occur, or both. In this context, risk handling includes both risk mitigation plans and contingency plans.

   Risk handling techniques are developed to avoid, reduce, and control adverse impact to project objectives and to bring about acceptable outcomes in light of probable impacts. Actions generated to handle a risk require proper resource loading and scheduling in plans and baseline schedules. This replanning should closely consider the effects on adjacent or dependent work initiatives or activities.

4. Establish a schedule or period of performance for each risk handling activity that includes a start date and anticipated completion date.

5. Provide a continued commitment of resources for each plan to allow the successful execution of risk handling activities.

6. Collect performance measures on risk handling activities.

> **TIP**
>
> To ensure that risk mitigation activities are performed properly, they must be planned, scheduled, and resourced, just like any other project activity.

RSKM

SOLICITATION AND SUPPLIER AGREEMENT DEVELOPMENT
A Project Management Process Area at Maturity Level 2

Purpose

The purpose of Solicitation and Supplier Agreement Development (SSAD) is to prepare a solicitation package, select one or more suppliers to deliver the product or service, and establish and maintain the supplier agreement.

Introductory Notes

The Solicitation and Supplier Agreement Development process area provides a set of practices that enables the acquirer to initialize and formalize a relationship with the supplier for the successful execution of the project. A supplier agreement is an agreement between the acquirer and supplier. This agreement can be a contract, license, or memorandum of agreement. The acquired product or service is delivered to the acquirer from the supplier according to the supplier agreement.

A supplier agreement created using these practices enables the acquirer to monitor and control supplier activities using other processes, such as the Project Monitoring and Control and Agreement Management processes.

The activities described in Solicitation and Supplier Agreement Development apply equally to initial supplier agreements and to subsequent change orders, task orders, or amendments related to those agreements.

The acquirer is responsible for establishing and maintaining ground rules for communicating with the supplier, documenting decisions, and resolving conflict through the life of the agreement. The acquirer facilitates these activities with relevant stakeholders. Roles and responsibilities of relevant stakeholders during the interaction with suppliers are defined, coordinated, and adhered to.

HINT

SSAD helps you prevent problems such as suppliers that fail to meet requirements, supplier agreements that prevent a proactive approach to supplier management, and suppliers that provide poor visibility into their activities.

X-REF

The entry point for SSAD is normally PP SP 1.1, once the acquisition strategy is established.

TIP

Maturing the approach to SSAD ensures that agreements can be reached more quickly. Uniform selection approaches and standardized agreements benefit both the acquisition organization and its suppliers. Effective emphasis on SSAD ensures that AM processes flow more easily.

HINT

Taking a broad view when applying SSAD can help reduce business-critical risks in obtaining products and services from suppliers.

SSAD

The specific goals and specific practices of this process area build on each other. The Prepare for Solicitation and Supplier Agreement Development specific goal and its associated specific practices identify potential suppliers and develop and distribute the solicitation package, including evaluation criteria and the statement of work. The solicitation package is developed using work products from other processes (e.g., requirements and design constraints from Acquisition Requirements Development processes, supplier project and technical measures and objectives from Project Planning and Measurement and Analysis processes).

The Select Suppliers specific goal and its associated specific practices use work products from the preparation of the solicitation to solicit responses from potential suppliers, evaluate these responses, negotiate with potential suppliers, and select a supplier who can best deliver. Subsequently, the Establish Supplier Agreements specific goal and its associated specific practices are used to establish and maintain the supplier agreement. In turn, data provided by the supplier and documented in the supplier agreement (e.g., cost, schedule, risks) are used by Project Planning processes to update the project plan.

This process area contains many lists of examples to include in work products. As in other process areas, these lists are not all-inclusive and the acquirer should rely on other related lists when building work products. Considerations for supplier agreement content are described throughout the process areas.

Although this process area describes acquisition practices for a project, an acquirer would use the same practices in establishing a supplier agreement for multiple projects. The requirements included in the solicitation package and the supplier agreement would reflect a broader scope, and the evaluation and selection process would require an appropriate level of review before a selection is made.

> **TIP**
>
> In some cases, agreements with the customer may also be necessary—particularly when the customer organization is significantly different from the acquisition organization. If a customer agreement is useful, the practices in SSAD can be tailored to facilitate the creation of these agreements as well. The acquirer, in these cases, may be viewed as the supplier to the ultimate customer.

Related Process Areas

Refer to the Agreement Management process area for more information about ensuring that the supplier and the acquirer perform according to the terms of the supplier agreement.

Refer to the Acquisition Requirements Development process area for more information about developing and analyzing customer and contractual requirements.

Refer to the Decision Analysis and Resolution process area for more information about analyzing possible decisions using a formal evaluation process that evaluates identified alternatives against established criteria.

Refer to the Measurement and Analysis process area for more information about aligning measurement and analysis activities.

Refer to the Project Planning process area for more information about establishing estimates, developing a project plan, and obtaining commitment to the plan.

Refer to the Requirements Management process area for more information about managing requirements of the project's products and product components and identifying inconsistencies between those requirements and the project's plans and work products.

Specific Goal and Practice Summary

SG 1 Prepare for Solicitation and Supplier Agreement Development
   SP 1.1   Identify Potential Suppliers
   SP 1.2   Establish a Solicitation Package
   SP 1.3   Review the Solicitation Package
   SP 1.4   Distribute and Maintain the Solicitation Package
SG 2 Select Suppliers
   SP 2.1   Evaluate Proposed Solutions
   SP 2.2   Establish Negotiation Plans
   SP 2.3   Select Suppliers
SG 3 Establish Supplier Agreements
   SP 3.1   Establish an Understanding of the Agreement
   SP 3.2   Establish the Supplier Agreement

Specific Practices by Goal

SG 1 PREPARE FOR SOLICITATION AND SUPPLIER AGREEMENT DEVELOPMENT

Preparation for solicitation and supplier agreement development is performed.

SP 1.1 IDENTIFY POTENTIAL SUPPLIERS

Identify and qualify potential suppliers.

Consistent with internal organizational policy, the acquisition strategy, and project scope and requirements, the acquirer identifies potential suppliers to receive the solicitation. The acquirer can identify suppliers from a variety of sources (e.g., staff, international seminars, market analysis reports, pre-established schedules).

In some organizations, acquirers may solicit proposals from a limited number of suppliers to reduce their cost and efforts for the solicitation. Acquirers should, however, ensure that they include suppliers who are capable of meeting the requirements and that a sufficient number of suppliers are included to provide a competitive environment. This competition enhances the leverage of the acquirer in achieving its objectives (e.g., providing different approaches to meeting requirements). In some

SSAD

TIP

Preferred supplier lists may exist within the organization that reduce the scope of the needed selection activities and the risks associated with unknown suppliers.

X-REF

The use of preferred suppliers is discussed further in "An Industry Perspective on CMMI-ACQ" in Chapter 6.

cases, the organization prequalifies preferred suppliers from which an acquirer can choose provided the preferred suppliers meet the specific needs of the project. Choosing from preferred suppliers can greatly reduce the effort and time required for solicitation.

Depending on applicable regulations and project characteristics, the acquirer can determine to pursue a sole-source acquisition rather than a competitive bid. Acquirers should document the rationale for determining potential suppliers, particularly in the case of sole-source selection.

Example Work Products

1. List of potential suppliers prepared to respond to the solicitation

Subpractices

1. Develop a list of potential suppliers.

   To develop a list of potential suppliers, the acquirer considers which suppliers have experience with similar systems or projects, the performance the acquirer has experienced with suppliers on previous projects, which suppliers are likely to provide the capabilities needed for the project, and the availability of critical resources to staff and support the project. In addition to assessing supplier capabilities, a risk assessment is prepared on the suppliers' financial capabilities (e.g., credit worthiness, financial stability, and access to capital and the impact to the supplier of a successful bid).

2. Communicate with potential suppliers concerning the forthcoming solicitation.

   The acquirer contacts suppliers to outline plans for the solicitation, including the projected schedule for releasing the solicitation package and expected dates for responses from suppliers. If a supplier expresses interest in responding to the solicitation, the appropriate confidentiality agreements are put in place.

Typical communication to candidate suppliers includes the following:
- Anticipated scope of the solicitation
- Schedule for release of the solicitation package
- Overall project schedule
- Approach and procedures to be used throughout the solicitation process
- High-level criteria for evaluating proposal responses
- Required supplier qualifications
- Schedule for the return of proposals
- Date when the supplier must indicate if it will or will not participate in the solicitation

---

3. Verify participants who will evaluate supplier proposals.

4. Verify participants in supplier negotiations.

SP 1.2 ESTABLISH A SOLICITATION PACKAGE

Establish and maintain a solicitation package that includes the requirements and proposal evaluation criteria.

Solicitation packages are used to seek proposals from potential suppliers. The acquirer structures the solicitation package to facilitate an accurate and complete response from each potential supplier and to enable an effective comparison and evaluation of proposals.

The solicitation package includes a description of the desired form of the response, the relevant statement of work for the supplier, and required provisions in the supplier agreement (e.g., a copy of the standard supplier agreement or non-disclosure provisions). In government acquisitions, some or all of the content and structure of the solicitation package can be defined by regulation.

The solicitation package typically contains the following:

- The statement of work for the supplier, including supplier process, product, and service level measures
- Guidance on how potential suppliers are to respond to the solicitation package
- A description of the evaluation process and criteria to be used to evaluate proposals
- Documentation requirements to submit with the response (e.g., project plans)
- The schedule for completing the solicitation process
- Procedures for addressing questions and contacts

The solicitation package is rigorous enough to ensure consistent and comparable responses but flexible enough to allow consideration of supplier suggestions for better ways to satisfy requirements. The acquirer can invite suppliers to submit a proposal that is wholly responsive to the request for proposal and to provide a proposed alternative solution in a separate proposal.

The complexity and level of detail of the solicitation package should be consistent with the value of, and risk associated with, the planned acquisition. In some cases, the solicitation may not include detailed requirements (e.g., it may be a solicitation for development of detailed requirements or it may include a statement of objectives to provide the supplier greater flexibility in addressing the scope of the project).

SSAD

Proposal and supplier evaluation criteria are identified and documented.

Example Work Products

1. Solicitation package
2. Supplier and proposal evaluation criteria

Subpractices

1. Develop the statement of work for the supplier.

The statement of work for the supplier defines, for those items being acquired, the portion of the project scope that is included in the related supplier agreement. The statement of work for a supplier is developed from the project scope, the work breakdown structure, and the task dictionary.

The statement of work for the supplier is written to be clear, complete, and concise. It describes the acquired product or service in sufficient detail to allow prospective suppliers to determine if they are capable of providing the product or service.

Example content in the statement of work for the supplier includes the following:

- Project objectives
- Requirements (including period of performance; milestones; work location; legal, statutory, and regulatory requirements; delivery format; quantities; content requirements)
- Design constraints
- Deliverables and rights (e.g., work breakdown structure of the supplier's work, detailed design, test results)
- An overview of the project with sufficient information for the supplier to understand the project environment and risks
- Expectations of the supplier's transition of the product to operations and support
- Expectations for process, product, and service level measures and reports that provide the acquirer visibility into supplier progress and performance
- Collateral services required (e.g. study reports, development of training materials, delivery of training to end users)
- Acquirer specified standard processes for the project (e.g., configuration management, issue escalation and resolution, corrective action for nonconformances, change management)
- The type of reviews to be conducted with the supplier and other communication processes and procedures

Continues

Continued

- Product acceptance criteria and required supplier involvement in the acquirer's validation and acceptance activities
- Post-project support

The statement of work for the supplier can be revised and refined as it moves through the solicitation, negotiation, and supplier agreement development processes until it is incorporated into a signed supplier agreement. For example, a prospective supplier can suggest a more efficient approach or a less costly product than what was originally specified.

2. Specify the process, product, and service level measures for acceptance.

The measures specify customer expectations and threshold values and are used to monitor the supplier and gauge the supplier's adherence to requirements.

Service levels are an indicator of service delivery performance relative to an agreed-on service level measure. Service levels are designed to support the acquisition strategy. (See the definitions of "service level" and "measure" in the glossary.)

3. Develop supplier evaluation and proposal evaluation criteria.

Evaluation criteria are developed and used to rate or score proposals. Evaluation criteria are included in the solicitation package. Evaluation criteria can be limited to purchase price if the acquisition item is readily available from a number of acceptable suppliers. Purchase price in this context includes both the cost of the item and ancillary expenses such as delivery. Other selection criteria can be identified and documented to support an evaluation of a more complex product or service (e.g., the individuals identified in the Project Planning resource plan develop and document criteria for evaluating potential suppliers and their proposals).

> **TIP**
>
> The criteria used to select a supplier depend on the project, its requirements, and other factors. If you enter "supplier selection criteria" into your favorite search engine, you will be amazed by both the commonality and the variety of supplier selection criteria used in different industries.

> **TIP**
>
> Risks are typically included as criteria in a formal evaluation.

Examples of areas used to evaluate a potential supplier's ability and proposal include the following:

- Compliance to stated requirements contained in the solicitation package
- Experience with similar products or services (e.g., data on most recent similar projects with the associated cost, schedule, and performance and the degree to which requirements were fulfilled)
- Familiarity with acquirer processes, the technical environment, and the core business
- Total ownership and lifecycle costs
- Technical capability (e.g., expected compliance to functional and quality attribute requirements, criteria given the architecture and technical solution proposed)

Continues

SSAD

Continued

- Management, development, and delivery processes and procedures
- Proposed technical methodologies, techniques, solutions, and services
- Financial capability
- Production capacity and interest (e.g., staff available to perform the effort, available facilities, other available resources)
- Business size and type
- Intellectual property and proprietary rights

4. Document the proposal content that suppliers must submit with their response.

Examples of proposal content required for suppliers to submit include the following:

- Compliance with requirements
- References, company overview, and case studies
- Evidence of the supplier's organizational processes on which supplier processes for the project will be based and the commitment to execute those processes from project inception
- Plan describing how the supplier will carry out the scope and content of the solicitation package, including any improvements of execution capability over the duration of the supplier agreement
- Understanding of the size and complexity of the requested work based on requirements
- The pricing and compensation methodology that enables calculation of charges for the services being provided to the acquirer pursuant to supplier agreement terms and conditions, including taxes, credits, foreign currency translation, licenses, pass-through costs, and travel reimbursements
- Pricing and compensation schedules that provide for charges for the products and services provided, including frequency, term, and pricing type (e.g., fixed price, lump sum, time and materials) as well as rate cards, and a skills matrix
- Compliance with acquirer travel reimbursement policies
- References and experience validating the capability of the supplier's proposed approach to meet proposed funding, schedule, and quality targets
- Risk management plan describing how the supplier will periodically manage risks throughout the life of the project and how risks documented in the solicitation package will be managed
- Methods for early defect identification and the prevention of defects in delivered products
- The supplier's approach to assuring the quality of the product
- Approach to the escalation and resolution of issues

Continues

Continued

- Description of the supplier's proposed use of COTS products and rationale for the supplier's confidence that COTS products can achieve the requirements
- Description of the supplier's proposed reuse of previously developed hardware and software, rationale for the supplier's confidence that re-use can be achieved, and associated information about data rights
- Approach to providing visibility of development progress and costs at a level appropriate for the type of agreement and commensurate with the degree of risk
- Retention of critical staff during the project
- Identification of work to be performed by subcontractors

5. Incorporate the acquirer's (standard) supplier agreement, terms and conditions, and additional information into the solicitation package.

Supplier agreement terms and conditions typically include the following:
- Recitals
- Deliverables and rights
- Compensation and payments
- Confidentiality
- Privacy statements
- Continuous improvement and best practices
- Exclusive services, key staff, supplier staff at acquirer sites
- Information gathering practices and ethical representation
- Force majeure
- Term
- Termination for insolvency, breach, or non-performance
- Termination for convenience
- Termination assistance
- Indemnification
- Insurance
- Right to audit
- Notices

Typical considerations for additional instructions and general information to help the supplier when responding to the solicitation package include the following:
- Submission of intent to submit proposal
- Submission due date, time, and destination

Continues

Continued

- Number of proposal copies that must be submitted
- Proposal format
- Non-complying proposals
- Proposal ownership
- Bidder inquiries
- Key dates and activities
- Discretionary selection and potential modifications of the solicitation process
- No implied offer
- Response constitutes an offer to do business
- Confidentiality of information
- Publicity
- Use of subcontractors
- Due diligence
- Incurred costs
- Language requirements
- Statutory units
- Warranty provisions
- Licensing provisions

SP 1.3 *REVIEW THE SOLICITATION PACKAGE*

Review the solicitation package with relevant stakeholders to obtain commitment to the approach.

The solicitation package is reviewed with stakeholders to ensure requirements have been accurately and sufficiently stated so that the solicitation can lead to a manageable agreement. The acquirer establishes traceability between requirements and the solicitation package. Suppliers can be included as stakeholders in the review of the solicitation package. The acquirer wants the solicitation package to attract a variety of responses and encourage competition. The acquirer also wants the solicitation package to be legally inclusive of all qualified suppliers.

Refer to the Perform Peer Reviews specific goal in the Acquisition Verification process area for more information about conducting peer reviews.

The acquirer can use standard templates and checklists to verify that the necessary components (e.g., skills, standards, verification and validation methods, measures, acceptance criteria) are covered in the solicitation package.

Refer to the Organizational Process Definition process area for more information about establishing organizational process assets.

The independent cost and schedule estimates for the supplier's project work are reviewed.

Example Work Products

1. Record of the reviews of the solicitation package

SP 1.4 DISTRIBUTE AND MAINTAIN THE SOLICITATION PACKAGE

Distribute the solicitation package to potential suppliers for their response and maintain the package throughout the solicitation.

The solicitation package is distributed to potential suppliers in accordance with approved acquirer solicitation policies and procedures.

Refer to the Project Monitoring and Control process area for more information about monitoring the project against the plan.

Refer to the Project Planning process area for more information about establishing and maintaining plans that define project activities.

Example Work Products

1. Responses to supplier questions
2. Amendments to the solicitation package

Example Supplier Deliverables

1. Supplier proposals
2. Supplier questions and requests for clarification

Subpractices

1. Finalize a list of potential suppliers.
2. Distribute the solicitation package to potential suppliers.
3. Document and respond to supplier questions according to the instructions in the solicitation package.
   Verify that all potential suppliers have equal access and opportunity to provide feedback on the solicitation package. Provide the opportunity for selected potential suppliers and stakeholders to clarify points of ambiguity in requirements as well as disconnects or concerns with requirements.
4. Acknowledge the receipt of supplier proposals according to the schedule identified in the solicitation package.
5. Verify conformance to requirements and completeness of supplier responses.

The suppliers should be contacted for corrective action if the response is non-conforming or incomplete.

6. Issue amendments to the solicitation package when changes are made to the solicitation.

SG 2 SELECT SUPPLIERS

Suppliers are selected using a formal evaluation.

Suppliers are selected according to approved acquirer selection policies and procedures.

Refer to the Decision Analysis and Resolution process area for more information about analyzing possible decisions using a formal evaluation process that evaluates identified alternatives against established criteria.

SP 2.1 EVALUATE PROPOSED SOLUTIONS

Evaluate proposed solutions according to documented proposal evaluation criteria.

Proposals submitted in response to solicitation packages are evaluated in accordance with an overall established timeline, preliminary project plans, and proposal evaluation criteria. Proposal evaluation criteria are used to evaluate potential supplier responses to the solicitation. Evaluation results and decision-making notes (e.g., advantages and disadvantages of potential suppliers, scoring against criteria) should be documented and maintained.

For task orders or changes in the terms of an existing supplier agreement, the acquirer uses documented evaluation criteria to evaluate task order responses or proposed changes to terms of the agreement. In a sole-source or change order environment, this practice is critical to enable relevant stakeholder understanding of the intent of the effort or changes before placing additional work against the supplier agreement.

Example Work Products

1. Clarification correspondence between the acquirer and potential suppliers
2. Evaluation results and rationale
3. List of candidate suppliers

Example Supplier Deliverables

1. Proposal revisions based on clarifications

X-REF

If a supplier is using CMMI-DEV, supplier capability evaluations can be aided by the types of activities outlined in the technical report "Understanding and Leveraging a Supplier's CMMI Efforts: A Guidebook for Acquirers" (CMU/SEI-2007-TR-004).

X-REF

Capability evaluation methods associated with CMMI include the SCAMPI B and C appraisal methods. See www.sei.cmu.edu/cmmi/tools/appraisals/index.cfm for more information.

TIP

Some organizations hire a cadre of supplier selection personnel to facilitate these processes. Selection personnel are most effective when teamed with acquisition personnel who manage the agreement responsibly.

2. Supplier documentation of their approach to the project work, their capabilities, and a preliminary technical solution

Subpractices

1. Distribute supplier proposals to individuals identified by the acquirer to perform the evaluation.

2. Schedule an acquirer evaluation review of supplier proposals to consolidate questions, concerns, and issues.

3. Schedule supplier presentations.

4. Confirm the mutual understanding of the statement of work.

   A good practice is to compare the supplier's estimates to the estimates developed in project planning; this comparison provides a means to determine if there is a mutual understanding of requirements and the associated work to fulfill them.

5. Evaluate supplier proposals and document findings.

6. Execute due diligence.

   Due diligence provides an opportunity for the acquirer to further clarify requirements, particularly the ones related to the acquirer's existing environment and products in use. Potential suppliers ask questions and gain understanding, which enables them to make realistic proposals. It also enables the acquirer to gain insight into the capability of the potential suppliers' proposed solutions to meet requirements.

   Due diligence helps to eliminate assumptions and replace them with facts, to identify and document risks and their mitigation plans or effect on the agreement, and to list issues and dependencies between the acquirer and supplier to include in the agreement.

   > Examples of typical due diligence activities include the following:
   > - Reviews of requirements with the current supplier or acquirer resources maintaining the products or providing the services
   > - Reviews of interfaces of a system with other systems maintained by the acquirer
   > - Reviews and validations of supplier references
   > - Reviews of the operating environment's facilities and capabilities
   > - Reviews of regulatory and security requirements
   > - Reviews of supplier capabilities

7. Document candidate supplier recommendations based on the proposal evaluation.

SP 2.2 ESTABLISH NEGOTIATION PLANS

Establish and maintain negotiation plans to use in completing a supplier agreement.

The acquirer develops and refines a negotiation plan for each of the candidate suppliers based on the evaluation of the suppliers and their proposals.

The proposal evaluation and negotiations with suppliers provide the basis for selecting the supplier best able to meet the requirements of the solicitation.

The size of a negotiation team depends on the size and complexity of the project. Typically, the team is led by acquirer management and includes individuals who have detailed knowledge of the statement of work documented in the solicitation package. The negotiation team is typically supported by a legal staff, a financial analyst, purchasing, and the project manager.

Negotiations between acquirers and suppliers can be restricted by regulation. Review all regulations affecting negotiations before entering into them with a supplier.

X-REF

Establishing (and revising) an agreement often requires *negotiation skills. See Getting to Yes: Negotiating Agreement Without Giving In*, revised second edition, by William Ury, Roger Fisher, and Bruce Patton (Penguin USA).

Examples of items included in a negotiation plan include the following:
- Roles and responsibilities of negotiation team members
- Key issues to be negotiated from supplier responses
- Negotiation "levers" and where and when they should be used
- The sequence of events to negotiate issues
- Fall-back or compromise positions as necessary on given issues (possible concessions and trades)
- List of items that are non-negotiable
- External factors that could influence negotiations (e.g., other pending deals and strategic plans)
- Prior experiences with supplier agreements to discover previous positions and issues (and negotiating styles)
- Schedule and sequence of supplier negotiation meetings
- Objectives for each negotiating session
- Risks, consequences, and mitigation alternatives

Example Work Products

1. Negotiation plan for each candidate supplier

SP 2.3 SELECT SUPPLIERS

Select suppliers based on an evaluation of their ability to meet specified requirements and established criteria.

Proposal evaluation results are used to finalize a supplier selection based on the outcome of negotiations or responses to acquirer questions provided by potential suppliers. Negotiations enable the acquirer to select the best supplier for the project. In some cases, the acquirer can take the top two proposals and use negotiations to make the final selection decision.

Evaluation results and negotiation results support the selection decision or cause the acquirer to take other action as appropriate. If the return on investment is not sufficient, the acquirer can decide to defer or cancel the project.

Example Work Products

1. Revisions due to negotiations
2. Supplier selection decision
3. Evaluation reports

Subpractices

1. Evaluate supplier proposals.

   The evaluation of supplier proposals includes an evaluation of past performance. The acquirer's evaluation of past supplier performance is carried out primarily to document the supplier's competency relative to performing similar work on the project or other projects.

2. Negotiate with suppliers to determine the best fit for the project.

   Negotiate with the selected supplier or candidate suppliers to resolve issues identified during due diligence and to address remaining issues with requirements. Revise requirements to be fulfilled by the supplier as appropriate.

3. Select a supplier to be awarded the supplier agreement.

   Refer to the Decision Analysis and Resolution process area for more information about analyzing possible decisions using a formal evaluation process that evaluates identified alternatives against established criteria.

4. Document the selection.

SG 3 ESTABLISH SUPPLIER AGREEMENTS

Supplier agreements are established and maintained.

A supplier agreement is established and maintained based on the supplier selection decision.

SP 3.1 ESTABLISH AN UNDERSTANDING OF THE AGREEMENT

Establish and maintain a mutual understanding of the agreement with selected suppliers and end users based on acquisition needs and the suppliers' proposed approaches.

HINT

Strongly consider using DAR when evaluating potential suppliers. These subpractices describe some of what is involved in such an evaluation.

HINT

Select a capable supplier that can meet your requirements with a quality product that is delivered on time and within budget.

TIP

A proactive approach provides benefits such as addressing the capability gap of the organization uniformly, reducing the time that projects take to select suppliers, establishing a more efficient umbrella agreement with a preferred supplier, and protecting core competencies.

SSAD

To assist in establishing a mutual understanding of the agreement, the acquirer should review requirements of the agreement with the supplier and end user. Because points of clarification and ambiguities can arise after award of the supplier agreement, the acquirer should work with the supplier and end user to ensure that a mutual understanding is maintained through the life of the project (e.g., supplier workshops, executive meetings).

Example Work Products

1. Correspondence clarifying elements of the agreement
2. Frequently asked questions (for use with end users and other suppliers)

SP 3.2 ESTABLISH THE SUPPLIER AGREEMENT

Establish and maintain the supplier agreement.

The agreement can be either a stand-alone agreement or part of a master agreement. When part of a master agreement, the project agreement can be an addendum, work order, or service request to the master agreement.

Example Work Products

1. Supplier agreement (including terms and conditions)

Subpractices

1. Establish the supplier agreement.

> Supplier agreement provisions typically include the following:
> - The statement of work, specification, terms and conditions, list of deliverables, schedule, budget, and acceptance process
> - Product acceptance criteria to be satisfied by the supplier
> - Mechanisms and deliverables that provide sufficient data to allow the acquirer to evaluate and analyze acquired products
> - Which acquirer and supplier representatives are responsible and authorized to make changes to the supplier agreement
> - How requirements changes and changes to the supplier agreement are determined, communicated, and addressed
> - Standards and procedures to be followed (e.g., configuration management, escalation, nonconformances, conflicts, issues)
> - Requirements for the supplier to establish a corrective action system that includes a change control process for rework and reevaluation
> - Critical dependencies between the acquirer and supplier
>
> *Continues*

HINT

If it's not documented in the supplier agreement, don't count on it happening! Renegotiating an agreement can be expensive, so make sure the initial agreement covers everything that is important to you for managing the supplier and receiving the product that you are expecting.

HINT

The supplier agreement should be documented in a form suitable to the nature of the business transaction. The supplier agreement is the basis for monitoring your supplier and accepting the product—so make sure it covers all critical information.

Continued

- Documentation of what the acquirer will provide to the supplier (e.g., facilities, tools, software, documentation, services)
- Analysis methods and acceptance criteria for designated supplier deliverables
- The types of reviews to be conducted with the supplier
- The supplier's responsibilities to execute corrective actions when initiated by project monitoring and control processes
- Non-hire and non-compete clauses
- Confidentiality, non-disclosure, and intellectual capital clauses pertaining to process and product quality assurance, measurement data, and staff who would perform audits or are authorized to validate measurement data
- The supplier's responsibilities for preparing the site and training the support and operations organizations according to acquirer specified standards, tools, and methods
- The supplier's responsibilities for ongoing maintenance and support of acquired products and their role as a stakeholder
- Requirements for the supplier to maintain bi-directional traceability to requirements provided in the supplier agreement
- Requirements for the supplier to be involved in deployment as necessary
- Warranty, ownership, usage, and data rights for acquired products
- Schedule for supplier compensation
- Security and legal penalty recoveries
- Dispute resolution procedures

2. Verify that all parties to the agreement understand and agree to all requirements by signing the supplier agreement.

    The acquirer should ensure that the supplier makes a commitment in the agreement to execute its proposed processes.

3. Notify the suppliers not selected for the award.

4. Communicate the supplier agreement in the organization as required.

5. Maintain the supplier agreement as required.

    After establishment of the supplier agreement, the acquirer can find requirements that are no longer optimal or applicable based on the supplier's progress or environment changes. Examples include the availability of new technology, overly burdensome documentation, and reporting requirements. Changes to supplier agreements can also occur when the supplier's processes or products fail to meet agreed-to criteria. The supplier agreement and project documents should be revised to reflect changes in conditions as appropriate. This includes updating cost, schedule, and budget documents as needed.

TIP

The acquirer must engage the supplier in reviews, monitoring, and evaluations to a depth and breadth appropriate to the circumstances and risks. The supplier agreement must cover the details of these reviews.

X-REF

The project's progress and milestone reviews are covered in PMC SPs 1.6 and 1.7. Management reviews of the supplier are covered in AM SP 1.1, and technical reviews of the supplier's technical solutions are covered in ATM SP 1.3.

SSAD

TIP

Especially with long-term agreements (i.e., a duration of more than one year), technical and nontechnical requirements may change. It is necessary to document these changes in the supplier agreement because it is often the legal document that will make these significant changes binding.

All changes are formally documented and approved by both the acquirer and supplier before being implemented by this specific practice. Approved change requests can include modifications to terms and conditions of the supplier agreement, including the statement of work, pricing, and the descriptions of products, services, or results to be acquired.

Refer to the Configuration Management process area for more information about tracking and controlling changes.

6. Ensure that all records related to the supplier agreement are stored, managed, and controlled for future use.

PART THREE

The Appendices

APPENDIX A

REFERENCES

Ahern 2005   Ahern, Dennis M.; Armstrong, Jim; Clouse, Aaron; Ferguson, Jack R.; Hayes, Will; & Nidiffer, Kenneth E. *CMMI SCAMPI Distilled: Appraisals for Process Improvement.* Boston: Addison-Wesley, 2005.

Ahern 2008   Ahern, Dennis M.; Clouse, Aaron; & Turner, Richard. *CMMI Distilled: A Practical Introduction to Integrated Process Improvement, 3rd Edition.* Boston: Addison-Wesley, 2008.

Beck 2001   Beck, Kent; et al. Manifesto for Agile Software Development. 2001. http://agilemanifesto.org/.

Chrissis 2011   Chrissis, Mary Beth; Konrad, Mike; & Shrum, Sandy. *CMMI: Guidelines for Process Integration and Product Improvement, 3rd Edition.* Boston: Addison-Wesley, 2011.

Crosby 1979   Crosby, Philip B. *Quality Is Free: The Art of Making Quality Certain.* New York: McGraw-Hill, 1979.

Curtis 2009   Curtis, Bill; Hefley, William E.; & Miller, Sally A. *The People CMM: A Framework for Human Capital Management, 2nd Edition.* Boston: Addison-Wesley, 2009.

Deming 1986   Deming, W. Edwards. *Out of the Crisis.* Cambridge, MA: MIT Press, 1986.

Dodson 2006   Dodson, Kathryn M.; et al. *Adapting CMMI for Acquisition Organizations: A Preliminary Report* (CMU/SEI-2006-SR-005, ADA453524). Pittsburgh: Software Engineering Institute, Carnegie Mellon University, June 2006. www.sei.cmu.edu/library/abstracts/reports/06sr005.cfm.

EIA 2002a   Electronic Industries Alliance. *Systems Engineering Capability Model* (EIA/IS-731.1). Washington, DC, 2002.

EIA 2002b   Government Electronics and Information Technology Alliance. *Earned Value Management Systems* (ANSI/EIA-748). New York, 2002. http://webstore.ansi.org/RecordDetail.aspx?sku=ANSI%2FEIA-748-B.

EIA 2003   Electronic Industries Alliance. *EIA Interim Standard: Systems Engineering* (EIA/IS-632). Washington, DC, 2003.

Forrester 2011   Forrester, Eileen; Buteau, Brandon; & Shrum, Sandy. *CMMI for Services: Guidelines for Superior Service, 2nd Edition.* Boston: Addison-Wesley, 2011.

Gallagher 2011   Gallagher, Brian; Phillips, Mike; Richter, Karen; & Shrum, Sandy. *CMMI-ACQ: Guidelines for Improving the Acquisition of Products and Services, 2nd Edition.* Boston: Addison-Wesley, 2011.

GEIA 2004   Government Electronic Industries Alliance. *Data Management* (GEIA-859). Washington, DC, 2004. http://webstore.ansi.org/RecordDetail.aspx?sku=ANSI%2FGEIA+859-2009.

Gibson 2006   Gibson, Diane L.; Goldenson, Dennis R.; & Kost, Keith. *Performance Results of CMMI-Based Process Improvement* (CMU/SEI-2006-TR-004, ADA454687). Pittsburgh: Software Engineering Institute, Carnegie Mellon University, August 2006. www.sei.cmu.edu/library/abstracts/reports/06tr004.cfm.

Glazer 2008   Glazer, Hillel; Dalton, Jeff; Anderson, David; Konrad, Mike; & Shrum, Sandy. *CMMI or Agile: Why Not Embrace Both!* (CMU/SEI-2008-TN-003). Pittsburgh: Software Engineering Institute, Carnegie Mellon University, November 2008. www.sei.cmu.edu/library/abstracts/reports/08tn003.cfm.

Humphrey 1989   Humphrey, Watts S. *Managing the Software Process.* Boston: Addison-Wesley, 1989.

IEEE 1991   Institute of Electrical and Electronics Engineers. *IEEE Standard Computer Dictionary: A Compilation of IEEE Standard Computer Glossaries.* New York: IEEE, 1991.

ISO 2005a   International Organization for Standardization. *ISO 9000: International Standard.* 1987. www.iso.org/iso/iso_catalogue/catalogue_tc/catalogue_detail.htm?csnumber=42180.

ISO 2005b   International Organization for Standardization and International Electrotechnical Commission. *ISO/IEC 20000-1 Information Technology—Service Management, Part 1: Specification; ISO/IEC 20000-2 Information Technology—Service Management, Part 2: Code of Practice*, 2005. www.iso.org/iso/iso_catalogue/catalogue_tc/catalogue_tc_browse.htm?commid=45086.

ISO 2006a   International Organization for Standardization and International Electrotechnical Commission. *ISO/IEC 15504 Information Technology—Process Assessment Part 1: Concepts and Vocabulary, Part 2: Performing an Assessment, Part 3: Guidance on Performing an Assessment, Part 4: Guidance on Use for Process Improvement and Process Capability Determination, Part 5: An Exemplar Process Assessment Model*, 2003–2006. www.iso.org/iso/iso_catalogue/catalogue_tc/catalogue_tc_browse.htm?commid=45086.

ISO 2006b   International Organization for Standardization and International Electrotechnical Commission. *ISO/IEC 14764 Software Engineering—Software Life Cycle Processes—Maintenance,* 2006. www.iso.org/iso/iso_catalogue/catalogue_tc/catalogue_tc_browse. htm?commid=45086.

ISO 2007   International Organization for Standardization and International Electrotechnical Commission. *ISO/IEC 15939 Systems and Software Engineering—Measurement Process,* 2007. www.iso.org/iso/ iso_catalogue/catalogue_tc/catalogue_tc_browse. htm?commid=45086.

ISO 2008a   International Organization for Standardization and International Electrotechnical Commission. *ISO/IEC 12207 Systems and Software Engineering—Software Life Cycle Processes,* 2008. www.iso. org/iso/iso_catalogue/catalogue_tc/catalogue_tc_browse. htm?commid=45086.

ISO 2008b   International Organization for Standardization and International Electrotechnical Commission. *ISO/IEC 15288 Systems and Software Engineering—System Life Cycle Processes,* 2008. www.iso. org/iso/iso_catalogue/catalogue_tc/catalogue_tc_browse. htm?commid=45086.

ISO 2008c   International Organization for Standardization. *ISO 9001, Quality Management Systems—Requirements,* 2008. www.iso.org/iso/ iso_catalogue/catalogue_tc/catalogue_tc_browse.htm?commid=53896.

IT Governance 2005   IT Governance Institute. *CobiT 4.0.* Rolling Meadows, IL: IT Governance Institute, 2005. www.isaca.org/ Content/NavigationMenu/Members_and_Leaders/COBIT6/Obtain_ COBIT/Obtain_COBIT.htm.

Juran 1988   Juran, Joseph M. *Juran on Planning for Quality.* New York: Macmillan, 1988.

Lapham 2010   Lapham, Mary Ann; Williams, Ray C.; Hammons, Charles; Burton, Daniel; & Schenker, Fred. *Considerations for Using Agile in DoD Acquisition* (CMU/SEI-2010-TR-022). Pittsburgh: Software Engineering Institute, Carnegie Mellon University, April 2010. www.sei.cmu.edu/library/abstracts/reports/10tn002.cfm.

McFeeley 1996   McFeeley, Robert. *IDEAL: A User's Guide for Software Process Improvement* (CMU/SEI-96-HB-001, ADA305472). Pittsburgh: Software Engineering Institute, Carnegie Mellon University, February 1996. www.sei.cmu.edu/library/abstracts/reports/ 96hb001.cfm.

McGarry 2001   McGarry, John; Card, David; Jones, Cheryl; Layman, Beth; Clark, Elizabeth; Dean, Joseph; & Hall, Fred. *Practical Software Measurement: Objective Information for Decision Makers.* Boston: Addison-Wesley, 2001.

Richter 2008   Software Engineering Institute. *CMMI for Acquisition (CMMI-ACQ) Primer, Version 1.2* (CMU/SEI-2008-TR-010). Pittsburgh: Software Engineering Institute, Carnegie Mellon University, May 2008. www.sei.cmu.edu/library/abstracts/reports/08tr010.cfm.

Office of Government Commerce 2007a   Office of Government Commerce. *ITIL: Continual Service Improvement.* London: Office of Government Commerce, 2007.

Office of Government Commerce 2007b   Office of Government Commerce. *ITIL: Service Design.* London: Office of Government Commerce, 2007.

Office of Government Commerce 2007c   Office of Government Commerce. *ITIL: Service Operation.* London: Office of Government Commerce, 2007.

Office of Government Commerce 2007d   Office of Government Commerce. *ITIL: Service Strategy.* London: Office of Government Commerce, 2007.

Office of Government Commerce 2007e   Office of Government Commerce. *ITIL: Service Transition.* London: Office of Government Commerce, 2007.

SEI 1995   Software Engineering Institute. *The Capability Maturity Model: Guidelines for Improving the Software Process.* Reading, MA: Addison-Wesley, 1995.

SEI 2002   Software Engineering Institute. *Software Acquisition Capability Maturity Model (SA-CMM) Version 1.03* (CMU/SEI-2002-TR-010, ADA399794). Pittsburgh: Software Engineering Institute, Carnegie Mellon University, March 2002. www.sei.cmu.edu/library/abstracts/reports/02tr010.cfm.

SEI 2007a   CMMI Product Team. *CMMI for Acquisition, Version 1.2* (CMU/SEI-2007-TR-017). Pittsburgh: Software Engineering Institute, Carnegie Mellon University, November 2007. www.sei.cmu.edu/library/abstracts/reports/07tr017.cfm.

SEI 2007b   CMMI Guidebook for Acquirers Team. *Understanding and Leveraging a Supplier's CMMI Efforts: A Guidebook for Acquirers* (CMU/SEI-2007-TR-004). Pittsburgh: Software Engineering Institute, Carnegie Mellon University, March 2007. www.sei.cmu.edu/library/abstracts/reports/07tr004.cfm.

SEI 2010a   CMMI Product Team. *CMMI for Development, Version 1.3* (CMU/SEI-2010-TR-033). Pittsburgh: Software Engineering Institute, Carnegie Mellon University, November 2010. www.sei.cmu.edu/library/abstracts/reports/10tr033.cfm.

SEI 2010b   CMMI Product Team. *CMMI for Services, Version 1.3* (CMU/SEI-2010-TR-034). Pittsburgh: Software Engineering

Institute, Carnegie Mellon University, November 2010. www.sei. cmu.edu/library/abstracts/reports/10tr034.cfm.

SEI 2010c   CMMI Product Team. *CMMI for Acquisition, Version 1.3* (CMU/SEI-2010-TR-032). Pittsburgh: Software Engineering Institute, Carnegie Mellon University, November 2010. www.sei.cmu.edu/ library/abstracts/reports/10tr032.cfm.

SEI 2010d   Caralli, Richard; Allen, Julia; Curtis, Pamela; White, David; & Young, Lisa. *CERT Resilience Management Model, Version 1.0* (CMU/SEI-2010-TR-012). Pittsburgh: Software Engineering Institute, Carnegie Mellon University, May 2010. www.sei.cmu.edu/ library/abstracts/reports/10tr012.cfm.

SEI 2011a   SCAMPI Upgrade Team. *Standard CMMI Appraisal Method for Process Improvement (SCAMPI) A, Version 1.3: Method Definition Document* (CMU/SEI-2011-HB-001). Pittsburgh: Software Engineering Institute, Carnegie Mellon University, expected January 2011. www.sei.cmu.edu/library/abstracts/reports/11hb001.cfm.

SEI 2011b   SCAMPI Upgrade Team. *Appraisal Requirements for CMMI, Version 1.2 (ARC, V1.3)* (CMU/SEI-2011-TR-001). Pittsburgh: Software Engineering Institute, Carnegie Mellon University, expected January 2011. www.sei.cmu.edu/library/abstracts/ reports/11tr001.cfm.

Shewhart 1931   Shewhart, Walter A. *Economic Control of Quality of Manufactured Product.* New York: Van Nostrand, 1931.

Information Assurance/Information Security Related Sources

DHS 2009   Department of Homeland Security. *Assurance Focus for CMMI (Summary of Assurance for CMMI Efforts),* 2009. https:// buildsecurityin.us-cert.gov/swa/proself_assm.html.

DoD and DHS 2008   Department of Defense and Department of Homeland Security. *Software Assurance in Acquisition: Mitigating Risks to the Enterprise,* 2008. https://buildsecurityin.us-cert.gov/swa/ downloads/SwA_in_Acquisition_102208.pdf.

ISO/IEC 2005   International Organization for Standardization and International Electrotechnical Commission. *ISO/IEC 27001 Information Technology—Security Techniques—Information Security Management Systems—Requirements,* 2005. www.iso.org/iso/iso_ catalogue/catalogue_tc/catalogue_detail.htm?csnumber= 42103.

NDIA 2008   NDIA System Assurance Committee. *Engineering for System Assurance.* Arlington, VA: NDIA, 2008. www.ndia.org/ Divisions/Divisions/SystemsEngineering/Documents/Studies/ SA-Guidebook-v1-Oct2008-REV.pdf.

APPENDIX B

ACRONYMS

ACQ   Acquisition constellation

AM   Agreement Management (process area)

ANSI   American National Standards Institute

API   application program interface

ARC   Appraisal Requirements for CMMI

ARD   Acquisition Requirements Development (process area)

ASR   alternative system review

ATM   Acquisition Technical Management (process area)

AVAL   Acquisition Validation (process area)

AVER   Acquisition Verification (process area)

CAR   Causal Analysis and Resolution (process area)

CCB   configuration control board

CDR   critical design review

CL   capability level

CM   Configuration Management (process area)

CMF   CMMI Model Foundation

CMM   Capability Maturity Model

CMMI   Capability Maturity Model Integration

CMMI-ACQ   CMMI for Acquisition

CMMI-DEV   CMMI for Development

CMMI-SVC   CMMI for Services

CMU   Carnegie Mellon University

CobiT   Control Objectives for Information and related Technology

COTS   commercial off-the-shelf

CPI   cost performance index

CPM   critical path method

DAR   Decision Analysis and Resolution (process area)

DEV   Development constellation

DHS   Department of Homeland Security

DoD   Department of Defense

EIA   Electronic Industries Alliance

EIA/IS   Electronic Industries Alliance/Interim Standard

EVM   earned value management

EVMS   earned value management system

FCA   functional configuration audit

FMEA   failure mode and effects analysis

GG   generic goal

GP   generic practice

IBM   International Business Machines

IBR   integrated baseline review

IDEAL   Initiating, Diagnosing, Establishing, Acting, Learning

IEC   International Electrotechnical Commission

IEEE   International Electrical and Electronics Engineers

INCOSE   International Council on Systems Engineering

IPD-CMM   Integrated Product Development Capability Maturity Model

IPM   Integrated Project Management (process area)

ISO   International Organization for Standardization

ISO/IEC   International Organization for Standardization and International Electrotechnical Commission

IT   information technology

ITIL   Information Technology Infrastructure Library

ITR   initial technical review

MA   Measurement and Analysis (process area)

MDD   Method Definition Document

ML   maturity level

NDIA   National Defense Industrial Association

OID   Organizational Innovation and Deployment (former process area)

OPD   Organizational Process Definition (process area)

OPF   Organizational Process Focus (process area)

OPM   Organizational Performance Management (process area)

OPP   Organizational Process Performance (process area)

OT   Organizational Training (process area)

OTRR   operational test readiness review

P-CMM   People Capability Maturity Model

PA   process area

PCA   physical configuration audit

PDR   preliminary design review

PERT   Program Evaluation and Review Technique

PMC   Project Monitoring and Control (process area)

PP   Project Planning (process area)

PPQA   Process and Product Quality Assurance (process area)

PRR   production readiness review

QFD   Quality Function Deployment

QPM   Quantitative Project Management (process area)

REQM   Requirements Management (process area)

RSKM   Risk Management (process area)

SA-CMM   Software Acquisition Capability Maturity Model

SCAMPI   Standard CMMI Appraisal Method for Process Improvement

SECAM   Systems Engineering Capability Assessment Model

SECM   Systems Engineering Capability Model

SEI   Software Engineering Institute

SFR   system functional review

SG   specific goal

SP   specific practice

SPI   schedule performance index

SRR   system requirements review

SSAD   Solicitation and Supplier Agreement Development (process area)

SSD   Service System Development (process area in CMM-SVC)

SSE-CMM   Systems Security Engineering Capability Maturity Model

SVC   Services constellation

SVR   system verification review

SW   software

SW-CMM   Capability Maturity Model for Software or Software Capability Maturity Model

TRA   technology readiness assessment

TRR   test readiness review

WBS   work breakdown structure

CMMI VERSION 1.3 PROJECT PARTICIPANTS

Many talented people were part of the product team that developed CMMI Version 1.3 models. Listed here are those who participated in one or more of the following teams during the development of CMMI Version 1.3. The organizations listed by members' names are those they represented at the time of their team membership.

The following are the primary groups involved in the development of this model:

- CMMI Steering Group
- CMMI for Services Advisory Group
- CMMI V1.3 Coordination Team
- CMMI V1.3 Configuration Control Board
- CMMI V1.3 Core Model Team
- CMMI V1.3 Translation Team
- CMMI V1.3 High Maturity Team
- CMMI V1.3 Acquisition Mini Team
- CMMI V1.3 Services Mini Team
- CMMI V1.3 SCAMPI Upgrade Team
- CMMI V1.3 Training Teams
- CMMI V1.3 Quality Team

CMMI Steering Group

The CMMI Steering Group guides and approves the plans of the CMMI Product Team, provides consultation on significant CMMI project issues, ensures involvement from a variety of interested communities, and approves the final release of the model.

Steering Group Members

- Alan Bemish, U.S. Air Force
- Anita Carleton, Software Engineering Institute
- Clyde Chittister, Software Engineering Institute
- James Gill, Boeing Integrated Defense Systems
- John C. Kelly, NASA
- Kathryn Lundeen, Defense Contract Management Agency
- Larry McCarthy, Motorola, Inc.
- Lawrence Osiecki, U.S. Army
- Robert Rassa, Raytheon Space and Airborne Systems (lead)
- Karen Richter, Institute for Defense Analyses
- Joan Weszka, Lockheed Martin Corporation
- Harold Wilson, Northrop Grumman Corporation
- Brenda Zettervall, U.S. Navy

Ex-Officio Steering Group Members

- Mike Konrad, Software Engineering Institute
- Susan LaFortune, National Security Agency
- David (Mike) Phillips, Software Engineering Institute

Steering Group Support

- Mary Beth Chrissis, Software Engineering Institute (CCB)
- Eric Hayes, Software Engineering Institute (secretary)
- Rawdon Young, Software Engineering Institute (Appraisal program)

CMMI for Services Advisory Group

The Services Advisory Group provides advice to the product development team about service industries.

- Brandon Buteau, Northrop Grumman Corporation
- Christian Carmody, University of Pittsburgh Medical Center
- Sandra Cepeda, Cepeda Systems & Software Analysis/RDECOM SED
- Annie Combelles, DNV IT Global Services
- Jeff Dutton, Jacobs Technology, Inc.
- Eileen Forrester, Software Engineering Institute
- Craig Hollenbach, Northrop Grumman Corporation (lead)
- Bradley Nelson, Department of Defense

- Lawrence Osiecki, U.S. Army ARDEC
- David (Mike) Phillips, Software Engineering Institute
- Timothy Salerno, Lockheed Martin Corporation
- Sandy Shrum, Software Engineering Institute
- Nidhi Srivastava, Tata Consultancy Services
- Elizabeth Sumpter, NSA
- David Swidorsky, Bank of America

CMMI V1.3 Coordination Team

The Coordination Team brings together members of other product development teams to ensure coordination across the project.

- Rhonda Brown, Software Engineering Institute
- Mary Beth Chrissis, Software Engineering Institute
- Eileen Forrester, Software Engineering Institute
- Will Hayes, Software Engineering Institute
- Mike Konrad, Software Engineering Institute
- So Norimatsu, Norimatsu Process Engineering Lab, Inc.
- Mary Lynn Penn, Lockheed Martin Corporation
- David (Mike) Phillips, Software Engineering Institute (lead)
- Mary Lynn Russo, Software Engineering Institute (nonvoting member)
- Sandy Shrum, Software Engineering Institute
- Kathy Smith, Hewlett-Packard
- Barbara Tyson, Software Engineering Institute
- Rawdon Young, Software Engineering Institute

CMMI V1.3 Configuration Control Board

The Configuration Control Board approves all changes to CMMI materials, including the models, the SCAMPI MDD, and introductory model training.

- Rhonda Brown, Software Engineering Institute
- Michael Campo, Raytheon
- Mary Beth Chrissis, Software Engineering Institute (lead)
- Kirsten Dauplaise, NAVAIR
- Mike Evanoo, Systems and Software Consortium, Inc.

- Rich Frost, General Motors
- Brian Gallagher, Northrop Grumman Corporation
- Sally Godfrey, NASA
- Stephen Gristock, JP Morgan Chase and Co.
- Eric Hayes, Software Engineering Institute (nonvoting member)
- Nils Jacobsen, Motorola
- Steve Kapurch, NASA
- Mike Konrad, Software Engineering Institute
- Chris Moore, U.S. Air Force
- Wendell Mullison, General Dynamics Land Systems
- David (Mike) Phillips, Software Engineering Institute
- Robert Rassa, Raytheon Space and Airborne Systems
- Karen Richter, Institute for Defense Analyses
- Mary Lou Russo, Software Engineering Institute (nonvoting member)
- Warren Schwoemeyer, Lockheed Martin Corporation
- John Scibilia, U.S. Army
- Dave Swidorsky, Bank of America
- Barbara Tyson, Software Engineering Institute
- Mary Van Tyne, Software Engineering Institute (nonvoting member)
- Rawdon Young, Software Engineering Institute

CMMI V1.3 Core Model Team

The Core Model Team develops the model material for all three constellations.

- Jim Armstrong, Stevens Institute of Technology
- Rhonda Brown, Software Engineering Institute (co-lead)
- Brandon Buteau, Northrop Grumman Corporation
- Michael Campo, Raytheon
- Sandra Cepeda, Cepeda Systems & Software Analysis/RDECOM SED
- Mary Beth Chrissis, Software Engineering Institute
- Mike D'Ambrosa, Process Performance Professionals
- Eileen Forrester, Software Engineering Institute
- Will Hayes, Software Engineering Institute
- Mike Konrad, Software Engineering Institute (co-lead)
- So Norimatsu, Norimatsu Process Engineering Lab, Inc.
- Mary Lynn Penn, Lockheed Martin Corporation

- David (Mike) Phillips, Software Engineering Institute
- Karen Richter, Institute for Defense Analyses
- Mary Lynn Russo, Software Engineering Institute (nonvoting member)
- John Scibilia, U.S. Army
- Sandy Shrum, Software Engineering Institute (co-lead)
- Kathy Smith, Hewlett-Packard
- Katie Smith-McGarty, U.S. Navy

CMMI V1.3 Translation Team

The Translation Team coordinates translation work on CMMI materials.

- Richard Basque, Alcyonix
- Jose Antonio Calvo-Manzano, Universidad Politecnica de Madrid
- Carlos Caram, Integrated Systems Diagnostics Brazil
- Gonzalo Cuevas, Universidad Politecnica de Madrid
- Mike Konrad, Software Engineering Institute
- Antoine Nardeze, Alcyonix
- So Norimatsu, Norimatsu Process Engineering Lab, Inc. (lead)
- Seven Ou, Institute for Information Industry
- Ricardo Panero Lamothe, Accenture
- Mary Lynn Russo, Software Engineering Institute (nonvoting member)
- Winfried Russwurm, Siemens AG
- Tomas San Feliu, Universidad Politecnica de Madrid

CMMI V1.3 High Maturity Team

The High Maturity Team develops high maturity model material.

- Dan Bennett, U.S. Air Force
- Will Hayes, Software Engineering Institute
- Rick Hefner, Northrop Grumman Corporation
- Jim Kubeck, Lockheed Martin Corporation
- Alice Parry, Raytheon
- Mary Lynn Penn, Lockheed Martin Corporation (lead)
- Kathy Smith, Hewlett-Packard
- Rawdon Young, Software Engineering Institute

CMMI V1.3 Acquisition Mini Team

The Acquisition Mini Team provides acquisition expertise for model development work.

- Rich Frost, General Motors
- Tom Keuten, Keuten and Associates
- David (Mike) Phillips, Software Engineering Institute (lead)
- Karen Richter, Institute for Defense Analyses
- John Scibilia, U.S. Army

CMMI V1.3 Services Mini Team

The Services Mini Team provides service expertise for model development work.

- Drew Allison, Systems and Software Consortium, Inc.
- Brandon Buteau, Northrop Grumman Corporation
- Eileen Forrester, Software Engineering Institute (lead)
- Christian Hertneck, Anywhere.24 GmbH
- Pam Schoppert, Science Applications International Corporation

CMMI V1.3 SCAMPI Upgrade Team

The SCAMPI Upgrade Team develops the Appraisal Requirements for CMMI (ARC) document and SCAMPI Method Definition Document (MDD).

- Mary Busby, Lockheed Martin Corporation
- Palma Buttles-Valdez, Software Engineering Institute
- Paul Byrnes, Integrated System Diagnostics
- Will Hayes, Software Engineering Institute (leader)
- Ravi Khetan, Northrop Grumman Corporation
- Denise Kirkham, The Boeing Company
- Lisa Ming, BAE Systems
- Charlie Ryan, Software Engineering Institute
- Kevin Schaaff, Software Engineering Institute
- Alexander Stall, Software Engineering Institute
- Agapi Svolou, Software Engineering Institute
- Ron Ulrich, Northrop Grumman Corporation

CMMI Version 1.3 Training Teams

The two training teams (one for CMMI-DEV and CMMI-ACQ and the other for CMMI-SVC) developed model training materials.

ACQ and DEV Training Team

- Barbara Baldwin, Software Engineering Institute
- Bonnie Bollinger, Process Focus Management
- Cat Brandt-Zaccardi, Software Engineering Institute
- Rhonda Brown, Software Engineering Institute
- Michael Campo, Raytheon
- Mary Beth Chrissis, Software Engineering Institute (lead)
- Stacey Cope, Software Engineering Institute
- Eric Dorsett, Jeppesen
- Dan Foster, PF Williamson
- Eric Hayes, Software Engineering Institute
- Kurt Hess, Software Engineering Institute
- Mike Konrad, Software Engineering Institute
- Steve Masters, Software Engineering Institute
- Robert McFeeley, Software Engineering Institute
- Diane Mizukami-Williams, Northrop Grumman Corporation
- Daniel Pipitone, Software Engineering Institute
- Mary Lou Russo, Software Engineering Institute (nonvoting member)
- Sandy Shrum, Software Engineering Institute
- Katie Smith-McGarty, U.S. Navy
- Barbara Tyson, Software Engineering Institute

SVC Training Team

- Drew Allison, Systems and Software Consortium, Inc.
- Mike Bridges, University of Pittsburgh Medical Center
- Paul Byrnes, Integrated System Diagnostics
- Sandra Cepeda, Cepeda Systems & Software Analysis/RDECOM SED
- Eileen Clark, Tidewaters Consulting
- Kieran Doyle, Excellence in Measurement
- Eileen Forrester, Software Engineering Institute (lead of SVC training)
- Hillel Glazer, Entinex
- Christian Hertneck, Anywhere.24 GmbH

- Pat Kirwan, Software Engineering Institute
- Suzanne Miller, Software Engineering Institute
- Judah Mogilensky, PEP
- Heather Oppenheimer, Oppenheimer Partners
- Pat O'Toole, PACT
- Agapi Svolou, Alexanna
- Jeff Welch, Software Engineering Institute

CMMI V1.3 Quality Team

The Quality Team conducts various quality assurance checks on the model material to ensure its accuracy, readability, and consistency.

- Rhonda Brown, Software Engineering Institute (co-lead)
- Erin Harper, Software Engineering Institute
- Mike Konrad, Software Engineering Institute
- Mary Lou Russo, Software Engineering Institute
- Mary Lynn Russo, Software Engineering Institute
- Sandy Shrum, Software Engineering Institute (co-lead)

APPENDIX D

GLOSSARY

The glossary defines the basic terms used in CMMI models. Glossary entries are typically multiple-word terms consisting of a noun and one or more restrictive modifiers. (There are some exceptions to this rule that account for one-word terms in the glossary.)

The CMMI glossary of terms is not a required, expected, or informative component of CMMI models. Interpret the terms in the glossary in the context of the model component in which they appear.

To formulate definitions appropriate for CMMI, we consulted multiple sources. We first consulted the *Merriam-Webster OnLine* dictionary (www.merriam-webster.com/). We also consulted other standards as needed, including the following:

- ISO 9000 [ISO 2005a]
- ISO/IEC 12207 [ISO 2008a]
- ISO/IEC 15504 [ISO 2006a]
- ISO/IEC 15288 [ISO 2008b]
- ISO/IEC 15939 [ISO 2007]
- ISO 20000-1 [ISO 2005b]
- IEEE [IEEE 1991]
- CMM for Software (SW-CMM) v1.1
- EIA 632 [EIA 2003]
- SA-CMM [SEI 2002]
- People CMM (P-CMM) [Curtis 2009]
- CobiT v. 4.0 [IT Governance 2005]
- ITIL v3 (Service Improvement, Service Design, Service Operation, Service Strategy, and Service Transition) [Office of Government Commerce 2007]

We developed the glossary recognizing the importance of using terminology that all model users can understand. We also recognized that words and terms can have different meanings in different contexts and environments. The glossary in CMMI models is designed to document the meanings of words and terms that should have the widest use and understanding by users of CMMI products.

Even though the term "product" includes services as well as products and the term "service" is defined as a type of product, many of the terms in the glossary contain both the words "product" and "service" to emphasize that CMMI applies to both products and services.

Every glossary entry has two to three components. There is always a term and always a definition. Sometimes additional notes are provided.

The definition appears first in a type size similar to the term listed. Glossary notes follow the definition and are in a smaller type size.

acceptance criteria   The criteria that a deliverable must satisfy to be accepted by a user, customer, or other authorized entity. (See also "deliverable.")

acceptance testing   Formal testing conducted to enable a user, customer, or other authorized entity to determine whether to accept a deliverable. (See also "unit testing.")

achievement profile   A list of process areas and their corresponding capability levels that represent the organization's progress for each process area while advancing through the capability levels. (See also "capability level profile," "target profile," and "target staging.")

acquirer   The stakeholder that acquires or procures a product or service from a supplier. (See also "stakeholder.")

acquisition   The process of obtaining products or services through supplier agreements. (See also "supplier agreement.")

acquisition strategy   The specific approach to acquiring products and services that is based on considerations of supply sources, acquisition methods, requirements specification types, agreement types, and related acquisition risks.

addition   A clearly marked model component that contains information of interest to particular users.

In a CMMI model, all additions bearing the same name can be optionally selected as a group for use. In CMMI for Services, the Service System Development (SSD) process area is an addition.

allocated requirement   Requirement that results from levying all or part of a higher level requirement on a lower level architectural element or design component.

More generally, requirements can be allocated to other logical or physical components including people, consumables, delivery increments, or the architecture as a whole, depending on what best enables the product or service to achieve the requirements.

appraisal   An examination of one or more processes by a trained team of professionals using an appraisal reference model as the basis for determining, at a minimum, strengths and weaknesses.

This term has a special meaning in the CMMI Product Suite besides its common standard English meaning.

appraisal findings   The results of an appraisal that identify the most important issues, problems, or opportunities for process improvement within the appraisal scope.

Appraisal findings are inferences drawn from corroborated objective evidence.

appraisal participants   Members of the organizational unit who participate in providing information during an appraisal.

appraisal rating   The value assigned by an appraisal team to (a) a CMMI goal or process area, (b) the capability level of a process area, or (c) the maturity level of an organizational unit.

This term is used in CMMI appraisal materials such as the SCAMPI MDD. A rating is determined by enacting the defined rating process for the appraisal method being employed.

appraisal reference model   The CMMI model to which an appraisal team correlates implemented process activities.

This term is used in CMMI appraisal materials such as the SCAMPI MDD.

appraisal scope   The definition of the boundaries of an appraisal encompassing the organizational limits and CMMI model limits within which the processes to be investigated operate.

This term is used in CMMI appraisal materials such as the SCAMPI MDD.

architecture   The set of structures needed to reason about a product. These structures are comprised of elements, relations among them, and properties of both.

In a service context, the architecture is often applied to the service system.

Note that functionality is only one aspect of the product. Quality attributes, such as responsiveness, reliability, and security, are also important to reason about. Structures provide the means for highlighting different portions of the architecture. (See also "functional architecture.")

audit An objective examination of a work product or set of work products against specific criteria (e.g., requirements). (See also "objectively evaluate.")

This is a term used in several ways in CMMI, including configuration audits and process compliance audits.

baseline A set of specifications or work products that has been formally reviewed and agreed on, which thereafter serves as the basis for further development, and which can be changed only through change control procedures. (See also "configuration baseline" and "product baseline.")

base measure Measure defined in terms of an attribute and the method for quantifying it. (See also "derived measure.")

A base measure is functionally independent of other measures.

bidirectional traceability An association among two or more logical entities that is discernable in either direction (i.e., to and from an entity). (See also "requirements traceability" and "traceability.")

business objectives (See "organization's business objectives.")

capability level Achievement of process improvement within an individual process area. (See also "generic goal," "specific goal," "maturity level," and "process area.")

A capability level is defined by appropriate specific and generic goals for a process area.

capability level profile A list of process areas and their corresponding capability levels. (See also "achievement profile," "target profile," and "target staging.")

A capability level profile can be an "achievement profile" when it represents the organization's progress for each process area while advancing through the capability levels. Or, it can be a "target profile" when it represents an objective for process improvement.

capability maturity model A model that contains the essential elements of effective processes for one or more areas of interest and describes an evolutionary improvement path from ad hoc, immature processes to disciplined, mature processes with improved quality and effectiveness.

capable process A process that can satisfy its specified product quality, service quality, and process performance objectives. (See also "stable process" and "standard process.")

causal analysis The analysis of outcomes to determine their causes.

change management Judicious use of means to effect a change, or a proposed change, to a product or service. (See also "configuration management.")

CMMI Framework The basic structure that organizes CMMI components, including elements of current CMMI models as well as rules and methods for generating models, appraisal methods (including associated artifacts), and training materials. (See also "CMMI model" and "CMMI Product Suite.")

The framework enables new areas of interest to be added to CMMI so that they will integrate with the existing ones.

CMMI model A model generated from the CMMI Framework. (See also "CMMI Framework" and "CMMI Product Suite.")

CMMI model component Any of the main architectural elements that compose a CMMI model.

Some of the main elements of a CMMI model include specific practices, generic practices, specific goals, generic goals, process areas, capability levels, and maturity levels.

CMMI Product Suite The complete set of products developed around the CMMI concept. (See also "CMMI Framework" and "CMMI model.")

These products include the framework itself, models, appraisal methods, appraisal materials, and training materials.

commercial off-the-shelf Items that can be purchased from a commercial supplier.

common cause of variation The variation of a process that exists because of normal and expected interactions among components of a process. (See also "special cause of variation.")

configuration audit An audit conducted to verify that a configuration item or a collection of configuration items that make up a baseline conforms to a specified standard or requirement. (See also "audit" and "configuration item.")

configuration baseline The configuration information formally designated at a specific time during a product's or product component's life. (See also "product lifecycle.")

Configuration baselines plus approved changes from those baselines constitute the current configuration information.

configuration control An element of configuration management consisting of the evaluation, coordination, approval or disapproval, and implementation of changes to configuration items after formal establishment of their configuration identification. (See also "configuration identification," "configuration item," and "configuration management.")

configuration control board   A group of people responsible for evaluating and approving or disapproving proposed changes to configuration items and for ensuring implementation of approved changes. (See also "configuration item.")

Configuration control boards are also known as "change control boards."

configuration identification   An element of configuration management consisting of selecting the configuration items for a product, assigning unique identifiers to them, and recording their functional and physical characteristics in technical documentation. (See also "configuration item," "configuration management," and "product.")

configuration item   An aggregation of work products that is designated for configuration management and treated as a single entity in the configuration management process. (See also "configuration management.")

configuration management   A discipline applying technical and administrative direction and surveillance to (1) identify and document the functional and physical characteristics of a configuration item, (2) control changes to those characteristics, (3) record and report change processing and implementation status, and (4) verify compliance with specified requirements. (See also "configuration audit," "configuration control," "configuration identification," and "configuration status accounting.")

configuration status accounting   An element of configuration management consisting of the recording and reporting of information needed to manage a configuration effectively. (See also "configuration identification" and "configuration management.")

This information includes a list of the approved configuration, the status of proposed changes to the configuration, and the implementation status of approved changes.

constellation   A collection of CMMI components that are used to construct models, training materials, and appraisal related documents for an area of interest (e.g., acquisition, development, services).

continuous representation   A capability maturity model structure wherein capability levels provide a recommended order for approaching process improvement within each specified process area. (See also "capability level," "process area," and "staged representation.")

contractor   (See "supplier.")

contractual requirements   The result of the analysis and refinement of customer requirements into a set of requirements suitable to be included in one or more solicitation packages, or supplier agreements. (See also "acquirer," "customer requirement," "supplier agreement," and "solicitation package.")

Contractual requirements include both technical and nontechnical requirements necessary for the acquisition of a product or service.

corrective action   Acts or deeds used to remedy a situation or remove an error.

customer   The party responsible for accepting the product or for authorizing payment.

The customer is external to the project or work group (except possibly in certain project structures in which the customer effectively is on the project team or in the work group) but not necessarily external to the organization. The customer can be a higher level project or work group. Customers are a subset of stakeholders. (See also "stakeholder.")

In most cases where this term is used, the preceding definition is intended; however, in some contexts, the term "customer" is intended to include other relevant stakeholders. (See also "customer requirement.")

End users can be distinguished from customers if the parties that directly receive the value of products and services are not the same as the parties that arrange for, pay for, or negotiate agreements. In contexts where customers and end users are essentially the same parties, the term "customer" can encompass both types. (See also "end user.")

customer requirement   The result of eliciting, consolidating, and resolving conflicts among the needs, expectations, constraints, and interfaces of the product's relevant stakeholders in a way that is acceptable to the customer. (See also "customer.")

data   Recorded information.

Recorded information can include technical data, computer software documents, financial information, management information, representation of facts, numbers, or datum of any nature that can be communicated, stored, and processed.

data management   The disciplined processes and systems that plan for, acquire, and provide stewardship for business and technical data, consistent with data requirements, throughout the data lifecycle.

defect density   Number of defects per unit of product size.

An example is the number of problem reports per thousand lines of code.

defined process   A managed process that is tailored from the organization's set of standard processes according to the organization's tailoring guidelines; has a maintained process description; and contributes process related experiences to the organizational process assets. (See also "managed process.")

definition of required functionality and quality attributes   A characterization of required functionality and quality attributes obtained through "chunking," organizing, annotating, structuring, or formalizing the requirements (functional and nonfunctional) to facilitate further refinement and reasoning about the requirements as well as (possibly, initial) solution exploration, definition, and evaluation. (See also "architecture," "functional architecture," and "quality attribute.")

As technical solution processes progress, this characterization can be further evolved into a description of the architecture versus simply helping scope and guide its development, depending on the engineering processes used; requirements specification and architectural languages used; and the tools and the environment used for product or service system development.

deliverable   An item to be provided to an acquirer or other designated recipient as specified in an agreement. (See also "acquirer.")

This item can be a document, hardware item, software item, service, or any type of work product.

delivery environment   The complete set of circumstances and conditions under which services are delivered in accordance with service agreements. (See also "service" and "service agreement.")

The delivery environment encompasses everything that has or can have a significant effect on service delivery, including but not limited to service system operation, natural phenomena, and the behavior of all parties, whether or not they intend to have such an effect. For example, consider the effect of weather or traffic patterns on a transportation service. (See also "service system.")

The delivery environment is uniquely distinguished from other environments (e.g., simulation environments, testing environments). The delivery environment is the one in which services are actually delivered and count as satisfying a service agreement.

derived measure   Measure that is defined as a function of two or more values of base measures. (See also "base measure.")

derived requirements   Requirements that are not explicitly stated in customer requirements but are inferred (1) from contextual requirements (e.g., applicable standards, laws, policies, common practices, management decisions) or (2) from requirements needed to specify a product or service component.

Derived requirements can also arise during analysis and design of components of the product or service. (See also "product requirements.")

design review   A formal, documented, comprehensive, and systematic examination of a design to determine if the design meets the applicable requirements, to identify problems, and to propose solutions.

development   To create a product or service system by deliberate effort.

In some contexts, development can include the maintenance of the developed product.

document   A collection of data, regardless of the medium on which it is recorded, that generally has permanence and can be read by humans or machines.

Documents include both paper and electronic documents.

end user   A party that ultimately uses a delivered product or that receives the benefit of a delivered service. (See also "customer.")

End users may or may not also be customers (who can establish and accept agreements or authorize payments).

In contexts where a single service agreement covers multiple service deliveries, any party that initiates a service request can be considered an end user. (See also "service agreement" and "service request.")

enterprise   The full composition of a company. (See also "organization.")

A company can consist of many organizations in many locations with different customers.

entry criteria   States of being that must be present before an effort can begin successfully.

equivalent staging   A target staging, created using the continuous representation that is defined so that the results of using the target staging can be compared to maturity levels of the staged representation. (See also "capability level profile," "maturity level," "target profile," and "target staging.")

Such staging permits benchmarking of progress among organizations, enterprises, projects, and work groups, regardless of the CMMI representation used. The organization can implement components of CMMI models beyond the ones reported as part of equivalent staging. Equivalent staging relates how the organization compares to other organizations in terms of maturity levels.

establish and maintain   Create, document, use, and revise work products as necessary to ensure they remain useful.

The phrase "establish and maintain" plays a special role in communicating a deeper principle in CMMI: work products that have a central or key role in work group, project, and organizational performance should be given attention to ensure they are used and useful in that role.

This phrase has particular significance in CMMI because it often appears in goal and practice statements (though in the former as "established and maintained") and should be taken as shorthand for applying the principle to whatever work product is the object of the phrase.

example work product An informative model component that provides sample outputs from a specific practice.

executive (See "senior manager.")

exit criteria States of being that must be present before an effort can end successfully.

expected CMMI components CMMI components that describe the activities that are important in achieving a required CMMI component.

Model users can implement the expected components explicitly or implement equivalent practices to these components. Specific and generic practices are expected model components.

findings (See "appraisal findings.")

formal evaluation process A structured approach to evaluating alternative solutions against established criteria to determine a recommended solution to address an issue.

framework (See "CMMI Framework.")

functional analysis Examination of a defined function to identify all the subfunctions necessary to accomplish that function; identification of functional relationships and interfaces (internal and external) and capturing these relationships and interfaces in a functional architecture; and flow down of upper level requirements and assignment of these requirements to lower level subfunctions. (See also "functional architecture.")

functional architecture The hierarchical arrangement of functions, their internal and external (external to the aggregation itself) functional interfaces and external physical interfaces, their respective requirements, and their design constraints. (See also "architecture," "functional analysis," and "definition of required functionality and quality attributes.")

generic goal A required model component that describes characteristics that must be present to institutionalize processes that implement a process area. (See also "institutionalization.")

generic practice An expected model component that is considered important in achieving the associated generic goal.

The generic practices associated with a generic goal describe the activities that are expected to result in achievement of the generic goal and contribute to the institutionalization of the processes associated with a process area.

generic practice elaboration   An informative model component that appears after a generic practice to provide guidance on how the generic practice could be applied uniquely to a process area. (This model component is not present in all CMMI models.)

hardware engineering   The application of a systematic, disciplined, and quantifiable approach to transforming a set of requirements that represent the collection of stakeholder needs, expectations, and constraints, using documented techniques and technology to design, implement, and maintain a tangible product. (See also "software engineering" and "systems engineering.")

In CMMI, hardware engineering represents all technical fields (e.g., electrical, mechanical) that transform requirements and ideas into tangible products.

higher level management   The person or persons who provide the policy and overall guidance for the process but do not provide the direct day-to-day monitoring and controlling of the process. (See also "senior manager.")

Such persons belong to a level of management in the organization above the immediate level responsible for the process and can be (but are not necessarily) senior managers.

incomplete process   A process that is not performed or is performed only partially; one or more of the specific goals of the process area are not satisfied.

An incomplete process is also known as capability level 0.

informative CMMI components   CMMI components that help model users understand the required and expected components of a model.

These components can be examples, detailed explanations, or other helpful information. Subpractices, notes, references, goal titles, practice titles, sources, example work products, and generic practice elaborations are informative model components.

institutionalization   The ingrained way of doing business that an organization follows routinely as part of its corporate culture.

interface control   In configuration management, the process of (1) identifying all functional and physical characteristics relevant to the interfacing of two or more configuration items provided by one or more organizations and (2) ensuring that proposed changes to these characteristics are evaluated and approved prior to implementation. (See also "configuration item" and "configuration management.")

lifecycle model   A partitioning of the life of a product, service, project, work group, or set of work activities into phases.

managed process   A performed process that is planned and executed in accordance with policy; employs skilled people having adequate resources to produce controlled outputs; involves relevant stakeholders; is monitored, controlled, and reviewed; and is evaluated for adherence to its process description. (See also "performed process.")

manager   A person who provides technical and administrative direction and control to those who perform tasks or activities within the manager's area of responsibility.

This term has a special meaning in the CMMI Product Suite besides its common standard English meaning. The traditional functions of a manager include planning, organizing, directing, and controlling work within an area of responsibility.

maturity level   Degree of process improvement across a predefined set of process areas in which all goals in the set are attained. (See also "capability level" and "process area.")

measure (noun)   Variable to which a value is assigned as a result of measurement. (See also "base measure," "derived measure," and "measurement.")

The definition of this term in CMMI is consistent with the definition of this term in ISO 15939.

measurement   A set of operations to determine the value of a measure. (See also "measure.")

The definition of this term in CMMI is consistent with the definition of this term in ISO 15939.

measurement result   A value determined by performing a measurement. (See also "measurement.")

memorandum of agreement   Binding document of understanding or agreement between two or more parties.

A memorandum of agreement is also known as a "memorandum of understanding."

natural bounds   The inherent range of variation in a process, as determined by process performance measures.

Natural bounds are sometimes referred to as "voice of the process."

Techniques such as control charts, confidence intervals, and prediction intervals are used to determine whether the variation is due to common causes (i.e., the process is predictable or stable) or is due to some special cause that can and should be identified and removed. (See also "measure" and "process performance.")

nondevelopmental item   An item that was developed prior to its current use in an acquisition or development process.

Such an item can require minor modifications to meet the requirements of its current intended use.

nontechnical requirements   Requirements affecting product and service acquisition or development that are not properties of the product or service.

Examples include numbers of products or services to be delivered, data rights for delivered COTS and nondevelopmental items, delivery dates, and milestones with exit criteria. Other nontechnical requirements include work constraints associated with training, site provisions, and deployment schedules.

objectively evaluate   To review activities and work products against criteria that minimize subjectivity and bias by the reviewer. (See also "audit.")

An example of an objective evaluation is an audit against requirements, standards, or procedures by an independent quality assurance function.

operational concept   A general description of the way in which an entity is used or operates.

An operational concept is also known as "concept of operations."

operational scenario   A description of an imagined sequence of events that includes the interaction of the product or service with its environment and users, as well as interaction among its product or service components.

Operational scenarios are used to evaluate the requirements and design of the system and to verify and validate the system.

organization   An administrative structure in which people collectively manage one or more projects or work groups as a whole, share a senior manager, and operate under the same policies.

However, the word "organization" as used throughout CMMI models can also apply to one person who performs a function in a small organization that might be performed by a group of people in a large organization. (See also "enterprise.")

organizational maturity   The extent to which an organization has explicitly and consistently deployed processes that are documented, managed, measured, controlled, and continually improved.

Organizational maturity can be measured via appraisals.

organizational policy   A guiding principle typically established by senior management that is adopted by an organization to influence and determine decisions.

organizational process assets   Artifacts that relate to describing, implementing, and improving processes.

Examples of these artifacts include policies, measurement descriptions, process descriptions, process implementation support tools.

The term "process assets" is used to indicate that these artifacts are developed or acquired to meet the business objectives of the organization and that they represent investments by the organization that are expected to provide current and future business value. (See also "process asset library.")

organization's business objectives   Senior-management-developed objectives designed to ensure an organization's continued existence and enhance its profitability, market share, and other factors influencing the organization's success. (See also "quality and process performance objectives" and "quantitative objective.")

organization's measurement repository   A repository used to collect and make measurement results available on processes and work products, particularly as they relate to the organization's set of standard processes.

This repository contains or references actual measurement results and related information needed to understand and analyze measurement results.

organization's process asset library   A library of information used to store and make process assets available that are useful to those who are defining, implementing, and managing processes in the organization.

This library contains process assets that include process related documentation such as policies, defined processes, checklists, lessons learned documents, templates, standards, procedures, plans, and training materials.

organization's set of standard processes   A collection of definitions of the processes that guide activities in an organization.

These process descriptions cover the fundamental process elements (and their relationships to each other such as ordering and interfaces) that should be incorporated into the defined processes that are implemented in projects, work groups, and work across the organization. A standard process enables consistent development and maintenance activities across the organization and is essential for long-term stability and improvement. (See also "defined process" and "process element.")

outsourcing   (See "acquisition.")

peer review   The review of work products performed by peers during the development of work products to identify defects for removal. (See also "work product.")

The term "peer review" is used in the CMMI Product Suite instead of the term "work product inspection."

performance parameters   The measures of effectiveness and other key measures used to guide and control progressive development.

performed process   A process that accomplishes the needed work to produce work products; the specific goals of the process area are satisfied.

planned process   A process that is documented by both a description and a plan.

The description and plan should be coordinated and the plan should include standards, requirements, objectives, resources, and assignments.

policy   (See "organizational policy.")

process   A set of interrelated activities, which transform inputs into outputs, to achieve a given purpose. (See also "process area," "subprocess," and "process element.")

There is a special use of the phrase "the process" in the statements and descriptions of the generic goals and generic practices. "The process," as used in Part Two, is the process or processes that implement the process area.

The terms "process," "subprocess," and "process element" form a hierarchy with "process" as the highest, most general term, "subprocesses" below it, and "process element" as the most specific. A particular process can be called a subprocess if it is part of another larger process. It can also be called a process element if it is not decomposed into subprocesses.

This definition of process is consistent with the definition of process in ISO 9000, ISO 12207, ISO 15504, and EIA 731.

process action plan   A plan, usually resulting from appraisals, that documents how specific improvements targeting the weaknesses uncovered by an appraisal will be implemented.

process action team   A team that has the responsibility to develop and implement process improvement activities for an organization as documented in a process action plan.

process and technology improvements   Incremental and innovative improvements to processes and to process, product, or service technologies.

process architecture   (1) The ordering, interfaces, interdependencies, and other relationships among the process elements in a standard process, or (2) the interfaces, interdependencies, and other relationships between process elements and external processes.

process area   A cluster of related practices in an area that, when implemented collectively, satisfies a set of goals considered important for making improvement in that area.

process asset   Anything the organization considers useful in attaining the goals of a process area. (See also "organizational process assets.")

process asset library   A collection of process asset holdings that can be used by an organization, project, or work group. (See also "organization's process asset library.")

process attribute   A measurable characteristic of process capability applicable to any process.

process capability   The range of expected results that can be achieved by following a process.

process definition   The act of defining and describing a process.

The result of process definition is a process description. (See also "process description.")

process description   A documented expression of a set of activities performed to achieve a given purpose.

A process description provides an operational definition of the major components of a process. The description specifies, in a complete, precise, and verifiable manner, the requirements, design, behavior, or other characteristics of a process. It also can include procedures for determining whether these provisions have been satisfied. Process descriptions can be found at the activity, project, work group, or organizational level.

process element   The fundamental unit of a process.

A process can be defined in terms of subprocesses or process elements. A subprocess is a process element when it is not further decomposed into subprocesses or process elements. (See also "process" and "subprocess.")

Each process element covers a closely related set of activities (e.g., estimating element, peer review element). Process elements can be portrayed using templates to be completed, abstractions to be refined, or descriptions to be modified or used. A process element can be an activity or task.

The terms "process," "subprocess," and "process element" form a hierarchy with "process" as the highest, most general term, "subprocesses" below it, and "process element" as the most specific.

process group   A collection of specialists who facilitate the definition, maintenance, and improvement of processes used by the organization.

process improvement   A program of activities designed to improve the process performance and maturity of the organization's processes, and the results of such a program.

process improvement objectives   A set of target characteristics established to guide the effort to improve an existing process in a specific, measurable way either in terms of resultant product or service characteristics (e.g., quality, product performance, conformance to standards) or in the way in which the process is executed (e.g., elimination of redundant process steps, combination of process steps, improvement of cycle time). (See also "organization's business objectives" and "quantitative objective.")

process improvement plan   A plan for achieving organizational process improvement objectives based on a thorough understanding of current strengths and weaknesses of the organization's processes and process assets.

process measurement   A set of operations used to determine values of measures of a process and its resulting products or services for the purpose of characterizing and understanding the process. (See also "measurement.")

process owner   The person (or team) responsible for defining and maintaining a process.

At the organizational level, the process owner is the person (or team) responsible for the description of a standard process; at the project or work group level, the process owner is the person (or team) responsible for the description of the defined process. A process can therefore have multiple owners at different levels of responsibility. (See also "defined process" and "standard process.")

process performance   A measure of results achieved by following a process. (See also "measure.")

Process performance is characterized by both process measures (e.g., effort, cycle time, defect removal efficiency) and product or service measures (e.g., reliability, defect density, response time).

process performance baseline   A documented characterization of process performance, which can include central tendency and variation. (See also "process performance.")

A process performance baseline can be used as a benchmark for comparing actual process performance against expected process performance.

process performance model   A description of relationships among the measurable attributes of one or more processes or work products that is developed from historical process performance data and is used to predict future performance. (See also "measure.")

One or more of the measurable attributes represent controllable inputs tied to a subprocess to enable performance of "what-if" analyses for planning, dynamic re-planning, and problem resolution. Process performance models include statistical, probabilistic, and simulation based models that predict interim or final results by connecting past performance with future outcomes. They model the variation of the factors, and provide insight into the expected range and variation of predicted results. A process performance model can be a collection of models that (when combined) meet the criteria of a process performance model.

process tailoring   Making, altering, or adapting a process description for a particular end.

For example, a project or work group tailors its defined process from the organization's set of standard processes to meet objectives, constraints, and the environment of the project or work group. (See also "defined process," "organization's set of standard processes," and "process description.")

product   A work product that is intended for delivery to a customer or end user.

This term has a special meaning in the CMMI Product Suite besides its common standard English meaning. The form of a product can vary in different contexts. (See also "customer," "product component," "service," and "work product.")

product baseline   The initial approved technical data package defining a configuration item during the production, operation, maintenance, and logistic support of its lifecycle. (See also "configuration item," "configuration management," and "technical data package.")

This term is related to configuration management.

product component   A work product that is a lower level component of the product. (See also "product" and "work product.")

Product components are integrated to produce the product. There can be multiple levels of product components.

Throughout the process areas, where the terms "product" and "product component" are used, their intended meanings also encompass services, service systems, and their components.

This term has a special meaning in the CMMI Product Suite besides its common standard English meaning.

product component requirements   A complete specification of a product or service component, including fit, form, function, performance, and any other requirement.

product lifecycle   The period of time, consisting of phases, that begins when a product or service is conceived and ends when the product or service is no longer available for use.

Since an organization can be producing multiple products or services for multiple customers, one description of a product lifecycle may not be adequate. Therefore, the organization can define a set of approved product lifecycle models. These models are typically found in published literature and are likely to be tailored for use in an organization.

A product lifecycle could consist of the following phases: (1) concept and vision, (2) feasibility, (3) design/development, (4) production, and (5) phase out.

product line   A group of products sharing a common, managed set of features that satisfy specific needs of a selected market or mission and that are developed from a common set of core assets in a prescribed way. (See also "service line.")

The development or acquisition of products for the product line is based on exploiting commonality and bounding variation (i.e., restricting unnecessary product variation) across the group of products. The managed set of core assets (e.g., requirements, architectures, components, tools, testing artifacts, operating procedures, software) includes prescriptive guidance for their use in product development. Product line operations involve interlocking execution of the broad activities of core asset development, product development, and management.

Many people use "product line" just to mean the set of products produced by a particular business unit, whether they are built with shared assets or not. We call that collection a "portfolio," and reserve "product line" to have the technical meaning given here.

product related lifecycle processes   Processes associated with a product or service throughout one or more phases of its life (e.g., from conception through disposal), such as manufacturing and support processes.

product requirements   A refinement of customer requirements into the developers' language, making implicit requirements into explicit derived requirements. (See also "derived requirements" and "product component requirements.")

The developer uses product requirements to guide the design and building of the product or service.

product suite   (See "CMMI Product Suite.")

project   A managed set of interrelated activities and resources, including people, that delivers one or more products or services to a customer or end user.

A project has an intended beginning (i.e., project startup) and end. Projects typically operate according to a plan. Such a plan is frequently documented and specifies what is to be delivered or implemented, the resources and funds to be used, the work to be done, and a schedule for doing the work. A project can be composed of projects. (See also "project startup.")

In some contexts, the term "program" is used to refer to a project.

project plan   A plan that provides the basis for performing and controlling the project's activities, which addresses the commitments to the project's customer.

Project planning includes estimating the attributes of work products and tasks, determining the resources needed, negotiating commitments, producing a schedule, and identifying and analyzing project risks. Iterating through these activities may be necessary to establish the project plan.

project progress and performance   What a project achieves with respect to implementing project plans, including effort, cost, schedule, and technical performance. (See also "technical performance.")

project startup   When a set of interrelated resources for a project are directed to develop or deliver one or more products or services for a customer or end user. (See also "project.")

prototype   A preliminary type, form, or instance of a product, service, product component, or service component that serves as a model for later stages or for the final, complete version of the product or service.

This model of the product or service (e.g., physical, electronic, digital, analytical) can be used for the following (and other) purposes:

- *Assessing the feasibility of a new or unfamiliar technology*
- *Assessing or mitigating technical risk*
- *Validating requirements*
- *Demonstrating critical features*
- *Qualifying a product or service*
- *Qualifying a process*
- *Characterizing performance or features of the product or service*
- *Elucidating physical principles*

quality   The degree to which a set of inherent characteristics fulfills requirements.

quality and process performance objectives   Quantitative objectives and requirements for product quality, service quality, and process performance.

Quantitative process performance objectives include quality; however, to emphasize the importance of quality in the CMMI Product Suite, the phrase "quality and process performance objectives" is used. "Process performance objectives" are referenced in maturity level 3; the term "quality and process performance objectives" implies the use of quantitative data and is only used in maturity levels 4 and 5.

quality assurance   A planned and systematic means for assuring management that the defined standards, practices, procedures, and methods of the process are applied.

quality attribute A property of a product or service by which its quality will be judged by relevant stakeholders. Quality attributes are characterizable by some appropriate measure.

Quality attributes are nonfunctional, such as timeliness, throughput, responsiveness, security, modifiability, reliability, and usability. They have a significant influence on the architecture.

quality control The operational techniques and activities that are used to fulfill requirements for quality. (See also "quality assurance.")

quantitative management Managing a project or work group using statistical and other quantitative techniques to build an understanding of the performance or predicted performance of processes in comparison to the project's or work group's quality and process performance objectives, and identifying corrective action that may need to be taken. (See also "statistical techniques.")

Statistical techniques used in quantitative management include analysis, creation, or use of process performance models; analysis, creation, or use of process performance baselines; use of control charts; analysis of variance; regression analysis; and use of confidence intervals or prediction intervals, sensitivity analysis, simulations, and tests of hypotheses.

quantitative objective Desired target value expressed using quantitative measures. (See also "measure," "process improvement objectives," and "quality and process performance objectives.")

quantitatively managed (See "quantitative management.")

reference model A model that is used as a benchmark for measuring an attribute.

relevant stakeholder A stakeholder that is identified for involvement in specified activities and is included in a plan. (See also "stakeholder.")

representation The organization, use, and presentation of a CMM's components.

Overall, two types of approaches to presenting best practices are evident: the staged representation and the continuous representation.

required CMMI components CMMI components that are essential to achieving process improvement in a given process area.

Specific goals and generic goals are required model components. Goal satisfaction is used in appraisals as the basis for deciding whether a process area has been satisfied.

requirement (1) A condition or capability needed by a user to solve a problem or achieve an objective. (2) A condition or capability that must be met or possessed by a product, service, product component, or service component to satisfy a supplier agreement, standard, specification, or other formally imposed documents. (3) A documented representation of a condition or capability as in (1) or (2). (See also "supplier agreement.")

requirements analysis   The determination of product or service specific functional and quality attribute characteristics based on analyses of customer needs, expectations, and constraints; operational concept; projected utilization environments for people, products, services, and processes; and measures of effectiveness. (See also "operational concept.")

requirements elicitation   Using systematic techniques such as prototypes and structured surveys to proactively identify and document customer and end-user needs.

requirements management   The management of all requirements received by or generated by the project or work group, including both technical and nontechnical requirements as well as those requirements levied on the project or work group by the organization. (See also "nontechnical requirements.")

requirements traceability   A discernable association between requirements and related requirements, implementations, and verifications. (See also "bidirectional traceability" and "traceability.")

return on investment   The ratio of revenue from output (product or service) to production costs, which determines whether an organization benefits from performing an action to produce something.

risk analysis   The evaluation, classification, and prioritization of risks.

risk identification   An organized, thorough approach used to seek out probable or realistic risks in achieving objectives.

risk management   An organized, analytic process used to identify what might cause harm or loss (identify risks); to assess and quantify the identified risks; and to develop and, if needed, implement an appropriate approach to prevent or handle causes of risk that could result in significant harm or loss.

Typically, risk management is performed for the activities of a project, a work group, an organization, or other organizational units that are developing or delivering products or services.

senior manager   A management role at a high enough level in an organization that the primary focus of the person filling the role is the long-term vitality of the organization rather than short-term concerns and pressures. (See also "higher level management.")

A senior manager has authority to direct the allocation or reallocation of resources in support of organizational process improvement effectiveness.

A senior manager can be any manager who satisfies this description, including the head of the organization. Synonyms for senior manager include "executive" and "top-level manager." However, to ensure consistency and usability, these synonyms are not used in CMMI models.

This term has a special meaning in the CMMI Product Suite besides its common standard English meaning.

service A product that is intangible and non-storable. (See also "product," "customer," and "work product.")

Services are delivered through the use of service systems that have been designed to satisfy service requirements. (See also "service system.")

Many service providers deliver combinations of services and goods. A single service system can deliver both types of products. For example, a training organization can deliver training materials along with its training services.

Services may be delivered through combinations of manual and automated processes.

This term has a special meaning in the CMMI Product Suite besides its common standard English meaning.

service agreement A binding, written record of a promised exchange of value between a service provider and a customer. (See also "customer.")

Service agreements can be fully negotiable, partially negotiable, or non-negotiable, and they can be drafted either by the service provider, the customer, or both, depending on the situation.

A "promised exchange of value" means a joint recognition and acceptance of what each party will provide to the other to satisfy the agreement. Typically, the customer provides payment in return for delivered services, but other arrangements are possible.

A "written" record need not be contained in a single document or other artifact. Alternatively, it may be extremely brief for some types of services (e.g., a receipt that identifies a service, its price, its recipient).

service catalog A list or repository of standardized service definitions.

Service catalogs can include varying degrees of detail about available service levels, quality, prices, negotiable/tailorable items, and terms and conditions.

A service catalog need not be contained in a single document or other artifact, and can be a combination of items that provide equivalent information (such as web pages linked to a database). Alternatively, for some services an effective catalog can be a simple printed menu of available services and their prices.

Service catalog information can be partitioned into distinct subsets to support different types of stakeholders (e.g., customers, end users, provider staff, suppliers).

service incident   An indication of an actual or potential interference with a service.

Service incidents can occur in any service domain because customer and end-user complaints are types of incidents and even the simplest of services can generate complaints.

The word "incident" can be used in place of "service incident" for brevity when the context makes the meaning clear.

service level   A defined magnitude, degree, or quality of service delivery performance. (See also "service" and "service level measure.")

service level agreement   A service agreement that specifies delivered services; service measures; levels of acceptable and unacceptable services; and expected responsibilities, liabilities, and actions of both the provider and customer in anticipated situations. (See also "measure," "service," and "service agreement.")

A service level agreement is a kind of service agreement that documents the details indicated in the definition.

The use of the term "service agreement" always includes "service level agreement" as a subcategory and the former may be used in place of the latter for brevity. However, "service level agreement" is the preferred term when it is desired to emphasize situations in which distinct levels of acceptable services exist, or other details of a service level agreement are likely to be important to the discussion.

service level measure   A measure of service delivery performance associated with a service level. (See also "measure" and "service level.")

service line   A consolidated and standardized set of services and service levels that satisfy specific needs of a selected market or mission area. (See also "product line" and "service level.")

service request   A communication from a customer or end user that one or more specific instances of service delivery are desired. (See also "service agreement.")

These requests are made within the context of a service agreement.

In cases where services are to be delivered continuously or periodically, some service requests may be explicitly identified in the service agreement itself.

In other cases, service requests that fall within the scope of a previously established service agreement are generated over time by customers or end users as their needs develop.

service requirements   The complete set of requirements that affect service delivery and service system development. (See also "service system.")

Service requirements include both technical and nontechnical requirements. Technical requirements are properties of the service to be delivered and the service system needed to enable delivery. Nontechnical requirements may include additional conditions, provisions, commitments, and terms identified by agreements, and regulations, as well as needed capabilities and conditions derived from business objectives.

service system   An integrated and interdependent combination of component resources that satisfies service requirements. (See also "service system component" and "service requirements.")

A service system encompasses everything required for service delivery, including work products, processes, facilities, tools, consumables, and human resources.

Note that a service system includes the people necessary to perform the service system's processes. In contexts where end users perform some processes for service delivery to be accomplished, those end users are also part of the service system (at least for the duration of those interactions).

A complex service system may be divisible into multiple distinct delivery and support systems or subsystems. While these divisions and distinctions may be significant to the service provider organization, they may not be as meaningful to other stakeholders.

service system component   A resource required for a service system to successfully deliver services.

Some components can remain owned by a customer, end user, or third party before service delivery begins and after service delivery ends. (See also "customer" and "end user.")

Some components can be transient resources that are part of the service system for a limited time (e.g., items that are under repair in a maintenance shop).

Components can include processes and people.

The word "component" can be used in place of "service system component" for brevity when the context makes the meaning clear.

The word "infrastructure" can be used to refer collectively to service system components that are tangible and essentially permanent. Depending on the context and type of service, infrastructure can include human resources.

service system consumable   A service system component that ceases to be available or becomes permanently changed by its use during the delivery of a service.

Fuel, office supplies, and disposable containers are examples of commonly used consumables. Particular types of services can have their own specialized consumables (e.g., a health care service may require medications or blood supplies).

People are not consumables, but their labor time is a consumable.

shared vision   A common understanding of guiding principles, including mission, objectives, expected behavior, values, and final outcomes, which are developed and used by a project or work group.

software engineering   (1) The application of a systematic, disciplined, quantifiable approach to the development, operation, and maintenance of software. (2) The study of approaches as in (1). (See also "hardware engineering" and "systems engineering.")

solicitation   The process of preparing a package to be used in selecting a supplier. (See also "solicitation package.")

solicitation package   A collection of formal documents that includes a description of the desired form of response from a potential supplier, the relevant statement of work for the supplier, and required provisions in the supplier agreement.

special cause of variation   A cause of a defect that is specific to some transient circumstance and is not an inherent part of a process. (See also "common cause of variation.")

specific goal   A required model component that describes the unique characteristics that must be present to satisfy the process area. (See also "capability level," "generic goal," "organization's business objectives," and "process area.")

specific practice   An expected model component that is considered important in achieving the associated specific goal. (See also "process area" and "specific goal.")

The specific practices describe the activities expected to result in achievement of the specific goals of a process area.

stable process   The state in which special causes of process variation have been removed and prevented from recurring so that only common causes of process variation of the process remain. (See also "capable process," "common cause of variation," "special cause of variation," and "standard process.")

staged representation   A model structure wherein attaining the goals of a set of process areas establishes a maturity level; each level builds a foundation for subsequent levels. (See also "maturity level" and "process area.")

stakeholder   A group or individual that is affected by or is in some way accountable for the outcome of an undertaking. (See also "customer" and "relevant stakeholder.")

Stakeholders may include project or work group members, suppliers, customers, end users, and others.

This term has a special meaning in the CMMI Product Suite besides its common standard English meaning.

standard (noun)   Formal requirements developed and used to prescribe consistent approaches to acquisition, development, or service.

Examples of standards include ISO/IEC standards, IEEE standards, and organizational standards.

standard process   An operational definition of the basic process that guides the establishment of a common process in an organization.

A standard process describes the fundamental process elements that are expected to be incorporated into any defined process. It also describes relationships (e.g., ordering, interfaces) among these process elements. (See also "defined process.")

statement of work   A description of work to be performed.

statistical and other quantitative techniques   Analytic techniques that enable accomplishing an activity by quantifying parameters of the task (e.g., inputs, size, effort, and performance). (See also "statistical techniques" and "quantitative management.")

This term is used in the high maturity process areas where the use of statistical and other quantitative techniques to improve understanding of project, work, and organizational processes is described.

Examples of non-statistical quantitative techniques include trend analysis, run charts, Pareto analysis, bar charts, radar charts, and data averaging.

The reason for using the compound term "statistical and other quantitative techniques" in CMMI is to acknowledge that while statistical techniques are expected, other quantitative techniques can also be used effectively.

statistical process control   Statistically based analysis of a process and measures of process performance, which identify common and special causes of variation in process performance and maintain process performance within limits. (See also "common cause of variation," "special cause of variation," and "statistical techniques.")

statistical techniques   Techniques adapted from the field of mathematical statistics used for activities such as characterizing process performance, understanding process variation, and predicting outcomes.

Examples of statistical techniques include sampling techniques, analysis of variance, chi-squared tests, and process control charts.

subpractice   An informative model component that provides guidance for interpreting and implementing specific or generic practices.

Subpractices may be worded as if prescriptive, but they are actually meant only to provide ideas that can be useful for process improvement.

subprocess   A process that is part of a larger process. (See also "process," "process description," and "process element.")

A subprocess may or may not be further decomposed into more granular subprocesses or process elements. The terms "process," "subprocess," and "process element" form a hierarchy with "process" as the highest, most general term, "subprocesses" below it, and "process element" as the most specific. A subprocess can also be called a process element if it is not decomposed into further subprocesses.

supplier   (1) An entity delivering products or performing services being acquired. (2) An individual, partnership, company, corporation, association, or other entity having an agreement with an acquirer for the design, development, manufacture, maintenance, modification, or supply of items under the terms of an agreement. (See also "acquirer.")

supplier agreement   A documented agreement between the acquirer and supplier. (See also "supplier.")

Supplier agreements are also known as contracts, licenses, and memoranda of agreement.

sustainment   The processes used to ensure that a product or service remains operational.

system of systems   A set or arrangement of systems that results when independent and useful systems are integrated into a large system that delivers unique capabilities.

systems engineering   The interdisciplinary approach governing the total technical and managerial effort required to transform a set of customer needs, expectations, and constraints into a solution and to support that solution throughout its life. (See also "hardware engineering" and "software engineering.")

This approach includes the definition of technical performance measures, the integration of engineering specialties toward the establishment of an architecture, and the definition of supporting lifecycle processes that balance cost, schedule, and performance objectives.

tailoring   The act of making, altering, or adapting something for a particular end.

For example, a project or work group establishes its defined process by tailoring from the organization's set of standard processes to meet its objectives, constraints, and environment. Likewise, a service provider tailors standard services for a particular service agreement.

tailoring guidelines   Organizational guidelines that enable projects, work groups, and organizational functions to appropriately adapt standard processes for their use.

The organization's set of standard processes is described at a general level that may not be directly usable to perform a process.

Tailoring guidelines aid those who establish the defined processes for project or work groups. Tailoring guidelines cover (1) selecting a standard process, (2) selecting an approved lifecycle model, and (3) tailoring the selected standard process and lifecycle model to fit project or work group needs. Tailoring guidelines describe what can and cannot be modified and identify process components that are candidates for modification.

target profile   A list of process areas and their corresponding capability levels that represent an objective for process improvement. (See also "achievement profile" and "capability level profile.")

Target profiles are only available when using the continuous representation.

target staging   A sequence of target profiles that describes the path of process improvement to be followed by the organization. (See also "achievement profile," "capability level profile," and "target profile.")

Target staging is only available when using the continuous representation.

team   A group of people with complementary skills and expertise who work together to accomplish specified objectives.

A team establishes and maintains a process that identifies roles, responsibilities, and interfaces; is sufficiently precise to enable the team to measure, manage, and improve their work performance; and enables the team to make and defend their commitments.

Collectively, team members provide skills and advocacy appropriate to all aspects of their work (e.g., for the different phases of a work product's life) and are responsible for accomplishing the specified objectives.

Not every project or work group member must belong to a team (e.g., a person staffed to accomplish a task that is largely self-contained). Thus, a large project or work group can consist of many teams as well as project staff not belonging to any team. A smaller project or work group can consist of only a single team (or a single individual).

technical data package   A collection of items that can include the following if such information is appropriate to the type of product and product component (e.g., material and manufacturing

requirements may not be useful for product components associated with software services or processes):
- Product architecture description
- Allocated requirements
- Product component descriptions
- Product related lifecycle process descriptions if not described as separate product components
- Key product characteristics
- Required physical characteristics and constraints
- Interface requirements
- Materials requirements (bills of material and material characteristics)
- Fabrication and manufacturing requirements (for both the original equipment manufacturer and field support)
- Verification criteria used to ensure requirements have been achieved
- Conditions of use (environments) and operating/usage scenarios, modes and states for operations, support, training, manufacturing, disposal, and verifications throughout the life of the product
- Rationale for decisions and characteristics (e.g., requirements, requirement allocations, design choices)

technical performance   Characteristic of a process, product, or service, generally defined by a functional or technical requirement.

Examples of technical performance types include estimating accuracy, end-user functions, security functions, response time, component accuracy, maximum weight, minimum throughput, allowable range.

technical performance measure   Precisely defined technical measure of a requirement, capability, or some combination of requirements and capabilities. (See also "measure.")

technical requirements   Properties (i.e., attributes) of products or services to be acquired or developed.

traceability   A discernable association among two or more logical entities such as requirements, system elements, verifications, or tasks. (See also "bidirectional traceability" and "requirements traceability.")

trade study   An evaluation of alternatives, based on criteria and systematic analysis, to select the best alternative for attaining determined objectives.

training   Formal and informal learning options.

These learning options can include classroom training, informal mentoring, web-based training, guided self-study, and formalized on-the-job training programs.

The learning options selected for each situation are based on an assessment of the need for training and the performance gap to be addressed.

unit testing   Testing of individual hardware or software units or groups of related units. (See also "acceptance testing.")

validation   Confirmation that the product or service, as provided (or as it will be provided), will fulfill its intended use.

In other words, validation ensures that "you built the right thing." (See also "verification.")

verification   Confirmation that work products properly reflect the requirements specified for them.

In other words, verification ensures that "you built it right." (See also "validation.")

version control   The establishment and maintenance of baselines and the identification of changes to baselines that make it possible to return to the previous baseline.

In some contexts, an individual work product may have its own baseline and a level of control less than formal configuration control may be sufficient.

work breakdown structure (WBS)   An arrangement of work elements and their relationship to each other and to the end product or service.

work group   A managed set of people and other assigned resources that delivers one or more products or services to a customer or end user. (See also "project.")

A work group can be any organizational entity with a defined purpose, whether or not that entity appears on an organization chart. Work groups can appear at any level of an organization, can contain other work groups, and can span organizational boundaries.

A work group together with its work can be considered the same as a project if it has an intentionally limited lifetime.

work plan   A plan of activities and related resource allocations for a work group.

Work planning includes estimating the attributes of work products and tasks, determining the resources needed, negotiating commitments, producing a schedule, and identifying and analyzing risks. Iterating through these activities can be necessary to establish the work plan.

work product   A useful result of a process.

This result can include files, documents, products, parts of a product, services, process descriptions, specifications, and invoices. A key distinction between a work product and a product component is that a work product is not necessarily part of the end product. (See also "product" and "product component.")

In CMMI models, the definition of "work product" includes services, however, the phrase "work products and services" is sometimes used to emphasize the inclusion of services in the discussion.

work product and task attributes Characteristics of products, services, and tasks used to help in estimating work. These characteristics include items such as size, complexity, weight, form, fit, and function. They are typically used as one input to deriving other resource estimates (e.g., effort, cost, schedule).

work startup When a set of interrelated resources for a work group is directed to develop or deliver one or more products or services for a customer or end user. (See also "work group.")

Book Contributors

BOOK AUTHORS

Brian P. Gallagher

Division Director, Engineering
Northrop Grumman—Information Systems Sector
Intelligence Systems Division

Brian P. Gallagher is the division director of engineering within the Intelligence Systems Division, Information Systems Sector, Northrop Grumman where he is responsible for providing leadership for all enterprise engineering activities across the division. Prior to this position, he was director, Acquisition Support at the Software Engineering Institute where he was responsible for building teams from across the SEI's disciplines to support the needs of DoD and other government agency acquisition programs. He was previously employed with the Aerospace Corporation where he worked as a software acquisition and engineering advisor for several Air Force and NRO projects. He retired from the Air Force in 1996. During his Air Force career, he was the deputy chief of Software Engineering with an Air Intelligence Agency remote intelligence site, chief software engineer on the Range Operations Control Center Project at Cape Canaveral AFS, FL, a software project manager for the Titan IV Program Office, and a software engineer with Strategic Air Command. He received his B.S. in management information systems from Peru State College and M.S. in computer science/software engineering from Florida Institute of Technology.

Mike Phillips

Program Manager
CMMI Initiative
Software Engineering Institute

Mike Phillips is the program manager for CMMI at the Software Engineering Institute (SEI), a position created to lead the Capability Maturity Model Integration (CMMI) product suite evolution. He has led the team, which spans government, industry, and the SEI, through three significant upgrades to the original version of the integrated model, which now covers engineering, acquisition, and services. He was previously responsible for Transition Enabling activities at the SEI. He has authored technical reports, technical notes, CMMI columns, and various articles, in addition to presenting CMMI material at conferences around the world. He is a coauthor of the first edition of the Addison-Wesley book on CMMI for Acquisition.

Prior to his retirement as a colonel from the Air Force, he was the program manager of the $36 billion development program for the B-2 stealth bomber in the B-2 System Program Office at Wright-Patterson AFB, OH. In addition to more than five years of B-2 experience, he has four years of experience guiding acquisition programs in the Pentagon for both the Air Force and the Office of the Secretary of Defense. His bachelor's degree in astronautical engineering is from the Air Force Academy, and his master's degrees are in nuclear engineering from Georgia Tech, in systems management from the University of Southern California, and in international affairs from Salve Regina College and the Naval War College. He is a graduate of the Program Management Course at the Defense Systems Management College and of the Air Force Test Pilot School.

Dr. Karen J. Richter

Research Analyst and Senior Project Leader
Institute for Defense Analyses

Dr. Karen Richter is a research analyst and senior project leader at the Institute for Defense Analyses (IDA), a research and development "think tank" for the Department of Defense. She has led numerous projects for the Office of the Under Secretary of Defense for Acquisition, Technology, and Logistics [OUSD(AT&L)] in acquisition management; systems and software engineering, integration, and interoperability; system lifecycle process management; integrated product and process development (IPPD) and concurrent engineering; advanced manufacturing practices and virtual enterprises; system quality, reliability, and maintainability; design and manufacturing technology including modeling and simulation; and lifecycle affordability. She also led or participated in projects for the Office of the Under Secretary of Defense for Policy [OUSD(P)] and the Assistant Secretary of Defense for Networks and Information Integration [ASD(NII)]. She was a member of the development teams for the CMMI SE/SW/IPPD and CMMI-DEV models and co-chair of the development team for CMMI-ACQ. She has served on the CMMI Configuration Control Board and the CMMI Steering Group. She helped develop international standards on lifecycle process management, systems engineering, software engineering, and quality management as a member of both ISO/JTC1/Subcommittee 7 (Software and Systems Engineering) Working Group 7 (Life Cycle Management) and ISO/TC176 (Quality). She taught in the Department of Engineering Mechanics at the University of Wisconsin–Madison and in the Departments of Mechanical Engineering at The Ohio State University and the University of Maryland at College Park. She is the coauthor of three college engineering textbooks. She earned a B.A. in mathematics from Knox College and an M.S. and Ph.D. in engineering mechanics from the University of Wisconsin–Madison.

Sandy Shrum

Senior Writer/Editor
Communications
Software Engineering Institute

Sandy Shrum is a senior writer/editor and communications point of contact for the Software Engineering Process Management program at the Software Engineering Institute. Besides this book, she has coauthored two other CMMI books: *CMMI for Services: Guidelines for Superior Service* and *CMMI: Guidelines for Process Integration and Product Improvement*, first and second editions. She has been with the SEI since 1995 and has been a member of the CMMI Development Team since the CMMI project's inception in 1998. Her roles on the project have included model author, small review team member, reviewer, editor, model development process coordinator, and quality assurance process owner. Before joining the SEI, she worked for eight years as a document developer with Legent Corporation, a Virginia-based software company. Her experience as a technical communicator dates back to 1988, when she earned her M.A. in professional writing from Carnegie Mellon University. Her undergraduate degree, a B.S. in business administration, was earned at Gannon University, Erie, Pennsylvania.

CONTRIBUTING AUTHORS

Claude M. Bolton

Executive-in-Residence
Defense Acquisition University

Claude M. Bolton, Jr., became the Executive-in-Residence for the Defense Acquisition University (DAU) on January 3, 2008. In this position, he supports the DAU president, faculty, and students with strategic planning, course development, and mentoring. His primary focus is assisting the DAU president in achieving the congressional direction to recruit, retain, train, and educate the DoD acquisition workforce. He is also the first chair of the University of Nebraska Space and Telecommunications Law Advisory Board. In addition, he is an independent management consultant specializing in DoD program management, providing his expertise to DoD organizations and the defense industry. Prior to becoming the DAU Executive-in-Residence, he served as the Assistant Secretary of the Army for Acquisition, Logistics and Technology (ASAALT).

George Richard Freeman

Technical Director
Air Force Center for Systems Engineering
Air Force Institute of Technology

George Richard Freeman is the technical director of the Air Force's Center for Systems Engineering (SE), located at the AF Institute of Technology. He has more than 30 years of experience in process and systems engineering and has held numerous positions in civilian industry and government, including AF MAJCOM chief, Concept Development and Process Engineering; senior executive vice president and board member for EICON Inc.; and numerous positions with General Electric (GE) and United Nuclear and UNC Aerospace, including director of Expansion Programs (Manufacturing Plant Manager), materials manager, manufacturing systems manager, and engineering systems manager. He retired from the U.S. Air Force with the rank of Colonel. He was responsible for bringing the first GE robotic assembly system into production and has led the successful installation of two enterprise resource planning (ERP) systems for GE and UNC Aerospace, and the web-based AF enterprise-wide Reduction of Total Ownership Cost Decision Support System; all of these systems were based on service-oriented architectures and employed shared authoritative data. He also led the successful development and fielding of the Air Force's first SE process assessment model, which is based on the tenets of Capability Maturity Model Integration (CMMI). He holds a B.S. in computer science and aviation, an M.S. in engineering/industrial management, and an M.A. in national security strategy, and is a Certified Systems Engineering Professional (CSEP & CSEP-Acq).

Richard Frost

Global Director
Identity and Access Management
General Motors

Richard Frost is the global director of Identity and Access Management for General Motors. In this role, he is developing and implementing a global strategy to manage the identity, authentication, access, and security to GM's systems and intellectual property.

Previously, he was the global director of Systems Development for General Motors, where he streamlined the devolvement process and spearheaded numerous initiatives to accelerate business innovation and cost savings. These efforts include incremental and agile development lifecycles, requirements visualization, and outsourcing optimization. He is a member of the advisory board for CMMI for Acquisition (CMMI-ACQ) at the SEI and remains a driving force in its global implementation at GM.

Prior to joining General Motors, he was an executive at Volkswagen of America, where he focused on streamlining development and aligning IT and business strategies. His tenure at Volkswagen included executive leadership of Systems Development, along with executive business positions in Supply Chain, Marketing, and CRM.

His background includes more than 25 years of leadership in a variety of technologies. He received a Ph.D. in systems engineering from Oakland University and bachelor's and master's degrees in computer science from the University of Michigan.

Ashok Gurumurthy

Delivery Executive
Global Application Integration Management
Hewlett-Packard

Ashok Gurumurthy is currently a delivery executive at Hewlett-Packard, managing the Global Application Integration Management group for one of HP's clients. He has 15 years of experience in IT governance, program management, and process improvements in the areas of CMMI, Six Sigma, ITIL, and ISO 9000. He was one of the reviewers of the initial CMMI-ACQ model. He managed the first CMMI-ACQ pilot by one of HP's clients in 2006. He was also invited by the Software Engineering Institute to participate in the CMMI-ACQ Pilot Panel at the SEPG 2007 Conference in Texas and in the CMMI-ACQ rollout panel at the SEPG 2008 conference in Florida. He has presented 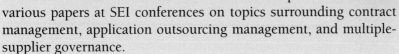 various papers at SEI conferences on topics surrounding contract management, application outsourcing management, and multiple-supplier governance.

Steve Kelley

Process Lead
Missile Systems
Strike and Surveillance Systems Division
Aerospace Systems, Northrop Grumman

Steve Kelley is the process lead for Missile Systems within the Strike and Surveillance Systems Division, Aerospace Systems, Northrop Grumman, where he is responsible for organizing and maintaining process documentation to enable the organization to acquire complex missile components and integrate them on behalf of government customers. As a Lean Six Sigma Master Black Belt, his roles have encompassed process engineering and continuous improvement disciplines, engineering planning, finance, financial and accounting system design and implementation, program management, systems engineering, and training. Before joining Northrop Grumman, he spent eight years at United Technologies Chemical Systems, where he developed and maintained a validated earned value management system. His bachelor's degree in chemistry and his M.B.A. are both from Baylor University.

Tom Keuten

Process Improvement Consulting Executive

Tom Keuten is a results-oriented management consulting executive who is focused on earning clients' trust through meaningful and

valuable engagements. He was a member of the CMMI-ACQ Model Team and has been trained as a SCAMPI Lead Appraiser. He led teams at General Motors that drove significant improvements in the way the company acquires information technology. He works with organizations to improve strategy execution, and specializes in organizational project management, quality assurance, and process improvement. His background includes executive roles in both start-up and established technology consulting organizations. Throughout his career, he has been passionate about delivering successful projects that have meaningful bottom-line improvements. In addition to earning an MBA from the University of Notre Dame and a bachelor of science degree from

Central Michigan University, he has also achieved the Certified Management Consultant (CMC) designation.

Mary Ann Lapham

Senior Member of the Technical Staff
Acquisition Support Program
Software Engineering Institute

Mary Ann Lapham is a senior member of the technical staff in the Software Engineering Institute's Acquisition Support Program (ASP). She is currently supporting or has in the past supported Air Force programs such as 3DELRR, CCS-C, AEHF, TSAT, GPS-OCX, and GBS to improve acquisition practices in acquiring these software-intensive systems. She is also currently conducting research in the application of Agile methods in the DoD environment. In addition, she has participated in and/or led ITAs for both DoD and non-DoD clients and is an instructor for the Software Acquisition Survival Skills course. Prior to joining SEI, she was a director for SchlumbergerSema, managing large system integration programs for utilities. Prior to that, she was a director at Computer Technology Associates (CTA), where she established and directed two satellite offices supporting the Naval Computer and Telecommunications Station in New Orleans and the state of Nebraska's Y2K program. While at CTA, she also served as a program manager, system engineer, test engineer, and security engineer for a variety of DoD programs. She received her B.A. and M.A. in mathematics from the State University of New York. She also is a PMP.

Dan Lutrell

Systems Engineering and Process Manager
Information Systems' Defense Systems Division
Northrop Grumman

Dan Luttrell is a systems engineering and process manager for Northrop Grumman Information Systems' Defense Systems Division. With more than 30 years of experience, he has held positions as a software engineer, systems engineer, process engineer, and program manager in several product fields, including engineering services, semiconductors, satellites, communications, and control systems. He is a Certified High Maturity Lead Appraiser and Six Sigma Black Belt.

Dominique Luzeaux
Director for Land Systems Acquisition
Direction Générale de l'Armement (DGA)

Dominique Luzeaux graduated from École Polytechnique (1987) and École Nationale Supérieure des Techniques Avancées (1989), and completed a Ph.D. from University Paris XI (1991) and a Faculty Habilitation (2001). He has been employed by the DGA for more than 20 years and was promoted to the rank of Brigadier General in 2009. He has held a variety of positions, such as director of the Complex System Engineering Department from 2002 to 2004 and chief information officer from 2005 to 2007. He is currently director for Land Systems acquisition. He teaches graduate-level students and has also coauthored several books on system-of-systems engineering published in French (Éd. Hermès Lavoisier, 2008, 2009) and English (Wiley, 2010).

B. Craig Meyers
Senior Member of the Technical Staff
Research, Technology, and System Solutions
Software Engineering Institute

Dr. B. Craig Meyers is a senior member of the technical staff at the Software Engineering Institute. He works in the Research, Technology and System Solutions group at the SEI and is concerned with architecture and interoperability, including interoperability in the acquisition process. He has also served on a number of review teams for various major government acquisition programs. Previously he worked in the area of real-time distributed systems. He was a member of the SEI project that transitioned the use of rate-monotonic analysis, and was involved in the development of IEEE standards for real-time distributed communication. Prior to joining the SEI, he was head of the Advanced Software Technology Group at the Naval Surface Warfare Center in Dahlgren, Virginia.

Eric Million-Picallion
Management Systems Division
Direction Générale de l'Armement (DGA)

Eric Million-Picallion graduated from École Polytechnique (1985) and École Nationale Supérieure de l'Aéronautique et de l'Espace (1987), and has been employed by the DGA for more than 20 years. He has held a variety of positions in the field of military aircraft systems dealing with depot-level maintenance, weapon system development, export program control, and armament programs expertise. He held the Project Management Division from 2005 to 2009. He is currently head of the Management Systems Division, in charge of defining, implementing, and promoting the applicable methods and standards in the field of quality and performance within the DGA.

Madhav Panwar
Senior Level Technologist
U.S. Government Accountability Office

Madhav Panwar is a senior level technologist at the U.S. Government Accountability Office (GAO). He has led a number of software acquisition and software development related evaluations using the Software Engineering Institute's Capability Maturity Models. He has an M.S. in computer science from California State University, Chico, and an undergraduate degree in chemical engineering from Columbia University, New York. He has more than 30 years of systems and software engineering experience. At GAO, he leads and/or assists on various audits of federal

agencies' efforts to acquire, install, or upgrade information systems and technology. Prior to working for GAO, he was responsible for managing the U.S. Navy's operations and maintenance budget for airborne avionics and software and related acquisitions. Currently he is responsible for evaluating various technologies related to greenhouse gas reductions, power plant efficiencies, automotive fuel economy, weapon systems software, and a host of other issues that require software and engineering expertise.

Jean-René Rualt
Direction Générale de l'Armement (DGA)

Jean-René Rualt completed a master's degree in experimental social psychology and graduate-level training in industrial engineering. After more than 10 years as a consultant on software engineering and human–computer interaction, he was hired in 2004 by the DGA as an expert in systems engineering, standardization, and human factors. With Dominique Luzeaux, he has coauthored books on systems of systems published in French (Éd. Hermès Lavoisier, 2008) and English (Wiley, 2010).

Anthony W. Spehar
Division Vice President and Program Manager
Strike and Surveillance Systems Division
Northrop Grumman Aerospace Systems

Anthony W. Spehar is vice president and program manager of the Intercontinental Ballistic Missile (ICBM) Prime Integration Contract and leads a multicorporation industry team given the responsibility by the Air Force to sustain and modernize the nation's ICBMs. The ICBM Prime Team's contract was awarded on December 23, 1997, and is headquartered in Clearfield, Utah, adjacent to Hill AFB. Since joining Northrop Grumman in 1979, he has served in other program management and engineering roles spanning nuclear hardness and survivability, program acquisition, hardware and software development, production, and deployment. He earned his bachelor's degree in physics and his master's degree in nuclear engineering from the University of Utah. He also completed the Advanced Program Management course at the Defense Systems Management College in Fort Belvoir, Virginia.

INDEX

A

Accept the Acquired Product practice, 195–196
Acceptance criteria
    defined, 536
    for measurements, 308
Acceptance levels in solicitation packages, 503
Acceptance testing, 536
Achieve Specific Goals goal, 173
Achievement profiles, 40–41, 536
Acquirers
    in Agile development, 147–148
    defined, 536
Acquisition Mini Team, 532
Acquisition Module, 10
Acquisition process, 536
Acquisition Requirements Development (ARD)
        process area, 47–48, 50
    Acquisition Technical Management relation,
        216
    Acquisition Validation relation, 230
    Acquisition Verification relation, 238
    ACS program, 104–105
    Analyze and Validate Requirements goal,
        209–214
    Develop Contractual Requirements goal,
        204–207
    Develop Customer Requirements goal,
        201–204
    developer agility, 146–148
    DGA system, 96, 99–100

government acquisition, 73
introductory notes, 199–200
IPIC experience, 84
operational agility, 145–146
Project Planning relation, 412
purpose, 199
related process areas, 201
Requirements Management relation, 472
Solicitation and Supplier Agreement
        Development relation, 498
supplier agreements, 131–132
Acquisition strategy
    defined, 536
    establishing and maintaining, 414–418
Acquisition Technical Management (ATM)
        process area, 50
    Acquisition Requirements Development
        relation, 201
    Acquisition Validation relation, 230
    Acquisition Verification relation, 238
    Agreement Management relation, 191
    Evaluate Technical Solutions goal, 217–225
    government acquisition, 73–74, 135–136
    introductory notes, 215–216
    operational agility, 145
    Perform Interface Management goal, 225–227
    Project Planning relation, 412
    purpose, 215
    related process areas, 216–217

The SEI Partner Network:
Helping hands with a global reach

Do you need help getting started with adoption of SEI tools and methods in your organization? Or are you an experienced professional in the field who wants to join a global network of SEI service providers?

The SEI Partner Network is a world-wide group of licensed organizations with individuals qualified by the SEI to deliver SEI services. SEI Partners can provide you with the training courses, adoption assistance, appraisal methods, and teamwork and management processes that you need to succeed.

To find an SEI Partner near you, or to learn more about this global network of professionals, please visit the SEI Partner Network website at *http://www.sei.cmu.edu/partners*

ESSENTIAL GUIDES TO CMMI®

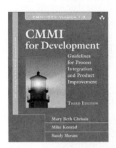

**CMMI® for Development:
Guidelines for Process Integration
and Product Improvement,
Third Edition**

Mary Beth Chrissis, Mike Konrad,
and Sandy Shrum

ISBN-13: 978-0-321-71150-2

The definitive guide to CMMI—now
updated for CMMI v1.3. Whether you are
new to CMMI or already familiar with
some version of it, this book is the essential resource for managers, practitioners,
and process improvement team members
who to need to understand, evaluate,
and/or implement a CMMI model.

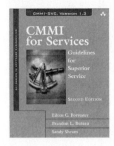

**CMMI® for Services:
Guidelines for Superior Service,
Second Edition**

Eileen C. Forrester, Brandon L. Buteau,
and Sandy Shrum

ISBN-13: 978-0-321-71152-6

The authoritative guide to CMMI for
Services v1.3, a model designed to help
service-provider organizations improve
their processes and thereby gain business
advantage. This book, which contains
the complete model, also includes helpful commentary by the authors and case
studies to illustrate how the model is
being used.

**CMMI® for Acquisition:
Guidelines for Improving the
Acquisition of Products and
Services, Second Edition**

Brian P. Gallagher, Mike Phillips,
Karen J. Richter, and Sandy Shrum

ISBN-13: 978-0-321-71151-9

The official guide to CMMI-ACQ—an
extended CMMI framework for improving product and service acquisition
processes. In addition to the complete
CMMI-ACQ itself, the book includes tips,
hints, and case studies to enhance your
understanding and to provide valuable,
practical advice.

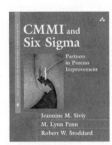

**CMMI® and Six Sigma:
Partners in Process Improvement**

Jeannine M. Siviy, M. Lynn Penn, and
Robert W. Stoddard

ISBN-13: 978-0-321-51608-4

Focuses on the synergistic, rather than
competitive, implementation of CMMI
and Six Sigma—with synergy translating
to "faster, better, cheaper" achievement
of mission success.

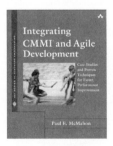

**Integrating CMMI® and Agile
Development: Case Studies and
Proven Techniques for Faster
Performance Improvement**

Paul E. McMahon

ISBN-13: 978-0-321-71410-7

Explains how combining an Agile
approach with the CMMI process
improvement framework is the fastest,
most effective way to achieve your
business objectives.

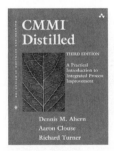

**CMMI® Distilled: A Practical
Introduction to Integrated Process
Improvement, Third Edition**

Dennis M. Ahern, Aaron Clouse,
and Richard Turner

ISBN-13: 978-0-321-46108-7

Updated for CMMI version 1.2, this
third edition again provides a concise
and readable introduction to the model,
as well as straightforward, no-nonsense
information on integrated, continuous
process improvement.

**For more information on these and other CMMI-related books, as well as on all
titles in The SEI Series in Software Engineering, please visit informit.com/seiseries.**

The SEI Series in Software Engineering

ISBN 0-321-46108-8

ISBN 0-321-22876-6

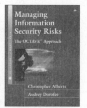

ISBN 0-321-11886-3

ISBN 0-201-73723-X

ISBN 0-321-50917-X

ISBN 0-321-15495-9

ISBN 0-321-17935-8

ISBN 0-321-27967-0

ISBN 0-201-70372-6

ISBN 0-201-70482-X

ISBN 0-201-70332-7

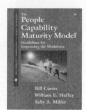

ISBN 0-201-60445-0

ISBN 0-201-60444-2

ISBN 0-321-42277-5

ISBN 0-201-52577-1

ISBN 0-201-25592-8

ISBN 0-321-47717-0

ISBN 0-201-54597-7

ISBN 0-201-54809-7

ISBN 0-321-30549-3

ISBN 0-201-18095-2

ISBN 0-201-54610-8

ISBN 0-201-47719-X

ISBN 0-321-34962-8

ISBN 0-201-77639-1

ISBN 0-201-73-1134

ISBN 0-201-61626-2

ISBN 0-201-70454-4

ISBN 0-201-73409-5

ISBN 0-201-85-4805

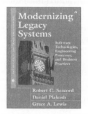

ISBN 0-321-11884-7

ISBN 0-321-33572-4

ISBN 0-321-51608-7

ISBN 0-201-70312-2

ISBN 0-201-70-0646

ISBN 0-201-17782-X

Please see our web site at informit.com/seiseries for more information on these titles.

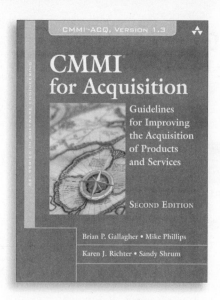

FREE Online Edition

Your purchase of *CMMI® for Acquisition, Second Edition,* includes access to a free online edition for 45 days through the Safari Books Online subscription service. Nearly every Addison-Wesley Professional book is available online through Safari Books Online, along with more than 5,000 other technical books and videos from publishers such as, Cisco Press, Exam Cram, IBM Press, O'Reilly, Prentice Hall, Que, and Sams.

SAFARI BOOKS ONLINE allows you to search for a specific answer, cut and paste code, download chapters, and stay current with emerging technologies.

Activate your FREE Online Edition at www.informit.com/safarifree

> **STEP 1:** Enter the coupon code: CMRPFDB.

> **STEP 2:** New Safari users, complete the brief registration form. Safari subscribers, just log in.

If you have difficulty registering on Safari or accessing the online edition, please e-mail customer-service@safaribooksonline.com

Process Areas by Maturity Level

Maturity Level 2

Agreement Management (AM)
Acquisition Requirements Development (ARD)
Configuration Management (CM)
Measurement and Analysis (MA)
Project Monitoring and Control (PMC)
Project Planning (PP)
Process and Product Quality Assurance (PPQA)
Requirements Management (REQM)
Solicitation and Supplier Agreement Development (SSAD)

Maturity Level 3

Acquisition Technical Management (ATM)
Acquisition Validation (AVAL)
Acquisition Verification (AVER)
Decision Analysis and Resolution (DAR)
Integrated Project Management (IPM)
Organizational Process Definition (OPD)
Organizational Process Focus (OPF)
Organizational Training (OT)
Risk Management (RSKM)

Maturity Level 4

Organizational Process Performance (OPP)
Quantitative Project Management (QPM)

Maturity Level 5

Causal Analysis and Resolution (CAR)
Organizational Performance Management (OPM)